Jacob van Ruisdael

Jacob van Ruisdael

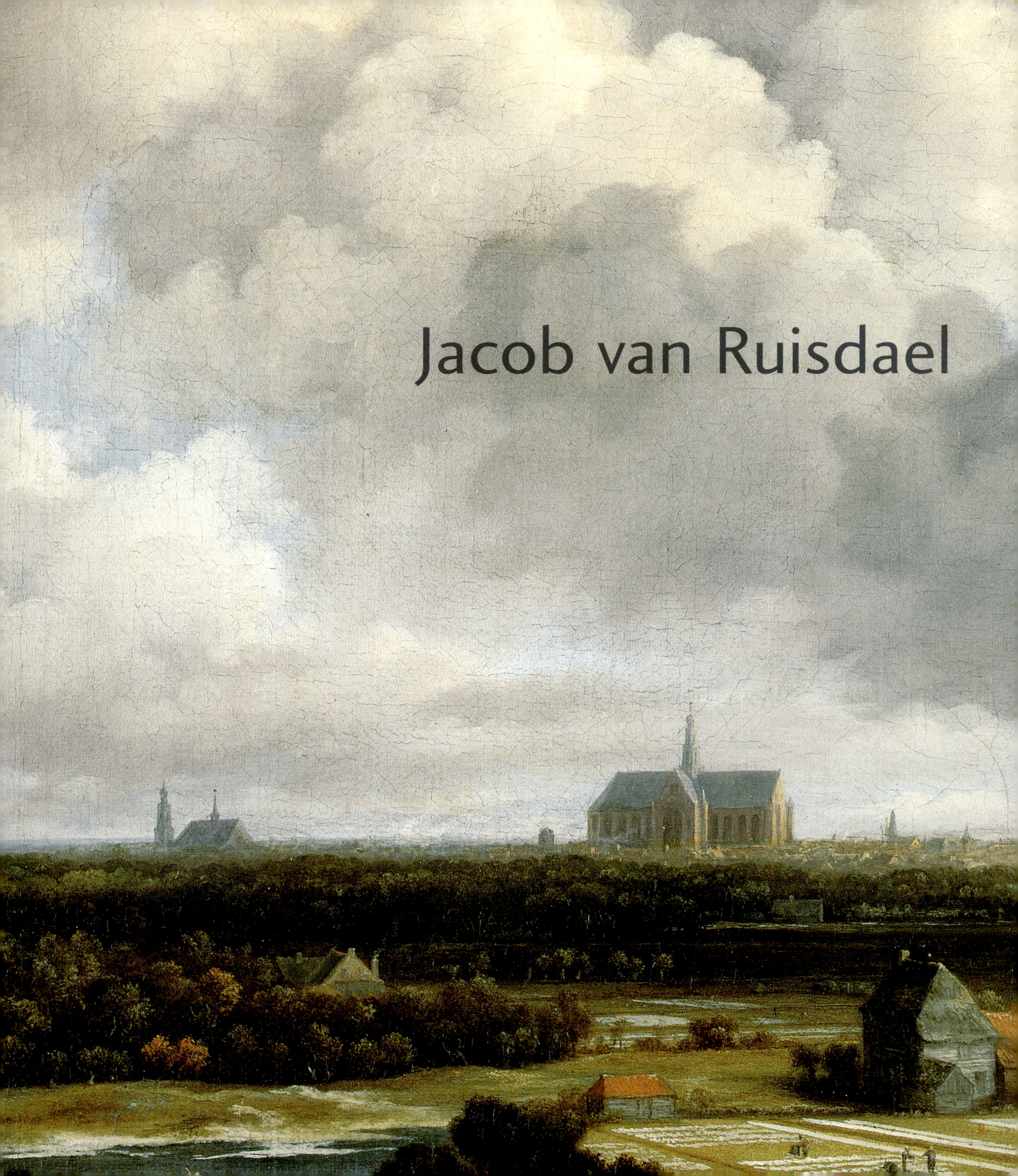

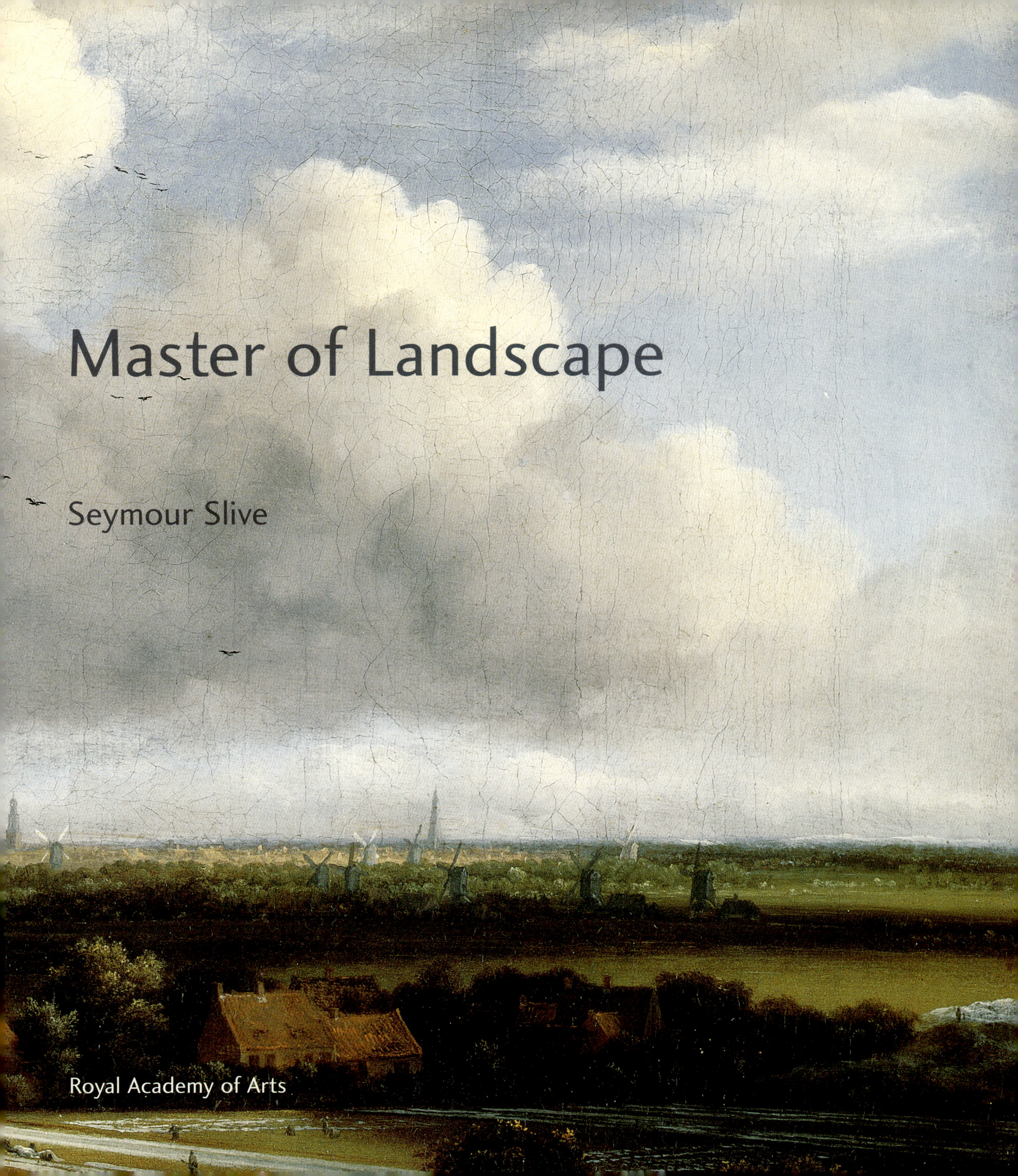

Master of Landscape

Seymour Slive

Royal Academy of Arts

First published on the occasion of the exhibition
'Jacob van Ruisdael: Master of Landscape'
Los Angeles County Museum of Art, 26 June – 18 September 2005
Philadelphia Museum of Art, 23 October 2005 – 5 February 2006
Royal Academy of Arts, London, 25 February – 4 June 2006

The Royal Academy of Arts is grateful to Her Majesty's Government for agreeing to indemnify this exhibition under the National Heritage Act 1980, and to Resource, The Council for Museums, Archives and Libraries, for its help in arranging the indemnity.

CATALOGUE PRODUCTION
by Yale University Press
Design: Sally Salvesen
Printed in Singapore by CS Graphics

TITLEPAGE ILLUSTRATION
View of Haarlem with Bleaching Grounds (detail), Kunsthaus Zürich, Stiftung Prof. Dr. L. Ruzicka, cat. 49

British Library Cataloguing-in-Publication Data
A catalogue record for this book is available from the British Library
ISBN 1-903973-74-0 (paperback)
ISBN 1-903973-24-4 (hardback)

Distributed in the United States and Canada by Yale University Press, New Haven
Distributed outside the United States and Canada by Thames & Hudson Ltd, London

Contents

Lenders to the Exhibition

AUSTRIA
Albertina, Vienna
Gemäldegalerie der Akademie der Bildenden Künste, Vienna
Kunsthistorisches Museum, Gemäldegalerie, Vienna

BELGIUM
Musées Royaux des Beaux Arts de Belgique, Brussels

FRANCE
Collection Frits Lugt, Institut Néerlandais, Paris
Ecole Nationale Supérieure des Beaux-Arts, Paris
Musée Jacquemart-André, Institut de France, Paris
Musée du Louvre, Paris

GERMANY
Staatliche Museen zu Berlin, Gemäldegalerie
Staatliche Museen zu Berlin, Kupferstichkabinett
Herzog Anton Ulrich-Museum, Braunschweig
Gemäldegalerie Alte Meister, Staatliche Kunstsammlungen Dresden
Kupferstich-Kabinett, Staatliche Kunstammlungen Dresden
Städelsches Kunstinstitut, Frankfurt am Main
Hamburger Kunsthalle
Staatliche Kunsthalle Karlshruhe
Museum der Bildenden Künste, Leipzig
Bayerische Staatsgemäldesammlungen, Alte Pinakothek, Munich

HUNGARY
Szépművészeti Múzeum, Budapest

IRELAND
The National Gallery of Ireland, Dublin

THE NETHERLANDS
Gemeentearchief, Amsterdam
Amsterdams Historisch Museum
Rijksmuseum, Amsterdam
Frans Hals Museum, Haarlem
Teylers Museum, Haarlem
Museum Bredius, The Hague
Royal Cabinet of Paintings Mauritshuis, The Hague
Collection Noro Foundation

RUSSIA
The State Hermitage Museum, St Petersburg

SPAIN
Museo Thyssen-Bornemisza, Madrid

SWITZERLAND
Kunsthaus Zürich

UNITED KINGDOM
The Duke of Buccleuch and Queensberry KT
Fitzwilliam Museum, Cambridge
The Torrie Collection, University of Edinburgh
The British Museum, London
The National Gallery, London
Worcester College, Oxford
The McEwan Collection, Polesden Lacey (The National Trust)

UNITED STATES OF AMERICA
Maida and George Abrams Collection, Boston, Massachusetts
Museum of Fine Arts, Boston
Mrs Edward W. Carter
Fogg Art Museum, Harvard University Art Museums, Cambridge, Massachusetts
The Art Institute of Chicago
The Cleveland Museum of Art
The Hascoe Collection
Kimbell Art Museum, Fort Worth
Los Angeles County Museum of Art
The J. Paul Getty Museum, Los Angeles
Currier Museum of Art, Manchester, New Hampshire
The Metropolitan Museum of Art, New York
The Pierpont Morgan Library, New York
Philadelphia Museum of Art
Thaw Collection, New York
Toledo Museum of Art
The National Gallery of Art, Washington DC

and others who wish to remain anonymous

Foreword

More than two decades have passed since Jacob van Ruisdael, one of the most influential figures of the Golden Age of painting in the Netherlands, was last the subject of a major monographic exhibition. We are delighted, therefore, to be able to introduce this remarkable artist to a new generation of viewers and admirers. That we can do so in collaboration with one of the undisputed authorities on Ruisdael's art, Professor Seymour Slive, gives us even greater pleasure. We are honoured that Professor Slive, whose comprehensive catalogue raisonné of Ruisdael's oeuvre has been justly acclaimed since its publication by Yale University Press in 2001, has brought his many years of expertise to the selection of the present exhibition and the writing of its catalogue. We are profoundly indebted to him for the energy he has devoted to the project.

The work of Jacob van Ruisdael has shaped landscape painting traditions from the English School to Barbizon in France, and the Hudson River School in the United States, as well as generations of Dutch landscape artists. His influence stems from his innovative treatment of the most straightforward subject-matter: the landscape of Holland and neighbouring parts of Northern Europe. Since the last retrospective, which was held in 1981–82 at the Fogg Art Museum in Cambridge, Massachusetts, and the Mauritshuis in The Hague, Ruisdael's paintings have been the subject of much discussion and debate. That they are so pregnant with meaning (hidden or otherwise) should come as no surprise when we consider the artist's acquisitive, roaming intellect. It is the hope of those responsible for the present exhibition that Ruisdael's handling of paint, his treatment of light, colour and compositional structure and his remarkable powers of observation – the formal qualities that contributed so much to his greatness and that so captivated earlier generations of admirers – will once again be affirmed.

In organizing *Jacob van Ruisdael: Master of Landscape*, the Royal Academy of Arts is proud to present the first exhibition of the artist's work in Great Britain. In the present catalogue, Professor Slive explores the character of Ruisdael's achievement, and his critical reception and posthumous reputation. The freshness and force of Ruisdael's landscapes were admired by the Academy's first President, Sir Joshua Reynolds, when he journeyed through Holland in 1781, an appreciation shared by other Academicians, including Gainsborough, J. M. W. Turner and Constable, who was particularly moved by the Dutch master's works.

The exhibition opens in Los Angeles at an auspicious time, celebrating the significant gift of twelve Dutch seventeenth-century paintings from the collection of Hannah L. Carter and the late Edward W. Carter, including a major painting by Ruisdael. For Philadelphia, the exhibition highlights the strengths of the Museum's extensive holdings of Dutch seventeenth-century painting and in particular the collection of the lawyer John G. Johnson. Johnson's collection, bequeathed to the City of Philadelphia in 1917, included five paintings by Ruisdael; four were added through the generosity of other donors.

It is with pleasure and great appreciation that we thank the many people who have contributed to the realization of the exhibition and catalogue. Our greatest debt of gratitude is of course to those institutions and individuals who have so willingly lent their works. We are also grateful to the many people who have helped in other ways: Noël Annesley,

Monica Bachtler, Ronni Baer, Christoph Becker, Suzanne Benfield, Mària van Berge-Gerbaud, Marian Bisanz-Prakken, Christopher Brown, Michael Clarke, The Rt Hon. The Earl of Crawford and Balcarres, Anthony Crichton-Stuart, Charles C. Cunningham Jr., Rhoda Eitel-Porter, George Gordon, Bob Haboldt, Nicholas V. Iljine, Christina Jansen, Pieter Klein, Christian Klemm, Anna Konivets, Tom Krens, Alastair Laing, Christopher Lloyd, Julia Lloyd Williams, Harald Marx, Andrew McLean, John Nicoll, Nadine Orenstein, Mikhail Piotrovsky, Wolfgang Prohaska, Martin Royalton-Kisch, Francis Russell, Zoya Slive, Irina Sokolova, Peter Sutton, Christopher White and Martha Wolff.

This exhibition has been realized through the efforts of MaryAnne Stevens, Norman Rosenthal, Cecilia Treves, Emeline Winston, Hillary Taylor and Andreja Brulc of the Royal Academy of Arts. Its presentation in the United States is entirely due to the enthusiasm and commitment of the Los Angeles County Museum of Art and the Philadelphia Museum of Art. We wish to offer sincere thanks to J. Patrice Marandel, Ayako Yoshida, Irene Martín, Joseph Fronek and Renée Montgomery in Los Angeles and to Joseph Rishel, Lloyd DeWitt, Suzanne F. Wells, Mark Tucker and Amy Dowe in Philadelphia for helping to ensure the exhibition's success.

The Royal Academy of Arts is grateful to Her Majesty's Government for agreeing to indemnify the exhibition and to The Museums, Libraries and Archives Council for its help in arranging the indemnity. In the United States the exhibition is supported by an indemnity from the Federal Council on the Arts and the Humanities. The Royal Academy also wishes to thank His Excellency Count Jan de Marchant et d'Ansembourg, Ambassador of the Kingdom of the Netherlands, for his advice and support.

In Los Angeles, the exhibition was made possible in part by Los Angeles County Museum of Art's Wallis Annenberg Director's Endowment Fund. In Philadelphia, the exhibition is supported by a grant from The Pew Charitable Trusts, by the Robert Montgomery Scott Fund for Exhibitions at the Philadelphia Museum of Art, and by the generous and timely support of an anonymous admirer of Jacob van Ruisdael's work.

Sir Nicholas Grimshaw
President,
Royal Academy of Arts, London

Andrea L. Rich
President and Wallis Annenberg Director,
Los Angeles County Museum of Art

Anne d'Harnoncourt
The George D. Widener Director and C.E.O.,
Philadelphia Museum of Art

Author's Acknowledgements

My deepest debt, by far, is to all the lenders who generously agreed to part with their works for a long period of time. I also am particularly beholden to members of the organizing committee for their indispensable help: Norman Rosenthal, MaryAnne Stevens, Cecilia Treves and Hillary Taylor of the Rcyal Academy of Arts, Patrice Marandel and Irene Martin of the Los Angeles County Museum of Art, and Lloyd de Witt and Suzanne Wells of the Philadelphia Art Museum.

Once again I acknowledge with deep gratitude the meticulous editorial assistance received from Alice I. Davies. Sally Salvesen of Yale University Press is offered special thanks for her expert supervision of the catalogue's production and its handsome design and layout.

Finally I am indebted to the directors of Yale University Press for permission to reprint material, in an amended form, published in my Ruisdael catalogue that appeared under their imprint in 2001.

SS
20 October 2004
Cambridge, Massachusetts

Editorial Note

Works in each medium are catalogued in an order that approximates their date of execution. Where external evidence permits, a firm date is cited. All paintings are in oil. Dimensions of all works are cited in centimetres (cm), height preceding width. Works are shown in Los Angeles, Philadelphia and London, unless otherwise indicated.

Comparative figures in the entries are identified by the catalogue number of the exhibited work and a letter (*e.g.*, fig. 28a). The *Bibliography Cited in Abbreviated Form*, pp.265–71, offers bibliographical information regarding shortened references in the text. Details of exhibitions are cited in *Exhibitions Cited in Abbreviated Form*, pp.272–74.

Reference is made throughout to "grain" and "grainfield" instead of "corn" and "cornfield" because the last named terms refer specifically in North American usage to "maize" or "Indian corn", not, as in British usage, to any edible grain. Ruisdael of course never depicted a field of maize or Indian corn, a grain that was not cultivated in the Netherlands in his day.

Following Dutch usage patronymics have been abbreviated in the text. Those ending in "sz" or "sdr" should be read as "zoon" or "dochter", *i.e.*, the son of or daughter of. Put another way, Isaacksz means Isaackszoon (the son of Isaack), and Isaacksdr means Isaacksdochter (the daughter of Isaack).

Ruisdael's works are identified by the number assigned to them in Seymour Slive, *Jacob van Ruisdael: A Complete Catalogue of His Paintings, Drawings and Etchings*, New Haven and London, 2001. The following abbreviations are used to refer to works listed there.

- S followed by a number, *e.g.*, S 41, refers to a painting
- S followed by a D and a number, *e.g.*, S D27, refers to a drawing
- S followed by an E and a number, *e.g.*, S E10, refers to an etching
- S followed by dub and a number, *e.g.*, S dub34, refers to a painting that has a dubious status or has been wrongly ascribed to the artist
- S followed by dubD and a number, *e.g.*, S dubD15, refers to a drawing that has a dubious status or has been wrongly attributed to the artist

Chronology

1628 or 1629 Born in Haarlem. Ruisdael's statement made on 9 June 1661 (see below) that he was thirty-two years old establishes 1628 or 1629 as the year of his birth.

1646 Year of his earliest existing dated works.

1648 Joins Haarlem's St. Lucas guild of painters.

early 1650s Travels to the border region between the eastern provinces of the Netherlands and western Germany, most probably with his friend and sometime collaborator Nicolaes (Claes) Berchem.

14 March 1652 A small landscape (*een cleijn lantschapien*), a wooded landscape (*een bosschage*), and a view of Weesp by "Ruysdael" are cited in the posthumous inventory made in Amsterdam on 14 March 1652 of the effects of Carel Niellius de jonge (1608–52); the three paintings were in ebony frames. If the citations refer to works by Jacob Isaacksz van Ruisdael, they are the earliest existing inventory references to his paintings. If they were his, it would be notable that they found their way to Amsterdam as early as 1652. However, it is possible that they were by his uncle Salomon van Ruysdael, his cousin Jacob Salomonsz van Ruysdael or his father Isaack van Ruisdael. We can only speculate if the pictures' ebony frames were made by Isaack who also was an ebony-framemaker.

14 June 1657 Requests baptism into the Calvinist Reformed Church while living in Amsterdam near the Dam on Beursstraat (today the Rokin) in "de Silvere Trompet." The document is the earliest known reference to the artist's residency in Amsterdam.

17 June 1657 Baptized in Ankeveen, a village near Naarden.

15 January 1659 Becomes a burgher of Amsterdam.

about 1660 Probable date of *The Arrival of Cornelis de Graeff and Members of His Family at Soestdijk, His Country Estate*, National Gallery of Ireland, Dublin (fig. 23), the only existing work among more than 800 attributable to the artist today that can be related to a specific patron. The painting, however, is not solely by Ruisdael. Thomas de Keyser (1596/7–1667) portrayed all the figures, the animals and de Graeff's handsome coach; Ruisdael contributed the landscape and Soestdijk's country house.

18 March 1660 Maria van Ruisdael, Jacob's half sister, is baptized in Haarlem at the age of seventeen; she was the daughter of Isaack and his third wife, Barbertje Hoevernaels.

8 July 1660 Meindert Hobbema testifies before a notary in Amsterdam that he spent several years serving and studying (*eenige jaren gedient en geleert*) with Ruisdael. Hobbema is Ruisdael's only documented pupil.

9 June 1661 Testifies before an Amsterdam notary on the authenticity of a shore scene allegedly by Jan Porcellis. The artists Barent Kleeneknecht, Allart van Everdingen and Willem Kalf also testify. All four agree the painting cannot be attributed to Porcellis, but there is no consensus on an alternative attribution. Ruisdael's statement upon this occasion that he is thirty-two years old is the source for offering 1628 or 1629 as his birth year.

10 May 1664 A large Ruisdael landscape sold for sixty guilders at an Amsterdam sale. More than twenty other paintings by seventeenth-century Dutch artists, including Adriaen van de Velde and Jan van der Heyden, fetched prices that ranged from twelve to forty-two guilders. Only a pair of pictures attributed to "Bassant" (Bassano?) brought more; they sold for 400 guilders.

23 May 1667 Ruisdael, sick in body but with his understanding, memory and faculty of speech intact, made a will designating his half sister Maria his sole beneficiary with the obligation to support their father Isaack, who was to have the income from the artist's estate. Ruisdael is described as a bachelor, living in the Kalverstraat, near the Dam, across from "'t Hoff van Hollant."

27 May 1667 After revoking all previous wills, Ruisdael made his father Isaack his sole beneficiary; he was to receive the income from his estate. If his father became incapacitated, his executors were instructed to provide a decent place (*civiele plaetse*) for him for the rest of his life. He named his uncle Salomon van Ruysdael and his cousin Jacob Salomonsz van Ruysdael his executors.

11 April 1668 Isaack van Ruisdael transfers all his possessions to Jacob in return for loans he received from his son.

2 October 1668 Witness at the marriage of Meindert Hobbema and Eeltje Pietersdr Vinck from Gorkum.

3 November 1670 Burial of Jacob's uncle Salomon van Ruysdael in St. Bavo's Church, Haarlem.

11 October 1671 Godfather to the twins of the fruit and flower painter Cornelis Simonsz Kick and his wife Cornelia Spaaroogh.

12 January 1672 Burial of his stepmother, Barbertje Hoevernaels, third wife of Isaack van Ruisdael.

3 February 1673 Witness at the marriage declaration of his cousin Jacob Salomonsz van Ruysdael and his second wife Annetje Jansdr Colijn.

12 November 1673 Marriage in Haarlem of Joost van der Hulst and Jacob's half sister Maria van Ruisdael.

1674 Assessed the special "200th penny tax" Amsterdam levied on its citizens in 1674 to help pay for the costly war that drove Louis XIV from the gates of the city in 1672. The tax of ½% was demanded only from citizens whose effects were worth more than 1000 guilders. Ruisdael paid 10 guilders; thus his possessions were appraised at 2000 guilders.

24 July 1674 Pieter Cornelisz de Graef (1638–1707), oldest son of the mighty Amsterdam burgomaster Cornelis de Graeff (1599–1664), in the presence of a notary, commissioned Ruisdael to repaint (*overschilderen*) and improve (*verbeteringh*) landscapes of de Graef estates at Soestdijk and Polsbroek. For work on one painting Ruisdael was to receive a fee of thirty guilders, for the other forty guilders. Neither painting has been identified.

15 October 1676 The name "Jacobus Ruijsdael" is inscribed in the List of Amsterdam Doctors with the notation that he received his medical degree at Caen University on 15 October 1676. The name has been vigourously scratched out. It is the only name in Amsterdam's *Series Nominum Doctorum* of the period which has been expunged. Whether or not the deleted name refers to the artist Jacob Isaacksz van Ruisdael is debatable.

2 October 1677 Opening of a grave in the Nieuwe Kerk, Haarlem, for Isaack van Ruisdael, Jacob's father.

9 July 1678 Date on a bond made to secure a loan of 400 guilders that Ruisdael made to Dr. Jan Baptist van Lamsweerde, physician of the Catholic Maagdenhuis (an orphanage for girls), in the Spui, Amsterdam (see 5 October 1682 below).

21 January 1682 Begins proceedings to sequester Dr. Jan Baptist van Lamsweerde's goods because payment of the interest on the loan cited above is overdue (see 5 October 1682 below).

***c.* 10 March 1682** Ruisdael dies in Amsterdam.

14 March 1682 A grave is opened for Ruisdael in the south transept (no. 177) of St. Bavo, Haarlem.

2 June 1682 A commission of ten guilders is charged by Haarlem's St. Lucas guild for auctioning paintings by "Ruysdael" and "[Hendrick] Mommer[s]", a follower of Nicolaes Berchem.

5 October 1682 A notorial document states that Maria van Ruisdael, Jacob's half sister and sole beneficiary, will receive 150 guilders as partial settlement of the debt that Dr. Jan Baptist van Lamsweerde owes the late Jacob van Ruisdael. It also states that the deceased Ruisdael made his loan of 400 guilders to Lamsweerde on 9 July 1678 and he started action on 21 January 1682 to confiscate his debtor's goods because the interest on the loan was overdue.

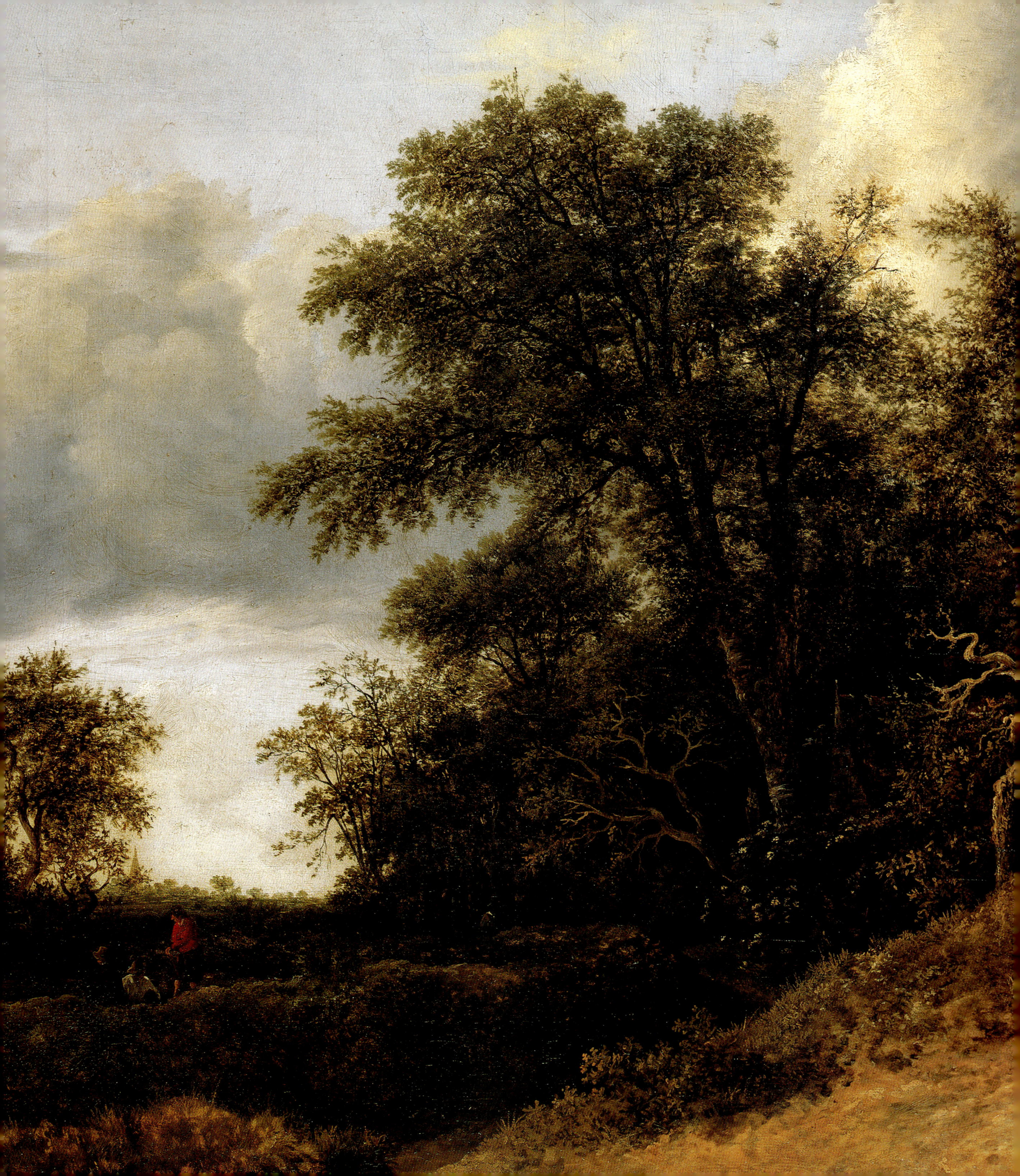

1

Jacob van Ruisdael: Master Landscapist

No old master or modern artist begins to match the astonishing variety of landscapes Jacob van Ruisdael depicted during the course of his career. His themes include identifiable sites, grainfields, woods and forests, rivers, bridges, sluices, rushing torrents, Scandinavian waterfalls, hills and mountains, views of the countryside with churches, ruins, lofty castles as well as modest cottages with ramshackle privies, dunes, country roads, beach and shore scenes, seascapes, winterscapes, windmills, water mills and more. He even made a drawing of a rarely represented mudmill (cat. 85), a contraption employed by the Dutch to dredge mud and muck from silted waterways or to help reclaim land from fresh water or the sea. Reference to a *Limekiln Burning Fiercely at Night*, the provenance of which dates back to 1760, suggests he also may have painted at least one nocturnal scene. Regrettably, today there is no way to appraise that picture's authenticity. Its original design virtually disappeared after it suffered irreparable water damage in the 1980s; a photo made before the accident is unknown.[1]

To judge from the artist's existing work there are, however, a few subjects he never touched. Notable is the absence of historiated landscapes, a subject favoured, as every gallery-goer knows, by Claude and Poussin and not infrequent in the work of some seventeenth-century Netherlandish landscapists. An anonymous later painter, called by the sharp French art historian Louis Viardot in 1855 a *barbouilleur de figures* (bungler of figures), attempted to fill the gap by adding Christ and the disciples going to Emmaus to a Ruisdael landscape which included Bentheim Castle.[2]

On the other hand, figures painted by Ruisdael himself or a collaborator that have nothing to do with biblical, mythological or historical subjects play a role in the artist's landscapes from the beginning. The group of dancing and sporting peasants in his *Landscape with a Grainfield and Farmhouses*, signed and dated 1646 (figs. 1, 2), the year he appears on the scene in his native Haarlem as a phenomenal seventeen- or eighteen-year-old, fully formed artist, are attributable to an unidentified follower of Adriaen van Ostade.[3] Recent study has revealed two additional early joint efforts. Both are dated 1647; one is at the Louvre (S 401), the other at Kassel (S 328). The Louvre landscape also includes rollicking country folk, among them a conspicuous amorous couple, by Gerrit Lundens, best known for his copy of Rembrandt's *Night Watch* before it was cut down. The Kassel painting is embellished by a pair of lovers perhaps also by Lundens; the lovers had been painted out and only reappeared when the painting was cleaned about a generation ago. Restoration of other Ruisdael landscapes may reveal additional painted out figures, but odds are high that they will not depict biblical characters, gods or classical heroes by Jacob or a fellow artist.

Another subject that did not attract Ruisdael is Italianate landscape. None by his hand has been identified. To our knowledge he never visited Italy; however, this does not explain the absence of Italian motifs seen in the warm shimmering light of the south

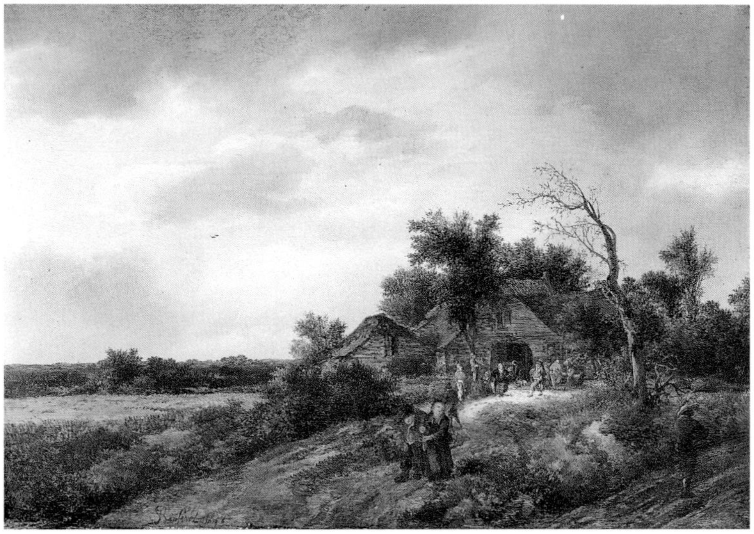

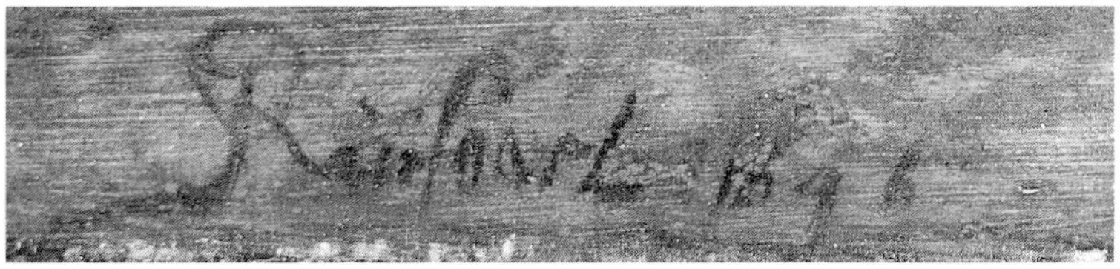

Fig. 1 Jacob van Ruisdael, *Landscape with a Grainfield and Farmhouses*, 1646. Viscount Allendale, Bywell Hall, Northumberland.

Fig. 2 Detail of signature and date on fig. 1.

Facing page Detail of cat. 3, *Dune Landscape*

Fig. 3 Jacob van Ruisdael, *Extensive Landscape with Trees, a Grainfield, Dunes and a Distant View of a Town*, 1648. 31.5 x 57.8 cm. Museum of Fine Arts, Springfield, Massachusetts.

Fig. 4 Rembrandt, *The Three Trees*, 1643. Etching.

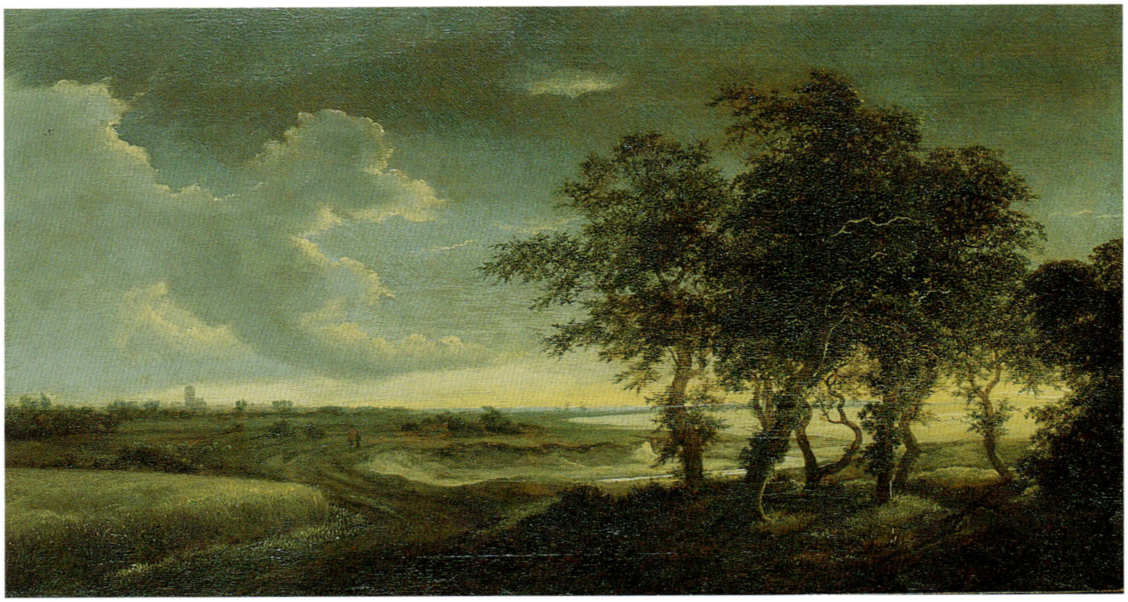

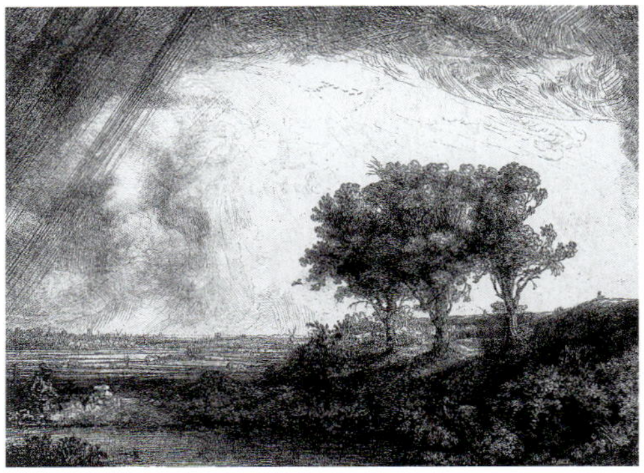

from his vast repertoire. After all, there is no documentary evidence that Nicolaes Berchem, who, Arnold Houbraken tells us, was Jacob's great friend, ever crossed the Alps, and there is no convincing reason to believe he made the trip. Yet Berchem specialized in pictures of Italianate pastoral and arcadian scenes. Ruisdael achieved a similar accomplishment in the numerous persuasive Scandinavian landscapes he began to paint in his early maturity and continued to produce until his last years. It is not news that Ruisdael ceaselessly observed nature intensely and then accurately incorporated what he saw in his works, but this was not his invariable working method. As far as we know he never set foot on Norwegian or Swedish soil. The art of Allart van Everdingen, who made the trip from Holland to the north, was his source. If it is still needed, good proof that seventeenth-century Dutch artists were not apes of nature is provided by Ruisdael's rushing waterfalls in northern mountainous landscapes and Berchem's Italianate views.

Diversity of subject characterizes the artist's work from his early phase. So does a prodigious proficiency. There is not a sign of fumbling or groping in the fifteen existing landscapes he signed and dated in 1646.[4] Nineteen equally expert landscapes are signed and dated 1647.[5] Documented works done during these two years establish that young Jacob was intensely active as an independent artist even before he joined the artists' guild of Haarlem in 1648.

Not the slightest trace of the struggle normally associated with a budding artist's formative phase is seen in the sparkling pointillist-like effect of the black chalk sketches known as the 'Dresden Sketchbook Drawings' (see cat. 59–64), which were probably done in 1646 or perhaps a trifle earlier. His three tiny oval landscape etchings (cat. 102–04) are contemporary with the Dresden sketches. They tell another story. Their tangled hatching, lack of spatial clarity and amorphous forms show less than full control of the etcher's technique and hint that though Ruisdael was wondrously precocious he does not qualify as a prodigy who, as has been said of Lucas van Leyden, was an artist before he left his mother's womb.

Who was Jacob's teacher? We have no idea who introduced the teenager to the art of etching. His father Isaack van Ruisdael, an ebony-framemaker, occasional dealer, and gifted but, apparently, not very prolific painter, and his uncle Salomon van Ruysdael,[6] a leading Haarlem landscapist, are the best candidates for the distinction of introducing him to the crafts of drawing and painting. However, neither was a printmaker. Their credentials as his teachers are not based on written records, but on commonsense – granted, not always a reliable source.

In Jacob's early paintings traces of the impact of his father's and uncle's pictures are seldom conspicuous, and it is impossible to say what his drawings owe to them since not a single drawing by Isaack or Salomon has been identified. Nevertheless, it seems perverse not to accept the notion that the boy was trained at home or in his uncle's studio – or in both places, particularly when it is recalled that Jacob's father most probably did not have a *stuiver* to pay for his son's apprenticeship. From a series of legal

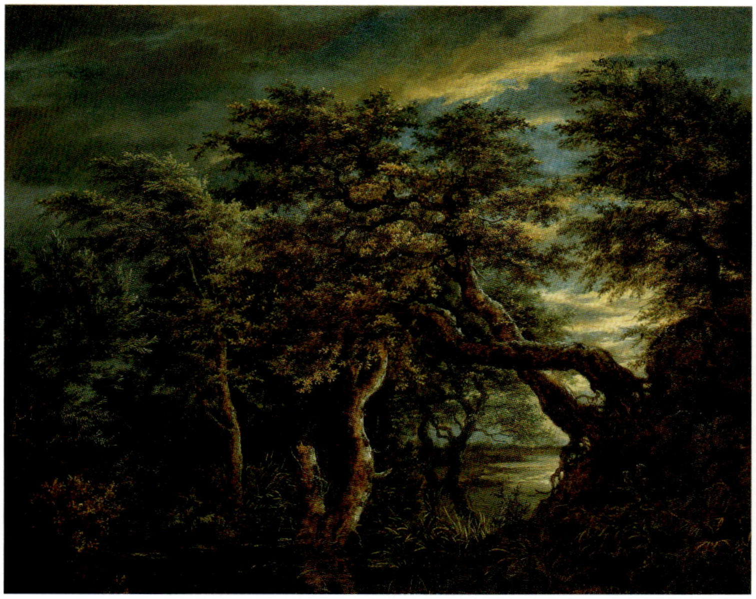

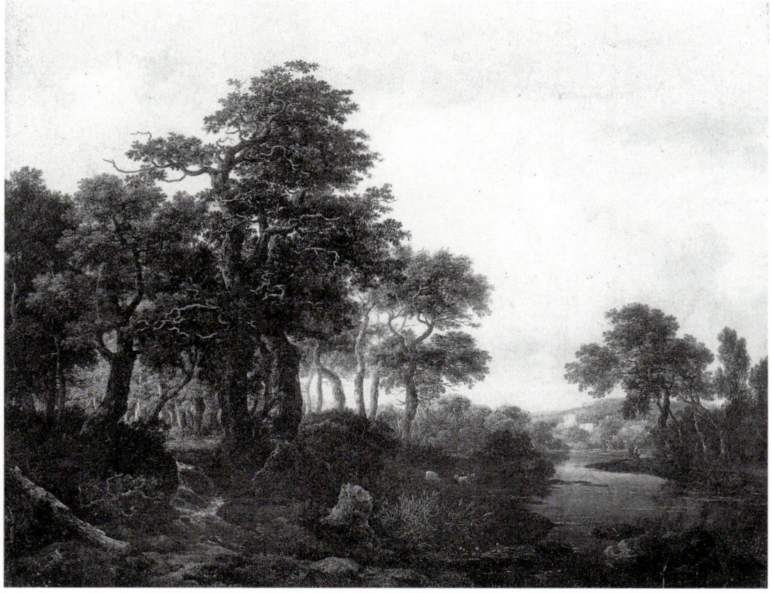

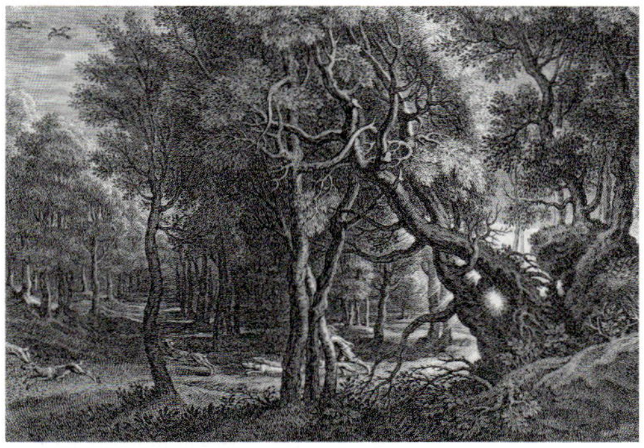

Fig. 5 Jacob van Ruisdael, *Marsh in a Wood at Dusk*. 78 x 92.5 cm. Museo de Bellas Artes de Bilbao.

Fig. 6 Schelte à Bolswert after Rubens, *Forest at Dawn with a Deer Hunt*. Engraving.

Fig. 7 Jacob van Ruisdael, *Wooded Landscape with a River*. 75 x 96.2 cm. private collection, New York.

Fig. 8 Hieronymus Cock, based on a drawing by Pieter Bruegel, *The Temptation of Christ*. Etching.

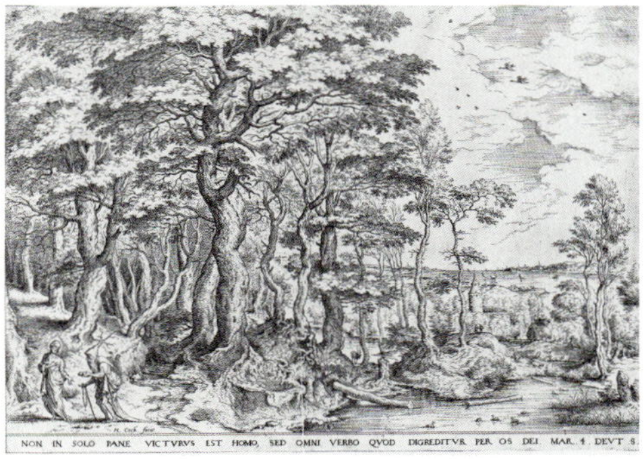

proceedings we know Isaack and his wife were living in grinding poverty when Jacob was born in about 1628 or 1629, and the father's financial affairs remained in a wretched state until his son began to work as an independent artist in 1646. If Isaack sent his young son to Salomon for instruction it is not unreasonable to assume he asked his brother to give the boy free tuition or that Salomon, out of the goodness of his heart, volunteered his services to his nephew who came from an impoverished family.

By the time young Ruisdael began to work on his own a host of astonishingly innovative seventeenth-century Dutch artists had firmly established the tradition of naturalistic landscape painting in the northern Netherlands. Esaias van de Velde and Hendrick Avercamp were the leading pioneers; by the first decades of the century both were producing pictures of an unprecedented freedom and simplicity of setting. Among the outstanding landscapists of the following generation were Jacob's uncle Salomon, Jan van Goyen and Pieter de Molyn. It is not hard to imagine Ruisdael seizing every opportunity to absorb what he could from his predecessors and older contemporaries, but little of what specifically impressed him is patent.

Apart from the impetus he received around the mid-1650s from Allart van Everdingen's Nordic landscapes and, as we shall see, from at least one of his seascapes, Ruisdael's large output offers little satisfaction to hunters of who begat whom. We have already heard that his uncle Salomon's and his father's pictures had a modicum of effect on his early efforts. More conspicuous is his reaction to the tender mood and filagree-like foliage in Cornelis Vroom's poetic wooded landscapes; his adaptation of them is recognizable in pictures done in the 1640s and early 1650s. It also can be shown in a handful of paintings that he was inspired during various phases of his career by landscape schemes invented by Rembrandt, Rubens, Pieter Bruegel and Roelandt Savery (see figs. 3–8; cat. 37, fig. 37a). These were virtually one-time responses to these masters – they hardly occur again.

Among the rare exceptions is Rembrandt – an artist, it seems, who is always an exception. Seventeenth-century Dutch art would certainly be painfully poorer if Rembrandt had not become an artist but its history, as Kenneth Clark observed, would be much tidier if he had followed a different vocation. Reminiscences of Rembrandt's *Three Trees* of 1643 (fig. 4; Bartsch 212), his most famous etched landscape, are evident in Ruisdael's 1648 *Extensive Landscape with Trees* (fig. 3) and his etching of *Three*

Oaks (cat. 108), dated a year later. More intriguing is the connection of Ruisdael's quick black chalk sketch of the *Montelbaanstoren at Amsterdam* (cat. 70) to Rembrandt's powerful reed pen and wash drawing of the structure (fig. 70b). Both depict the late medieval tower without the high, elaborate steeple it acquired in 1606 (see fig. 70a) and which it still has today. More about the two sheets is offered in the commentary to cat. 70.

A crucial part of Ruisdael's way of making landscapes is his astonishingly accurate portrayal of natural phenomena, a quality that has been stressed at least since 1721 when Houbraken's thumbnail account of the artist's life and work in *De Groote Schouburgh* was posthumously published (for its translation see p. 23 below). I was made keenly aware of his amazing power of observation while trying to determine whether three colossal trees in the Norton Simon Foundation's mountainous river landscape were birch or beech trees (S 475). They had been called both in the early literature. My attempt failed. Peter Ashton, Professor of Forestry, Harvard University, and sometime director of Harvard's Arnold Arboretum, solved the problem when asked if the three trees were birches or beeches. After an instantaneous glance at a photo of the painting he responded, 'Neither. The huge tree on the right is unmistakably a beech. The other two are oaks.' Ashton was amazed by the almost incredible accuracy of Ruisdael's portrayal of the trees. Later, he identified other trees and shrubs in his work. Among them were elms, willows, a pruned apple tree and elder shrubs, all found in the Netherlands and all faithfully done.

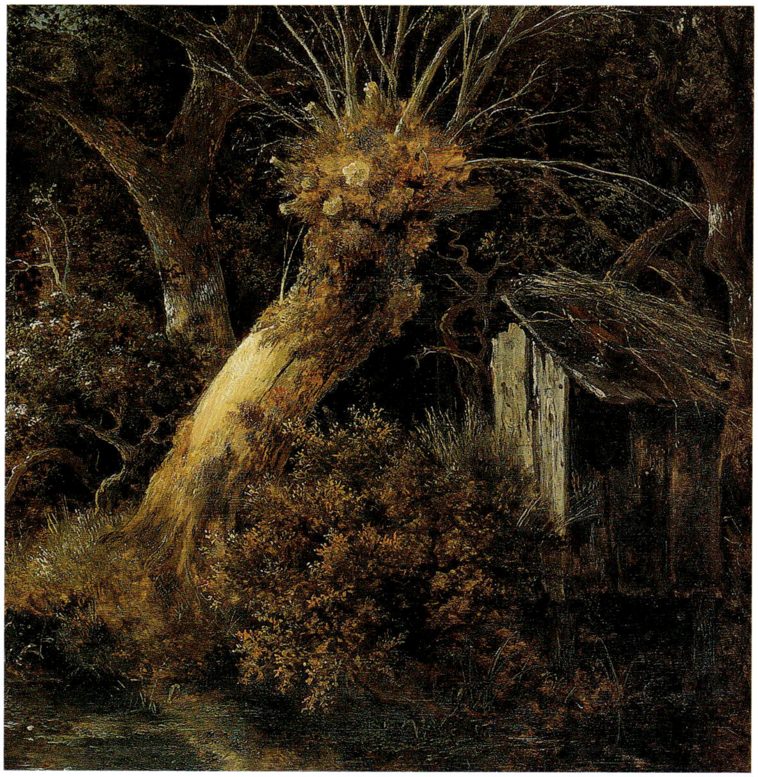

Fig. 9 Jacob van Ruisdael, detail of *Landscape with Cottage and Trees*. Kunsthalle, Hamburg (cat. 1).

Perhaps Ashton's most surprising botanical observation regarding Ruisdael's landscapes is his identification of the small dense shrub with dark foliage and cream-coloured flowers on the bank in the artist's *Dunes by the Sea*, dated 1648 (cat. 9 and fig. 9b). He recognized it as the wayfaring tree, *viburnum lantana*. It belongs to the same family as the elder and is very local to Haarlem. By including it young Jacob observed an exceedingly uncommon plant that the brilliant Swedish botanist Carolus Linnaeus failed to spot when he worked in Haarlem's vicinity during the following century.[7] Ruisdael also portrayed Norway spruces, trees he probably never saw; those that populate his Scandinavian landscapes were derived from Everdingen.[8]

Ashton writes that Ruisdael is the first Western artist to depict a variety of trees and shrubs which are unequivocally recognizable to the botanist on account of his faithful representation of their shape and characteristic growth.[9] His conclusion is beautifully supported by a close view of the blasted pollard willow, oak tree and blooming elder bush in Hamburg's *Landscape with a Cottage and Trees* (fig. 9; see also cat. 1), inscribed 1646, the year, as we have heard, his first dated pictures appear. Judging from the startling accuracy of his portrayal of the trees and thick undergrowth he most probably made careful drawings of the structure and epidermis of individual trees and shrubs, and plants and grasses similar to those by Leonardo and Dürer, and a few more modest ones by his own countrymen, Simon de Vlieger and Aelbert Cuyp (fig. 10). If he did, none have survived.

The total absence of meticulous drawings of various species of trees and close views of plants by Ruisdael is not the only indication that there are huge gaps in our knowledge of his achievement as a draughtsman. It is unarguable that our existing sample of his draughtsmanship (today almost 140 drawings are known) is badly skewed. When we recall that the two themes that occur most frequently in his painted *oeuvre* (it consists of a total of more than 690 paintings) are waterfalls in northern landscapes and woodland scenes, yet only a single drawing of a northern waterfall is known (cat. 90) and only one preliminary drawing for a wooded landscape has been identified (cat. 68). These examples are not unique. There is but a single sketch of a marine and because it is a calm, not an agitated sea, it is uncharacteristic (cat. 64). There are no drawings of mountain scenes, none of winter landscapes and none of Bentheim Castle which he depicted in more than a dozen paintings from various sides and vantage points from at least 1651 until his last years. If these numbers represent a fair account of his output as a draughtsman, it follows that in Ruisdael's case the law of probability has crumbled.

Happily, in a couple of instances, a clutch of drawings of the same motif has survived. Four sketches of the very same overshot water mill seen from different points of view exist. He used them as preparatory studies for four paintings; two are in the exhibition (cat. 74, 75). One or perhaps two drawings also can be related to his *View of Naarden* of 1647 (see cat. 6), his earliest extant painted panoramic view. The painting and at least one of the drawings establish that by the time he was eighteen or nineteen he was a master at depicting vast expanses of distant plains and the towering sky as well as representing nature seen close-up. Variations on the theme of the push and pull of distant and near natural forms remain a passionate preoccupation during the following decades.

Young Ruisdael favoured distant views for his paintings of Egmond aan Zee, a fishing village on the North Sea about thirty-five kilometres northwest of Haarlem. One, which includes a memorable portrait of a blasted elm in the foreground, is dated 1648 (cat. 8); three others are datable about the same time.[10] He also included a distant panoramic view in his glorious *Banks of a River* of 1649 (cat. 12). The vast sky of this six-footer and its mirror-smooth river flanked by mighty trees on one bank and on the other by a bright sandy cove, rolling hills and a road that winds until it is lost in the distance makes it the most imposing landscape he painted before leaving Haarlem a year or two later for a journey to the border area between the eastern United Provinces and Westphalia in western Germany.

The time Ruisdael spent on his trip to the east has been called his *Wanderjahre*. A glance at a map indicates he did not wander very far. As the crow flies, it is only about 175 kilometres from Haarlem to the border region he visited. The journey is not documented; however, ample visual evidence indicates he travelled to the area and explored the surrounding countryside in the early 1650s. It is principally offered by his views of the picturesque castle at Bentheim (see cat. 14–16), a small town in Westphalia about ten kilometres from the Dutch border. The date of 1651 inscribed on his painting (cat. 14) that includes the castle in an imaginary, enchanted forest that could serve as a setting for a tale of chivalrous horsemen *en route* to a fortress where they free a lovely imprisoned princess indicates he must have visited Bentheim by that year. Support for the notion that he most probably travelled with his friend and sometime collaborator Nicolaes Berchem is offered by Berchem's drawing of the castle dated 1650 (fig. 14a). In 1656 Berchem painted two arcadian landscapes that incorporate it from the same viewpoint as his drawing,[11] and Ruisdael painted several that offer a similar view; one is in the exhibition (cat. 15).

Jacob's most impressive painting of the castle is the view now at Dublin, dated 1653 (cat. 16). Four additional paintings dated in the same year are mentioned below. After 1653 he virtually stopped inscribing a year on his efforts; why he ceased a practice he began in 1646 is an unsolved mystery. As for his drawings and etchings, he apparently stopped dating them as early as 1649. Only a few subsequent works can be given more-or-less firm dates on the basis of their partially legible inscriptions or topographical and other probative evidence. Though there is general agreement about the development of his art from the 1650s until his final phase, with so few pegs to establish a chronology, the dates assigned to his production during the last three decades of his life cannot be more than approximate.

Turning again to the magnificent *Bentheim Castle* of 1653, the artist has enlarged Bentheim's unimposing low hill (fig. 16a) into a wooded mountain providing the castle with a commanding position. His invention is a superb expression of his aggrandizement of forms during these years. The spatial clarity is new, as are the strong colors, the energetic brushwork and unification of the close view of a nearly overwhelming wealth of detail with the most distant parts of the landscape into a consistent whole. Some of the vegetation in the foreground is as inventive as the mountain he created for the castle. The distinctive small plants blooming with creamy white flowers on a mound near the centre foreground are unmistakably wayfaring trees. We have heard that the artist showed his familiarity with this plant, found upon occasion in the neighbourhood of Haarlem, in *Dunes by the Sea* of 1648. The rare lime-loving plant does not grow in Bentheim. Apparently Jacob's desire for intense light accents on the foreground mound accounts for its transplantation.

Another motif Ruisdael discovered on his trip to the Dutch-German border region was the water mill. The type of half-timbered overshot and undershot mills he favoured was used in the eastern provinces of the Netherlands and in the area near Bentheim. Of course, earlier artists included water mills in their pictures but he was first to make them the principal theme of a painting. The subject became a specialty of Meindert Hobbema, his only documented pupil, and today, when we think of them, his paintings, not Ruisdael's, come to mind. But in judging their respective accomplishments it should be stressed that Ruisdael

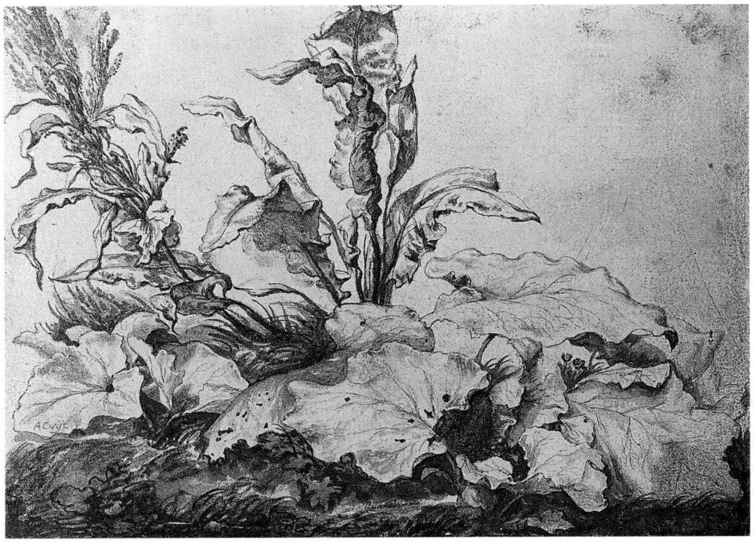

Fig. 10 Aelbert Cuyp, *Study of Leafy Plants (possibly sorrel and butterbur)*. Black chalk, grey wash, touched with red, yellow and green watercolour, heightened with white gum arabic. British Museum, London.

painted powerful ones, such as *Two Water Mills and an Open Sluice*, dated 1653 (cat. 17), at the Getty Museum, with its unmatched cohesion of forms and clear daylight effect, before Hobbema held a brush in his hand.

The distinctive half-timbered construction and vertical plank gable of the conspicuous water mill in the Getty painting is characteristic of Bentheim's vernacular architecture and of buildings in a small area in the western part of Westphalia and in eastern sections of the Netherlands. Conspicuous half-timbered houses of this type are depicted in two of his other pictures dated 1653;[12] they quickly became part of his repertoire and he continued to use them in his landscapes until his last years.

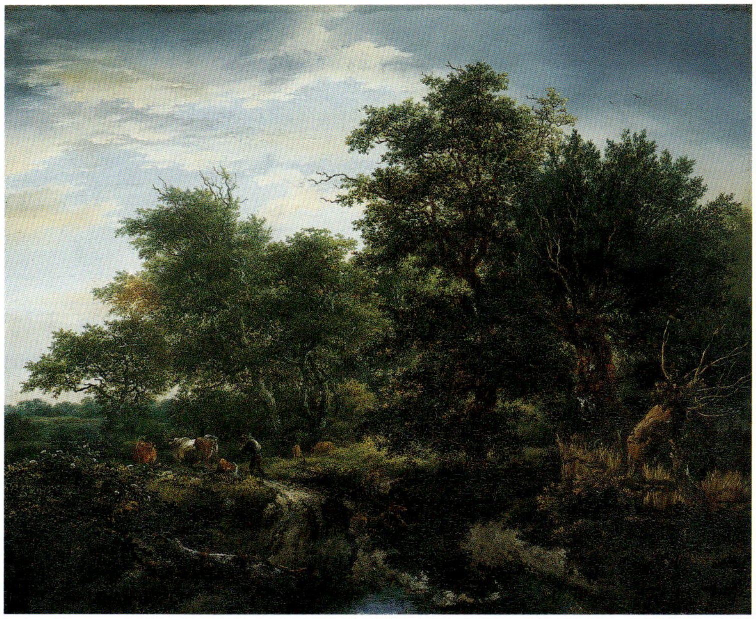

The fifth picture of 1653 is a small *Forest Scene* at the Rijksmuseum, Amsterdam (fig. 11). Its heavy, grainy paint and vivid color give the panel a rich quality but the composition is a bit tangled and rather crowded. Though Ruisdael's tendency in his woodland scenes is to proceed from dense, knotted views to those with greater clarity, the Amsterdam forest is a helpful reminder that deviations in the progression exist. If they did not, the *Great Oak* at Los Angeles (cat. 20), with its spaciousness, would postdate it by a considerable number of years. But it does not. It is dated 1652. The example does not surprise. Like many artists, Ruisdael, now and then, turns to schemes he employed earlier or anticipates a new strain by more than a few years. Cross currents also exist. However, the general development of his grand painted views of woods and dense forests of the 1650s remains clear. He helps untangle his early dense spatial relationships by pushing back masses of trees and stressing large motifs. Sharp light accents are introduced and openings to distant vistas are provided. As in the *Edge of a Forest with a Grainfield*, Worcester College, Oxford (cat. 23), and *Wood with a Flooded Road*, Kunsthistorisches Museum, Vienna (fig. 12; S 437), a new order and stateliness begin to express the nobility and peaceful beauty of forests and woods.

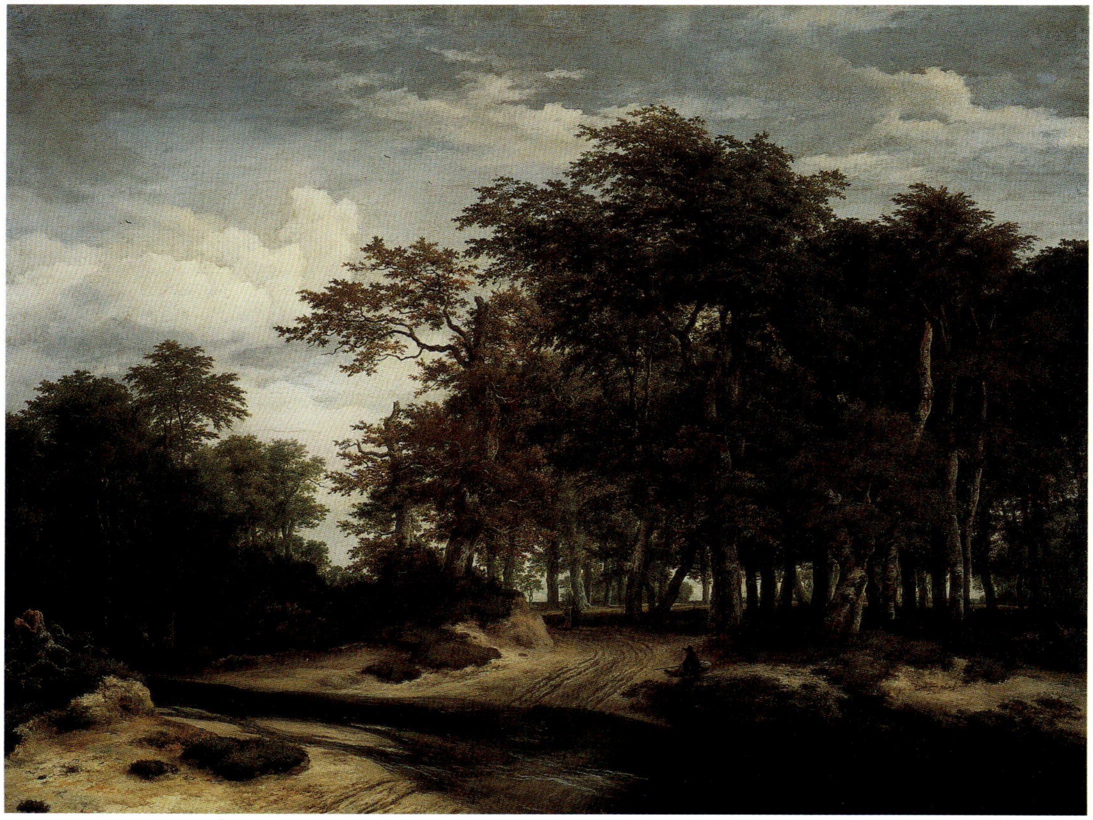

Fig. 11 Jacob van Ruisdael, *Forest Scene*, 1653. 42 x 49 cm. Rijksmuseum, Amsterdam.

Fig. 12 Jacob van Ruisdael, *Wood with a Flooded Road*. 139.5 x 180 cm. Kunsthistorisches Museum, Vienna.

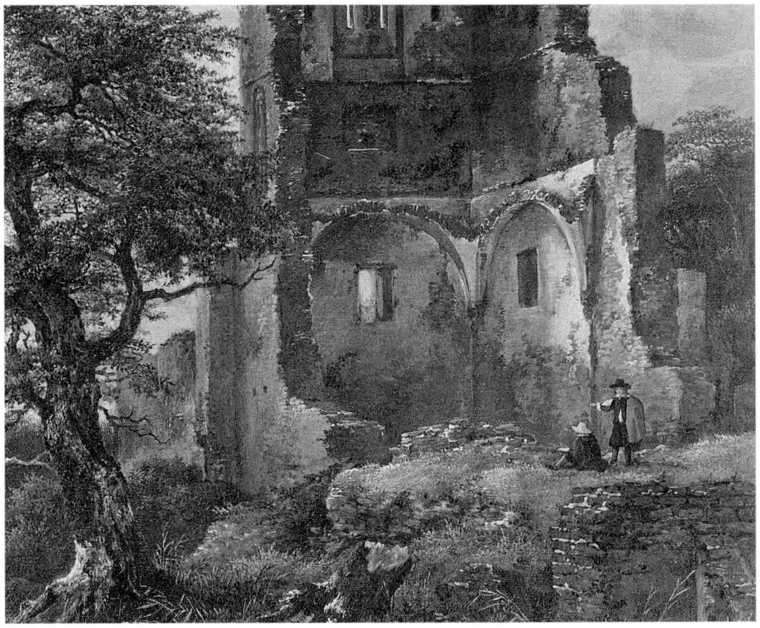

Fig. 13 Jacob van Ruisdael, detail of *Ruins in a Wood*. Formerly Gemäldegalerie, Danzig.

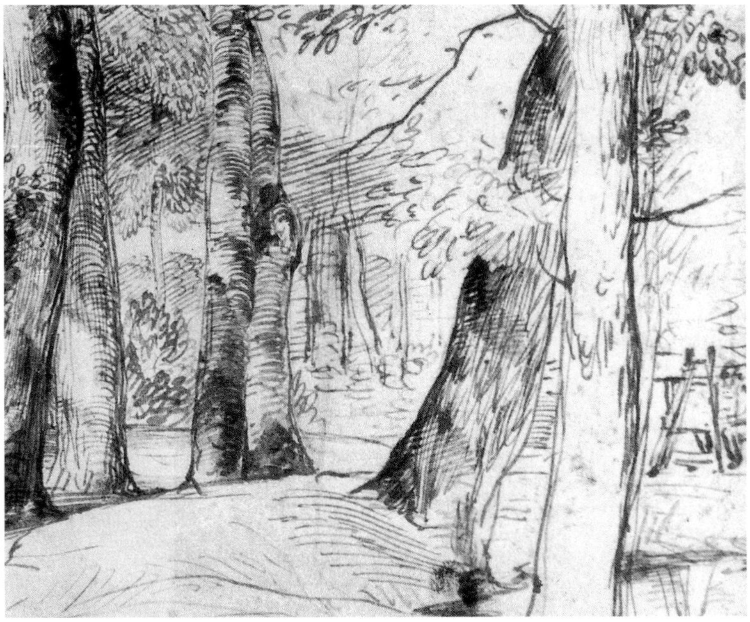

Fig. 14 Jan Lievens, detail of *Wooded Landscape with an Artist Seated at an Easel*. Reed pen on Japanese paper. Städelsches Kunstinstitut, Frankfurt a. M.

Vienna's *Wood* receives boundless praise from the protagonist of *Nachkommenschaften* (*Descendants*), a novella by the popular Austrian author and gifted painter Adelbert Stifter (1805–68):

> There is a landscape in Vienna. A clear stream courses over the loam in the foreground, then there are trees, a little wood, and between the trunks one again sees the open air. The sky has a simple cloud structure. Such scenes have existed in the world more than one hundred million times and yet this landscape is the most powerful and moving that can exist.[13]

Markedly different from the weighty, monumental effects of forest scenes of the 1650s is a group, done in the same decade, of unpretentious, small paintings of plain Dutch scenes. Their subjects are simple motifs: a riverbank and modest cottage (cat. 25), a glimpse of a beach seen from a high dune (cat. 26), or merely the scrubby dunes themselves (cat. 27). They are characterized by a relatively bright palette, a tendency to open up space and often an intensification of light and shadow. Some appear to be hardly modified excerpts of nature done from life. There is, however, no evidence that Ruisdael ever set up his easel outdoors and painted from nature. Following the general practice of seventeenth-century artists, he made drawings, not paintings, *naar het leven* (from life); the former were then used often as studies for landscapes painted in his studio. The depiction of a seated artist drawing a motif in a landscape is not rare in Dutch art of the period. About a half-dozen are known by Ruisdael. A close view of one is illustrated here (fig. 13); a tiny draughtsman also is seen in the lower right foreground of Zurich's superb *View of Haarlem with Bleaching Grounds* (cat. 49). But representations of an artist painting outdoors at an easel are rarities that can be counted on the fingers of one hand; among them is Jan Lievens's vigorous reed pen sketch of the subject[14] (fig. 14); Ruisdael is not among those who left a representation of the theme.

Ruins also begin to find a predominant role in the fifties. Fine examples are Chicago's majestic *Landscape with the Ruins of Egmond Castle* (cat. 18) and a pair of finished drawings at the Rijksmuseum of the same castle's ruins, almost certainly made as autonomous works (cat. 82, 83). Their large forms, emphasis on solid masses and the colorful accents in the painting place them in the first half of the decade. Philadelphia's oil sketch of a *Ruined Entrance Gate of Brederode Castle* (cat. 29) can be grouped with them as well.

Datable to about the mid-fifties are the artist's celebrated version of *The Jewish Cemetery* at Dresden (cat. 22) and the larger, more elaborate one at Detroit (fig. 22a), which include ruins that are part of a deliberate allegorical programme. The combination of their conspicuous ruins, even more conspicuous tombs, large dead beech trees, broken trunks and rushing streams alludes to the familiar themes of transience, the vanity of life and the ultimate futility of all human endeavour. On the other hand, the burst of light that breaks through the ravening clouds in each painting, their rainbows and the luxuriant growth that contrasts with the dead trees offer a promise of hope and new life.

The iconographical programme of Ruisdael's versions of *The Jewish Cemetery* leaves no doubt that they were intended as moralizing landscapes. The artist's unpretentious *Wooded Landscape with a Pond* at Downton Castle (fig. 15) may be another; it includes an

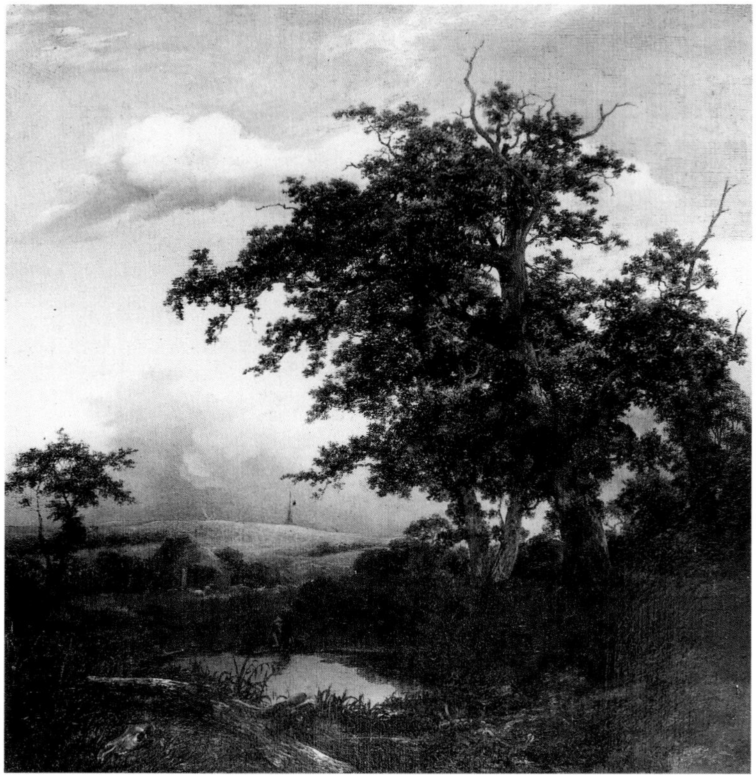

Fig. 15 Jacob van Ruisdael, *Wooded Landscape with a Pond*. 43.2 x 38.1 cm. D. P. H. Lennox, Downton Castle, near Ludlow, Shropshire.

animal skull on one side of its foreground and animal bones on the other. Taken together they possibly refer to the *memento mori* theme – only human skulls and bones are more familiar allusions to the *topos*. If they were indeed intended as references to the transitory character of all life and the inexorable need to prepare for death, to my knowledge, the Downton Castle picture and the two versions of *The Jewish Cemetery* are the only works in Ruisdael's vast *oeuvre* that include overt referential objects of this sort.

He depicts bones in two other landscapes (I cannot cite any others): *The Great Oak* at Los Angeles (cat. 20), in which a few animal bones are scattered at the head of the crossroad just below the mound that supports the monumental tree, and *Wooded Landscape with a Pool and Figures* at Pasadena (S 408), where some bones are on a path that leads to a road. Neither picture includes a skull. In my view there is no reason to call the bones in these landscapes allegorical symbols, nor do I see the crossroads in them as references to two ways of life, one leading to salvation and the other to damnation; nor the broken wheel and goat near the bones in the Pasadena painting as allusions to idleness and lasciviousness. The context in which these elements are found in pictures by other artists may permit such interpretations but, in my opinion, they do not in the Los Angeles and Pasadena paintings. When considering these matters it is salutary to bear in mind Luther's comment on his own foolish youthful tendency to allegorize everything, even chamber pots.[15]

Ruisdael made numerous pictures that include identifiable or imaginary ruins, dead and broken trees, rushing streams, rivers and waterfalls. Were these motifs invariably intended by the artist as symbols of transience and the vanity of life? It has been argued that this is indeed the case, and that these motifs not only offer the iconographical essence of Ruisdael's landscapes but also the key to the meaning of seventeenth-century Dutch landscape painting. According to this interpretation they were intended as visual sermons to convey the biblical message that man lives in a transient world beset by sinful temptation, but may hope for salvation.[16]

Now, there may have been some devout Dutchmen who chose to interpret these motifs as homilies or metaphors for biblical messages, but it is noteworthy that not a single contemporary source indicates that landscape paintings were viewed this way. Equally important, motifs in these landscapes, like those in so many Dutch pictures, can be given different readings. They are not devoid of ambiguities that permit multiple interpretations. Ruins were also included in pictures as parts of topographical views for their historical associations or, as in Ruisdael's *Reconstruction of the Ruins of Kostverloren* (cat. 31), as a painting of a stage of the renewal of an identifiable building. Dead trees juxtaposed to live ones and luxuriant growth have their natural share in an undiluted image of nature.

It strains credulity to breaking point to accept the notion that every river, torrent and waterfall, every ruin and tumbledown cottage, every withered tree in Dutch landscapes is an intentional allusion to transience and the *vanitas* theme, that forests were depicted because they represent the dangerous world through which man must pass before he reaches the goal of eternal life, that every wayfarer in a Dutch landscape is an image of man on the road of life, and, since bridges can be read as symbols of Christ, that every image of a person crossing one must needs allude to man *en route* to salvation. An interpretation of Dutch landscape that admits one and only one reading impoverishes the subject. Additionally, it fails to take into account how skimpy and flimsy is our knowledge of the intentions of Dutch artists. Broad generalizations based on it are correspondingly shaky.

About the time Ruisdael moved from Haarlem and settled in Amsterdam around 1656–57, he began to represent waterfalls and rushing torrents in mountainous northern valleys and they soon became an important theme in his *oeuvre*. Today more than 150 are attributable to him. They form the largest category of his existing paintings. Pictures of forests and woodlands run a very close second; there are almost the same number of this type.

Ruisdael, as we have heard, derived his northern landscapes from Allart van Everdingen's work, not his own firsthand study of the motif. Everdingen travelled to Norway and Sweden in 1644. He was back in Holland by February, 1645, and settled in Haarlem with a stock of Scandinavian themes which he soon incorporated into his paintings and graphic work. His earliest

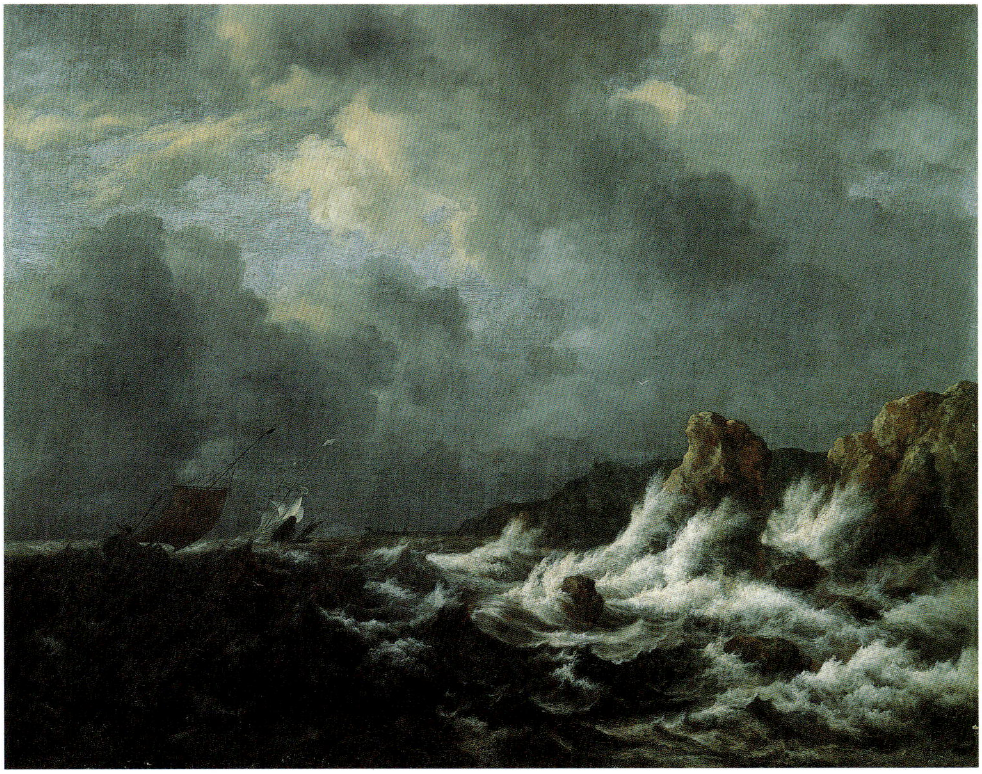

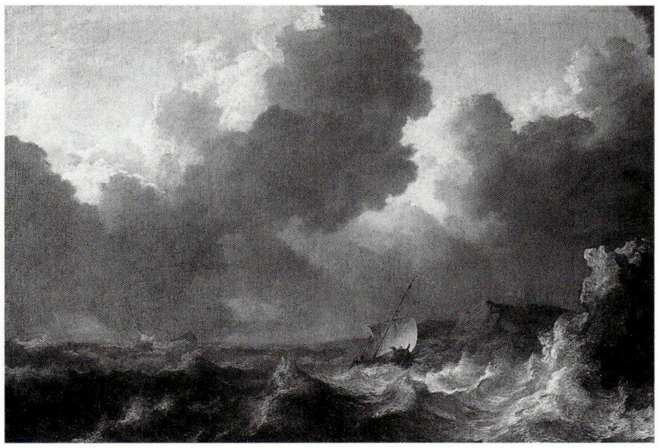

Fig. 17 Allart van Everdingen, *Storm on a Rocky Coast*. 139.3 x 98.4 cm. Städelsches Kunstinstitut, Frankfurt a. M.

Fig. 16 Jacob van Ruisdael, *Rough Sea with Sailing Vessels off a Rocky Coast*. 101 x 123 cm. Foundation Calouste Gulbenkian, Lisbon.

dated painted Nordic waterfall is inscribed 1646, the very year seventeen- or eighteen-year-old Ruisdael appears on the scene in Haarlem. Even before Everdingen moved to Amsterdam in 1652 he had evolved the Nordic landscapes that served as a point of departure for Jacob's paintings of them.[17]

Ruisdael may have had an opportunity to see Everdingen's first Scandinavian pictures when he was an exceptionally active young artist in his native city. If he did, he apparently felt no compulsion whatsoever to add northern landscapes to his stock-in-trade during the first phases of his career. None of his landscapes with waterfalls and torrents are datable to the forties and those that can be placed in the early and mid-fifties do not have a Scandinavian setting. Evidently he only began to use Everdingen's cascading waterfalls in northern scenery in works datable toward the end of the fifties, not long after he, like Everdingen, moved from Haarlem and settled in Amsterdam. It seems a vogue for them in the leading city of the United Provinces, sparked by Everdingen, induced Jacob to devote part of his energy to the subject.

At first he closely followed Everdingen's example by employing rather thin fir trees, an over-abundance of rocky cliffs and fallen trees, and the older artist's somewhat sweet colour harmonies of pinky reds and pale greens. By the mid-sixties he began a series of waterfalls that outstrip even Everdingen's finest Nordic scenes. An outstanding example is at the Fogg Art Museum (cat. 33); others are at Amsterdam (S 139), Braunschweig (S 156, S 157) and Kettwig (S 207). In these works the wide torrents that wildly rush over large boulders are seen close, filling more than the lower third of the paintings. The spaces behind are built high with towering trees, dense masses of rocky wooded hills and precipitous mountainous cliffs surmounted by castles or watchtowers. Although their formats are vertical (his favourite one for Nordic scenes during this period), the height of the landscape and the expanse of the waterfall are in equilibrium. They impress through the variations he achieves by differing the height of the drop of the falls, the direction of the rushing water, the character of the boiling foam, the formation of the rocks and terrain, the variation of colour and the organization of the powerful contrasts of light and dark areas.

Young Ruisdael seems to have been as uninspired by the group of seascapes Everdingen painted during his first phase as he was by Allart's early Nordic landscapes. The total number of marines known by each artist is about twenty. The only existing one by Jacob that shows an unequivocal use of an Everdingen is his *Rough Sea with Sailing Vessels off a Rocky Coast*, Gulbenkian Collection, Lisbon (fig. 16), which is clearly indebted to Allart's *Sailboats in a Storm off a Rocky Coast*, Städelsches Kunstinstitut, Frankfurt a.M. (fig. 17), and a closely related drawing at the Albertina.[18] The Gulbenkian Ruisdael is datable to the 1660s; there is consensus that Everdingen's painting and drawing were done in the 1640s.

A familiar word of caution is called for: not one seascape by Ruisdael is dated and only two by Everdingen bear dates, one inscribed 1640, the other 1643.[19] The reasoning that accounts for

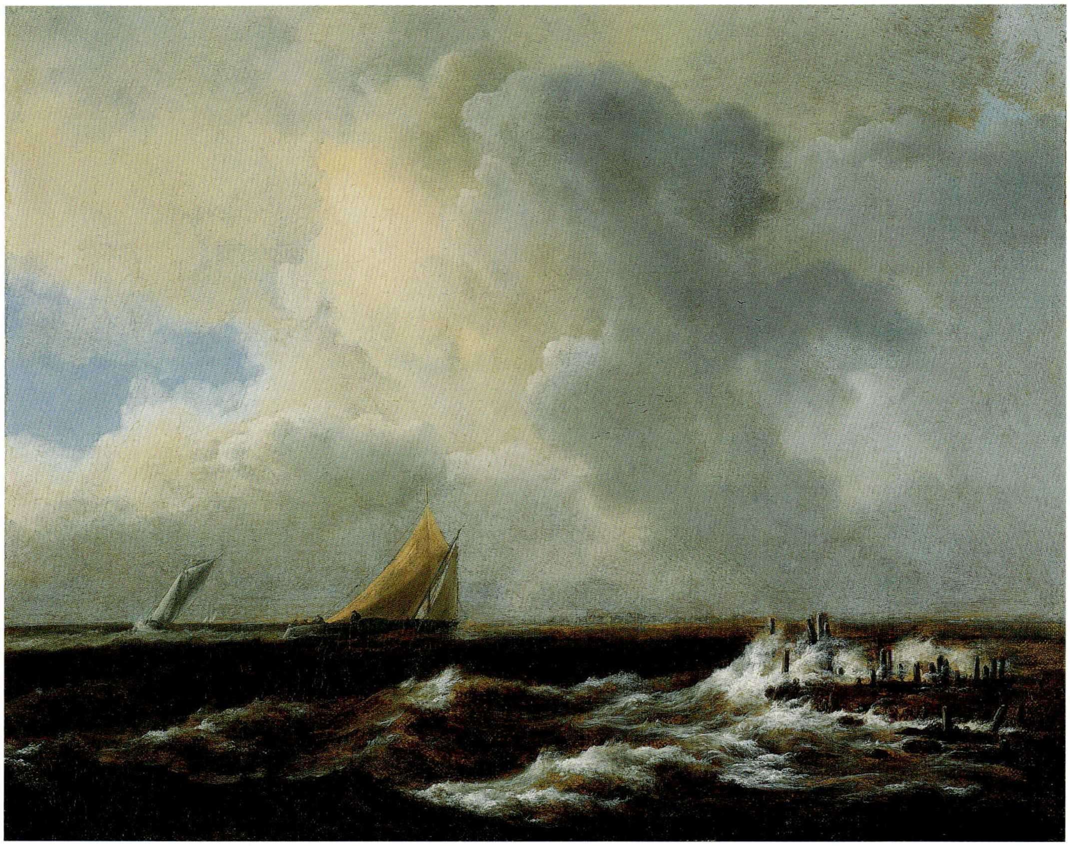

Fig. 18 Jacob van Ruisdael, *Sailing Vessels in a Fresh Breeze*. 44.5 x 54.6 cm. The National Gallery, London.

the chronology offered here for Ruisdael's treatment of the theme is based on the hypothesis that his marines at the Netherlands Institute for Cultural Heritage, Amsterdam (S 646), and at Stockholm (S 657) were done in the late forties or a few years later because of their unmistakable connection to the epoch-making, mature seascapes by Jan Porcellis, the leading marine painter of an earlier generation, and his follower Simon de Vlieger. In my view, they are not at all indebted to Everdingen's marines. Not long afterward, I propose, Jacob evolved a personal scheme he often employed during the course of the following decades. It consists of a high sky filled with clouds that tower over a relatively narrow band devoted to an expanse of agitated sea affected by winds that range from fresh to almost gale force; in the foreground waves either play or pound against rocks, pilings, a jetty or wharf that projects from one side of the painting. Sailing vessels are seldom overly prominent and are confined to the middle and far distance. The scheme is used for a marine in the National Gallery, London (fig. 18); the marked absence of fine gradations in the dark areas makes the contrast between its dark and light areas of water rather sharp while limiting the spatial effect, suggesting that it is probably one of the earliest existing paintings of the type. Perhaps it was painted in the early or mid-fifties. A variant on the arrangement introduces a wharf, jetty or spit of land in the foremost part of the painting. Fort Worth's *Rough Sea at a Jetty* (cat. 24) is the most impressive work that uses this scheme. Its highly dramatic effects, strong contrasts of ominous darks and brilliant light, and limited palette suggest this masterwork was done in the mid-fifties.

The relative chronology offered here assumes there is greater restraint in the use of deep darks in seascapes datable to the late fifties and sixties; in them gusts of fresh silvery air seem to bind water and sky. It is also assumed that a richer variety of contrasts and more subtle differentiation of points of reference from the foreground to the far distance characterizes marines of the 1670s (see cat. 51).

A document that offers a rare glimpse of Ruisdael's activities apart from his own practice focuses upon an alleged beachscape by Jan Porcellis, whose relation to Jacob's earliest known marines has been mentioned. It tells us that Ruisdael was one of four painters who gave opinions before a notary in Amsterdam on 9 June 1661 regarding the authenticity of a beachscape with cliffs and figures that had been attributed to Porcellis (at this hearing Jacob testified he was thirty-two years old, thereby providing the one and only source for the year of his birth). The other artists were the little-known Barent Kleeneknecht, Allart van Everdingen and Willem Kalf whose reputation as a leading Amsterdam painter of exquisite still lifes was already secure. Ruisdael's pupil Meindert Hobbema signed the document as one of the witnesses. Kleeneknecht declared that probably almost the entire picture was painted by Hendrick van Anthonissen, pupil and brother-in-law of Porcellis. Everdingen maintained that Porcellis, at most, had done something to the cliffs. Kalf was more negative; he concluded it had nothing to do with Porcellis's paintings, either in detail or in general. In Ruisdael's opinion Porcellis had perhaps begun it, but in its present condition it must not be sold as his work.[20]

The alleged Porcellis obviously was not borderline. However, there was no agreement regarding an alternative conclusion. To people of our time who attempt to determine the authorship of Dutch paintings done almost four centuries ago, the case is humbling. What are our chances of finding definitive attributions for marginal works if four expert witnesses, who had knowledge of the art scene of their time which we can never match, fail to find one? However, a measure of comfort can be taken in the affair. It is consoling to learn that experts of the period shared our frequent inability to give firm names to substandard pictures.

Among the artist's most personal creations are his forest scenes of the 1660s. Clearings and open vistas combined in varying degrees with large-scale forms and massive trees no longer virtually sealing off middle ground and distant views are now found. The Hermitage's majestic *Marsh* (cat. 37) is a high point of this new trend. Only one of Ruisdael's forest scenes of its type is dated, and its date is only partially visible. It is the *Wooded Landscape with a Pond* (fig. 37b; S 393), which is inscribed: 166[?]. This supports the date in the 1660s given to Jacob's forest paintings which join powerful forms seen close-up with open spaces.[21] While mindful that experimentation must be taken into account when considering an artist of Ruisdael's originality, it is nevertheless reasonable to propose that his forest scenes with more open compositions were done later in the decade than those that stress their massiveness.

The magnificent *Stag Hunt* at Dresden (cat. 38) is a woodland scene datable late in the decade. Here Ruisdael creates a vast expanse of space by filling the entire front plane with a smooth, broad marsh virtually devoid of luxuriant growth, lifting the powerful beeches out of the context of the forest, and, not least, placing large middle-ground forms against tangible distant views. In contrast to his earlier wooded landscapes we now see further into the picture, higher up and more around the volume of individual trees. The differentiation between light and shadow also is heightened and richer, particularly in the touches of sparkling, silvery white on the giant dead beech seen against the bronze-brown and deep-green background of the trees and in the strong pulse of light in the distant vistas and on the marsh and low hill.

Not long after Ruisdael painted Dresden's *Stag Hunt* he created the *Windmill at Wijk bij Duurstede*, his most celebrated picture (cat. 39). It is appropriate that a windmill, the best known symbol of the Dutch landscape, should be its subject but to judge from the small number of times the artist made a mill a major accent in his paintings, he was not particularly partial to the motif. Only about ten are known today. Apart from the *Mill at*

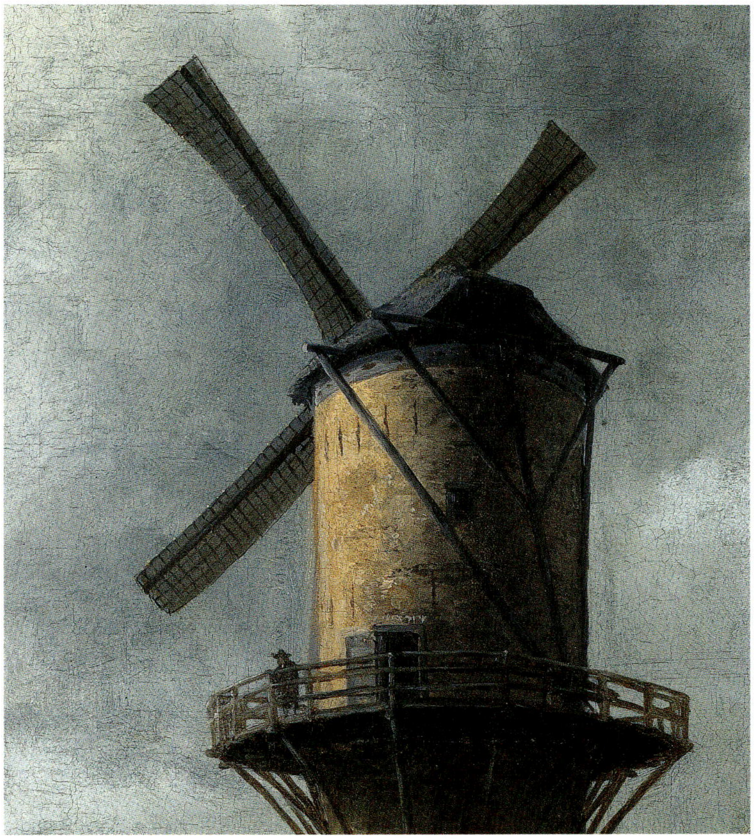

Fig. 19 Jacob van Ruisdael, detail of *Windmill at Wijk bij Durstede*, Rijksmuseum, Amsterdam (cat. 39).

Wijk, all are datable to the first ten or twelve years of his activity. None of them even hint at what he achieved in his classical pronouncement on the subject. Mysterious? Not at all. Artists of great creative power are capable of reaching a towering height without leaving a trace of the path they followed to reach it.

As so often occurs in the artist's work, the masterful pictorial organization of the *Mill at Wijk* is coupled with scrupulous attention to natural phenomena. An expert oceanographer has observed that in the foreground Ruisdael depicted crossing wave fronts, indicating two independent wave sources; this is the kind of detail normally caught by hydrologists, not artists.[22] The phenomenon Ruisdael records in the painting could be the result of the Lek River and the Crooked (Kromme) Rhine merging at Wijk bij Duurstede or by pilings along the shore. Here the artist was equally attentive to man-made contrivances, as can be seen in a detail view of the windmill (fig. 19). In his time, there could have been few Dutchmen who did not know that the vanes of a windmill move counterclockwise: Hence, when spars were used, they were either placed in the middle of the frames of the vanes or forward toward their leading edges. If placed aft they produced vibration – too much vibration could be catastrophic.[23] The close view of Ruisdael's mill shows the spars in an usable position, forward toward the vanes' leading edges. According to an historian of the aerodynamics of windmills who is also an aeronautic engineer, it shows more: to his knowledge, it is the earliest existing representation of a spar at quarter-chord, a position that seventeenth-century windmill makers happily found by trial and error, and which modern engineers have established is near the vane's (or rotor's) aerodynamic centre, its best position.[24]

On one level the *Mill at Wijk* is accessible to everyone as a characteristic scene of the Dutch countryside. For the notion that it may have had another meaning for some of the artist's contemporaries, see cat. 39, and for the possibility that the great mill's owner may have commissioned the picture as a portrait of his prize possession see p. 19 below.

During the second half of the 1660s and early 1670s Ruisdael painted a group of waterfalls in a large horizontal format. The most magnificent one in a heroic Scandinavian setting is in a private collection, Scotland (cat. 34). In others the scene shifts to a more temperate zone. Giant boulders still occur in their foregrounds but they no longer include stately firs and spruces, and towering heights do not prevail over breadth. The countryside has become flatter and long, open vistas create an effect of great distance. Despite the relatively low terrains, the waterfalls retain their force and power as their rushing movement and the froth of their lower torrents decisively broaden the view. A splendid painting exemplifying this new development is the Rijksmuseum's *Waterfall near an Oak Wood* (cat. 35), the artist's largest waterfall.

Datable to his full maturity are extraordinary imaginary mountain views as well as scenes of the Netherlands in its various aspects, particularly vast fertile plains, the sea and the shore, and all are viewed under majestic skies. Winter landscapes and panoramas of Amsterdam and the plains of Haarlem, with its bleaching grounds, also are important subjects.

An unmistakable prophecy of the effects of the artist's mature extensive, flat landscapes is offered by *View of Naarden*, dated 1647 (cat. 6), merely a year after he makes his first documented appearance in Haarlem. It and a panoramic view of an unidentified distant town dated 1648 (fig. 3) are the only paintings of the type that bear dates but it is evident that other antecedents for his classic panoramas are found in dunescapes done in the early or mid-1650s and in grainfields with skies that have yet to attain a full degree of height and openness, which are datable to the fifties as well.

To judge from his existing paintings, it was in the 1660s that Ruisdael began to create panoramas of the distinctive extensive skyline of Haarlem, its nearby plains and bleaching grounds, works now widely accepted as the most characteristic views of the Dutch countryside. Put another way, Ruisdael began to use his native town as a subject only after he left it and settled in Amsterdam about 1656 or 1657. Two bits of documentary evidence help support this supposition. An inventory reference to a painting of Haarlem by Ruisdael is found in a list compiled in Amsterdam in 1664 and another inventory complied in the same city in 1669 makes reference to a *Haerlempje* (little view of Haarlem) by Ruisdael.[25]

There is no way of determining whether the small, exceptionally well-preserved *View of Haarlem with Bleaching Grounds* (cat. 46) was the painting of the city listed in the 1664 or 1669 inventory, but it qualifies as a candidate because it is datable to the first half of the 1660s on the basis of its emphatic horizontal layout, the relative lack of articulation into depth on the left side of the picture and, not least, the thick, grainy paint. Ruisdael has taken more than usual delight in the patterns created on the bleaching grounds by the long strips and smaller pieces of linen. The bleachery depicted is De Mol near Bloemendaal, a village that lies northwest of Haarlem; another view of the same bleachery from a different vantage-point is seen in cat. 47.[26] In the distance to the left, the roof and two chimneys of the country house Hartelust can be discerned. It was built by Michiel de Wael who owned the bleaching fields around it from 1631 to 1652; de Wael was portrayed in about 1627 by Frans Hals (fig. 47a) as a captain flushed by drink and bursting with energy in a group portrait of Haarlem civic guards celebrating at a banquet.[27]

Frans Hals also made a portrait of Lucas de Clercq (fig. 48a) while he owned the bleachery depicted in the foreground of the *View of Haarlem with Bleaching Fields* at the Mauritshuis (cat. 48).[28] The pitched roof and two chimneys of the house in the right middle ground of the painting belonged to Huis Clercq en Beeck, a manor Lucas de Clercq owned with his brother-in-law Lucas van Beeck. The Mauritshuis picture is datable to about 1670–75, when Ruisdael produced his classic *Haarlempjes*; other outstanding examples are at Amsterdam, Berlin and Zurich.

The Zurich painting (cat. 49) can serve as a paradigm of the group. Its sky, as those in many of them, takes up more than two-thirds of the canvas. Here the impression of height is increased by the pronounced vertical format, and even more by the dominant part the towering clouds play in the awe-inspiring aerial zone. The prospect of Haarlem's broad plain is seen from a more distant and elevated viewpoint than in the earlier examples. As a result there is a reduction both in scale and overlappings of cottages, rich woods and tracts of land. The eye can explore the extensive bleaching fields and vast expanse of land richly differentiated by gradations of alternating bands of light and shadow into the distance toward the view of the city on the horizon dominated by St Bavo, its great church. Viewers familiar with the city would have readily recognized, from left to right, Haarlem's Bakenesse Church, St John Church, Clock Tower, Town Hall and New Church.

The same viewers would also have recognized whether some of Ruisdael's panoramas show Haarlem's countryside and bleaching fields as seen from the range of dunes which served as a natural dike protecting Haarlem from the North Sea, from the northwest, west or southwest of the city. We have heard that specific bleacheries and houses are identifiable in a few *Haarlempjes*, while others are not exact representations of particular prospects. Bird's-eye views, for example, could never have been seen from any vantage points near Haarlem. In addition, the artist occasionally invents or takes considerable liberties with the buildings depicted in these paintings.

Ruisdael's *Haarlempjes* made an impression on his contemporary Jan Vermeer II van Haarlem, and a deeper one upon his younger, frequent follower, Jan van Kessel, who was possibly his pupil. Vermeer van Haarlem painted six or eight that belong to the category; one is helpfully dated 1675.[29] Kessel produced about a half-dozen paintings that include bleaching grounds and a distant view of Haarlem and around another six that concentrate on bleacheries without a view of the urban centre.

Haarlem's bleaching industry was inextricably linked to its linen industry. Both originated in the late fifteenth century and both gained enormously in scale and international importance from the large wave of skilled Flemish bleachers, linen manufacturers and merchants who fled from their homeland and settled in the city after the fall of Antwerp to the Spanish in 1585. The dune region in the neighbourhood was ideally suited for bleaching. Its ample supply of clear spring water that emerged at the foot of the area's young dunes furnished the needed water – it also was the water used for brewing Haarlem's famous beer. Equally important, Holland's rich dairy farms, which did not process the buttermilk they produced in their operations but considered it waste, offered bleacheries a ready, near-by supply of the millions of litres of buttermilk needed to produce 'Haarlem Bleach', a term regarded from the late sixteenth until the early nineteenth century (when chemical discoveries destroyed the old industry completely) as being epithetic of the best that could be achieved in the way of refining processes for yarn and linen fabrics.[30]

In her fundamental history of the industry Regtdoorzee Greup-Roldanus notes that its outward appearance did not appeal only to artists.[31] She cites references to the bleaching fields in poems by Karel van Mander, Hendrick Laurensz Spiegel and Elisabeth Koolaart. Samuel Ampzing rhapsodizes about the bleacheries in his descriptive history of the city published in 1628. Haarlem's visitors made special trips to its environs to see the wondrous sight of long white linen strips on the fresh green meadows, just as tourists in our time make pilgrimages to view Holland's celebrated tulip fields which now occupy the very grounds that formerly supported the bleacheries.

There is a record of a son and daughter-in-law of Joan Wolfert van Brederode, the highest ranking military officer of the new republic after the death of Willem II, visiting the bleaching grounds in 1659, and in the early summer of the following year young Willem III, the Prince of Orange, later King William III of England, and his mother Mary Stuart, the widowed princess, viewed them. A contemporary chronicler, who wrote a detailed account of their five-day visit to Haarlem, informs us that they were escorted to the environs of the city to see the 'pleasurable

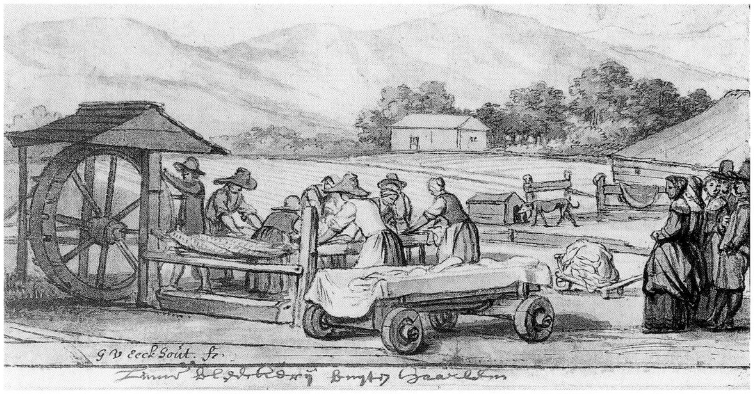

Fig. 20 Gerbrand van der Eckhout, *Linen Bleachery outside Haarlem.* Watercolour, over black chalk, touches of pen, brown ink, brush, black ink. Rijksprentenkabinet, Amsterdam.

sight of the bleacheries'.[32] Haarlem's most important industry understandably was not part of their itinerary – the chronicler makes no reference to a visit by the princess and the ten-year-old prince to one of Haarlem's breweries. As a fitting complement to the visit of the prince and princess, the city fathers gave them a large set of fine Haarlem table linen. The gift included seventy-six napkins and three table cloths; the largest of the latter measured *c.*280 by 630 cm, suitable for a table set for about fifty guests.[33] If the relative chronology offered here for Ruisdael's *Haarlempjes* is correct, the city's officials would have been unable to offer their distinguished visitors one of Ruisdael's views of Haarlem and its bleaching grounds in 1660 as another souvenir of their visit; he did not begin to produce them until a bit later in the decade.

Contemporary sources report that city folk enjoyed Sunday excursions to see the bleaching grounds.[34] Although Gerbrand van den Eeckhout does not tell us if the signed watercolour he inscribed 'Linen bleachery outside Haarlem' (*Linne bleeckerij buiten Haarlem*) was made on a Sunday, there is no doubt that the fashionably dressed women and their companions taking a close look at working bleachers in it are excursionists (fig. 20).

In light of the wider public's interest in the spectacle of Haarlem and its bleacheries, some of Ruisdael's *Haarlempjes* and those by Kessel and Vermeer van Haarlem were probably made for the tourist trade. It also seems reasonable to assume that Haarlemers who took pride in their city and an industry that brought it wealth and fame bought views of the city's bleacheries. However, inventories of paintings compiled in Haarlem from Ruisdael's day until 1740 do not support this notion; not one is listed in inventories which have been examined (see pp. 19–20 below).

During the seventeenth century numerous Dutch artists were portraying other cities and towns of the Netherlands, particularly Dordrecht and its environs and Rhenen, whose skyline dominated by St. Cunera's elegant late Gothic tower made it a special

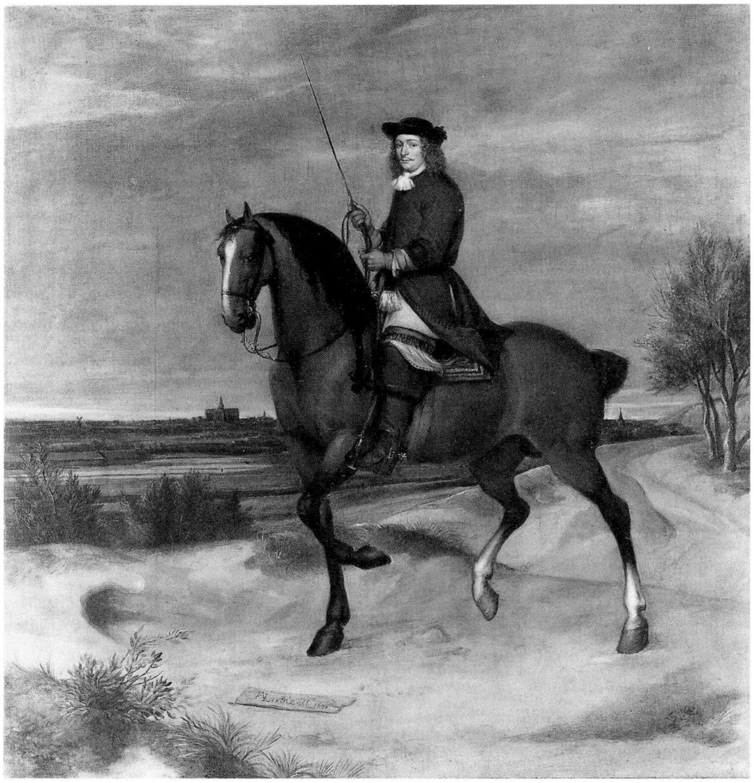

Fig. 21 Jan Andrea Lievens, *Equestrian Portrait of Dirck Decker in the Dunes with a View of Bleaching Grounds and Haarlem*, 1671. 137.8 x 131.4 cm. Fitzwilliam Museum, Cambridge.

favourite;[35] for Ruisdael's beautiful brush drawings of Rhenen at St Petersburg and Berlin see cat. 71, 72. Some of these views were also most likely made for the tourist trade as well as local markets. The greatest demand was understandably for paintings and prints of Amsterdam. Ruisdael himself helped satisfy the vigorous, long-lived craze for both paintings and prints of the new republic's leading metropolis that began again about 1660 after the hiatus that followed the first burst of interest in views of the new nation's towns and its countryside during the early decades of the century (see cat. 57, 58, 86). In 1670 prints were made after Ruisdael's topographical drawings of the *Portuguese-Jewish Cemetery at Ouderkerk*, a site to which John Evelyn dashed during his brief visit to Amsterdam in 1641 (see cat. 79, 80). During these decades, the very decades that Ruisdael and his followers painted their *Haarlempjes*, there is little indication that printmakers and their publishers had a market, or attempted to generate one, for prints of Haarlem and its bleacheries. The fact that none of their paintings or drawings of the subject were reproduced by contemporary printmakers indicates that popular demand for them was not brisk.

Workers in the bleaching fields, whose miserable average weekly wage ranged between Dfl.1½ and Dfl.4, hardly could have been prospective customers for inexpensive prints of the grounds, not to mention paintings of them. But proprietors of the bleacheries and linen merchants, who often owned bleaching fields, and traded in yarn and ash as well, can be considered likely potential clients for the paintings of the motif done by Ruisdael and his followers. Here a question arises: were any of these artists' pictures commissioned specifically by owners as portraits of their own grounds? Commissioned landscapes of estates are uncommon in seventeenth-century Dutch art but they do occur; one by Ruisdael and inventory references to other untraceable ones he painted are discussed on pp. 17, 18, and 29, note 9 below. Although the reappearance of the same manors, cottages, sheds and parcels of land in more than one of the bleaching ground paintings indicates that a few were derived from specific sites and, as we have heard, the sometime owners of two of them (Lucas de Clercq and Michiel de Wael) have been identified, no evidence corroborates that any were done to order as portrayals of individual properties.

There is, however, a painting which may be a viable contender for the distinction of being a commissioned portrait of a specific bleaching field with an unmistakable depiction of Haarlem in the background. It is Jan Andrea Lievens's *Equestrian Portrait of Dirck Decker*, signed and dated 1671 (fig. 21). Dirck Decker was born in 1644 (or perhaps 1642), probably at Bloemendaal where his father Cornelis was a bleacher. Though it cannot be proved, it is reasonably likely that Jan Andrea depicted elegant Dirck riding in the dunes with a view of his family's bleaching grounds at Bloemendaal behind him.[36]

Ruisdael's views of Haarlem with bleaching grounds have not been ignored by people searching for meanings in Dutch landscape painting which, they contend, were patent to seventeenth-century Dutchmen but are overlooked or remain hidden to modern viewers until they are signalled. For example, it has been noted that in seventeenth-century emblem books references to bleaching, accompanied by references to biblical passages, could refer to the purity of the soul, which is God's gift. Thus, the argument continues, in a *Haarlempje*, such as the one at The Hague (cat. 48) where the bleaching ground receives great emphasis, Ruisdael's intent is to extol the soul's purity.[37] Unless one is prepared to read the picture as a painted emblem, which I am unable to do, this proposal must be rejected. The painting's emblematic reading can also be rejected because a symbolic interpretation demands that all the picture's principal elements be considered. Since the view of Haarlem on the horizon is as important in The Hague painting as the bleaching fields, the emblematic reference cannot allude only to the soul's purity but must be extended to the purity of the city of Haarlem itself, a proposition there is no reason to believe that Ruisdael or his contemporaries would have been prepared to propose or defend.[38]

In 1672, just about the time Ruisdael was creating his grandiose *Haarlempjes* and Kessel and Vermeer van Haarlem were following his lead, and a year after Jan Andrea Lievens painted Dirck Decker as a fashionable horseman *cum* bleaching fields and

Haarlem, a country seat in the dune region of the city was offered at auction. As a special recommendation it was advertised as having a beautiful view of bleaching fields,[39] a reminder that it is not anachronistic to credit a seventeenth-century Dutchman with urging his countrymen to enjoy a dune with a view without reference to pride in a local industry, a man's patrimony, emblematic or religious meanings.

During Ruisdael's final decade the pastoral effect that characterizes a considerable number of the artist's works of these years also affects his treatment of waterfalls, a subject that hardly seems to lend itself to the new tendency. In these late works the falls do not become insignificant, but they are subdued, not least by the gentle beginning of their drop from broad, quiet rivers or pools. The crushing heights of the earlier waterfalls have been eliminated. Hills are levelled almost to horizontals imbuing views with a soothing sense of breadth, while a delicate treatment of trees often seen against the pinks and delicate blues of an evening sky add to the effect of peace and quiet. There must have been a good market for the idyllic mood of these works since there is a sizable number of them. Among the best is Berlin's *Waterfall with a Wooded Hill* (fig. 22; S 150), which is still on its original, unlined canvas secured to its original seventeenth-century stretcher – a rare, happy circumstance.

Wooded landscapes become even more open in their spatial setting during Jacob's final phase. Trees become thinner and lighting more diffuse. It is customary to speak of a decline in Jacob's power during these years. To be sure, when works of this phase are juxtaposed to the imposing forest scenes done a decade earlier there is an unmistakable lessening of grandeur. However, they gain a pastoral intimacy and many attain a new poetic quality.

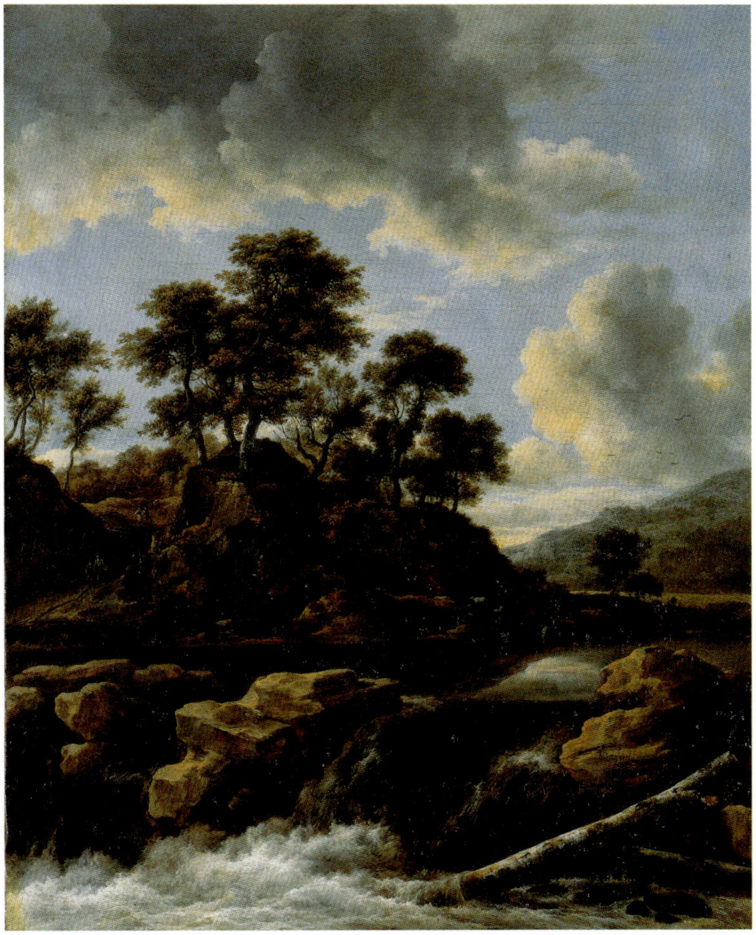

Fig. 22 Jacob van Ruisdael, *Waterfall with a Wooded Hill*. 69 x 53 cm. Staatliche Museen, Gemäldegalerie, Berlin.

Ruisdael died in Amsterdam probably on or about 10 March 1682.[40] His body was sent to Haarlem, where a grave was opened for it on 14 March at St Bavo,[41] the great church that invariably appears on the horizon in his extensive panoramic view of the skyline of his native city. When he died he had reached the age of fifty-four or fifty-five. Not a letter he wrote or a note he scribbled during the course of his life has been found, nor has any correspondence directed to him been discovered. To our knowledge he did not keep a diary or a daybook – would that he had. Neither a self-portrait nor portrait of him has surfaced. However, there can be no doubt that he was very productive as a landscapist. Today the grand total of his known painted, drawn and etched landscapes numbers more than eight hundred. But he did not die rich. His name does not appear in the register of death duties listed by Amsterdam's authorities upon the estate of a citizen who died, as he did, without direct descendents. Its absence indicates he did not possess real estate or securities at the time of his death. Not a single record of the payment he received for any of his works has been discovered. As indicated in the following essay, the scant existing data regarding appraisals given during his lifetime to his paintings cited in inventories shows they were valued on the low side. Yet it seems safe to say he earned his bread until the end. He earned enough to be assessed the special '200th penny tax' the city levied on its citizens in 1674 to help pay for the costly war that drove Louis XIV from the gates of Amsterdam in 1672. The tax of ½ % was demanded only from citizens whose effects were worth more than 1,000 guilders. Jacob paid ten guilders, indicating that his possessions were appraised at 2,000 guilders.[42]

As late as 1678 he had enough money on hand to lend 400 guilders to Dr Jan Baptist van Lamsweerde, physician at an Amsterdam orphanage for girls (Maagdenhuis). His debtor proved to be a bad risk. On 21 January 1682, less than two months before his own death, Ruisdael brought suit in Amsterdam against the doctor and had him distrained of his goods because he had not paid the required interest. To his half-sister Maria the artist bequeathed the note of debt as a legacy in the form of a letter of credit for which she was paid 150 guilders.[43]

To us Ruisdael bequeathed his precious landscapes. The intent here is to show their unrivalled range and quality.

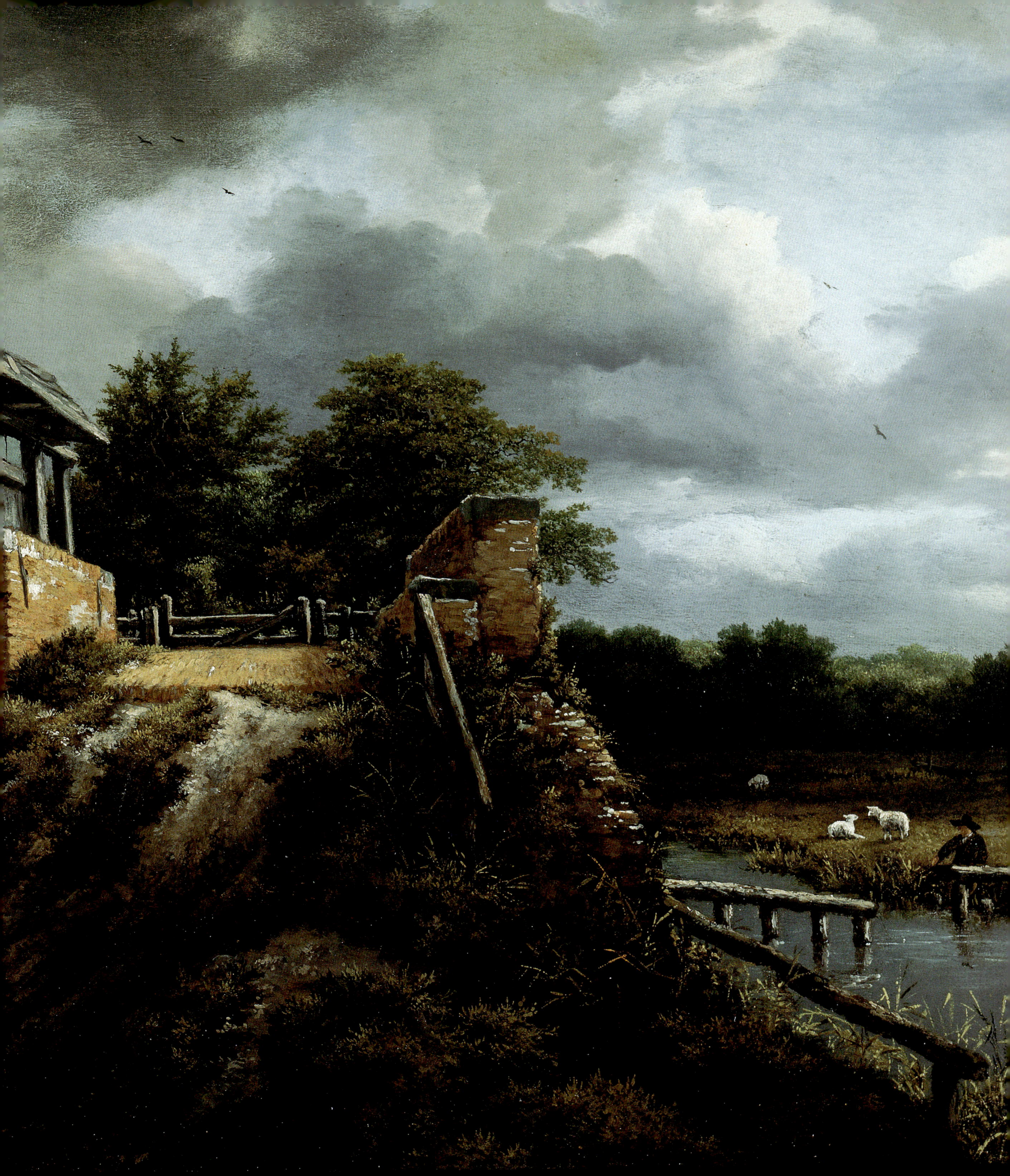

2 Ruisdael's Clientele, Early Collectors and Critics

Ruisdael's clientele and early reception by collectors and critics do not offer a clue that in our time he would be given an unshakeable place, by common consent, as the pre-eminent landscapist of the heroic age of Dutch painting. Nothing whatsoever has been discovered about what his contemporaries thought of his work or the way his clients acquired the more than eight hundred landscapes he created. We can guess if he kept a stock on hand to sell directly to customers or worked through dealers – of course there is no reason to maintain he did not do both.

The ground is a only wee bit firmer when we consider his commissions. The name of one patron is known. He was the extremely wealthy and powerful Amsterdam burgomaster Cornelis de Graeff (1599–1664), Lord van Zuidpoelsbroek, Pumerland and Ilpendam. Ruisdael's effort for him can be spotted in the National Gallery of Ireland's painting of de Graeff and members of his family arriving at Soestdijk, his country estate about fifteen kilometres from Utrecht (fig. 23).[1] The picture, however, is not solely by Ruisdael. It is a collaborative effort between him and Thomas de Keyser (1586/7–1667), the leading Amsterdam portraitist before Rembrandt arrived there in the early 1630s. De Keyser did the lion's share of the group portrait which qualifies as an early example of a conversation piece: the characteristic small-scale, highly finished figures, the richly appointed carriage, the horses and prominent dogs who have had as much care lavished on their portraits as those of their masters. Ruisdael was responsible for the landscape and the portrait of the country house in the background.[2] The ages of the family members portrayed as well as the style of the figures and landscape date the picture about 1660, three or four years after Ruisdael moved from his native Haarlem and settled in the principal metropolis of the Netherlands.

De Graeff played a key role in his city's and the new republic's politics. Indeed, during the last decades of his life he was the guiding political force in Amsterdam and the close advisor and confidant of Johan de Witt, Holland's leading statesman; but no attention is called to these aspects of his life in the artists' joint effort.

In 1660, about the time the picture was painted, Joost van den Vondel, the foremost seventeenth-century Dutch poet, published his verse translation of Virgil's *Aeneid* which he dedicated to de Graeff. In *Parnasloof*, the work's dedicatory poem, Vondel wrote that de Graeff sought welcome relaxation in Soestdijk's bucolic setting after slaving day and night at the service of his city and country in the burgomasters' chamber of Amsterdam's town hall.[3] De Graeff must have felt equally at home in the glorious New Town Hall. It was not only the seat of his power. He was a member of the committee that planned its programme and served on the one that had selected Jacob van Campen as its architect. He also gave financial support for its construction and composed the inscription on the panel in its high court chamber that commemorates the laying of its cornerstone.

The Dublin picture shows de Graeff in his carriage (monograms that include the letter 'G' are employed in its decoration) with his second wife Catharina Hooft (1618–91). Their two sons follow behind on horseback: first Pieter (1638–1707) and then Jacob (1642–90).[4] The latter son inherited Soestdijk from his father and, in turn, sold it to the stadholder Willem III, later William III, King of England. A royal Dutch palace still stands at Soestdijk.

As for the painting, it found a home in Pieter de Graeff's Ilpendam manor, a seigniory the elder son inherited from his father. In 1670, among the notes he made in his East India

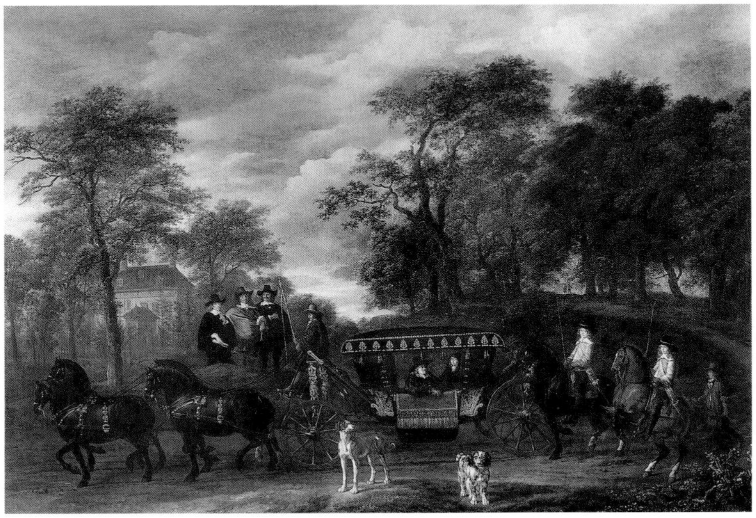

Fig. 23 Jacob van Ruisdael, *The Arrival of Cornelis de Graeff and Members of His Family at Soestdijk, His Country Estate*. National Gallery of Ireland, Dublin.

Facing page Detail of cat. 8, *Brick Bridge with a Sluice*

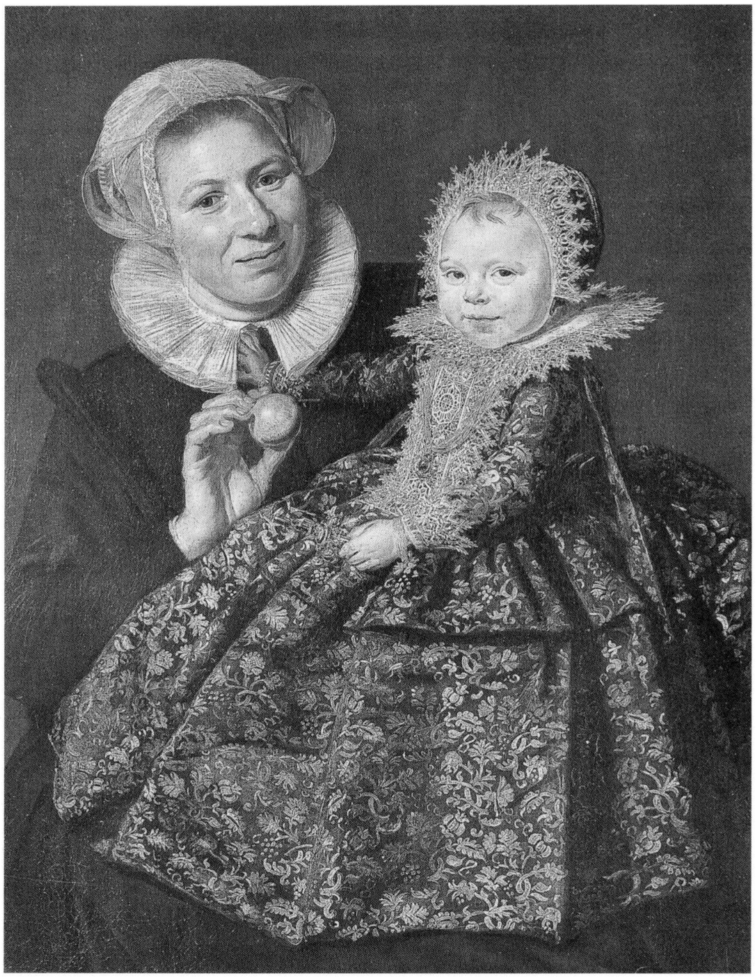

Fig. 24 Frans Hals, *Catharina Hooft with Her Nurse*. 86 x 65 cm. Staatliche Museen, Gemäldegalerie, Berlin.

Company (V.O.C.) almanac regarding the few pictures he had at the estate, he gave the painting's dimensions and described it as a landscape by de Keyser of Soestdijk, with his late father, his state carriage and a few other portraits.[5] Pieter did not say a word about Ruisdael's contribution.

Neither de Keyser nor Ruisdael is mentioned by the compiler of the 1691 estate inventory of Catharina Hooft, Pieter's mother; at the time of her death the picture was mounted in Ilpendam's salon called the *Johan de Wittzaal*.[6] Frans Hals's sympathetic double portrait of a nurse and a young child (fig. 24), now in Berlin, was displayed in the same room. Like the Dublin painting it is a family portrait; Hals's picture portrays Catharina Hooft, about the age of two, with her nurse[7] – perhaps the double portrait was part of young Catharina's dowry when she married Cornelis de Graeff in 1635. And like the Dublin painting, Hals's double portrait was inherited by Pieter – according to Dutch custom, family portraits normally pass to the eldest son.

In 1709, two years after Pieter's death, inventories were made of his effects at Ilpendam manor and his grand home on the Herengracht in Amsterdam. The Dublin painting was still in the manor, described in an inventory, without mention of either of its artists, as in the *Roozaal*:

> 1 large painting with portraits of the late Burgomaster Cornelis de Graeff, his wife, and two sons.[8]

The posthumous inventory made of Pieter's effects in his Amsterdam home tells us that he owned two additional depictions by Ruisdael of de Graeff estates:

> One painting of Zuidpolsbroek by Jacob Ruijsdael *f.*36
> One ditto of Soestdijk *f.*36[9]

These paintings are now unidentified or untraceable, but they, as well as the Dublin picture, offer a precious clue to a category of commissions Rusidael received. They establish that at least one family owned views by Jacob of their properties. It is evident that the de Graeff family had a penchant for views of this type. In addition to those by Ruisdael, Pieter de Graeff's 1709 inventory lists almost a dozen others, including two by Isaac de Moucheron (1667–1744), one of Ilpendam, the other of Zuidpolsbroek.[10]

No monetary appraisal is given in Pieter de Graeff's inventory for the painting now in Dublin, but, as noted above, his lost views of Zuidpolsbroek and Soestdijk were valued at Dfl.36 each, not high valuations, and, as we shall see, comparable to the appraisals and prices Ruisdael's pictures generally fetched during the following half-century. However, each view was appraised more than Frans Hals's double portrait of *Catharina Hooft with Her Nurse* which was also in Pieter de Graeff's 1709 inventory; it was valued at merely Dfl.30. The inventory also lists a gold bell that was appraised at 57 guilders, 18 stuivers,[11] almost twice the price of Hals's painting as well as Ruisdael's lost views of two de Graeff estates. It could very well have been the fine gold rattle Pieter's mother holds in her fist in Hals's heart-warming portrayal of her when she was still a toddler.

Ruisdael's work on a painting of Soestdijk and inventory references to two additional pictures of de Graeff's estates that are either lost or unidentified raise a reasonable question. Are there other works by the artist that can be identifed as commissioned portraits of specific properties? Several candidates come to mind but none offer open and shut cases.

For example, John Smith, who complied the pioneer catalogue of Ruisdael's paintings published in 1835, wrote of the artist's majestic *Bentheim Castle* (cat. 16), now a major accent in the National Gallery of Ireland: 'Tradition states it to have been painted expressly for the Count of Bentheim, in whose family it is said to have remained until the entrance of the French into Germany, about which time [*c.*1792–94] it was taken to Paris [...]'.[12] As far as I know there is not a shred of evidence to support the tradition a Count of Bentheim commissioned the mighty masterwork and it is apparent from Smith's carefully worded account of the painting's early provenance he had none either.

During recent decades Ruisdael's painting at Dublin of Bentheim Castle and more than a dozen of his other pictures which include the castle have been given various symbolic interpretations (for instance, an allusion to the cardinal sin of pride; a reference to the eternal city of Zion).[13] Some of Ruisdael's contemporaries may have entertained such notions but an image of Bentheim must have conjured up other thoughts in the minds of the Dutch merchants who imported Bentheim limestone from Westphalian quarries to Amsterdam. During the first half of the century it was used as a building material in the city and as such it reached its peak when, along with Italian marble, it was a favoured building material for Amsterdam's New Town Hall. Merchants who handsomely profited by providing hundreds of tons of Bentheim limestone used in the construction of 'the world's eighth wonder' had good reason to have fond memories of the site.

The earliest documented reference I know to a painting of Bentheim was made two years before Ruisdael died. It is found in the posthumous inventory, dated 2 May 1680, of the effects of Pieter van Lutsen (*c.*1612–79): '1 painting of the house of Bentheim' ('*1 schilderij het huis van Benthem*').[14] Although no artist's name is cited, in view of the rarity of paintings of the castle other than those by Ruisdael, the chance that the inventory refers to one of his pictures seems better than even. As for van Lutsen, it is known that he was an affluent Amsterdam merchant with international contacts and his family's business may very well have originated in the eastern Netherlands not far from Bentheim.[15] But in the end, we can only speculate if part of his wealth was related to Bentheim limestone transactions and if his painting of Bentheim Castle was in fact by Ruisdael.

What is known about the history of the Manor of Kostverloren in Ruisdael's day raises the possibility that the artist's intriguing painting of its reconstruction, now at the Amsterdam Historical Museum[16] (cat. 31), was a commissioned work. The bald facts are these. In about 1650 the old manor was badly damaged by fire, a very bad storm or a flood. However, the fabric of its tower remained sound. In the late 1650s or early 1660s the ruined manor was acquired by new owners. Their intent was to rehabilitate it by demolishing, and then rebuilding the ruined parts. After completion they proposed to rent out the restored manor, thereby deriving income for the estate.[17]

Was the Kostverloren painting commissioned from Ruisdael by the new owners to serve as a record of an early stage of their project? Possibly. But I find it unlikely that they ordered a view of either partial demolition or the initial phase of the reconstruction of their property. More probable is the hypothesis that the picture was made in response to the artist's own impulse to paint a landscape that incorporated a record of the beginning of the manor's new life when the white paint that formed a wondrous pattern on a side of its naked tower was visible. Ruisdael's addition of three naked men cavorting in the manor's moat adds an unusual note to the landscape. In Dutch pictures of the period naked male figures who are not gods, saints or classical heroes are almost as scarce as hen's teeth.

Another possible contender for a work that was made to order is Ruisdael's untraceable drawing known from Abraham Blooteling's etching *Mr Huydecoeper's House from the Rear* (*De Heer Huydecoepers Huis van achteren*; see p. 212 below). In my opinion, however, the lost drawing can be dismissed as a non-starter. It hardly qualifies as a commission given to the artist by Mr. Huydecoeper or another person with a special interest in the house since it is one of a series of Blooteling's six etched *Small Views of the Amstel by Jacob van Ruisdael* (*Amstel-Gesichjes door Jacob van Ruisdael*; see under cat. 86). The print's unmistakable emphasis is on the large site where workmen are preparing land for Amsterdam's dramatic expansion in about 1663. Like other identifiable Amsterdam structures in etchings of the *Amstel-Gesichjes* series, Mr Huydecoeper's house is an element in a broad topographical view, not the subject of the print.

It is tantalizing to think that some of the artist's celebrated panoramic views of bleaching fields with the skyline of Haarlem on the distant horizon may qualify as commissioned works. Extensive bleaching grounds in Ruisdael's *Haarlempjes* are generally seen adjacent to the buildings of a bleachery: a lye house, a dairy, living quarters and stables. Some of the bleacheries have been identified,[18] but it has not been possible to determine if any of them were ordered by their proprietors. Portraits of properties are not common in seventeenth-century Dutch art but we have seen they exist; Cornelis de Graeff's painting of his estate at Soestdijk has been mentioned and so have those owned by his son Pieter. Better known is Allart van Everdingen's huge panoramic view of the Trip family's *Cannon Foundry at Julitabroeck, Södermanland, Sweden*, the principal source of the family's fabulous wealth.[19] More unusual is the large, meticulous 'pen painting' Jacob van Matham did in 1627 of Johan van Loo's brewery 'De Drie Lilien' on the Spaarne in Haarlem and his country manor; in the picture the manor is transported from its actual site about five kilometres from the city to a spot a stone's throw from van Loo's brewery.[20] Considering the interest of some Dutch patrons in property portraits (in the nineteenth and twentieth centuries the appetite for them spread to other countries and was satisfied by an international group of photographers), it is conceivable that the Rijksmuseum's grandiose *Windmill at Wijk bij Duurstede* (cat. 39), Ruisdael's most famous picture, was commissioned as a portrait of the great mill by its proud owner.

Finding material to support the hunch cited above is exceedingly difficult. The mill depicted in the painting no longer stands, the name of its owner in about 1670 when the masterpiece was created is unknown and nothing unequivocal can be stated about its provenance until it was purchased by Adriaan van der Hoop from Albertus Brondgeest for the sensational price of Dfl.4,000 as late as 1833.

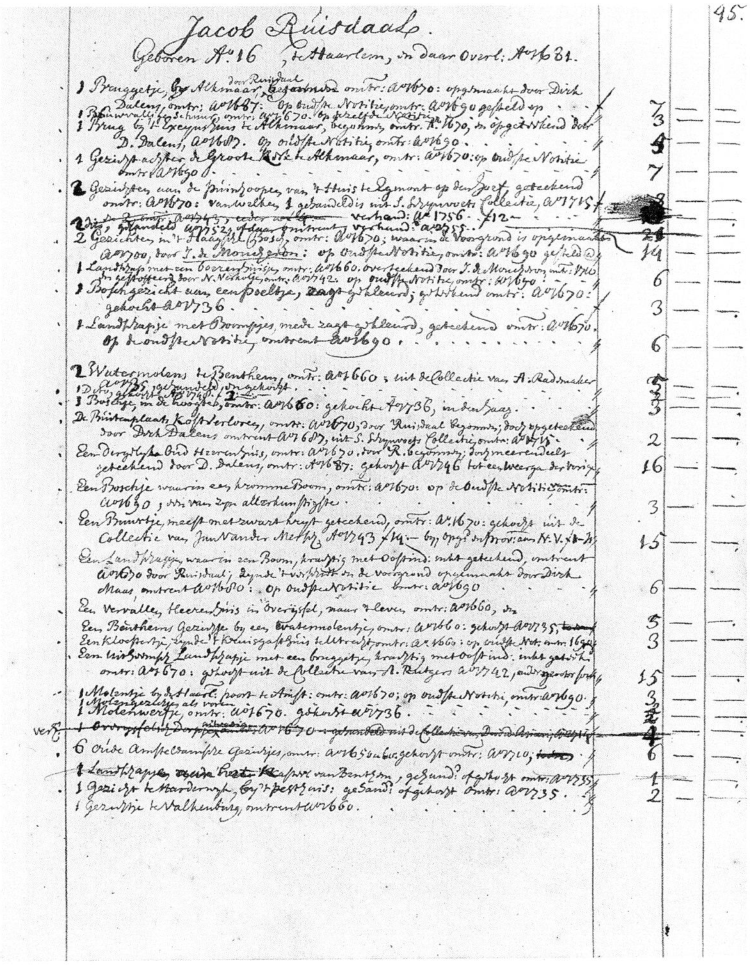

Fig. 25 List of Ruisdael drawings in *Notitie der Teekeningen (Notes on Drawings)* by Sybrand Feitama II. Rijksbureau voor Kunsthistorisch Documentatie, The Hague.

As for pinpointing a view by Ruisdael of a Haarlem bleachery commissioned by its owner, there is little reason to be optimistic. Not a single painting by the artist of the subject is listed in an exhaustive study of Haarlem probate inventories compiled from 1572 until 1740[21] (naturally only those dated in 1646, the year Ruisdael burst on the scene in Haarlem, or later, are pertinent here). By contrast, eight are cited in Amsterdam inventories made from 1664 until 1740.[22] The dates are not surprising. The artist only began to depict *Haarlempjes* in the early 1660s – less than a decade after he moved from Haarlem to settle in Amsterdam – and he continued to paint them until his final years. Unexpected, however, is the indication that Amsterdamers had a greater interest in his views of Haarlem than did citizens of his native city. Whether any Amsterdamers who had *Haarlempjes* in their possession owned or had investments in Haarlem bleacheries remains to be determined.

Finally, a word about proposals that Ruisdael's magisterial versions of *The Jewish Cemetery* at Dresden and Detroit (cat. 22 and fig. 22a) were commissioned works. It has been suggested that they were probably ordered specifically as portraits of the tombs and that their obvious symbolic references were added for good measure.[23] It also has been proposed that one of the versions may have been ordered by the family of Eliahu Montalto (*d.* 1616), the famous doctor of Ferdinand I, Grand Duke of Tuscany, and then of Marie de' Medici, whose white marble sarcophagus is prominent in both paintings, and that the other version (and perhaps a third untraceable one) was probably ordered afterwards by other members of Amsterdam's Jewish community.[24]

Proposals that the cemetery paintings were commissioned will remain hypothetical until evidence is found regarding the relation between the artist and the person or persons who acquired them. Once again, there is hardly reason to believe it will turn up soon. Nothing firm is known about the early ownership of the Dresden version until it is recorded in a Dresden inventory of 1754. The Detroit picture's history is more elusive; the earliest solid reference to its existence is in an 1828 London auction catalogue. We can say, however, it is highly unlikely that the paintings were done for Jewish patrons, as has been suggested,[25] because the inscriptions on the pictures' tombs (apart from Ruisdael's own beautiful signature on gravestones in the lower right of each painting) are painted in pseudo-Hebraic letters, not Hebrew. It is improbable that members of Amsterdam's Jewish community would have commissioned or accepted paintings with gibberish inscriptions instead of faithful transcriptions of the Hebrew texts on the sarcophagi.[26]

Similarly, the inscriptions on Abraham Blooteling's two engravings done after the artist's drawings of tombs at the Portuguese-Jewish Cemetery are in mumbo-jumbo, not Hebrew, and so are the inscriptions on the artist's drawings that served as their models (see cat. 79, 80). The engraved captions 'Burial place of the Jews outside Amsterdam' ('*Begraef-plaets der Joden buyten Amsteldam*') on both prints also are telling. They indicate that they were almost certainly made to help satisfy the wider public's interest in topographical views and not commissioned by the members of the Portuguese-Jewish community the cemetery served. If the latter were the case, it is reasonable to propose that the captions would have included a specific reference to the name of the cemetery (*Beth Haim*) that houses the tombs.

It is patent that an attempt to learn about Ruisdael's transactions with his clients brings us to a frontier of knowledge quickly. Facts about early collectors of his paintings are sparse as well. There are not many references to them in Dutch inventories and auction catalogues compiled before the middle of the eighteenth century, and it has already been noted that appraisals of their monetary worth as well as the prices they fetched on the art market are never high (also see Appendix, pp. 260 below). The conclusion that during this period they simply did not generate much interest is inescapable. Unlike Gerrit Dou, Ruisdael never had a Pieter Spiering who, according to a contemporary, paid Dou 500 guilders annually to have first choice of his pictures (another contemporary

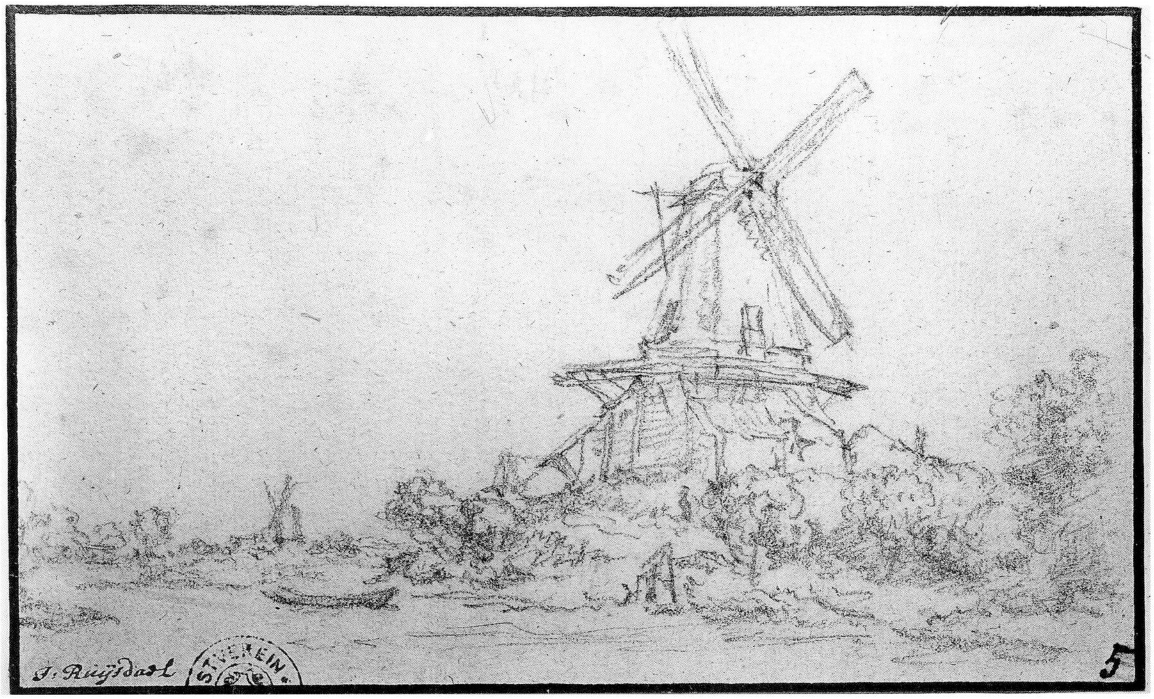

Fig. 26 Jacob van Ruisdael, *Windmills near a Body of Water.* 9.4 x 15.7 cm. Black chalk. Kunsthalle, Bremen.

states Spiering paid Dou 1,000 guilders annually for the privilege) and no Dutchman acquired Ruisdael's paintings engross, the way the Delft printer Jacob Dissius managed to have twenty-one of Vermeer's pictures in his possession when he died in 1695.

The few existing inventories of collections owned by contemporary Dutch artists indicate that none of his colleagues developed a passion for his work. Consider the significant case of Jacob's almost exact contemporary, Jan van de Cappelle (1624/26–79), Holland's outstanding marine painter of mirror-smooth waters and silvery atmospheric effects. Van de Cappelle did not devote all of his time to painting. He also helped manage, and then inherited his father's profitable Amsterdam dye-works. At his death he was worth a fortune of more than 90,000 guilders, and owned substantial holdings in real estate, a pleasure yacht and a vast collection of more than 200 paintings and about 6,000 drawings. He collected large quantities of works by artists he favoured, among them sixteen paintings by Porcellis, nine paintings and more than 1,300 drawings by Simon de Vlieger, ten paintings and over 400 drawings by van Goyen. He also possessed paintings by Rembrandt, Rubens, Frans Hals, Van Dyck, Brouwer, Hercules Segers and Avercamp. He had almost 900 drawings by Avercamp and more than 500 by Rembrandt. But no Ruisdael. Not a single one of his paintings, drawings or prints is listed in the posthumous inventory of van de Cappelle's awesome collection.[27]

The well-known 1656 inventory of Rembrandt's property drawn up by Amsterdam's insolvency court, which, apart from Rembrandt's own paintings, drawings and etchings, includes more than 2,000 works on paper and about fifty paintings by Netherlandish and Italian artists. It would be nice to learn that the mature Rembrandt recognized Ruisdael's genius early and owned his works by 1656. But Rembrandt's inventory tells the same story as van de Cappelle's. Nothing by Ruisdael is mentioned.[28] The fact that during the course of the following decades a handful of Ruisdael's paintings are listed in inventories of a few Dutch artists or their heirs hardly alters the picture.[29]

More is known about late seventeenth-century collectors of the artist's drawings, thanks to the rare manuscript inventory of almost 1,500 drawings compiled by Sybrand Feitama II (1694–1758). The valuable inventory comprises sheets that were in or passed through his collection and it also documents drawings acquired by his grandfather Sybrand Feitama I (1620–1701) and his father Isaac Feitama (1666–1709). Entitled *Notitie der Teekeningen* (*Notes on Drawings*), the inventory covers the period from 1685, three years after Ruisdael's death, until 1758, the year Sybrand II died.[30]

No less than forty-one Ruisdael drawings are listed in his inventory (fig. 25). He carefully notes that thirteen of them were in the collection formed by his grandfather and father as early as about 1690. Eight of the thirteen have been identified and five outstanding ones are included here (cat. 76, 77, 84, 95, 96).

A close look at two of his small, quick black chalk drawings of windmills, now at Bremen, shows that both are clearly inscribed in the lower left corner, in brown ink, 'J. Ruijsdael' (fig. 26 reproduces one of them; also see p. 168, fig. 46).[31] These signatures are not in Jacob van Ruisdael's hand. They probably were written by an unknown collector or dealer (today known as the 'J. Ruijsdael collector') who must have been active even before the sketches were acquired for the Feitama collection about 1690. Proof that the pair was inscribed before this time is offered by their unbro-

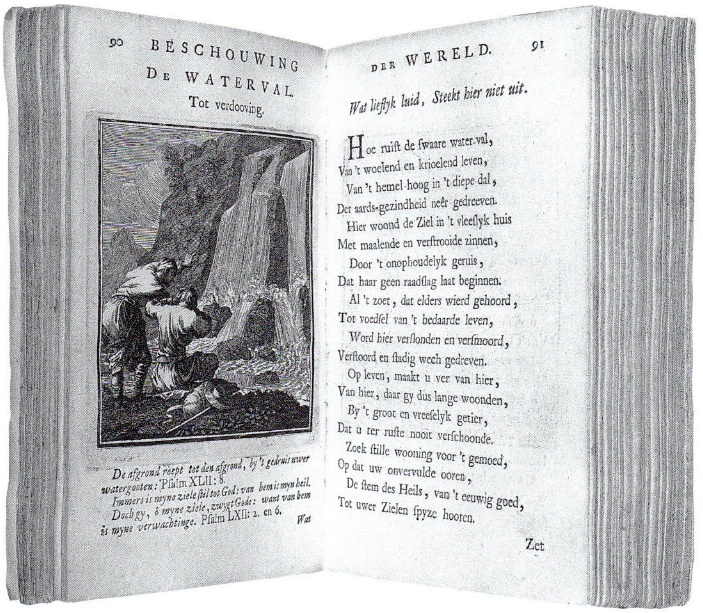

90 BESCHOUWING

DE WATERVAL.

Tot verdooving.

De afgrond roept tot den afgrond, by 't gedruis uwer watergooten: Pſalm XLII: 8.
Immers is myne ziele ſtil tot God: van hem is myn heil. Doch gy, ô myne ziele, zwygt Gode: want van hem is myne verwachtinge. Pſalm LXII: 2. en 6.

Wat

DER WERELD. 91

Wat lieflyk luid, Steekt hier niet uit.

Hoe ruiſt de ſwaare water-val,
Van 't woelend en krioelend leven,
Van 't hemel-hoog in 't diepe dal,
Der aards-gezindheid neêr gedreeven.
Hier woond de Ziel in 't vleeſlyk huis
Met maalende en verſtrooide zinnen,
Door 't onophoudelyk geruis,
Dat haar geen raadſlag laat beginnen.
Al 't zoet, dat elders wierd gehoord,
Tot voedſel van 't bedaarde leven,
Word hier verſlonden en verſmoord,
Verſtoord en ſtadig wech gedreven.
Op leven, maakt u ver van hier,
Van hier, daar gy dus lange woonden,
By 't groot en vreeſelyk getier,
Dat u ter ruſte nooit verſchoonde.
Zoek ſtille wooning voor 't gemoed,
Op dat uw onvervulde ooren,
De ſtem des Heils, van 't eeuwig goed,
Tot uwer Zielen ſpyze hooren.

Zet

Fig. 27 "De Waterval" ("The Waterfall"), emblem by Jan Luiken in his *Beschouwing der wereld* (Contemplation of the World), Amsterdam, 1708.

ken history from around 1690 until 1782 and by the fact that specialists have identified sixteen other sketches, inscribed 'J. Ruijsdael', that were in different collections and never part of the Feitama family holdings; see, for example, cat. 68, 70. The suggestion that the 'J. Ruijsdael collector' may have procured some of the eighteen sketches that bear his inscription soon after Ruisdael's death in 1682 – or even earlier – is not improbable.[32] In any event, to our knowledge, the anonymous 'J. Ruijsdael collector' earns the honour of being the first person to assemble a sizeable group of the artist's works.

Sybrand II records in his *Notes on Drawings* that two of the Ruisdael sheets in his collection were acquired by his father or grandfather in about 1690 and that they were retouched by Dirk Dalens II (1658–88), a minor Dutch landscapist, around 1687, and a third Ruisdael, acquired from a different source, was embellished by Dalens in about 1687 as well.[33] Now, the declaration that Dalens worked on three of his Ruisdael drawings merely five years after the master died (and only a year before Dalens's death) may indicate that Dalens had them in his possession around 1687 and that he even may have acquired them directly from Jacob or his estate. If this is indeed the case, Dalens would qualify as the earliest identifiable owner of drawings by Ruisdael. But the case is not that simple. Despite statements by Sybrand Feitama II about Dalens's participation in the three drawings, finding an indubitable trace of his hand in them is as difficult as hearing the grass grow.[34]

Gérard de Lairesse (1640–1711), the leading Dutch classical artist and theorist, famously remembered for confessing he once had a special preference for Rembrandt, but at a time when he had hardly begun to understand the infallible rules of art, is the first to mention Ruisdael's name in a text. In 1707 he refers to him in his *Het groot schilderboek*, an encyclopedic handbook that includes ideas promulgated by seventeenth-century French academic artists and theorists. His section on landscape painting does no more than include the artist's name in his short list of artists ('[...] the famous painters Everdingen, Pynacker, Ruisdael, Moucheron [...]') who followed what he calls the modern manner by depicting unembellished nature in contrast to those who work, according to him, in the antique, perfect manner by judiciously adorning improved nature with references to classical antiquity.[35] Though Lairesse's passing reference to Ruisdael is not of great moment, it tells us that twenty-five years after Jacob's death his name comes easily to the lips of the theorist-painter his contemporaries trumpeted as the 'Dutch Apelles', the 'Dutch Raphael', and the 'Dutch Poussin'.

Yet another indication of Ruisdael's name recognition in the Netherlands at the very same time is found in the emblem book *Beschouwing der wereld* (Contemplation of the World) published in

Fig. 28 Biography of Ruisdael in Arnold Houbraken, *De groote schouburgh der nederlantsche Konstschilders en schilderessen (The Great Theatre of Netherlandish Painters and Painteresses)*, vol. 3, pp. 65–6, Amsterdam, 1721.

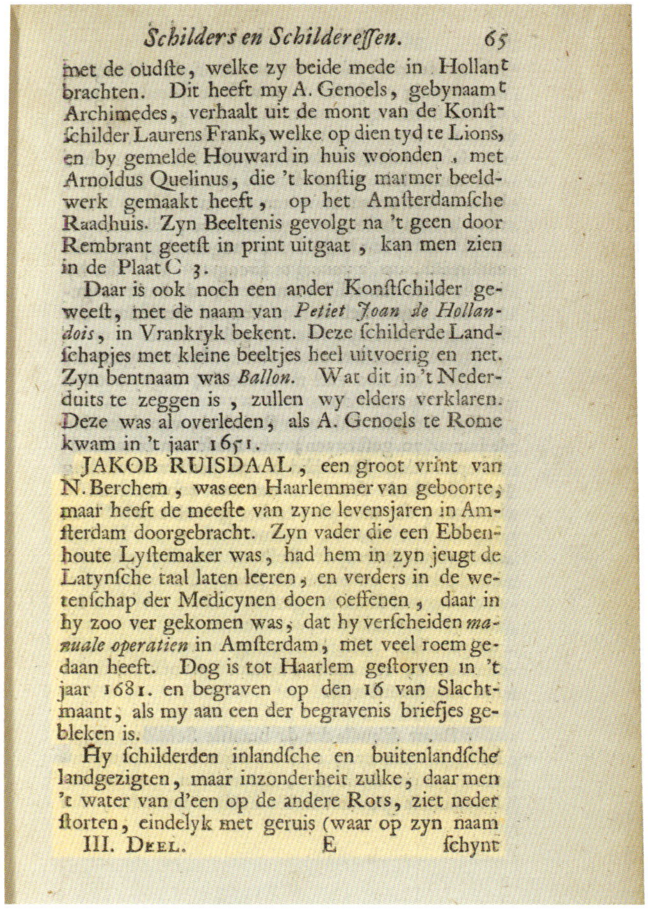

Schilders en Schildereſſen. 65

met de oudſte, welke zy beide mede in Hollant brachten. Dit heeft my A. Genoels, gebynaamt Archimedes, verhaalt uit de mont van de Konſtſchilder Laurens Frank, welke op dien tyd te Lions, en by gemelde Houward in huis woonden, met Arnoldus Quelinus, die 't konſtig marmer beeldwerk gemaakt heeft, op het Amſterdamſche Raadhuis. Zyn Beeltenis gevolgt na 't geen door Rembrant geetſt in print uitgaat, kan men zien in de Plaat C 3.

Daar is ook noch een ander Konſtſchilder geweeſt, met de naam van *Petiet Joan de Hollandois*, in Vrankryk bekent. Deze ſchilderde Landſchapjes met kleine beeltjes heel uitvoerig en net. Zyn bentnaam was *Ballon*. Wat dit in 't Nederduits te zeggen is, zullen wy elders verklaren. Deze was al overleden, als A. Genoels te Rome kwam in 't jaar 1651.

JAKOB RUISDAAL, een groot vrint van N. Berchem, was een Haarlemmer van geboorte, maar heeft de meeſte van zyne levensjaren in Amſterdam doorgebracht. Zyn vader die een Ebbenhoute Lyſtemaker was, had hem in zyn jeugt de Latynſche taal laten leeren, en verders in de wetenſchap der Medicynen doen oeffenen, daar in hy zoo ver gekomen was, dat hy verſcheiden *manuale operatien* in Amſterdam, met veel roem gedaan heeft. Dog is tot Haarlem geſtorven in 't jaar 1681. en begraven op den 16 van Slachtmaant, als my aan een der begravenis briefjes gebleken is.

Hy ſchilderden inlandſche en buitenlandſche landgezigten, maar inzonderheit zulke, daar men 't water van d'een op de andere Rots, ziet neder ſtorten, eindelyk met geruis (waar op zyn naam

III. DEEL. E ſchynt

1708 by Jan Luiken (1649–1712; hereafter spelled Luyken, the orthography he himself most often used for his surname). Luyken, a fanatical Pietist, etched and engraved more than 3,000 prints mainly of religious and moralizing subjects. His *Beschouwing der wereld* consists of one hundred emblems that employ all sorts of natural phenomena to expound notions related to the Divine.

The main focus of Luyken's emblem of special interest here is a waterfall (fig. 27).[36] The emblem, like virtually all those published since the long-lived European fashion for them began in the sixteenth century, is a combination of three parts used collectively: a motto, a picture and an epigram, and, as was Luyken's practice, it is embellished with a few short quotations from Scripture. The emblem's motto '*Tot verdooving*' ('Until deafening') is accompanied by Luyken's etching of a crashing waterfall witnessed by two men, one pointing to the falls and the other clapping his hands over his ears to shut out its deafening noise. The emblem's epigram in the form of a poem uses the waterfall as a symbol of earthly uproar and contrasts it with the silence of God. The poem also includes a clever play on Ruisdael's surname twice as an allusion to the world as a noisy dale or valley (*Ruis* [noise] – *dal* [dale]). Here, the artist's name stands for one of his best known products: a roaring waterfall.[37] I agree with the critics of our day who reject the idea that Ruisdael's more than one hundred waterfall pictures were intended by the artist as visual sermons or had a moralizing intent. The idea that the noisy dale (*Ruisdal*) alludes to the commotion of the world is Luyken's invention, not Ruisdael's.

Arnold Houbraken (1660–1719), the artist's earliest biographer, makes a similar play on Ruisdael's surname in his discussion of Jacob's waterfalls in his short account of the artist published in 1721 (fig. 28).[38] Houbraken's biography appears in his *De groote schouburgh der Nederlantsche konstschilders en schilderessen* (The Great Theatre of Netherlandish Painters and Painteresses), a still indispensable three-volume compendium of lives of more than 550 seventeenth-century Dutch and Flemish male painters and about a dozen women artists. He writes:

> Jakob Ruisdaal, a great friend of N. Berchem, was a Haarlemer by birth, but spent most of his life in Amsterdam. His father, an ebony-framemaker, had him taught Latin in his youth, and then had him trained in the science of medicine, in which he came so far as to perform various operations in Amsterdam, for which he received great fame. Yet, he died in Haarlem in 1681 and was buried on 16 November, as I have seen on a burial notice. He painted both native and foreign landscapes, but especially those in which water is seen dashing from one rock to another, finally ending with a noise [*geruis*] (as his name seems to intimate) down through the dales [*dalen*]. And he could depict water splashing and foaming as it dashed upon the rocks so naturally clear and transparent, that it appears to be nothing less than real water. He also could depict the sea, and when he chose, a tempestuous sea with violent waves lashing against rocks and dunes. In this type of painting he was one of the best. However, I cannot say he had luck as his friend.
>
> He remained unmarried until the end of his life; it is said, in order to be of greater service to his father.
>
> His brother Salomon van Ruysdael, who pre-deceased him in 1670 also was a good landscape painter.

Houbraken does not include another word about Salomon's art. He does add, however, a few lines about Salomon's invention of an artificial marble that was so close to genuine stone that one could not help believe it was the real thing.

Ruisdael's native landscapes are not glossed by Houbraken, but it seems he was in accord with public taste when he singles out the naturalism of the artist's turbulent waterfalls and seascapes for special praise. To judge from the small sample of subjects of Jacob's landscapes that are mentioned in Dutch sale catalogues from the 1690s to the 1760s, his admiration for the waterfalls was shared by contemporary collectors; thirteen are specifically cited and ten marines are mentioned (winterscapes run a close third

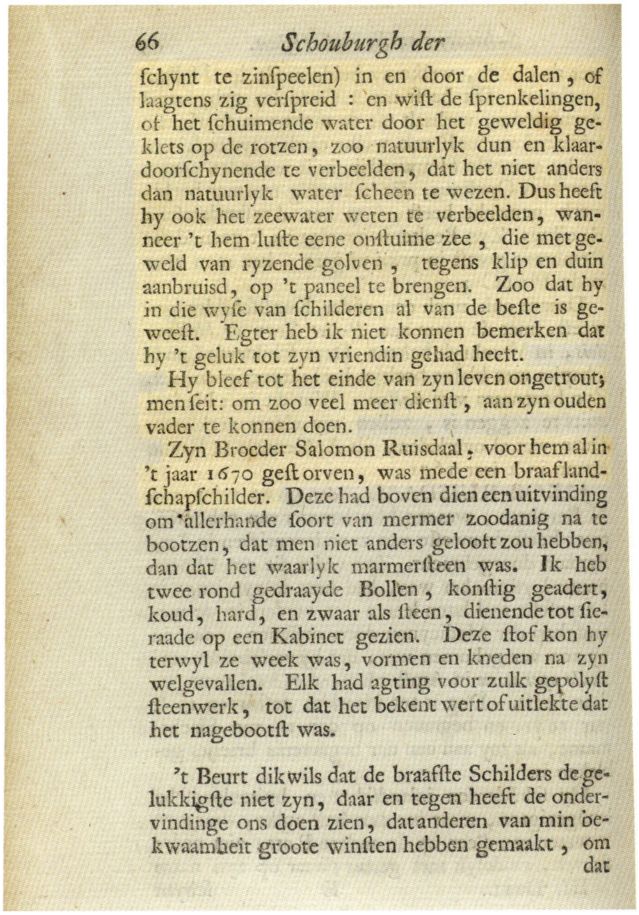
66 *Schouburgh der*

ſchynt te zinſpeelen) in en door de dalen, of laagtens zig verſpreid: en wiſt de ſprenkelingen, of het ſchuimende water door het geweldig geklets op de rotzen, zoo natuurlyk dun en klaardoorſchynende te verbeelden, dat het niet anders dan natuurlyk water ſcheen te wezen. Dus heeft hy ook het zeewater weten te verbeelden, wanneer 't hem luſte eene onſtuime zee, die met geweld van ryzende golven, tegens klip en duin aanbruisd, op 't paneel te brengen. Zoo dat hy in die wyſe van ſchilderen al van de beſte is geweeſt. Egter heb ik niet konnen bemerken dat hy 't geluk tot zyn vriendin gehad heeft.

Hy bleef tot het einde van zyn leven ongetrout; men ſeit: om zoo veel meer dienſt, aan zyn ouden vader te konnen doen.

Zyn Broeder Salomon Ruisdaal, voor hem al in 't jaar 1670 geſtorven, was mede een braaf landſchapſchilder. Deze had boven dien een uitvinding om allerhande ſoort van mermer zoodanig na te bootzen, dat men niet anders gelooft zou hebben, dan dat het waarlyk marmerſteen was. Ik heb twee rond gedraayde Bollen, konſtig geadert, koud, hard, en zwaar als ſteen, dienende tot ſieraade op een Kabinet gezien. Deze ſtof kon hy terwyl ze week was, vormen en kneden na zyn welgevallen. Elk had agting voor zulk gepolyſt ſteenwerk, tot dat het bekent wert of uitlekte dat het nagebootſt was.

't Beurt dikwils dat de braafſte Schilders de gelukkigſte niet zyn, daar en tegen heeft de ondervindinge ons doen zien, dat anderen van min bekwaamheit groote winſten hebben gemaakt, om dat with nine).[39] Existing references to waterfall paintings by Ruisdael in princely collections also speak for their early popularity. Two are recorded in an inventory made of Augustus the Strong's holdings at Dresden in 1722, just a year after Houbraken's life of Ruisdael appeared.[40] In 1738 Duke Karl I of Braunschweig, acquired two of the artist's waterfalls as well as his monumental *Hilly Landscape with a Great Oak and Grainfield* (cat. 21) for the gallery at Salzdahlum Castle.[41] Landgrave Wilhelm VIII of Hessen-Kassel acquired a Ruisdael waterfall in 1750 when he purchased *en bloc* the collection of Cornelia Röver van der Dussin of Delft; her deceased husband bought the waterfall in Amsterdam as early as 1716.[42]

Subsequent studies confirm or support other points Houbraken makes. For instance, the artist was indeed a native Haarlemer, spent most of his life in Amsterdam, was Berchem's friend and remained a bachelor. His father was an ebony-framemaker, and Jacob's two wills made in 1667 indicate his touching concern for his father's well-being.

Despite the convincing testimony of Ruisdael's two wills it is fair to ask if there were factors other than Houbraken's remark that 'He remained unmarried until the end of his life [...] to be of greater service to his father.' Did the age of forty-eight or forty-nine that he had reached in 1677, the year his father died, stop him from considering marriage? Or was he a life-long victim of unrequited love as well as a devoted son? Or did his sexual orientation preclude marriage? And what was Houbraken hinting when he wrote, 'I cannot say he had luck as his friend'? I have found no way to tease out answers to these personal questions.

Returning to Houbraken's biography, not all of it is fully reliable. His claim that Jacob studied Latin and became a renowned surgeon is moot.[43] He also got a couple of facts wrong. Jacob van Ruisdael did not die in Haarlem in 1681 and was not buried there on 16 November of that year. These vital statistics belong to his cousin Jacob Salomonsz van Ruysdael. Furthermore Salomon van Ruysdael was not Jacob's brother, but his uncle.

Notice of Houbraken's errors here is not impelled by scholarly *schadenfreude*. They are signalled because they, as well as some of the reliable data Houbraken presents, were shamelessly plagerized, pilfered and embroidered by later biographers, first by Jacob Campo Weyerman (1729), and then by Dézallier d'Argenville (1752), James Burgess (1754), Dirk Schrevel (1754; also called Theodorus Schrevelius), Jean-Baptiste Descamps (1754) – the list can be extended. Fresh archival research on Ruisdael and his family only began in the nineteenth century. It proceeded slowly. The muddle Houbraken made when he confused our Jacob's death date with his cousin Jacob Salomonsz van Ruysdael's was corrected as late as 1870.[44]

By the middle of the eighteenth century new interest in Ruisdael's pictures and naturalistic landscapes by other seventeenth-century Dutch painters is evident beyond the borders of the Netherlands. In 1760 the French painter, better remembered as an historian, Jean-Baptiste Descamps (1706–91) wrote in his *La vie des peintres flamands, allemands et hollandais* that Ruisdael's paintings are beginning to be known in France where they are also esteemed as much as they are in Holland.[45] He cites five paintings by Ruisdael in contemporary French collections.[46] He also briefly mentions Salomon van Ruysdael whom he considers vastly inferior to Jacob. Salomon is dismissed by him as 'un froid imitateur' of Jan van Goyen and Johannes Schoeff. According to Descamps, Salomon's landscapes are not comparable to Jacob's, except by *demi-connoisseurs* who buy only by name.[47]

The new interest is seen also in England where Thomas Gainsborough (1727–88) made a faithful, carefully finished chalk drawing (fig. 29; Whitworth Art Gallery, University of Manchester) after Ruisdael's *Wooded Landscape with a Flooded Road*. Jacob's original (fig. 30) belongs to the Louvre and is now on extended loan to the Musée de la Chartreuse, Douai.[48] The drawing is datable to about 1747, when young Gainsborough also studied pictures by other Dutch landscapists (Wynants, Waterloo, Hobbema). The impact of Ruisdael's composition on his work is clearly apparent in major paintings he made about the same time.[49]

Gainsborough's model for the Manchester drawing is unknown. If he made it from a print, no impression has survived; the earliest known print after the painting was engraved more than a decade after Gainsborough's death. The possibility that he drew his copy from Ruisdael's original cannot be excluded, and its closeness to its model suggests this may be the case. Perhaps Ruisdael's original made a round trip across the Channel before it found a home in the Louvre. At least one landscape attributed to Ruisdael appeared in an English sale as early as 1722. His pictures, and a surprising number of works by other seventeenth-century Dutch landscapists, showed up with ever increasing frequency during the following decades when dealers began to import what they could after combing continental collections for stock.

In Britain the taste for classical landscapists, especially Claude and Poussin, and Italianate ones, notably Nicolaes Berchem and Jan Both, did not wane until well into the nineteenth century but it began to exist alongside a growing appreciation of painters of naturalistic Dutch landscapes. The painting ascribed to Ruisdael that was sold in 1722 appeared in a sale of pictures that belonged to Mr Van Huls: 'no. 21. A Landskip, figures Bathing'; it was purchased by Mr Dean for £4 15*s*. This entry is included in a valuable two volume manuscript collection of 176 transcriptions of English sale catalogues dating from 1711 to 1759.[50] The two volumes have never been exhaustively published or analysed. However, a helpful survey of their Dutch material is available; it includes references to thirty-two artists (from Berchem to Wynants) and cites more than 150 of their pictures.[51] Nine paintings called Ruisdael that appeared in five sales from 1722 until 1757 are mentioned in the survey. My trawl through the sale catalogues in the volumes compiled from 1722 to 1759 concentrated

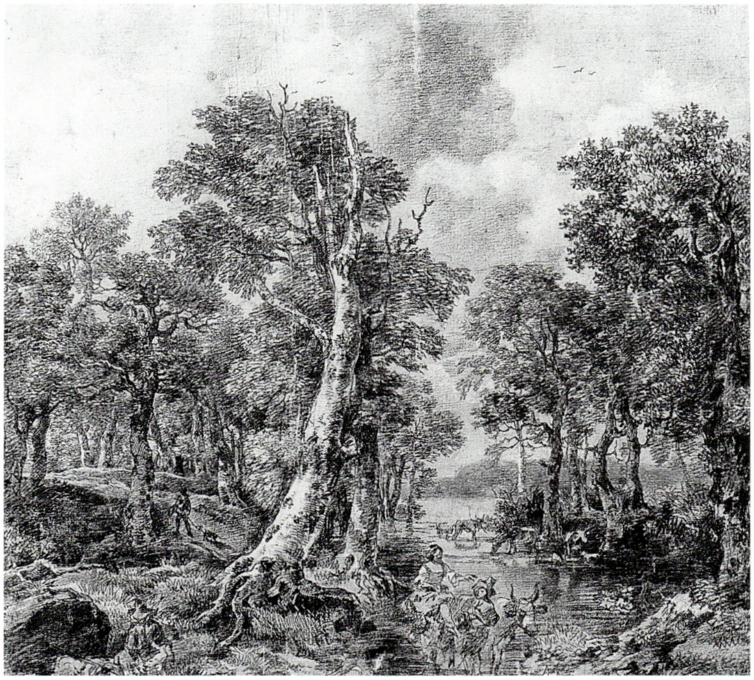

Fig. 29 Thomas Gainsborough, copy of Ruisdael's *Wooded Landscape with a Flooded Road* (see fig. 30). Black and white chalks, heightened with white., Whitworth Art Gallery, University of Manchester.

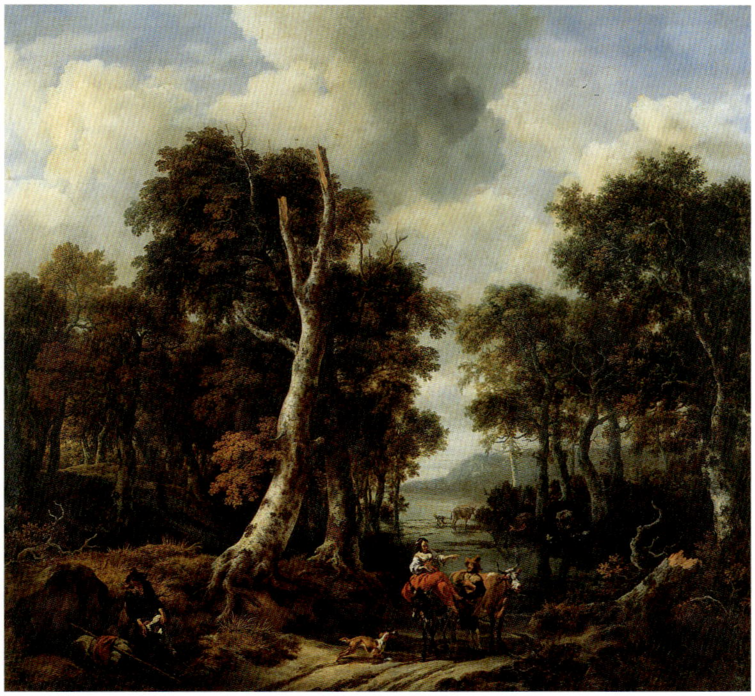

Fig. 30 Jacob van Ruisdael, *Wooded Landscape with a Flooded Road*. 171 x 194 cm. Musée du Louvre, Paris (on extended loan to the Musée de la Chartreuse, Douai).

on Ruisdael; it produced references to ninety-six paintings attributed to him in twenty sales. Of special note is the sale in London of John van Spangen's 253 pictures held in 1748, which included an unexpected eighteen works called Ruisdael; they brought a total of £362 18s. 18d. Their buyers included the Duke of Rutland, Lords Ashburton, Londonderry, Petersham and Sir W. Beauchamp.[52] Although the sample is small, it is fair to say the manuscript transcriptions of sales indicate Ruisdael's stock began to rise during these years.

As we shall see, Sir Joshua Reynolds (1723–92), who was to become England's greatest eighteenth-century collector of pictures, made his first recorded appearance at a sale in the 1740s. During the following decades, when his pockets became deeper thanks to a large clientele willing to pay top prices to the artist recognized as England's leading portraitist, his collecting activity and that of his agents increased enormously. The principal posthumous sale of his collection of paintings (1795) included 466 pictures and, when his drawings came to the auction block (1794; 1798), they numbered more than 6,000 sheets.[53] It is not surprising that the collection of the first president of The Royal Academy and author of the celebrated *Discourses* mainly comprised works attributed to Italian High Renaissance and Baroque artists but most other continental schools were well represented, including the seventeenth-century Dutch.

The earliest existing reference to Reynolds as a buyer of pictures is at the London sale of John Glover in 1745 where he is recorded as purchasing at least five Dutch paintings: Jan van Goyen's *View in Holland*, Rembrandt's *Boy's Head*, Jan Lievens's *Girl's Head*, [?Dirk] Dalens's *Large Landscape* and Wouwerman's *Horse Market*. They fetched a total of £26 5*s*.[54]

At first blush Reynolds's purchases appear to be a very auspicious start to his grand career as a collector. However, second thoughts can lead to another conclusion. It has reasonably been argued that Reynolds, who lived from hand to mouth until his almost immediate success as a portraitist soon after returning to England after a two-year stay in Italy and setting up his own London studio in 1753, would not have had the needed £26 5*s*. in 1745 to pay for the pictures. The amount suggests that young Reynolds was not buying for himself, but acting as the agent for another buyer, probably Thomas Hudson, the artist who supervised Reynolds's apprenticeship.[55]

By the second half of the 1750s Reynolds's financial situation had radically changed. His meteoric rise as a popular portraitist provided funds that allowed him to become an active player in London's sale rooms. Records of his acquisitions are incomplete and, if the low prices he paid for some works are an indication of quality, his collecting was uneven. Nevertheless, available documents and annotated sale catalogues are telling. They reveal that between 1755 and 1760 he began collecting in earnest. During this brief period he acquired at least eighty paintings at a total cost of more than £700.[56] Most significant was his acquisition in 1758 of Poussin's magnificent *Landscape with Orion*, now at the Metropolitan Museum of Art. For our account it is remarkable

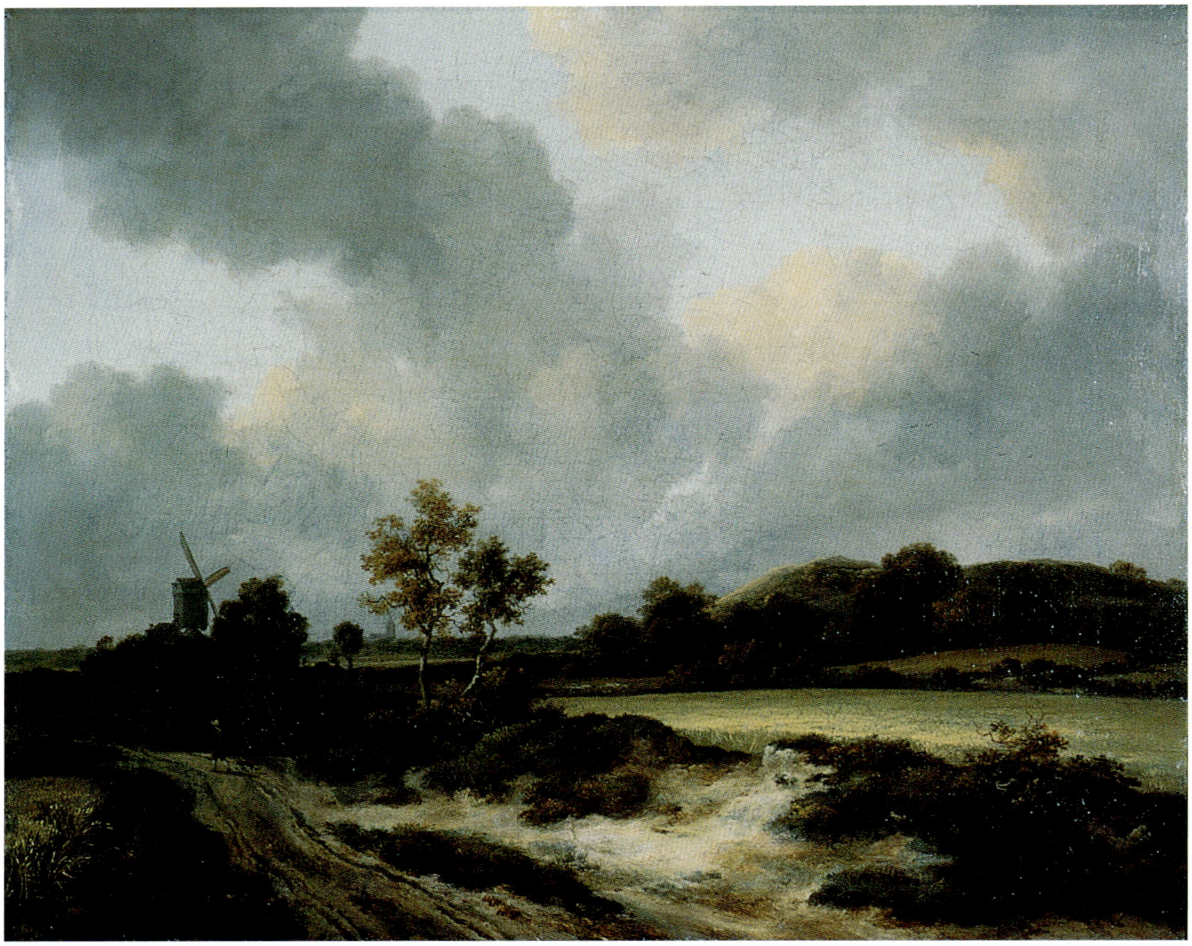

Fig. 31 Jacob van Ruisdael, *Grainfields near a Road*. 47 x 57.2 cm. The Friedsam Collection, The Metropolitan Museum of Art, New York.

that from 1755 until 1759 he is recorded as the buyer of no less than five Ruisdael landscapes,[57] one of which was almost certainly Ruisdael's fine *Grainfield* (fig. 31), at the Metropolitan Museum.[58] Reynolds's interest in Ruisdael was not a passing fancy. He wrote in *A Journey to Flanders and Holland*, a record of his impressions of a tour made in 1781: 'The landscapes of Ruysdael have not only great force, but have a freshness which is scarce seen in any other painter.'[59]

While in the Low Lands in 1781, among the pictures Reynolds commissioned an agent to buy on his behalf was Ruisdael's *View of Het IJ on a Stormy Day* (fig. 32), now at the Worcester Art Museum. He had instructed his agent to bid no higher than Dfl. 250; the painting fetched Dfl. 450, thus he lost it.[60] At the time, the price was rather high but not exaggerated. The artist's prices began to rise in Holland as well as in England after the middle of the century. The Getty Museum's *Bridge with a Sluice* (cat. 7), for example, was acquired in The Hague by a *marchand-amateur* in 1744 for Dfl. 57. In his posthumous sale of 1763, held in the same city, it brought Dfl. 200, and his untraceable Ruisdael 'Landscape with a Handsome Distant View' sold for Dfl. 310.[61]

Prices for Ruisdael's drawings did not lag behind. Sybrand II records in his 'Notes on Drawings' that in about 1710 he acquired all six of the drawings Jacob made as *modelli* for the etched series of *Small Views of the Amstel* for Dfl. 6. When they appeared as successive lots in his 1758 posthumous Amsterdam sale, they were knocked down for a total of Dfl. 218.30, an increase of more than thirty-six times the price he originally paid for them (see cat. 86).

The small boom Ruisdael and other seventeenth-century Dutch artists enjoyed in sale rooms ended abruptly when general economic conditions in Britain and on the continent were depressed by the upheavals of the French revolutionary and Napoleonic wars. A few years before these dramatic events occurred Joseph Holden Pott (1759–1847), who does not rank today among the renowned eighteenth-century art critics, gave modest expression to the new positive reaction and familiarity with the Dutch School in England in *An Essay on Landscape Painting* that appeared in 1782. Pott published poetry and his *Essay* before he took orders and long before he became Archdeacon of London. By the time his *Essay* appeared he was a well-informed amateur

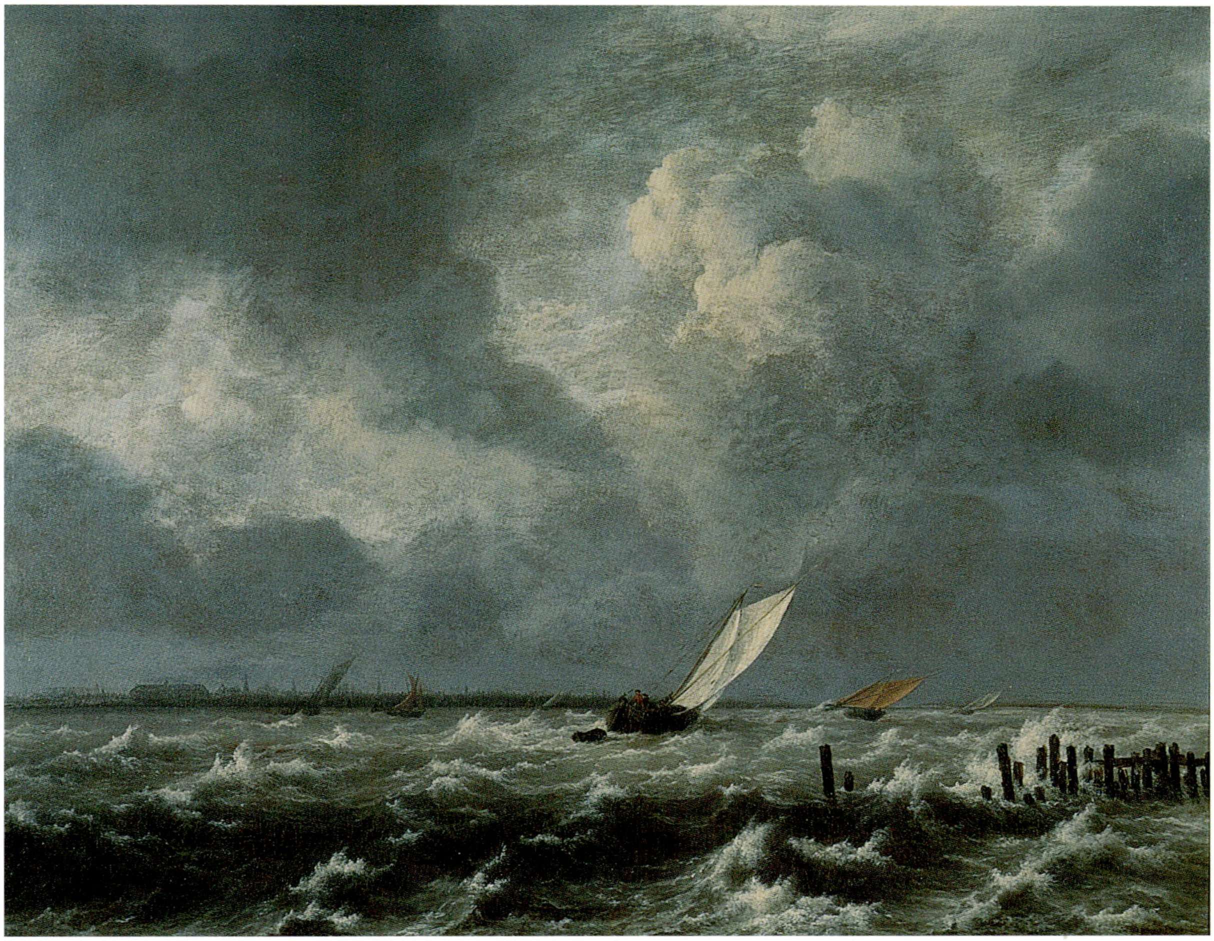

Fig. 32 Jacob van Ruisdael, *View of Het IJ on a Stormy Day*. 65.8 x 82.7 cm. The Worcester Art Museum, Massachusetts.

able to include references in his pages to Jan van Goyen, Pieter de Molyn, Cornelis Decker and Meindert Hobbema, landscapists who found a place neither in Houbraken's three volumes dedicated to the lives of seventeenth-century Dutch artists nor in Reynolds's account of thoughts generated by his visits to collections in Holland.

Pott sensed he was tilling new ground. In his prefatory note to the reader he states his material is personal and not 'as a celebrated writer expresses it, swelled by the passing of contents of one vessel to another'. Regarding Ruisdael he writes:

> Berghem and Both, are particularly eminent among these [artists who have adopted the clear, warm manner of painting], as Rysdael is among those who painted more in the Dutch manner. In treating of landscape particularly, I am almost induced to give a very material preference to Rysdael. He united the exquisite truth of the Dutch manner, with a degree of taste not surpassed even in the Italian School. Rysdael is never vulgar or inelegant, always natural, frequently beautiful and picturesque, and sometimes unites grandeur of taste with each of the foregoing excellencies. To Berghem he is in many respects undoubtedly inferior; but, though Berghem was always elegant in his designs, and admirable in the perspective propriety, delicacy of touch, and brilliancy of his pictures, yet there is a sameness in his landscapes, many of which are entirely subordinate to his cattle and figures. There is not that endless variety which is seen in Rysdael's choice. In all the lists of painters, no one so constantly produces that delight, which we, in a former part of this work, described as arising from the strong resemblance of nature, in all its delicate familiar characters.[62]

Whether young John Constable (1776–1837) ever had Pott's book in his hands is unknown. There is, however, no question that Constable admired Ruisdael's work before he left his family's Suffolk home in 1799 to settle in London where he attended the Royal Academy Schools. His early admiration became a lifelong passion. The story of his devotion to the Dutch master is told in the following essay.

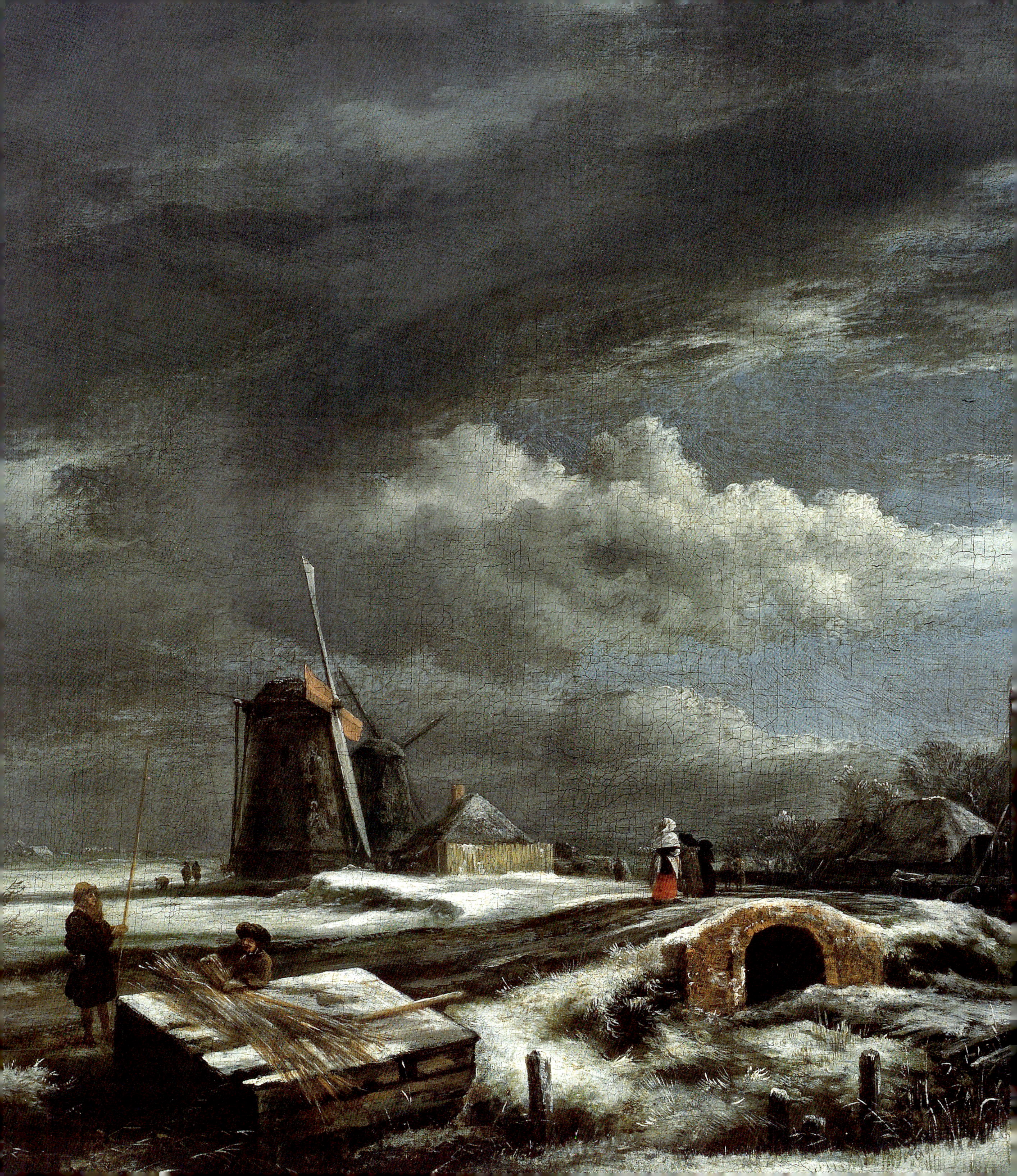

3

Constable and Ruisdael

> I have seen an affecting picture this morning by Ruysdael.
> It haunts my mind and clings to my heart . . .
>
> Constable to Archdeacon Fisher, 28 November 1826.[1]

John Constable expressed a keen interest in Ruisdael's work even before he obtained parental permission to study art in London. On 16 January 1797 the twenty-year-old fledgling artist, still in his family's grain and coal business, wrote to his tutor, John Thomas 'Antiquity' Smith:

> I have a great mind to copy one of Rysdael's etchings, I have seen one at your house where there are two trees standing in the water, and there is one which your Father copied, either of these I should like very much, but as they are very scarce and dear, perhaps you would not like to [en]trust them [to me], if not any one which is not so.[2]

Whether he managed to get Ruisdael's print of 'two trees standing in the water,' which must refer to the master's etching *Forest Marsh with Travellers on a Bank* (cat. 112), or another one to copy at this time is unknown, but it is evident from Constable's earliest existing etching, *The Deserted Cottage*, dated 1797, that in the beginning, he emulated Smith's prints, not Ruisdael's. The fact is not astonishing. Smith taught him the art of etching.[3]

A letter Constable wrote on 4 February 1799 to John Dunthorne Sr., his mentor and teacher before Smith, establishes that by this date Constable either owned or had a copy of a painting attributed to Ruisdael that had been copied in reverse by a printmaker; his letter was written soon after he settled in London (in the following month he was admitted as a probationer to the Royal Academy Schools):

> I shall begin painting as soon as I have a loan of a sweet little picture by Jacob Ruysdael to copy. Since I have been in town I have seen some remarkably fine ones by him, indeed I never saw him before; yet don't think, by this, I am out of conceit with my own, of which I have seen a print, 'tis of the same size and reversed.[4]

Constable was evidently satisfied with his Ruisdael, but the remarkably fine ones he saw in London made him confess: 'indeed I never [really] saw him before.'[5]

Joseph Farington records in his *Diary* on 2 March 1799: 'Constable called – shewed him Ruysdael,'[6] and on 16 April of the same year he notes: 'Constable called and brot. a Copy He had made from Ruysdael.'[7] Perhaps he brought his replica of the sweet little Ruisdael he wanted to copy a few months earlier. In any event, Farington's entry establishes that by April 1799 Constable had copied a Ruisdael.

In the spring of the following year Constable informed Dunthorne Sr. that he was copying yet another Ruisdael that he had purchased with a friend:

> I have likewise begun to copy a very fine picture by Ruysdael, which Mr. Reinagle and myself have purchased in partnership for £70 [. . .] I have finished my copy from Ruysdael, all but the glazing, which cannot be done till the picture is dry. It has been roasting in the sun these two or three days.[8]

At this time Constable shared lodgings with Ramsay Richard Reinagle (1775–1862), a fellow student at the Academy's schools, and later an Academician. They soon parted company, and by 1801 the Ruisdael painting they jointly owned was sold. Reinagle attempted to renew contact with Constable, but the latter, who found Reinagle's character reprehensible, resolved never again to establish a close relationship with him.[9] Reinagle became a picture cleaner and dealer with a shabby reputation that became much worse in 1848 when he submitted a marine painting to the Academy's exhibition by a young, little-known artist, which he had slightly altered and signed with his own name; when the cheat was discovered he was asked to resign as an Academician. Ruisdael's impressive *Waterfall in a Hilly Landscape*, at Indianapolis (S 205), passed through his hands; so did the dubious *Ruined Cottage* formerly at Boston (S dub120). Ramsay's father, Philip Reinagle, R.A. (1749–1833), was also a restorer and picture dealer; he made copies of paintings by Ruisdael, Hobbema, Wijnants and Wouwerman, reputedly so skilful that they passed for originals.

The Ruisdael copy that Constable showed Farington in 1799 and the one he made in 1800 have not been identified. It is certain that neither one can be his 1832 copy of *Winter Landscape* (fig. 45), a painting now in the Johnson Collection, Philadelphia Museum of Art (cat. 43), and it is highly unlikely that either is

Facing page Detail of cat. 43, *Winter Landscape*

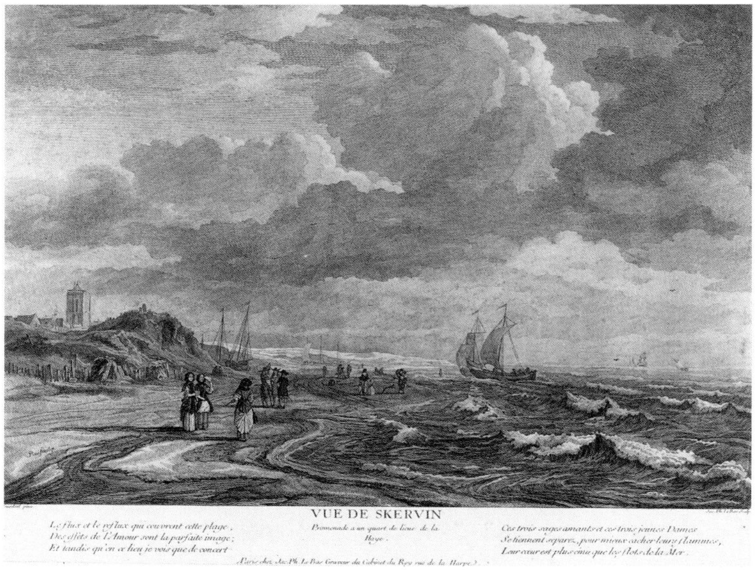

Fig. 33 J. P. Le Bas, engraving (in reverse) of Jacob van Ruisdael, *The Shore at Egmond aan Zee*.

identical with *Windmills* (fig. 43), his only other existing painted copy of a Ruisdael landscape, which, as we shall see, was done after a picture in the Dulwich Gallery. *Windmills* is an improbable contender, because it is unlikely that Constable, who was employed as a youth in his father's mills, would have failed to mention to Dunthorne Sr., a man able to give time to his art only after he finished his work as a glazier, plumber and odd-jobber, that he was copying a painting of windmills by Ruisdael. Mills were in Constable's blood. His younger brother Abram recognized this and was proud of it. Abram remarked to C.R. Leslie, Constable's first biographer: 'When I look at a mill painted by John, I see that it will *go round*, which is not always the case with those by other artists.'[10] Moreover there is reason to believe that Constable's copy of *Windmills* is not an early work but, as we shall see, may have been done as late as about 1830.

Constable remained attached to his early copies of Jacob's work. In 1819 his intimate friend Archdeacon John Fisher asked: 'Would you part with your copy of your Reysdale? not for myself. & price.'[11] 'I should hardly like to part with my copy of Ruysdael,' he responded. 'Its being an old school exercise (of which I have too few) gives it a value to me beyond what I could in conscience ask for it.'[12]

As a young man Constable followed the accepted tradition of first copying prints and then paintings by earlier artists. In addition to Ruisdael, Claude was a favourite. Mature Constable continued to copy, testimony of his firm belief that he could still learn from his predecessors. Copying also was a time-honoured way of paying homage to respected Old Masters – Constable never lost the fine feeling for those he admired as a young man. On the other hand, his contempt for landscapists he despised was outspoken. Before giving a lecture on landscape at the Royal Institution in 1836 he wrote to a friend 'I hope to murder Both and Berghem on Thursday next [. . .]' and in the lecture he savaged these Italianates:

> [. . .] Both and Berghem, who by an incongruous mixture of Dutch and Italian taste, produced a bastard style of landscape, destitute of the real excellence of either [. . .] Their art is destitute of sentiment or poetic feeling, because it is factitious, though their works being specious, their reputation is still kept up by the dealers, who continue to sell their pictures for high prices.[13]

After his lecture, one of Constable's listeners, a gentleman possessing a fine collection of pictures, said to him: 'I suppose I had better sell my Berchems.' To which Constable replied: 'No, sir, that will only continue the mischief, *burn them*.'[14]

What would Constable have said if his listener had responded: 'Mr. Constable, are you aware that Arnold Houbraken, Ruisdael's first biographer, tells us that he was a great friend of Berchem, that they most probably travelled together from Haarlem as far as Bentheim in Westphalia during the early 1650s, and they certainly collaborated on landscapes during the course of their careers? If Ruisdael, who you adore, found aspects of Berchem's efforts worthwhile, perhaps you, sir, have overlooked some of their qualities.' *The Great Oak* (cat. 20), dated 1652, Los Angeles County Museum of Art, is a beautiful example of their joint effort; another, datable almost two decades later, *Wooded Landscape with a Flooded Road*, is on extended loan to the Musée de la Chartreuse, Douai, from the Louvre (fig. 30).

Constable's thoughts turned to love after viewing a print that reproduces a Ruisdael shore scene he called 'a view of the shoar at Skeveling' in a letter he wrote in 1812 to Maria Bicknell, who became his wife four years later. The print was almost certainly Jacques Philippe Le Bas's (1707–83) engraving (in reverse; fig. 33) of Ruisdael's *Shore at Egmond aan Zee*, now at the National Gallery, London (see fig. 52a). The print is inscribed 'Vue de Skervin. Promenade a un quart de lieue de la Haye' and includes a six-line poem that tells the viewer:

> Le flux et le reflux qui couvrent cette plage,
> Des effets de l'Amour sont la parfaite image;
> Et tandis qu'en ce lieu je vois que de concert,
> Ces trois sages amants et ces trois jeunes Dames
> Se tiennent separez, pour mieux cacher leurs flammes,
> Leur coeur est plus ému les flots de la Mer.
>
> (The ebb and flow that covers this beach
> Is the perfect image of the effects of Love;
> And while I see here that, by mutual agreement,
> These three prudent lovers and these three young Women
> Keep apart, to better conceal their ardours,
> Their hearts are more agitated than the waves of the Sea.)

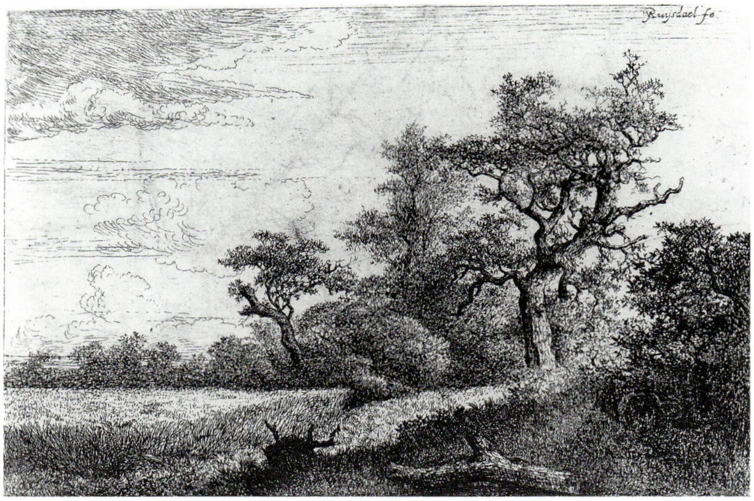

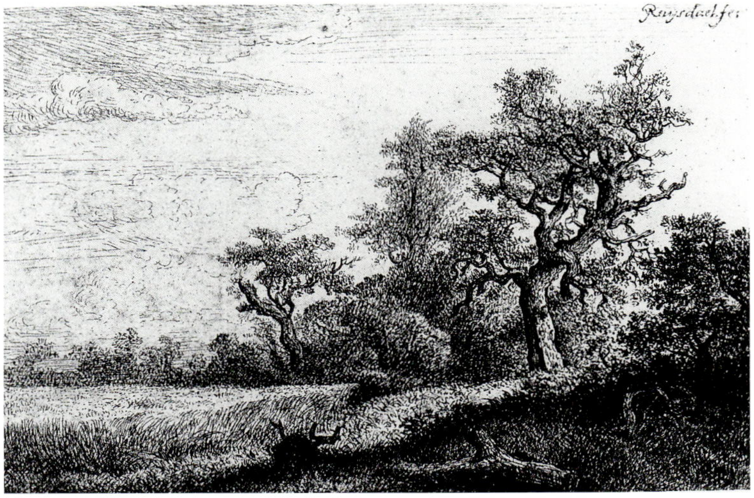

Fig. 34 Jacob van Ruisdael, *Grainfield at the Edge of a Wood*, 1648. 9.9 x 14.8 cm. Etching (cat. 107).

Fig. 35 John Constable, copy of cat. 107. Pen and ink, 1818. London, Victoria and Albert Museum.

Constable wrote to his 'dearest Maria':

> I am quite pleased you have taken up drawing again, and I hope you have not let the fine weather pass altogether without sketching the scenes about Bognor. I do not know if it be a beautifull place or otherwise, but a sea coast is always a subject enough for a pencil. I have a print hanging up in the room where I am now writing, a view of the shoar at Skeveling by Ruisdael, which gives me great pleasure. The waves are so well done that it is impossible to look at it without thinking on Bognor and all that is dear to me.[15]

In 1818, at the age of forty-two, Constable made a close pen and ink copy of Ruisdael's 1648 etching of *Grainfield at the Edge of a Wood* (fig. 34; cat. 107). His copy (fig. 35) includes the print's spurious 'JvRuysdael' signature and even simulates its plate mark but misses some of the delicacy of the original.[16] It has been reasonably suggested that he very well may have had Archdeacon Fisher in mind when he made his copy of the etching.[17] The year Constable made it, Fisher sent a letter by hand to the artist's new quarters at 1 Keppel Street, London; he addressed it to 'Reysdale House.' A few days later Fisher sent a note to the same address, slightly more correctly directed to 'Ruysdale House.'[18] Fisher was well aware of Constable's steadfast admiration for Ruisdael, and it was with the name of Ruisdael that he would link Constable's own when he was attempting to console or please the artist: 'You are painting for a name to be remembered

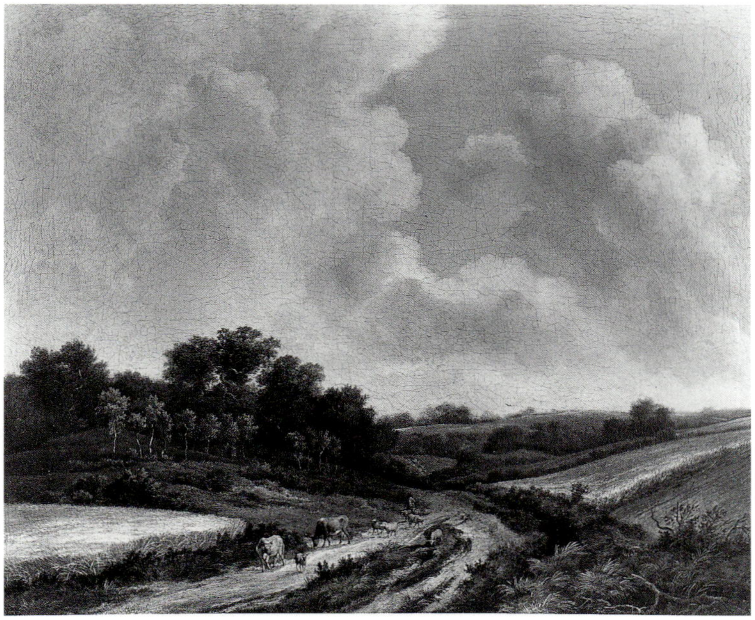

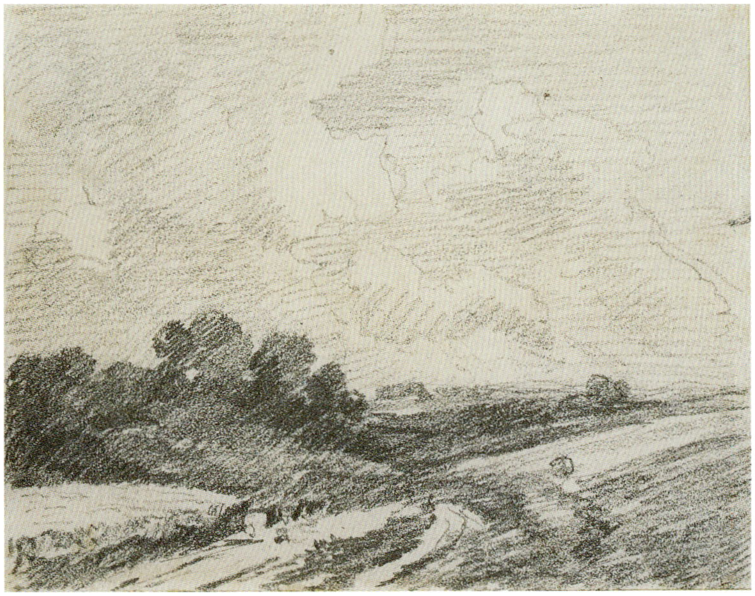

Fig. 36 Jacob van Ruisdael, *Landscape with a Grainfield*. 45.7 x 54.6 cm. Krefeld-Forstwald, Wolfgang Leufen.

Fig. 37 John Constable, copy of fig. 36. Graphite, 1819. Toronto, David Thomson.

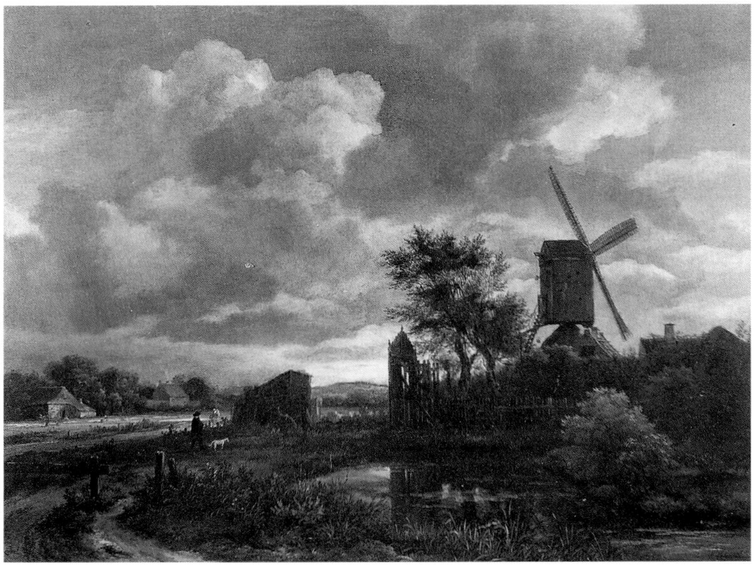

Fig. 38 Jacob van Ruisdael, *Evening Landscape: A Windmill by a Stream*. Collection Her Majesty Queen Elizabeth II.

hereafter: for the time when men shall talk of Wilson & Vanderneer & Ruisdale & Constable in the same breath,' he wrote in 1822, after Constable had been overwhelmingly defeated in the election at the Academy by Richard Cook, a minor painter who married a rich wife and never exhibited again after 1819.[19]

Constable was attracted by Ruisdael's *Landscape with a Grainfield* (fig. 36; S 93) when it was exhibited in 1819 at the British Institution and made a quick pencil copy of it (fig. 37).[20] Until his sketch was identified by Robert Hooze it had been regarded as one of Constable's own Suffolk views.[21] At the same exhibition he also made pencil copies of at least six other Old Master landscapes and marines, among them works by Claude, Aelbert Cuyp, and Willem van de Velde II. On the back of several, including his copy of the Ruisdael, he carefully noted their dimensions and the heights of their horizons (see p. 264, note 20). A good case has been made to support the hypothesis that the measurements are related to Constable's studies for *Waterloo Bridge*, a motif that engaged him at the time, and which culminated in *Whitehall Stairs*, a painting finished and exhibited at the Academy in 1832.[22]

Another Ruisdael painting that intrigued Constable was *Evening Landscape: A Windmill by a Stream* (fig. 38; S 130), which had been bought for the Prince Regent, later George IV, in 1810, and is still in the Royal Collection. In a letter dated 20 September 1821 Constable told Archdeacon Fisher that he had seen it at the Academy and wanted to copy it: 'The beautiful Ruisdael of the 'Windmill and log-house' which we admired at the Gallery is left there for the use of the students – I trust I shall be able to procure a memorandum of it.'[23]

Regarding this brief passage David Lucas, the printmaker and artist's friend, wrote that Constable expressed special admiration for the picture 'in which he said he could all but see the ells [*sic*] in the pools of water – that there were acres of sky expressed.'[24] In the same letter Constable also gave high praise to a Poussin which had been lent to the Academy, *Landscape: A Man Washing His Feet at a Fountain*, now at The National Gallery, London (no. 40). Students of Constable's works have been uncertain as to whether Lucas's comment refers to the Ruisdael or the Poussin, though it is usually assumed the Poussin is meant. However, the Poussin landscape cannot be characterized as a work with acres of sky and is hardly one that conjures up images of eels in pools; thus, it seems safe to assume that Lucas's comment refers to Constable's reaction to the Ruisdael, not the Poussin. Whether Constable managed 'to procure a memorandum' of Ruisdael's painting is not known; in any event, a copy of it by him has not been identified.

Constable saw Ruisdael's *Thatch-Roofed House with a Water Mill* (fig. 39; S 121), now at The Boijmans Van Beuningen Museum, Rotterdam, in 1826, when it was with the London dealer John Smith (who published the first catalogue of the Dutch master's paintings nine years later). A letter Constable sent Archdeacon Fisher the very day he saw it testifies how deeply it moved him:

> I have seen an affecting pucture this morning, by Ruisdael. It haunts my mind and clings to my heart – and has stood between me & you while I am now talking to you. It is a watermill, not unlike '*Perne's Mill*' – a man & boy are cutting rushes in the running stream (in the '*tail* water') – the whole so true clear & fresh – & as brisk as champagne – a shower has not long passed. It was beside the large one at Smiths – & showed Ruisdaels compass of mind in landscape.[25]

His remarks as well as Ruisdael's *Thatch-Roofed House with a Water Mill* recall well-known, similarly moving lines he sent to Fisher about his own art:

> [. . .] the sound of water escaping from Mill dams, so do Willows, Old rotten Banks, slimy posts, & brickwork. I love such things – Shakespeare could make anything poetical [. . .] As long as I do paint I shall never cease to paint such Places. The have always been my delight [. . .][26]

The unique impression of Ruisdael's early small etching of *Willows on a Bank* (fig. 40; cat. 102) served as a model for Constable's pen and black ink drawing of it (fig. 41) in 1827.[27] The precious original was lent to him by the Leeds industrialist and avid collector John Sheepshanks (1787–1863); it was acquired in 1836 by the British Museum as one of the treasures in his collection of more than 7,500 prints and 800 drawings for £5,000, a bargain-basement price deliberately set well below their market value to help the museum make the acquisition.[28] Constable knew the modest print was rare (a fact he probably learned from the exceptionally well-informed Sheepshanks); the label attached to the backboard of the framed drawing, written in the artist's hand, reads: 'Hampstead. Febr 21. 1827./ Copied from a scarce

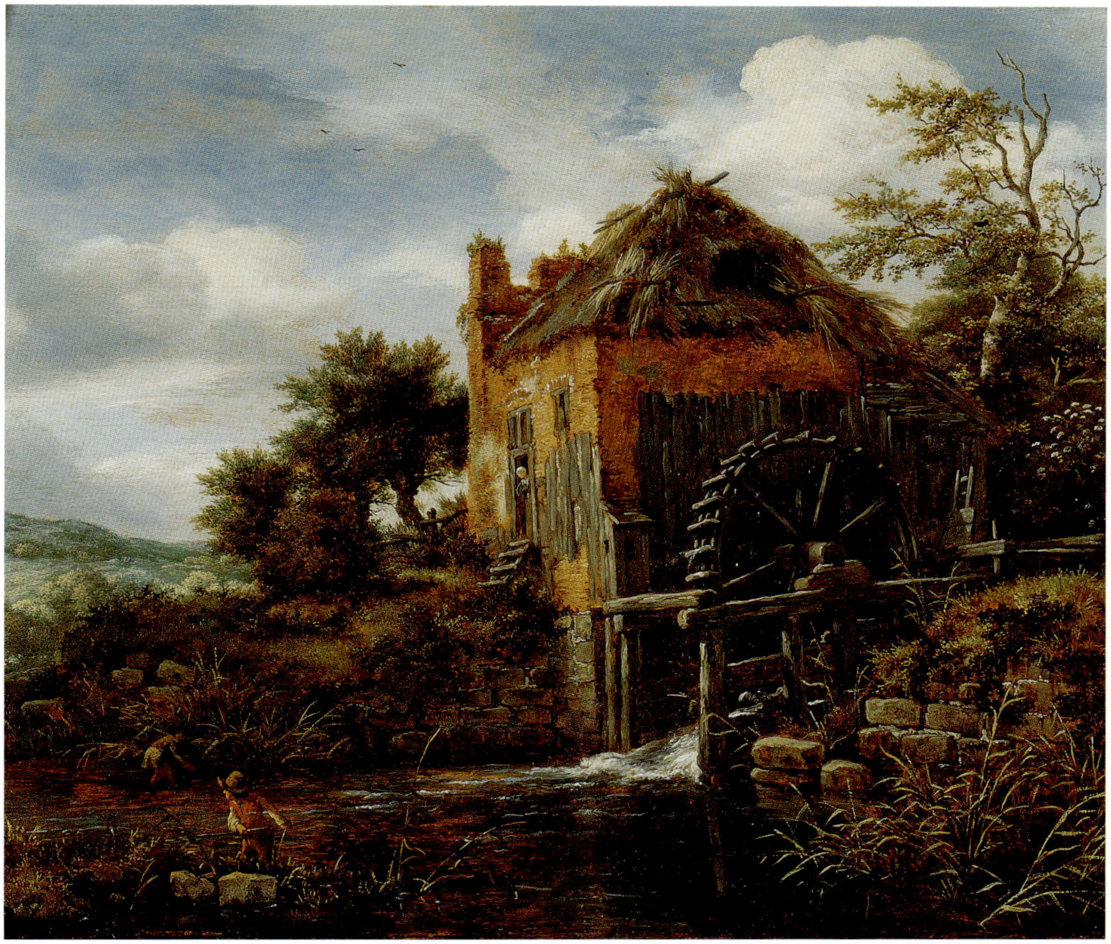

Fig. 39 Jacob van Ruisdael, *Thatch-Roofed House with a Water Mill*. 36 x 42 cm. The Boijmans Van Beuningen Museum, Rotterdam.

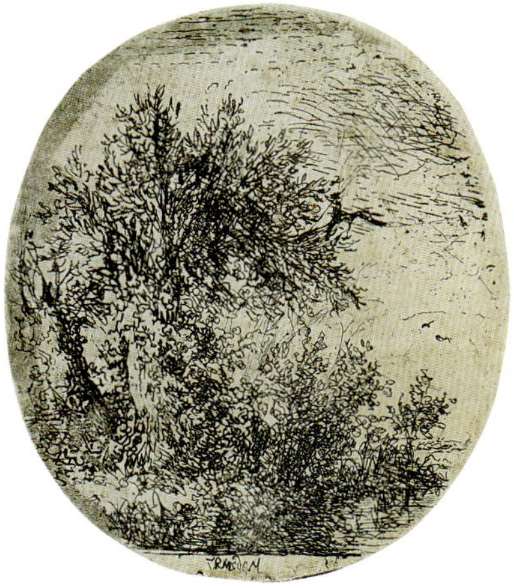

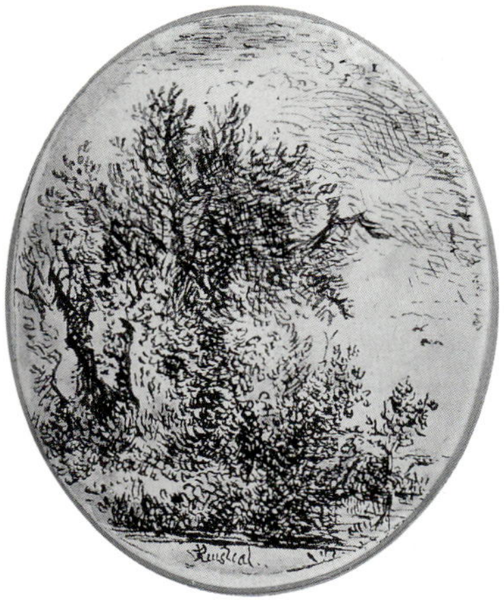

Fig. 40 Jacob van Ruisdael, *Willows on a Bank*. Etching (cat. 102).

Fig. 41 John Constable, copy of fig. 40. Pen and ink, 1827. Private collection.

etching/ by J. Ruysdael/ Lent to me by Mr. Sheepshanks/ John Constable.' A year later Sheepshanks lent Constable a rare etching by Herman van Swanevelt to copy.[29]

The copy by Constable of Ruisdael's *Landscape with Two Windmills* (fig. 43) is in the T.A. Gore Browne collection;[30] we have already heard the original is at Dulwich (fig. 42; S 131). The copy has been dated about 1797.[31] Although we know that young Constable wrote as early as 1797 that he wanted to copy Ruisdael's etchings and that he made copies of Ruisdael's paintings in 1799 and again in 1800, the style of the Gore Browne painting does not place it with the artist's *juvenilia*. In fact, there is no reason to believe that Constable laid eyes on it before the Dulwich Picture Gallery opened the doors of its new museum to the public in 1814.[32] Moreover, a partially legible inscription on the verso of the panel (not in Constable's hand) offers a clue to a much later date: '[. . .] by Constable, R.A. f. 1831. The Windmill from the original painting by J. Ruysdael in the Dulwich Gallery' (kind communication from T. A. Gore Browne). The fact that Constable visited Dulwich in 1830 and again in 1831 lends a shred of support to the late date. In a letter posted 29 July 1830 to David Lucas, Constable wrote 'I go to Dulwich to fetch pictures from the Gallery'[33] (pictures were being lent from the Dulwich Gallery to the Royal Academy). In July 1831, Constable informed Lucas that he would visit Dulwich again, this time to attend a dinner given by the Governors of Dulwich College to the President and Council of the Royal Academy.[34]

The artist's last reference to copying Ruisdael is in a letter he sent to Leslie on 4 September 1832, less than a fortnight after the death of his dearest friend Archdeacon Fisher:

> I cannot say but this very sudden and awfull event has strongly affected me. The closest intimacy has subsisted for many years between us – we loved each other and confided in each other entirely – and his loss makes a sad gap in my life & worldly prospects – he would have helped my children, for he was a good adviser though impetuous, and a truly religious man – God bless him until we meet again – I cannot tell how

singularly his death has affected me. I shall pass this week at Hampstead to copy the Winter – for which indeed my mind is in a fit state.[35]

The winter piece to which he referred is Ruisdael's painting of a *Winter Landscape*, then in the collection of Sir Robert Peel and now in the Johnson Collection, Philadelphia Museum of Art (fig. 44; cat. 43). Constable's copy is now in a private collection[35] (fig. 45). He inscribed on its stretcher:

> Copied from the Original Picture by Ruisdael in the possession of Sir Robt Peel, Bart. by me John Constable R.A. at Hampd. Sep. 1832. P.S. Color [. . .] Dog added [. . .] only [. . .] Size of the Original [. . .] and 'Showed this Picture to Dear John Dunthorne Octr. 30. 1832 [. . .] this was the last time I [. . .] poor J. Dunthorne died on friday (all Saints) the 2d of November. 1832 – at 4 o clock in the afternoon Aged 34.Years.

The latter inscription refers to the premature death of his one-time assistant Johnny Dunthorne, son of his first mentor in art.

It is not known when Constable first saw Peel's outstanding collection (in 1871 more than seventy of his paintings were acquired by The National Gallery, London; among them were two splendid Ruisdael landscapes [S 215, S 372], Rubens's *Chapeau de Paille*, and Hobbema's masterpiece, *Avenue at Middleharnis*) or how he persuaded Peel to allow him to copy the picture at his studio in Hampstead.[37] Apart from the addition of a dog on the left, Constable's copy is an exceptionally faithful one; like the copies he made of Ruisdael's etchings *Landscape with Two Willows* and *A Grainfield at the Edge of a Wood*, it even imitates the signature inscribed on the work. According to a note written by Lucas in his annotated volume of Leslie's *Memoirs of the Life of Constable*, 1843, the addition of the dog was not the artist's whim but was introduced to fill a demand made by Peel:

> The loan of this picture was accompanied by a condition that some addition or omission should be made in order that the composition might be some what different he complied by introducing a dog behind the princepal [*sic*] figure in all other respects the imitation was so perfect that looking on the surface only few could detect any difference.[38]

Lucas's note provides a rare account of the conditions that compelled a copyist to deviate from his model.

Soon after Constable copied the *Winter Landscape* he used it and an untraceable copy of an unidentified Ruisdael seascape in an 1836 lecture at the British Institution on Dutch and Flemish painting to bolster his maxim that 'We see nothing till we truly understand it.'[39] Pointing to his copy of the *Winter* he said:

> This picture represents an approaching thaw. The ground is covered with snow, and the trees are still white; but there are two windmills near the centre; the one has the sails furled, and is turned in the position from which the wind blew when the mill left off work; the other has the canvas on the poles, and is

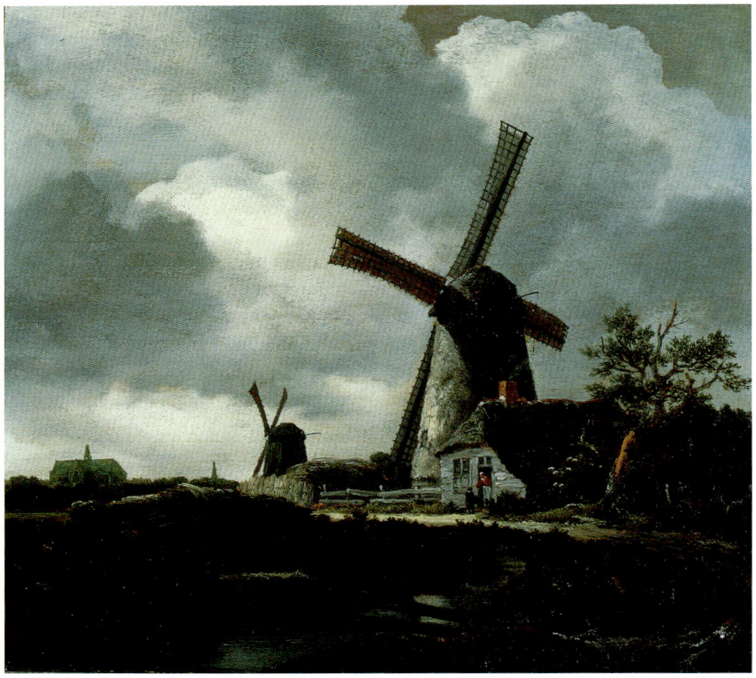

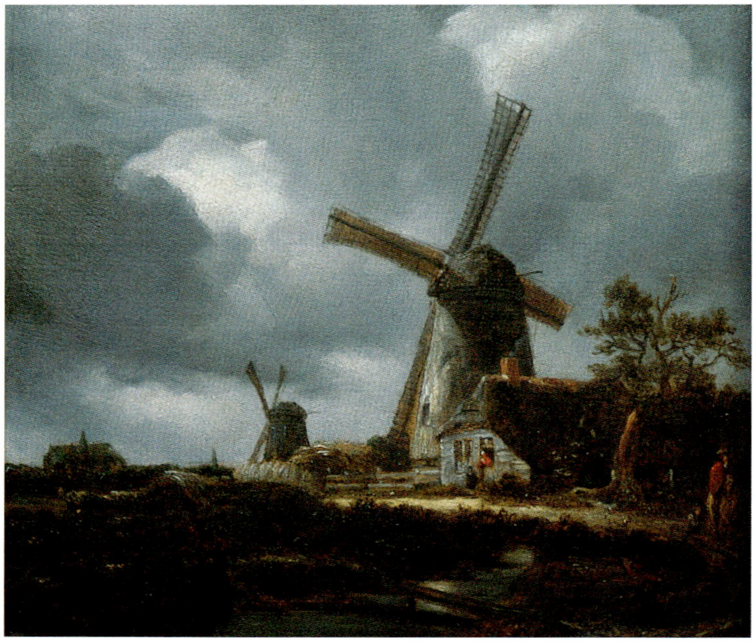

Fig. 42 Jacob van Ruisdael, *Landscape with Windmills*. 31.5 x 33.9 cm. Dulwich Picture Gallery, London.

Fig. 43 John Constable, copy of fig. 42. T. A. Gore Brown, London.

turned another way, which indicates a change in the wind. The clouds are opening in that direction, which appears by the glow in the sky to be the south (the sun's winter habitation in our hemisphere), and this change will produce a thaw before morning. The concurrence of these circumstances shows that Ruysdael *understood* what he was painting.[40]

In the same lecture he told his audience that Ruisdael's *Allegory of the Life of Man* was a failure because in the work he attempted to tell with symbolic references that which is outside the reach of art; for support of the suggestion that he almost certainly was referring to the Detroit version of *The Jewish Cemetery* (see cat. 22, pp.87–88).

At the time of his death in 1837 Constable's copies of Peel's *Winter Landscape* and Dulwich's *Windmills* as well as two others were still in his possession. They appeared in the posthumous sale of his paintings, London (Foster), 15–16 May 1838:[41]

No. 45 A Winter Scene, from the original, by Jacob Ruysdael, in the possession of Sir Robert Peel (£15.15).
No. 47 The Windmill[s], from the original picture, by Jacob Ruysdael, in the Dulwich Gallery (£5.15.6).
No. 50 A small upright Landscape, after Ruysdael (£4.4).
No. 52 The Cornfield, after Jacob Ruisdael (£9.9).

The small upright landscape (no. 50) and the painting called a *Cornfield* (no. 52) have not been identified.[42]

Three paintings catalogued in the sale were listed as Ruisdael originals:

No. 10 A small Landscape with chateau (£8.18.6).
No. 15 Woody Landscape and figures reposing (£4.14.6).
No. 16 Landscape with cottage and figures (£5.5).

None is traceable today. Perhaps one of them hung in his bedroom four years before his death. In 1833 he wrote to Rev. Henry Scott Trimmer, an amateur painter: 'I have your little picture of a Wreck and Storm at sea, over the chimney peice [*sic*] of my bed room, above the beautifull Ruysdael, so that I am daily reminded of you [. . .]'[43]

A letter Constable wrote to his wife in 1823 tells us he also had in his possession a copy of a Ruisdael waterfall by Sir George Beaumont: 'Will you take the trouble to measure the inside of the gilt frame which contains the sketch of the waterfall from Ruysdael by Sir G – it hangs over the sofa in the drawing room [. . .] I think you will find it about 18 by 15 inches more or less.'[44] Whether it was one of the seven landscapes by Beaumont that appeared in the 1838 sale of Constable's estate cannot be determined. Beaumont's works are baldly catalogued as: no. 42 Three Landscapes; no. 43 Four ditto.[45]

It is evident that Constable's interest in Ruisdael's etchings continued until the end; four of them were in his collection when he died. Three were offered as one lot in the posthumous sale of his works on paper held in Foster's London rooms, 10–12 May 1838, no. 401: *The Little Bridge*, *The Two Peasants and their dog*; *The Cottage on the Hill* (cat. 109–11). The fourth was offered independently: no. 402 *The Travellers* (cat. 112). It is touching to learn that by the time of his death he had managed to acquire what the compiler of his posthumous sale catalogue described as a 'fine and extremely rare' impression of the very Ruisdael etching young Constable told 'Antiquity' Smith in 1797 he had 'a great mind to copy'.

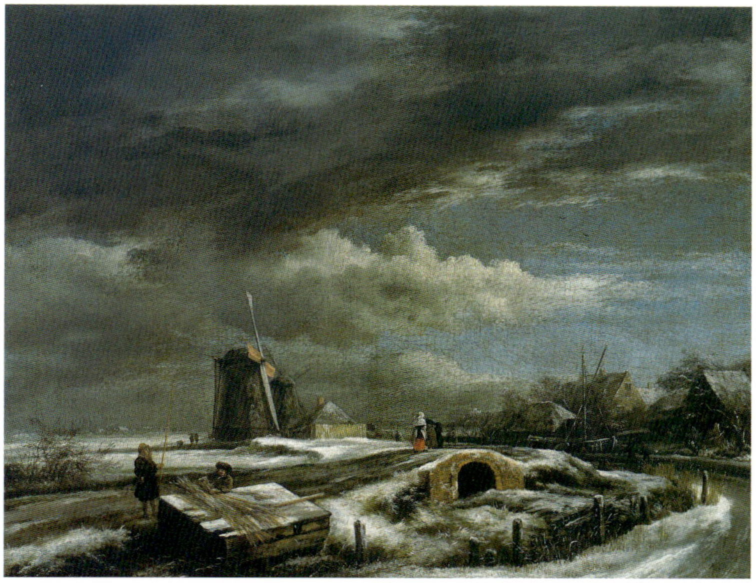

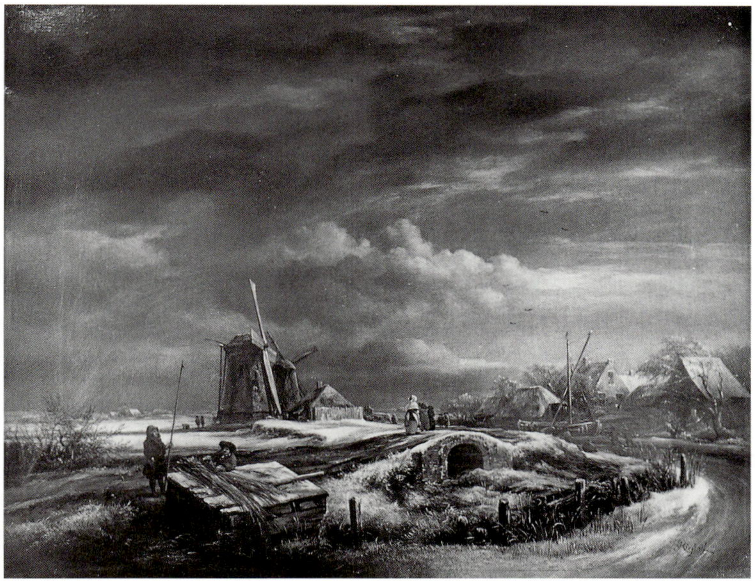

Fig. 44 Jacob van Ruisdael, *Winter Landscape*. 55.2 x 66.6 cm. Philadelphia Museum of Art, John G. Johnson Collection (cat. 43).

Fig. 45 John Constable, copy of cat. 43. 1832. Private collection.

Overleaf Detail of cat. 18 *Landscape with the Ruins of Egmond Castle*

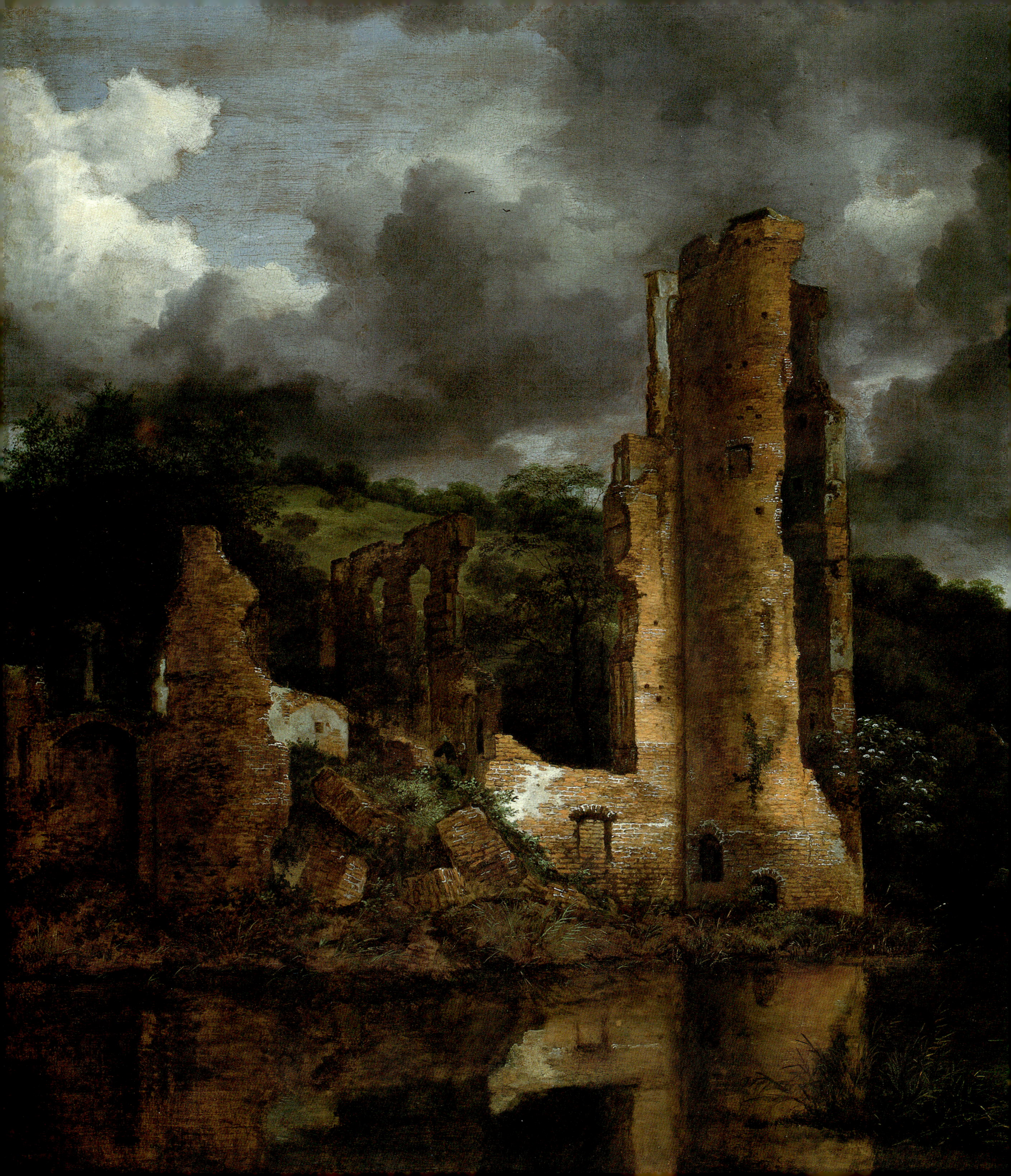

Catalogue • Paintings

1

Landscape with a Cottage and Trees

Signed and dated 1646, lower left. Panel,[1] 71.8 × 101 cm
Hamburger Kunsthalle, 159

PROVENANCE: Collection Wortmann, Hamburg; collection Sillem, Hamburg; Johannes Amsinck, Hamburg, 1836; he bequeathed it to the Kunsthalle, 1879.

EXHIBITIONS: The Hague–Cambridge 1981–82, no. 1, repr.; Hamburg–Haarlem 2002, no. 10, repr.

LITERATURE: Manuscript Catalogue of the Collection of Johannes Amsinck, 1836, no. 10; Kunsthalle Hamburg, Inventory, 1880, p.22, no. 148 (staffage by A. van de Velde); Bredius 1890, p.191 (staffage by Berchem); HdG 806 (staffage by Berchem); Ros 503 (staffage by Berchem); Simon 1930, p.15 (staffage by Berchem); Kunsthalle, Hamburg, Catalogue, 1956, no. 159; Schaar 1958, p.36, note 32; Ashton *et al.* 1982, pp.18ff., pl. 17 (detail); Walford 1991, pp.59–61, repr.; Slive 2001, no. 569, repr.

LACMA and PMA

The year 1646 inscribed on the painting has a particular claim as Ruisdael's *annus mirabilis*. It is the year when the seventeen- or eighteen-year-old youth appears on the scene in Haarlem as an accomplished master with a large group of dated landscapes – fifteen have been identified.[2] Among them the Hamburg landscape near dunes with a modest cottage and a ramshackle plank privy takes a special place. It already has the unmitigated density of vegetation that remains characteristic of so many of his later paintings; his ardor for nature is expressed repeatedly by a massive crowding of closely packed trees and thick undergrowth. To judge from the astonishingly accurate portrayal of the blasted pollard willow, the blooming elder bush and the oak tree in the painting, young Jacob must have made drawings of individual trees and shrubs that had an almost microscopic attention to detail. But if he did, not one has survived.

The figures and animals in the picture, which have partly disappeared through cleaning, have been variously attributed to Ruisdael, A. van de Velde and Nicolaes Berchem, but during the course of a 1934 restoration it was reported that only the two women and man in a black jacket on the left are contemporaneous with the landscape; the rest of the staffage, including the ducks, are painted by another artist, possibly in the early eighteenth century.[3] William W. Robinson noted (private communication) that the cowherd blowing his horn and resting his arm on the back of one of his animals, also later additions, are almost identical to figures that appear in an early painting by Adriaen van de Velde (1636–72), dated 1655, and an etching (in reverse), dated 1659.[4] Apparently, the anonymous staffage painter pilfered part of his contribution from Adriaen van de Velde.

1. The dendrochronological analysis made by Peter Klein, Hamburg University (private communication), in 1994 of the work's three oak boards from the Baltic region that form its support indicates that the painting's creation is plausible about 1640 or later.
2. Fourteen are listed in Slive 2001, "Chronological List of Dated Works," p.5. The fifteenth work reappeared in 2003; see p.1, above, and figs. 1, 2.
3. The restoration report, dated 25 April 1934, is in the curatorial files of the Kunsthalle.
4. The painting is *Herdsman and Other Figures in a Meadow*, with the dealer H. Schaeffer, Berlin, 1932 (HdG, A.v.d.Velde, 4, p.537, no. 201; photo RKD). The print is *Herdsman with a Bull*, title sheet to a series of ten prints depicting various animals (Bartsch 1978–: 1, 1978, p.223, repr.).

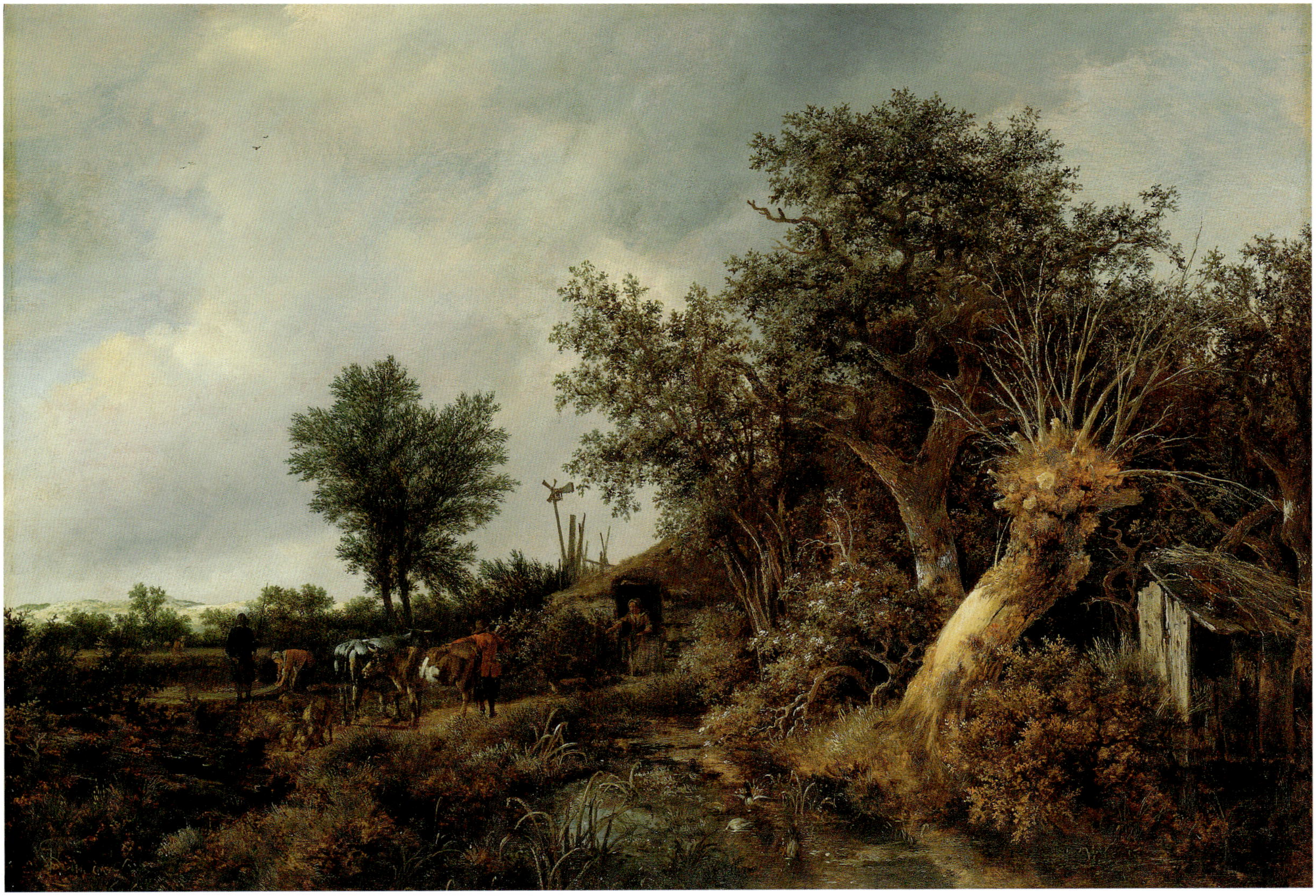

2

A Windmill near Fields

Monogrammed and dated 1646, lower right. Panel,[1] 49.5 × 68.5 cm
The Cleveland Museum of Art, Mr. and Mrs. William Marlatt Fund 1967.19

PROVENANCE: Sir Francis Cook (1817–1901), Doughty House, Richmond; by descent to his son Sir Frederick Cook (1844–1920), Doughty House, Richmond; by descent to his son Herbert Cook (1868–1939), Doughty House, Richmond; Sir Francis Ferdinand Maurice Cook (1907–78), Le Coin, Jersey, Channel Islands; sale, Trustees of the Cook Collection, London (Christie's), 25 November 1966, no. 55 (as follower of Ruisdael); dealer F. Kleinberger, New York; acquired by The Cleveland Museum of Art, Mr. and Mrs. William H. Marlatt Fund, 1967.19.

EXHIBITIONS: Lincoln 1946, no. 43; Manchester, City Art Gallery, 1964–66; Hamburg–Haarlem 2002, no. 12, repr. (not exhibited at either venue).

LITERATURE: HdG 180; Kronig 1914, p.94, no. 350 (certainly not by Ruisdael, but by an unknown close follower who differs from him by a black untransparent tonality in the foliage and a clumsy handling; the monogram and date are not mentioned); Ros 119 (signed and dated 1647); Simon 1930, p.79 (dated 1646); Stechow 1968, pp.250ff.; Slive 1981, p.47, repr. p.46; Cleveland Museum, Catalogue, 1982, 3, p.266, no. 117, repr.; Walford 1991, pp.55–57, repr.; Slive 2001, no. 127, repr.

Engraved by Joh[ann]. Georg Hertel, who can be identified as an Augsburg engraver who was still active in 1760, or his identically named son (see *Thieme-Becker*, 16, p.552). The print, which crops the composition at the top, is inscribed: No. 39 (Slive 2001, fig. 127a). The painting was also engraved in reverse by P[ierre Jacques] Duret (1729–about 1800) as "Le Moulin Flamand" (Slive 2001, fig. 127b).

LACMA and RA

In this work dated 1646 the mother-of-pearl pink, blue, grey and white of the streaky clouds and late afternoon sky recall effects achieved by Jacob's uncle Salomon van Ruysdael. However, the deep, dark tonality and dense massing on the right of the house, trees, gate and fence dominated by the windmill are highly original. *The Road in a Village with a Windmill*, also dated 1646, in a private collection (Slive 2001, no. 135, repr.), which is less tightly knit, may represent the same site seen from a closer and different point of view.

A copy of the Cleveland picture, in reverse, is at the Hermitage;[2] it is probably based on Duret's reversed print after the picture. A painting by an imitator in an octagonal format bears some resemblance to the present work, but it may be a variant or a dim reflection of a lost original that showed the same site (formerly dealer A. J. Schreuder, Amsterdam; photo RKD). Of greater consequence is the *Windmill* at Buckingham Palace (Slive 2001, no. 130, repr.) painted about 1650. It is a brilliant variation on the Cleveland picture, but less well preserved.

For early drawings of windmills by Ruisdael, see cat. 61, 62.

1. The panel consists of two oak boards originating from the Baltic/Polish region. Dendrochronological analysis of the sapwood rings of the youngest board indicates that the creation of the painting is plausible from 1641 upwards (information kindly provided by Peter Klein, Hamburg University, private communication, 8 April 1993).
2. No. 3139, uncatalogued; panel, 22.5 × 31.2. Provenance: P. Semenov, St. Petersburg, until 1915 when it entered the Imperial Hermitage, Petrograd. Literature: Semenov 1906, p.cxxii, no. 303 (anonymous Dutch, *c.*1640–45).

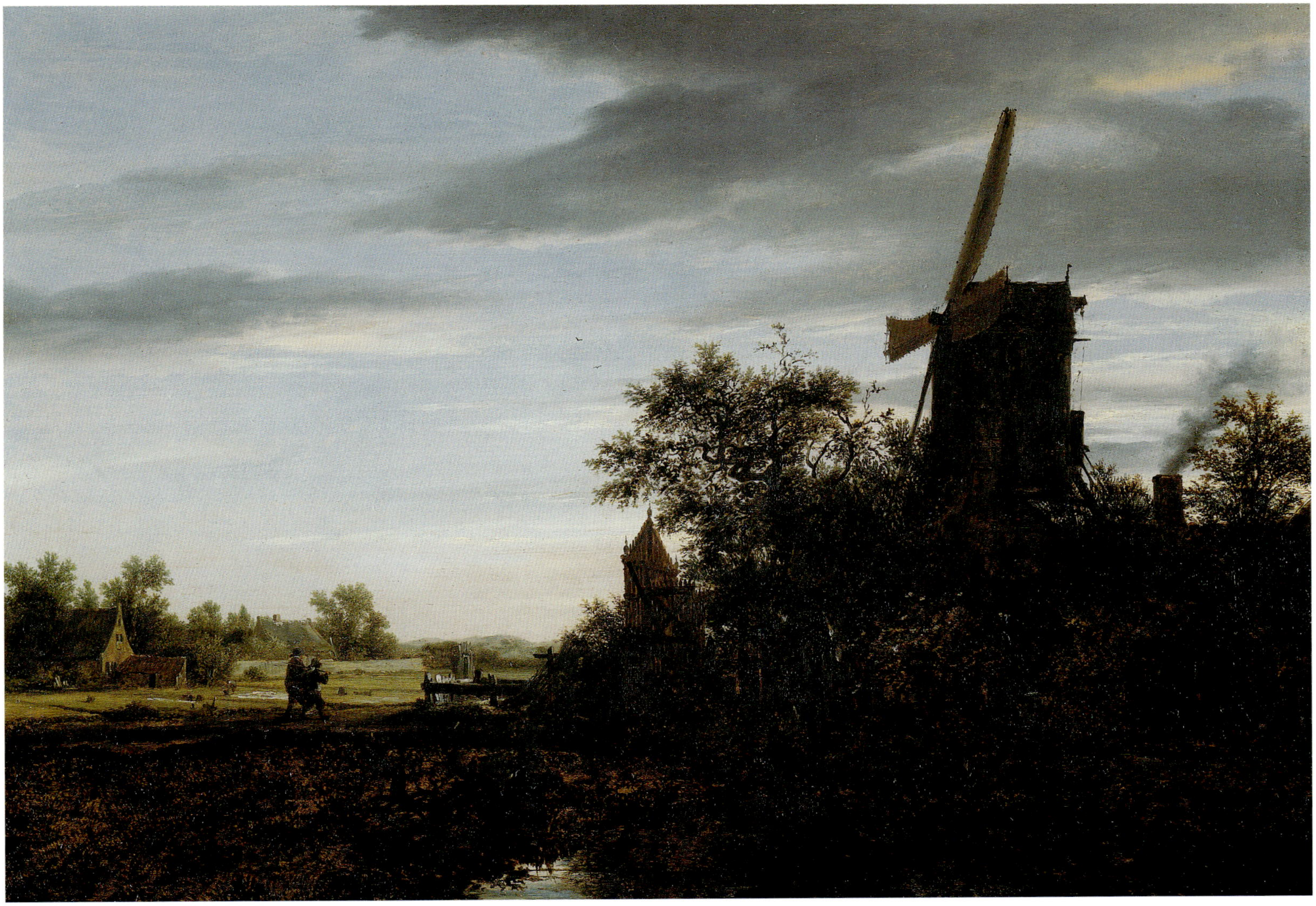

3

Dune Landscape

Signed and dated 1646, right centre near the bottom. Canvas, 105.5 × 163 cm
The State Hermitage Museum, St. Petersburg, 939

PROVENANCE: Acquired for the Imperial Hermitage, 1859.

EXHIBITIONS: The Hague–Cambridge 1981–82, no. 3, repr. (shown in The Hague only); New York–Chicago 1988, no. 28; Hamburg–Haarlem 2002, no. 13, repr. (not exhibited in either venue).

LITERATURE: Waagen 1864, p.243; Hermitage, St. Petersburg, Catalogue, 1895, 2, no. 1143; HdG 895; Shcherbachova 1924, p.21; Pappé 1926, p.200 (by Ruisdael, not F. Knibbergen as W. Martin stated on a recent visit to the Hermitage); Ros 552; Simon 1935, p.189 (staffage by Isaack van Ruisdael); Simon 1935a, p.17 (staffage by Isaack van Ruisdael); Hermitage, Leningrad, Catalogue, 1958, 2, p.246, no. 939; Fechner 1958, p.6; Fechner 1963, pp.93, 170; Hermitage, Leningrad, Catalogue, 1981, 2, p.162, no. 939; Liedtke 1989, p.160; Slive 2001, no. 615, repr.

The painting manifests the astonishing velocity with which Ruisdael gave novel effects to a traditional scheme. By 1646 both Salomon van Ruysdael and Jan van Goyen had produced numerous broad views of dunes with a house crowded by trees set on an elevation in the middle ground and distant vistas on either side of the main motif. New in the painting is the greater solidity Ruisdael gives to the high dune and the dominating tree group and the way the trees stand out forcibly against the sky. The concentration of strong light on the sandy road introduces an unusually emphatic contrast in the foremost plane, where the grainy paint and rugged touch characteristic of Jacob's works done in the forties and early fifties is particularly evident. The large size of the canvas also is exceptional; it is an index of the youthful artist's ambition.

At the time of writing, an old yellowed surface coating which distorts the colours of the original paint layer of this early master work is being removed during the course of its restoration in the Hermitage's conservation laboratory. A detail of the painting during its restoration is illustrated on p. xiv.

A smaller, autograph version of the dunescape, also signed and dated 1646 [not 1645], is at the Gouverneurs Huis, Paramaribo, Surinam (Slive 2001, no. 610). Simon's (1935, p.189, and 1935a, p.17) conclusion that the staffage in both works is by Isaack, the artist's father, is unconvincing. The larger scale, more monumental effect and greater clarity of the vista on the right side of the house and large clump of trees of the Petersburg landscape suggests it postdates the Paramaribo painting.

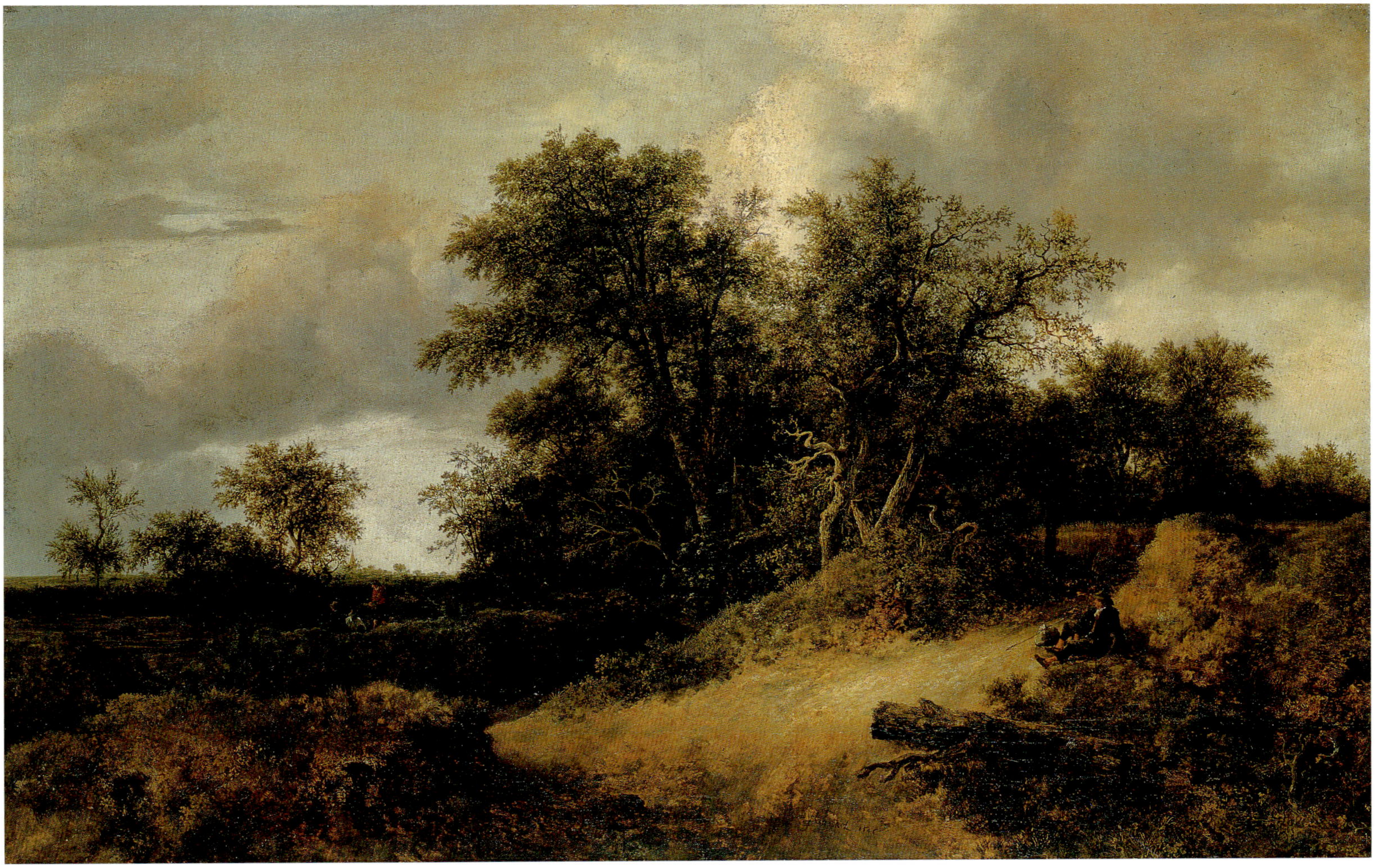

4

Entrance to a Wood

Monogrammed, lower right. About 1646. Panel, 57.5 × 47 cm
Gemäldegalerie der Akademie der bildenden Künste, Vienna, 1368

PROVENANCE: Acquired by a Viennese private collector from the English art market about 1924; acquired for the Akademie in 1924.

EXHIBITION: Brussels 1977–78, p.71, repr.; Minneapolis–Houston–San Diego 1985, no. 32, repr.

LITERATURE: Eigenberger 1927, 1, pp.363f.; Ros 386; Münz 1948, p.26, no. 50; Münz 1955, p.36, no. 55; Akademie der bildenden Künste, Vienna, Catalogues, 1961, p.46, no. 58, and 1972, p.107, no. 191; Walford 1991, pp.58–59; Trnek 1992, pp.324–28, no. 106; Slive 2001, no. 434, repr.

LACMA and PMA

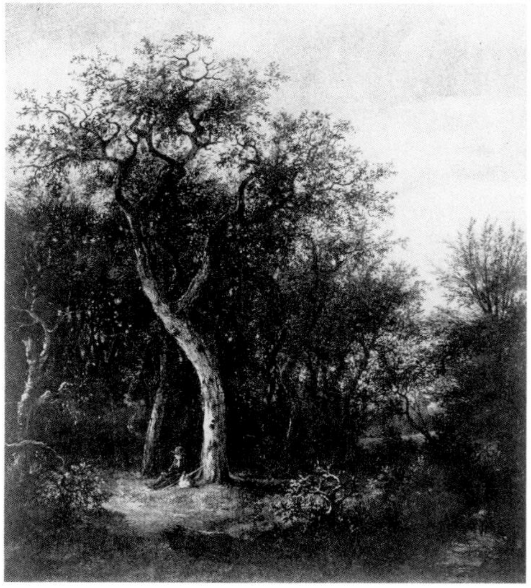

Fig. 4a Jacob van Ruisdael, *Wood with a Sunlit Path*, 1646. Formerly A. C. J. A. Stöcker, Amsterdam.

Today the painting is accepted as an unchallenged early woodland scene by Ruisdael. It was, however, acquired by the Akademie as a work by Gillis Rombouts. On the basis of its close similarity to Ruisdael's *Wood with a Sunlit Path*, signed and dated 1646, formerly in the A. C. J. A. Stocker collection, Amsterdam (fig. 4a; Slive 2001, no. 308), Rosenberg (1928, p.17) correctly attributed it to Ruisdael and assigned it to the same phase of the artist's career. In both works young Ruisdael depicts a path in a dense wood with a view of the sky. The lacey effect of the crowns of the prominent trees in both works indicate the young artist's early familiarity with Cornelis Vroom's highly personal, serene landscapes. The Akademie's painting is also related to the right half of Jacob's drawing of *Hunter with Three Dogs entering a Wood* of 1646 at Berlin (cat. 65) and the unique impression of his etching of *Willows on a Bank* at the British Museum (cat. 102), datable about the same time.

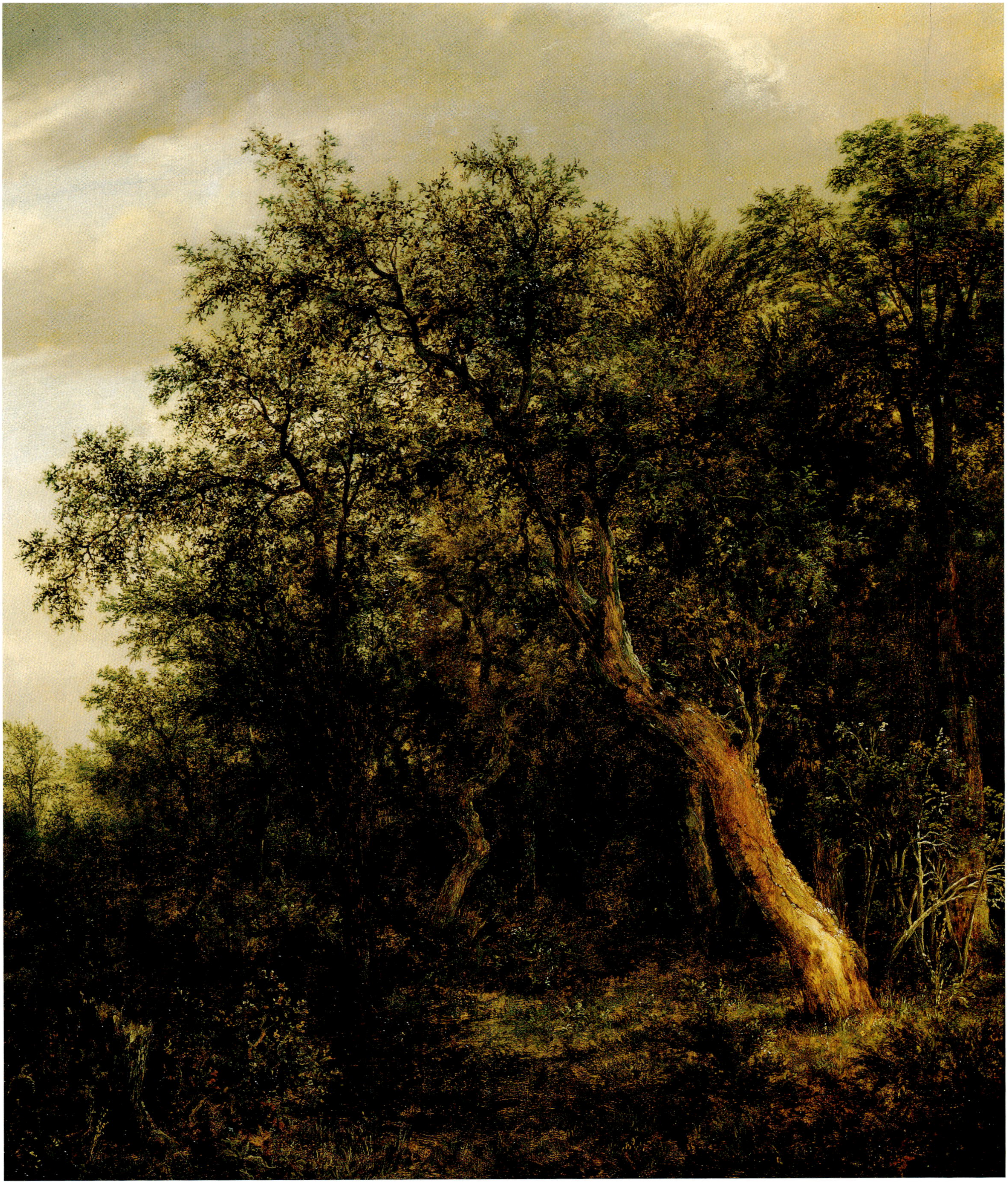

5

Oak Tree and Dense Shrubbery at the Edge of a Pond

About 1646–48. Panel, 66 × 48.9 cm
Szépművészeti Múzeum, Budapest, 263

PROVENANCE: Collection Esterházy, by 1812.

EXHIBITIONS: The Hague–Cambridge 1981–82, no. 4, repr.; Tokyo and elsewhere 1992–93, no. 52, repr.

LITERATURE: *Catalog der Gemählde-Gallerie des durchlauchtigen Fürsten Esterházy von Galantha zu Laxenburg bey Wien*, 1812, 8, no. 9; Frimmel 1891–92, 1, p.173 (probably by Ruisdael; birds by D. Wijntrack); Ros 279a; A. Pigler, *Katalog der Galerie Alter Meister*, Budapest, 1967, pp.601f., no. 263; Czobor 1967, no. 23; Kouznetsov 1973, pp.35ff; *Summary Catalogue*, vol. 2, Budapest, 2000, p.147, no. 263; Slive 2001, no. 325, repr.

Etched by Friedrich Loos (1797–1890).

For young Ruisdael foregrounds could become paramount, and in early works such as this close view of a sharply lit, battered oak engulfed by dense undergrowth near the edge of a pond, or the unique impression at the British Museum of his small etching of a similar subject (cat. 105), distant views have been virtually eliminated.

Jacob's innate acuteness as a draughtsman, invariably seen to some extent in his paintings, is particularly evident in the tangled growth near the edge of the still pond. Equally remarkable is his expressive portrait of the half-barren, blasted oak. The birds were done by another hand.[1]

Ágnes Czobor (1967) mentions that the old tree trunk and owl in the tree allude to the mortality of life. Iouryi Kouznetsov (1973, p.39), well aware of the many symbolic meanings that have been assigned to trees since ancient times, proposes that, in this case, the tree symbolizes fragility and corruptibility. Kouznetsov further writes that the owl perched on a broken limb of the tree is being attacked by two small birds. This motif, he adds, traditionally alludes to strife and hate in the world, and it may have this meaning in Ruisdael's painting.[2] His interpretation of the motif is questionable because it is not clear if the two little birds are attacking the owl. The case for their attack is not strengthened by the presence of two other air-borne small birds, who are oblivious to it. Kouznetsov does not insist upon the point. He notes that the owl may allude to the *vanitas* theme, as Czobor suggests, or to *melancholia*. He further proposes that the owl and other birds may have been added to the painting by one of Ruisdael's contemporaries without the artist's knowledge to give the landscape added meaning.

The symbolic possibilities for battered trees and owls can be enlarged upon. Whether Ruisdael himself intended them to have one of the multitudinous meanings that have been assigned to them since the tree of life and tree of knowledge appeared in the garden of Eden and Athena appeared in Athens with her owl remains moot.

1. T. Frimmel (1891–92) attributed them to Dirck Wijntrack (before 1625–87), a painter who specialized in birds, particularly ducks. I am unable to confirm his attribution.
2. The best-known treatments of this theme are found in Hieronymus Bosch's drawings. For a discussion of the iconography of the motif in Bosch's time that centers on the well-known drawing of *Owls in a Tree* at the Boijmans Van Beuningen Museum, see Jakob Rosenberg, "On the Meaning of a Bosch Drawing," *De Artibus Opuscula XL, Essays in Honor of Erwin Panofsky*, ed. Millard Meiss, 1, New York, 1961, pp.422ff.

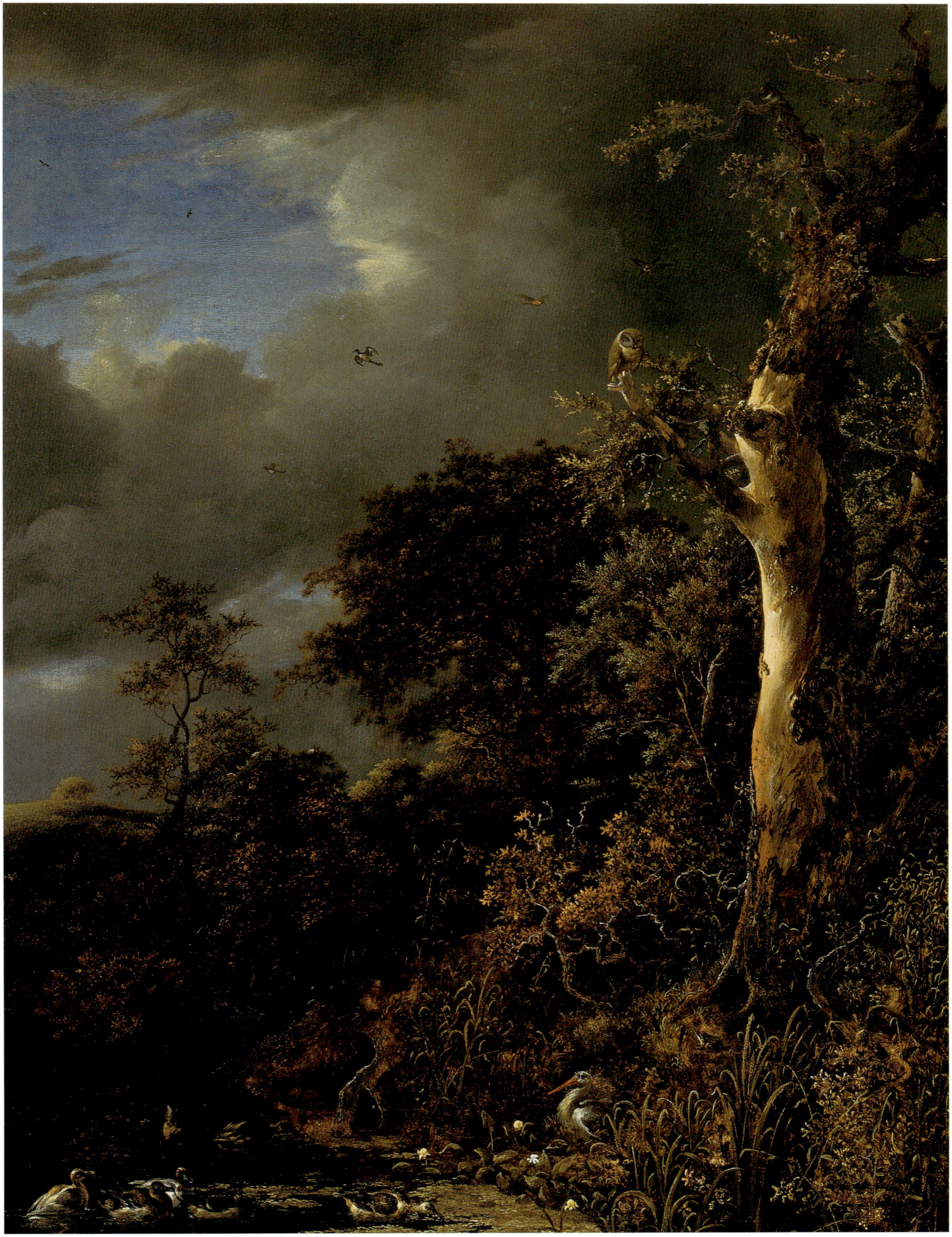

6 View of Naarden

Signed and dated 1647, bottom left. Panel, 34.8 × 67 cm
Museo Thyssen-Bornemisza, Madrid, 1930.99

PROVENANCE: Possibly Richard Grosvenor, 2nd Marquess of Westminster (d.1869); possibly his widow, Elizabeth, Dowager Marchioness of Westminster (d.1891); possibly Hugh, 3rd Marquess (from 1874, 1st Duke) of Westminster (d.1899); inherited by Lady Theodora Guest (née Grosvenor; d.1924), daughter of the 2nd Marquess, Inwood House, near Henstridge, Somerset; possibly among the works sold by her privately to dealer Robert Langton Douglas, London, *c.*1917; dealer Galerie Matthiesen, Berlin, from whom acquired by Baron Heinrich Thyssen-Bornemisza, in or before 1928; thence by descent.

EXHIBITIONS: London 1929, no. 190; Düsseldorf 1929, no. 57; Munich 1930, no. 283, repr. (erroneously as dated 1667); Rotterdam–Essen 1959–60, no. 92, repr.; London 1961, no. 95; The Hague–Cambridge 1981–82, no. 6, repr.; Madrid 1994–95, no. 50, repr.; Amsterdam 2000, no. 82, repr.

LITERATURE: Ros 73; C. Linfert, "Eine Landschaft des Haarlemer Vermeer im Wallraf-Richartz-Museum zu Köln," *Kunstchronik und Kunstliteratur*, appendix to *Zeitschrift für bildende Kunst*, January 1930, pp.113–14, repr.; Gerson 1934, p.79, repr.; Simon 1935, p.191; Gerson 1936, p.19; Schloss Rohoncz, Lugano, Catalogues, 1937, no. 364, repr., and 1958, no. 364; Stechow 1966, pp.42, 45, repr.; *The Thyssen-Bornemisza Collection, Catalogue of the Paintings*, Castagnola–Ticino, 1969, p.295, no. 296, repr.; *Thyssen-Bornemisza Collection, Catalogue of the Exhibited Works of Art*, Castagnola, 1981, p.274, no. 269, repr.; Gaskell 1990, pp.374–77, no. 86; Walford 1991, pp.64–65, repr.; Davies 1993, pp.110–11, under no. 16, repr.; Slive 2001, no. 78, repr.

RA

Naarden lies about twenty kilometres southeast of Amsterdam on the Zuider Zee (in 1932 the name of the sea was changed to the IJsselmeer). The sea can be seen on the extreme right of the painting. The small sunlit building in the far distance on the horizon is the ruined church of Muiderberg. Naarden and its environs had a particular attraction for Ruisdael; his grandfather settled there late in the sixteenth century, and it was the birthplace of his father Isaack and his uncle Salomon. A year after the Thyssen picture was painted, Jacob made a finished drawing of a coastal scene that includes a view of the ruined church of Muiderberg with Naarden in the background (cat. 66; for Ruisdael's other works that include Muiderberg's church, see cat. 68 and fig. 68a).

The 1647 painting takes pride of place as the artist's earliest existing flat landscape, a theme he later took up for some of his most original and impressive pictures. It and his *Extensive Landscape with Trees, a Grainfield, Dunes and a Distant View of a Town*, of 1648 at the Springfield Museum of Art, Springfield, Massachusetts, (fig. 3; Slive 2001, no. 66), are his only existing dated panoramic views.

The landscape shows his debt to earlier Netherlandish artists in the low, oblong shape he chose for his painting; it was the format favoured by his predecessors for their extensive views. The mound on the left, beautifully balanced in the picture by the dramatically lit field in the middle ground and by the lighted area on the horizon, was also a device often used by earlier landscapists to help frame and fix the foremost plane of their panoramas. Original to Ruisdael is the subtlety with which he suggests movement into depth through the obliquely arranged fields and the broad road winding its way to the town.

A black chalk drawing, extensively retouched with grey wash by another hand, which may have served as a preliminary study for the *View of Naarden* is at the Rijksbureau voor Kunsthistorische Documentatie, The Hague (fig. 6a; Slive 2001, no. D71). The close correspondence of the drawing to the painting supports its ascription to Ruisdael; however, the later touches of wash, which obscure the light chalk sketch, make it difficult to give the sheet an unqualified attribution. A bolder chalk and wash panoramic drawing of Naarden and the church at Muiderberg from a slightly different and lower point of view is at Darmstadt (fig. 6b; Slive 2001, no. D42). The drawing does not contain the lateral mound on the left in the Thyssen painting; however, it includes the distant view of the Zuider Zee seen on the right of the picture. In it the proportion of the view devoted to the sky also is closer to the painting than the relation of the sky to earth in the Hague drawing, an indication that the latter may have been cropped at the top.

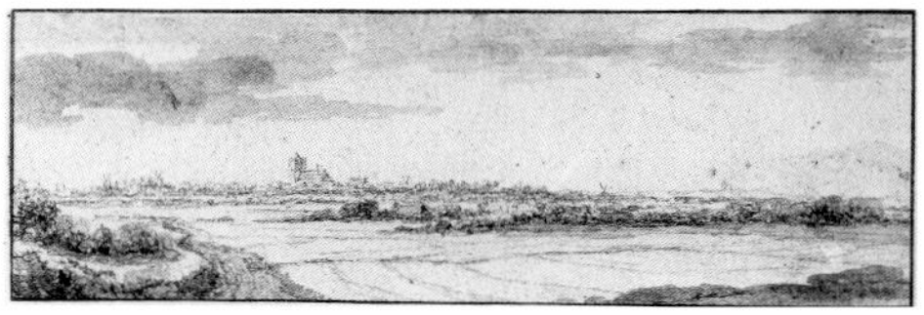

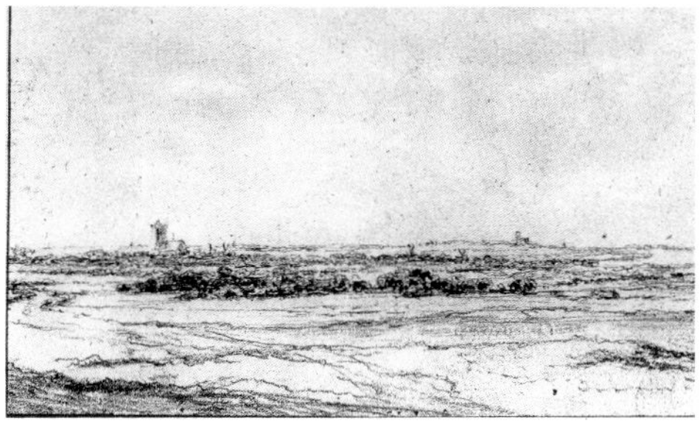

Fig. 6a Jacob van Ruisdael, *View of Naarden and the Church at Muiderberg*. Black chalk, grey wash. Rijksbureau voor Kunsthistorische Documentatie, The Hague.

Fig. 6b Jacob van Ruisdael, *View of Naarden and the Church at Muiderberg*. Black chalk, grey wash. Hessiches Landesmuseum, Darmstadt.

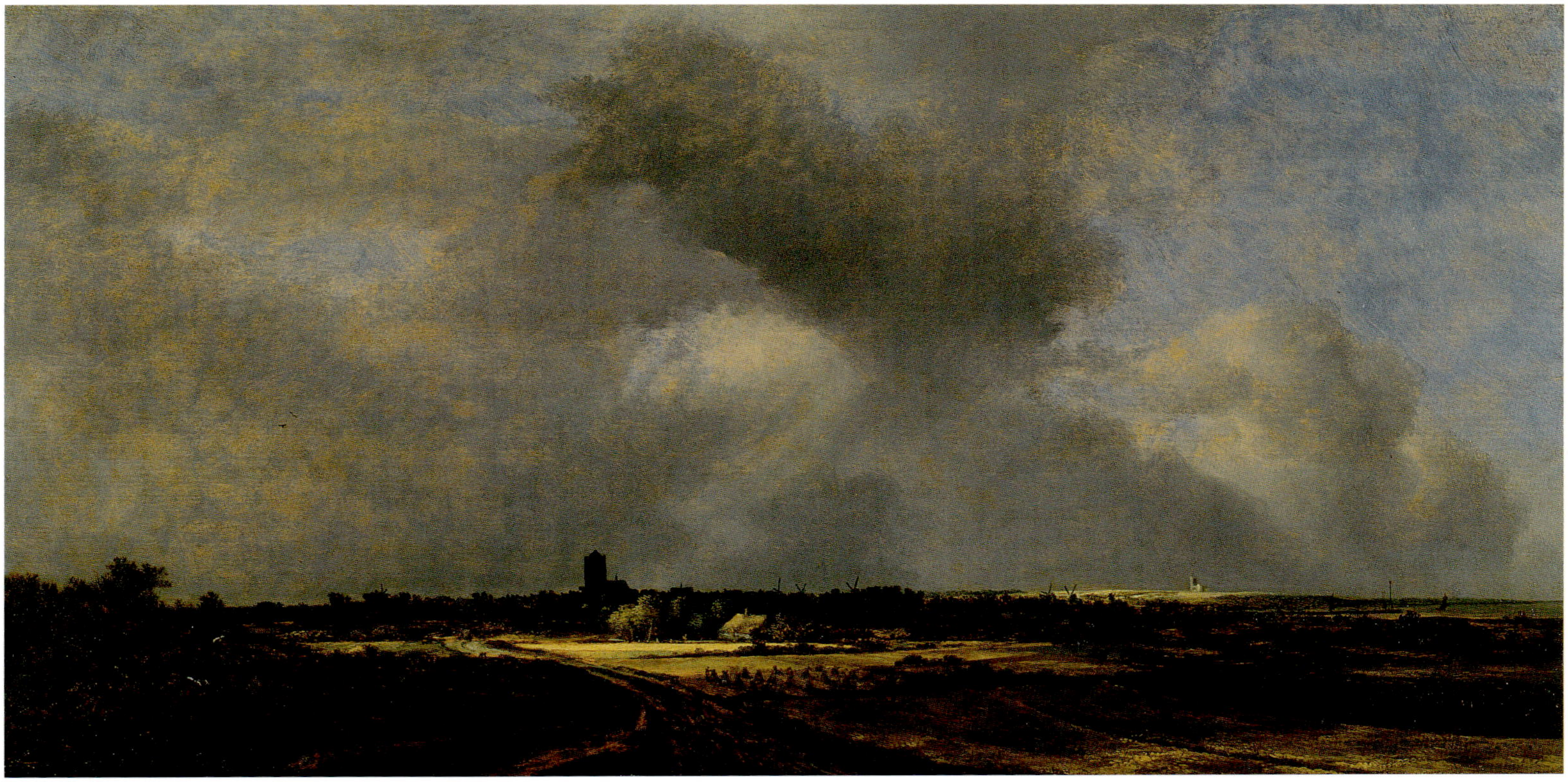

7

Brick Bridge with a Sluice

About 1647. Panel, 39.5 × 52.1 (original dimensions); 39.5 × 56.2 cm (existing dimensions)
The J. Paul Getty Museum, Los Angeles, 86.PB.597

PROVENANCE: Purchased by the Hague banker, diplomatic agent and dealer Willem Lormier (1682–1758) at the sale, The Hague (Verheyden), 25 February 1744, no. 6 (Dfl.57);[1] sale, Willem Lormier, The Hague (Francken), 4 *sqq.* July 1763 (Terw. 328), no. 226 (Dfl.200); sale, Duc de Choiseul, Paris, by about 1770; his sale, Paris (Boileau), 6 *sqq.* April 1772, no. 66 (fr.706); sale, Prince de Conti, Paris (Remy), 8 April–6 June 1777, no. 406 (with a painting by Lucas van Uden; fr.2400, Count d'Ossieu); sale, Count de Merle, Paris (Paillet), 1 March 1784, no. 5 supplement (with a painting by van Uden; fr.1900, Paillet); sale, Morel a.o., Paris (Lebrun), 19 April 1786, no. 54 (fr.1450, Lebrun); sale, Lebrun, Paris (Lebrun), 1–30 April 1791, no. 52 (fr.2123); sale, G. Th. A. M. Baron van Brienen van de Grootelindt of The Hague, Paris (Leroy), 8 May 1865, no. 32; sale, E. Secrétan, Paris (Drouot), 1 July 1889, no. 160; collection Mrs. John W. Simpson, New York; dealer Knoedler, New York, 1942, who sold it to Harold E. Montag of Atlanta, Georgia, in 1943; bequeathed by his widow to the Georgia Tech Foundation, Inc., Atlanta, Georgia; sold by the latter to dealer French and Co., New York, in 1985; acquired by the Getty Museum, 1986.

EXHIBITIONS: New York 1909, no. 109, repr.; New York 1942, no. 54, repr.

LITERATURE: *Catalogus van Schilderyen van den Heer Agent Willem Lormier...*, The Hague [1752], p.23; the catalogue was compiled by Lormier himself. In a copy at the RKD, he writes he paid Dfl. 60 for the painting; the catalogue is transcribed in Hoet 1752, vol. 2, pp.415–50; Descamps 1753–64, 2, p.12; Smith 25 and Smith 45; HdG 663; Ros 448; Watson 1963, p.9; Snowman 1966, p.149 [appendix by Watson]; Slive 1981, p.118, sub no. 40; Slive 2001, no. 505, repr.; Altes 2000–01, p.267, note 60; Altes 2003, pp.77–78, note 60.

Engraved in reverse by R. A. Wieth in Basan 1771, no. 24.

The picture is in very good condition. A strip 4.1 cm wide has been added to at the left edge, making the existing dimensions of the panel 39.5 by 56.2. The addition is certainly not by Ruisdael's hand. Since it is not included in Wieth's 1771 engraving of the picture, the strip was almost certainly added after his print was published. The painting is normally exhibited with the addition covered by the frame's rabbet; it is illustrated here with the addition deleted.

The same bridge and sluice depicted from a more conventional viewpoint is seen in a landscape dated 1647, at the Rijksmuseum Twenthe, Enschede (fig. 7a; Slive 2001, no. 497). The Getty picture is datable about the same time. It is reasonable to assume Ruisdael made preliminary drawings of the motif from various points of view which are now lost.

According to Watson (1963) a very tiny miniature of the present painting appears along with other pictures on one of the panels that depict five interiors of the richly appointed hôtel in Paris of the Duc de Choiseul, who had a passion for Dutch painting. The small panels, painted by Louis-Nicholas van Blarenberghe (1716 [1719?]–94) in about 1770, were used to decorate a fine gold snuff-box that is in the Baron Elie de Rothschild collection, Paris. Watson (*ibid.*) also writes another landscape that belonged to Choiseul appears in the same panel; it is a miniature copy of a dubious Ruisdael woodland scene now in the National Gallery, London (no. 2563; see Slive 2001, no. dub70). Additionally, Choiseul owned a *Landscape with a View of Huis ten Bosch* which was wrongly attributed to Ruisdael when it was in his collection. Watson (*ibid.*, p.11) states it too is depicted in a view of a room on the snuff-box. Choiseul's *Huis ten Bosch* is, in fact, by Jan van der Heyden and is now in Museum Wuyts-van Campen, Lier (no. 56; HdG, 8, van der Heyden, nos. 80 and 257; Wagner 1971, no. 139).[2]

When the Getty painting appeared in Choiseul's Paris sale in 1772, it was sold as one lot. In the Paris sale of the Prince de Conti, held five years later, it was sold as one lot with Lucas van Uden's *Landscape with Woods and Water*, with staffage attributed to David Teniers.[3] Both pictures are described as on panel and given the same dimensions; however, the compiler of the Conti sale catalogue did not suggest the pictures were pendants and there is no reason to propose that they were intended as mates.

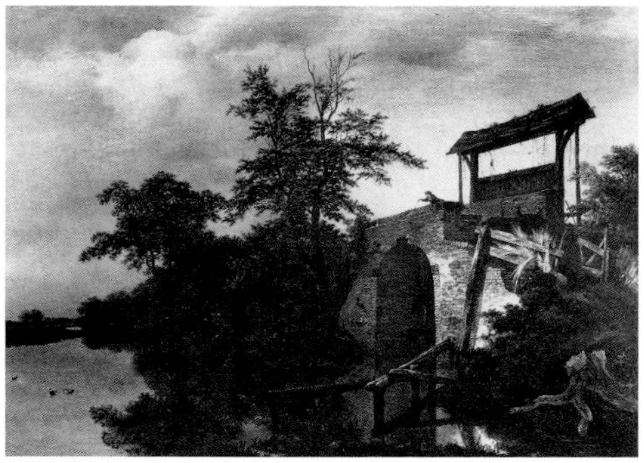

Fig. 7a Jacob van Ruisdael, *Stone Bridge with a Sluice*, 1647. Rijksmuseum Twenthe, Enschede.

1. Altes 2000-01, p.267, note 60; Altes 2003, pp.77–78, note 60.
2. For a full discussion of the snuff-box see Watson 1963 (publication of his Charlton Lecture delivered in 1961). Watson also is author of an appendix on the box published in Snowman 1966, pp.145–58. His appendix is a bibliographical anomaly; it was written before he gave his Charlton Lecture in 1961 (*ibid.*, p.147, note 2). The illustrations of the box in Watson (1963), Snowman (1966) and Jean Feray, *Architecture intérieure et décoration en France*, Paris, 1988, are not clear enough to distinguish the Getty's *Bridge with a Sluice*, Slive 2001, no. dub70, or the van der Heyden, now in Lier. I have not had an opportunity to make a firsthand examination of the box.
3. Sale, Prince de Conti, Paris, 8 *sqq.* April 1777, no. 406, Ruisdael and Lucas van Uden: "Deux tableau: l'une par Ruysdael . . . l'autre par Van Uden, représente un bois, & à droite une piece d'eau. David Teniers y a peint sur le premier plan quatre hommes & deux chiens".

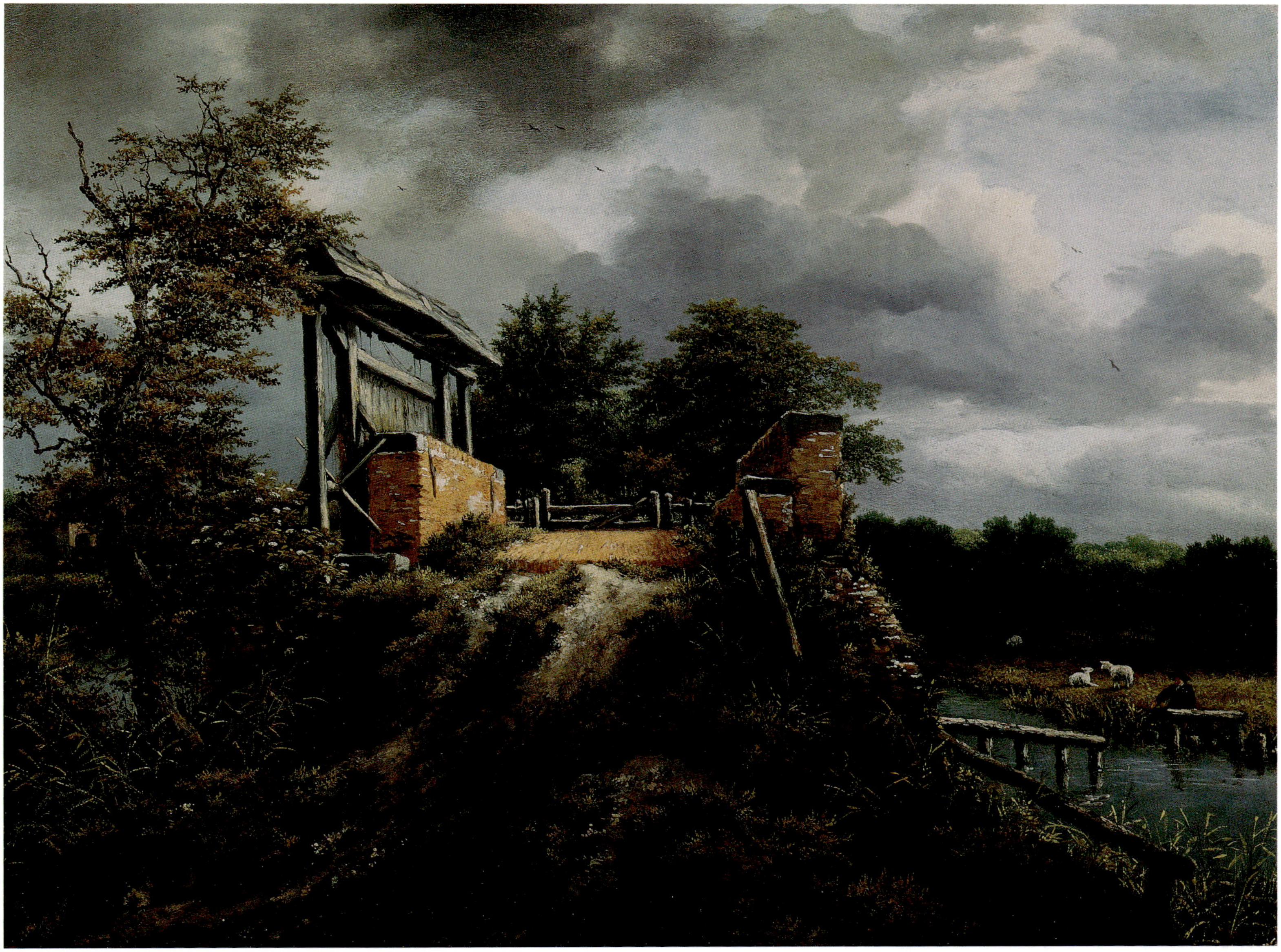

8

View of Egmond aan Zee with a Blasted Elm

Signed and dated 1648, lower left.[1] Panel, 65.09 × 49.85 cm
Currier Museum of Art, Manchester, New Hampshire.
Museum purchase, Currier Funds, 1950.4

PROVENANCE: Sir Francis Cook (1817–1901), Doughty House, Richmond; by bequest to his son Frederick Cook (1844–1920), Doughty House, Richmond; by bequest to his son Sir Herbert Cook (1868–1939), Doughty House, Richmond; Walter Dunkels, Walhurst Manor, Cowfold; dealer E. Speelman, London, 1946; sale, Walter Dunkels, London (Christie's), 12 March 1948, no. 124, repr. (the sale catalogue erroneously states that the painting is dated 1645 [£1680, Partridge]); acquired by the gallery in 1950.

EXHIBITIONS: Worcester 1951, no. 24; New York–Toledo–Toronto 1954–55, no. 69; Amsterdam–Toronto 1977, no. 121; The Hague–Cambridge 1981–82, no. 7, repr.; Hamburg–Haarlem 2002, no. 21, repr.

LITERATURE: HdG 49; Kronig 1914, p.94, no. 351, repr. (painted about 1660; figures by Adriaen van de Velde); Rosenberg 1928, p.116, note 1 (Jan van Kessel); Simon 1930, p.81 (by a contemporary Haarlem artist); Elizabeth Smith, "An Early Landscape by Ruisdael," *A.Q.*, 14, 1951, pp.359f.; Stechow 1966, p.105; Bol 1973, p.279; Ashton *et al.* 1982, p.17, pl. 15 (detail); Sutton 1986, p.147 (dubious); Walford 1991, pp.66–67, repr.; Slive 2001, no. 32, repr.

PMA and RA

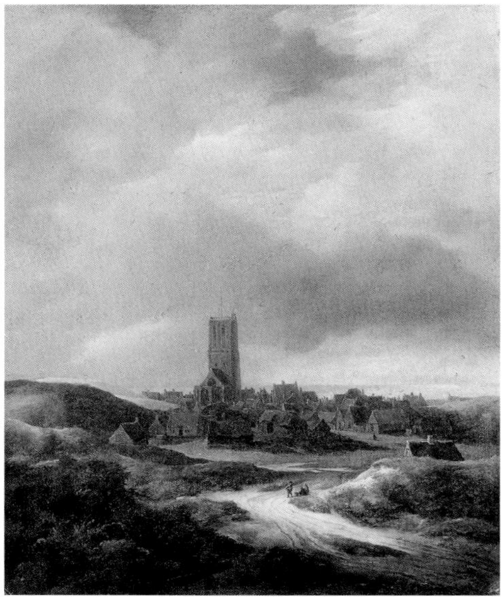

Fig. 8a Jacob van Ruisdael, *View of Egmond aan Zee*. State Pushkin Museum of Fine Arts, Moscow.

The fishing village of Egmond aan Zee is on the North Sea, east of Alkmaar, about twenty-five kilometres from Haarlem. Its prominent church and modest houses are included in beach and dunescapes by Jacob's father Isaack, his uncle Salomon van Ruysdael and Jan van Goyen. Younger artists, among them Claes Molenaer and Aelbert Cuyp, also depicted the village's site.

Identification of the Manchester painting's extraordinary blasted tree as an elm was made by Peter S. Ashton, professor of dendrology and botany at Harvard University and sometime director of the Arnold Arboretum. He finds it is an excellent example of the characteristic twisted, fissured trunks of elms; the surfaces between the fissures are wide and flake irregularly. Identity is also confirmed by a few persisting asymmetrical leaves that hang curled up along the midrip or down at the ends (Ashton *et al.* 1982). Ruisdael's beautiful drawing of an elm made about the same time is at The Morgan Library (Slive 2001, no. D94). For a note on the possible symbolism of the conspicuous battered tree, see cat. 5.

At first, it appears that Ruisdael chose an upright format for this unusual picture because it seemed most appropriate for his full-length portrait of the ancient, shattered elm. However, a closely related version of the painting at the State Pushkin Museum of Fine Arts, Moscow (fig. 8a; Slive 2001, no. 33), which has the same format but eliminates the tree, indicates that the tree did not necessarily determine the shape of the picture. The Moscow variant has other differences. The figures in it have been used to help set the scale of the scene rather than create a diversity of attraction, the patches of light are more effectively concentrated, and the movement into the picture over the complicated terrain is accomplished with greater ease. These alterations suggest that it probably was painted a bit later than the Manchester painting.

1. Examination of the painting when it was exhibited at the Fogg Museum in 1982 revealed that the "R" of the signature is normally hidden by the frame's rabbet; the remainder of the signature is hardly legible. The date of 1648 is visible with the aid of a tungsten lamp. Rosenberg (1928, p.116, note 1) and Simon (1930, p.81) doubted the authenticity of the picture. Rosenberg later informed me that he changed his opinion when a cleaning done not long before the painting was acquired by the Currier Gallery in 1950 brought out its qualities and revealed the unpublished signature and date. To judge from its almost strident colours, the cleaning was a harsh one that removed some of the original glazes.

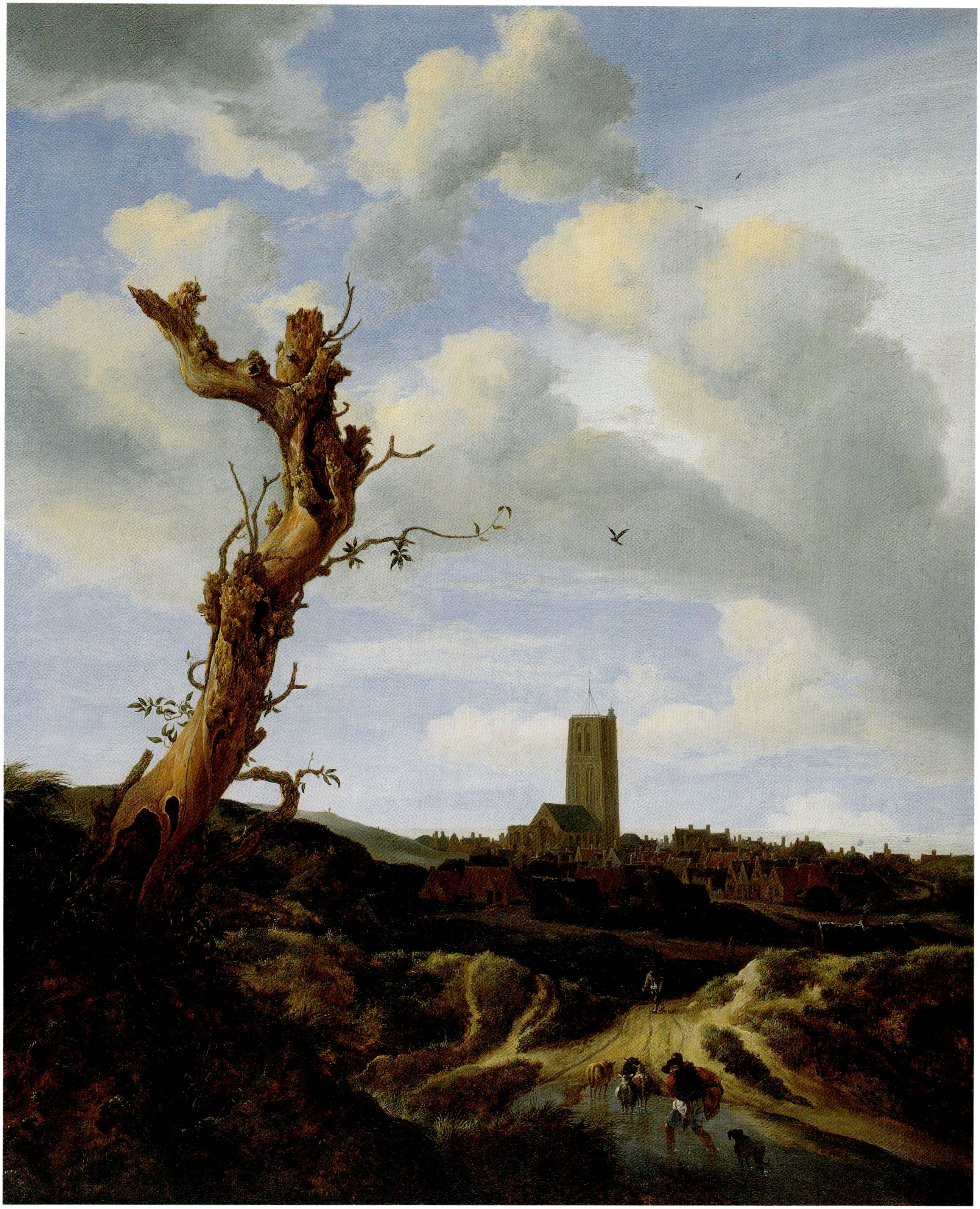

9

Dunes by the Sea

Signed and dated 1648, right centre at bottom. Panel, 46 × 61 cm
The Hascoe Collection

PROVENANCE: Richter Oelrich, Bremen, about 1820; Bernhard Hausmann, Hannover, by 1831; Provinzial-museum, Hannover; sale, Duke of Cumberland, Berlin (Lepke), 31 March 1925, no. 63, repr.; Düsseldorf art market, 1948; private collection, Cologne; dealer Waterman Art Gallery, Amsterdam, 1982.

EXHIBITIONS: Cologne 1954, no. 19, repr.; The Hague–Cambridge 1981–82, no. 8, repr.; on loan to the Museum of Art, Rhode Island School of Design, Providence, Rhode Island, 1983–87; Greenwich, Connecticut 2003–04, pp. 24–25, 88–89, repr.; Greenwich, Connecticut 2005, no. 8, repr.

LITERATURE: *Verzeichnis der Hausmann'schen Gemälde-Sammlung in Hannover*, Braunschweig, 1831, no. 270; Parthey 1864, 2, p.461, no. 135; Provenzialmuseum, Hannover, Catalogue, 1891, no. 474; HdG 925 (dimensions reversed); Moes 1913, p.296; Ros 567; Stechow 1966, p.29; Ashton *et al.* 1982, pp.19–21, pl. 21 (detail); Slive 2001, no. 635, repr.

LACMA and PMA

A subject young Ruisdael tried a couple of times and then apparently abandoned was a view of a coast flanked by a spit of land supporting hardy trees and shrubs that have been whipped by the wind and sea. Today only two paintings of the theme are known: the present one dated 1648 and another one dated 1647, now in a private Westphalian collection (fig. 9a; Slive 2001, no. 627).[1] The latter has the compact, falling diagonal composition ending with a vista into the distance that Ruisdael favoured during his first phase. Its bright, far view of the sea gives a small foretaste of his marines.

The changes Ruisdael rang on the motif in the 1648 picture indicate by the time it was done the artist had assimilated the elegant fashioning of forms that Cornelis Vroom (1591/92–1661) had introduced into Dutch landscape painting more than a decade earlier. Vroom's impact is seen in the more transparent and fine filigree treatment of the foliage and in the lighter, more tender palette of the painting.

Ruisdael's highly finished drawing, signed and dated 1648, of a coastal scene that includes a view of Muiderberg and the town of Naarden at the British Museum (cat. 66) is another variation on the compositional scheme used for the two paintings and also betrays Vroom's influence in the treatment of the foliage.

Peter Ashton made a significant observation about the Hascoe picture. He noted that the small dense shrub with dark foliage and cream coloured flowers which the artist depicted on the right, near the base of the dune, is the wayfaring tree, *viburnum lantana* (fig. 9b). It is a plant that belongs to the same family as the elder, and like it is a glutton for good fertile ground, but keeps to old vegetation and is not associated with habitations. The wayfaring tree is very local in Haarlem.[2] By including it Ruisdael seems to have observed a plant the brilliant botanist Carolus Linnaeus (1707–78) missed when he worked in the vicinity. By showing it:

> [. . .] where rich flushes of groundwater, arising from shell accumulations in the old beach sand, form limy patches, and in precisely the habitat at which it occurs at present, Ruisdael seems to have demonstrated exceptional mastery of his local flora. The great Linnaeus, who stayed as a young man at Hartekamp, estate of George Clifford, to compile the celebrated *Hortus Cliffortianus*, completed in 1737, included this species. However, he cited it from Alsace, England, France, Switzerland, Etruria, and Italy, but apparently was not aware that it grew within a few miles from where he wrote! Indeed, it was first recorded in the Netherlands only in 1861, and then at St. Pietersberg in the extreme southeast.[3]

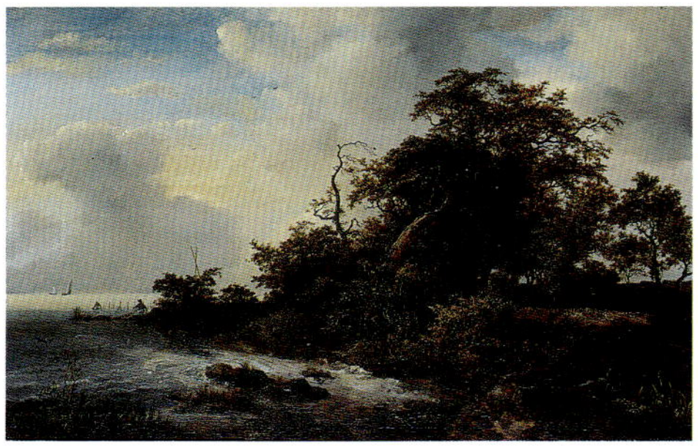

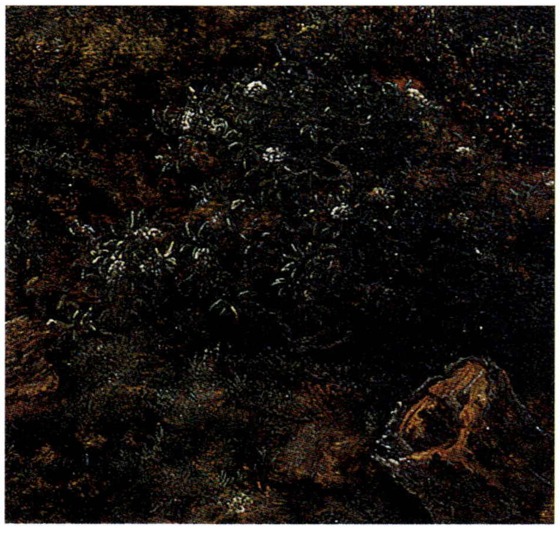

Fig. 9a Jacob van Ruisdael, *Wooded Bank by the Sea*, 1647, private collection.

Fig. 9b Detail of cat. 9.

1. After the painting appeared in the sale of the late Col. S.J.L. Hardie of Ballathie, Perthshire, at London (Sotheby's), 3 December 1969, no. 73, repr., its whereabouts were unknown in the literature until it was published in the exh. cat. *Sammlerlust. Europäische Kunst aus fünf Jahrhundert. Gemälde, Zeichnungen und Kunsthandwerk aus einer westfälischen Privatsammlung* (ed. Monika Bachtler), Westfälischen Landesmuseum für Kunst und Kulturgeschichte, Münster, 18 May–24 August 2003, no. 38 (entry by U. Middendorf).
2. Ashton observes that in H. Henkel, *De flora van Nederland*, 3 vols., Leiden, 1910, it is recorded from some seven localities, one of which is Haarlem, another Santpoort a few kilometres to the north. He also points out that the only reliable records prior to 1950 are two near Haarlem and three, hundreds of kilometres away, in the chalk hills in the extreme southeast of the country; see Ashton *et al.* 1982, p.20.
3. Ashton *et al.* 1982, pp.20–21 (in this publication, which was a collaborative effort, its botanical observations, the core of the article, were made by Peter Ashton).

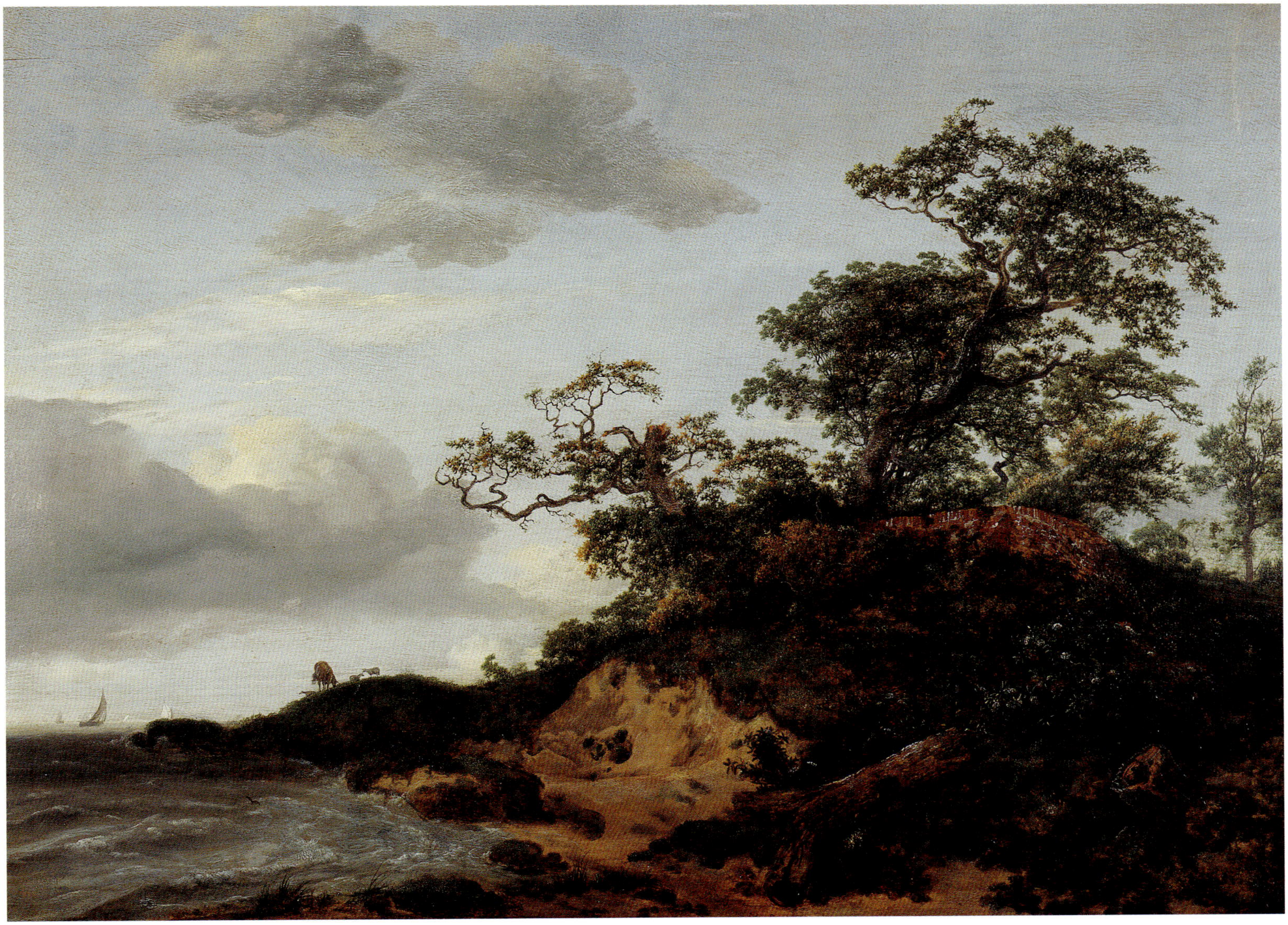

10

Bleaching Ground (near Haarlem?) in a Hollow by a Cottage

Signed at the bottom towards the right. Late 1640s. Panel, 52.5 × 67.8 cm
The National Gallery, London, NG44

PROVENANCE: Possibly sale, Marin, Paris (Lebrun), 22 March 1790, no. 147; bequeathed in 1847 by General Sir John May to the National Gallery, with a life interest to Lady May, who ceded it to the Gallery in 1854.

LITERATURE: HdG 95; Ros 63; Simon 1930, p.79; MacLaren 1960, p.335, no. 44; MacLaren and Brown 1991, p.380, no. 44; Slive 2001, no. 43, repr.

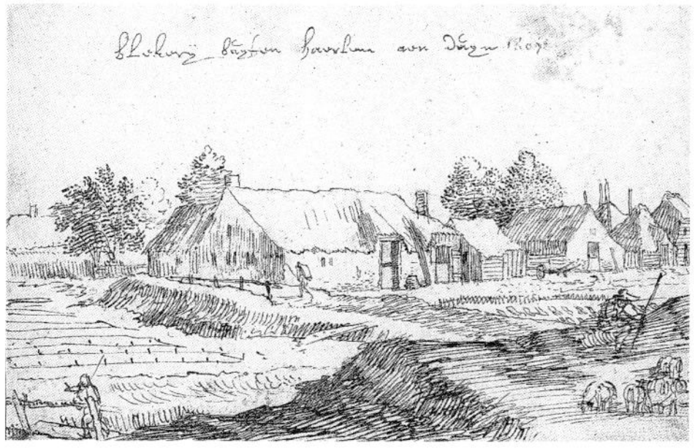

Fig. 10a Claes Jansz Visscher, *Bleachery in the Dunes outside Haarlem*, 1607. Pen and brown ink. Municipal Archives, Haarlem.

This unusual, close view of a modest bleaching field nestled in high dunes is datable to the late forties. The deep green, filagree-like foliage of the tree on the left shows the distinct impact of Vroom's work on Ruisdael during these years.

A three-line inscription appears on a label on the back, apparently in a seventeenth-century hand. The only decipherable words are the last two: *op harlem* (at Haarlem). If the inscription is trustworthy the picture was based on one of the numerous small bleacheries that were situated in the dune area near Haarlem. It is Ruisdael's only existing painting that includes a bleaching ground as a central motif which does not provide an identifiable topographical reference.

There is some precedence for depictions of bleacheries near Haarlem. Claes Jansz Visscher, a leading pioneer of realistic Dutch landscapes, showed one in a drawing as early as 1607 (fig. 10a; Municipal Archives, Haarlem; inscribed: *Blekerij buyten haerlem aen duyn/1607*; Simon 1958, no. 39); it served as the preliminary drawing for one of his two etchings of bleacheries that appeared in a series of eleven prints of *Plaisante Plaetsen* (Pleasant Spots) near Haarlem, published about 1611 (*ibid.*, nos. 134, 137; repr. in de Groot 1979, nos. 30, 33). On a sheet that includes a view of Leiden's skyline and two large studies of trees Pieter Jansz Saenredam made a sketch dated 1617 of bleachers' houses outside the city; it depicts meadows in front of them without linen spread to bleach (inscribed: *eenige bleyckers huijsen aende duijnkant buyte Haerlem 1617*).[1] Pictures of small bleacheries became a favourite subject of the Haarlemer Claes Molenaer about the time Ruisdael painted the present one; his 1647 painting of a bleaching field that includes a view of Haarlem is at Leipzig. The Haarlem landscapist Willem Gras also painted one which is now at Rotterdam, signed and dated 1648.

The rough, hilly terrain Ruisdael selected for the present picture distinguishes it from the depictions of the theme cited above. His predecessors and contemporaries most often show fields at the edge of a village or near clusters of cottages; compared to the uncultivated ground that flanks this sloping bleaching field those depicted by earlier artists and his contemporaries appear manicured. Other artists usually showed more extensive bleaching grounds. Here the lawn-like size of the bleaching field is appropriate to the size of cloth the workers are treating. They are laying out small pieces of linen to air, bleach and be sprinkled, not the long strips of cloth seen so often in Jacob's later *Haarlempjes*. Although workers appear in the latter paintings and in some of his other landscapes, he rarely gives such a close view of their activities; for another notable exception to the general rule, see the men repairing the river bed of an inoperative sluice in his landscape at Toledo (cat. 40) painted about two decades later

1. Berlin, Staatliche Museen Preussischer Kulturbesitz, Kupferstichkabinett, no. 5707. The drawing of Leiden is dated 1625. For the entire sheet see Utrecht 1961, no. 207, repr., and Schwartz and Bok [1990], p.33, fig. 20 and pp.296–97, no. 207.

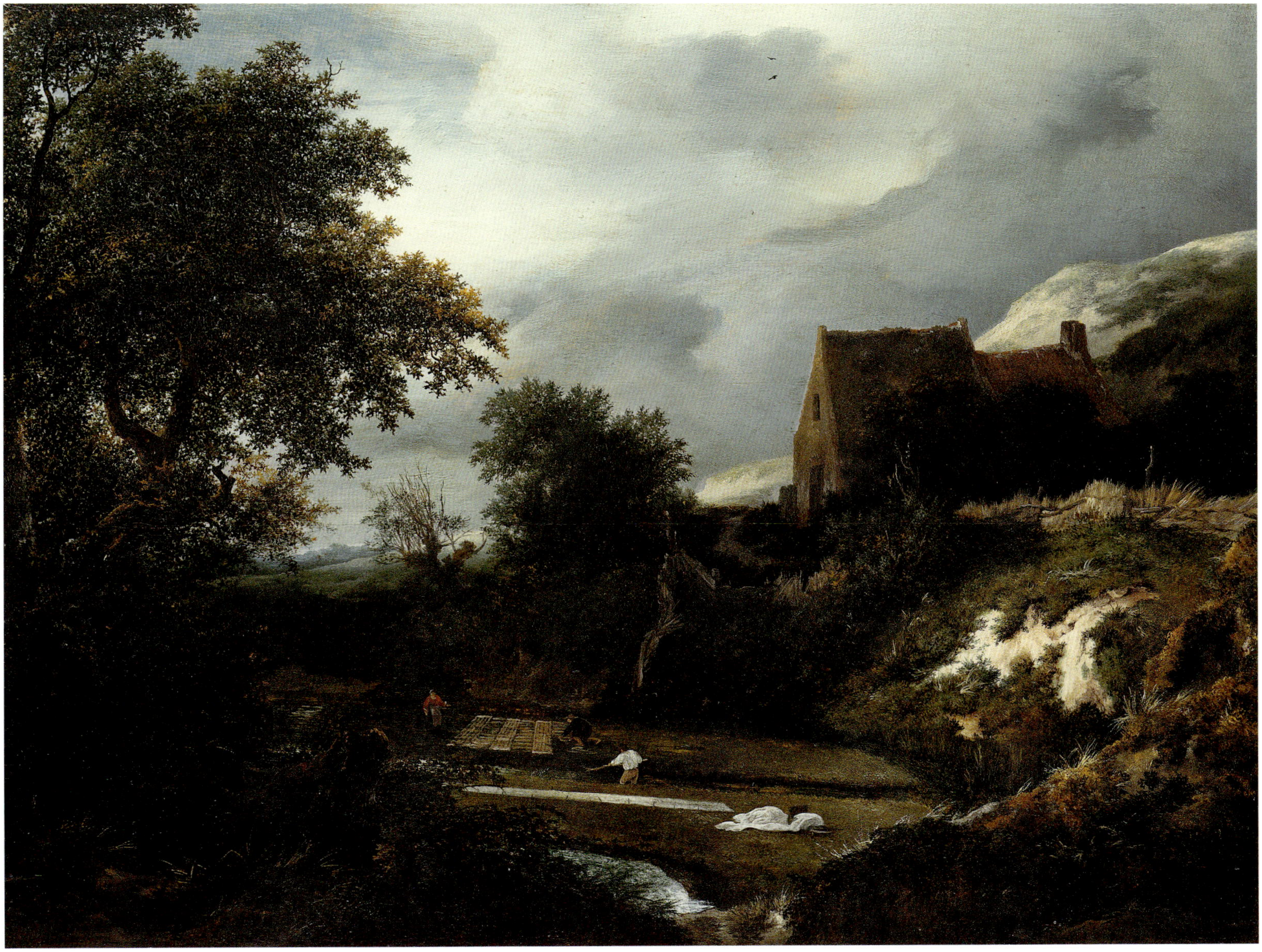

11

River Landscape with the Entrance to a Vault

Signed and dated 1649, lower right. Panel, 69.8 × 92 cm
Kunsthistorisches Museum, Gemäldegalerie, Vienna, 9807

PROVENANCE: Acquired by Graf Johann Nepomuk Ernst from Stöber in Vienna, 1823; Harrach Gemäldegalerie, Vienna, until 1982 when it was acquired by the Kunsthistorisches Museum.

LITERATURE: Parthey 1863–64, 2, p.457, no. 479 (signed and dated 1679); Waagen 1866–67, 1, p.323, no. H.52 (although signed and dated 1679 I think it is the work of a good pupil); Harrach Gemäldegalerie, Vienna, Catalogue, 1897, no. 315 (dated 1679); HdG 687 (dated 1649, not 1679); Ros 457; Simon 1930, p.20; Harrach Gemäldegalerie, Vienna, Catalogue, 1960, p.66, no. 18; Slive 2001, no. 522, repr.

LACMA and PMA

Before Hofstede de Groot (687) correctly read the painting's date as 1649 this marvellously well-preserved picture was catalogued as dated 1679.

The elevated viewpoint Ruisdael used for the landscape enabled him to silhouette almost the full length of the grove of trees on the right against the light sky. The arrangement recalls the scheme Ruisdael employed in his *Extensive Landscape with Trees, a Grainfield and a Distant View of a Town* painted a year earlier, now at the Museum of Fine Arts, Springfield (see p.2, fig. 3). In the present landscape reminiscences of Rembrandt's etching of *Three Trees* (p.2, fig. 4), evident in the Springfield picture, are less conspicuous.

A nameless *River Landscape with a Brick Vault and a Ruin* is at The Bowes Museum, Barnard Castle, Co. Durham[1] (repr. Slive 2001, p.382, fig. 522a); it may have been based on studies made at the site of the Vienna picture, but more probable is the assumption that it is a variant based on Ruisdael's landscape.

1. No. 154. At Barnard Castle it is called "Dutch School". Christopher Wright (Newcastle 1983, p.90) attributes it to Roelof van Vries; I find it too crude for his hand.

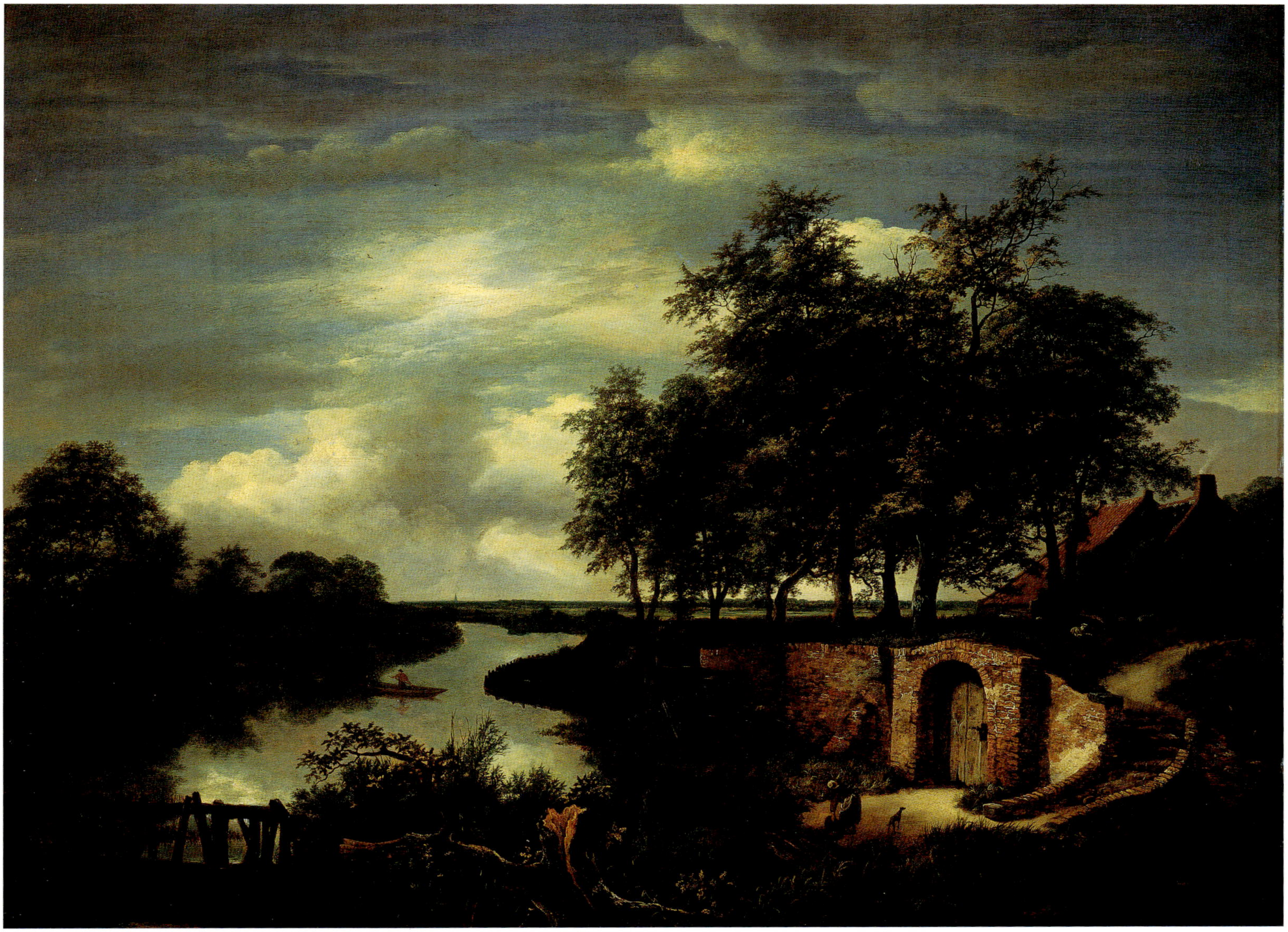

12

Banks of a River

Signed and dated 1649, lower left. Canvas, 134 × 193 cm
Torrie Collection, University of Edinburgh, 734

PROVENANCE: Sir James Erskine of Torrie, who bequeathed it in 1825 to the University of Edinburgh which received the picture in 1836; placed on loan in 1845 to the Board of Manufactures, Edinburgh, first at the Royal Institution, then at the National Gallery of Scotland for its opening in 1859 where it has remained.[1]

EXHIBITIONS: The Hague–Cambridge 1981–82, no. 9, repr. (shown in Cambridge only); London 1986, no. 105, repr.; Edinburgh 1992, no. 56, repr.; Madrid 1994–95, no. 51, repr.

LITERATURE: Smith Suppl. 32 (the principal figures by Wouwerman); Waagen 1854, 3, pp.273–74 (principal figures by Wouwerman); Hofstede de Groot 1893, p.133 (an important rather early work; figures probably by Berchem, not Wouwerman); HdG 703 (figures possibly by Berchem); Moes 1913, p.295; Ros 431; Simon 1930, pp.20, 23; The National Gallery of Scotland, Edinburgh, *Fifty-Sixth Report of the Board of Trustees*, 1962 (1963), p.5; The National Gallery of Scotland, Edinburgh, Catalogue, 1978, p.94, no. 75 (staffage based on those of Wouwerman done during this period; see especially his *Water-place*, HdG, 2, no. 71, with Böhler, Lucerne, 1949); Walford 1991, pp.71–72; Walsh 1991, p.106; Slive 2001, no. 496, repr.

A cleaning in 1962 revealed the signature and date of 1649. As references cited in the Literature indicate, the staffage has been attributed with varying degrees of conviction to Nicolaes Berchem and Philips Wouwerman; attribution to the latter is possibly correct.

Ruisdael's poorly preserved *River Landscape with a High Sandy Bank*, dated 1647, in the Hage Collection, Nivaagaard, Denmark (Slive 2001, no. 513), most likely provided an early idea for the painting, but it offers no indication that two years later he would transform it into the most imposing landscape he created before his departure from Haarlem about 1650 for his travels in the Dutch-German border region. A hint of a longing for journeys to far-off places already is evident in the vast imaginary panorama of rolling hills and the prominent road that winds along the bank of the mirror-smooth river until it is lost in the distance.

As in other works of the forties, there are reminiscences of Cornelis Vroom in the majestic painting. Here they are evident in the poetic mood as well as in the refined, airy treatment of the foliage of the half-bare, split beech and in the elegant trees in the distant vista. Transcending Vroom are the tremendous scale of the landscape, the heroic treatment of the commanding group of trees against the towering sky and the grouping of a great wealth of motifs into powerful rhythms, all of which show Jacob's growing desire for monumental effect.

Moes (1913) asserts Arnhem is depicted on the horizon and Walford (1991) states that the painting is an imaginative view of the area near Rhenen. More convincing than these proposals is Walsh's (1991) observation that the painting's huge double branch cloud is a meteorological anomaly; it is another example of the artist taking liberties with nature.

1. Data from Edinburgh 1992, no. 56.

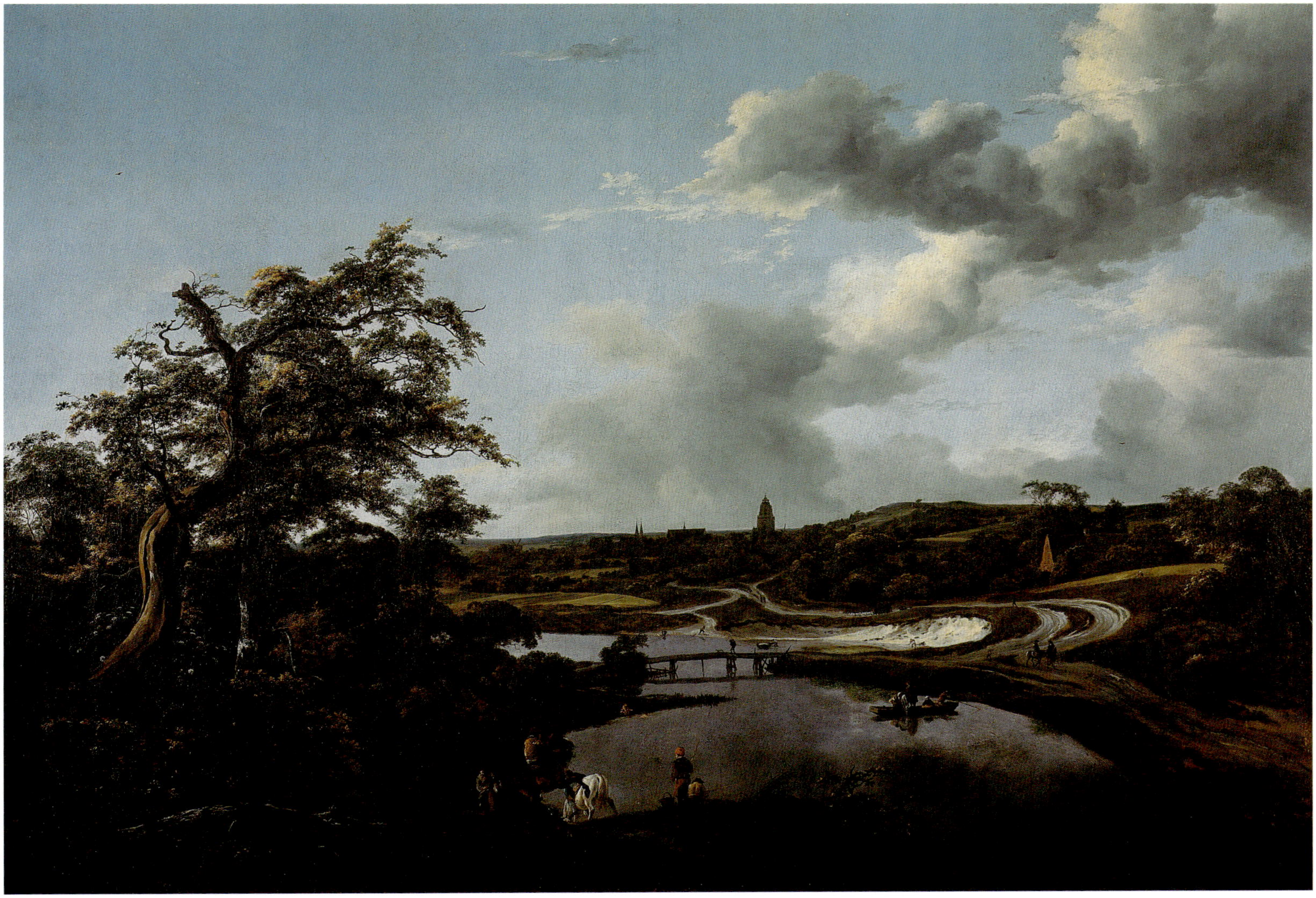

13

Landscape with a Windmill Near a Town Moat

Signed on the gunwale of the boat on the left. Early 1650s. Canvas, 63 × 76.5 cm
Private collection

PROVENANCE: Sale, P. Locquet, Amsterdam (v.d. Schley), 22 September 1783, no. 317 (Dfl.600, Gildemeester); sale, Jan Gildemeester, Amsterdam (v.d. Schley), 11 June 1800, no. 189 (Dfl.1000, Labouchère); by 1808 in the collection of Earl Gower (1785–1833), 2nd Marquess of Stafford, who became 1st Duke of Sutherland shortly before his death in 1833; bequeathed in 1833 to Lord Francis Edgerton who became the Earl of Ellsmere in 1846; thence by descent to the present owner.

LITERATURE: Britton 1808, no. 225 ("View of the old gate at Amsterdam, with a canal, bridge, windmill, etc."); Stafford Gallery 1818, no. 121; Westmacott 1824, p.203, no. 225; Stafford Gallery 1825, no. 125; Smith 135; Waagen 1837, 1, p.348; Jameson 1844, p.149, no. 227; Bridgewater Collection, London, Catalogue, 1851, no. 197; Waagen 1854, 2, p.49; Cust 1903, no. 95; HdG 174 (more or less in the style of Hobbema), identical with HdG 16 (*View of the Ramparts of Amsterdam*); Moes 1913, p.295; Ros 113; Simon 1930, pp.64 (late fifties), 74; Slive 2001, no. 133, repr.

Engraved by I. H. Wright in Stafford Gallery 1818, no. 121, and again by an unidentified artist in Stafford Gallery 1825, no. 125.

RA

The meticulously painted old brick supports of the makeshift footbridge in this picturesque view of a town moat are not unusual notes in the artist's *oeuvre*. Ruisdael seemed to enjoy finding ways of depicting ample displays of bricks and mortar, without boring himself or his viewer, as he took in painting superabundant displays of foliage. Among the exhibited pictures that show his passion for painting brickwork are his *River Landscape with the Entrance to a Vault*, Vienna, Kunsthistorisches Museum, *Ruins of Egmond Castle*, Art Institute of Chicago, and *Reconstruction of the Ruins of the Manor Kostverloren*, Amsterdam Historical Museum (cat. 11, 18, 31).

The claim made by various cataloguers that the Sutherland painting is a view of Amsterdam has not been substantiated; the site has not been identified. Ruisdael's drawing of a *Bulwark with a Footbridge Across a Moat* at the Hermitage, St. Petersburg (cat. 88) has also been called a view of Amsterdam's ramparts, but that identification has not been confirmed either.

The painting figures prominently in Adriaan de Lelie's (1755–1820) portrait done in 1794–95 of the prominent Amsterdam collector Jan Gildemeester with friends and visitors in his crowded private picture gallery in his house on the Herengracht where framed pictures virtually cover the walls from floor to ceiling.[1]

1. For a discussion of Gildemeester's collection and an illustration of de Lelie's painting, now in the Rijksmuseum, Amsterdam, as well as other identifiable paintings in it see C. J. de Bruyn Kops, "De Amsterdamse verzamelaar Jan Gildemeester Jansz," *Bulletin van het Rijksmuseum*, 13, 1965, pp.79–114; also Slive 1995, pp.298, 317 and fig. 417.

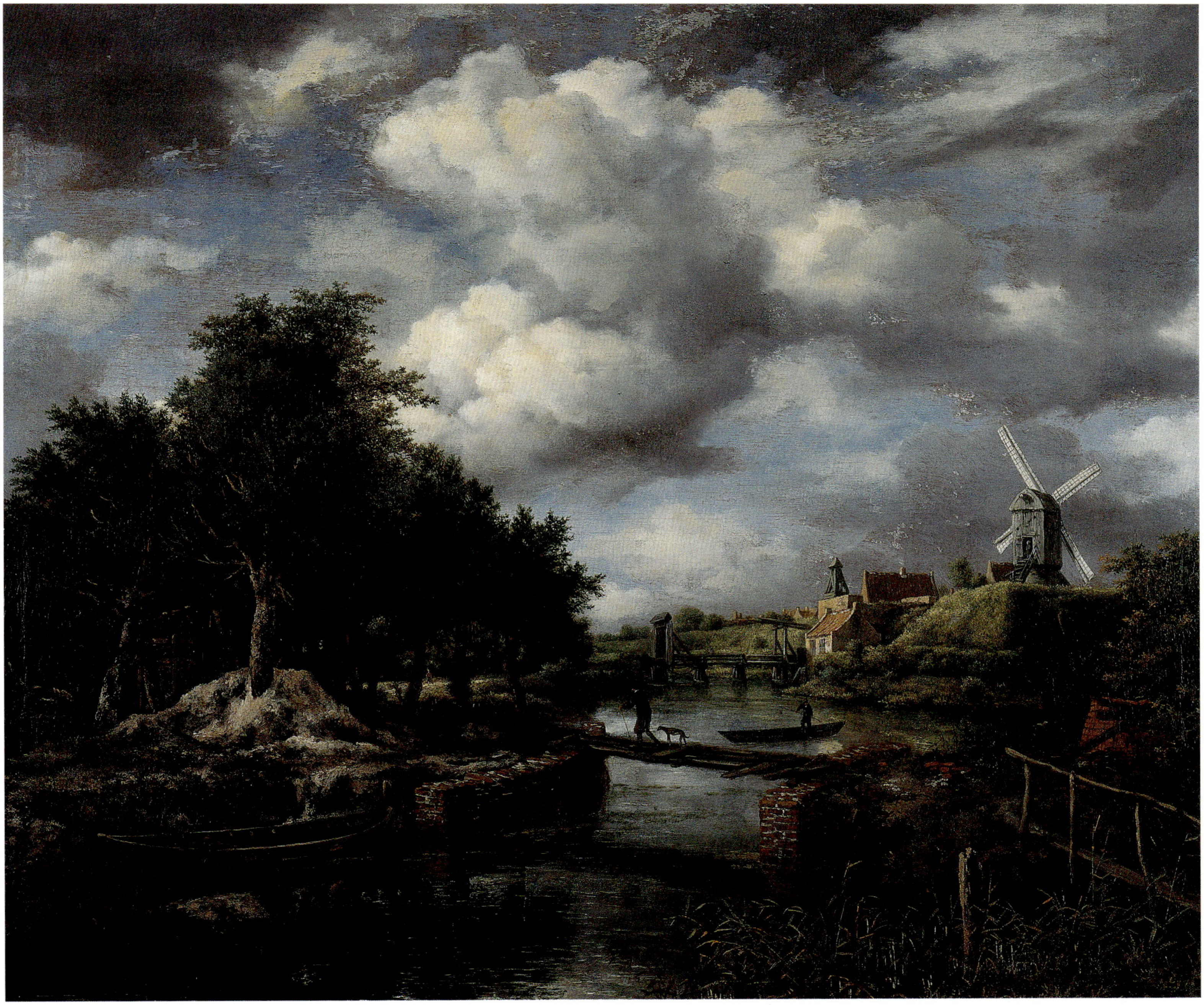

14

Bentheim Castle

Signed and dated 1651, bottom left centre. Canvas, 96.5 × 80 cm
Private collection

PROVENANCE: Possibly sale, John Hickman, London (Christie's), 14 July 1828, no. 59 ("A romantic View upon a Road, through a woody pass, on the approach to the Castle of Bentheim, with figures"; £46.40, Michael Peacock). Purchased 19 March 1859 from the Munro Collection by the dealer J. Rutley for J. S. Beckett (£300 plus £15 commission for Rutley); John Staniforth Beckett; inherited by Sir H. B. Bacon about 1890; Sir Hickman Bacon, Gainsborough; Sir Edmund Bacon, Raveningham Hall, Norfolk.

EXHIBITIONS: London 1938, no. 273, repr. (wrong provenance); London 1952–53, no. 318, repr.; London 1976, no. 99, repr.; The Hague–Cambridge 1981–82, no. 12, repr.; London 1986, no. 106, repr.; Madrid 1994–95, no. 52; Hamburg–Haarlem 2002, no. 30, repr.

LITERATURE: HdG 24; Ros 15; Keith Roberts, *B.M.*, 119, 1977, p.515; Maschmeyer 1978, p.69; Walford 1991, pp.75–76, repr.; Büttner and Unverfehrt 1993, pp.103–04, no. 7, repr.; Slive 2001, no. 24, repr.

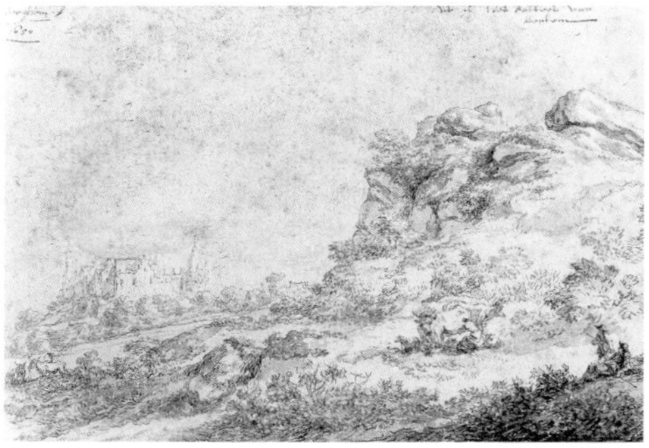

Fig. 14a Nicolaes Berchem, *Bentheim Castle*, 1650. Black chalk, grey wash. Städelsches Kunstinstitut, Frankfurt a. M.

The year Ruisdael inscribed on the marvellous painting indicates that by 1651 he made a trip to Bentheim, a small town in Westphalia near the border between the United Provinces and Germany. Support for the hypothesis that he most probably travelled there a year earlier with his friend Nicolaes Berchem[1] is offered by Berchem's drawing of Bentheim, dated 1650 (fig. 14a; Städelsches Kunstinstitut, Frankfurt a. M.) and by Ruisdael's painting of a similar but more ambitious view, formerly in Bremen and presumably lost in World War II (Slive 2001, no. 12, repr.), which is datable about the same time. Additional evidence of their contact during these years is found in Ruisdael's *Great Oak*, dated 1652 (cat. 20) and his *Forest Scene*, of 1653 (fig. 11); Berchem painted the figures in both landscapes.

During the course of his career Ruisdael depicted the castle more than a dozen times from various points of view. Here it is seen from the southwest; Dublin's monumental *Bentheim* of 1653 (cat. 16), Ruisdael's only other existing dated painting of the site, shows it from the same direction.

As in most of the artist's paintings of the castle, the setting is imaginary. There is no height near Bentheim comparable to the one Jacob shows on the left. The almost impenetrable, heavily wooded hill in the middle distance also is the artist's invention. Primary emphasis is on the naturalistic detail of dense trees, the thick undergrowth and the gargantuan fallen beech tree that dwarfs the two horsemen. The huge scale of the dead beech and the lush growth near it suggest that by 1651 Ruisdael was inspired by motifs in Roelandt Savery's fantastic forest scenes (or Egeidius Saedler's prints after them), but had no interest in Roelandt's distinctive ornamental effects.

1. According to an old, often repeated tradition Pieter Claesz, the prominent still-life painter who was Nicolaes Berchem's father, was born in Burgsteinfurt (also Steinfurt) near Bentheim and that family business brought Berchem to the area. Tradition also has it that the two friends travelled to Pieter Claesz's birthplace together or met *en route*. Irene van Thiel-Stroman proved the old tradition is wrong when she discovered a document in Haarlem's Municipal Archive which establishes that Pieter Claesz is not a native of Burgsteinfurt but of Berchem (probably the village near Antwerp). The place accounts for the surname invariably used by the son; following a well-established custom Berchem adopted the name of his father's origin. For a transcription of documents pertinent to van Thiel-Stroman's archival find see Slive 2001, p.27, note 3.

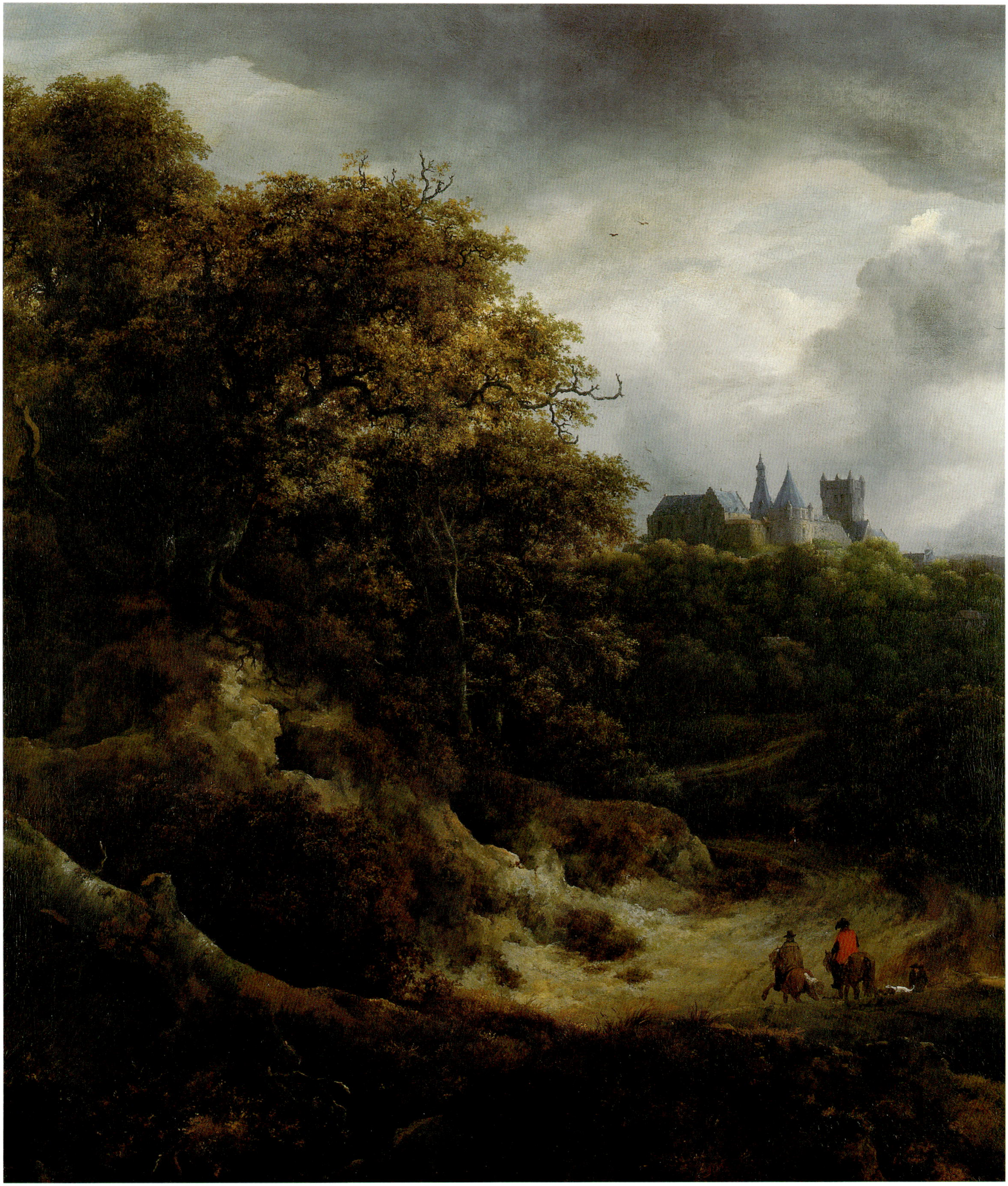

15

Bentheim Castle

Signed, lower right. About 1651–55. Canvas, 37 × 44.4 cm
Private collection

PROVENANCE: Purchased in 1850 for £120 from the London dealer Norton by John Staniforth Beckett; inherited by Sir H. B. Bacon about 1890; Sir Hickman Bacon, Gainsborough; Sir Edward Bacon, Raveningham Hall, Norfolk.

EXHIBITIONS: London, The Guild Art Gallery, 1890, no. 76; London 1952–53, no. 298; Utrecht 1953, no. 81, repr.; The Hague–Cambridge 1981–82, no. 13, repr.

LITERATURE: HdG 23; Ros 14; Maschmeyer 1978, p.69; Büttner and Unverfehrt 1993, p.103, no. 5, repr.; Slive 2001, no. 25, repr

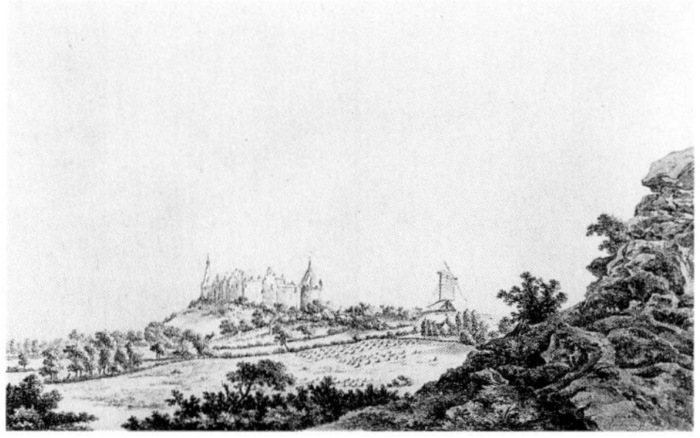

Fig. 15a Frederik de Moucheron, *Bentheim Castle*. Black chalk, grey wash. Österreichische Nationalbibliothek, Vienna (Atlas van der Hem).

The painting, which shows the castle from the northwest, is one of the rare ones by Ruisdael that most likely offers a topographically accurate view of the site in the artist's day. Berchem's 1650 drawing of the castle shows it from the same viewpoint (fig. 14a) and so does the topographical drawing Frederik de Moucheron (1633–86) made of Bentheim for Laurens van der Hem's monumental atlas (fig. 15a) which is also called the Blaeu Atlas.[1]

It has been noted that not a single drawing by Ruisdael of Bentheim is known (see p.4, above). A detail in the present painting, also found in a few of Ruisdael's other depictions of the site (for example, cat. 16), offers good proof that he made sketches of Bentheim that are now untraceable. The clue is the huge, unmistakable sandstone pylon that still stands at the northwest corner of the castle's mound. It is seen here just below the painting's optical center. Most probably his own drawings recorded the position and shape of the unusual geological formation, known locally as "The Devil's Cushion" or "Drusus's Rock", from various points of view, and then were used as *aides-mémoires* in the studio for his paintings.

1. Vienna, Österreichische Nationalbibliothek, Blaeu Atlas, vol. 29, p.16, 35 × 52.7, pen and wash; inscribed, lower right: Moucheron f [?]/Benthem. The Blaeu Atlas (also known as Atlas van der Hem) was assembled by the Amsterdam attorney and collector Laurens van der Hem (1621–78). It contained drawings by older artists (Roelandt Savery) as well as contemporary ones in addition to Moucheron (Willem Schellinks, Lambert Doomer, Jan Hackaert, *et al.*).

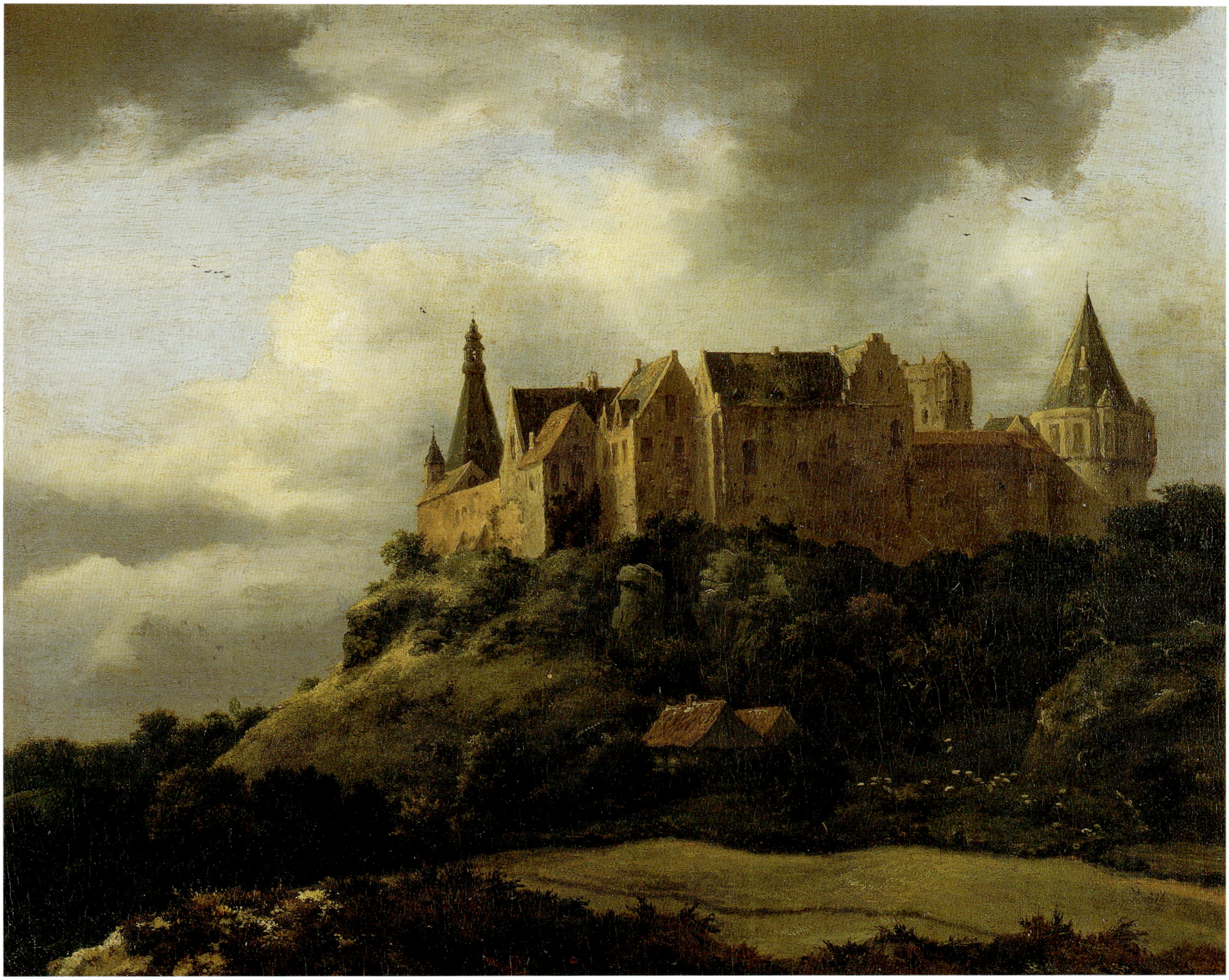

16

Bentheim Castle

Monogrammed and dated 1653, lower left. Canvas, 110.4 × 144 cm
National Gallery of Ireland, Dublin, NGI 4531

PROVENANCE: John Smith (258) states that according to tradition Ruisdael painted the picture "expressly for the Count of Bentheim, in whose family it is said to have remained until the entrance of the French into Germany [*c.* 1792–94] about which time it was taken to Paris . . .". He adds that from Paris it passed into England and became the property of William Smith, MP. In Paris it is said to have been in the collection of Le Noire (see below). John Bligh, 4th Earl of Darnley; his sale, London (Christie's), 8 May 1802, no. 54: "A Landscape, View of the Castle of Bentheim – a very capital and surprising Performance, finished in a very exquisite masterly Stile, with a noble brilliant Sky, admirably suited to the grandeur of the Scene; considered as the finest Picture known from the Pencil of Ruysdael; – from the Collection of Mons. Le Noire, at Paris" (£315 to Caleb Whitefoord for William Smith). Collection William Smith (1756–1835), MP for Norwich. Buchanan (1824, 2, p.360) writes it was consigned by William Smith to him and by 1824 had passed into the possession of a gentleman at Bristol, valued at £500. Thomas Kebble of Green Trees, near Tonbridge, Kent, by 1835; sale, a nobleman [according to Lugt, *Répertoire*, 2, no. 23035, Thomas Kibble, *sic*], London (Christie's), 2 June 1856, no. 54 (£1270.10, Woodin for J. Walter); John Walter, Bearwood; Sir Otto Beit, London; by descent to Sir Alfred Beit. Presented by Alfred and Lady Beit to The National Gallery of Ireland, 1987.

EXHIBITIONS: London, British Institution, 1815 (William Smith, MP); Manchester 1857, no. 708; London, British Institution, 1861, no. 50 (Walter); Leeds 1868, no. 792; London 1929, no. 95; Brussels 1935, no. 764; Cape Town, National Gallery, 1949 (on loan from Beit collection); The Hague–Cambridge 1981–82, no. 14, repr.; Chicago and elsewhere 1992–93, no. 32, repr.; Madrid 1994–95, no. 53, repr; Amsterdam 2000, no. 156, repr.

LITERATURE: Josi 1821, 2, [n.p.], under "Jacob Ruisdael"; W. Buchanan, *Memoirs of Painting, with a Chronological History of the Importation of Pictures by the Great Masters into England Since the French Revolution*, vol. 2, London, 1824, p.360; Smith 258; Bürger 1865, p.295; Frimmel 1896, p.64, note 1; Michel 1910, pp.148ff., repr. pl. 9; HdG 25, identical with HdG Zus. 28c; Bode 1913, no. 50, repr.; Ros 18; Götker 1964, pp.96–100; Hagels 1968, p.46; Maschmeyer 1978, p.69; Ashton *et al.* 1982, pp.6, 7, 19–21, fig. 2 (detail); Bruyn 1987–88, pp.98–99, repr.; A. Le Harivel *et al.*, *National Gallery of Ireland, The Beit Collection*, Dublin, 1988, no. 14; Norfolk 1988, under no. 99, repr.; Walford 1991, pp.86–87, repr.; Sutton 1992, p.167, note 5, repr.; Büttner and Unverfehrt 1993, p.104, no. 8, repr.; Slive 2001, no. 15, repr.; Slive 2004, pp.180–81, repr..

No support has been found for the tradition, related by John Smith (258) in 1835, that Ruisdael painted the picture "expressly for the Count of Bentheim". The tradition is probably groundless. If not, in view of the imaginary setting and vegetation Ruisdael introduced in the painting (see below), his putative patron was neither a stickler for topographical nor for botanical accuracy. According to the 1802 Darnley sale catalogue cited above, before the painting passed to England from Paris it belonged to a Monsieur Le Noire. A possible candidate for the not uncommon name is the notoriously difficult Alexandre Lenoir, founder of the Musée des Monuments Français, but whether the masterwork was ever in his personal collection remains to be determined.

Today there is universal agreement that the picture is Ruisdael's most imposing painting of Bentheim and that it ranks with the artist's most impressive works. However, as late as 1856 Samuel Mawson, the dealer who often served as an agent of the 4th Marquess of Hertford, principal builder of the Wallace Collection, recommended to Hertford that he try to buy Teniers's "very tip top" *Egg Dance* rather than the Ruisdael when both appeared in the Kibble sale. Evidently buyers at the sale did not share Mawson's opinion; the Teniers fetched £700 while the Ruisdael brought £1,270.10 (see Ingamells 1981, pp.86–87). It is not known if Hertford, whom Thoré-Bürger characterized about a decade later as "le plus grand collectionneur de l'Europe" (Bürger 1867, p.537), bid for either painting. In any event, neither picture entered his collection.

Dublin's painting of Bentheim, seen from the southwest, is dated 1653; Ruisdael's only other dated picture of it, done in 1651 (cat. 14), shows a more distant view of the castle from the same direction.

Jakob Rosenberg demonstrated how Ruisdael heightened and enhanced the unimposing site when he juxtaposed a photograph of it (fig. 16a; repr. from Rosenberg 1928, fig. 46) with the Dublin painting. Comparison of photographs of landscapes depicted by artists with their works is common practice today, but to my knowledge the comparison that Rosenberg made in 1928 is the first time an art historian used a camera to clinch a point regarding a landscapist's transformation of an actual site.

As the photograph shows, the hill at Bentheim is a low one. In the majestic Dublin picture Ruisdael vastly enlarged it into a wooded mountain, which provides the castle with a commanding position. The dense mass of the mountain, obliquely stretching away into depth, and the coulisses on either side of the front edge of the painting are reminiscent of some compositions painted by the generation of his teachers, but the spatial clarity is new, as is the way he unifies the close view of a nearly overwhelming wealth of detail with the most distant parts of the landscape into a consistent whole. The impact of the broad prospect is as intense as that of the vegetation seen close-up. Some of the vegetation in the foreground is as imaginary as the mountain Ruisdael invented for the castle; the distinctive small plants blooming with creamy white flowers on a mound near the center of the front plane are unmistakably *Viburnum lantana*, the wayfaring tree. Early in his career Ruisdael became familiar with this lime-loving plant in the neighbourhood of Haarlem; it does not grow in the vicinity of Bentheim.[1] Artistic licence accounts for its transplantation.

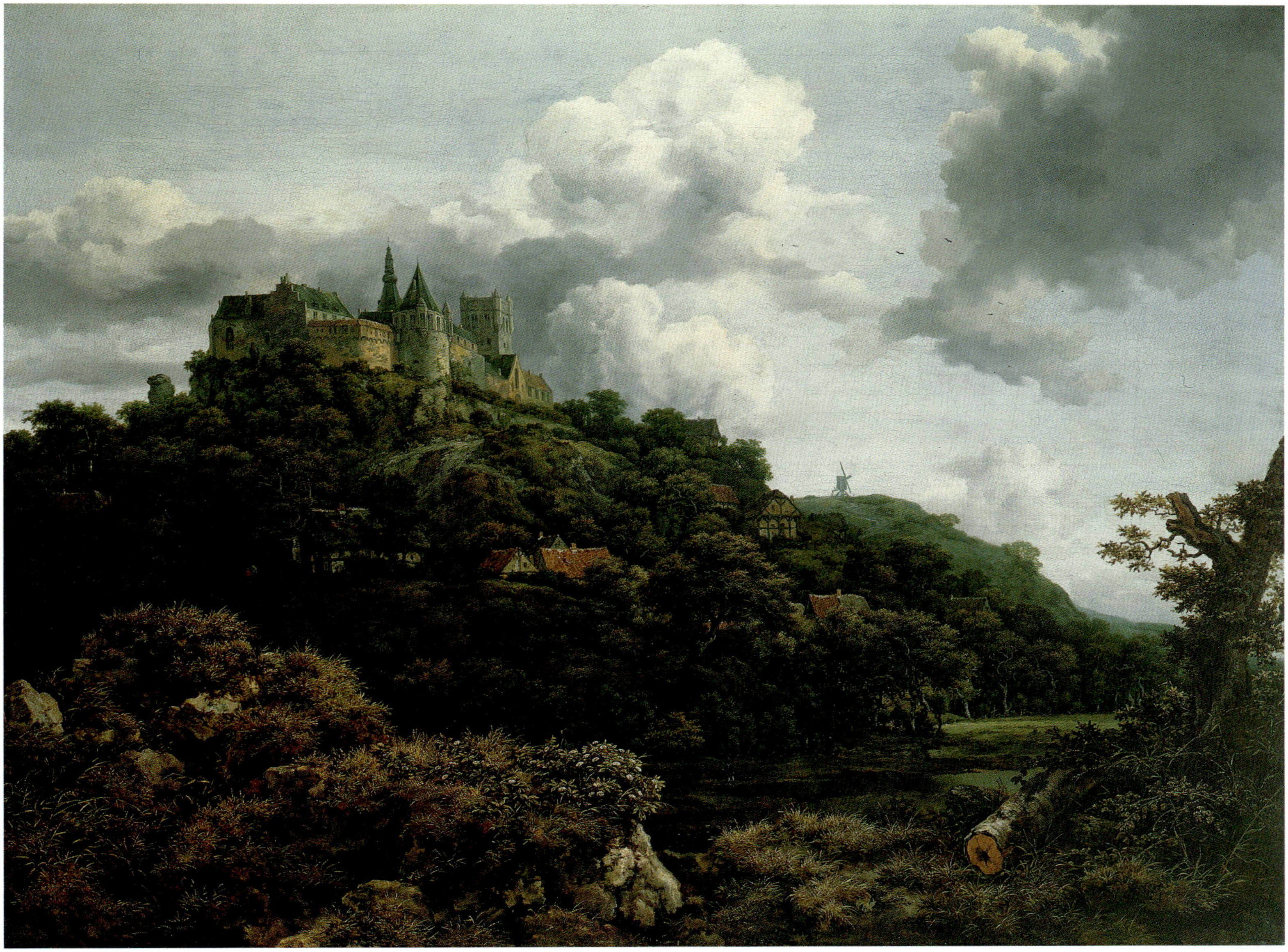

A quick, small pencil sketch after the painting by the Norwich artist John Sell Cotman (1782–1842), which includes his notes regarding its colour and handling, is at the Leeds City Art Galleries (S. D. Kitson Bequest 1938, no. 9.51/49; Moore 1988, no. 99, repr.). Andrew W. Moore (*ibid.*) rightly proposes that Cotman almost certainly made his copy when the picture was lent by William Smith to the exhibition of Netherlandish art held at the British Institution in 1815. Among the other Dutch paintings Smith lent to that exhibition were Rembrandt's *Windmill*, now in the National Gallery of Art, Washington (no. 1942.9.62), a Berchem (HdG, vol. 9, 159e), and Aelbert Cuyp's *Horsemen and Herdsmen*, the National Gallery of Art, Washington (no. 1942.9.16).

1. Ashton *et al.* 1982, pp.6, 7, 19–21; also see cat. 9, above.

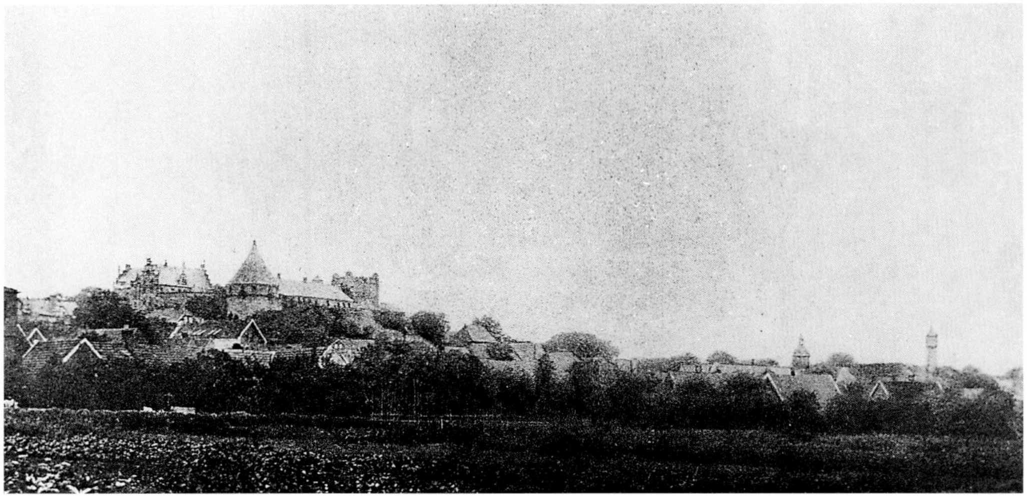

Fig. 16a Photograph of Bentheim, *c.* 1925.

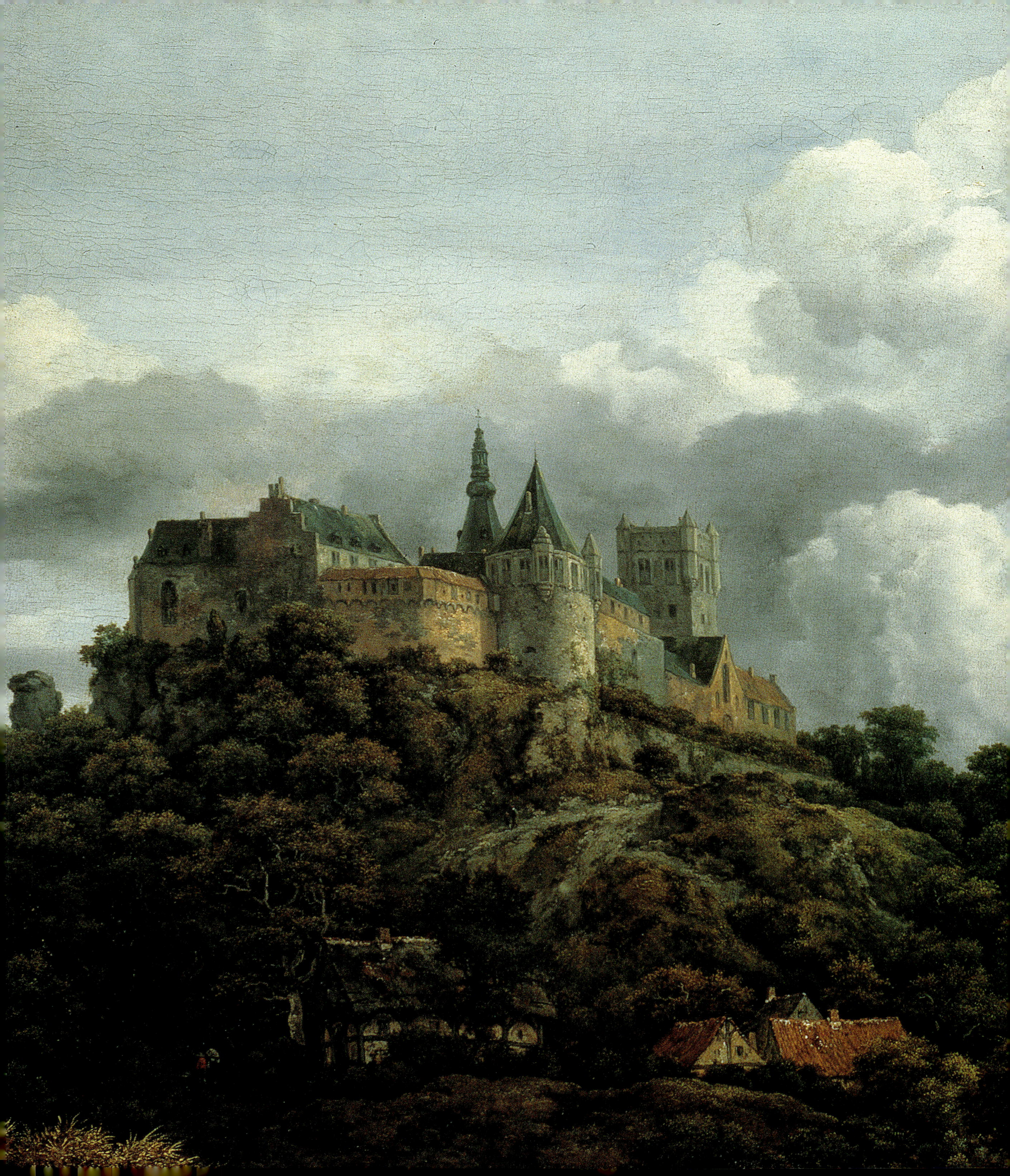

17

Two Water Mills and an Open Sluice

Monogrammed and dated 1653 on the stone embankment on the left. Canvas, 66 × 84.5 cm
J. Paul Getty Museum, Los Angeles, 82.PA.18

PROVENANCE: Sale, Jhr. J. Goll van Franckenstein, Amsterdam (de Vries), 1 July 1833, no. 70 (Dfl.1980, Clarke for C. J. Nieuwenhuis); sale, Casimir Périer, London (Christie's), 5 May 1848, no. 13 (£367.10, Gardner); sale, J. D. Gardner of Bottisham Hall, Cambridgeshire, London (Christie's), 25 March 1854, no. 71 (£451.10, Brown; a manuscript note in the RKD annotated copy of the catalogue states that the painting is dated 1653); sold by Brown to Edmund Foster, Clewer Manor, near Windsor; sale, Richard Foster of Clewer Manor, London (Christie's), 3 June 1876, no. 13 (£1837.10, Durlacher); Alfred de Rothschild, 1876; Baroness Mathilde von Rothschild, Frankfurt a.M.; art market, Berlin, 1923–25; dealer Kleykamp, The Hague, Catalogue, 1927, no. 34, repr.; H. M. Clark, London, *c.*1930; private collection, Switzerland, 1945; sale, anon., Laren, N. H. (Christie's), 20 October 1980, no. 252, repr.; dealer Hoogsteder, The Hague; Manfred R. Mayer; purchased by the museum from Hoogsteder or from Manfred R. Mayer through Hoogsteder, 1982.

EXHIBITIONS: Basel 1945, no. 79; The Hague–Cambridge 1981–82, no. 23, repr.; Amsterdam–Boston–Philadelphia 1987–88, no. 81; Madrid 1994–95, no. 54.

LITERATURE: Smith 250; Waagen 1857, 4, p.287 (wrong dimensions and support); HdG 169d; Ros 102 (wrong dimensions; wrongly said to be identical with HdG 171); Simon 1930, p.81; MacLaren 1960, pp.359 and 360, note 7; H. Hagens, "Jacob van Ruisdael, Meindert Hobbema en de identificatie-zucht," *'t inschrien*, 14, no. 1, 1982, pp.7–12; J. Paul Getty Museum, *Handbook of the Collections*, 1986, p.98, repr.; MacLaren and Brown 1991, pp.384 and 385, note 8; Walford 1991, pp.87–89; Hagens and Elling 1991, pp.25 and 33, note 46.; Slive 2001, no. 119, repr.

The types of water mills Ruisdael depicted (single and double, undershot and overshot; often half-timbered) were found in the eastern provinces of Gelderland and Overijssel as well as western Westphalia, areas the artist toured in the early 1650s when he travelled to Bentheim and the borderland between the Netherlands and Germany. He discovered the theme during the course of his trip.

The present work of 1653 is the artist's sole surviving, fully dated picture of the subject. Most of the artist's water mill paintings are datable to the 1650s. The complex spatial arrangement and greater openness of the 1653 Getty picture of a downstream view of two half-timbered, undershot water mills suggest it postdates a group with similar themes. In each the right-hand mill is in a different state of preservation, but it is not possible to rely on that mill's deterioration to establish a relative chronology for them, since there is no reason to believe that Ruisdael faithfully transcribed precisely what he saw at mill sites. The liberties he took with the setting of Bentheim Castle are also evident in his water mill paintings.

Because it is seldom known how a particular mill looked in the artist's time and, as is frequently noted in the present catalogue, Ruisdael often selected, rearranged and invented motifs to suit his needs. Attempts to identify precise sites of the water mills in his paintings remain tentative. On the other hand, the existence of four sketches of different views of the same overshot water mill, which served as preparatory drawings for four paintings (see cat. 74, 75), indicates that he made various studies of at least one mill *in situ*.

The rushing cascade falling from the broad open sluices in the Getty picture is among the artist's first successful attempts to portray a powerful torrent and seething foam. It stood him in good stead in the late fifties and early sixties when he began painting a motif he had never seen: tumultuous Scandinavian waterfalls. It was during the 1660s that pictures of water mills in a landscape became one of the specialties of Meindert Hobbema, Ruisdael's only documented pupil.

The monogram and date of 1653 on the Getty picture are painted in two colours to give them a three-dimensional effect. Ruisdael used the same device on a few other landscapes dated or datable in the early fifties.[1]

1. *Wooded Landscape with a Ruined Mill Run and a Ruined Building in the Middle Distance*, Gallery of South Australia, Adelaide (Slive 2001, no. 109, repr.); *Wooded Valley with a Footbridge*, 1652, The Frick Collection, New York (Slive 2001, no. 511, repr.); *Thatch-Roofed House with a Water Mill*, The Boijmans Van Beuningen Museum, Rotterdam (fig. 39; Slive 2001, no. 121); *Hilly Wooded Landscape with Cattle*, The Duke of Buccleuch and Queensberry, Selkirk, Bowhill (cat. 19).

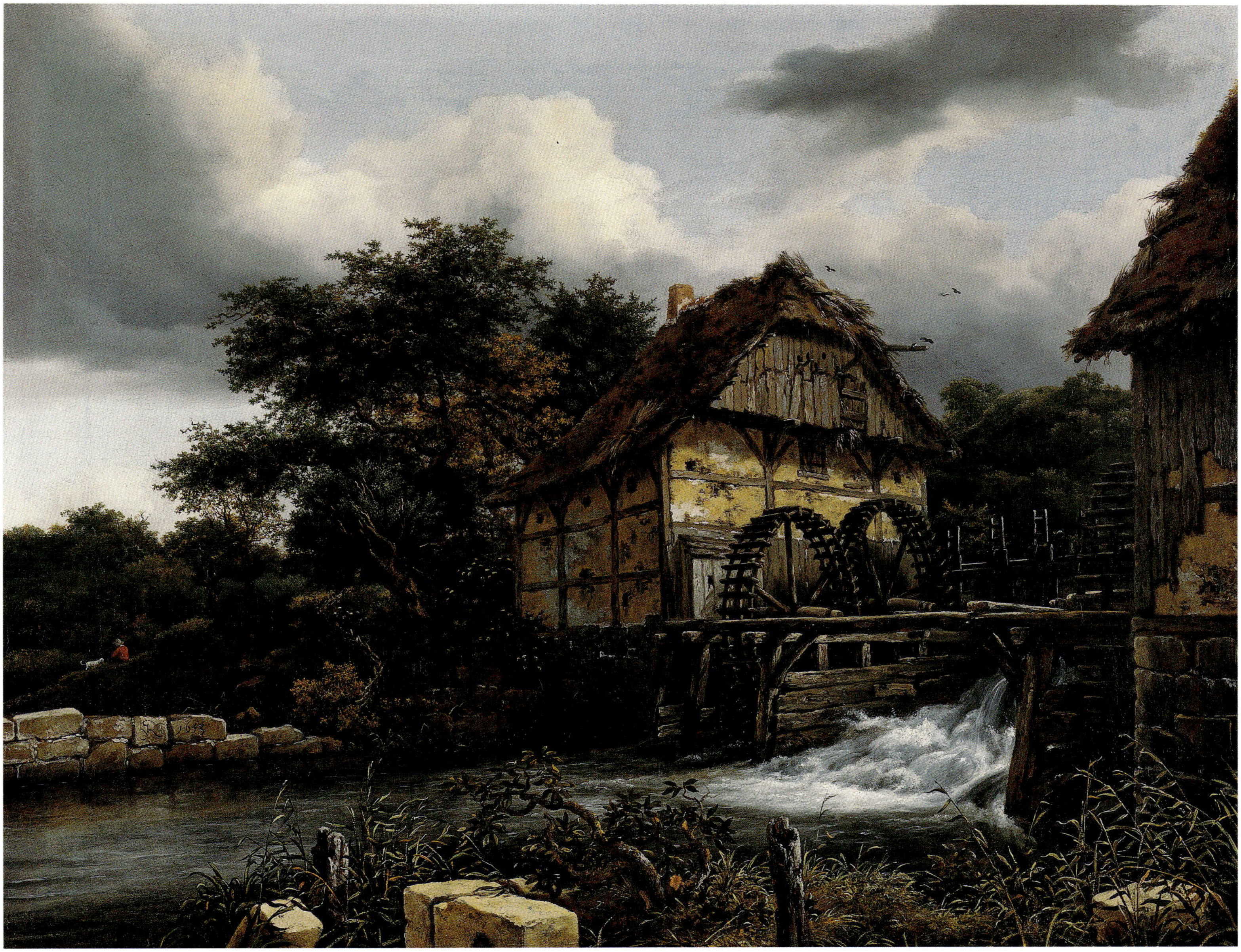

18

Landscape with the Ruins of Egmond Castle at Egmond aan den Hoef

Monogrammed, lower right. About 1650–53. Canvas, 95 × 125 CM (original dimensions); 98 × 129.9 cm (existing dimensions)[1]
The Art Institute of Chicago, Potter Palmer Collection, 1947.475

PROVENANCE: Sale, Baron Étienne Martin de Beurnonville (d.1881), Paris (Drouot), 9 May 1881, no. 451 (fr.10,000; erroneously called *Ruins of the Castle of Brederode*); G. von Ráth, Budapest; Oscar Huldschinsky, Berlin, purchased from P. & D. Colnaghi, London by 1906; sale, Oscar Huldschinsky, Berlin (Cassirer), 10–11 May 1928, no. 29 (DM61,000, Boehler, bought in); dealer J. Goudstikker, Rotterdam and Amsterdam, Catalogue no. 36, 22 December 1928–28 February 1929, no. 67; dealer Kurt Walter Bachstitz, Berlin by 1929; dealer Paul Cassirer, London, 1947, as agent for an anonymous family with Otto Reichenheim as intermediary; sold to The Art Institute of Chicago, 1947.

EXHIBITIONS: Berlin 1906, no. 117, repr.; London 1932, no. 27; The Hague–Cambridge 1981–82, no. 19, repr.

LITERATURE: Frimmel 1891–92, p.261; Bode 1909, no. 26; HdG 51 (Egmond?); Ros 34 (Egmond?); *Bulletin of the Bachstitz Gallery*, The Hague, 1929, pp.36–7; A. L. Romdahl, "Barock, Kontrabarock och Akademism," *Tidskrift för Konstvetenskap*, 20, 1937, pp.39–40; Renaud 1940, pp.339–41; D. C. Rich, "Two Great Romantic Landscapes," *Bulletin, Art Institute of Chicago*, 42, 1948, pp.20–22; *Paintings in the Art Institute of Chicago*, 1961, pp.408–09; Kouznetsov 1973, p.35; Ashton *et al.* 1982, p.19, pl. 19 (detail); Keyes 1989, pp.168–69 (more Romantic than seventeenth century in mood; perhaps after a Ruisdael invention); Slive 1991, p.598, note 2 (rejects Keyes's suggestion that the painting is not by Ruisdael); Slive 2001, no. 29, repr.

Egmond Castle at Egmond aan den Hoef, situated near Alkmaar, was the seat of the counts of Egmond. Spanish troops occupied it during their invasion of Holland in 1573–74. To prevent the Spanish from again using it as an encampment, in the year they departed it was destroyed at the command of Willem the Silent, Prince of Orange, by the troops of Diederik Sonoy, governor of the northern quarter of Holland. Since that time the castle has remained a ruin; only a few modest remains are visible today.

The ruins and their site, easily accessible from Haarlem, attracted Ruisdael in the early and mid-fifties when monumental forms began to play a key role in his work. Firm identification of most of the artist's paintings and drawings of the ruins was first made by Renaud (1940). Here, he notes, Ruisdael shows the remains of the southeastern corner tower of the castle's main building and the adjacent wall of its south façade. A drawing formerly at Bremen, presumably lost in World War II (Slive 2001, no. D33, repr.), may have been used by the artist for a section of the ruins depicted in the picture.

The painting is an example of Jacob's urge in the early fifties to heighten large forms, emphasize solid masses, and create solidly constructed compositions. Apart from the huge trailing cloud formations, Ruisdael's approach to the landscape was a lateral one. The far bank of the castle moat provides a firm base for the surging power of the towering ruin and the massiveness of the long, low hill close behind it. Compared to his earlier works, colours have gained in freshness and concentration. As remarkable as his treatment of the light terracotta red of the noble ruin is his handling of white. The strongest patch of the latter is on the low wall. Smaller strokes of white and near-white have been gathered together very restrainedly to animate other portions of the ruin, while a few gentle touches appear as blossoms on the large elder bush, sheep on the bank, moss on the oak stump in the foreground, and reflections in the water. There is only a single, small point of intense colour in the painting: the shepherd's red jacket.

Although the powerful impact of the large picture recalls nothing in Cornelis Vroom's oeuvre, reminiscences of the older artist's landscapes are still perceptible in it. Even though the delicate lacy foliage of the small tree on the right is slightly abraded, it still could pass as a quotation from one of Vroom's works, and the oblique slope of the prominent hill that stretches across the middle ground recalls a compositional scheme that Vroom often favoured. The hill also indicates that here Ruisdael was not concerned with offering a topographically accurate view of the castle's site. Like the hill he introduced in his versions of *The Jewish Cemetery* (cat. 22, fig. 22a), it is his invention.

1. The tacking margins of the painting's original support have been turned out on all four sides, extending the picture. The original support with its tacking margins have been secured to a new lining. Its original dimensions have been determined with the help of x-radiographs in the Institute's conservation laboratory and were kindly communicated (October 2003) by Martha Wolff, Curator of European Painting before 1750. I also am beholden to her for data regarding the picture's provenance.

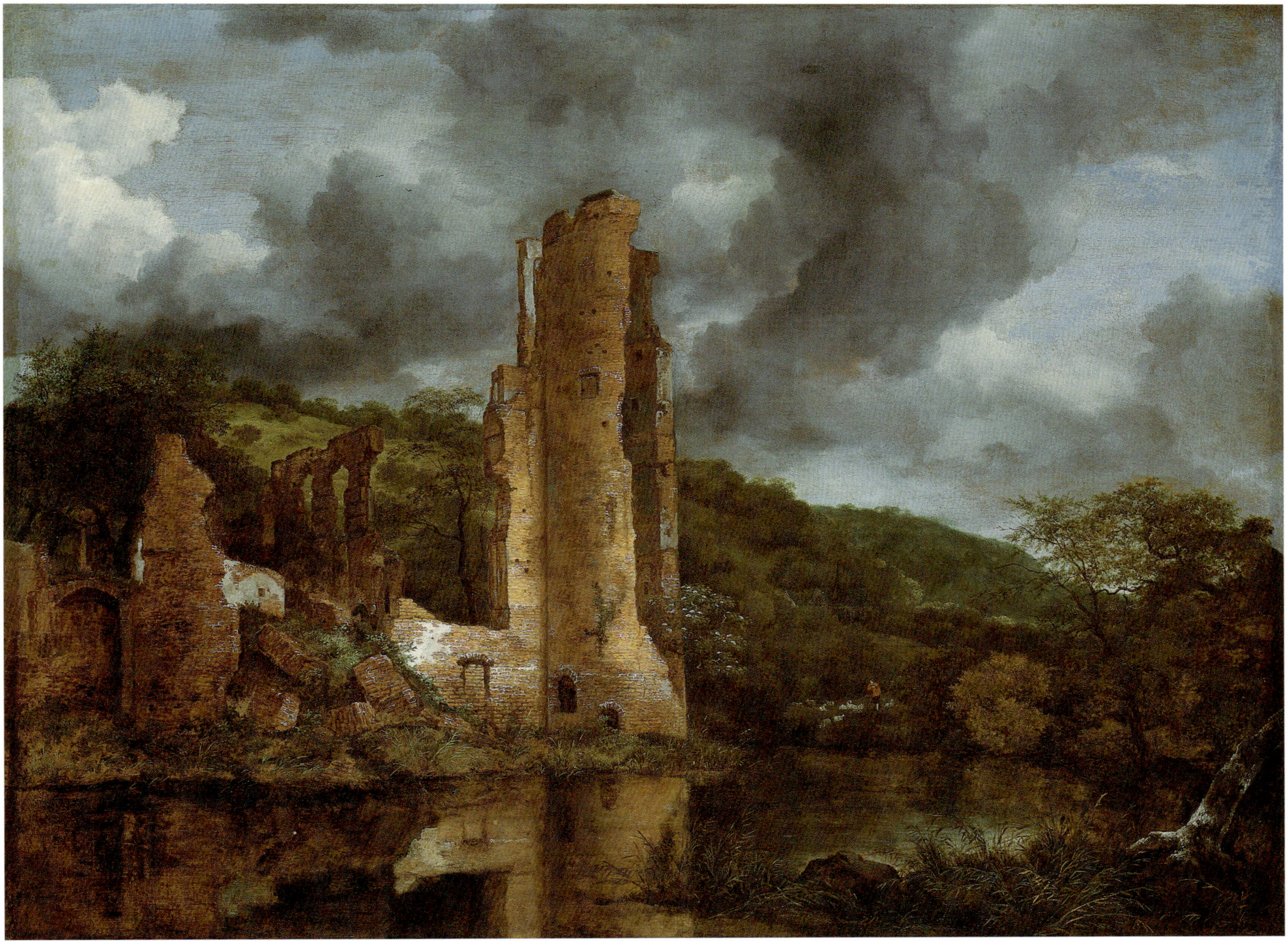

19

Hilly Wooded Landscape with Cattle

Monogrammed at the left edge, about 30 cm above the canvas's bottom. Early 1650s.
Canvas, 98 × 124 cm
In the collection of the Duke of Buccleuch and Queensberry KT, DH 176

PROVENANCE: According to Francis Russell (Washington 1985–86, no. 321), the landscape may be the "good Ruysdael" cited in 1768 by Walpole (Toynbee 1927–28, p.66) in the gallery at Adderbury in Oxfordshire, the house rebuilt by John Campbell (1680–1743), 2nd Duke of Argyll and 1st Duke of Greenwich, and inherited by his elder daughter, Caroline, Countess of Dalkeith, mother of the 3rd Duke of Buccleuch. Russell notes that other pictures from Adderbury are known to have been taken to Dalkeith Palace near Edinburgh, where the present painting is first certainly recorded [by Smith 283] in the possession of the 5th Duke of Buccleuch in 1835.

EXHIBITIONS: London 1978, no. 37, repr.; The Hague–Cambridge 1981–82, no. 15, repr.; Washington 1985–86, no. 321, repr. (entry by Francis Russell).

LITERATURE: Smith 283; Waagen 1854, 3, p.313; Waagen 1857, p.436; Steuart 1890, p.48; Hofstede de Groot 1893, p.213; Dalkeith Palace Collection, Catalogue, 1911, no. 176; HdG 546; Ros 402; Slive 2001, no. 477, repr.

RA

In the early 1650s Ruisdael began to use the compositional scheme of hills rising high on either side of a vista into the distance. However, in none of his existing variations on the theme are the multifarious geological formations and luxuriant mass of foliage and vegetation on either edge of the cleavage brought so close to the foreground. The close-up view intensifies the feeling of their density, massive solidity and weight, while the sky that comes deep down into the landscape accents the distant prospect. As in the outstanding *Bentheim Castle* of 1653 at Dublin (cat. 16), the closely observed near and far views have been united into a consistent whole.

The excellently preserved painting shows the granular quality of the artist's paint during the early fifties as well as the rich variety of his ochres and browns, and the vivid green he favoured for distant foliage in his youth and early maturity. A minor detail regarding the monogram on the picture is worth mentioning. Ruisdael gave it special emphasis by painting it in two colours to give it a three-dimensional effect. He used the same device for monograms and signatures on other paintings of the early fifties.[1] A similar stress upon his authorship also occurs on a few of his etchings.

1. See cat. 17, note 1.

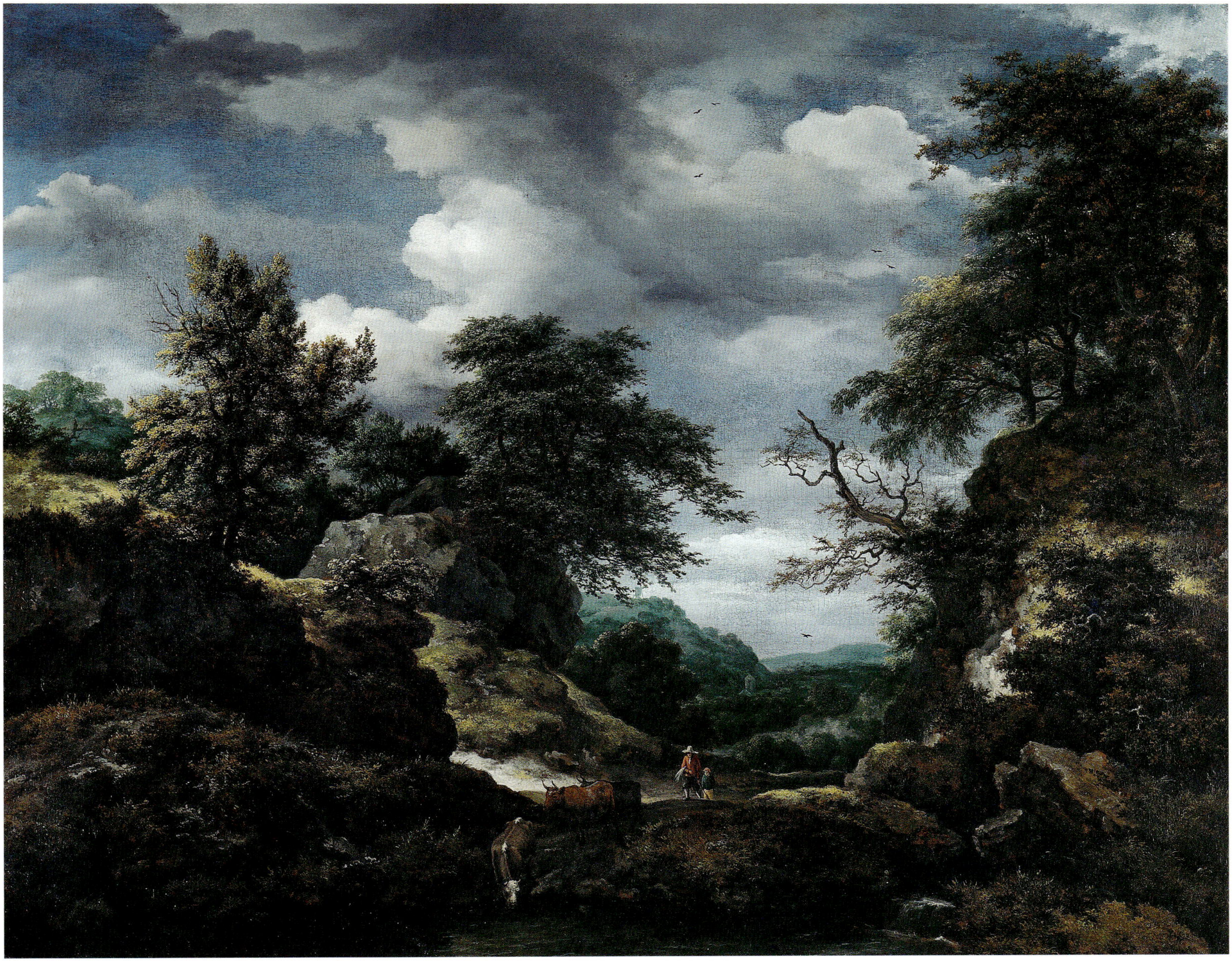

20

The Great Oak

Signed and dated 1652, bottom left of centre. Canvas, 85.1 × 104.3 cm
Los Angeles County Museum of Art. Gift of Mr and Mrs Edward William Carter in honor of the museum's twenty-fifth anniversary, M 91.164.1

PROVENANCE: Collection Cardinal Silvio Valenti Gonzaga (1690–1756), Rome, by 1749; posthumous manuscript inventory of his painting collection, datable 1756–63, no. 154 (as Berchem);[1] sale, Cardinal Valenti, Amsterdam (de Leth and de Winter), 18 May 1763, no. 39 (as Berchem; canvas secured to panel; Dfl.1000, Fouquet; 1763 sale catalogue reprinted in Terwesten 1770, pp.289–309, see p.296, no. 39); sale, Pierre de Grand-Pré, Paris (Paillet), 16–24 February 1809, no. 98 (as Ruisdael, with figures by Berchem; canvas; fr.7001, la Fontene), private sale, Duchesse de Berry, London (Christie's), April 1834, no. 37 (as Ruisdael, with figures by Berchem); sale, [Duchesse de Berry], Paris (Paillet), 4–6 April 1837, no. 26 (fr.8000); Samuel Wheeler, Brighton and Barrow Hills, Surrey, 1867; his sale, London (Christie's), 29 July 1871, no. 105 (£792.15, King; figures and animals "admirably introduced by N. Berchem." Signed by both artists, and dated 1652); G. Cavendish Bentinck, 1876; sale, G. A. F. Cavendish Bentinck, London (Christie's), 8–14 July 1891, no. 566 (£1470, Colnaghi); Arthur Sanderson, Edinburgh; F. Fleischmann, London, acquired from Colnaghi, 1897; by descent to F. N. [Noel] Ashcroft (née Fleischmann), London; private collection, England; private collection, The United States, 1984; dealers Harari and Johns, London, 1984; sold to Mr. and Mrs. Edward William Carter, 1985, who gave it to the museum, 1991.

EXHIBITIONS: London, British Institution, 1856, no. 22, and 1867, no. 54 (lent by Samuel Wheeler); London, Royal Academy, Winter Exhibition, 1876, no. 67 (lent by G. Cavendish Bentinck); London, Royal Academy, 1890, no. 73 (lent by G. C. Bentinck); dealer Lawrie, London, Catalogue, 1903, no. 4; London, Grafton Galleries, October 1911, no. 69 (lent by Mrs. Fleischmann); London 1949, no. 142; subsequently placed on anonymous loan to the City Museums and Art Gallery, Birmingham, England; The Hague–Cambridge 1981–82, no. 16, repr.; Los Angeles 1992–93, pp.132–37, no. 33, repr.

LITERATURE: Smith 103 (signed by both Ruisdael and Berchem) and Smith Suppl. 54; Blanc 1857–58, 2, pp.423–24; Hofstede de Groot 1893, pp.211–12; HdG 550 (the English translation of Hofstede de Groot notes the work is signed by both Ruisdael and Berchem); Ros 339 (signed by both Ruisdael and Berchem); Schaar 1958, p.36 (staffage by Berchem); Ashton *et al.* 1982, pl. 6 (detail); Slive 1987, pp.169f., repr.; Montreal 1990, p.15, repr.; Walford 1991, pp.80–81; Slive 1995, p.225, repr.; Slive 2001, no. 380, repr.

The sky is reasonably intact. There are several scattered areas of flake losses and damages (*e.g.*, in the trees and along the bottom). Apart from these passages the masterwork is in excellent condition. Its date of 1652 makes it a documented example of the artist's use of heroic trees as protagonists in the early fifties. For a comment on the crossroad and the animal bones on it see p. 8 above.

Inclusion of the landscape in the lower left of Giovanni Paolo Panini's monogrammed *Interior of a Picture Gallery Showing the Collection of Cardinal Silvia Valenti Gonzaga* (figs. 20a, b), dated at Rome in 1749, Wadsworth Atheneum, Hartford, establishes that it was in the Cardinal's collection by that date.[2] Its presence in Rome by 1749 makes it the earliest known instance of a work by Ruisdael in an Italian collection. To my knowledge, apart from a *Waterfall*, collection of the heirs of Hans P. Wertitsch, said to have been acquired in Rome in 1752 (Slive 2001, no. 291, repr.), no other work by the artist found a home in Italy until 1797 when his *Landscape with a Grainfield* entered the Uffizi (Slive 2001, no. 87, repr.). However, there is excellent reason to believe Cardinal Valenti thought *The Great Oak* was by Nicolaes Berchem, not Ruisdael; it is listed as a Berchem in his posthumous inventory, compiled between 1756–63,[3] and again when it appeared in his estate sale held in Amsterdam in 1763.[4]

The Great Oak's wrong attribution to Berchem at this time is not as wild as it might seem at first blush. As Berchem did on more than one occasion, he made an unmistakable contribution to Ruisdael's landscape; he painted the lovely figures and animals on either side of the great oak. Moreover, during the eighteenth century, when Nicolaes was much better known than Jacob, most collectors preferred a Berchem to a Ruisdael. This was the time when Dutch landscapists of idyllic scenes that capture the shimmering bright light and warm air of the Roman *campagna* were preferred to those who derived motifs from a study of Holland's countryside. Of all the Dutch artists who painted Italianate scenes, Berchem was the one most avidly collected.[5]

Ruisdael's name is associated with the picture only during the first decade of the nineteenth century, when he began to acquire his reputation as Holland's greatest seventeenth-century landscapist. During these years the earliest references to *The Great Oak* as a landscape by Ruisdael with figures introduced by Berchem are found. They occur in catalogues prepared for sales held in 1809 at Paris and in 1834 at London (see provenance).

When Smith (103) published the painting as a landscape by Ruisdael with figures by Berchem, he flatly stated: "This picture is signed by both artists, and dated 1652". Hofstede de Groot (550) and Rosenberg (339) repeat Smith's assertion that it bears both autographs. I have been unable to determine if the painting was, in fact, doubly signed. Today it bears only Ruisdael's signature and date, and not a trace of Berchem's name.

The Great Oak fetched 8,000 francs when it appeared in the sale of the Duchesse de Berry's pictures at Paris in 1837. Someone wrote after the price "C'est pour rien" in the copy of the catalogue from which Blanc (1857–58, 2, p.424) compiled a selected list of paintings that appeared in the sale. At the same sale Gerard ter Borch's famous *Signing of the Peace at Münster*, The National Gallery, London (no. 896), brought 45,500 francs, Paulus Potter's *Seven Cows in a Meadow*,

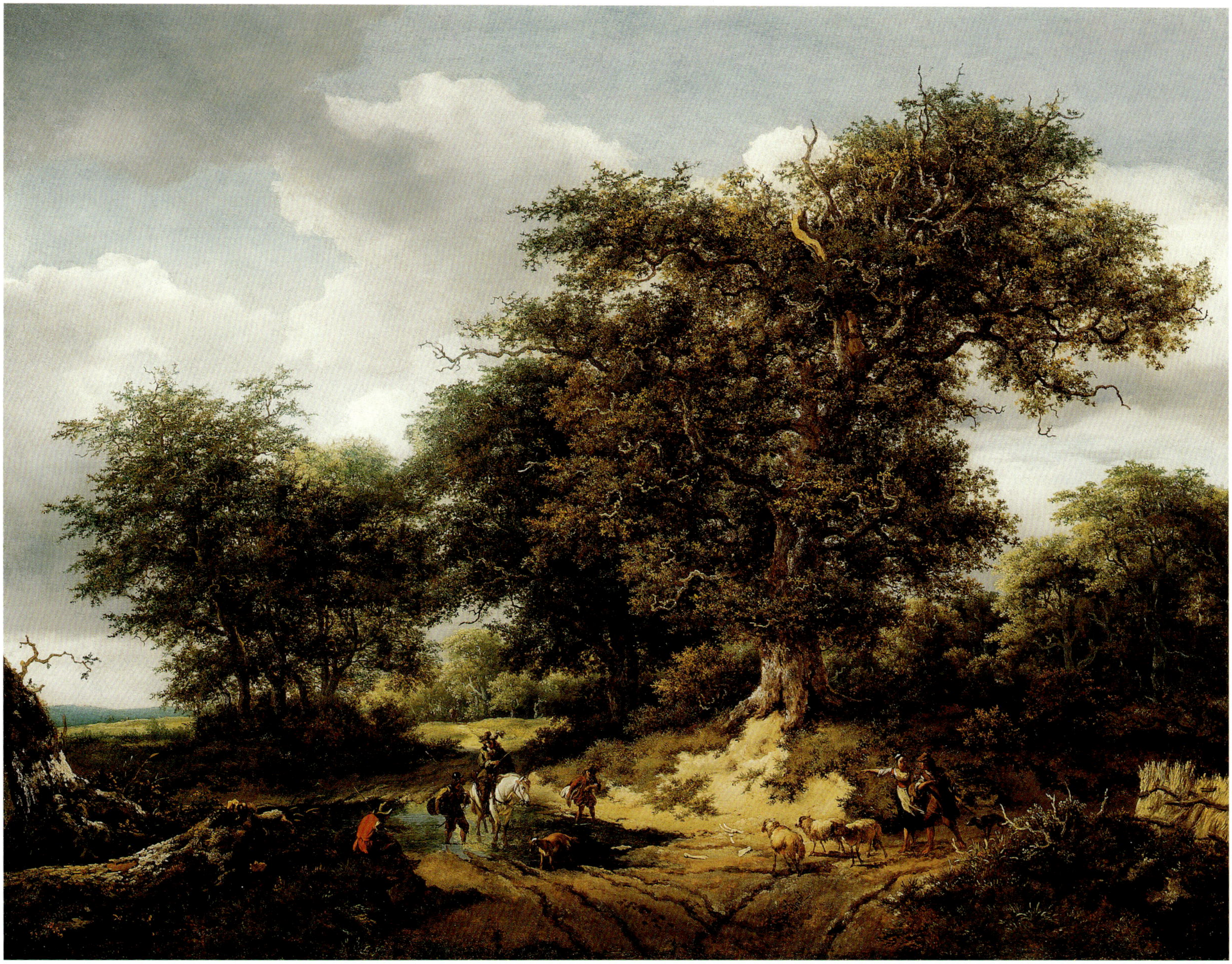

Philips-de Jongh Collection, Eindhoven (HdG, 4, no. 45), was sold for 37,100 francs, and Isack van Ostade's *Travellers Outside an Inn*, Mauritshuis, The Hague (no. 789; HdG, 3, no. 22), fetched 31,000 francs. In view of these prices we agree that *The Great Oak* went "for nothing" at the sale. Another picture in that auction would today be considered a far greater bargain: Vermeer's *Woman with a Maid Servant*, now in The Frick Collection, New York (no. 19.1.126), was purchased for 415 francs.

James Stark (1794–1859) made a copy of *The Great Oak* which is now at Picton Castle, Haverfordwest, Pembrokeshire, where it is called "Rabbiting in Windsor Forest".[6]

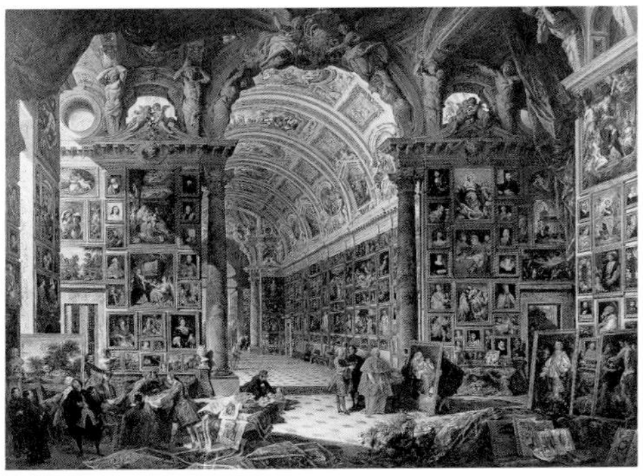

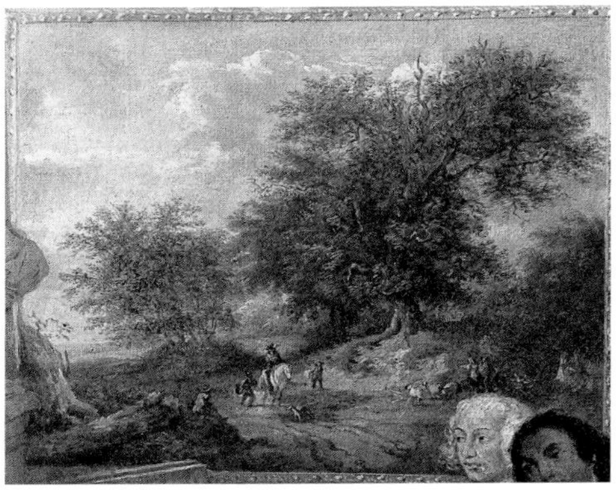

Fig. 20a Giovanni Paolo Panini, *Interior of a Picture Gallery Showing the Collection of Cardinal Silvia Valenti Gonzaga*, 1749. Wadsworth Atheneum, Hartford.

Fig. 20b Detail of fig. 20a.

1. *Catalogo dei quadri, tuttavia essistenti nella galleria della Ch. Mem. Dell' Emo Sig. Cardinale Silvio Valenti*, no. 154: "Quadro di palmi 4, once 9 per larghezza, e palmi 3, once 3 per altezza, rappresentante un paese, con figure, in tavola, di Berclem [*sic*]". The catalogue is in the Biblioteca Communale, Mantua, misc. 109.1; a typescript is at the Wadsworth Atheneum, Hartford.
2. For Cardinal Valenti and his collection of Dutch pictures see Slive 1987, pp.169–90.
3. See note 1 above.
4. See PROVENANCE. Valenti's second sale was held in Amsterdam (de Winter), 28 September 1763.
5. For a survey of Berchem's eighteenth-century reputation see Slive 1987, pp.176–80.
6. Stark's copy can be distinguished in a photo of Picton Castle's drawing room in *Picton Castle in Photographs*, Haverfordwest [n.d., unpaginated], a booklet of views of the castle. Stark, a pupil of James Crome and painter of the Norwich school, is better known for his Hobbema-like landscapes than for works done after Ruisdael.

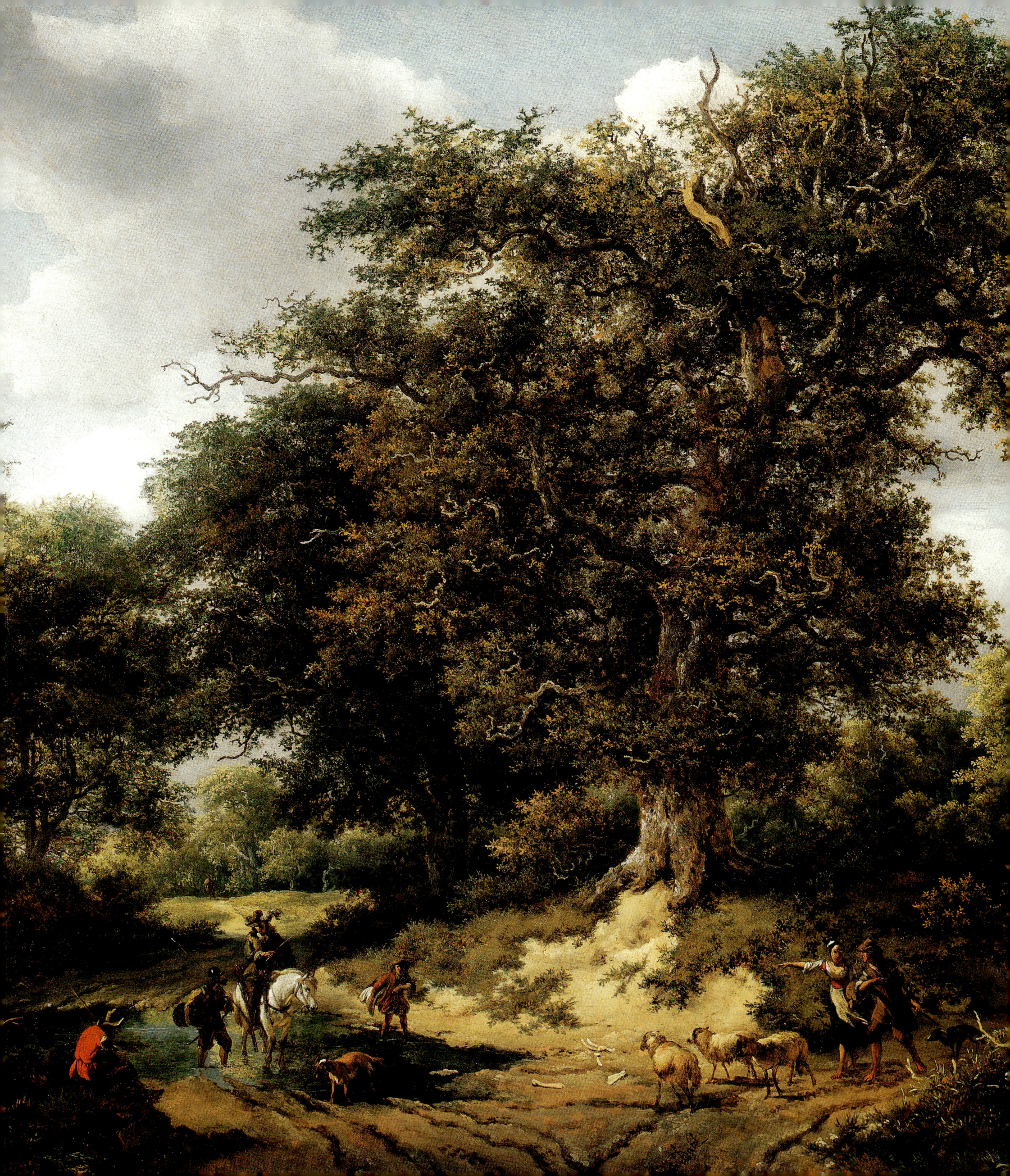

21

Hilly Landscape with a Great Oak and a Grainfield

About 1652–55. Canvas, 106 × 138 cm
Herzog Anton Ulrich-Museum. Kunstmuseum des Landes Niedersachsen, Braunschweig

PROVENANCE: Acquired by Duke Karl I (1713–80) for the Gallery at Salzdahlum Castle in 1738; taken by Napoléon to Paris, 1807–15; returned by 1816.

EXHIBITIONS: Paris, Musée Napoléon, 1807, no. 558; Krefeld 1938, no. 107; The Hague–Cambridge 1981–82, no. 17, repr.; Amsterdam–Boston–Philadelphia 1987–88, no. 82, repr.; Hamburg–Haarlem 2002, no. 32, repr.

LITERATURE: Manuscript Catalogue, Ducal Collection, Salzdahlum, 1744; Ducal Collection, Salzdahlum, Catalogue (French edition), 1776, p.311, no. 16; P. C. Ribbentrop, *Beschreibung der Stadt Braunschweig*, 1789, 1, p.337, no. 16; Filhol 1810, 7, 74th livraison, p.7, repr. ("Ce joli tableau est dû aux conquêtes de 1806"); Emeperius 1816, column 45; Duchesne ainé [n.d.; *c.*1825], 2, p.A116, repr.; Smith 299 and Smith 331; Parthey 1864, 2, p.455, no. 13; Riegel 1882, 2, pp.367f.; Riegel 1885, no. 83; Michel 1887, p.23; Michel 1890, p.83; Michel 1906, pp.187, 193; HdG 107; Ros 74; Simon 1930, p.24; Fink 1954, pp.53–54, 90; Herzog Anton Ulrich-Museum, Catalogue, 1976, p.51, no.376; Korn 1978, p.114; Maschmeyer 1978, pp.64–66; Klessmann 1983, pp.177–78, no. 376, repr.; Walford 1991, pp.84–85, repr.; Slive 2001, no. 84, repr.

An etching of the painting begun by Jean Desaulx and finished by Niquet after a drawing by Vasserot is in Filhol 1810, 7, 74th livraison, plate 442. Also engraved by Jean de Saulx (= Desaulx) after a drawing by Storelly in Duchesne ainé [n.d., *c.*1825], 2, facing p.A116.

RA

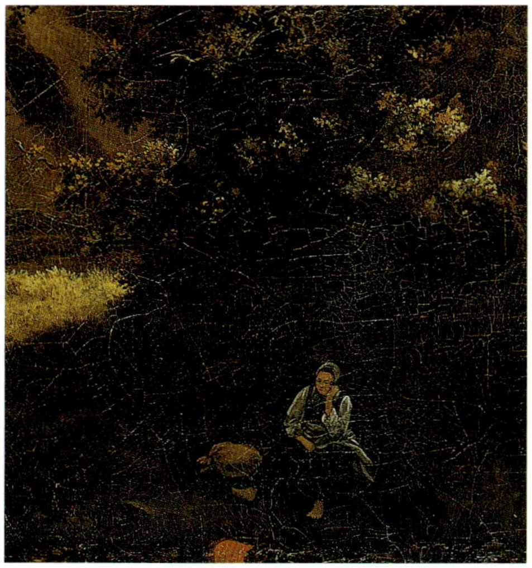

Fig. 21a Detail of cat. 21.

The large canvas has been cut on all four sides, principally on the upper edge (the top of the crown of the huge oak and a strip of sky above it originally may have been visible) and on the right side. Where the sky has become thin on the right it is apparent to the naked eye that it covers foliage. Lead white paint that coats the back of the canvas makes it exceedingly difficult to discover more about the work's pentimenti and underpainting by radiographic examination.

Duke Karl I (1713–80) acquired this great landscape, two of Ruisdael's splendid waterfalls (Slive 2001, nos. 158, repr.; 159, repr.) and an untraceable dunescape (Slive 2001, no. 594) in 1738; the four paintings were procured along with more than two hundred other paintings (about one third were Netherlandish) for the Gallery at Salzdahlum (Fink 1954, pp.53–54). The only Ruisdael landscapes known to have been acquired for a royal European collection at an earlier date are two northern waterfalls (Slive 2001, nos. 182, repr.; 183, repr.) which are listed in a 1722 manuscript inventory of Dresden's holdings; they are still in Dresden.

Not the grainfield, but the giant oak, which seems to embody the vital forces of growth in nature, is the major accent in this hilly landscape. The tree's powerful twisted roots claw into the cliff upon which it grows, much the way a beech in his etching datable to the first half of the 1650s clings precariously to its bluff (see cat. 110). Its massive, curved dark brown trunk is brightened by a reddish-ochre bare patch – the most vivid hue in the picture – and its great crown spreads across the middle of the large painting and reaches beyond its upper edge. Like *The Great Oak*, dated 1652, at the Los Angeles County Museum (cat. 20), there are vistas on either side of the awe-inspiring tree, but here they are richer. Instead of a fork in a road with views of subsidiary trees, one side opens up to the silvery yellow grainfield on a gently rolling slope with a village and castle[1] sharply silhouetted against the grey sky beyond, the other to a steeply rising road flanked by a half-timbered cottage. The more varied spatial organization of the painting and the greater amount of light that pierces and lightens the foliage suggest that it postdates the Los Angeles painting by a few years.

The eight small figures in the landscape were painted by Ruisdael. One is a solitary woman on the road; on the right a man enters the scene accompanied by a dog. More unusual is the pensive woman seated in the dark shadow of the oak (fig. 21a). The perfect accord of the contemplative woman, who qualifies as a Dutch Melancholia, and the other unobtrusive figures with the mood of the landscape makes one wonder why Ruisdael ever felt the need to call upon other artists to furnish staffage in his paintings.

1. Korn (1978) and Maschmeyer (1978) conclude that elements of the castle on the right are based on parts of Steinfurt Castle, at Burgsteinfurt (also Steinfurt), Westphalia. If they are correct, a contemporary engraving of the castle (see Slive 2001, p.409, fig. 572a) indicates that Ruisdael took much more than usual artistic licence in depicting it.

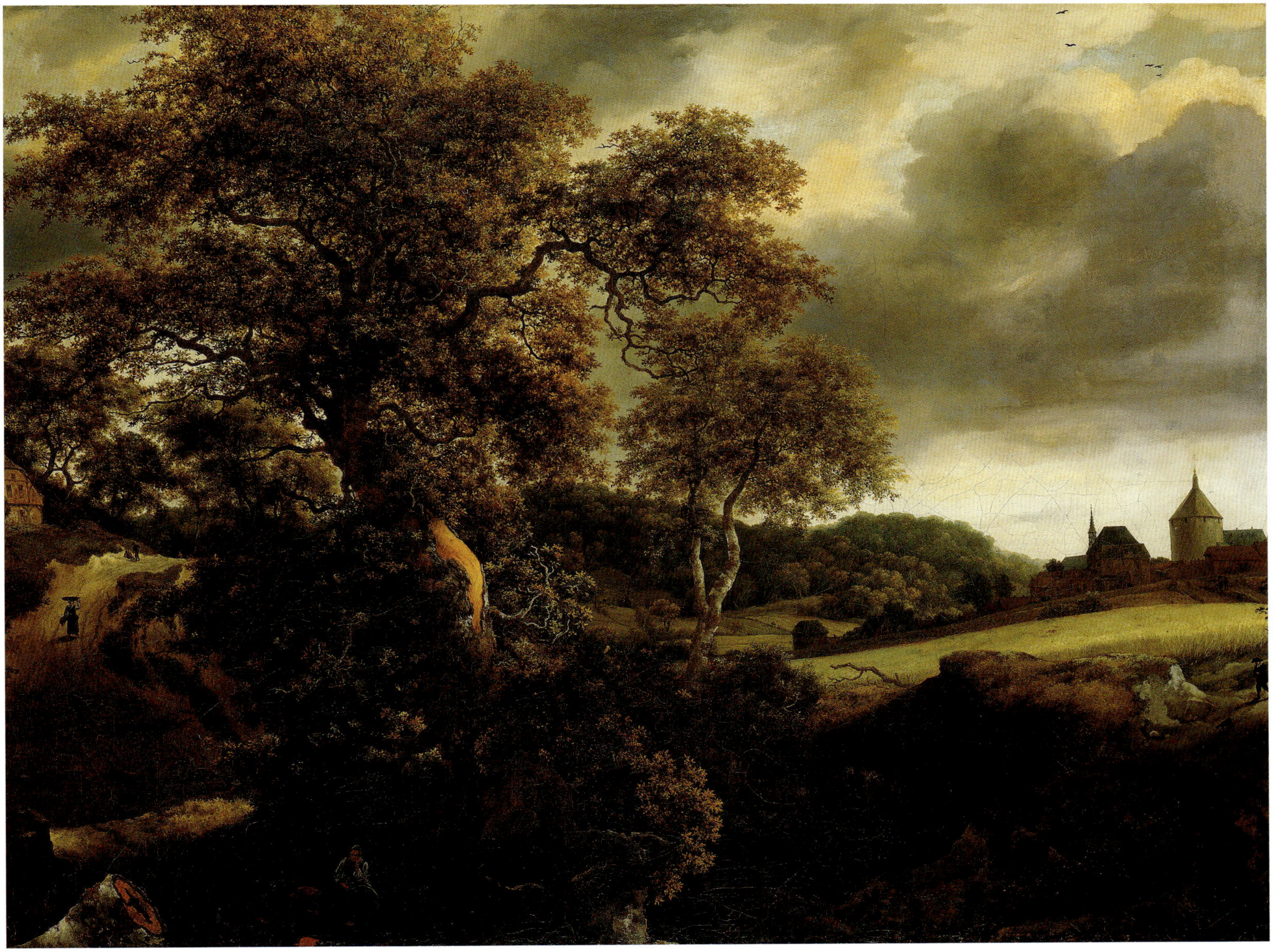

The Jewish Cemetery

Signed on the gravestone, lower left. About 1655. Canvas, 84 × 95 cm
Gemäldegalerie Alte Meister, Staatliche Kunstsammlungen, Dresden, 1502

PROVENANCE: Possibly sale, Amsterdam (Beukelaar), 16 September 1739, no. 88 ("Een Joode Begraafplaats, zeer natuurlyk, door denzelven [Ruisdaal]"; Dfl.11.10; see Hoet 1752, 1, p.604). In the Dresden manuscript inventory of 1754, 2, no. 490 ("Eine dunkele Landschaft, worauf ein Juden-Begräbnis, unten ein Wasserfall . . ."). In 1945, after the end of World War II, removed to the Soviet Union; returned to Dresden in 1955.

EXHIBITIONS: Berlin 1955–56, p.102; Zurich 1971, no. 41; Washington–New York–San Francisco 1978–79, no. 561, repr. (*c.*1660); The Hague–Cambridge 1981–82, no. 21, repr.; Tokyo and elsewhere 1992–93, pp.59f.; Hamburg–Haarlem 2002, no. 37, repr.

LITERATURE: Dresden, Catalogue, 1765, no. 548: "Un paysage orné de Tombeaux à l'antique, avec une Inscription en lettres hebraïques"; this entry is repeated in Lehninger 1782, p.423, no. 548, and Dresden, Catalogue, 1801, no. 546; Taillasson 1807, p.49; Goethe 1816 (reprinted in *Goethes Werke*, vol. 12, 1973, pp.141–42, 611–13); Deperthes 1822, p.445, note 1; under Smith 60 (describes the painting as "a duplicate, differing in size and inferior in quality, having become dark by time" of the version now in Detroit); Parthey 1864, 2, p.455, no. 11 ("Landschaft, bekannt unter dem Namen 'der Judenkirchof' "); Dresden, Catalogue, 1880, no. 1547; de Castro 1883, pp.17–18, note 34; Dresden, Catalogue, 1908, no. 1502; HdG 219; Ros 1926, pp.37ff. (Dresden version, 1660s; Detroit, probably late 1650s); Ros 154; Zwarts 1928, pp.232ff. (Dresden version, *c.*1679; Detroit version *c.*1678); Simon 1930, pp.31f. (both versions, 1653–55); Wijnman 1932, p.179 (*c.*1679; Detroit, 1678); Rosenberg, 1933, pp.217ff. (1650s); Gerson 1934, p.79 (1660s); Simon 1935c, pp.158f. (both versions, 1653–55); it is not possible to determine which version was done first); Martin 1935–36, 2, pp.300f., 516, note 412 (*c.*1665); Renaud 1940, p.140, note 1 (motifs taken from Egmond Castle); Gerson 1952, p.45 (*c.*1655); Carus [1955], pp.83–84; Rosenau 1958, pp.241f. (both versions after 1674); Stechow 1966, pp.139f. (both not far from 1660); Dubiez 1967, pp.206f. (both possibly after 1674); Wiegand 1971, pp.57–86 (no reason to date either after 1674); Kouznetsov 1973, pp.31f.; Vega 1975, *passim*; Scheyer 1977, pp.133–46 (both versions *c.*1653–55); Duparc 1981–82, pp.225–30; Sluijter-Seiffert 1984, "stelling" no. 3 (Dresden, mid-1650s; Detroit, at least a decade later); Mayer-Meintschel 1985, no. 101; Walford 1991, pp.97–102 (both paintings *c.*1653–54, the Dresden version the earlier of the two); Dresden, Catalogues, 1977, no. 1502 (after 1670); 1979, no. 1502 (1653–55); 1992, no. 1502 (1655–55); Slive 2001, no. 180, repr. (mid-1650s); Slive 2004, p.184.

Prints of the painting were made by J. Georg Primavesi (1774–1855), Johann Friedrich Franz Bruder (1782–1838), in reverse, after a drawing by Philipp Veith (1768–1837), Carl Straub (b.1805) and Ludwig Friedrich (1827–1916).

Another version, almost twice as large, is at Detroit (fig. 22a). The powerful cohesion between the broad expanse of the foregrounds of both and the wall-like impression of the bushes, trees and ruins beyond them, as well as the firm brushwork of their richly detailed forms, relate both pictures to Ruisdael's forest scenes and hilly landscapes datable to the mid-fifties. The brighter Detroit version shows the tombs closer and more to the side. Nature's luxuriant growth, ruins, clouds and rainbow are more strongly stressed in it than in the Dresden painting. The greater compactness and concentration on the motif of the tombs, and the bareness of the beech tree suggest the Dresden picture postdates the Detroit version; however, a long interval of time can hardly separate the two works.

Both pictures are among the rare landscapes by the artist that were painted with a deliberate allegorical intent. The combination of their conspicuous tombs, ruins, large dead beeches, broken tree trunks and small waterfalls alludes to the transience of all life and the ultimate futility of humankind's endeavours, a common theme in seventeenth-century Dutch art. On the other hand, the burst of light that breaks through the ravening clouds of each painting, their rainbows and the luxuriant growth that contrasts with the dead trees offer a promise of hope and renewed life. Their allegorical content has been recognized by virtually every author who has discussed them since they entered the literature early in the nineteenth century, but there has been neither unanimous approbation of these overtly moralizing landscapes nor a consensus on their meaning or the mood they evoke.

The Dresden version is the better known of the two paintings, thanks to its presence in one of Europe's leading picture galleries since at least 1754, and to Goethe's discussion of it in "Ruysdael als Dichter" published in 1816.[1] Goethe wrote that the painting is "entirely devoted to the past" and that the "tombs in their ruinous condition even point to something more than the past: they are tombstones to themselves". He did not emphasize a melancholy interpretation of the picture. On the contrary. He cited it as an example "where the artist, in the purity of his feeling and in the clarity of his thought, shows himself to be a poet, achieves a prefect symbolism, and at once delights, teaches, refreshes and revitalizes us by the wholeness of his inner and outward feelings."[2]

In 1807, nine years before Goethe published his essay praising the "thinking artist" as a poet of superb symbolism, the French artist and critic Jean Joseph Taillasson (1745/46–1809) wrote of the surpassing poetic qualities of Ruisdael's landscapes. "One cannot find," he asserted, "in the paintings of other artists of his country a poetry as moving as that which he puts into his own; he inspires a sweet melancholy; this comes, no doubt from the sensitivity of his soul, from the choice of the objects he painted, and perhaps from the dark colour of almost all his greens. Several times he painted the tombs of the Jews in Amsterdam. These silent resting places, surrounded by trees, and with a spirit of sadness, please the eye, with their unity, the simplicity of their form, and with their harmony of colour."[3]

Taillasson refers to the "sweet melancholy" inspired by Jacob's landscapes almost in the same breath that he mentions his paintings of the tombs of the Jews in Amsterdam. If he had the latter in mind when he wrote the phrase, he qualifies as the earliest critic to call them "melancholic" in print.

Taillasson's specific reference to several paintings by Ruisdael of the tombs of

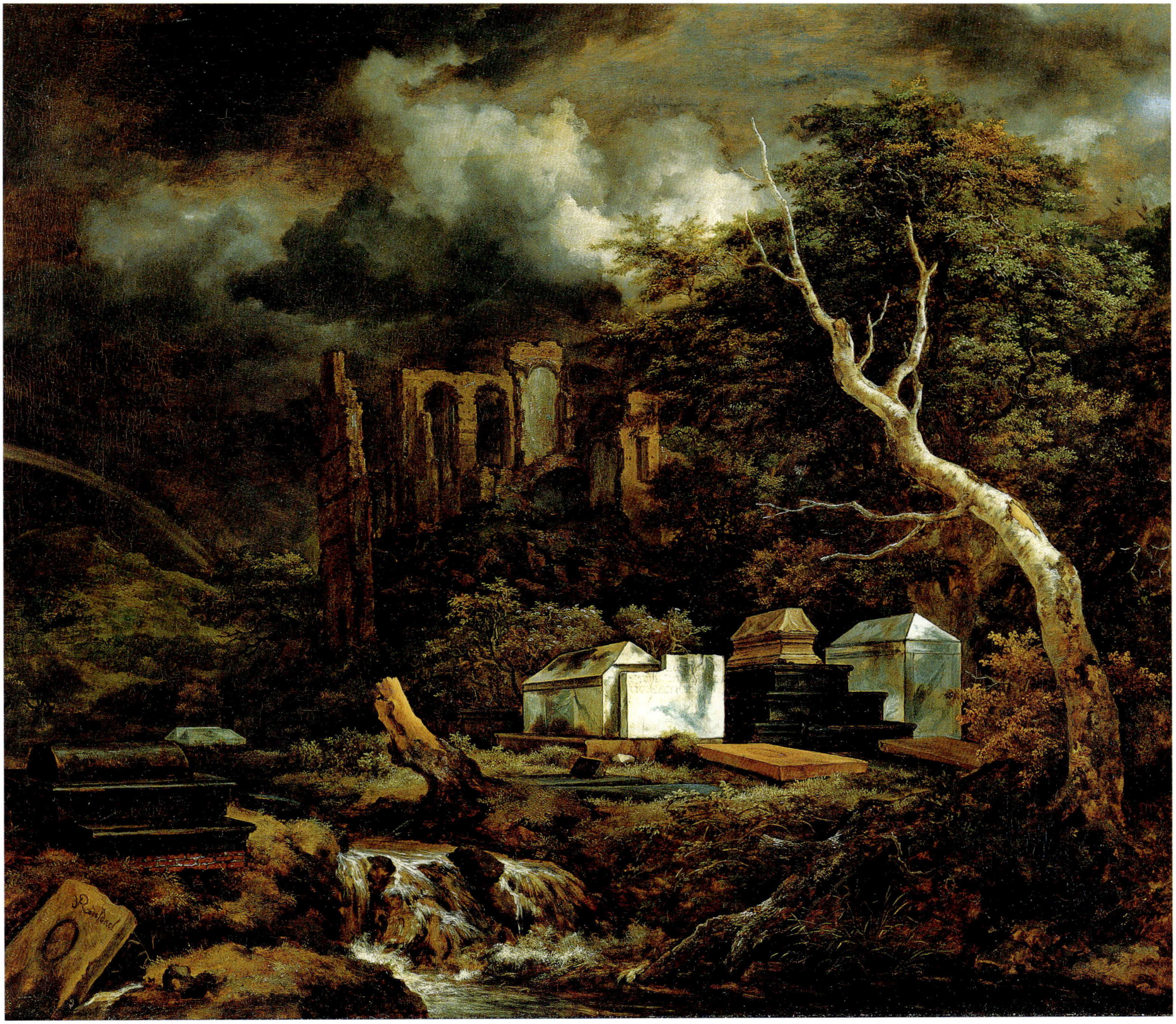

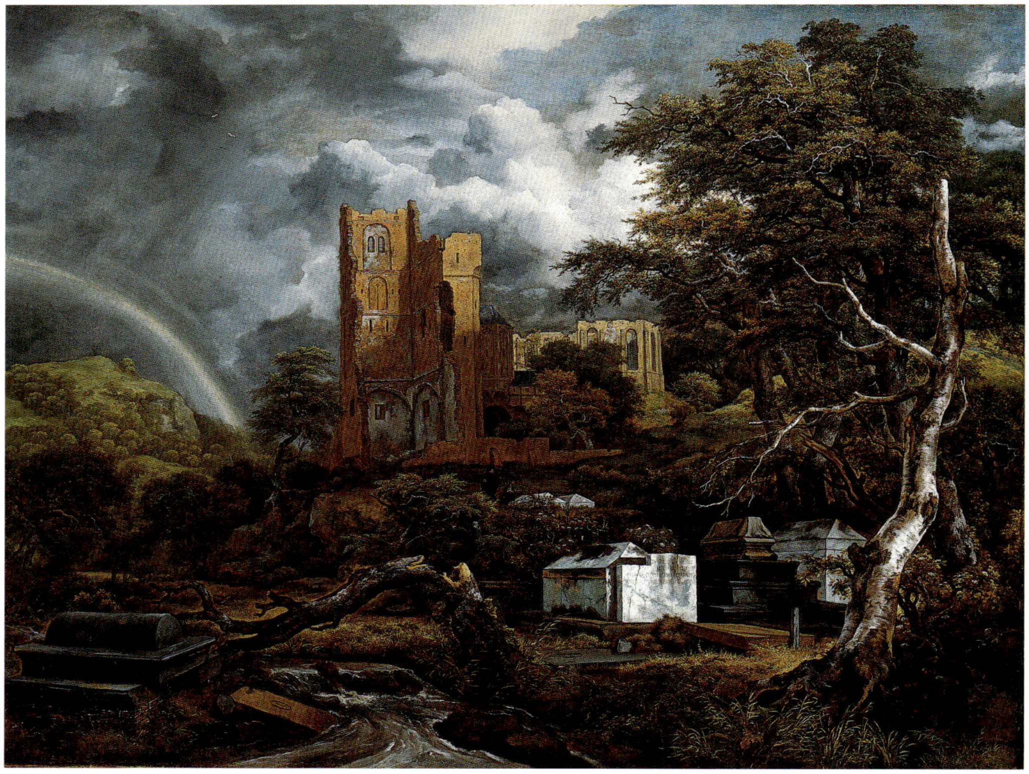

Fig. 22a Jacob van Ruisdael, *The Jewish Cemetery*. Detroit Institute of Arts.

the Jews of Amsterdam suggests that he had firsthand knowledge of the Detroit version of *The Jewish Cemetery*, which he could have seen in a Parisian private collection between 1790 (see its provenance in Slive 2001, p. 179) and 1807, the year his book was published, as well as of the Dresden *Cemetery*, perhaps through prints made by J. Georg Primavesi (1774–1855) or Johann Friedrich Franz Bruder (1782–1838). Since he explicitly states that the paintings show the "tombs of the Jews of Amsterdam," he may also have known the two prints Abraham Blooteling engraved in 1670 after Ruisdael's drawings of the site; they are inscribed "Begraefplaets der Joden buyten Amsterdam" (Burial place of the Jews outside Amsterdam; see figs. 79a, b).

Unlike Taillasson, Goethe had no idea that Ruisdael depicted Jewish tombs in the Dresden version. For Goethe, ruins of what was once a vast cathedral are seen in the background of the painting and the cemetery's imposing tombs "show how important the diocese was and what noble and wealthy families rest here."[4] An earlier compiler, though, described the Dresden painting in an inventory made there as early as 1754 (vol. 2, p.490) as "Eine dunkele Landschaft, worauf ein Juden-Begräbnis" (A dark Landscape with a Jewish Cemetery).[5]

The title of the Dresden painting given in the gallery's 1765 catalogue was more in accord with classical taste: "Un Paysage orné de Tombeaux à l'antique, avec une Inscription en lettres hebraïques" (*Catalogue des Tableaux de la Galerie Electorale à Dresde*, Dresden, 1765, p.108, no. 548). The same description of it is cited in *Abregé de la Vie des Peintres dont les Tableaux Composent la Galerie Electorale de Dresde . . .*, Dresden, 1782, p.423, no. 548. (Both cataloguers erroneously state the inscriptions are in Hebrew; the inscriptions in the Dresden as well as the Detroit picture are pseudo-Hebraic.)

Goethe made no remarks about the Dresden *Cemetery* in the catalogue he annotated during the course of his visit to the Dresden Gallery in 1790; evidently the

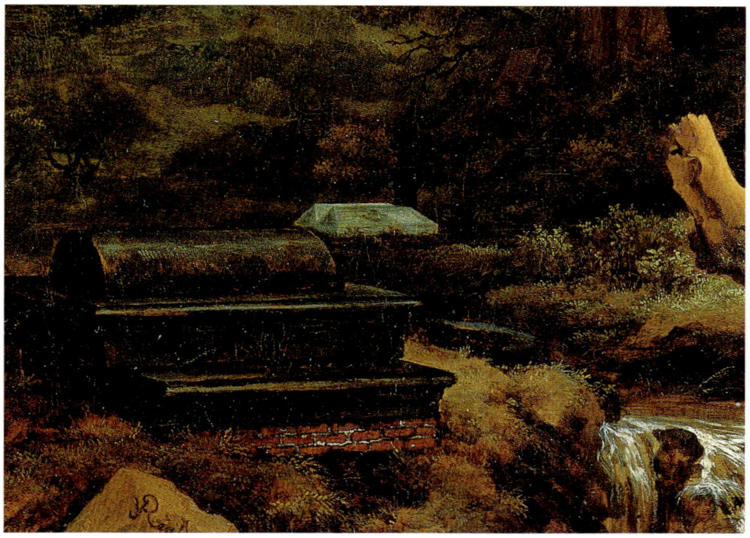

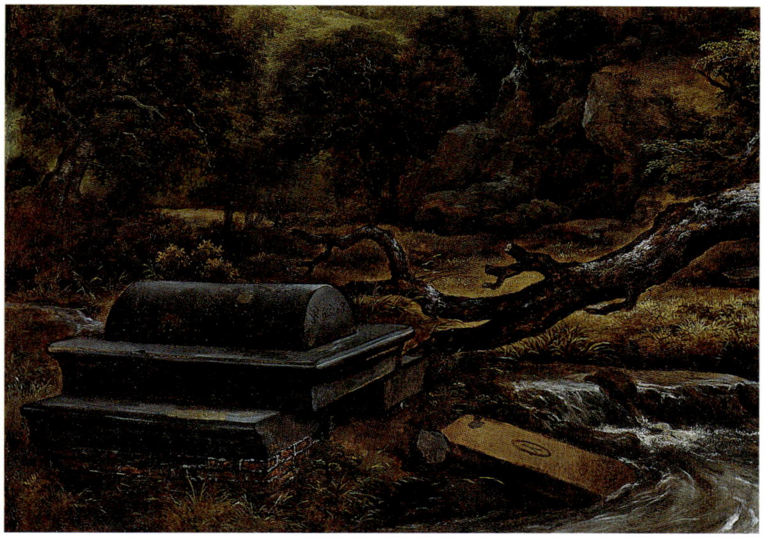

Fig. 22b Detail of cat. 22.

Fig. 22c Detail of fig. 22a.

work did not impress him on this early trip. He did, however, make notes about six other Ruisdaels in the collection.[6]

In 1835 John Smith introduced the version of the *Cemetery* now in Detroit to the literature in his pioneer catalogue of the artist's painted oeuvre (Smith 60). He provides us with word that the Detroit painting was imported from Paris into England about 1815 as well as most of what is known of its early history. Smith also knew the Dresden picture. In the introduction to his Ruisdael catalogue (1835, p.4) he wrote: "Two pictures also, of a highly classical character, merit particular notice: one of them is in the collection of Mr. Mackintosh; the other in the Dresden Gallery. They are styled 'The Jews' Burying Ground'; but are evidently intended as allegories of human life." Smith added in his catalogue entry (60) on the painting now in Detroit: "In this excellent picture, the artist has evidently intended to convey a moral lesson of human life; and in addition to this, there is a sublimity of sentiment and effect reigning throughout the composition which renders it worthy of the powers of Nicolo Poussin." Smith was less enthusiastic about the Dresden version; he called it "a duplicate . . . but differing in size, and inferior in quality, having become dark from time".

In 1835, the very year that Smith published the Detroit version of the *Cemetery*, Constable delivered his lecture on Dutch and Flemish landscape painting at the British Institution. Constable referred in his discourse to a Ruisdael painting which, he noted, was called during the artist's lifetime *An Allegory of the Life of Man*. If the Ruisdael painting that Constable had in mind is identical with the Detroit version of the *Cemetery*, which Smith characterized as evidently an allegory of human life intended to convey a moral lesson – and it is difficult to imagine it is not – he also knew the painting. Unlike Smith, he considered it a failure.

Constable did not give his low estimate of the picture before extolling the outstanding qualities of a winterscape and seascape by Ruisdael. To make his points he used his own copy of the artist's winterscape now in the Philadelphia Museum of Art (cat. 43), and an untraceable copy of an unidentified marine because they exemplified his maxim: "We see nothing till we truly understand it". Then Constable added, "In another instance he [Ruisdael] failed, because he attempted to tell that which is outside the reach of art. In a picture which was known, while he was living, to be called 'An Allegory of the Life of Man' [and it may therefore be supposed he so intended it], there are ruins to indicate old age, a stream to

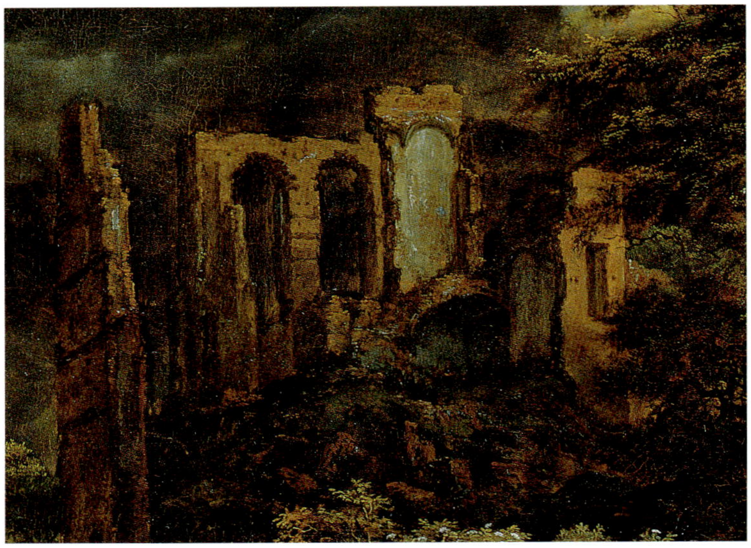

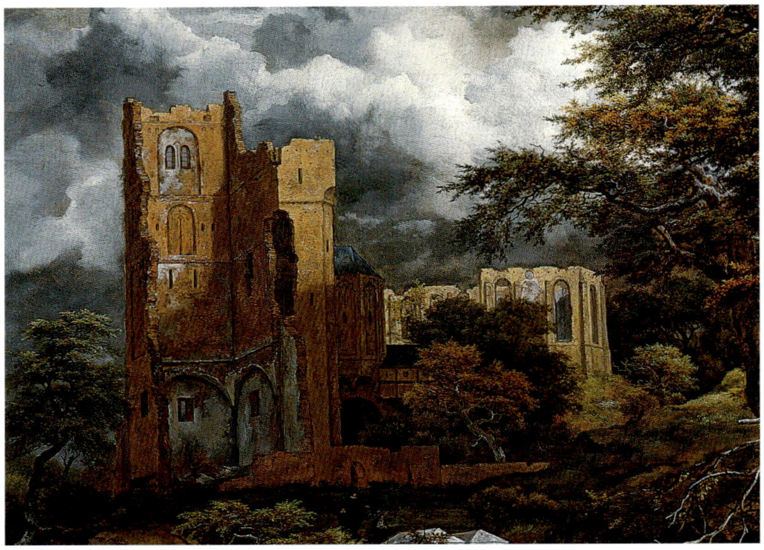

Fig. 22d Detail of cat. 22.

Fig. 22e Detail of fig. 22a.

signify the course of life, and rocks and precipices to shadow forth its dangers. But how are we to discover all this?"[7]

Not a word in seventeenth-century documents throws light on Constable's source for his statement that a painting by Ruisdael was known while the artist was living as "An Allegory of the Life of Man". In any event there can be no doubt that Constable concluded that Ruisdael failed when the intention of important elements in one of his landscapes could not be understood without an exegesis of their signification. Jakob Rosenberg (1928, p.30) voiced a similar sentiment almost a century later when he wrote of the Dresden *Cemetery*: "Today the symbolic burden of the picture no longer appears to be such a remarkable artistic achievement. We respect Ruisdael more when he solely allows the landscape to speak".

Since the Detroit version completely vanished from sight after Smith published it in 1835, and only reappeared in the London art market in the 1920s, during the intervening decades discussion centered naturally on the Dresden picture. In a study published in 1883, David Henrique de Castro (1883, pp.17–18, note 34) noted that the conspicuous tombs in the picture are identical with some early seventeenth-century sarcophagi that can still be seen at Beth Haim (House of Life), the cemetery at Ouderkerk on the Amstel River, a village about eight kilometres from Amsterdam. The cemetery is the burial place of the Portuguese–Jewish congregation of Amsterdam.

Castro, who knew the prints Blooteling made in 1670 after Ruisdael's drawings of the Jewish cemetery (figs. 80a, b), observed that the tombs in the Dresden painting are unmistakably related to those in Ruisdael's two drawings now at the Teyler Museum, Haarlem; for identification of the tombs depicted in them and a discussion of the burial site see cat. 79, 80. Castro rightly added that, apart from the monuments, the Dresden painting shows nothing of the actual site of the Portuguese–Jewish cemetery at Ouderkerk. When the Detroit version was rediscovered, it became patent that it also places the tombs at the site in an imaginary landscape. As a visit to the site and Ruisdael's two drawings show, the cemetery is in a flat landscape, not a hilly one, and no rushing stream runs through it. In addition, the site never had monumental ruins. The largest edifice in the vicinity is St. Urban's Church, an unimposing Romanesque structure which can be seen beyond the trees in the background of the Ruisdael drawing showing the tombs from the rear (cat. 80); it is the Oude Kerk (Old Church) from which the village of Ouderkerk received its name.

No scholar was better qualified than Castro to identify the tombs Ruisdael depicted and to discuss their setting. He was a member of the Portuguese–Jewish community that had established Beth Haim cemetery in the early seventeenth century, and was responsible for its nineteenth-century restoration. Castro spent more than two decades at the burial site identifying and restoring its monuments; the study he published in 1883 records his findings.

Ruisdael's drawing at Haarlem which depicts the tombs as they can be seen today from the east (cat. 79), or one very similar to it, served as a preparatory study for the tombs in the Detroit and Dresden paintings. The group of three imposing tombs is seen virtually the way they appear in both paintings. The tomb surmounted by a half-column in the right foreground of the drawing has been transposed in the paintings to the left, and, for pictorial reasons, shown from different points of view (figs. 22b, c).

The ruins in the background of the Dresden version (fig. 22d) were based on drawings Ruisdael made of the remains of the Castle of Egmond near Alkmaar (Renaud 1940, p.340, note 1). One, now at Stuttgart (Slive 2001, no. D120), depicts the ruins from a point of view that closely resembles that in the Dresden picture; another at Berlin (cat. 81) also is related to them.

A search for preliminary drawings which may have been used as studies for the more elaborate ruins in the Detroit picture (fig. 22e) has been fruitless. The ruins in it were most likely inspired by studies Ruisdael made of the noble remains of the Romanesque Abbey Church of Egmond and the Gothic Buurkerk at Egmond-Binnen, about three kilometres west of Alkmaar. Ruisdael included a more topographical view of the large ruin in the background of his small oil sketch of a windmill, now in the collection of the Earl of Northbrook (Slive 2001, no. 132).

Among the painted copies of the Dresden version is one by Ferdinand Georg Waldmuller (1793–1865), now in a private collection, Vienna.[8] Another, attributed to the Scottish artist Patrick Nasmyth (1787–1831), who occasionally worked in Ruisdael's as well as Hobbema's and Wijnants's manner, is at the Fine Arts Gallery, Florida State University, Tallahassee.[9] A partial copy by an anonymous artist is at Budapest where it is catalogued as *Forest with Ruins*.[10] It is based on the right part of the Dresden picture and includes the beech tree and part of the ruined church but eliminates the tombs. Parthey (1864, 2, p.462, no. 1) lists a copy (canvas, 3F. by 3F. 3Z.) in the Schloss, Hannover; its present whereabouts is unknown.

1. Goethe 1816 [reprinted in *Goethes Werke*, vol. 12, 1973], pp.141–42; for an excellent English translation see Gage 1980, pp.210–15.
2. Goethe's refusal to acknowledge a sorrowful note in the painting was emphasized again in his conversation in 1825 with Friedrich Förster about the *Monastery in Winter* by Karl Friedrich Lessing (1808–80). Goethe criticized the symbolism in Lessing's landscape as a "negation of life". Förster, in his attempt to defend young Lessing's picture, referred to Ruisdael's *Jewish Cemetery* and asked whether it does not show that an elegiac mood has a rightful place in landscape painting. Goethe responded: "Certainly – but only when the marble slabs of the tombs by the magic of the moonlight puts us in a benevolent, touching mood, and the trees with their green foliage, grass and flowers make us forget that we are on a burial ground" (see von Lorck 1936, p.205; Goethe 1816, pp.611–12).
3. Taillason 1807, p.49.
4. Goethe 1816, p.141.
5. An earlier reference to a painting by Ruisdael of a *Jewish Burial Place* is the one listed in an anonymous auction held at Amsterdam in 1739 [see PROVENANCE], but it is not possible to establish whether it refers to the Dresden or the Detroit picture or to one of the untraceable versions mentioned in Slive 2001, p.184, note 1.
6. The painting that made the strongest impression upon him in 1790 was the artist's *Stag Hunt* (cat. 38): "Vortrefflich und das beste von diesem Meister allhier"; see Goethe 1790, pp.368–87, for notes made in 1790. It was not cited in his essay on "Ruysdael als Dichter" published sixteen years later.
7. Beckett 1970, p.64. For further discussion of Constable's interest in Ruisdael see pp. 33–40, above.
8. Canvas, 84 × 95.5; signed and dated 1826; Grimschitz 1957, p.289, no. 154, repr.
9. Canvas, 76 × 94; for its possible provenance see Slive 2001, p.184, note 1.
10. Canvas, 67.5 × 55.5; Budapest, Catalogue, 1967, p.603, no. 53.410, repr. (follower of Ruisdael); *ibid.*, 2000, p.148, no. 53.410, repr. (nineteenth-century partial copy of the Dresden Painting).

23

Edge of a Forest with a Grainfield

Signed, lower right. About 1655. Canvas, 104.7 × 148.8 cm
Worcester College, Oxford

PROVENANCE: The Reverend Treadway Russell Nash, who bequeathed it to Worcester College in 1811.

EXHIBITIONS: Manchester 1857, no. 711; London, Royal Academy, Winter Exhibition, 1902, no. 100; London 1924, no. 12; London 1929, no. 145; Paris 1950–51, no. 72; London 1952–53, no. 300; The Hague–London 1970–71, no. 86, repr.; Oxford 1975, no. 34, repr.; The Hague–Cambridge 1981–82, no. 18, repr.; Hamburg–Haarlem 2002, no. 34, repr.

LITERATURE: Waagen 1854, 3, p.50; Bürger 1865, pp.294–95; HdG 121; Ros 89; Simon 1930, p.73 (*c.*1670); Stechow 1966, p.74 (1650s); Walford 1991, pp.131–33, 223, notes 21 and 23 (early sixties); Slive 2001, no. 394, repr.

In this outstanding landscape the artist uses the old scheme of a diagonal arrangement of a dense grove of trees ending in a prospect to the horizon, but he achieves a new effect by the small opening in the center that sharply contrasts the near view of the dark oak trees and the far vista of the terrain beyond them.

How deeply and intensely Ruisdael studied nature is seen in the diversified growth supported by the broad expanse of the smooth pond and its banks. The breadth of the foreground, accented by the sandy road that turns abruptly to the right and the horizontal stretch of the light golden grainfield, also sets the monumental wall of the wood sufficiently far back to allow its full contour to be viewed clearly. At the same time the oaks at the edge of the forest are seen near enough to impose a sense of their size and weight as well as afford an opportunity to scrutinize the lichen and moss growing on their great trunks.

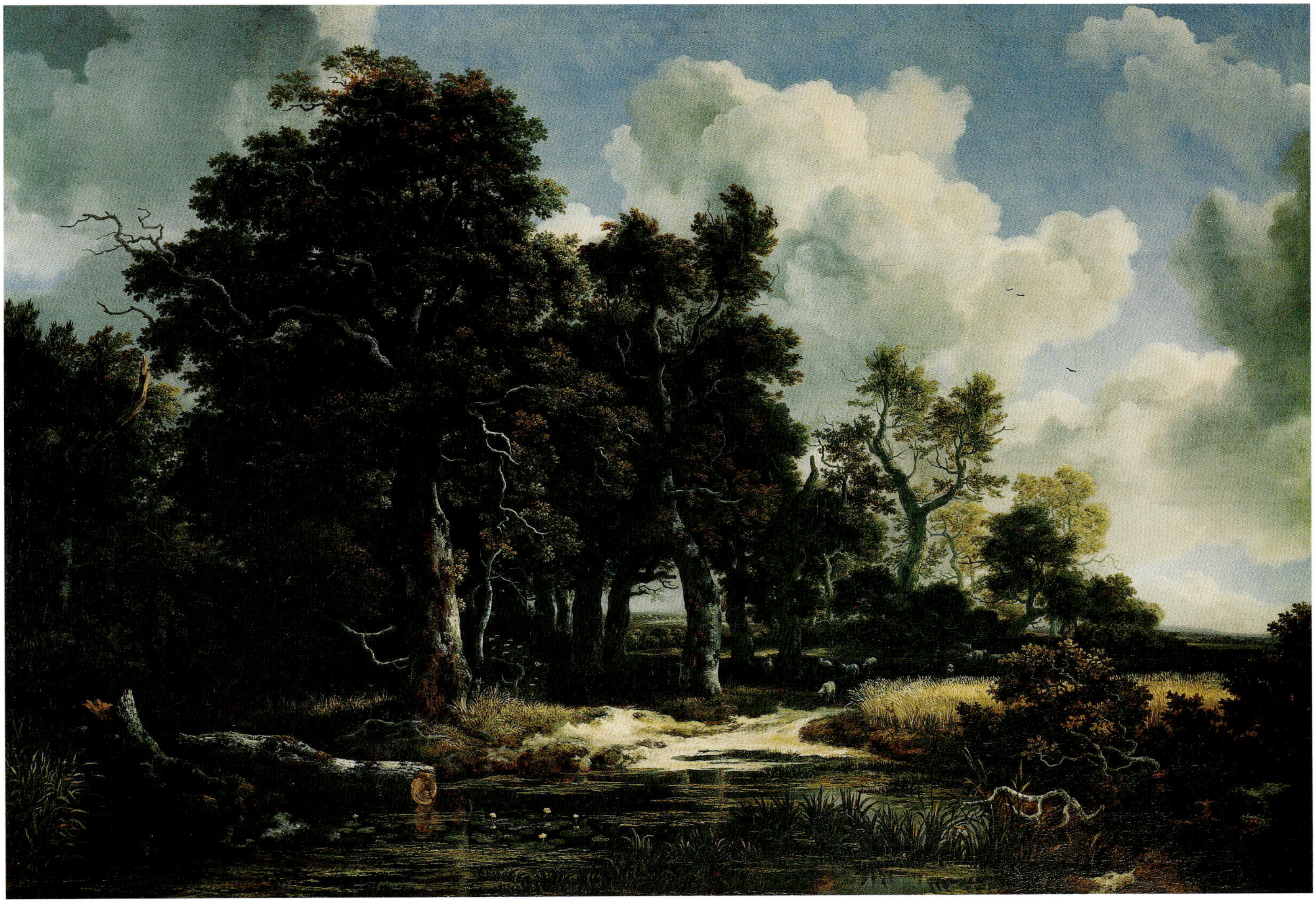

24

Rough Sea at a Jetty

Signed, lower right centre. About 1652–55. Canvas, 98.5 × 131.4 cm
Kimbell Art Museum, Fort Worth, Texas, AP 1989.01

PROVENANCE: The history of the picture, muddled by earlier cataloguers, was clarified by Bille.[1] Sale, widow Hoogeveen, Amsterdam (v. d. Linden), 5 June 1765, no. 36 (Dfl.214, Fouquet for Braamkamp; see Terwesten 1770, p.456); Gerard Braamkamp tried to sell the painting, Amsterdam (de Bosch), 4 June 1766, no. 6, as a work by Dubbels (Dfl.160, de Bosch for Braamkamp); that sale catalogue gives the same description and the same dimensions given to lot no. 198 in Braamkamp's 1771 sale (see below; moreover, a pencil note in a contemporary hand in an edition of the 1766 sale catalogue states that the painting is by Ruisdael; see Bille 1961, 2, pp.82, 117); sale, Gerard Braamkamp, Amsterdam (v. d. Schley), 31 July 1771, no. 198 (Dfl.264, P. Fouquet); sale, anon., Paris (Paillet), 18–25 April 1803, no. 199 (fr.1601, Rederne); bought privately by John Smith from the family of the Marquis Merialva, 1824 (fr.9000); from Smith to Robert Bankes, 2nd Earl of Liverpool, on 14 June 1826 (£500); his sale, London, 25 March 1829, no. 76 (£535, Lord Lansdowne); third to seventh Marquis of Lansdowne, Bowood, Calne, Wilts., 1829–1944; Baroness Nairne, Bignor Park, Pulborough, Sussex; dealer Th. Agnew, London, 1950; private collection, England; dealer Th. Agnew, London, 1977; private collection; sold to dealer Artemis, London, 1988; acquired by dealer French and Co., New York, 1988; acquired by the museum, 1989.

EXHIBITIONS: London, Royal Academy, Winter Exhibition, 1884, no. 191; The Hague–Cambridge 1981–82, no. 27, repr.; The Hague–San Francisco 1990–91, no. 54, repr; Rotterdam–Berlin 1996–97, no. 67, repr.

LITERATURE: Smith 2; Waagen 1838, 2, pp.296–97; Jameson 1844, pp.318–19, no. 86; Waagen 1854, 3, pp.158–59; HdG 945, identical with HdG 966; Ros 579; Bille 1961, pp.48, 48a, 82, 116–17; *A Dealer's Record: Agnew's 1967–81*, London, 1981, p.90, repr.; Goedde 1989, pp.191–93, 241–42, note 58; Walford 1991, pp.108–10, repr.; Edwards 1996, p.313; Slive 2001, no. 644, repr.

LACMA and RA

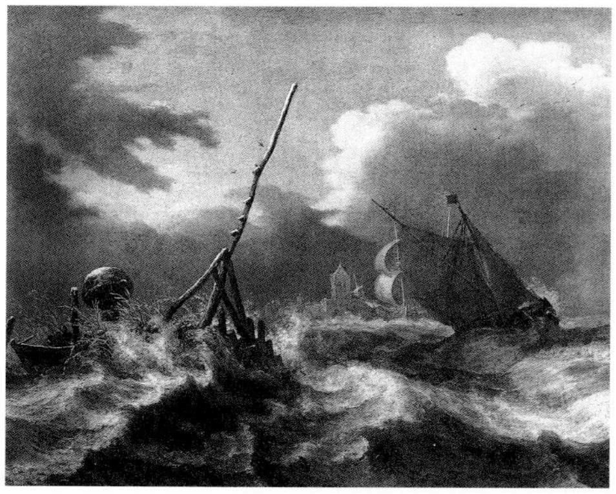

Fig. 24a Allart van Everdingen, *Snow Storm at Sea*. Chantilly, Musée Condé.

The pronounced contrast in this dramatic marine between the broad dark foreground and the band of wind-whipped waves beyond it illuminated by a brilliant burst of sunlight is still redolent of the seascapes Ruisdael painted in the Jan Porcellis-Simon de Vlieger tradition. A marine of this group datable to the late 1640s or early 1650s is at Stockholm (Slive 2001, no. 657, repr.); the much finer gradations in both the light and dark areas of the present painting, which heighten the spatial effect, suggest it postdates the Stockholm marine by a few years.

The artist employed an unusually restricted palette for the work: black, white, blue and some warm brown earth colours (probably ochre, burnt sienna and/or umber). A few slightly rubbed passages (for example, in the foreground of the breakwater that supports the tall beacon) indicate that in this case Ruisdael used a warm brown ground for a painting that has a predominantly cool tonality.

It has been noted that the picture is related to Allart van Everdingen's *Snow Storm at Sea* at Chantilly (fig. 24a), which probably predates Ruisdael's marine by a few years; however, significant differences between the works have been slighted by some critics.[2] Ruisdael offers a panoramic view not a close-up of the stormy sea; he devotes much more of his picture to the sky; and not least, his tall, firmly set beacon lends stability to his picture while Everdingen's askew beacon contributes significantly to the topsy-turvey effect of his melodramatic storm. Wolfgang Stechow put the matter in a nutshell when he wrote Everdingen's picture "somewhat overdoes it".[3]

It has been suggested that the beacons in Ruisdael's and Everdingen's paintings are related to those found in seventeenth-century Dutch emblems which allude to virtue, good understanding or guidance, and by implication to salvation.[4] However, there is no way of establishing that either Ruisdael or Everdingen intended them and their marines to convey such notions.

A copy of Ruisdael's painting by another hand, which misses the extraordinary range of greys of the original, is at The National Gallery of Ireland, Dublin (no. 916), where it was wrongly attributed to Ruisdael until 1981.[5] When the Dublin painting appeared in the 1927 sale of James Ross's paintings,[6] it was claimed that Turner had copied the picture when it was in the collection of his patron H. A. J. Munro, and that he called his copy, exhibited in 1827 and now at the Yale Center for British Art, *Port Ruysdael*.[7] This account is wrong. Although the Dublin picture was in Munro's collection, he only acquired it in 1856, twenty-nine years after Turner painted *Port Ruysdael* and five years after Turner's death.

1. Bille 1961, 2, pp.116–17.
2. Stechow (1966, p.209, note 53) writes the Fort Worth picture and a version now in Dublin (see below) seem especially indebted to the Chantilly Everdingen. Broos (The Hague–San Francisco 1990–91, p.398) flatly states that the Everdingen "unmistakably served as Ruisdael's model". Neither author refers to the independence of Ruisdael's invention.
3. Stechow 1966, pp.121–22.
4. Goedde 1989, pp.192–93.
5. See Slive 1981, no. 27.
6. Sale, James Ross of Montreal, London (Christie's), 8 July 1927, no. 24 (bought in).
7. See Butlin and Joll 1977, 1, pp.131–32, no. 237, repr.; rev. ed., 1984, 1, p.146. It has also been suggested (*ibid.*) that *Port Ruysdael* bears some resemblance to Ruisdael's *Storm off a Coast*, City Art Gallery, Manchester (Slive 2001, no. 651, repr.), but it is not known if Turner ever saw it.

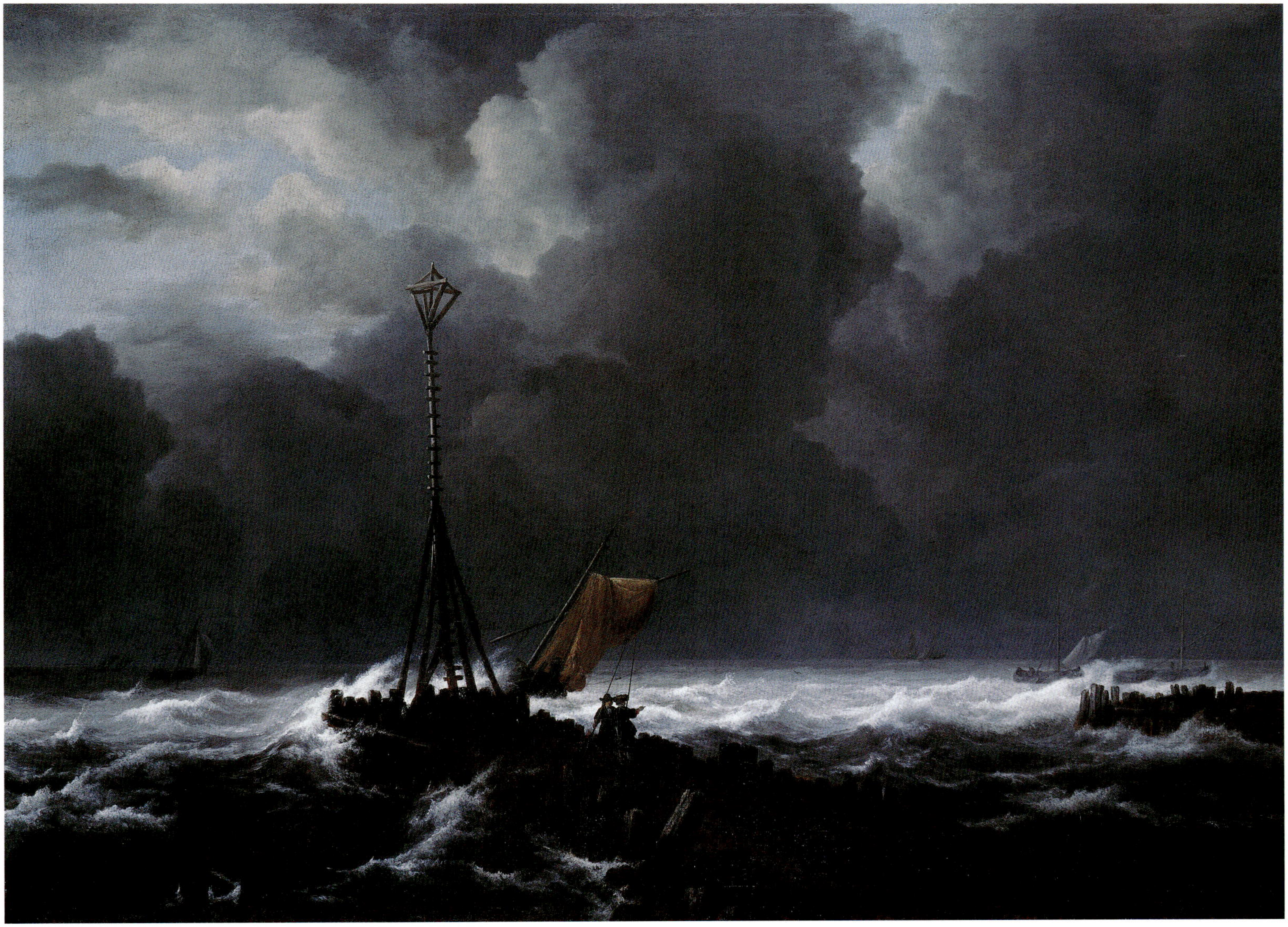

25

Wooded River Bank

Monogrammed, lower right. 1650s. Panel,[1] 26.4 × 35.5 cm
Staatliche Museen zu Berlin, Gemäldegalerie, 885H

PROVENANCE: According to the Berlin Catalogue, 1931, the painting was acquired by the Berlin Museum from a Paris dealer in 1896; since Sedelmeyer's seal is on the back of the cradled panel, at some time it almost certainly was with him.

LITERATURE: HdG 680; Ros 425; Staatliche Museen, Berlin, Catalogues, 1931, p.418 (*c.*1657), and 1986, p.67, no. 885H, repr.; Slive 2001, no. 491, repr.

The small landscape of trees, a cottage and path flanking a river exemplifies the qualities of a group of the artist's plain Dutch scenes datable to the fifties, that appear to be hardly modified excerpts from nature. *View from the Dunes to the Sea*, Zurich, *Dunes*, Philadelphia, and *Dune Landscape with a Rabbit Hunt*, Haarlem (cat. 26, 27, 28) also belong to the group. They are often characterized by a relatively bright palette and a tendency to open up and lighten space, markedly different from the monumental effects of many landscapes the artist produced during the decade, particularly during its first years. It formerly was thought that a firm reference point for dating them was provided by the year 1657 inscribed on a picture of a *Windmill and Cottage on a River Bank* at the Detroit Institute of Arts (Slive 2001, no. 129) which can be classified with these pictures as well; however, that date was spurious and came away with a cleaning, but it could not have been wide of the mark.

1. Peter Klein reported (private communication, 5 October 1992) that a dendrochronological analysis of the picture's panel is not possible ("Eine Messung der Gemäldetafel ist nicht möglich.").

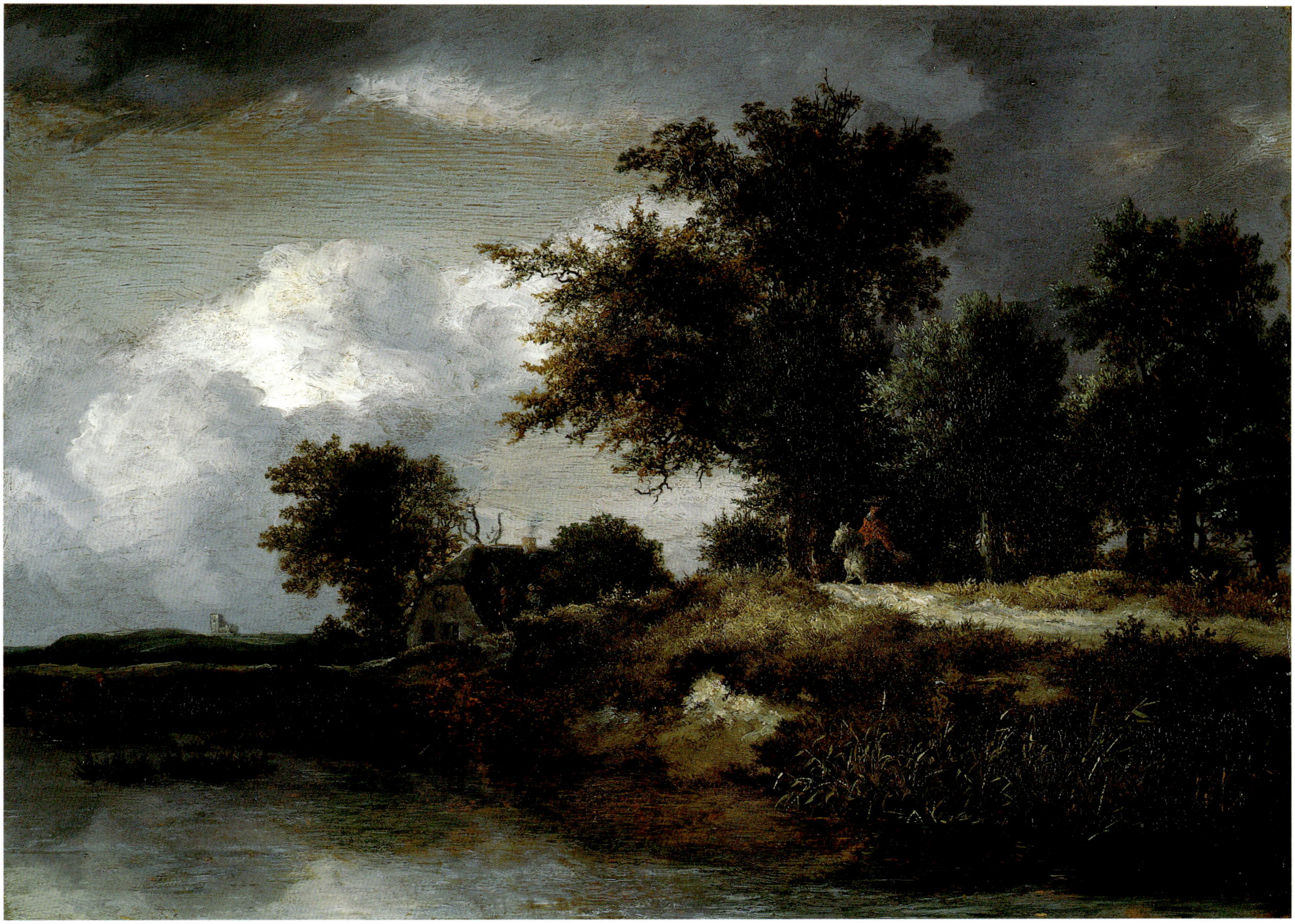

26

View from the Dunes to the Sea

Signed, lower right. 1650s. Canvas, 26 × 35.2 cm
Kunsthaus Zürich, Stiftung Prof. Dr. L. Ruzicka, R. 31

PROVENANCE: Purchased by the dealer Alexandre-Jaillet of Paris, in The Netherlands, 1777; sale, [A. Paillet], Paris (Paillet), 15 *sqq.* December 1777, no. 236; sale, [Trouard], Paris (Paillet), 22 *sqq.* February 1779, no. 132; Andrew Fountaine, Narford Hall, 1850; his sale, London (Christie's), 7 July 1894, no. 33; sale, Hope Edwardes a.o., London (Christie's), 27 April 1901, no. 57 (300gns., Wallis); Maurice Kann, Paris; dealer F. Kleinberger, Paris; A. de Ridder, Cronberg, near Frankfurt a. M.; sale, dealer F. Kleinberger, New York, November–December 1913, no. 57 (an extract of Bode's 1913 catalogue of the de Ridder Collection); sale, de Ridder, Paris (Petit), 2 June 1924, no. 63; dealer K. W. Bachstitz, The Hague; dealer Paul Cassirer, Amsterdam, 1957.

EXHIBITIONS: Zurich 1949–50, no. 31, repr.; Zurich 1950, p.22; Zurich 1953, no. 128; Rome 1954, no. 126; Milan 1954, no. 129, repr.; Cologne 1954, no. 22; The Hague–Cambridge 1981–82, no. 26, repr. (shown in The Hague only).

LITERATURE: Most probably Waagen 1854, 3, p.430, no. 4 ("A very small picture executed with singular truth. Quite a pearl."); Bode 1910, no. 81; HdG 922, identical with HdG 937, and most probably identical with HdG 1075e; Bode 1913, no. 57, repr.; Ros 573; Simon 1930, p.76; Stechow 1966, p.105, repr.; Walford 1991, p.111, repr.; Edwards 1996, p.53, repr.; Slive 2001, no. 634, repr.

RA

The little painting of a stretch of stormy sea and a high ominous sky seen from the dunes that are the natural dike between Holland and the sea is datable to the mid-fifties. Its compositional scheme of strata of dunes with a marine view beyond is reminiscent of beachscapes Jan van Goyen and Simon de Vlieger painted in the previous decade. However, Ruisdael's paint is heavier than theirs and his touch is more varied and vibrant. He also has introduced more emphatic contrasts; they increase the effect of solidity. Most striking is the luminous area of the sandy dunes in the centre seen against the dark grey sky. Few pictures capture greater freshness of sea air in a high wind.

Judging from his existing *oeuvre*, during the course of the following decades Ruisdael produced only one other painting of a beach scene seen from the dunes (Slive 2001, no. 636, repr.); it is datable to the 1670s. In it the vantage point is higher and more distant, and the view of the sea is far more extensive.

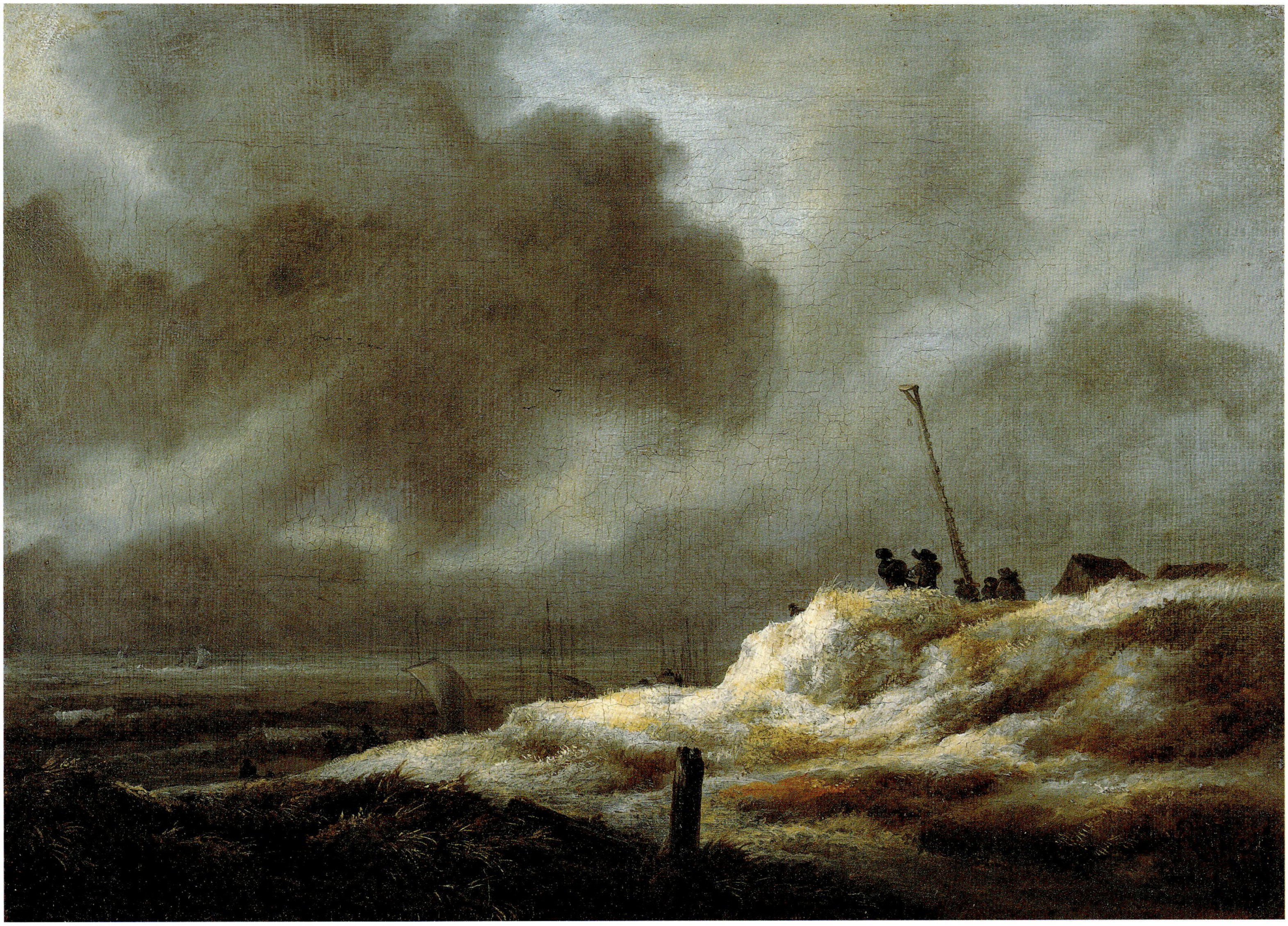

27

Dunes

Monogrammed, lower left. 1650s. Panel,[1] 33.5 × 49.2 cm
Philadelphia Museum of Art, John G. Johnson Collection, 1917, 563

PROVENANCE: Purchased in Paris by Smith in 1835 (fr.3200) and sold by him to Charles Brind; sale, Charles Brind, London (Christie's), 10 May 1849, no. 60 (£404.5, Rutley); Mrs. Lyne Stephens, Norfolk; sale, Lyne Stephens, London (Christie's), 9–20 May 1895, no. 344 (£315); John G. Johnson, Philadelphia, who bequeathed it to the City of Philadelphia, 1917.

EXHIBITIONS: London, British Institution, 1840, no. 49 (lent by Charles Brind); New York 1939, no. 340; Amsterdam–Boston–Philadelphia 1987–88, no. 80, repr.

LITERATURE: Smith Suppl. 53; HdG 897, identical with HdG 914; W. R. Valentiner, *Johnson Collection Catalogue*, Philadelphia, 1913, 2, p.123, no. 563, repr.; Ros 562; Simon 1930, p.76; Johnson Collection, Philadelphia, Catalogues, 1941, p.36, no. 563, *Flemish and Dutch Painting*, 1972, p.76, no. 563, and 1994, p.93, repr. (1651–55); Slive 2001, no. 612, repr.

Though Ruisdael, as many of his contemporaries, must have made landscape drawings from nature, it is virtually certain that he, like almost all of them, did not paint outdoors. Nevertheless, this superbly preserved painting, datable to the early 1650s, when the artist's forms become weightier and the contrast between light and shadow intensifies, has a startling *plein air* effect that anachronistically recalls fresh landscape oil sketches by Thomas Jones, Pierre-Henri de Valenciennes and Corot that actually were done in the open-air more than a century later.

The subject impresses by its simplicity: a solitary traveller and his lean hound making way on a track in hilly dunes, a remnant of a tumble-down fence and almost formless clouds. The painting is one of Jacob's rare ones that concentrates on dunes and their scrubby vegetation without a hint of fields cultivated by man. Another one, less well-preserved, is at Copenhagen.[2]

1. Peter Klein's private communication (7 April 1993) on his dendrochronological analysis of the single oak panel states that a creation date for the work is plausible from 1633 upwards.
2. Royal Museum of Fine Arts, Copenhagen, no. 3579; Slive 2001, no. 596, repr.

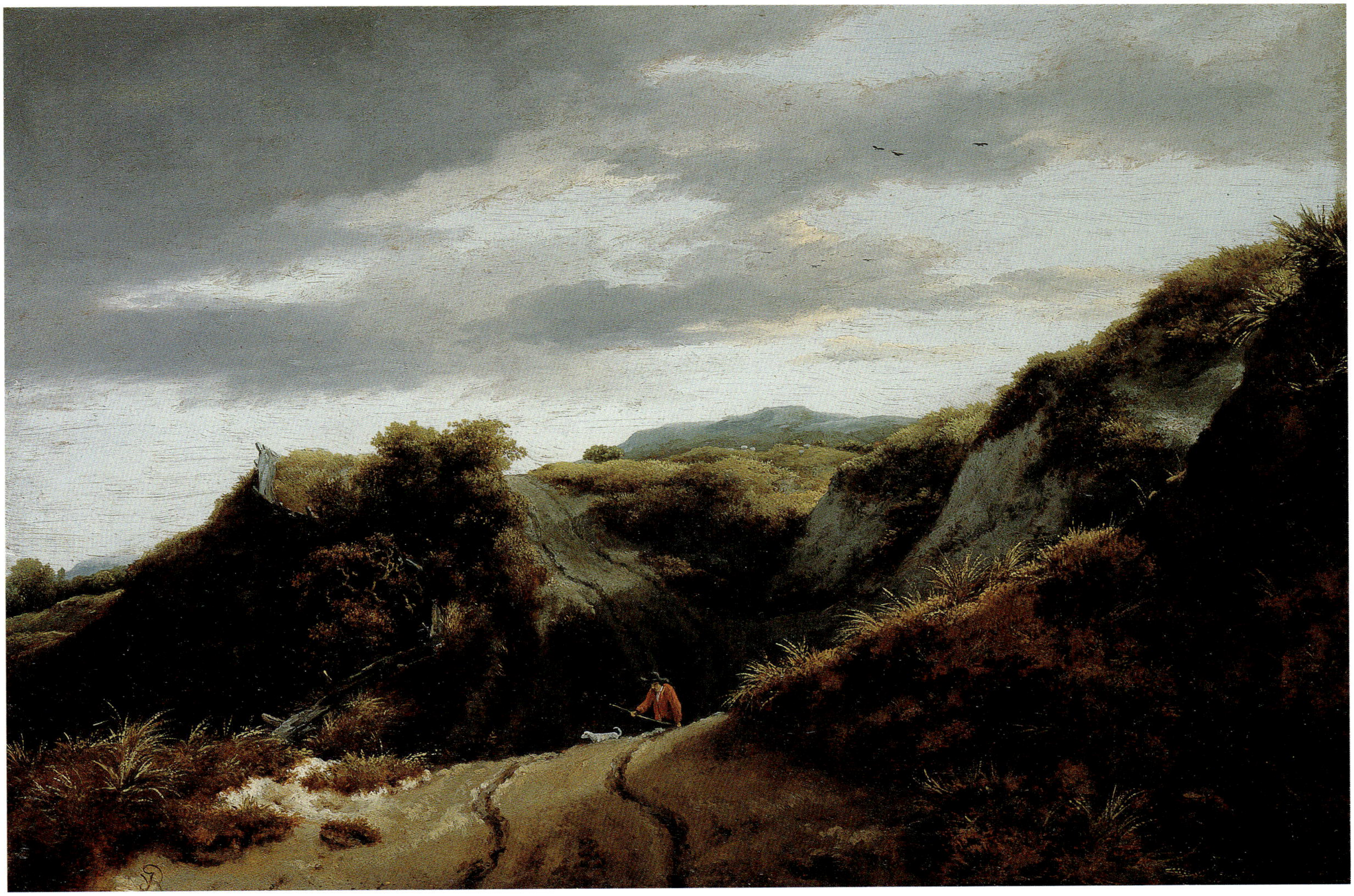

28

Dune Landscape with a Rabbit Hunt

Monogrammed, lower left. 1650s. Panel, 33.5 × 38 cm
Frans Hals Museum, Haarlem, os 1-299

PROVENANCE: Most probably sale, [Leboeuf], Paris (Lebrun), 8–12 April 1783, no. 25 (fr.800, Paillet); Amédée, Marquis de Pastoret, Paris; Marquess of Plessis-Bellière (daughter of the above), Paris; Château de Moreuil after 1870; sale, Plessis-Bellière, Paris (Drouot), 10 May 1897, no. 129; dealer E. Warneck, Paris; bought in Paris in 1900 for the museum by the Society for the Extension of the Art Collection and Antiquities in the Frans Hals Museum.

EXHIBITIONS: Brussels 1935, no. 765; Eindhoven 1948, no. 56; Paris 1950–51, no. 70; London 1952–53, no. 309; New York–Toledo–Toronto 1954–55, no. 70; The Hague–Cambridge 1981–82, no. 28, repr.; Hamburg–Haarlem 2002, no. 29, repr.

LITERATURE: Château de Moreuil, Catalogue, 1884, no. 195; HdG 885; *Ruysdael, Original-Abbildungen* [1920?], repr.; Ros 545; Simon 1930, p.76 (not by Ruisdael; probably painted at a later date); Simon 1935, p.192 (Kessel); Stechow 1966, pp.45, 195, note 41 (Simon doubted it without sufficient reason); Frans Hals Museum, Haarlem, Catalogue, 1969, p.58, no. 257; Burke 1974, p.7, repr.; Slive 2001, no. 600, repr.

The fresh colours and grainy paint of the delectable little flat landscape place it in the early or mid-fifties. Like many of the artist's small oil sketches done during the decade, it permits us to share his keen enjoyment of the observation of natural phenomena.

Simon's (1930 and 1935) doubts about the panel's authenticity were rightly rejected by Stechow (1966). Its style is compatible with that of other little pictures the artist painted during this phase of his career (see cat. 25, 26, 27). Here the format, the rich alteration of lights and darks in the fields, and the palpable clouds in its high sky anticipate his later panoramas.

A pastiche by an anonymous hand which substitutes a shepherdess with sheep for the horseman, dog, rabbit and other figures in the original, as well as changes the terrain a bit, was in the London art market, 1962, wrongly attributed to Jan Vermeer van Haarlem.[1]

1. Panel, 31.7 × 38.6. Provenance: Mrs. Heywood Johnstone, Bignor House, Pulborough; dealer L. Koetser, London, Catalogue, 27 April–31 May 1962, no. 10 (Jan Vermeer van Haarlem). Illustrated Slive 2001, fig. 600a. Pieter Biesboer's proposal (Hamburg-Haarlem 2001, no. 29) that the painting is probably Ruisdael's own autograph version of the composition is not compelling. The work lacks Jacob's vibrant touch.

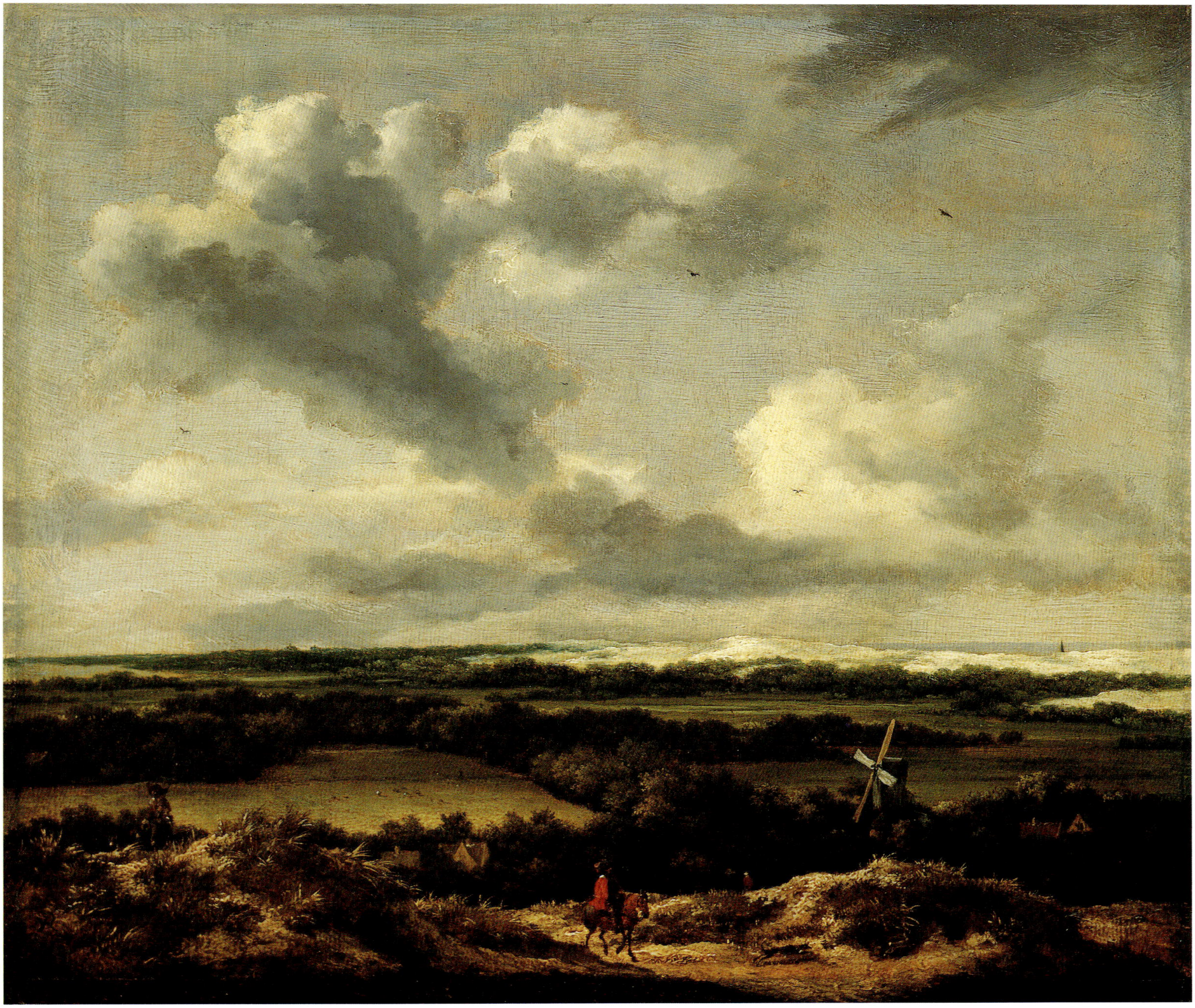

29

A Ruined Entrance Gate of Brederode Castle

Monogrammed, lower right. About 1655. Panel, 30.2 × 37.8 cm
Philadelphia Museum of Art, John G. Johnson Collection, 1917, 564

PROVENANCE: Sale, Chevalier de Clesle, Paris (Paillet), 4 December 1786, no. 18 (fr.1,000, Le Brun); sale, anon., Paris (Paillet), 9 April 1793, no. 44 (fr.764, Hamon); Samuel Wilberforce, Bishop of Winchester; sale, Wilberforce, London (Christie's), 10 June 1893, no. 61; John G. Johnson, Philadelphia, who bequeathed it to the City of Philadelphia, 1917.

LITERATURE: Smith 49; HdG 766; W. R. Valentiner, Johnson Collection Catalogue, Philadelphia, 1913, 2, p.123, no. 564; Ros 479; Johnson Collection Catalogue, Philadelphia, 1941, p.36, no. 564 (first identification as Brederode); John G. Johnson Collection, *Catalogue of Flemish and Dutch Paintings*, Philadelphia, 1972, p.76, no. 564; Haverkamp Begemann 1973, pp.37, 87, no. 40, repr.; Slive 1981, p.66, repr.; Amsterdam–Boston–Philadelphia 1987–88, sub no. 89, p.465, note 16 (wrongly identified as the ruins of Egmond Castle); Philadelphia 1994, p.93; Slive 2001, no. 28, repr.

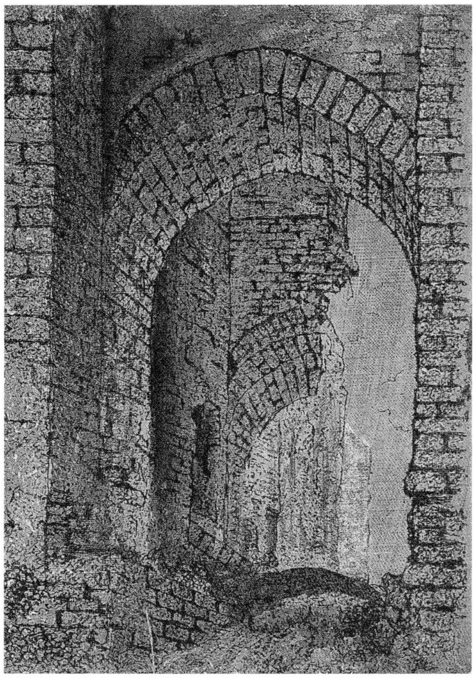

Fig. 29a Hercules Segers, *A Ruined Entrance Gate of Brederode Castle*. Etching, unique impression. Rijksprentenkabinet, Amsterdam.

Brederode Castle is situated near the village of Sandpoort about five kilometres northwest of Haarlem. Built by a member of the family that bore the name, it is mentioned as early as the thirteenth century. The castle comprised three parts contained within a large moat: an outer court, a thirteenth-century barbican (*voorbrucht*), and an early fourteenth-century square castle with a tower at each corner, one round and the other three rectangular. In 1351, and again in 1426, it was badly damaged by the Kabeljauws, a faction that had long internecine wars with the Hoeks. It suffered again in 1491 when Albrecht van Beieren's German soldiers made it a partial ruin. The Spanish made it a total ruin in 1573 during their seige of Haarlem. Restoration of it began in 1862; in its present restored state it offers a good idea of a Dutch medieval castle.[1]

The ruins of Brederode became a favourite motif of Dutch artists who discovered the delights of their native countryside about the beginning of the seventeenth century. As early as 1600 Goltzius made drawings of it and students of the work of Jacob Matham, Jan van de Velde, Buytewech, Saenredam, and Hercules Segers have catalogued depictions of the castle by their hands; for Segers's print of it see below. Later artists portrayed it as well: *e.g.*, Lievens, Simon de Vlieger, van Borssom, Berchem, Hobbema, and Kessel.[2]

Ruisdael's earliest existing representation of the ruin is a black chalk drawing at Dresden that belongs to a group of sketches the youthful artist made about 1646 (cat. 62). The sparkling effect of the draughtsman-like brushwork of Philadelphia's small painting, which depicts the eastern entrance gate seen from the outside, places it about a decade later. The gate, known as "de Poorthoog," was the principal entrance to Brederode. For other small oil sketches similar in style and handling that are datable about the same time see cat. 25–28.

Haverkamp Begemann (1973) first noted that Hercules Segers made an etching (in reverse) of the same gate, seen from a lower and more dramatic point of view; the unique impression of Segers's print is at the Rijksprentenkabinet, Amsterdam (fig. 29a; inv. no. OB 856). He also observed that a comparison of the two works confirms that both artists provided an accurate portrayal of the ruined gate.

1. For its history and occupants see van Reyen 1965, pp.71–73, 132; H. J. Calkoen, "Het Huis Brederode en zijn bewoners," *Velsen, grepen uit de gescheidenis van een oude woonplats in Kennemerland*, IJmuiden, 1967, pp.56–62; Groesbeek 1981, pp.73–81.
2. Jan van Kessel's panoramic *View of Bleaching Grounds with the Ruins of Brederode Castle* (Davies 1992, no. 13) was wrongly attributed to Ruisdael by Smith (200) and HdG (61). Rosenberg (1928, p.116, note 2) rightly gave it to Kessel; see Slive 2001, no. dub8, repr.

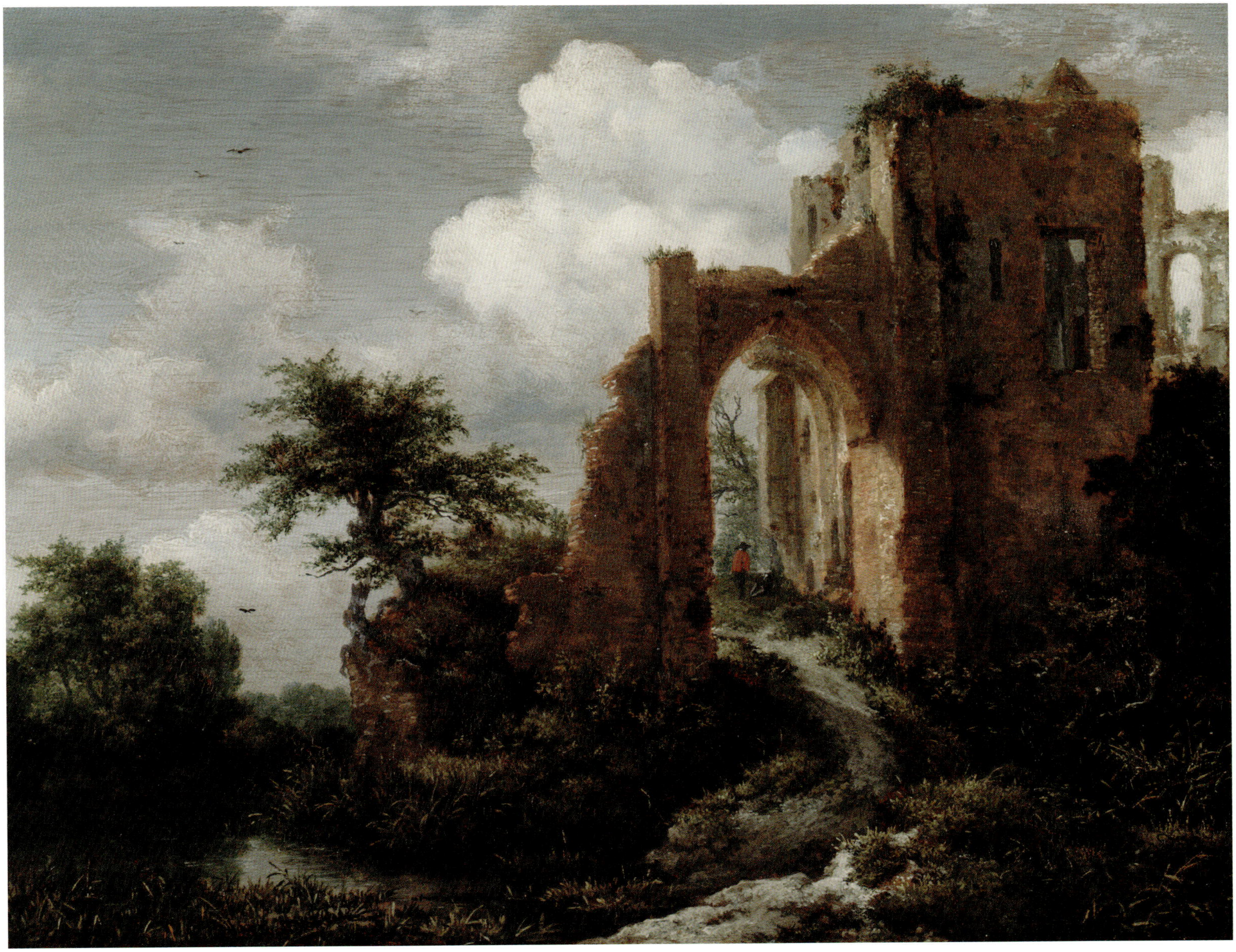

30

Cottage under Trees near a Grainfield

Monogrammed, lower right. About 1650–55. Canvas, 56.8 × 68.2 cm
Private collection, Hamburg

PROVENANCE: William Wells, Redleaf, Kent, by 1810; sale, W. Wells, London (Christie's), 12–13 May 1848, no. 97 (£273, Glendinning); but, according to Hofstede de Groot (120), purchased from Wells by John Smith who sold it to George Field in 1851; sale, George Field, London (Christie's), 10 June 1893, no. 33 (Sedelmeyer); dealer C. Sedelmeyer, Paris, *Catalogue of 300 Paintings*, 1898, no. 177, repr.; Rodolphe Kann, Paris, Catalogue, 1907, no. 76; bought *en bloc* in August 1907 by dealers Duveen Brothers, London; J. P. Morgan, New York, by 1909; (?) dealer Knowles, New York, *c.*1943; dealer Knoedler, New York, *c.*1946; dealer W. R. Drown, London; British Rail Pension Fund; their sale, London (Sotheby's), 5 July 1995, no. 46; dealer D. Koetser, Zurich, by 1996; dealer D. Koetser, Zurich, Catalogue, [1997], no. 26.

EXHIBITIONS: London, British Institution, London, 1824, no. 97; London, Marlborough House, 1856; Manchester 1857, no. 852; New York 1909, no. 108, repr.; on loan, Doncaster Museum and Art Gallery, 1977–93.

LITERATURE: Farington 1978–84, 11, pp.4004–05 (4 October 1811; on a list dated 2 November 1810, Wells states he paid £105 for the painting and his estimate of its future worth is £75); Smith 213; Waagen 1857, 4, p.194; Bürger 1865, p.292 (description of no. 852 [Manchester 1857] by Ruisdael, which he confuses with no. 845 by Hobbema, also at that time in G. Field's collection); HdG 120, identical with HdG 862 and HdG 1075a; Ros 88; Simon 1930, p.73; Slive 2001, no. 89, repr.

The landscape excels by its abundant display of lush, bosky growth and golden grain. A discussion of the interests and taste of William Wells (d.1847), the earliest known owner of the picture, make clear that Wells's interest in the painting was in accord with his personal "domesticated vision of sanitized rural charm".[1] Wells's taste for the picturesque was seen in the way he transformed his country estate Redleaf, near Penshurst, Kent, which he purchased in about 1808. The principal feature of the vista from the front view of his house was an especially constructed "woodman's cottage". In the words of a contemporary: "the effect of the woodman's cottage . . . which may be described as one of the aboriginal cottages of the country, is exceedingly good, as seen from the drawing room, by the strong contrast with its humble appearance, and the associations connected with it, afford to the richness and high art displayed in the house".[2] Ruisdael's *Cottage under Trees near a Grainfield* was one of the works Wells owned which "provided a model and a justification for the early Victorian urban capitalist Romantic and sentimental version of the countryside which he, Wells, constructed physically on his own domain" (*ibid.*, p.24).[3]

In addition to the present picture two other outstanding Ruisdael paintings appeared in Wells's 1848 posthumous sale: an unusual view of the dunes near Bloemendaal's bleaching fields with an imaginary ruined castle, walls and moat, now in the Bert and Mia Van Deun-Loyen collection, Oberrägeri, Switzerland,[4] and *Lily Pond in an Oak Wood with an Old Beech*, one of the artist's most beautiful woodland scenes which has been a treasure of the Staatliche Museen, Berlin, since 1891.[5]

1. Gaskell 1990, p.24.
2. J. C. Loudon, "Redleaf, the seat of William Wells, Esq., F. H. S.," *The Gardener's Magazine*, 15 (1839), pp.363–64 (cited by Gaskell 1990, p.24).
3. Gaskell's discussion focuses upon Isack van Ostade's *Traveller at Cottage Door*, Thyssen-Bornemisza Museum, Madrid, which could have been viewed by Wells and his guests as an equally effective referential object that helped contrast contrived life and art. However, it differs from Ruisdael's picture by its emphasis on rather large anecdotal figures: a traveller speaking to a man at a cottage door and a child hiding his face in a woman's lap.
4. Slive 2001, no. 58, repr.
5. *Ibid.*, no. 315, repr.

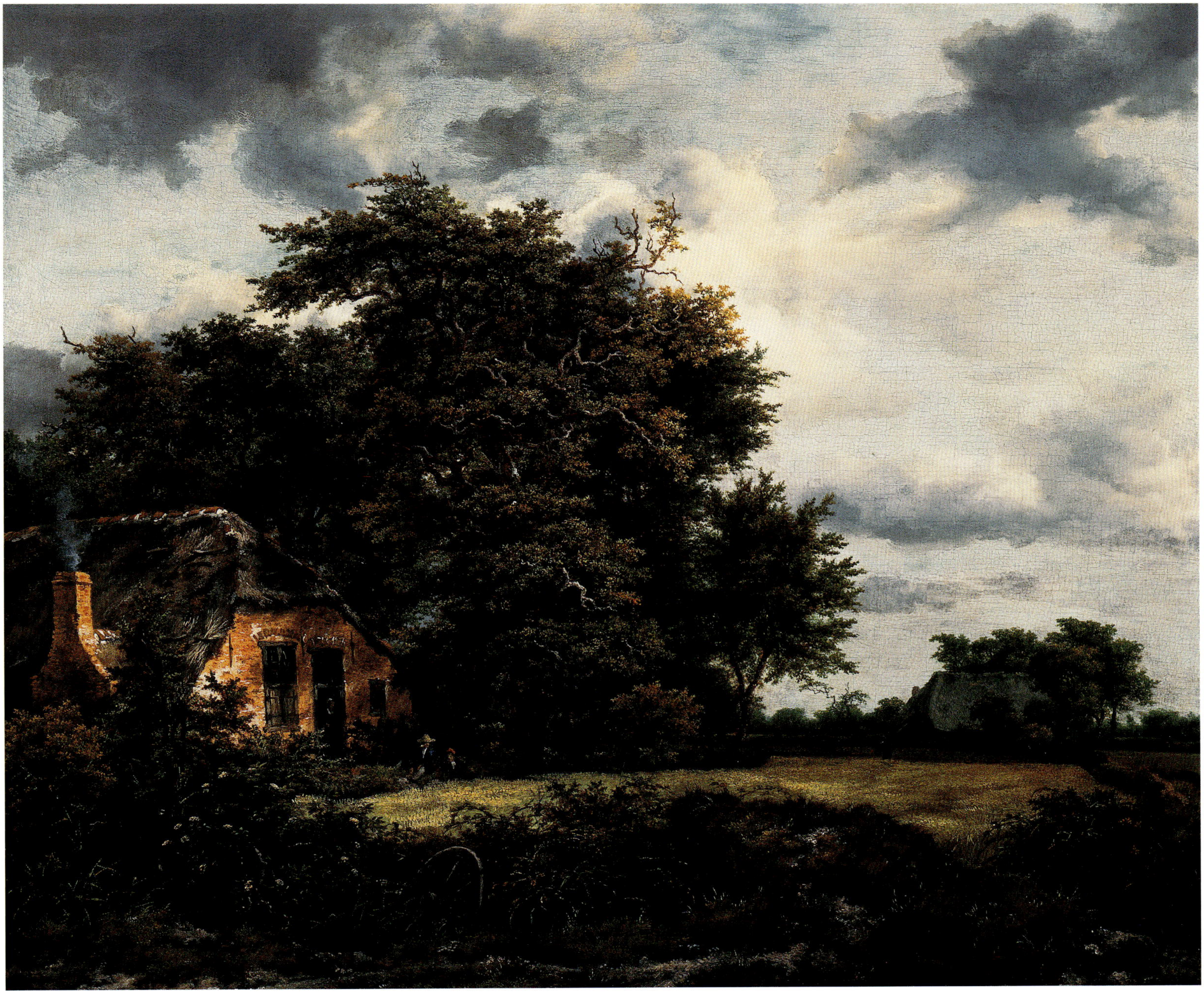

31

Reconstruction of the Ruins of the Manor Kostverloren

Monogrammed, lower left. About 1660. Canvas, 63 × 75.5 cm
Amsterdam Historisch Museum, acquired with aid from the Rembrandt Society, SA-38217

PROVENANCE: According to Haak (1981, p.91) possibly identical with *"Het Huis Kostverloren aan den Amstel* door Ruisdael" which appeared in the sale, Antoni Bierens, Amsterdam (de Stoppelaar), 20 July 1747, no. 20 (Dfl.37; Hoet, 2, p.200; HdG 100f [sale year wrongly listed as 1717]). This identification remains problematic because the sale catalogue offers neither a description of the painting nor its dimensions; the lot cited could refer to another painting by or attributed to Ruisdael of the manor. The painting may very well have been bought in at the 1747 sale since a picture listed as "Het huys Kostverloren aan den Amstel van Ruisdael" is cited in the inventory of Anthony Bierens of 28 August 1750, no. 18 ("In de Warmoestraat tegenover de Wijde Kerksteeg in de gekroonde star"; listed in a Getty Provenance Index print out, received December 1990). Sir Thomas Beauchamp Proctor, Langley Hall, Norfolk, 1815; Sir Ivor Beauchamp Proctor; Sir Christopher Beauchamp Proctor; sale, anon., London (Christie's), 12 December 1980, no. 108, repr. (bathers possibly by Adriaen van de Velde); dealer Robert Noortman, London, from whom it was acquired for Dfl.535,000 by the Museum with funds from the Vereniging Rembrandt in 1981.

EXHIBITIONS: The Hague–Cambridge 1981–82 (exhibited only at The Hague; not catalogued); Tokyo and elsewhere 1992–93, no. 57, repr; Hamburg–Haarlem 2002, no. 42, repr.

LITERATURE: Possibly HdG 100f; Haak 1981, pp.91–93 (in or soon after 1658); "Amsterdam Historisch Museum Koopt Ruisdael", *Tableau*, 4, no. 5, 1982, p.447; Slive 1988, pp.136–37, repr. p.132; Kloek and Niemeijer 1990, pp.65–66; Walford 1991, p.121, repr.; Davies 1992, p.145, sub no. 40; Slive 2001, no. 73, repr.; Slive 2004, pp.181–82, repr.

The manor Kostverloren, situated on a bend of the Amstel River about five kilometres south of Amsterdam, was built about 1500. Successive owners gave it various names, but by about 1525 it had already been called Kostverloren (literally "Lost Earnings" – the implication is "Money Down the Drain"). According to an old tradition the house acquired its nickname because of the seemingly endless cost of keeping its foundation intact in the marshy land in which it had been built.

Before the middle of the seventeenth century Kostverloren was the most conspicuous house in the vicinity. Its attractive location made it a notable landmark for people who saw it from boats that plied the Amstel and promenaders and travellers who used the road that followed the river. The manor's appeal was recorded amply by Dutch poets and artists. Among the latter, in addition to Ruisdael, were Jacob's pupil Hobbema, his close follower Jan van Kessel and Rembrandt.

In about 1650 the old manor was badly damaged by fire, a very bad storm or a flood. However, the fabric of its tower remained sound. In the late 1650s or early 1660s the ruined manor was acquired by new owners who rehabilitated it by demolishing, and then rebuilding the ruined parts. Their intent was to rent the manor after restoration to derive income for an estate.[1]

Ruisdael's painting shows the very first stages of the renovation of Kostverloren's tower. He himself most probably depicted the men working on the foundation of the house and the naked bathers cavorting in the manor's moat. Their activities as well as the newly applied, fresh white paint on the tower and the picture's luminous sky dispel associations of the ruins with the popular *vanitas* theme that is so often connected with depictions of ruined buildings. Here ruins allude to the resuscitation of an identifiable structure, not its inevitable demise.

1. For more on the chronology of the reconstruction of Kostverloren in Ruisdael's day see p.262, note 17, above.

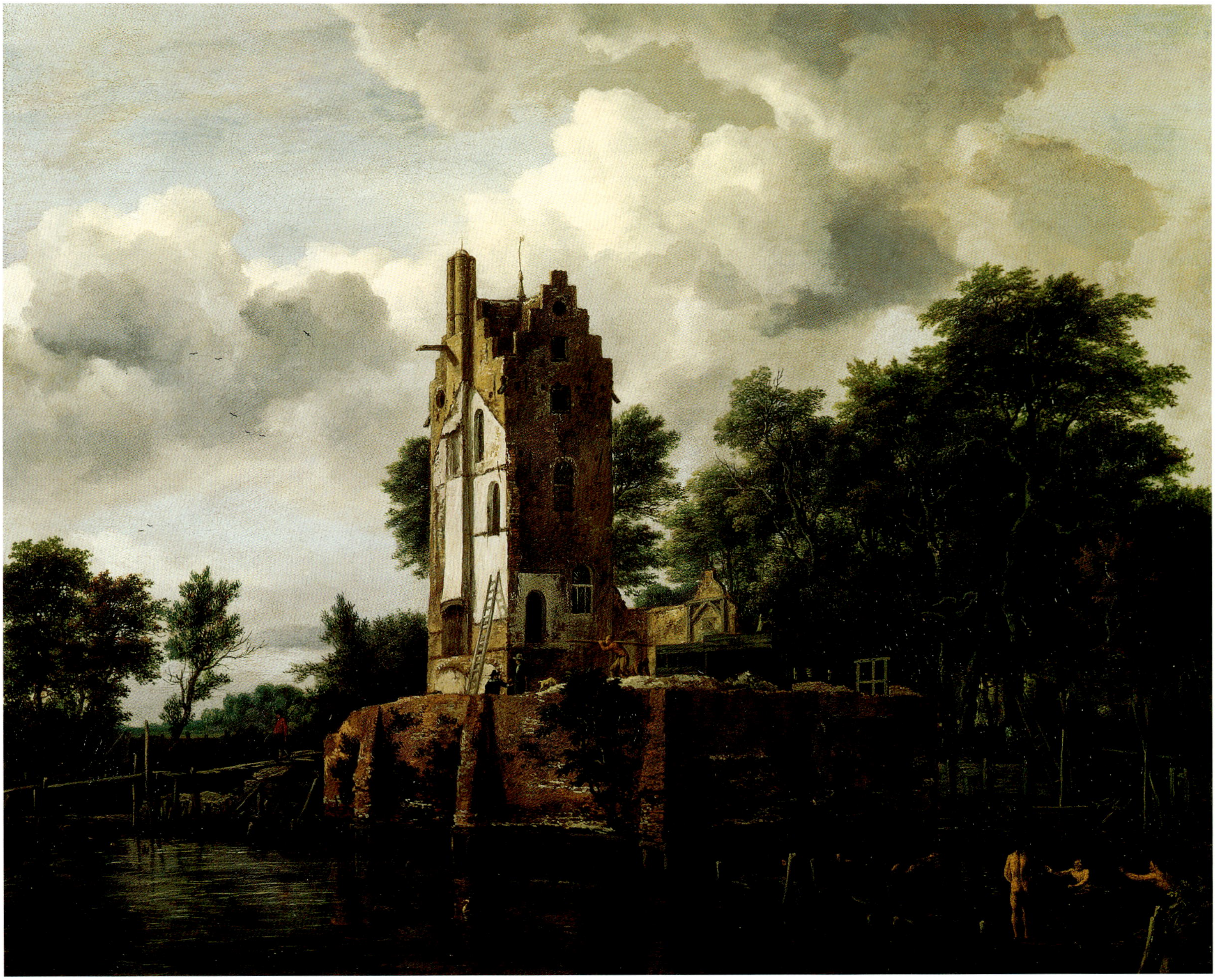

32 Waterfall in a Hilly Wooded Landscape

Signed, lower right. About 1660. Canvas, 105.5 × 123.4 cm
The National Gallery of Art, Washington DC, Widener Collection, 1942.9.80

PROVENANCE: Possibly Henry, 3rd Baron and 1st Marquess Conyngham (1766–1832), or his son, Francis Nathaniel, 2nd Marquess of Conyngham (1797–1876), Mount Charles, County Donegal and Minister Abbey, Kent; bought from the Marquess of Conyngham by Sir Hugh Hume Campbell or by Farrer (ms. note by Smith in his own copy of his Ruisdael catalogue; Smith does not state if the vendor was the father or the son); Sir Hugh Hume Campbell, Marchmont House, by 1857; his sale, London (Christie's), 18 June 1894, no. 48 (1250gns., Colnaghi); possibly dealer C. Sedelmeyer, Paris, Catalogue, 1895, no. 35, repr. (the entry is correct for this painting, however a different waterfall, now in Philadelphia [Slive 2001, no. 259, repr.] is erroneously illustrated); dealer M. Colnaghi, London; P. A. B. Widener, Lynnewood Hall, Elkins Park, Pennsylvania; Joseph E. Widener, who gave it to the Gallery in 1942.

EXHIBITIONS: Possibly London, British Institution, 1855, no. 54, and 1857, no. 79 (? lent by Campbell); London, British Institution, 1866, no. 59; London, Royal Academy, Winter Exhibition, 1877, no. 199.

LITERATURE: Waagen 1857, 4, pp.441–42; P. A. B. Widener, Catalogue, 1885–1900, no. 274; HdG 285, identical with HdG 367 and HdG 418 (probably not HdG 643c); Ros 196, identical with Ros 241; Simon 1930, p.74; National Gallery of Art, Catalogue, 1965, p.119, no. 676; Edinburgh 1992, p.176; Walford 1991, pp.102–04, repr. (mid-1650s); National Gallery of Art, Catalogue, 1995, pp.339–43, no. 1942.9.80[1] (*c.*1655; cat. by A. Wheelock); Slive 2001, no. 295, repr.

When the painting was treated in the gallery's conservation laboratory in 1999–2000, it was learned that apart from some retouching in the sky and thinning of a few dark areas in its lower part it is in remarkably good condition.

The picture, which ranks with the artist's best wooded landscapes with waterfalls, is datable to the late 1650s or early 1660s when the heightening of large forms and emphasis on solid masses, characteristic of works of the mid-fifties, begin to loosen and hint at the greater spatial effects of the sixties. Particularly fine are the accents made by the texture of the bark of the huge dead oak and the white trunk and stump of the even larger broken beech tree[2] on the right. A *Waterfall* in a New York private collection is a variant of the composition (Slive 2001, no. 243, repr.); it probably predates the present work.

1. Possible identification of the painting with HdG nos. 119, 134, 203 by Wheelock (National Gallery Catalogue, 1995, p.342) is erroneous. HdG 119 is the Benjamin Altman *Grainfield* at the Metropolitan Museum of Art (Slive 2001, no. 101; the painting, arguably Ruisdael's greatest representation of the theme, could not be considered for inclusion in the present exhibition because according to the terms of its bequest it cannot travel). HdG 134 is an untraceable *Grainfield*; HdG 203 is a *Waterfall* at Cologne (Slive 2001, no. 172).
2. Identification of the tree as a beech was made by Peter Ashton, sometime Professor of Botany, Professor of Dendrology and director of the Arnold Arboretum, Harvard University, in a private communication. Henry M. Cathey, director, U.S. National Arboretum, has identified it as a birch; see Wheelock 1995, p.342, note 4. Art historians are not the only specialists who have differences of opinion regarding attributions.

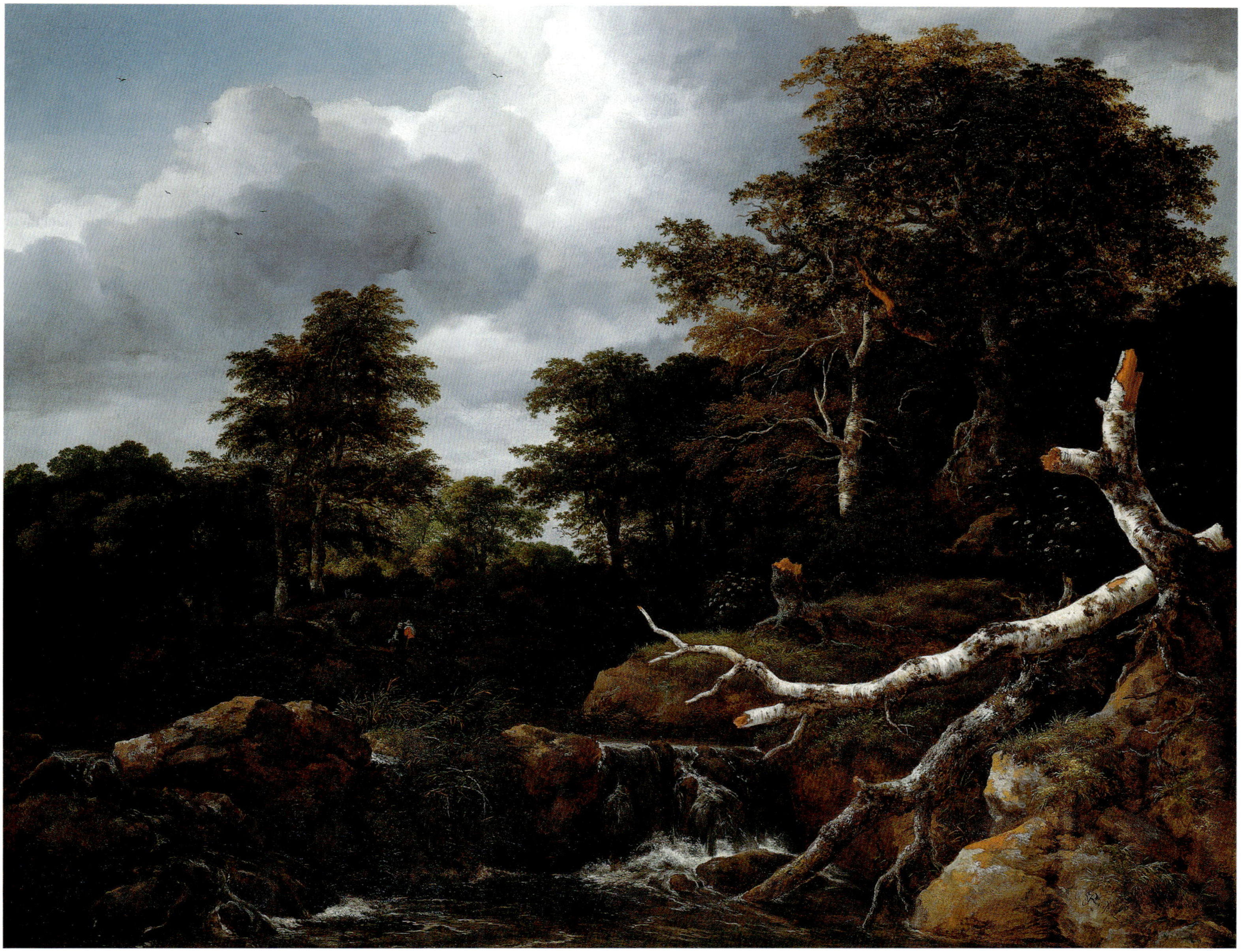

33

Waterfall with a Half-timbered House and Castle

Signed on a rock, lower right. About 1665. Canvas, 99.7 × 86.3 cm
Fogg Art Museum, Harvard University Art Museums, Cambridge, Massachusetts, gift of Helen Clay Frick, 1953.2

PROVENANCE: Edward R. Bacon, New York; Henry Clay Frick, Prides Crossing, Massachusetts; Miss Helen Clay Frick, New York, who presented it to the museum, 1953.

EXHIBITIONS: Chapel Hill 1958, no. 53, repr.; Baltimore 1968, no. 16, pp.32–33, repr.; The Hague–Cambridge 1981–82, no. 34, repr.; Amsterdam–Boston–Philadelphia 1987–88, no. 85, repr.

LITERATURE: Jakob Rosenberg, "A Waterfall by Jacob van Ruisdael," *Fogg Art Museum, Annual Report*, 1952–53, p.11, repr.; Stechow 1966, p.145, Fig. 288; Ashton *et al.* 1982, pp.8ff., pl. 3 (detail); Slive 1982, p.31, repr.; Bowron 1990, p.128, repr.; Slive 2001, no. 166, repr.

A prime example of the type of waterfall in a vertical format that the artist began to favour in the mid-1660s. The torrent wildly rushing over large boulders is seen close and fills more than the lower third of the painting. The space behind is built high, on one side with towering firs, and on the other side the dense mass of a rocky wooded hill, a cottage and, beyond, a precipitous mountain cliff surmounted by a castle. Though the format is vertical, the height of the landscape and the width of waterfall are in perfect equilibrium. The gigantic conifer on the left can serve as a model of a botanically correct Norway spruce (Ashton *et al.* 1982).

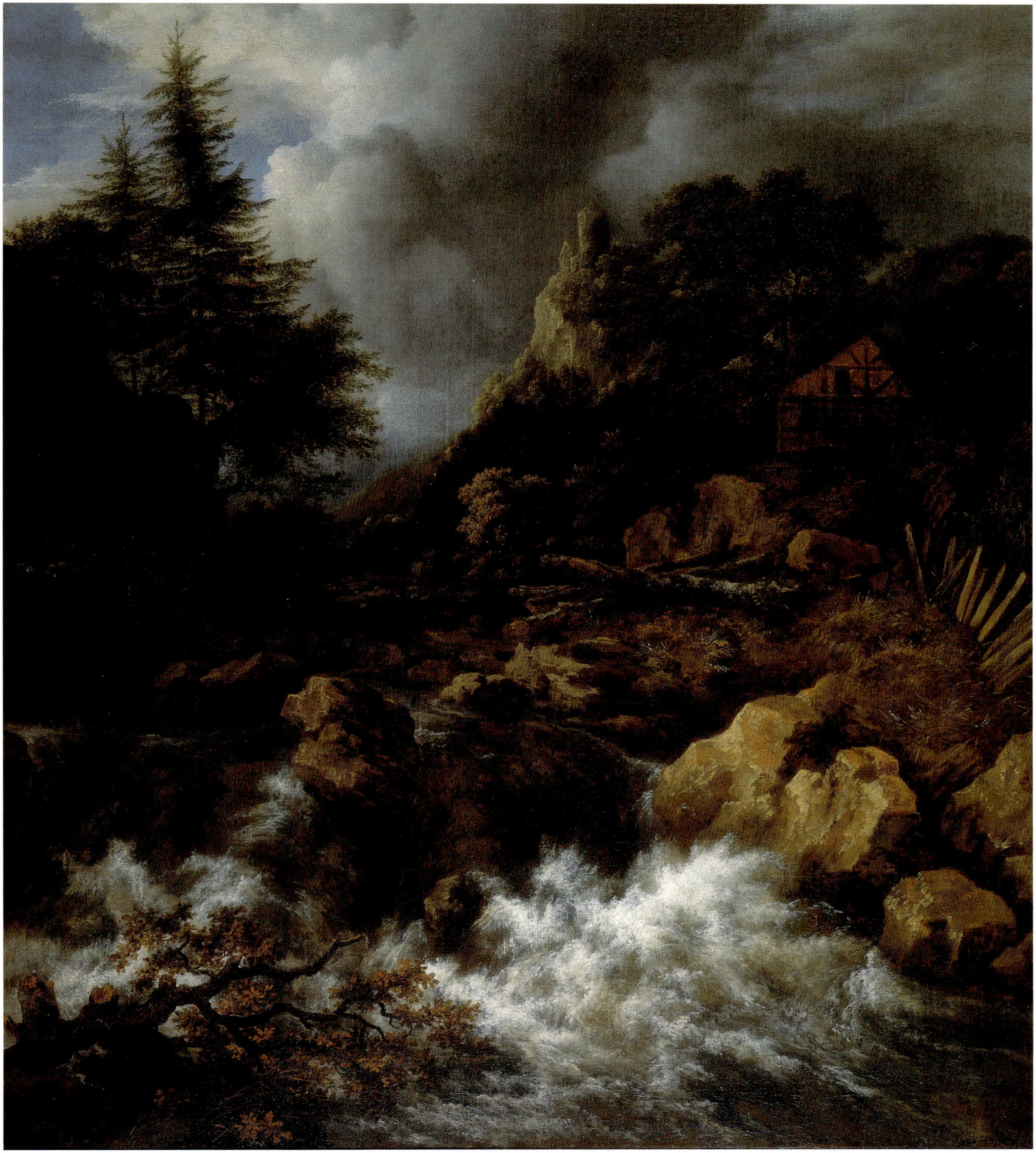

34

Waterfall in a Mountainous Landscape with a Ruined Castle

Signed, lower right. About 1665–70. Canvas, 119 × 180 cm
Private collection at Mount Stuart, B19

PROVENANCE: Almost certainly acquired by John Stuart, 3rd Earl of Bute (1713–92). It is first mentioned as being in the Bute collection at Luton in 1800.

EXHIBITIONS: London, British Institution, 1854, no. 19; Bethnal Green 1882–83, no. 219; Glasgow 1884, no. 145; Edinburgh 1949, no. 29; Edinburgh 1992, no. 59.

LITERATURE: Luton Hoo, Catalogue, 1800, no. 334; Smith 198; Waagen 1838, 2, pp.576–77; Waagen 1854, 3, pp.480–81; HdG 760; Ros 475; Walford 1991, p.104, repr. (c.1656–58); Slive 2001, no. 277, repr.; Russell 2004, pp.196, 203, 210.

Captain William Baillie (1723-1810) had this picture in mind when he told John Stuart, 3rd Earl of Bute: "Of this Painter your Lordship has ye very finest extant."[1] Baillie's enthusiasm was understandable. The magnificent, exceptionally large painting is a summit of the artist's wild, mountainous Scandinavian landscapes studded with live and fallen gigantic conifers and with immense, foaming waterfalls crashing on precipitous boulders. The artist's only existing drawing of a waterfall (The Pierpont Morgan Library, New York; cat. 90) is closely related to it.

In 2004–05 the painting was restored at the Los Angeles County Museum of Art's conservation laboratory by Joe Fronek, the museum's senior paintings conservator. The colour illustration opposite was made after the completion of its recent treatment.

1. Baillie's letter to Bute is dated 29 January 1791; see Russell 2004, pp.203, 210.

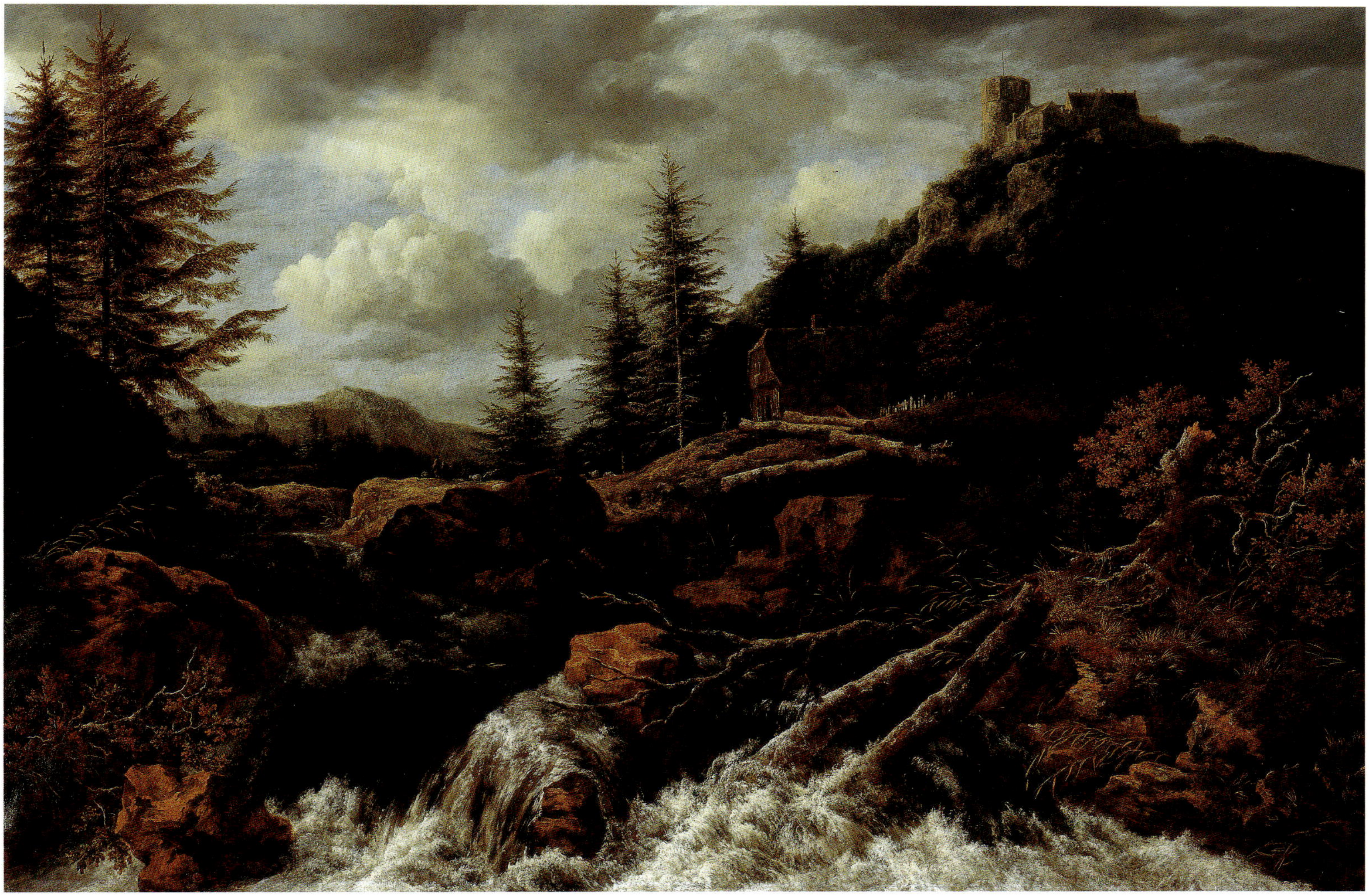

35

Waterfall near an Oak Wood

Signed, lower right. Late 1660s. Canvas, 142 × 195 cm
Rijksmuseum, Amsterdam; on loan from the City of Amsterdam, SK-C-210

PROVENANCE: According to Smith purchased on the continent around 1740 by an ancestor of Sir Charles Blount; Sir Charles Blount sold it to Smith in 1836; sold by Smith to A. van der Hoop, Amsterdam, 1837 (£1450), who bequeathed it to the City of Amsterdam, 1854; on loan at the Rijksmuseum since 1885.

EXHIBITIONS: Amsterdam, 1845, no. 134; Zurich 1953, no. 132; Rome 1954, no. 130; Milan 1954, no. 133.

LITERATURE: Smith Suppl. 1; Gower 1875, p.114; Musée van der Hoop, Amsterdam, Catalogue, 1883, p.41, no. 123 (erroneously accompanied by a facsimile of the signature and date which is on *Water Mill in a Wooded Landscape*, also in the Rijksmuseum; Slive 2001, no. 110, repr.); Bredius 1901–04, p.107, repr.; HdG 198; *Ruysdael, Original-Abbildungen* [1920?], repr.; Ros 120; Zwarts 1928, p.242; Rijksmuseum, Amsterdam, Catalogue, 1976, p.487, no. C 210; Slive 1981, p.107, repr.; Bruyn 1987–88, p.99, repr.; Walford 1991, pp.143–45, repr. (*c.*1660–65); Slive 2001, no. 138, repr.

LACMA and PMA

The painting is the artist's largest waterfall. Its horizontal format, scattered vistas, deep spatial effect and relatively open composition suggest a date in the late 1660s.

Zwarts's (1928) conclusion that the great waterfall is a preliminary study (*voorstudie*) for Ruisdael's *Jewish Cemetery* at Dresden is incomprehensible.[1] Bruyn's (1987–88) contention that Ruisdael intended the waterfall, woods and distant church in this picture, as well as others that use similar motifs, as *vanitas* symbols is a hypothesis that remains undemonstrated.

The Swiss landscapist Alexandre Calame (1810–64) was ecstatic about the painting when he saw it soon after it was acquired by Adriaan van der Hoop in 1837:

> Je ne dirai plusque Ruysdael n'est pas nature et qui'il est trop noir. Non, et cent fois non! Il est maître, et maître bien parfait! Quel moelleux surtout dans la touche du feuille sur le ciel, et quelle transparence! Comme l'on distingue bien les différents plans d'un même arbre![2]
>
> (I will never again say Ruysdael is not natural and that he is too dark. No, a hundred times no! He is a master, and an absolutely perfect master! What softness, particularly in the brushwork of the foliage against the sky, and what transparency! How well one is able to distinguish the different layers of the same tree!)

A reduced copy of the Amsterdam picture by an unidentified hand appeared in the sale, anon., London (Sotheby's), 22 February 1984, no. 53, repr. (canvas, 47 × 65); and again, in sale, anon., London (Sotheby's), 24 October 1984, no. 72, repr.

1. Zwarts's (1928, p.242) conclusion that the artist's *Stone Quarry* (Slive 2001, no. 484, repr.), now in Zurich, is a late work used as a preliminary study for the Dresden *Jewish Cemetery* is equally difficult to comprehend.
2. Cited in E. Rambert, *Alexandre Calame, sa vie et son oeuvre*, Paris, 1884, p.109; also see pp.95, 98, 562. For the possibility that Calame is the author of a landscape at Copenhagen that has been wrongly attributed to Ruisdael see Slive 2001, no. dub64, repr.

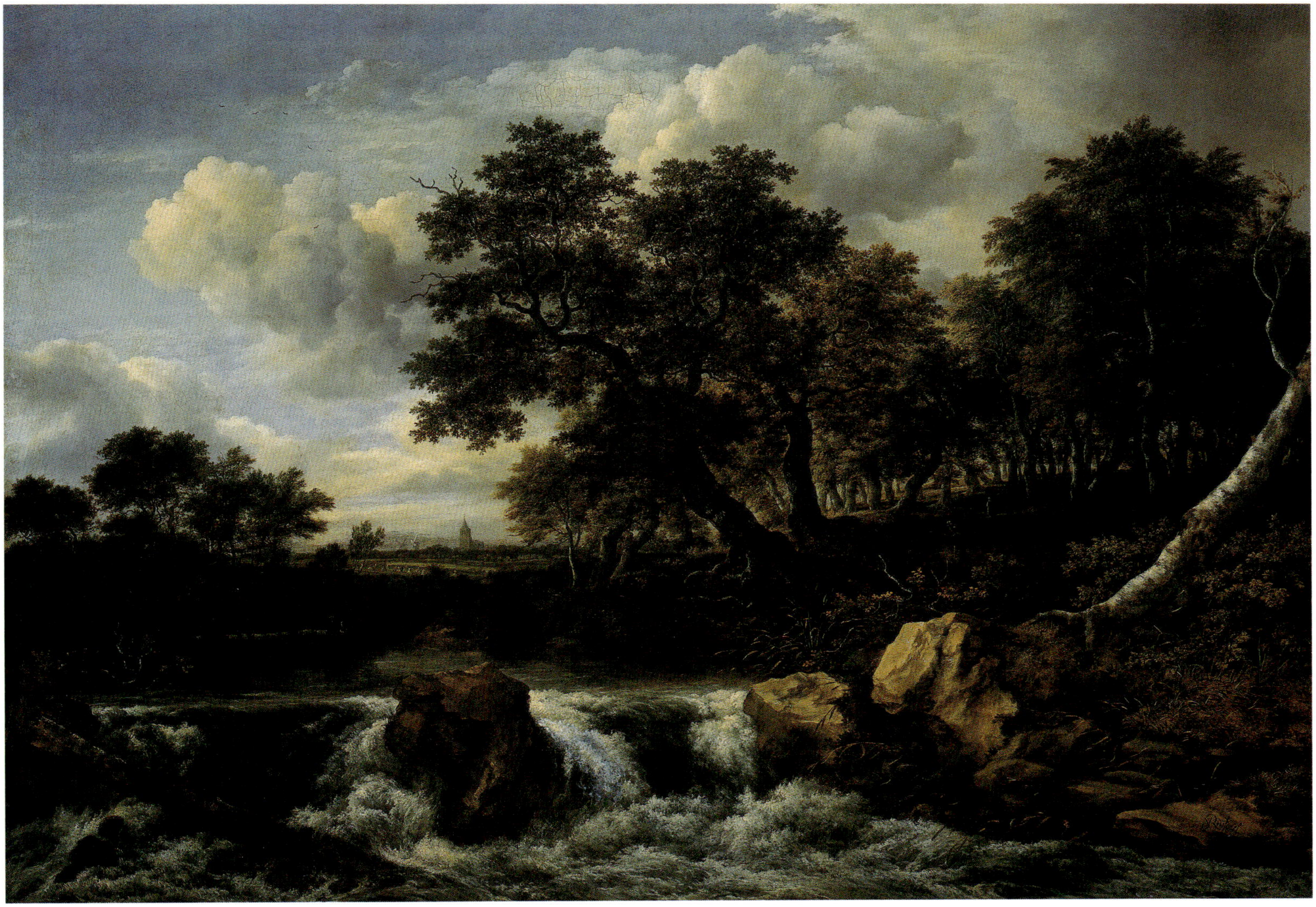

36

Grove of Large Oak Trees at the Edge of a Pond

Signed, lower right. About 1665. Canvas, 101 × 123 cm
Staatliche Kunsthalle, Karlsruhe, 2565

PROVENANCE: Sale, Cabinet de M . . . [Le Rouge], Paris (Laneuville), 16 January 1816, no. 22 (fr.10,000, Comte de Pourtalés); evidently Pourtalés sold the painting back to Le Rouge; in any event, it appeared in the sale, Mme. Le Rouge, Paris, 27 April 1818, no. 50 (fr.10,400, Laneuville); sold in 1826 by Comte de Pourtalés to Smith and Emmerson; bought back by Pourtalés in the same year; sale, Comte de Pourtalés, London (Phillips), 19–20 May 1826, no. 115 (300gns., Emmerson); sale, David McIntosh, London (Christie's), 16 May 1857, no. 56;[1] collection Bentley (?); sale, Sir Hugh Hume Campbell of Marchmont House, Berwickshire, London (Christie's), 8 June 1872, no. 56; sale, Paris (Palais Galliera), 3 December 1966, no. 25; acquired by the museum from dealers F. and P. Nathan, Zurich, 1967.

EXHIBITION: London, British Institution, 1857, no. 79.

LITERATURE: Smith 150; Waagen 1857, p.442; HdG 569; [Jan Lauts], *Jahrbuch der Staatlichen Kunstsammlungen in Baden-Württenburg*, 5, 1968, pp.162–63 (painted about the middle or the second half of the 1660s); Raupp 1980, pp.90–91, repr.; Slive 2001, no. 366, repr.

LACMA and PMA

The ancient colossal oak at the pond's edge manifests the commanding presence and enormous strength with which Ruisdael could endow trees. In accord with the poetic peace that suffuses the noble landscape, these qualities are portrayed with tactful restraint.

An untraceable copy by an anonymous hand with changes in the staffage and cut on the right surfaced in about 1940.[2]

1. The entry in the sale catalogue states: "This noble work is from the Collection of Madame Cattalin, of Paris". Hofstede de Groot (569) notes the picture appeared in the sale, De Catelan, Paris, 16 January 1816 (fr.10,000). Lugt *Repertoire* does not list a Cattalin or De Catelan sale catalogue; I have been unable to find a trace of either.
2. See Slive 2001, p.284, fig. 366a. An inscription on the verso of a photo in the Walther Bernt Archive, Fine Arts Library, Harvard University, reads "Lange [Berlin?] 1940."

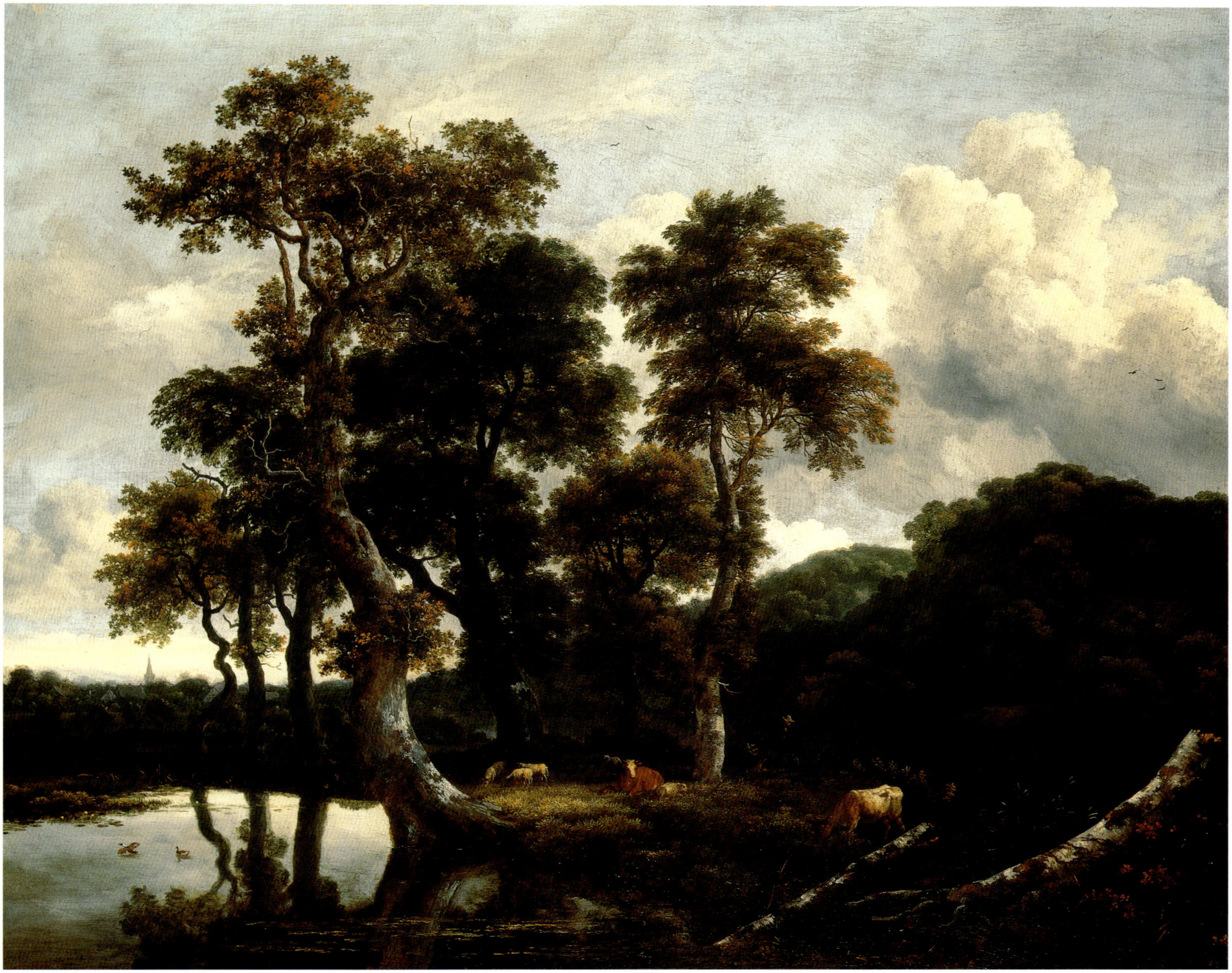

37

Marsh in a Forest

Signed, lower left. About 1665. Canvas, 72.5 × 99 cm
The State Hermitage Museum, St. Petersburg, 934

PROVENANCE: Acquired for the Imperial Hermitage, 1763–74.

EXHIBITIONS: Washington and elsewhere 1975–76, no. 23; The Hague–Cambridge 1981–82, no. 36, repr. (shown in The Hague only); Tokyo–Osaka 1983, no. 21; Rotterdam 1985, no. 25; Hamburg– Haarlem 2002, no. 41, repr.

LITERATURE: Smith 306; Waagen 1864, p.243; Hermitage, St. Petersburg, Catalogue, 1895, 2, no. 1136, repr.; Michel 1910, pp.150ff, repr. p.162; HdG 508; Roh 1921, p.331, note to fig. 158; Shcherbachova 1924, p.21; Ros 313; Hermitage, Leningrad, Catalogue, 1958, 2, p.250, no. 934; Fechner 1958, p.17; Fechner 1963, pp.93–94; 170–71; Kouznetsov 1973, p.33; Hermitage, Leningrad, Catalogue, 1981, 2, p.163, no. 934; Kuznetsov and Linnik 1982, no. 195; Gerszi 1986, p.142; Walford 1991, pp.133–34; Slive 2001, no. 414, repr.

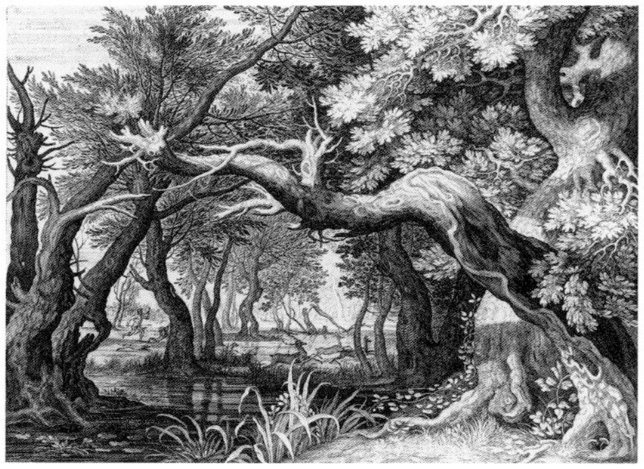

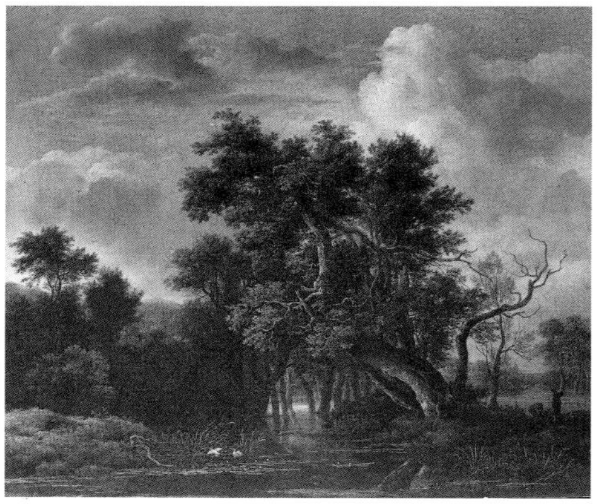

Fig. 37a Egidius Sadeler, after Roelandt Savery, *Stag Hunt in a Marsh*. Engraving.

Fig. 37b Jacob van Ruisdael, *Wooded Landscape with a Pond*, 166(?). Major H. S. L. Clowes, Norbury, Ashbourne, Derbyshire.

More than one student of Ruisdael's works has noted that the St. Petersburg *Marsh* was inspired by a composition of Roelandt Savery (1576–1639) engraved by Egidius Sadeler[1] (fig. 37a). Juxtaposition of the two works does not diminish Jacob's accomplishment one iota. The complex interweaving of Savery's wildly contorted trees and growth illustrates the fantastic, decorative trend of late mannerist landscapists. Savery's marshy woods could serve as a wondrous setting for a fairy tale as easily as it does for a hunting scene. Ruisdael's marsh in a forest could not. He has used Savery's composition to evoke the splendour and sublimity of the forest.

"An architectonic genius," in Jakob Rosenberg's words, "has blown over Savery's fantastic structure and has transformed it into a grown space of architectural order and solidity. Playful ornamentalism has been transformed into the mighty reality of the three-dimensional existence of things. The usual rich abundance of forms, their load of expression and their pressure of movement, has been pacified by the rhythm of the composition and by a sure feeling of what is possible in nature. It is the peace of controlled power, not the passive peace of the observed mood of the countryside to which we are accustomed in Dutch landscape painting."[2]

The close connection between The Hermitage's *Marsh* and Ruisdael's *Wooded Landscape with a Pond*, dated 166(?) (fig. 37b; H. S. L. Clowes collection, Ashbourne, Derbyshire[3]) is striking. The latter's date of 166(?; the last digit is no longer visible) supports the date in the 1660s given to the Hermitage picture and to stylistically related forest scenes with massive trees in the fore- or near-middle ground and with a lesser or greater degree of spaciousness. The Clowes painting is Jacob's only existing wooded landscape that bears a date in the sixties.

1. Roh 1921; Rosenberg 1928, pp.48f. After Rosenberg's publication of the relationship it became canonic in the literature.
2. Rosenberg 1928, p.49.
3. Slive 2001, no. 393, repr.

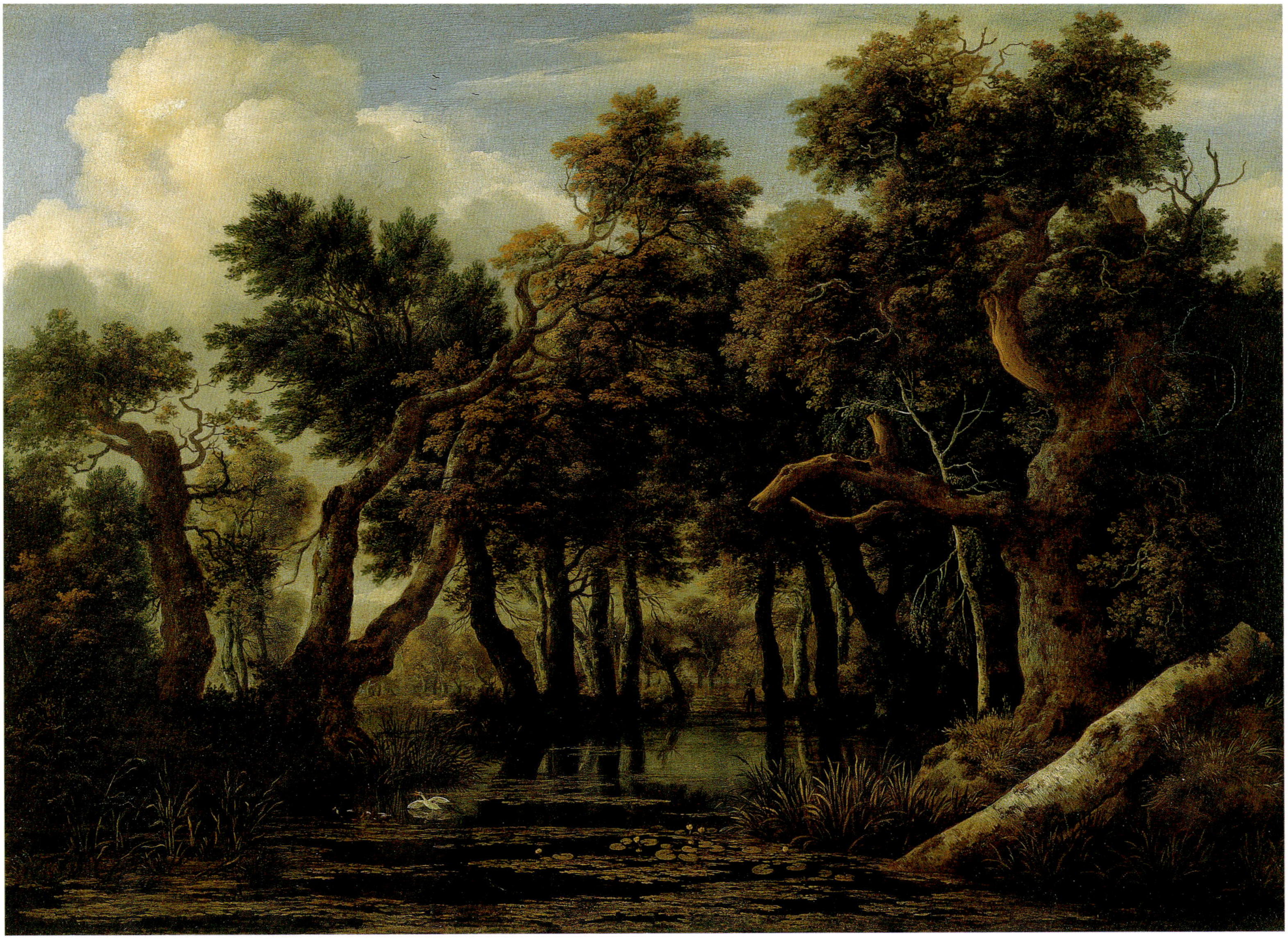

38

Stag Hunt in a Wood with a Marsh

Signed, lower left. About 1665–70. Canvas, 107.5 × 147 cm
Gemäldegalerie Alte Meister, Staatliche Kunstsammlungen, Dresden, 1492

PROVENANCE: In the Dresden manuscript inventory of 1754, 2, no. 205; removed to the Soviet Union in 1945, after the end of World War II; returned to Dresden in 1955.

EXHIBITIONS: Berlin 1955–56, p.103; Tokyo–Kyoto 1974–75, no. 60; The Hague–Cambridge 1981–82, no. 37, repr.

LITERATURE: Dresden, Catalogue, 1765, no. 196; Lehinger 1782, pp.422–23, no. 196; Goethe 1790, p.375, no. 196; Dresden, Catalogue, 1801, no. 196; Smith 230; Parthey 1863–64, 2, p.455, no. 15; Dresden, Catalogue, 1880, no. 1546; Michel 1890, p.57, repr.; Dresden, Catalogue, 1908, no. 1492; HdG 454; Ros 285; Dresden, Catalogue, 1930, no. 1492; Carus [1955], p.76; Dresden, Catalogues, 1956, no. 1492, and 1979, no. 1492 (*c.*1665–70); Walford 1991, pp.137–38; Dresden, Catalogue, 1992, no. 1492 (*c.*1665–70); Slive 2001, no. 338, repr.

Prints after the painting were made by Adrian Zingg (1734–1816; engraved [in reverse] in 1770 for his reception into Dresden's Academy); Christian August Günther (1759–1824); Johann Friedrich Frans Bruder (1782–1838) after a drawing by Philipp Veith (1768–1837); Friedrich Hohe (1801/02–70); Carl Krüger (1812–80); and Thomas Heawood (active *c.*1850).

The figures and animals are by Adriaen van de Velde. Although no mention is made of Adriaen's contribution in the entry on it in Dresden's 1754 inventory, Jean Antoine Reidel, author of the gallery's 1765 catalogue, not only recognized Adriaen's work but found it significant enough to list the painting as a joint effort by "Jacques Ruisdael, & Adr. v. Velde." Apart from Smith (230), who ascribes the staffage to Berchem, all cataloguers (some categorically, others more cautiously) have accepted Reidel's attribution. Like the figures and animals Berchem certainly added to Los Angeles's *Great Oak*, 1652 (cat. 20), the staffage in the Dresden painting can hardly be an afterthought. The spacious scene would have looked empty if it had not been enlivened by the stag hunt.

Efforts to discover whether the work was commissioned by a patron with a passion for hunting or if it was made for stock have been as fruitless as the attempts made to learn how Ruisdael and van de Velde planned their joint efforts. Adriaen's hand establishes that the noble landscape must have been painted before January 1672, when he died. Van de Velde also provided the staffage for Jacob's great panoramic view at The National Gallery, London (cat. 45), and a *Waterfall* at St. Petersburg (Slive 2001, no. 270, repr.). Both paintings are datable to the second half of the sixties; the Dresden *Stag Hunt* almost certainly was done during the same period.

When Goethe saw the painting in 1790 he called it superior and the best painting by the artist in Dresden's Gallery. He had second thoughts by the time he published "Ruysdael als Dichter" in 1816. His essay, devoted to three other paintings by the artist at Dresden, does not include a word about the *Stag Hunt*.[1]

1. Goethe's comment about the *Stag Hunt* was written in 1790 in his copy of Dresden's 1771 catalogue: "Vortrefflich und das beste von diesem Meister allhier" (Goethe 1790, p.375, no. 196). For Goethe's "Ruysdael als Dichter" see cat. 22.

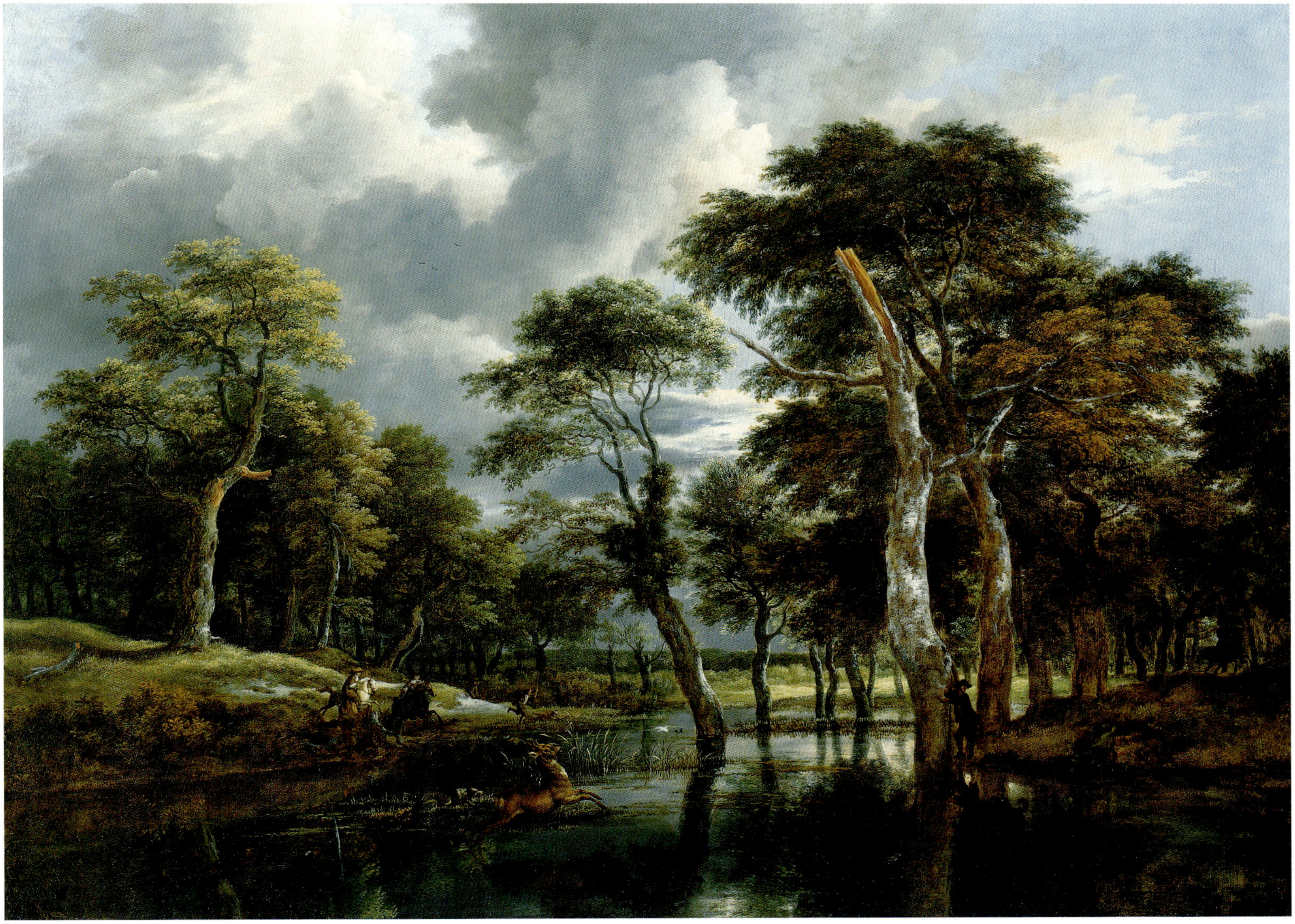

39

Windmill at Wijk bij Duurstede

Signed, lower right. About 1670. Canvas, 83 × 101 cm
Rijksmuseum, Amsterdam; on loan from the City of Amsterdam, no. SK-C-211

PROVENANCE: Probably sale, J. Juriaans, Amsterdam (v.d. Schley), 28 August 1817, no. 55 (Dfl.1,200, van Heijningen); perhaps sale, John Smith, London (Stanley), 2–3 May 1828, no. 41 (bought in at £262.10); purchased from Albertus Brondgeest in 1833 for Dfl.4,000 by Adriaan van der Hoop,[1] Amsterdam, who bequeathed it to the city of Amsterdam, 1854; Museum van der Hoop, Amsterdam; deposited on permanent loan to the Rijksmuseum, 1885.

EXHIBITIONS: Paris 1921, no. 91, repr.; London 1929, no. 207; Amsterdam 1945, no. 97; Rotterdam, Museum Boymans, Winter Exhibition, 1945–46, no. 39; Brussels–Antwerp 1946, no. 91, repr.; Paris 1950–51, no. 75; The Hague–Cambridge 1981–82, no. 39, repr.; Amsterdam–Boston–Philadelphia 1987–88, no. 88, repr; Amsterdam 2000, no. 154.

LITERATURE: Musée van der Hoop, Amsterdam, Catalogue, 1883, p.141, no. 124; HdG 105, probably identical with HdG 183; *Ruysdael, Original-Abbildung* [1920?], repr.; Ros 70; Hijmans 1951, pp.51–57; Rijksmuseum, Amsterdam, Catalogue, 1960, p.270, no. 2074; Stechow 1966, pp.59–60, fig. 115; Imdahl 1968; Rijksmuseum, Catalogue, 1976, p.487, no. 211; J. M. Drees, "Blade Twist, Droop Snoot, and Forward Spars," *Vertiflite*, September/October, 1976, pp.4–9; Kauffmann 1977, pp.379–97; Slive 1982, pp.26–28, repr.; Walford 1991, pp.150–51, repr.; Slive 2001, no. 81, repr.; Slive 2004, p.183.

Engraved by C. L. van Kesteren (1832–97), W. Steelink, Sr. (1826–1913) and J. M. Graadt van Roggen (b.1867).

RA

It is appropriate that a windmill, the best-known symbol of the Dutch landscape, should be the subject of Ruisdael's most famous picture, but to judge from the small number of times the artist made a mill the major accent in his paintings, he was not particularly partial to the motif. Only about ten are known today; apart from one, all are datable to the first ten or twelve years of his activity as a painter[2] (see Slive 2001, nos. 127–136). The remarkable exception is the present work, datable about 1670. It is his classical pronouncement on the subject.

The essence of the pictorial beauty of the magnificent painting is the firm cohesion of forms that harmonizes the dominant vertical mass of the mill's cylindrical body towering over the town with the high clouded sky, the breadth of the landscape, and the broad expanse of the river. The bond between the upper and lower parts of the landscape is strengthened by the counterplay between the cloud masses and countryside. Not only does the direction of the arms of the huge mill relate to the direction of the thick clouds, but almost every point on the ground and in the water is subtly connected to a corresponding spot in the vault of the heavy grey sky. Rhythmic tension is created between near and far by the strong emphasis on both the close and distant views, and by the contrasts between light and shadow which work together with the intensified concentration of mass and space.

It has long been recognized that the painting is a view of Wijk bij Duurstede, a small town situated about twenty kilometres southeast of Utrecht where the Lower Rhine divides into the Lek and the Crooked (Kromme) Rhine. Until Hijmans published his history of the town in 1951, it was assumed that the mill Ruisdael painted is the one that still exists there. Hijmans's research demonstrates that this supposition is incorrect. The existing windmill is a gate mill with a square base and lies north of the town. The one Ruisdael painted had a round base and was situated south of the town; today only some remnants of its foundation remain. An anonymous dated drawing of it at the Rijkskprentenkabinet (no. RP-T-AP 2.i), which depicts the mill from the opposite side, shows that it was still intact in 1750.

It is possible to identify two of the buildings Ruisdael saw from the bank of the Lek: to the left of the mill the late medieval castle of Wijk is clearly distinguishable; on the extreme right the squat tower of the Church of St. John the Baptist can be seen. In 1668 the town fathers ordered the installation of clock faces on the four sides of the church tower. Since Ruisdael painted the tower with the clock faces in place, the order for their installation provides a probable *terminus post quem* for the picture (Imdahl 1968, p.3).

On one level the *Mill at Wijk* is accessible to everyone as a characteristic scene of the Dutch countryside. Kauffmann's (1977) sensitive essay suggests that it may have had another level of meaning for some of the artist's contemporaries.

In Ruisdael's time, when people were more keenly aware of mankind's dependence upon the forces of nature that run windmills, water mills and sailing vessels than we are today – and when moralists were prone to read all of nature as symbolic of transcendental ideas – it was not uncommon for analogies to be made between the natural forces that power what man has made and the divine spirit that gives him life. A good example of this moralizing tradition is offered by an emblem published in Zacharias Heyns's *Emblemata, emblemes christienes, et morales.*

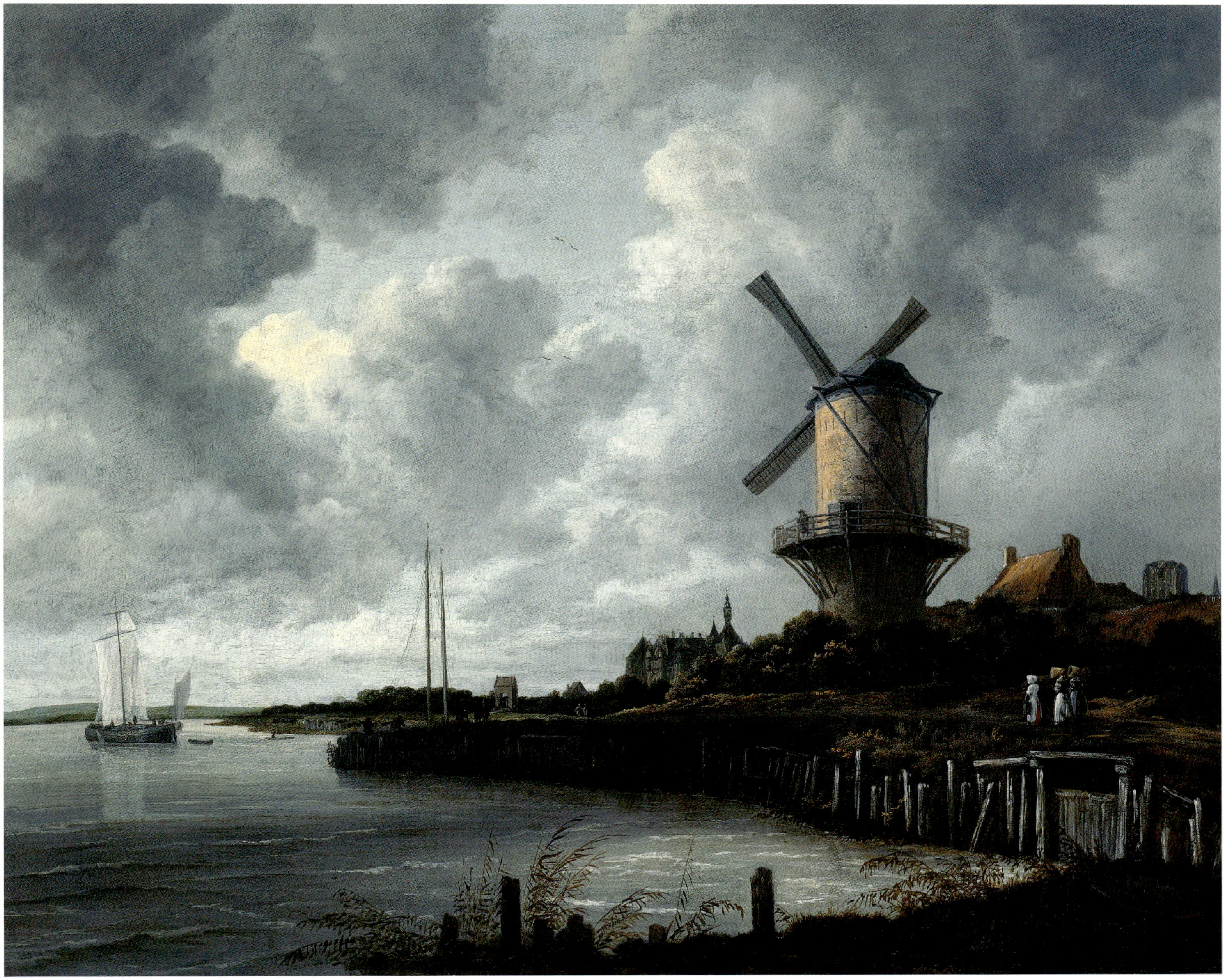

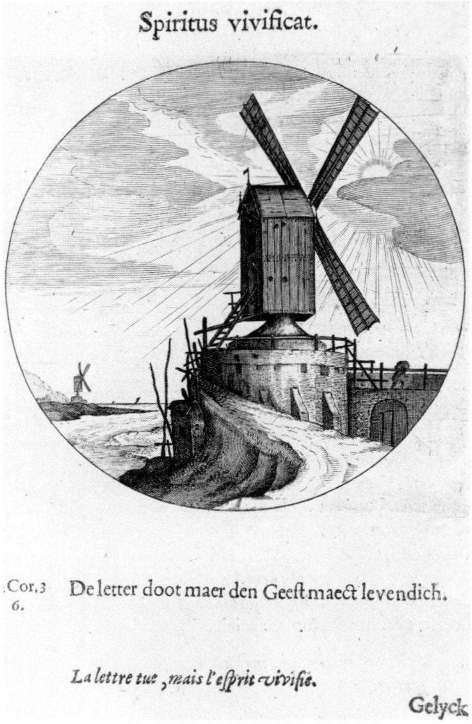

Fig. 39a Unidentified artist, *"Spiritus vivificat"* ("The spirit giveth life"). Emblem in Zacharias Heyns, *Emblemata, emblemes christienes, et morales...* Rotterdam, 1625. Engraving.

Sinne-Beelden streckende tot christelicke bedenkinghe ende leere der zedicheyt, Rotterdam, 1625 (fig. 39a; Kauffmann 1977, pp.382, 388). The emblem's motto "The letter killeth, but the spirit giveth life" (2 Cor. 3, 6) and the explanation that accompanies it, which elaborates on the similarity of the miller's dependence on the wind to grind his grain to man's dependence on the spirit of the Lord for life, is complemented by Jan Geeritsz Swelincks's engraving of a prominent windmill on a high bastion. Other epigrams and mottos were employed by moralists to express similar ideas: "Unless it breathes it is unmoved" (*Ni spiret immota*); "they are moved by the spirit" (*Aguntur Spiritu*; *ibid.*, p.392). In view of this visual and literary tradition, it is not hard to imagine that some of Ruisdael's contemporaries found a symbolic meaning in *The Windmill at Wijk bij Duurstede*. The extent to which the artist wanted his masterwork to convey this level of meaning has not yet been measured.

Matters easier to assess are Ruisdael's close observation of the gentle crossing wave fronts in the picture's foreground and his precise depiction of the construction of the mill's vanes. Both are discussed on pp. 11–12 above.

1. Bergveldt 1998, pp.153; 328, note 103; see Knoef 1948, pp.62–64 for a survey of the prices van der Hoop paid for his Dutch seventeenth-century paintings.
2. To be sure, windmills occasionally dot the artist's paintings of grainfields, panoramic views, winterscapes as well as other landscapes done during the course of his career, but in these works they are not principal motifs.

40

Landscape with a Sluice Gate

Signed, lower right. About 1665–70. Canvas, 104 × 87.5 cm
Lent by the Toledo Museum of Art. Purchased with funds from the Libbey Endowment, Gift of Edward Drummond Libbey, 1978.68

PROVENANCE: Collection Koucheleff Besborodko, St. Petersburg, by 1835; sale, Count Koucheleff Besborodko, Paris (Drouot), 5 June 1869, no. 30 (fr.26,500); Edmond de Rothschild, Paris; Maurice de Rothschild, Geneva; dealer Rosenberg and Stiebel, New York; dealer Agnew, London, 1963; Sidney J. van den Bergh, Wassenaer; sale, anon., London (Christie's), 10 December 1975, no. 73 (bought in); dealer G. Cramer, The Hague, 1976; dealer H. Schickman, New York, 1977; purchased by the museum.

EXHIBITIONS: Leiden 1965, no. 37; Tokyo–Kyoto 1968–69, no. 56; The Hague–London 1970–71, no. 86; Brussels 1971, no. 87; The Hague–Cambridge 1981–82, no. 40, repr.

LITERATURE: Smith 311; HdG 675; A. B. de Vries, "Old Masters in the Collection of Mr. and Mrs. Sidney van den Bergh," *Apollo*, 80, 1964, p.357, fig. 7; *Verzameling Sidney J. van den Bergh*, Wassenaar, 1968, no. 88; Hagens 1982, pp.11–12; Slive 2001, no. 519, repr.

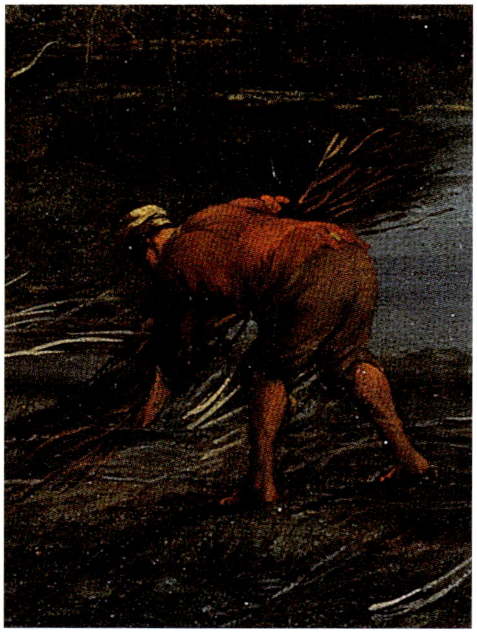

Fig. 40a Detail of cat. 40.

The landscape's paint surface is in an exceptionally fine state of preservation; its canvas support still has its original tacking margins. The work is datable to about 1665–70, when the artist combined powerful forms in the near and middle distance, in this case the cavernous sluice and a noble silvery beech, with fully developed receding spaces.

It has been suggested (Brussels 1971, no. 87) that the sluice is most likely identical with one at the manor house of Singraven near Denekamp, a village in the eastern part of the province of Overijssel. It is still used to regulate the level of the water of the Dinkel River, which serves the estate's water mills. Although the similarity is striking, the sluice cannot be identified with certainty; this type of sluice is common in the area.

The painting shows an inoperative sluice. The river's very low level enables a workman (fig. 40a) to lay bundles of reeds and branches in the river bed to protect it from the tremendous force of rushing water when the sluice functions. A second worker, silhouetted against the bright reflection in the water, is driving in a stake that will help support the bundles. In another riverscape the artist depicts men building a dam (Slive 2001, no. 520, repr.). These are rare notes in the artist's paintings. He seldom shows work people do. More familiar figures are the hunter and his dogs and the inconspicuous solitary traveller in this landscape.

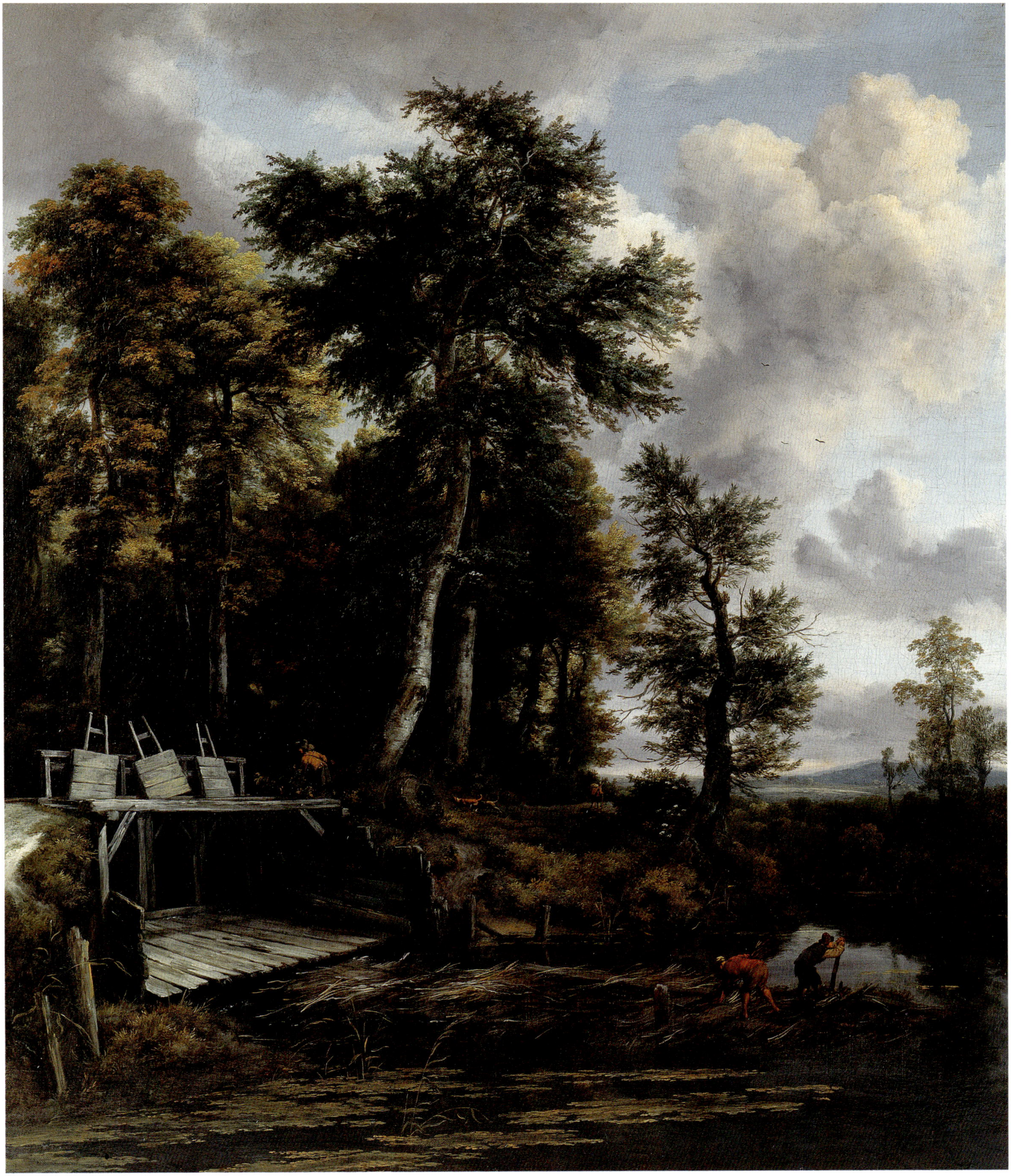

41

Sailing Vessels in a Choppy Sea

About 1665. Canvas, 43 × 43 cm
Private collection

PROVENANCE: Possibly sale, Count de Morny of Paris, London (Phillips), 20–21 June 1848, no. 19 (£126); Sir Hickman Bacon, Gainsborough, by 1912; Sir Edmund Bacon, Raveningham Hall, Norfolk.

EXHIBITIONS: London, Guildhall Art Gallery, 1890, no. 82; Norwich 1966, no. 37.

LITERATURE: HdG 948; Ros 583; Stechow 1966, p.209, note 55 (mid-sixties); Slive 2001, no. 660, repr.

The beautiful seascape is almost certainly identical with "une marine tout simple" that Eugène Delacroix described as a summit of art when he saw it in 1847 in the collection of his friend Comte de Morny (1811–65).[1] The marine he so highly praised is most probably listed in de Morny's sale catalogue of 1848 (no. 19), cited in the Provenance; it is described as "A Sea Piece. A fishing smack with a red sail is scudding before the wind; to the right a sand bank, on which some figures are walking. Canvas, 1 ft. 5 by 1 ft. 5½ [43.2 × 44]". On the same visit to de Morny's collection Delacroix was also deeply impressed by his friend's *Winter Landscape* by Ruisdael. He wrote these two works lessen the effect of de Morny's Watteau and Rubens. One can almost hear Delacroix sigh as he writes: "Avoir sous les yeux de semblables peintures dans sa chambre, serait la jouissance la plus douce."[2] ('To have such paintings before one's eyes in one's room, would be the sweetest pleasure').

Rosenberg (1928, p.15) dates the marine in the late 1640s and states it must have been modeled on a seascape by Salomon van Ruysdael similar to the one dated 1647 formerly in the Heilgendorff collection (illustrated in Rosenberg 1928, pl. 7; Stechow 1975, no. 285). Rosenberg rightly notes that the structure of Ruisdael's marine is very similar to Salomon's picture, itself reminiscent of Jan Porcellis with its lofty sky. He also justly stresses the difference in the treatment of the water; in the Salomon it is smooth and still, while in Jacob's seascape it is a more disturbed element. However, Ruisdael's marines datable to the late 1640s or early 1650s do not manifest the transparency of the sea air suggested by the fine gradations of tone in the present painting. I am inclined to accept Stechow's (1966) date of the mid-sixties for the work.

1. *Journal de Eugène Delacroix*, ed. André Joubin, Paris, I, 1932, p.213.
2. *Ibid.*, pp.212–13. For the possibility that the "effet de neige" by Ruisdael that Delacroix admired be the *Winter* formerly in the Michal Hornstein collection, Montreal, see fig. 43a below and Slive 2001, no. 683.

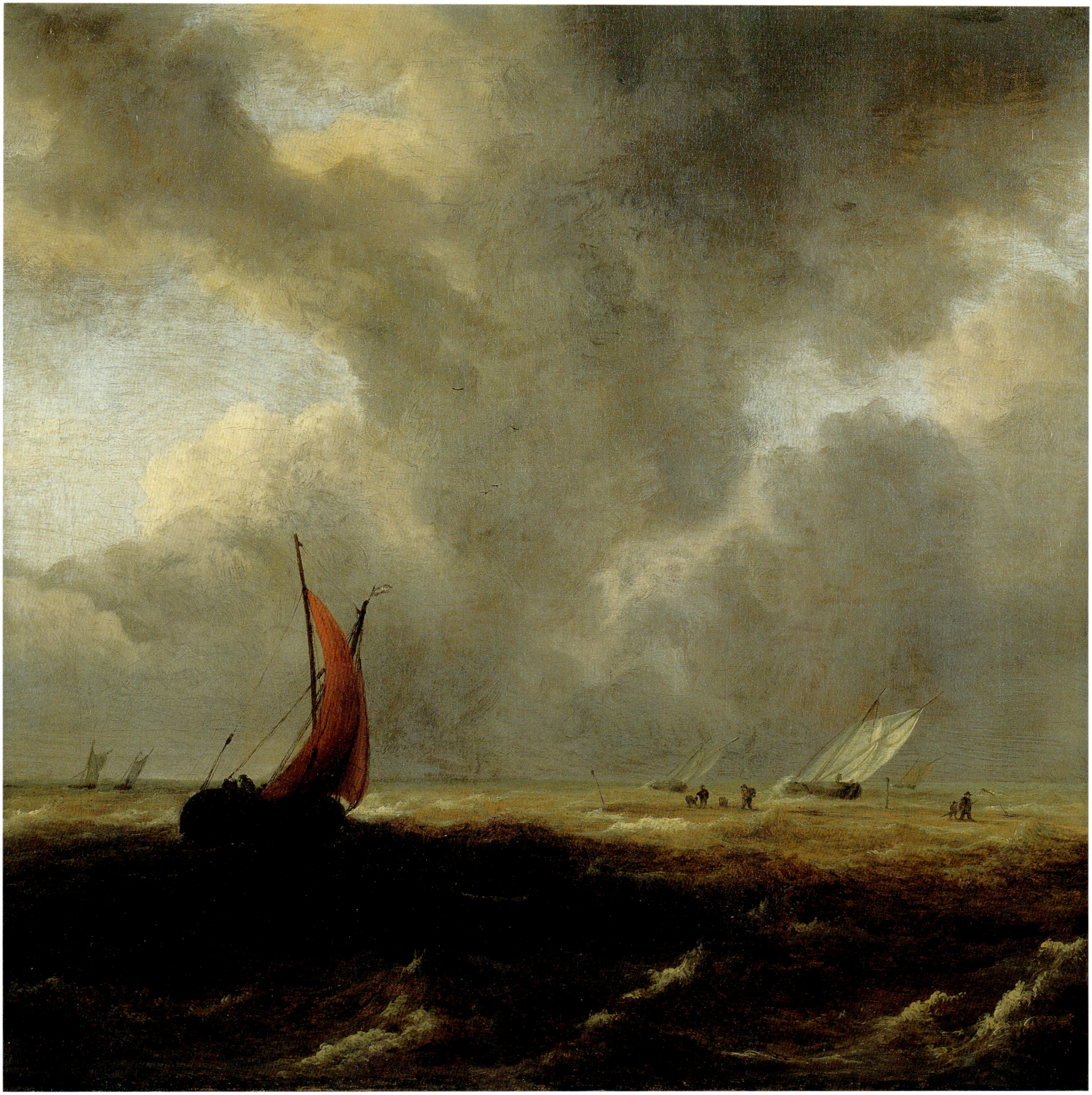

42

Village in Winter

Signed, lower right. About 1665. Canvas, 36.7 × 32.5 cm
Bayerische Staatsgemäldesammlungen, Alte Pinakothek, Munich, 117

PROVENANCE: Zweibrücken Gallery.

EXHIBITIONS: The Hague–Cambridge 1981–82, no. 41, repr.; Amsterdam–Boston–Philadelphia 1987–88, no. 84, repr.

LITERATURE: Smith 338; Parthey 1864, 2, p.459, no. 73; Altere Pinakothek, Munich, Catalogue, 1904, no. 549; Michel 1910, repr. p.163; HdG 999; Ros 618; Stechow 1966, p.97, repr. (early sixties); Alte Pinakothek, Munich, Catalogue, 1983, pp.476–77, inv. no. 117; Walford 1991, p.160, repr.; Slive 2001, no. 684, repr.

Lithographed (in reverse) by Joseph Anton Sedlmayr (1797–?); if his print (see Slive 2001, fig. 684a) is an accurate reproduction, it indicates the painting has been cut slightly on all four sides.

LACMA and PMA

None of the artist's winterscapes better succeeds in capturing the brooding mood of a winter day darkened by threatening storm clouds.

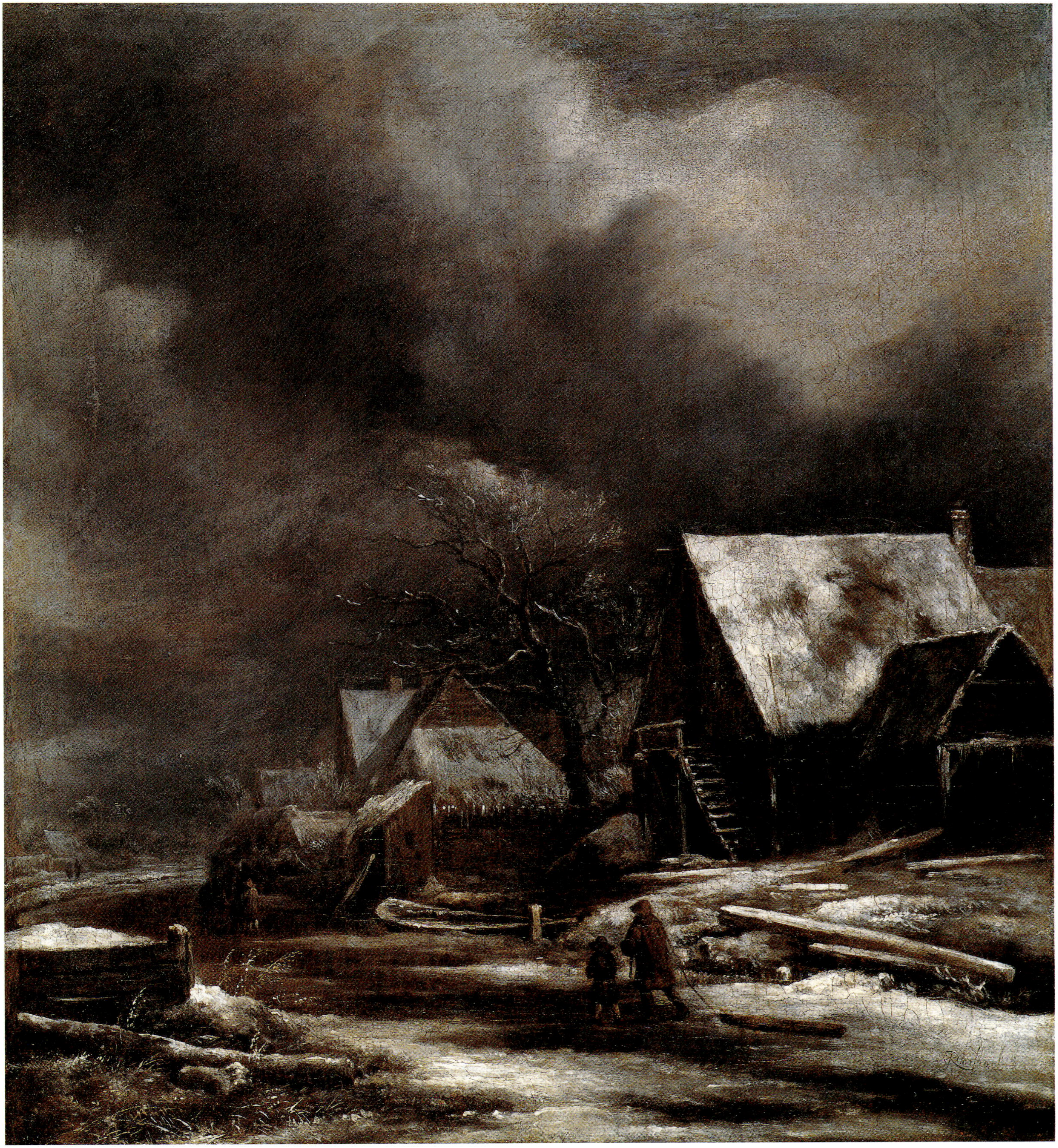

43

Winter Landscape

Signed, lower right. Late 1660s. Canvas, 55.2 × 68.6 cm
Philadelphia Museum of Art. John G. Johnson Collection, 1917, 569

PROVENANCE: According to Smith (210), sale, Anthony Sydervelt, Amsterdam (de Winter), 23–24 April 1766 (Dfl.249), but not mentioned in the sale catalogue or by Terwesten in his reprint of the sale catalogue; sale, Lapeyrière, Paris (Lebrun), 19 *sqq.* April 1825, no. 146 (fr.6755); sold to Sir Robert Peel in 1825 for £270 (cf. Jameson 1844, p.363); Constable noted it was in Peel's collection in 1832 (see below); Waagen (1837–39, 1, p.295) wrote that he saw it in 1835 at Peel's London residence and again notes it was with Peel when he visited his collection in 1850 (Waagen 1854, I, pp.397, 409); dealer F. Kleinberger, Paris; dealer E. Fischhof, Paris; in the John G. Johnson Collection, Philadelphia, 1909; bequeathed by John G. Johnson to the City of Philadelphia, 1917.

EXHIBITION: New York 1909, no. 111, repr.

LITERATURE: Smith 210; Waagen 1837–39, 1, p.295; Jameson 1844, p.363, no. 37; Waagen 1854, 1, p.409; HdG 1005; W. R. Valentiner, Johnson Collection, Catalogue, 1913, 2, p.125, no. 569; Ros 625; Stechow 1966, p.97 (second half of the sixties); Johnson Collection, Catalogue, 1972, p.77, no. 569 (erroneously listed as in the sale Lapeyrière, Paris, 14 March 1829, no. 88; there was no Lapeyrière sale in 1829); Slive 1981, pp.148–49, repr.; Reynolds 1984, p.242, no. 32.43, repr.; Walford 1991, pp.180, 190–92, repr.; Hove–Lincoln–Sudbury 1993, pp.7–8, repr.; Philadelphia 1994, p.93, repr.; Slive 2001, no. 688, repr.

The painting is one of a group of five winterscapes that show expansive open spaces with windmills set in the middle distance and scattered modest or more pretentious houses. The present picture, possibly the earliest of the group, is datable to the late sixties. Another, on a more intimate scale, probably done in the mid- or late 1670s, is also included here (cat. 55). The others, also datable to the 1670s, are illustrated figs. 43a–c.[1]

Philadelphia's picture has elicited highest praise from some of Ruisdael's earlier critics. When Waagen saw it in the collection of Sir Robert Peel in 1835 he (1837–39) wrote: "The feeling of winter is here expressed with more truth than I have ever seen." Valentiner (1913) considered it "the finest winter landscape by the artist, unsurpassed by any painting of similar motive in Dutch art".

Constable, who also greatly admired the work, painted a faithful copy in 1832 when it was in Peel's collection; his copy is now in a private collection (p. 35; fig. 45). On 4 September 1832, less than a fortnight after the death of his intimate friend Archdeacon Fisher, Constable wrote to his biographer Leslie:

> I cannot tell how singularly his death has affected me. I shall pass this week at Hampstead to copy the Winter – for which my mind is in a fit state.[2]

Since Constable's copy shows more of Ruisdael's original on all four sides and is slightly larger than the Philadelphia painting, the original was most probably cut down after the copy was painted. For additional remarks regarding Constable's high opinion of the original see pp. 34–35.

1. For the winterscapes formerly in the collection Michal Hornstein, Montreal; Collection Frits Lugt, Institut Néerlandais, Paris; private collection, The Netherlands, see Slive 2001, nos. 683, 686, 693, respectively.
2. Beckett 1968, 6, p.365.

Fig. 43a Jacob van Ruisdael, *Winter Landscape with a Windmill and a Manor House with Scaffolding.* Formerly Michal Hornstein collection, Montreal.

Fig. 43b Jacob van Ruisdael, *Winter Landscape with a Windmill.* Collection Frits Lugt, Institut Néerlandais, Paris.

Fig. 43c Jacob van Ruisdael, *Winter Landscape with a Windmill.* Private collection, The Netherlands.

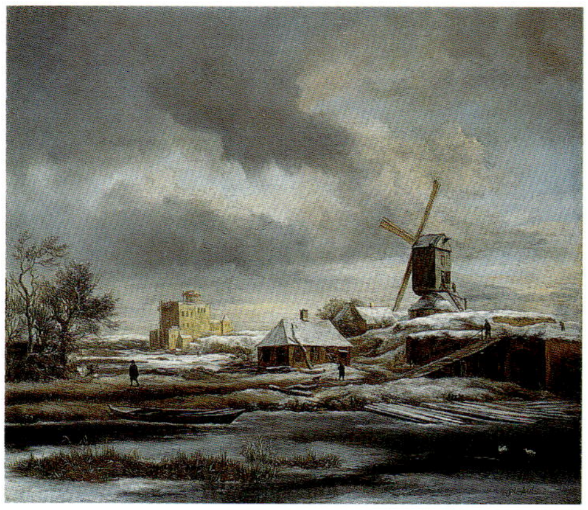

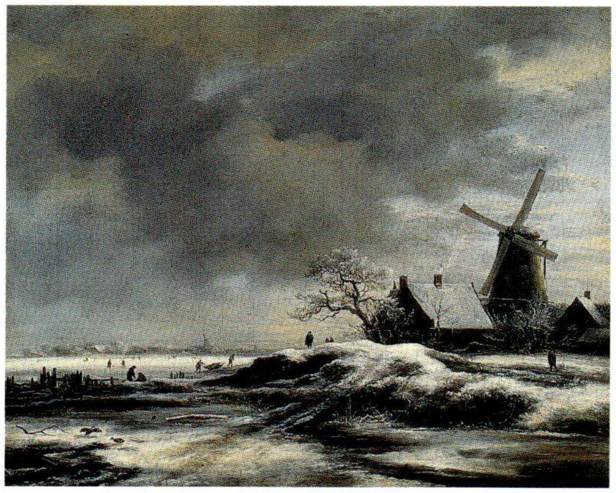

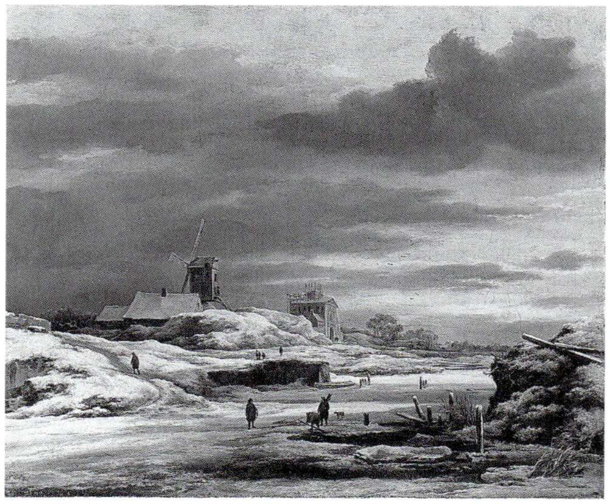

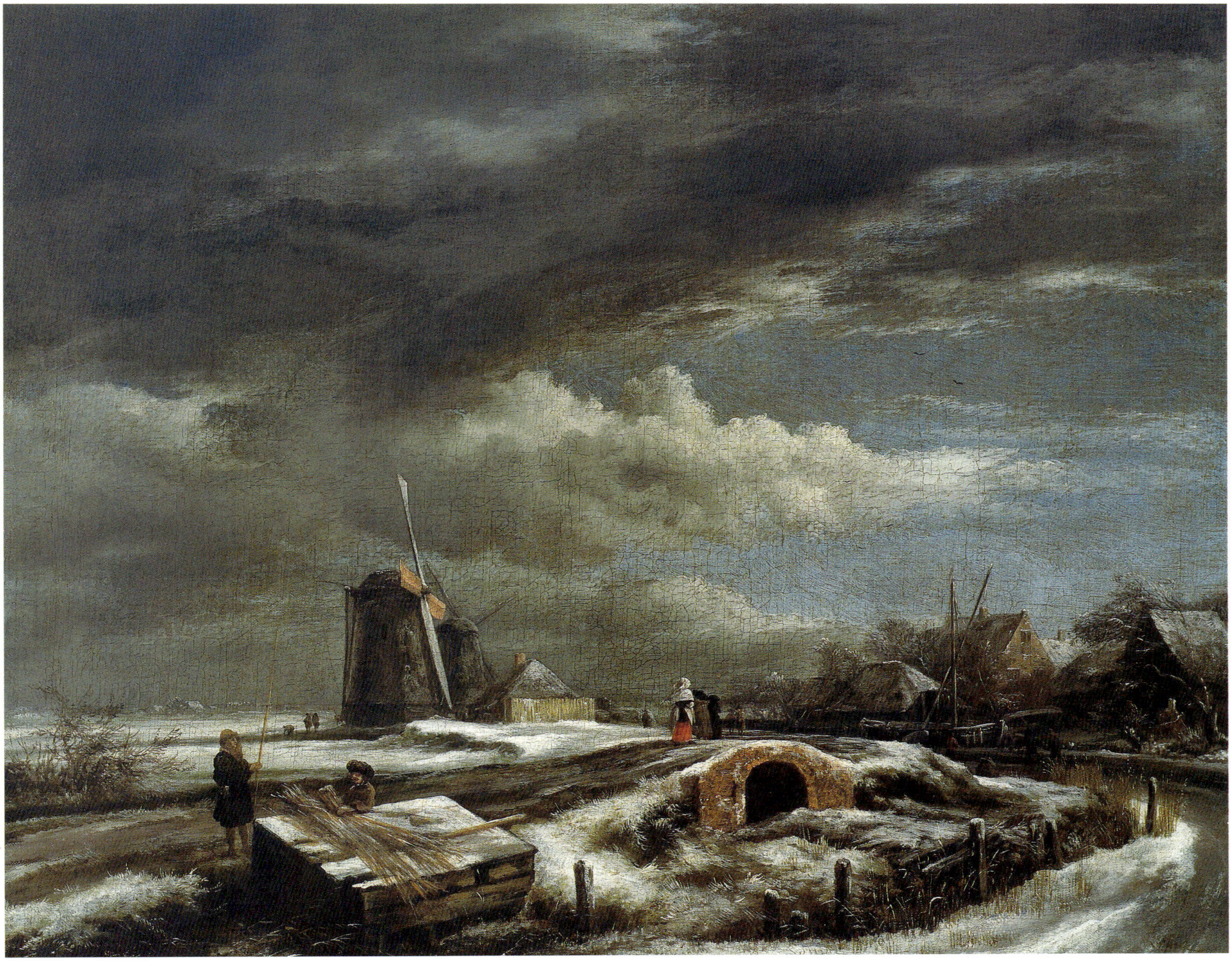

44

View of Grainfields with a Distant Town

Signed, lower left. About 1670. Canvas, 51.5 × 65 cm
Mrs. Edward W. Carter

PROVENANCE: Freiherr von Brabeck, Söder, until 1814; sale, Freiherr Andreas von Stolberg of Söder, Hannover (Rumpler), 31 *sqq.* October 1859, no. 230; Freiherr von Savigny, Berlin; dealer P. Cassirer, Berlin, who sold it in 1918 to a private Swedish collector; private collection, Norway; dealer Frederick Mont, New York, 1970.

EXHIBITIONS: Los Angeles–Boston–New York 1981–82, pp.84–87, no. 21, repr.; Los Angeles 1992–93, pp.84–87, no. 21, repr.

LITERATURE: F. W. B. von Ramdohr, *Beschreibung der Gemälde-Galerie des Freiherrn von Brabek zu Hildesheim*, Hannover, 1792, no. 264; HdG 139a; Slive 2001, no. 97, repr.

LACMA

The artist contrasts fields of uncut grain with stacks of bound sheaves as early as 1647 in his *View of Naarden* (cat. 6) and continues to juxtapose the two in later landscapes, but in no other is it as marked as it is in this beautiful painting done in the late sixties or early seventies.

A print (in reverse) of the painting by J. T. Prestel (1739–1808) is inscribed: "Peint par J. Ruijsdael . . . / Le Coup de Soleil/ D'après le Tableau original de la Galerie de Söder appartenant à Mr. le Pr. de Brabeck . . ." (see Slive 2001, fig. 97a). The title given to the work on the print did not stick; the Louvre's celebrated mountainscape (cat. 53) acquired it as early as 1804 and has been known as "Le Coup de Soleil" since then.

When Thoré-Bürger attended the Freiherr Andreas von Stolberg auction in 1859, he noted in his sale catalogue that the picture is "vrai et original" but also wrote it is "usé et dur?"; since it is neither "usé" nor "dur" his query suggests at the time the picture was either very dirty or hard to see.[1]

1. Cited in Los Angeles–Boston–New York 1981–82, p.86; however, the 1859 auction is wrongly listed as the Brabeck sale.

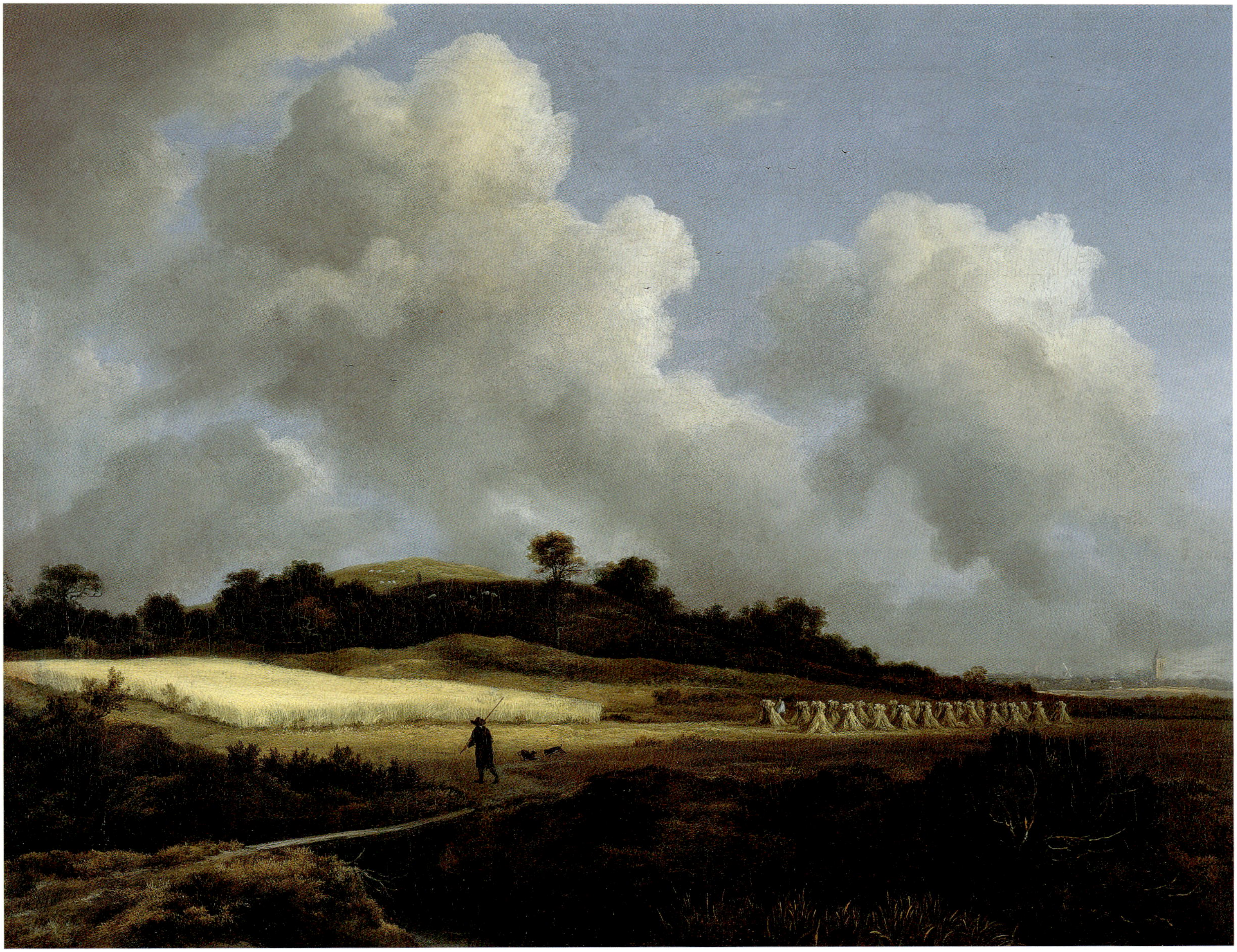

45

Extensive Landscape with a Ruined Castle and a Village Church

Signed in the water, lower right. About 1665–70. Canvas, 109 × 146 cm
The National Gallery, London, NG990

PROVENANCE: Sale, Jan Gildemeester, Amsterdam (v.d. Schley), 11 *sqq*. June 1800, no. 190 ("Vue en Gooiland"; Dfl.315, Thys); Marquis de Marialva, Paris, who died in 1823; bought privately by John Smith, apparently in 1825; sale, John Smith, London (Stanley), 2–3 May 1828, no. 78 (£472.10, Richard Abraham);[1] sale, Richard Abraham, London (Phillips), 28 June 1831, no. 69 (275gns.); Richard Sanderson, London, by 1835; his sale, London (Christie's), 17 June 1848, no. 23 (480gns., Brown); Wynn Ellis, London, by 1851; Wynn Ellis Bequest, 1876.

EXHIBITIONS: New York 1830, no. 2; London 1947–48, no. 75; London 1976, no. 98, repr.; The Hague–Cambridge 1981–82, no. 43, repr.

LITERATURE: Smith 214; Waagen 1838, 2 (English edition), p.399 (seen in the Richard Sanderson collection; described as the finest picture of this kind that he knew; figures by Adriaen van de Velde); Waagen 1854, 2, pp.288–89, 296–97 (MacLaren [1960, pp.364–65] notes that Waagen confused the provenance of the painting when he described it twice. He listed it in the Wynn Ellis Collection [pp.296–97] and again in the Richard Sanderson collection [pp.288–89]. Waagen's latter entry is incorrect. He rightly described the painting as in the Sanderson collection in *Works of Art and Artists in England*, 1838, 2, p.399 [the reference is cited above], and repeated this description in his 1854 volume in the erroneous belief that the painting was still there. The confusion was compounded by an erroneous entry in the provisional catalogue of the 1857 Manchester exhibition, which states that the picture was in the exhibition, lent by Sanderson. MacLaren has shown that it was not.); Bürger 1865, p.296 (Bürger's reference is erroneous; see MacLaren 1960, pp.364–65, note 20, which shows that Bürger was doubtless misled by the mistaken entry in the provisional Manchester catalogue); HdG 136, identical with HdG 758 (view of Beverwijk?) and HdG 844d; *Ruysdael, Original-Abbildung* [1920?], repr. (Landscape of a Wooded Region); Ros 24 (view of Beverwijk); Simon 1930, p.73; MacLaren 1960, pp.361–65, no. 990 (not a view of Beverwijk); Burke 1974, pp.8–9 (view of Beverwijk); MacLaren and Brown 1991, pp.387–90; Walsh 1991, p.103; Davies 1992, pp.62, 122, 135, 141, repr.; Slive 2001, no. 44, repr.

In this grandiose panorama the large cloud formations, which broaden and expand the view, appear as palpable as the landscape's firm tracts of land. Its heroic mood and strong chiaroscuro effect suggest it was painted about 1665–70. The two shepherds and the animals in the left foreground are by Adriaen van de Velde, whose death in January 1672 provides a *terminus ante quem* for the picture.

Several of Ruisdael's paintings appear to show the same vast plain, or part of it, from an elevated height. In the earlier literature they, and the present picture, have been described variously as views of Haarlem, or as views of Beverwijk, a small village which lies about twelve kilometres north of Haarlem. However, as MacLaren (1960) observed, the prominent church, which provides an important accent for the structure of the National Gallery picture and which figures in related paintings, is not compatible with the seventeenth-century appearance of St. Bavo at Haarlem or St. Agatha at Beverwijk. Thus, these paintings are views of neither Haarlem nor Beverwijk. Most probably they are invented sites.

An aspect of the present painting's history merits an additional word. It was exhibited by Richard Abraham (also called Abrams), along with a mixed lot of more than fifty old master originals and copies, at New York's American Academy of Fine Arts in March 1830; a catalogue accompanied the exhibition. There are only a few earlier references to Ruisdael's paintings in America. For example, according to the 1823 manuscript catalogue of the Baltimore collection of Robert Gilmor a "View of Haarlem, with a village + bleachground" by Ruisdael was in his possession; he acquired the painting in London in 1818.[2] Three Ruisdaels are also listed in a catalogue of pictures exhibited at the Boston Atheneum in 1827, and others were shown there in 1828 and 1829.[3] But these paintings as well as Gilmor's are untraceable and the reliability of their attributions is uncertain. Until an earlier reference to an identifiable work by Ruisdael is discovered, Richard Abraham can be credited with bringing the first work by the artist to the United States.

In 1834 William Dunlap (*History of the Rise and Progress of the Arts and Design in the United States*, New York, 1834, 1, p.362), chronicler of early nineteenth-century events on the American art scene, rightly asserted that the Abraham collection exhibited in New York was the best old master exhibition the country had seen. The little that is known about Abraham suggests that he did not win a reputation for other laudable deeds. Dunlap wrote:

> This man [Abrams] (as I was informed by an intelligent English gentleman, an amateur painter) was a picture dealer and cleaner in London; and having, in conjunction with another dealer, of the name of Wilmot, collected a number of good pictures, under various pretences, they concerted the scheme of flying with them to New York. Here they were stopped, and Abrams imprisoned. Wilmot, under the name of Ward, escaped the catchpoles, and embarked for Liverpool in the same vessel with my informant; and contrived, by cards and betting with the passengers, to gain upwards of three hundred guineas. On his arrival he was recognized before he could reach the great hiding place, London, and seized by those he had defrauded. Abrams made some compromise, by which he was permitted to exhibit the pictures for the benefit of the proprietors; and he did it adroitly, with an impudence worthy of a picture dealer.

By 28 June 1831 Ruisdael's landscape along with other works in Abraham's collection had been returned to London and auctioned. We can only conjecture what

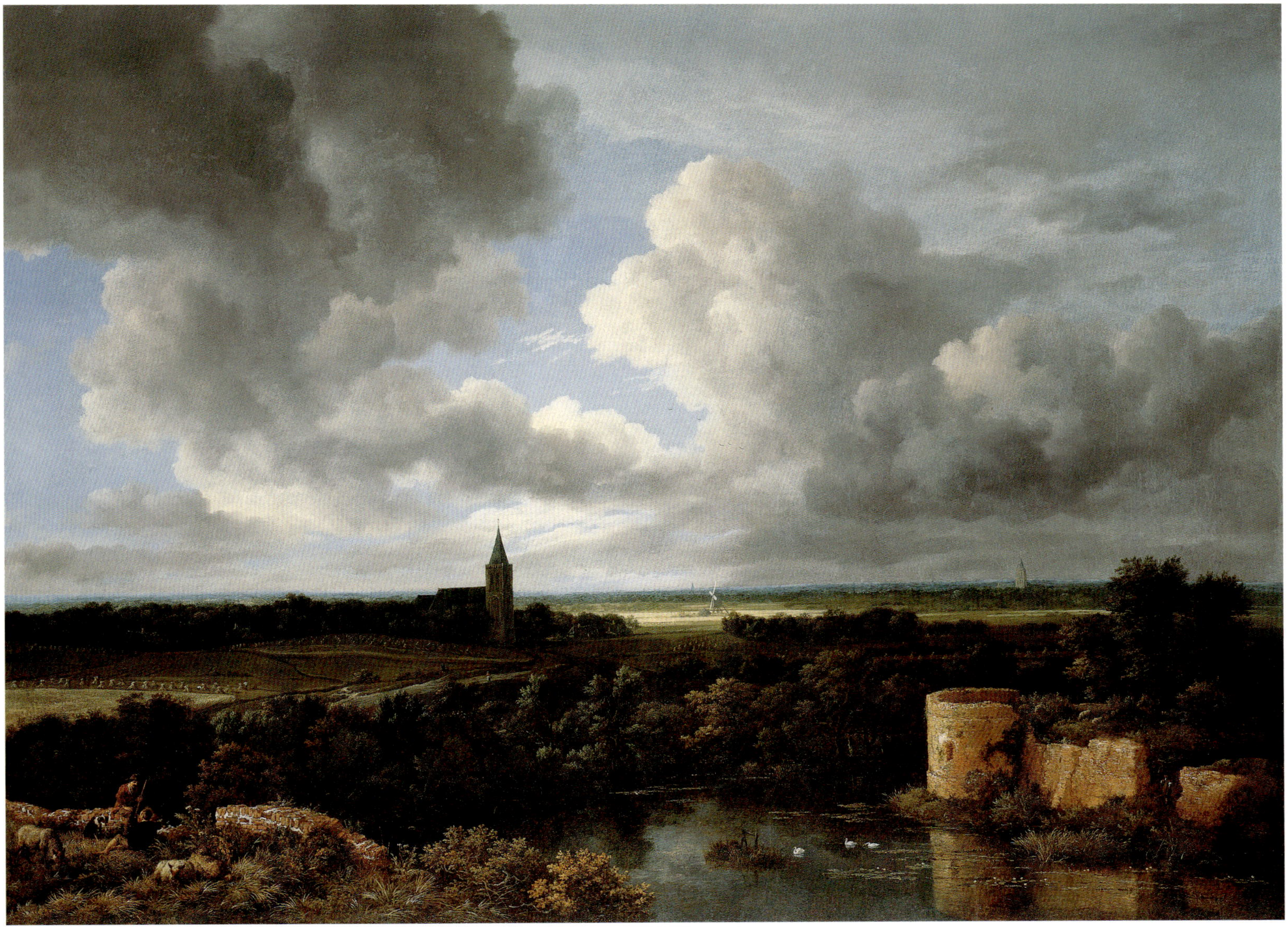

effect the noble picture would have had on American landscape painters if it had remained in the United States. However, we do know that when the American portraitist Thomas Sully (1783–1872) made brief notes on Abraham's collection in May 1830, he did not find Ruisdael's landscape worthy of notice (Dunlap 1834, 2, p.280). In Sully's opinion the best picture in the collection was a Murillo (no. 9); it is identical with a painting variously called *Four Figures on a Step*, *A Family Group* or *Group of Peasants*, which was acquired by The Kimbell Art Museum, Fort Worth, in 1984.[4] The only other paintings Sully cites are "a fine copy of Correggio's Magdelene" (no Correggio was exhibited; there was however a *Magdelene* attributed to Titian [no. 18]), a portrait by Velázquez which he called doubtful (no. 4), a Hobbema (there were two, nos. 10 and 13; the former is *The Water Mill*, now at Brussels; HdG, Hobbema, 155; Broulhiet 12; the latter was catalogued as a copy), and finally, a landscape which Sully wrote is "said to be by Claude" (no. 48; it is Claude's *Landscape with a Piping Shepherd* now in The Nelson-Atkins Museum of Art, Kansas City, no. 31–57).

1. MacLaren and Brown 1991, p.390, note 16, signal a nearly contemporary manuscript annotation in the copy of the Abraham 1831 sale catalogue in the RKD which states the picture belonged formerly to Marialva "& Mr Smith in whose Coll^{n} it was bo^{t} by Mr Abrahams for 420^{Gs} now in the Possession of Richd Sanderson Esqr sold by Mr Smith for 300£".
2. Gilmor purchased it at the sale, Robert Norman a.o., London (Christie's), 25 April 1818, no. 110 ("A View of a City in Holland with a Village, a bleaching ground and figures in the front, with a clean and brilliant sky – pure and very fine"; 70gns.). According to Gilmor's catalogue, it was on canvas, and measured 27 × 22 inches. EXHIBITIONS: Peale's Baltimore Museum, 1823, no. 53; Boston Athenaeum, 1828, no. 68. I am indebted to L. Humphries (private communication) for signalling Gilmor's Ruisdael and some of the data cited about it here.
3. *The Boston Athenaeum Art Exhibition Index: 1827–1874*, ed., Robert F. Perkins and William J. Gavin III, Boston, 1980, p.123. One of the pictures attributed to Ruisdael that was exhibited at the Atheneum was Gilmor's "View of Haarlem"; see note 2 above.
4. There is general agreement that the painting has some erotic overtones, but there is no consensus about their meaning; see *Bartolomé Esteban Murillo (1617–1682). Paintings from American Collections*, Kimbell Art Museum, Fort Worth–Los Angeles County Museum of Art, 2002, no. 31, repr. (cat. by Suzanne L. Stratton-Pruitt).

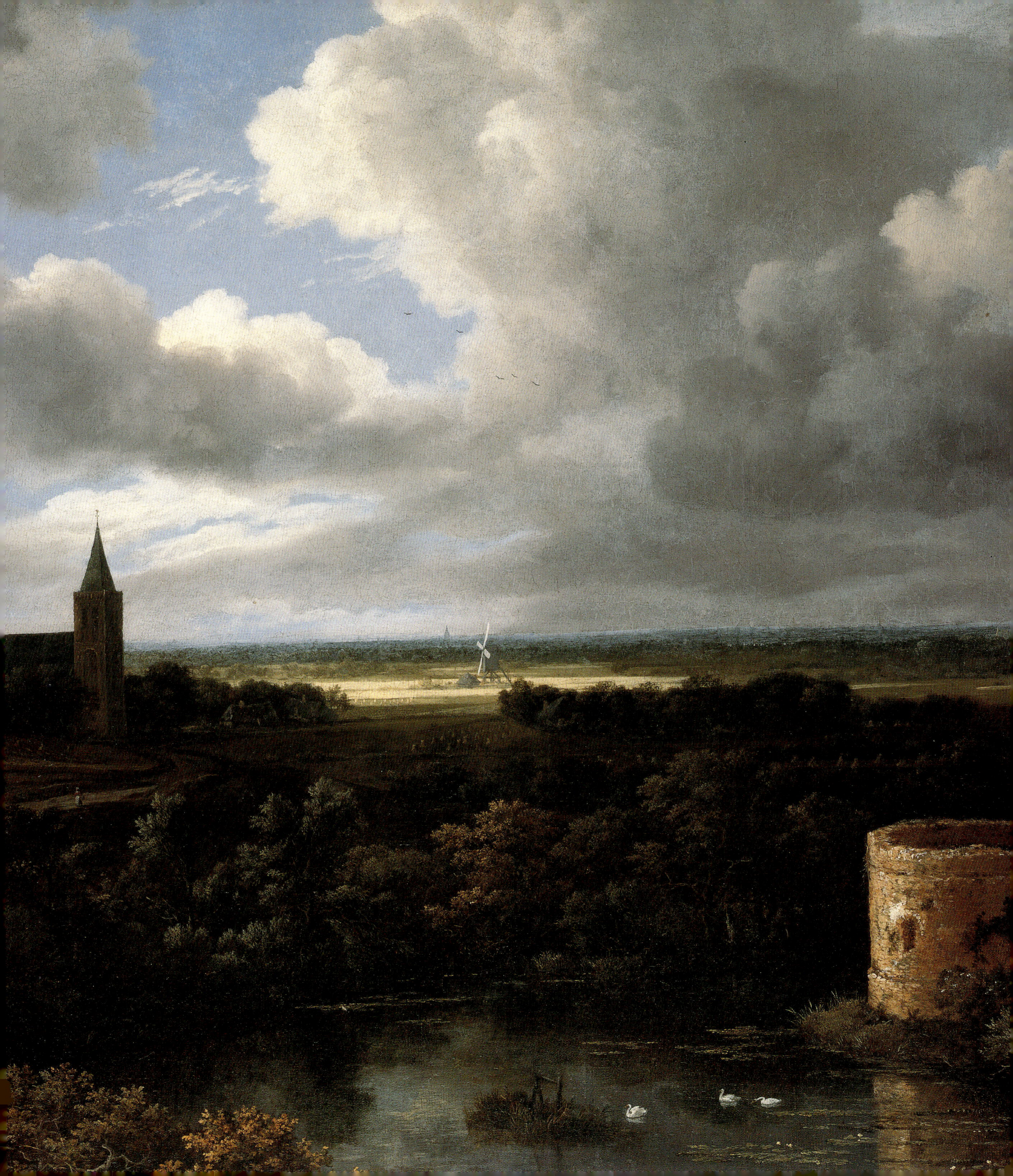

46

View of the Plain of Haarlem with Bleaching Grounds

Signed, lower left. Early 1660s. Canvas, 36.2 × 45 cm
Private collection

PROVENANCE: Earl of Beverly, London, by 1842; sold by him with his collection *en bloc* to J. M. and S. M. Smith, 7 June 1851; Thomas Baring, London, 1851, who bequeathed it to his nephew The Earl of Northbrook, London; hence by descent to Earls of Northbrook; dealer S. C. Dickinson, London, who sold it to the present owner in 2002.

EXHIBITIONS: London, Royal Academy, Winter Exhibition, 1872, no. 205; Winchester, Winchester College, *Exhibition of Old Masters from the Hampshire Houses*, 23 June–13 July 1938, no. 69.

LITERATURE: Smith, Suppl. no. 7; Waagen 1857, 4, p.99; Northbrook Collection, London, Catalogue, 1889, no. 93; HdG 72; Ros 56 (*c*.1660); Burke 1974, pp.7–8, 10, repr. (near 1660; St. Bavo seen from north-northwest); Biesboer 1995, p.38; Slive 2001, no. 46, repr.

The emphatic horizontal layout, the relative lack of articulation into depth on the left (the ruins of Huis ter Kleef are barely perceptible in the distance), and the thick grainy paint place the excellently preserved picture in the early sixties. In this view Ruisdael has taken more than usual delight in the patterns created on the bleaching grounds by the long strips of linen and smaller pieces of it.

With the aid of a watercolour map made by the surveyor Pieter Wils in 1643, Biesboer established that the bleaching operation De Mol near the village of Bloemendaal is depicted.[1] Its lyeing house, dairy, living quarters, and stables are on the left; its characteristic half-round bleaching field is near the end of the grounds on the right. In the distance to the left, the roof and two chimneys of the country house Hartelust can be discerned. It was built by Michiel de Wael, who owned the bleaching fields around it from 1631 to 1652. For reference to other depictions by Ruisdael of the site and Frans Hals's portraits of de Wael see cat. 47.

1. Biesboer 1995, pp.38, 288, fig. 6.

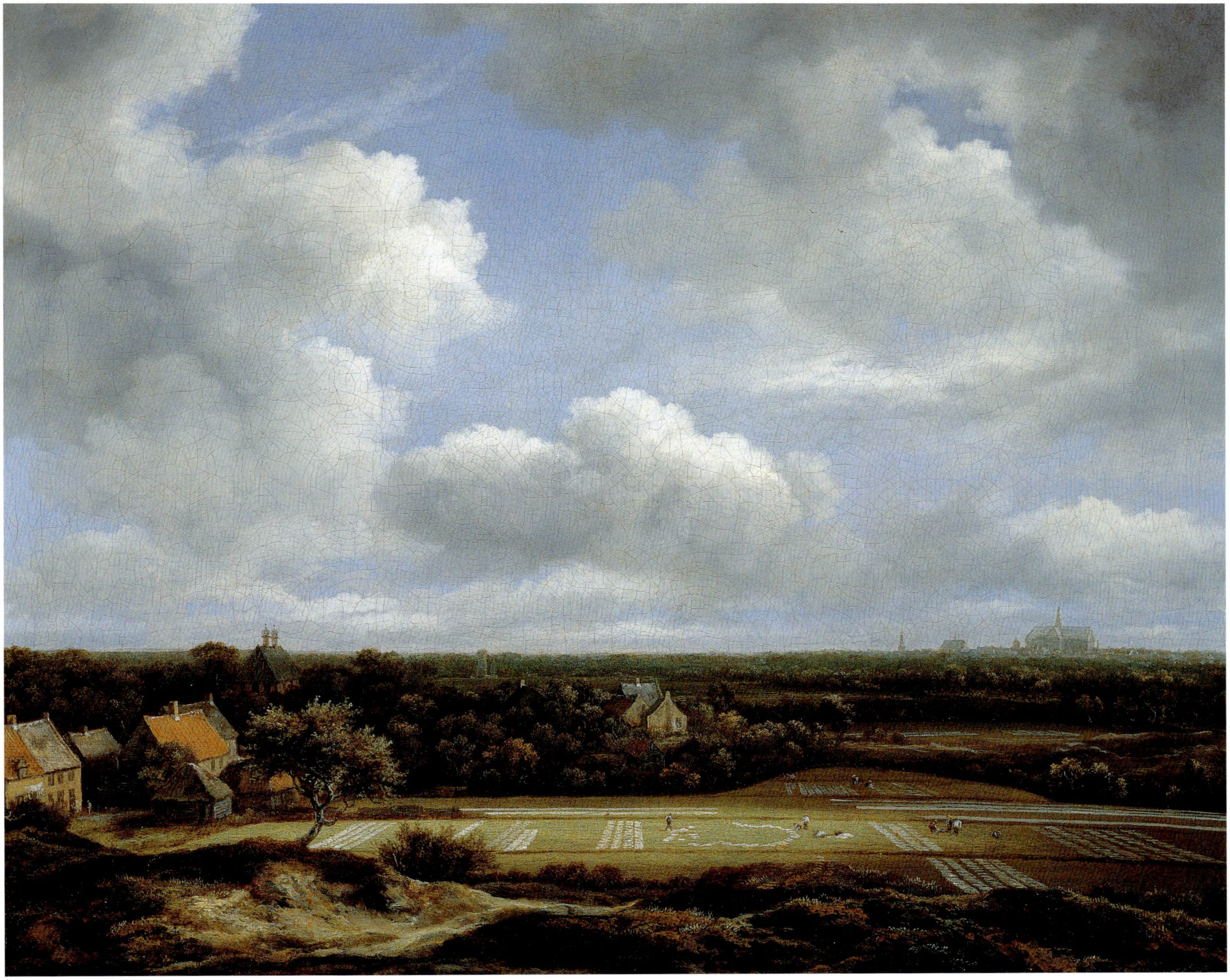

47

View of the Dunes near Bloemendaal with Bleaching Fields

Signed, lower left. Late 1660s. Canvas, 52 × 65.2 cm
Private collection

PROVENANCE: Sale, Evrad Rhoné, Paris (Drouot), 6 May 1861, no. 51 (fr.1950); sale, Galerie Péreire, Paris (Petit), 6 March 1872, no. 151 (fr.5550); Marquis du Blaisel, Paris; sale, Prince Demidoff, San Donato, 15 March 1880, no. 1034; dealer C. Sedelmeyer, Paris, *Catalogue of 300 Paintings*, 1898, no. 184, repr.; collection Rodolphe Kann, Paris, Catalogue, 1907, no. 77, repr.; bought *en bloc* by Duveen Brothers, London, in August 1907; Duveen Brothers, Paris; William Berg; Louis Kaplan, New York, by 1950; dealer L. Koetser, London, Catalogue, Autumn 1962, no. 12; sale, anon., London (Christie's), 23 March 1973, no. 76 (55,000gns., Brod); dealer A. Brod, London.

EXHIBITIONS: London, Royal Academy, Winter Exhibition, 1908, no. 42 (lent by Duveen Brothers); New York 1985, no. 12, repr.; New York 1988, no. 43.

LITERATURE: HdG 75 (bleaching fields of Overveen with Haarlem in the distance); Ros 64 (bleaching fields of Overveen); W. R. Valentiner and P. Wescher, *A Catalogue of Paintings in the Collection of Louis and Mildred Kaplan*, New York, 1950, unpaginated (bleaching grounds of Overveen near Haarlem); Gaskell 1990, p.384, note 9; Davies 1992, pp.68, note 12, 143, under no. 39; Biesboer 1995, pp.37–38; Slive 2001, no. 55, repr.

Etched by Leopold Lowenstam (also called Loewenstam; 1842–98).

Fig. 47a Frans Hals, Captain Michiel de Wael, detail from *Banquet of the Officers of the St. George Civic Guard*, c. 1627. Frans Hals Museum, Haarlem.

Datable to the late sixties. A smaller, less well preserved version of the composition is at Hartford and an extensively damaged variant of it is in the Museo Thyssen-Bornemisza, Madrid (Slive 2001, nos. 41, 50, respectively). Pieter Biesboer (1995) advanced knowledge of Ruisdael as a topographical artist by observing that in all three paintings, in addition to Bloemendaal's church, between the trees in the middle ground, a roof with two large chimneys is visible; they form part of Hartelust, a country house built by Michiel de Wael who owned the nearby bleaching fields from 1631 to 1652. Frans Hals portrayed de Wael as the liveliest man in his *Banquet of the Officers of the St. George Civic Guards*, *c.*1627 (fig. 47a); he appears again in Hals's group portrait of *Officers and Sergeants of the St. George Civic Guards* of *c.*1639.[1]

The bleaching field on the far right of the bleaching grounds in each of the three paintings has an unusual rounded shape which Biesboer observed was part of the De Mol bleaching operation that is identifiable on a map dated 1637; according to the map's inscription these fields flanked the Bloemendaalse Weg which makes a slight turn as it follows them.[2] The map shows the five parallel bleaching fields followed by the above-mentioned semi-circular field, all separated by small canals that are also visible in the three paintings. Beyond the fields on the left are the buildings of the bleachery: the lyeing house, dairy, living quarters and stable.

Another Ruisdael painting of the De Mol bleachery from a different vantage point, in another private collection, is also in the exhibition (cat. 46).

1. Slive 1970–74, 3, nos. 46 and 124.2.
2. Biesboer 1995, pp.37–38.

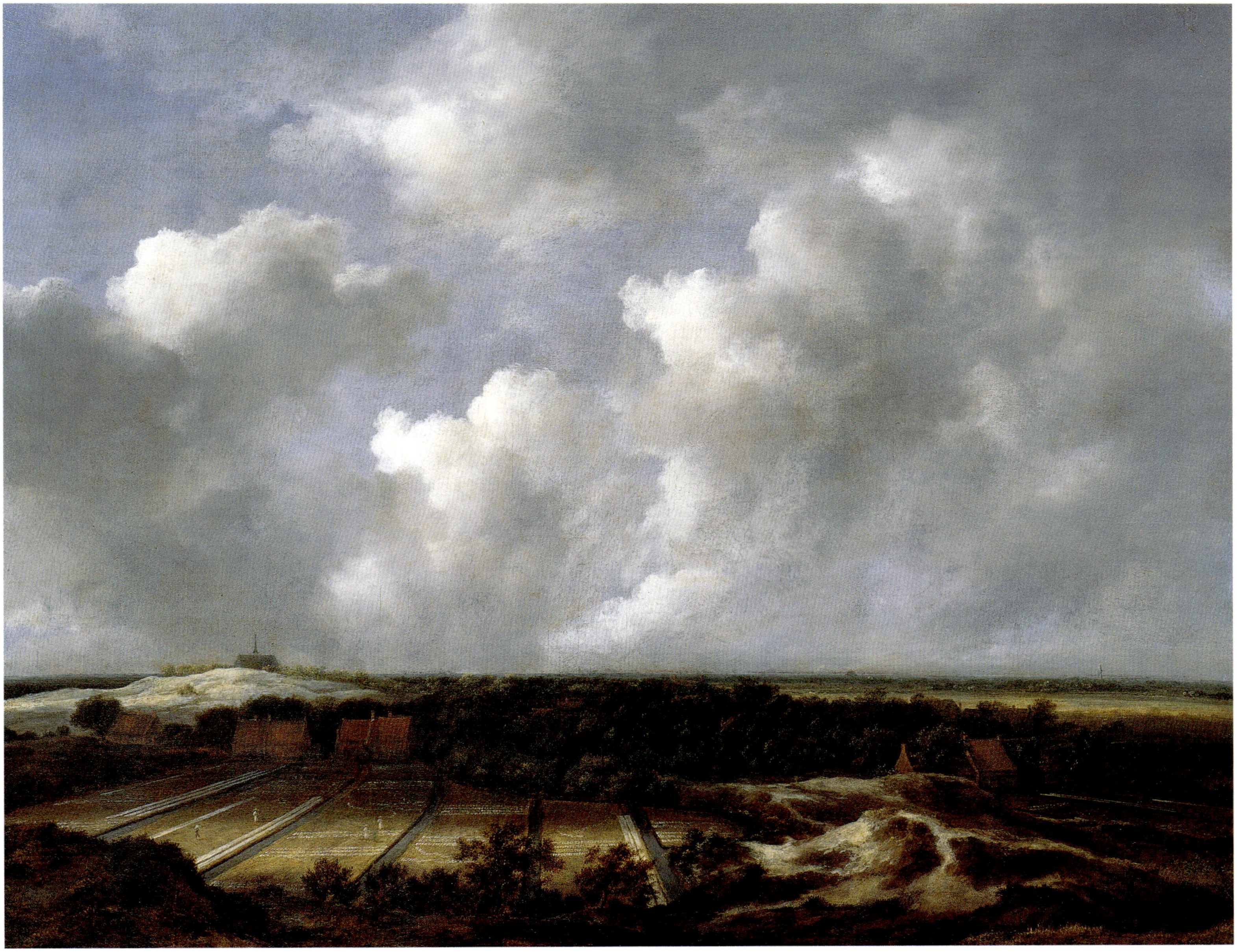

48

View of Haarlem with Bleaching Grounds

Signed, lower right. Early 1670s. Canvas, 55.5 × 62 cm
Royal Cabinet of Paintings Mauritshuis, The Hague, 155

PROVENANCE: Sale, Samuel Beyerman, Gouda (Boon), 21 April 1778, no. 3 (Lokhorst); Gerrit Muller, Amsterdam, by 1822; his sale, Amsterdam (de Vries and Roos), 2 April 1827, no. 59 (Dfl.6700, J. de Vries); purchased in 1827.

EXHIBITIONS: London 1929, no. 176; Amsterdam 1945, no. 98; Brussels–Antwerp 1946, no. 92, repr.; Eindhoven 1948, no. 58a; San Francisco–Toledo–Boston 1966–67, no. 57, repr.; Tokyo–Kyoto 1968–69, no. 54, repr.; The Hague–Cambridge 1981–82, no. 44, repr.; Washington–Fort Worth–Chicago–Los Angeles 1982–83, no. 30, repr.

LITERATURE: Josi 1821, 2, [n.p.] under "Jacob Ruisdael"; Ellis 1826, p.71 ("a curious bird's-eye 'View of Haarlem'" seen in Muller's collection, Amsterdam, 1822); *Les Principaux Tableaux du Musée Royal à la Haye*, Part 3, 1829, pp.24–25, no. 64; Smith 220; Bürger 1858, 1, pp.270–71; Gower 1875, p.34 ("a marvel of space on a small scale . . ."); HdG 65, identical with HdG 79m; *Ruysdael, Original-Abbildung* [1920?], repr.; Ros 48; Simon 1930, pp.49–52; Stechow 1966, p.47; Wiegand 1971, pp.99–106; Fuchs 1973, pp.284–85; Burke 1974, p.10 (St. Bavo seen from the north northwest); Mauritshuis, Catalogue, 1977, p.210, no. 155 (after *c.*1670); *Mauritshuis, Landschappen 17de eeuw*, Catalogue, 1980, pp.90–92 (*c.*1670–75); Slive 1982, p.128, repr.; Hoetink *et al.* 1985, pp.282–83, repr.; Broos 1987, pp.330–37, no. 55, repr.; Davies 1992, pp.67–69, 132, under no. 23, repr.; Mauritshuis, Catalogue, 1993, p.130, no. 155; Biesboer 1995, p.37; Slive 2001, no. 40, repr.

Engraved in outline by Frederik Lodewijk Huijgens (1802–87) in *Les Principaux Tableaux du Musée Royal à la Haye*, Part 3, 1829, facing p.24.

LACMA and PMA

This beautiful *Haarlempje* depicts the city from the northwest. Ruisdael's panorama of Haarlem and its bleaching grounds at the Rijksmuseum, Amsterdam (Slive 2001, no. 35, repr.), shows virtually the same view. Apart from its vertical format the pictorial organization of both works is similar, from the arrangement of the terrain in the foreground and the woods in the middle distance to the strong sunlight breaking through the clouds that illuminates areas of the vast plain.

Biesboer (1995) established that the bleaching operation seen in the foreground belonged for a time to Lucas de Clercq (d.1654) who was portrayed by Frans Hals in 1635[1] (fig. 48a). He also observed that in the lower left the bleachery's *droogberg* (a flattened sand dune studded with wooden stakes where linen yarn was stretched to dry) is depicted. Behind it, to the right, is the operation's lyeing house, dairy and stable, and on the right side of the painting, the roof and two chimneys, which rise above a large grove of trees, belonged to House Clercq en Beeck, a house Lucas de Clercq owned with his brother-in-law Lucas van Beeck.

Jacob's *Haarlempjes* at Berlin, Montreal and in a private collection, Scotland (Slive 2001, nos. 36, 52, 65, respectively), were inspired by the same spot. However, these works provide more extensive views and employ different compositional schemes. Instead of featuring one large series of bleaching fields grounds in the foreground Ruisdael depicts in them yet another extensive bleaching field to the left of the *droogberg*. His decision to eliminate the second bleaching ground in the Hague and Amsterdam paintings gives them a more concentrated effect, while the link he establishes in both works between the two brilliantly lit fields by keeping a wide opening in the woods gives the eye easier access to exploration of the extent of the plain and the cityscape in the far distance. These refinements suggest the Hague and Amsterdam pictures postdate the three *Haarlempjes* cited above.

The painting has been copied frequently. Among the copies one, formerly in the Cook Collection, Doughty House, Richmond, and another at the Calouste Gulbenkian Foundation, Lisbon, have been wrongly catalogued in the earlier literature as works by Ruisdael (see Slive 2001, under no. 46).

1. Amsterdam, Rijksmuseum, on loan from the City of Amsterdam, no. SK-C-556. Canvas, 126.5 × 93. Slive 1970–74, vol. 3, no. 104. The pendant to de Clercq's portrait is Hals's portrayal of his wife *Feynte van Steenkiste*, also at the Rijksmuseum, on loan from the City of Amsterdam, no. SK-C-557. Canvas, 123 × 93. *Ibid.*, no. 105, repr.

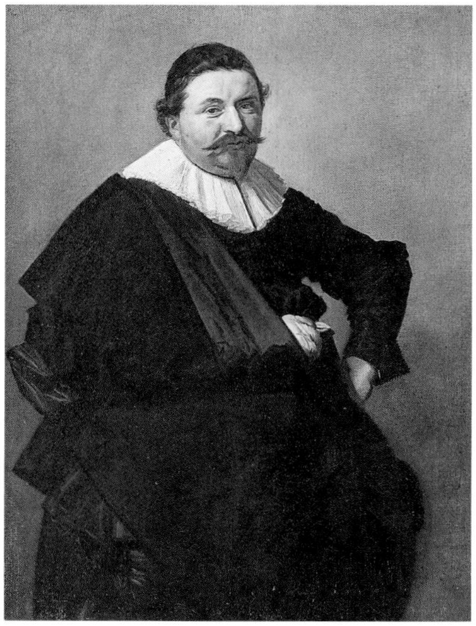

Fig. 48a Frans Hals, *Lucas de Clercq*, 1635. Rijksmuseum, Amsterdam (on extended loan from the City of Amsterdam).

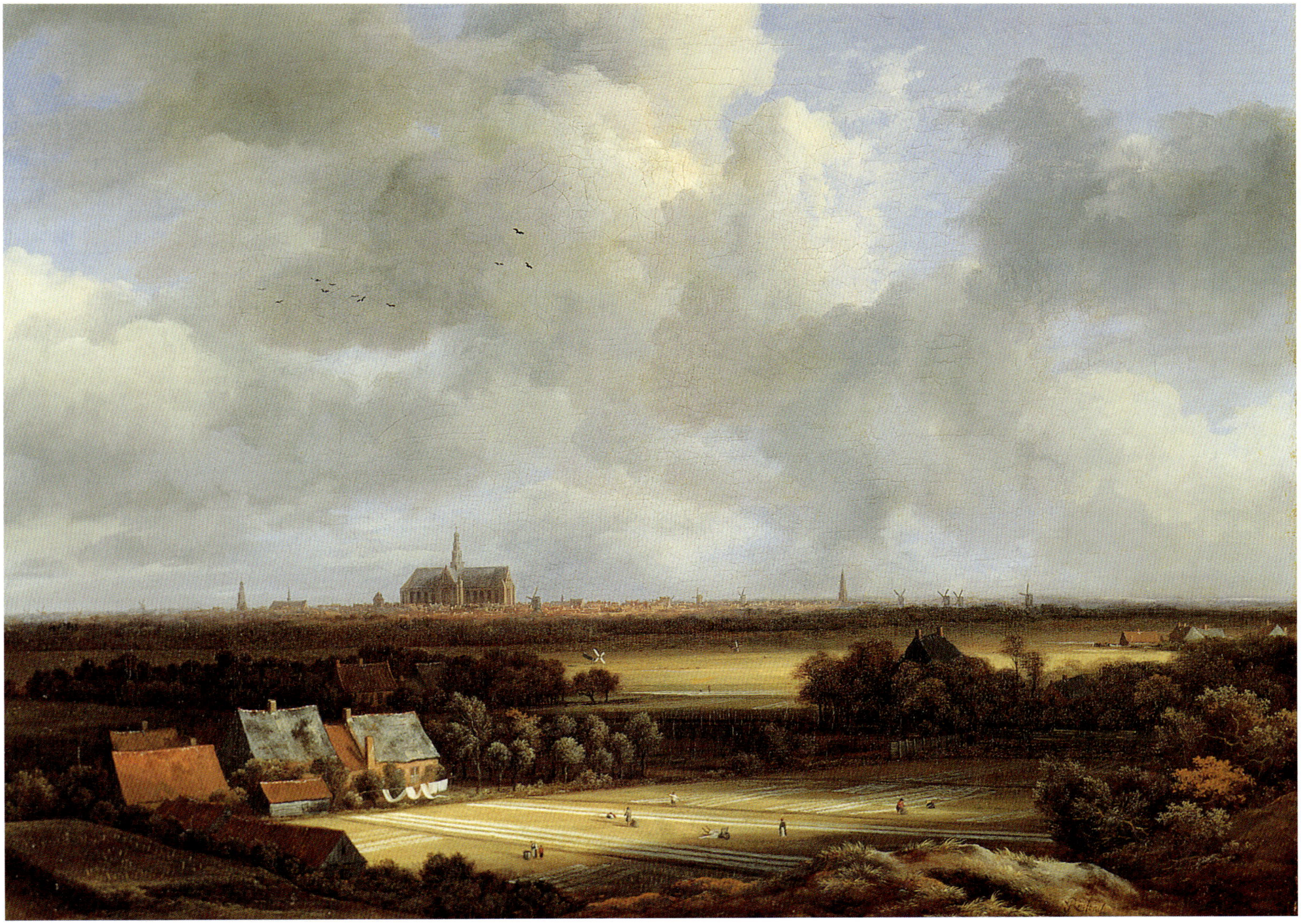

49

View of Haarlem with Bleaching Grounds

Signed, lower left. About 1670–75. Canvas, 62.2 × 55.2 cm
Kunsthaus Zürich, Stiftung Prof. Dr. L. Ruzicka, R.32

PROVENANCE: Count Sierstorpff, Schloss Driburg, by 1864; his sale, Berlin (Lepke), 19 April 1887, no. 67 (Vieweg); collection Vieweg, Braunschweig; sale, Vieweg, Berlin, 18 March 1930, no. 13, repr. (DM122,000, Cassirer); acquired for the Ruzicka collection in the Zurich art market, 1949.

EXHIBITIONS: Düsseldorf 1886, no. 288; Zurich 1949–50, no. 32, repr.; Zurich 1950, p.22; Neuchâtel 1953; Zurich 1953, no. 133; Rome 1954, no. 131; Milan 1954, no. 134; Cologne 1954, no. 23, repr.; Oslo 1959, no. 63; The Hague–Cambridge 1981–82, no. 45, repr. (shown in The Hague only); Basel 1987, no. 84, repr.; Madrid 1994–95, no. 59; Amsterdam 2000, no. 153; Hamburg–Haarlem 2002, no. 46, repr.

LITERATURE: Parthey 1864, 2, p.455, no. 5; HdG 59, identical with HdG 92; Moes 1913, p.296; Ros 44; Simon 1930, p.73; Valentiner 1930, no. 58; Stechow 1966, pp.45–47, repr.; Ruzicka Collection, Kunsthaus, Zurich, Catalogue, 1969, p.28, repr.; Burke 1974, p.10 (St. Bavo seen from the northwest); Davies 1992, pp.67, 69, 137, sub no. 29, repr.; Slive 2001, no. 70, repr.

RA

This peerless *Haarlempje* reaches an unparalleled degree of openness and height. The firm cohesion of the towering aerial zone gains in mass and significance from its relation to the diminutive forms on the extensive plain. Here the eye can explore, more than in Ruisdael's other views of Haarlem, the vast expanse of land richly differentiated by the gradation of alternating bands of light and shadow into the distance toward a horizon stretched taut as a sinew.

If there is place on Parnassus where pre-eminent Polish poets meet the best Dutch artists, Ruisdael will surely manage to tell Wisława Szymborska that he too believes, and in his paintings repeatedly tried to show, that it is in the nature of clouds:

> [...] never to repeat
> shapes, hues, poses and formations.
>
> Unburdened by the memory of anything,
> they float effortlessly above the facts.[1]

1. From "Clouds" in *Miracle Fair: Selected poems of Wisława Szymborska*, trans. by Joanna Trzeciak, New York–London, 2001.

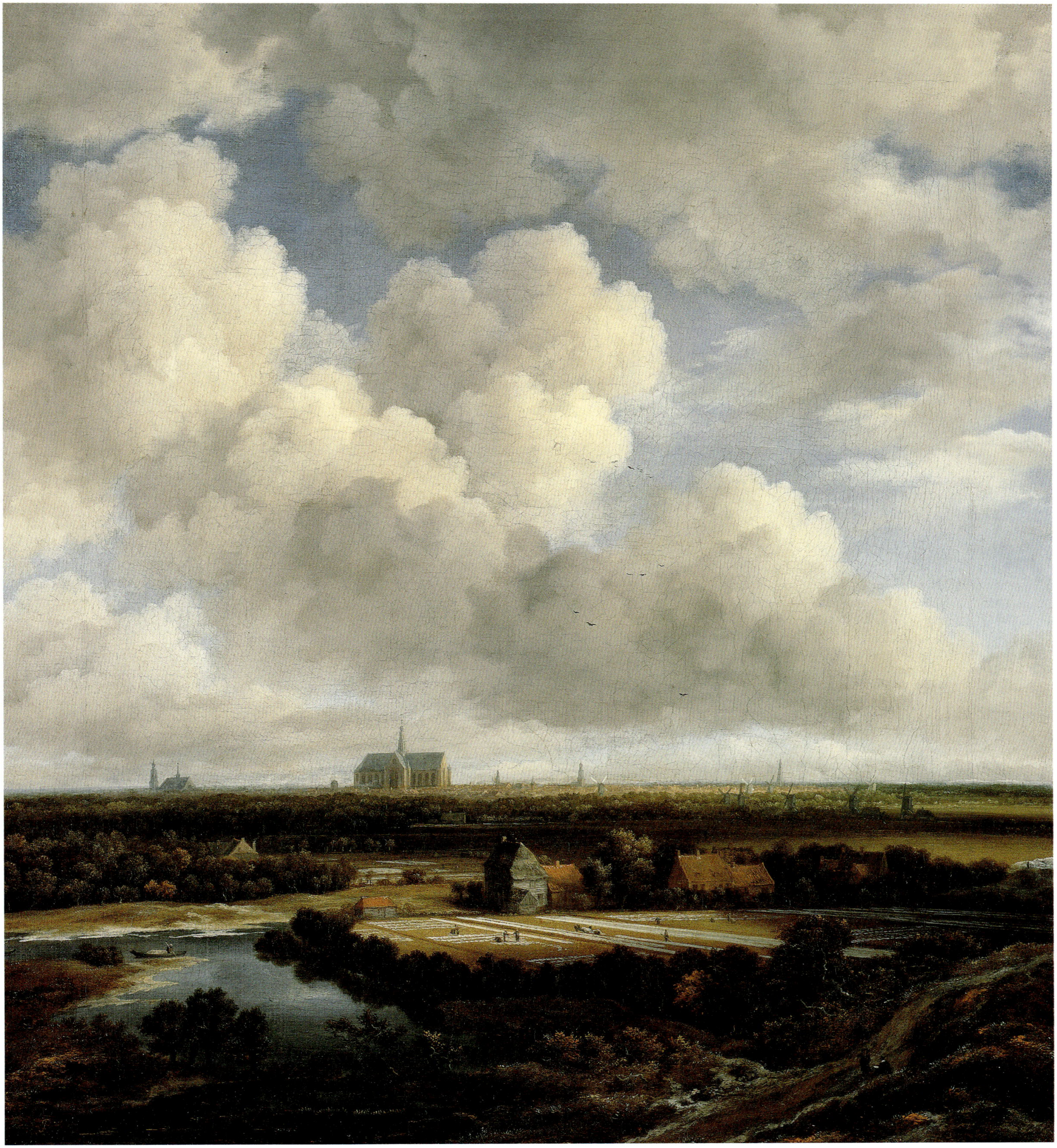

50

View of the Ruins of Huis ter Kleef and Haarlem

Signed, lower left. Second half of the 1670s. Canvas, 40 × 40 cm
Musée Jacquemart-André, Institut de France, Paris, 416

PROVENANCE: Collection Papin; sale, R. Papin, Paris (Drouot), 28 March 1873, no. 28 (as The Ruins of the Castle of Brederode near Haarlem; fr.25,000); sale, Prince Demidoff, San Donato near Florence, 15 March 1880, no. 1113; Edouard André; Madame Jacquemart-André, Paris, who bequeathed it to the Institut de France, 1912.

EXHIBITIONS: Paris 1911, no. 133; *Treasures of Musée Jacquemart-André*, Wildenstein Gallery, New York, 1956, no. 21.

LITERATURE: Martin 1911, p.506 (ruins of Brederode); HdG 76, identical with HdG 43 (ruins of Brederode); Moes 1913, p.295; Ros 60; Simon 1930, p.73; Musée Jacquemart-André, Paris, Catalogue, 8th ed., n.d., p.36, no. 416; Burke 1974, pp.9–10, repr. (St. Bavo seen from the northwest); Biesboer 1995, p.37; Slive 2001, no. 59, repr.

LACMA and PMA

The painting's powerful chiaroscuro effect makes it Ruisdael's most dramatic panoramic view of Haarlem's plains. Its exactly square format, a shape the artist hardly ever uses, also distinguishes the picture.

Haarlem's skyline can be identified on the horizon at the extreme right. Much more prominent are the ruins in the middle ground of the brightly lit plain. They are the remains of Huis ter Kleef, a castle north of Haarlem that must have been familiar to every citizen of the city. It served as the headquarters of Don Frederick de Toledo, the Spanish commander who finally managed to take Haarlem after conducting a devastating seven-month seige of the city in 1572–73. The Spanish destroyed the castle in 1573. It was partially restored in 1634 but in effect it remained a conspicuous ruin; only remnants of it are visible today.[1]

Biesboer (1995) notes that the two rows of trees to the right of the ruins flank the Kleverlaan and the small windmill to the left of the ruins was once situated on the Heussenvaart. Sharp eyes can also discern the ruins near the horizon, centre left, in Ruisdael's *View of the Plain of Haarlem with Bleaching Grounds*, now in a private collection (cat. 46). The ruins also figure in other works by and attributed to the artist.[2] Pioneer seventeenth-century landscapists who first depicted specific sites in the Dutch countryside respresented ter Kleef's ruins from various points of view.[3] After this first burst of interest in them, the remains did not attract much attention.[4]

1. For the castle's history see J. W. Groesbeek, *Huis ter Kleef, Serie Nederlandse Kastelen*, 29, 1977, and Groesbeek 1981, pp.23–27.
2. For example, ter Kleef's ruins, trees and some of the houses seen in the present picture appear on the left side of Jacob's *Haarlempje* in Montreal (Slive 2001, no. 52). The ruins and small windmill to their left in the painting also are apparent in the problematic view of the city formerly in the collection of the heirs of Ernest G. Rathenau and Ellen Rathenau Ettlinger (Slive 2001, no. dub20).
3. Claes Jansz Visscher included them in a print that belongs to a series of "Pleasant Places" near Haarlem published about 1611 (Simon 1958, no. 138). For Jan van de Velde's drawing of the ruins, datable *c.*1618-20, at the Teyler Museum, see Slive 2001, fig. 71a. Jan van de Velde also made prints of their appearance after his own designs (Franken and van der Kellen 1883, nos. 199, 228) and produced a print of them after a drawing by Pieter Saenredam that is included in Samuel Ampzing's *Beschryvinge ende lof der Stad Haerlem*, 1628 (Franken and van der Kellen 1883, no. 483). They also play a prominent role in his print of a *Large View of Haarlem* done after a drawing by Pieter de Molyn, 1621 (*ibid.*, no. 202–04; see Slive 2001, p. 52, fig. Haarlem d). Willem Buytewech devotes a print to the ruins in his series of "Various Landscapes" made about 1616 (Haverkamp Begemann 1959, p.174, no. vG 23).
4. To my knowledge the ruins are not included in any of Jan Vermeer II van Haarlem's panoramic views of the city. Jan van Kessel gave them a tiny place in his *Bleaching Grounds near Haarlem* now at Brussels (no. 3926; Slive 2001, p. 78, fig. 52a). The ruins are included in a few drawings that appear to have been done *naer het leven*: *e.g.*, an extensive view of the plains near Haarlem ascribed by van Regteren Altena (1954, p.4, repr.) to Willem Schellinks; but also attributable to Jan Baptist Weenix, and a signed drawing of the same subject by Willem's brother Daniel Schellinks; both sheets are at the Municipal Archives, Haarlem, inv. nos. Atlas 36/30, 36/31, respectively. A drawing by Vincent Laurensz van der Vinne, dated 11 April 1678, that concentrates on the ruins also is in Haarlem's archives, no. 4956.

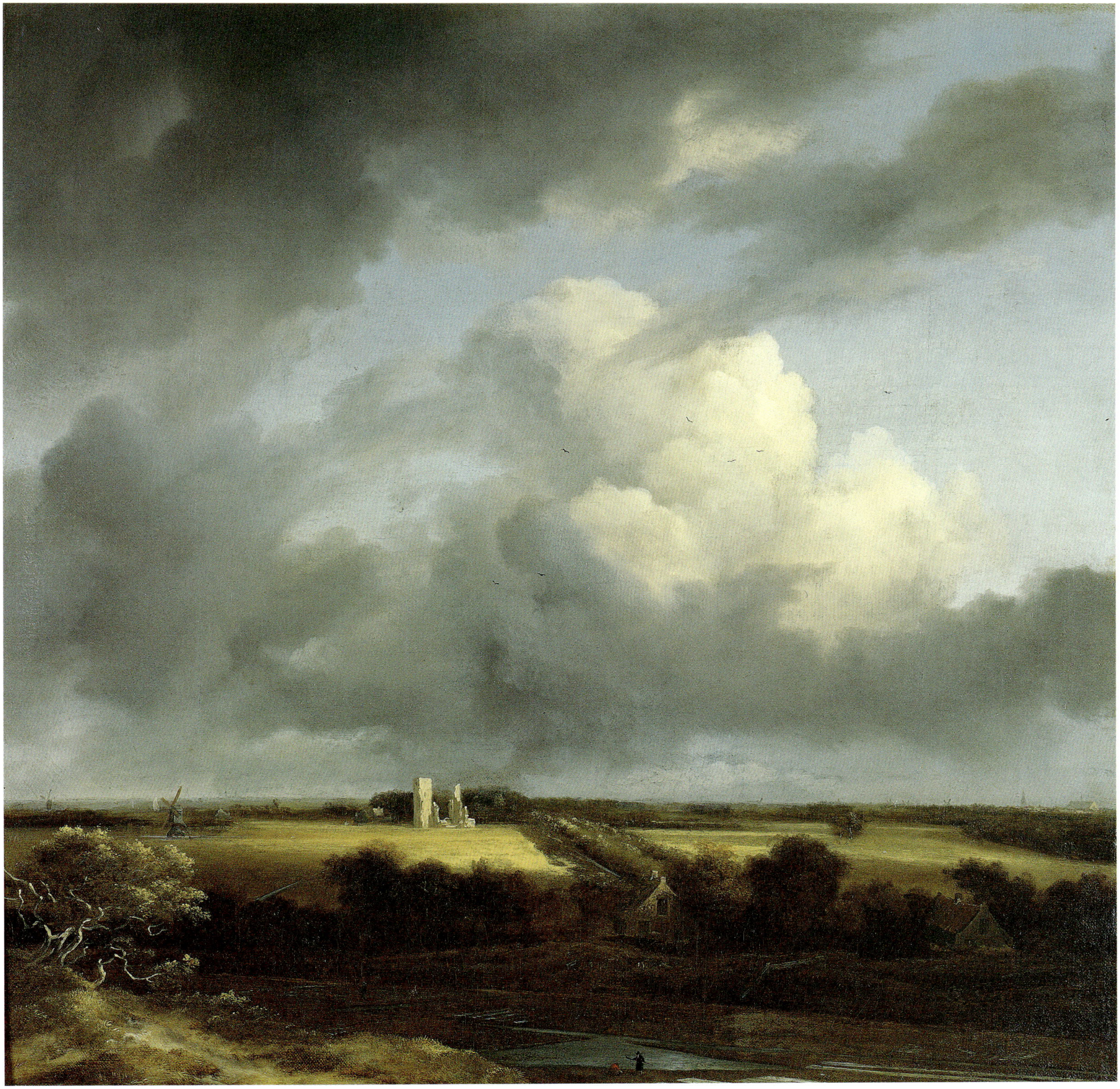

51

Vessels in a Choppy Sea

Signed, lower left. About 1670. Canvas, 107.1 × 125.8 cm
Museum of Fine Arts, Boston. William Francis Warden Fund, 57.4

PROVENANCE: Said by Waagen (1854) to have been discovered in Holstein by the Hamburg dealer Harzen; Edmund Forster; Richard Forster of Clewer Manor, Clewer Park; his sale, London (Christie's), 13 July 1895, no. 70 (£4410, Colnaghi); Sir Alfred Beit, London; dealer Duits Ltd., London; dealers Rudolf Heinemann, New York, and Th. Agnew, London, 1956; acquired by the museum in 1957.

EXHIBITIONS: Manchester 1857, no. 958; London, Royal Academy, Winter Exhibition, 1908, no. 57; London 1929, no. 100, repr.; San Francisco–Toledo–Boston 1966–67, no. 76, repr.; The Hague–Cambridge 1981–82, no. 48, repr.; Tokyo–Fukuoka–Kyoto 1983–84, no. 16, repr.; Minneapolis–Toledo–Los Angeles 1990–91, no. 25, repr.; Madrid 1994–95, no. 57, repr.

LITERATURE: Waagen 1854, 2, p.452; Bürger 1865, p.296; HdG 957 (about 1660); Bode 1913, no. 51, repr.; Ros 591; J. Rosenberg, "A Seascape by Jacob van Ruisdael," *Bulletin, Museum of Fine Arts, Boston*, 56, 1958, pp.145f.; Stechow 1966, p.122, repr.; Murphy 1985, p.255, repr.; Walford 1991, pp.154–55, note 16 (1660–65), repr.; Slive 2001, no. 646, repr.

The major accent in this great marine is the dark hull of the foremost boat and its white, sunlit sail seen against grey clouds, but equally impressive is the treatment of the foaming, feathery waves lapping against the ancient pilings and the atmospheric drama of the mighty sky. The great wealth of contrasts and the richly articulated differentiation of space in the seascape suggest that it was painted about 1670. As in his panoramic views of the extensive plains near Haarlem datable about the same time, Ruisdael provides the eye with subtle points of reference leading from the foreground to the middle and far distance.

Hofstede de Groot (957) wrote that the seascape was painted from the same place as the *View of Het IJ*, now at Worcester (fig. 32), but "the view is shifted more to the right; thus the town of Amsterdam is not visible." However, without the view of Amsterdam it is not possible to accept the suggestion that both seascapes were done from the same spot. Moreover, there is no reason to assume that Ruisdael painted any of his pictures out-of-doors, and the least likely candidates for this distinction are those devoted to the moods of the sky and sea.

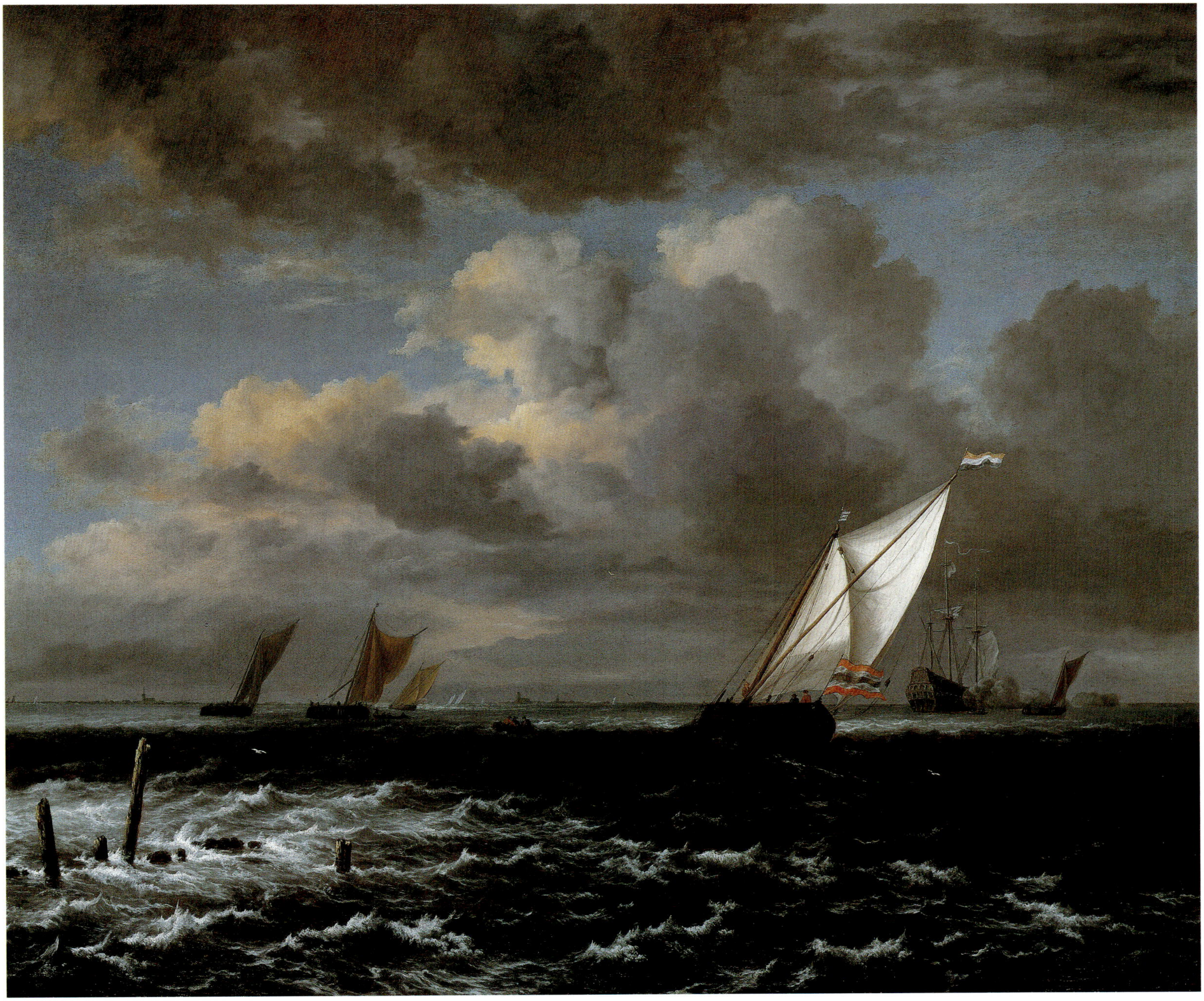

52

Beachscape with Dunes

Signed, lower left. 1670s. Canvas, 51.3 × 65.5 cm
Polesden Lacey, The McEwan Collection, The National Trust, POL.P.53

PROVENANCE: Sale, Duc de Choiseul, Paris (Boileau), 6 *sqq.* April 1772, no. 68 (fr.1701 [with the companion, no. 67], Boileau); sale, Prince de Conti, Paris (Remy), 8 *sqq.* April 1777, no. 400 (fr.2401 [with the companion], Langlier); sale, [Dulac and La Chaise], Paris (Paillet), 30 November *sqq.* 1778, no. 355 (fr. 2299 [with the companion]); Marquis de Marigny (later Marquis de Ménars, died 1781); his sale, Paris (Basan), 18 March–6 April 1782, no. 102 (fr.1851 [with the companion], Hamon); sale, B_ [of Caen], Paris (Pérignon), 3 December 1827, no. 10 (fr.2000, Delahante); Baron J. G. Verstolk van Soelen, The Hague, by 1835, whose collection was sold *en bloc* to Humphrey St. John Mildmay, Samuel Jones Loyd (later Lord Overstone) and Thomas Baring in 1846 (Chaplin acted on their behalf); this painting and its companion went to Mildmay; sale, Henry Bingham Mildmay, London (Christie's), 24 June 1893, no. 65 (£1785); bought by the Rt. Hon. E. McEwan and bequeathed by his daughter, the Hon. Mrs. Ronald Greville, London, to The National Trust in 1942.

EXHIBITIONS: London, Royal Academy, 1876, no. 164; London, The National Gallery, 1943; London 1945, no. 30, repr.; Paris 1950–51, no. 78; London 1952–53, no. 299; New York–Toledo–Toronto 1954–55, no. 72; The Hague–Cambridge 1981–82, no. 49, repr.

LITERATURE: Smith 20 ("view on the coast, with the town of Mayden [*sic*] and its berg"); Waagen 1857, 4, pp.154–55 ("view of the coast with the town of Muyden"); Weale and Richter 1889, pp.204–05; HdG 102 ("coast scene with Muiden and the Muiderberg"; described in reverse); Moes 1913, p.295 ("not Muiden; an unknown site"); Ros 572a ("beachscape supposedly with Muiden and the Muiderberg"); Polesden Lacey, Catalogue, 1955, no. 53 ("Zuiderzee Coast near Muiden"); Gore 1957, p.176; Stechow 1966, p.106; Edinburgh 1992, p.174; Edwards 1996, pp.18, 233; Slive 2001, no. 632, repr.

Engraved in reverse by an anonymous hand in Pierre François Basan, *Recueil d'estampes gravées d'après le Cabinet de Monseigneur le Duc de Choiseul*, Paris, 1771, no. 118 (see Slive 2001, fig. 632a). The wood engraving by John Quarterly (*c.*1835–67), which does not reverse the painting, may be a copy of Basan's print.

The extraordinarily beautiful beachscape has often been identified as the Zuider Zee coast with a view of Muiden and Muiderberg. Since I have been unable to spot these sites in it, I follow E.W. Moes's (1913) lead, and call the shore an unidentified one.

From the time the painting appeared in the 1772 sale of the collection of the Duc de Choiseul (1719–85) until 1893 it had the same history as Ruisdael's *Shore at Egmond aan Zee* now in the National Gallery, London (fig. 52a; Slive 2001, no. 631). On the basis of this association and their almost identical dimensions some specialists have concluded they were designed as companions. Visual evidence, however, does not make a compelling case for the hypothesis. Though both are datable to the seventies, they do not appear to have been intended as pendants. The pronounced perspective effect and the scudding clouds of the Polesden Lacey picture are not in accord with the treatment of space and aerial zone of its alleged companion. Additionally, the very small figures in the present painting are unlike the more conspicuous ones in the National Gallery picture. They do little more than provide a sense of scale to the vast panorama of sky, sea and dunes Ruisdael presents; whether they were painted by the same hand is moot.[1] Finally, auction sales of a pair of paintings as one lot do not establish that an artist intended the works as companion pieces.[2]

1. MacLaren (1960, p.365, no. 1390) writes the figures in the National Gallery picture are not by Ruisdael and seem to be by the same hand as those in the beachscape formerly in the Pannwitz collection and now in the collection of the Auroa Art Fund, New York (Slive 2001, no. 624, repr.); he adds that Rosenberg (1928, p.60) attributes those in the latter picture, probably correctly, to Gerard van Battem. These opinions are repeated in MacLaren and Brown 1991, p.391, no. 1390. I am not convinced they are by Van Battem; for the difficulty of attributing staffage in Ruisdael's paintings to him see cat. 57.
2. *E.g.*, see cat. 7 for Ruisdael's *Sluice*, now at the Getty Museum, which was sold without a mate in 1771 and then was offered in one lot with a Lucas van Uden landscape in a 1777 sale; by no stretch of the imagination can the two pictures be accepted as pendants. It is noteworthy that the Polesden Lacey beachscape and its putative companion were in the same 1771 and 1777 sales.

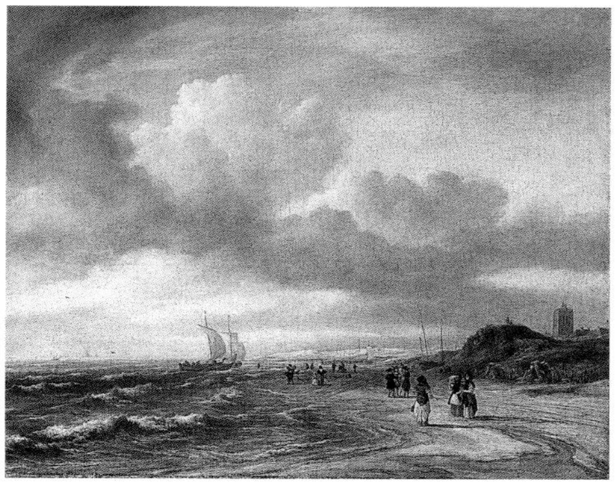

Fig. 52a Jacob van Ruisdael, *The Shore at Egmond aan Zee*. The National Gallery, London.

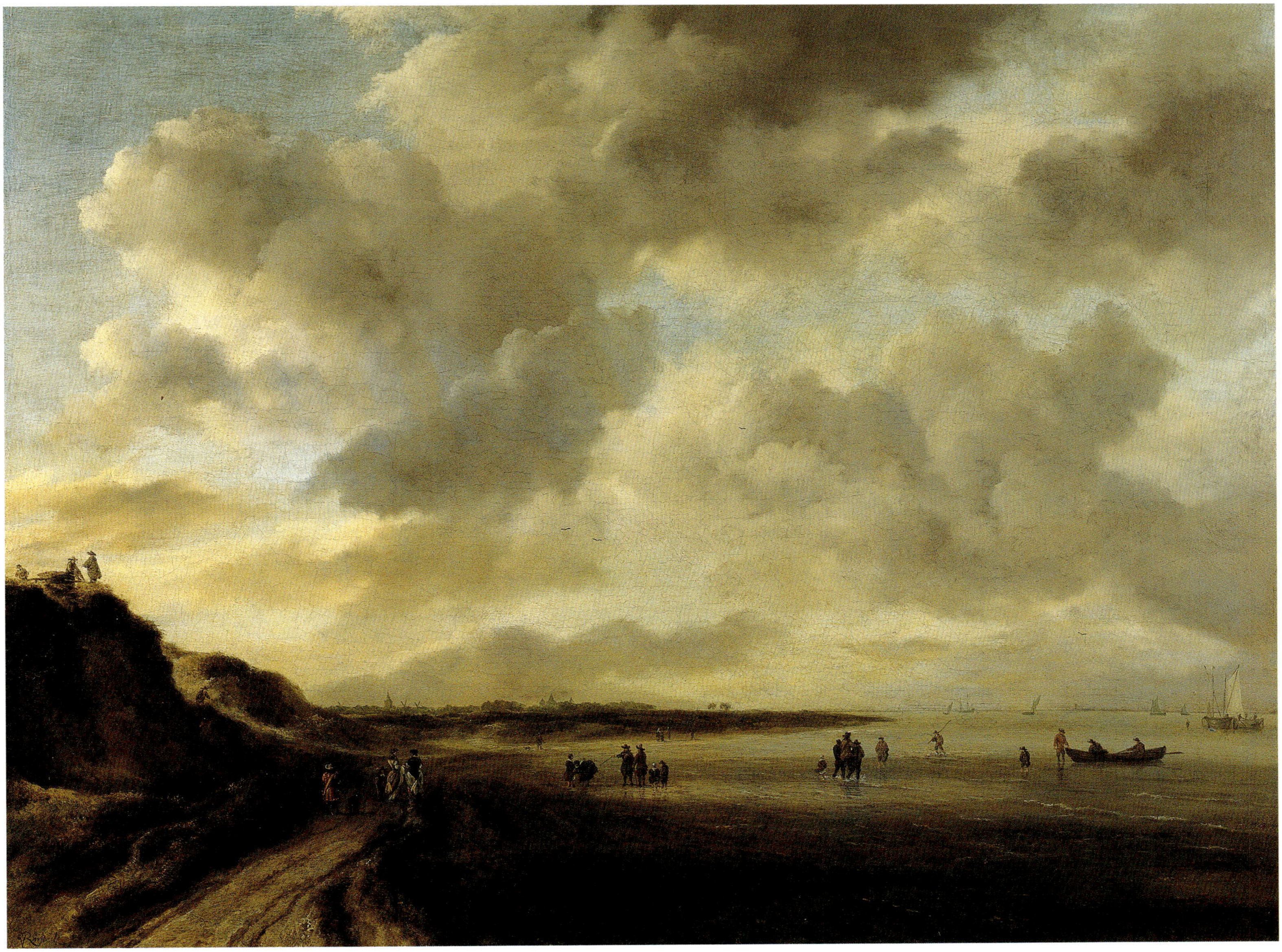

53

Le Coup de Soleil

Monogrammed, lower left corner. 1670s. Canvas, 83 × 99 cm
Musée du Louvre, département des Peintures, Paris, 1820

PROVENANCE: Sale, Comte de Vaudreuil, Paris (Lebrun), 24 November 1784, no. 61 (fr.4360, Paillet for Comte d'Angiviller who was buying on behalf of Louis XVI); collection Louis XVI, 1784.

EXHIBITIONS: Rome 1928, no. 104, repr.; Paris 1945, no. 60; Paris 1950–51, no. 76; Paris 1970–71, pp.198f., no. 191 (with a comprehensive bibliography); Amsterdam 1971, p.142, no. 58; The Hague–Cambridge 1981–82, no. 47, repr.

LITERATURE: Filhol 1804–15, 1, 12th livraison, p.5, repr. (figures by P. Wouwerman; "Voici l'un des plus beaux paysages connus dans les arts"); Landon 1805, 1, pp.29–30, repr.; Taillasson 1807, p.48; Landon 1815, 1, pp.29–30, repr.; Duchesne ainé [n.d.; *c*.1825], 2, p.A115, repr. (figures by P. Wouwerman); Landon 1825, 4, p.8, repr.; Smith 11 and Smith 39; Waagen 1839, 3, p.621; Louvre, Catalogue, 1852, no. 473; Blanc 1857–58, 2, p.100; Michel 1890, p.81; Engerand 1901, p.557; Riat [1905?], pp.37, 69, 93–95, repr. p.89; HdG 664, identical with HdG 701; *Ruysdael, Original-Abbildungen* [1920?], repr.; Louvre, Catalogue, 1922, no. 2560; Ros 413; Simon 1930, pp.53, 75; Simon 1935b, p.135; Stechow 1966, p.138; Gerson 1971, p.151 (late work); Louvre, Catalogue, 1979, p.123, no. *INV*. 1820; Walford 1991, p.171 (1670s or a little earlier); Edwards 1996, pp.114, 337, repr.; Slive 2001, no. 474, repr.

Etching begun by Jean Desaulx (also de Saulx) and finished by François Dequevaulier I (1745–1807) or his son and namesake (1783–1848) after a drawing by le Compte in Filhol 1804–15, 1, 12th livraison, pl. 70. An etching of it appears in Landon 1805 (pl. 13) and in other editions of Landon cited in LITERATURE; in all copies of the various editions examined the image of the print is bound so closely to the volume's gutter it is impossible to determine if the print bears its maker's name. Engraved by Pierre Laurent (1739–1809) after a drawing by Swebac in Duchesne ainé [n.d.; *c*.1825], 2, facing p.A115; etched by Charles-François Daubigny (1817–78) in 1860.

PMA and RA

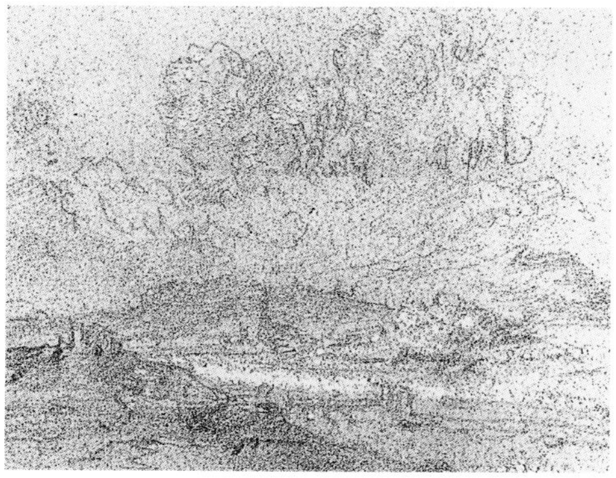

Fig. 53a J. M. W. Turner, copy of cat. 53, 1802. Graphite, heightened with white. London, British Museum.

Restored in 1991–92. Edwards (1996) notes the masterwork was one of the more than thirty paintings Alexandre-Joseph Paillet (1743–1814) purchased at the 1784 Comte de Vaudreuil sale where he represented the Directeur général de Bâtiments, Comte d'Angiviller (1730–1809), who was buying on behalf of the French Crown. At the sale the painting was described as: "Un superb paysage offrant une étendue de pays immense". It has been called *Le Coup de Soleil* at least since it was published in 1804 in Filhol's *Musée Napoléon*. Attempts that have been made to identify the site of the picture as a place in the province of Gelderland (Michel, cited in Paris 1970–71, p.199), the Rhine Valley (Riat [1905?], pp.93–94), or a view derived from scenery Jacob saw in France when he presumably was studying medicine at Caen late in life (Simon 1935b, p.135) are as futile as the efforts that have been made to pinpoint the precise geographical locations of the mountainous landscapes painted by Hercules Segers and Rembrandt. Like so many depicted by other Dutch masters of landscape, Ruisdael's *Le Coup de Soleil* is an imaginary scene.

The Louvre's landscape is datable to the 1670s, when the artist painted panoramic views of the Dutch countryside, beachscapes and marines that also appear to achieve almost the ultimate degree of openness and height. Particularly remarkable is the huge burst of sunlight that dramatically breaks through the clouds, from which the picture gets its popular name. It heightens the drama while stressing the horizontal character of the river valley and furthering the spatial effect.

Nicolaes Berchem, Philips Wouwerman and Ruisdael himself have been variously called the author of the landscape's staffage. None of these attributions is fully convincing.

Numerous copies have been made of the celebrated picture. The whereabouts of the one Hubert Robert painted is unknown (sale, Robert, Paris, 18 August 1821, no. 325). Turner made a quick pencil sketch of it when he visited the Louvre after the short-lived Peace of Amiens in 1802[1] (fig. 53a). Turner wrote in his sketchbook that he admired the landscape, but not without reservation. His interest in Ruisdael did not flag; for his *Port Ruysdael* (exhibited 1827) and *Fishing Boats Bringing a Disabled Ship into Port Ruysdael* (exhibited 1844), see Slive 2001, under no. 653. Testimony of his earlier attention to Ruisdael is offered by his drawing of about 1790 after a Ruisdael river scene discussed under Slive 2001, no. 528, repr.

There are references to ten other copies of the work.[2] The famous painting also was used as a motif on Sèvres porcelain during the 1830s.[3]

1. See Finberg 1909, p.193, no. LXXII, p.81).
2. Slive 2001, under no. 474.
3. See H. van der Tuin, "Reproduction et imitation de vieux tableaux flamands ou hollandais sur porcelain de Sèvres (1756–1847)," *O.H.*, 50, 1950, p.58; G. de Bellaigue, "Paintings in porcelain: Seventeenth-century Dutch and French landscapes seen through Sèvres eyes," *Apollo*, 2002, August, pp.40–7.

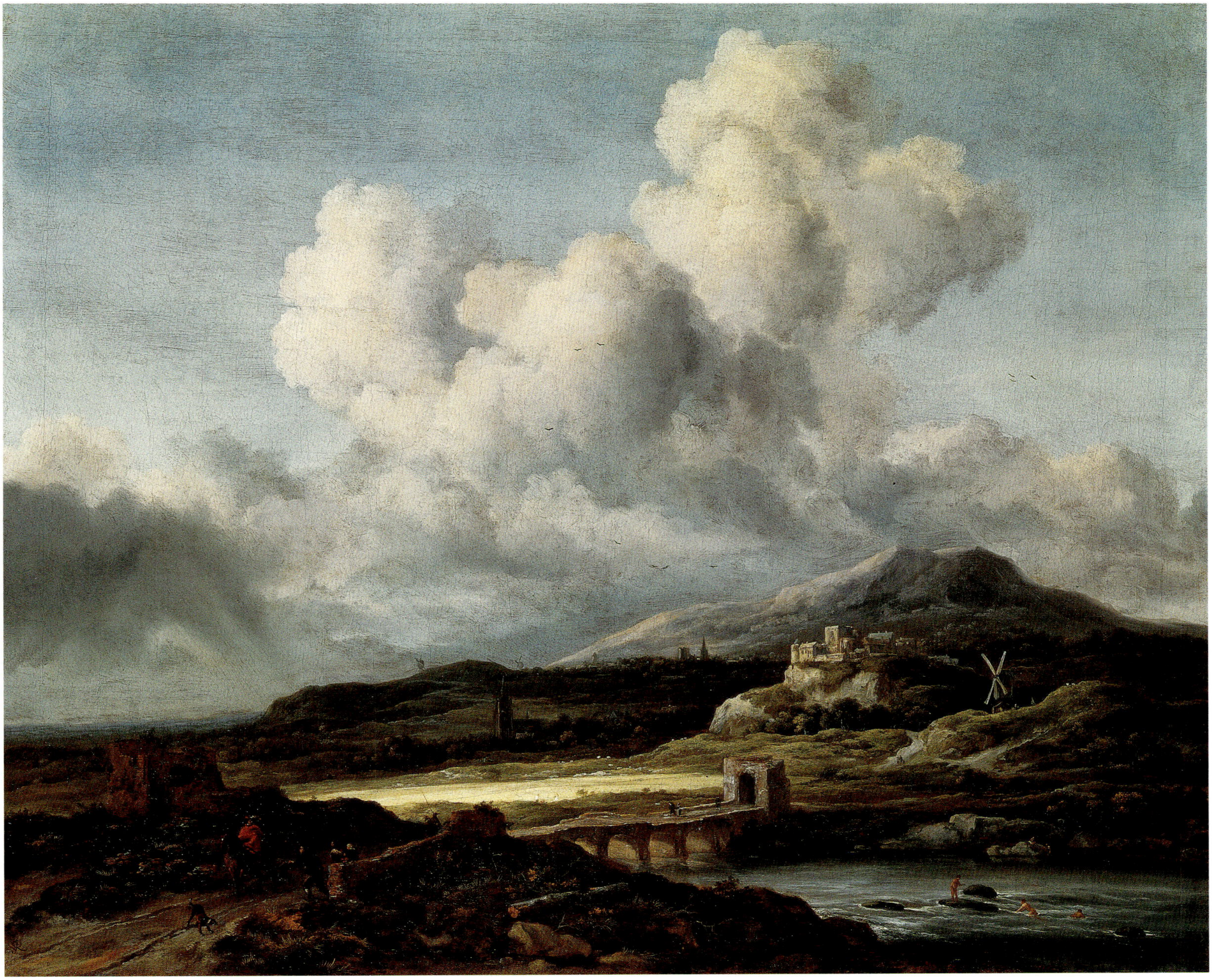

54

Mountainous and Wooded Landscape with a River

Late 1670s. Canvas, 99.5 × 137 cm
The State Hermitage Museum, St. Petersburg, 932

PROVENANCE: Collection Count Brühl, by 1752; acquired from Brühl for the Imperial Hermitage in 1769.

EXHIBITION: The Hague–Cambridge 1981–82, no. 52, repr. (shown in The Hague only).

LITERATURE: Smith 307; Waagen 1864, p.244; Hermitage, St. Petersburg, Catalogue, 1895, 2, no. 1147; HdG 155; Shcherbachova 1924, p.22; Ros 408; Hermitage, Catalogue, 1958, 2, p.244, no. 932; Fechner 1958, p.26; Fechner 1963, pp.95, 171; Hermitage, Catalogue, 2, 1981, p.163, no. 932; Walford 1991, pp.106–07; Slive 2001, no. 476, repr.

Engraved (in reverse) by P. E. Moitte (1722–80) in 1752 (see Slive 2001, fig. 476a). Moitte's print appears in *Recueil d'estampes gravées d'après les tableaux de la galerie . . . de Brühl*, Dresden, 1754, no. 5.

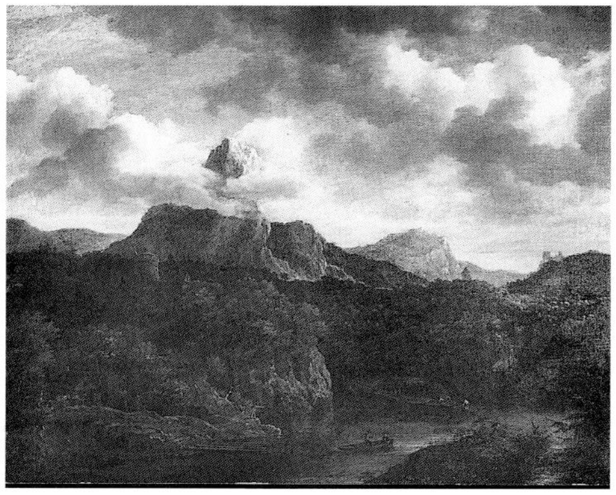

Fig. 54a Jacob van Ruisdael, *Mountainous Landscape with a River*. The Old Town House, Michaelis Collection, Cape Town.

This awesome painting and a comparable one in Cape Town (fig. 54a; Slive 2001, no. 462) are Ruisdael's most remarkable mountain landscapes. Both portray rugged mountain ranges as lofty as the Alps, with their highest peaks shrouded by clouds. The impulse that generated their creation was a new one for the artist. Mountains in his earlier pictures, grand as they may be, are part of the *mise-en-scène*. Only during his last years, did he employ them as the chief means of expressing the vastness and dominant power of nature.

The St. Petersburg and Cape Town mountainscapes are as unusual in seventeenth-century Dutch landscape painting as they are in the artist's *oeuvre*. Some precedents are found in the vast panoramas of mountain ranges with winding rivers in broad valleys by Pieter Bruegel and his followers and in works by Roelandt Savery and Allart van Everdingen, but one must turn to Poussin's rare mature landscapes and those done by members of his circle to find mountain scenes that evoke comparable moods. Possibly Jacob derived inspiration for these landscapes from pictures he saw by Poussin or Poussinesque painters in Holland; there are references to a few in seventeenth-century Dutch inventories.[1] Less probable is the possibility that he made contact with them during the course of his hypothetical journey through northern France about 1676 to study for a medical degree at the University of Caen.

The Hermitage painting is in quite good condition. Its surface coating is transparent, lies evenly and has not yellowed. The paint layer has darkened with time, an effect that may have become pronounced due to the dark priming layer.[2] Its darkening was noted as long ago as 1864 by Gustav Waagen. Despite it, Waagen wrote, the picture makes a sublime, poetic impression. There is no need to modify his comment today.

1. "Een lantschap van Poussin" is listed in the posthumous inventory, compiled in October 1661, of the effects of Willem van Campen (Bredius 1915–22, 4, p.1122, no. 106; he also owned "Een schets van Poussijn", *ibid.*, p.1122, no. 100, and "Een Buyten Amstel van Ruisdael", *ibid.*, p.1120, no. 31). Willem was the son of Nicolaes van Campen, the Amsterdam city councillor who commissioned or supervised the building of Amsterdam's theatre in 1637 and was a relative of Jacob van Campen, designer of Amsterdam's New Town Hall. For references in contemporary Dutch inventories to a handful of other works by or after Poussin see Bredius 1915–22, *passim*.
2. The account of the painting's condition is based on an examination made by Hermitage conservators in 2004 (kind communication from Irina Sokolova, Curator of Dutch Painting, The State Hermitage Museum).

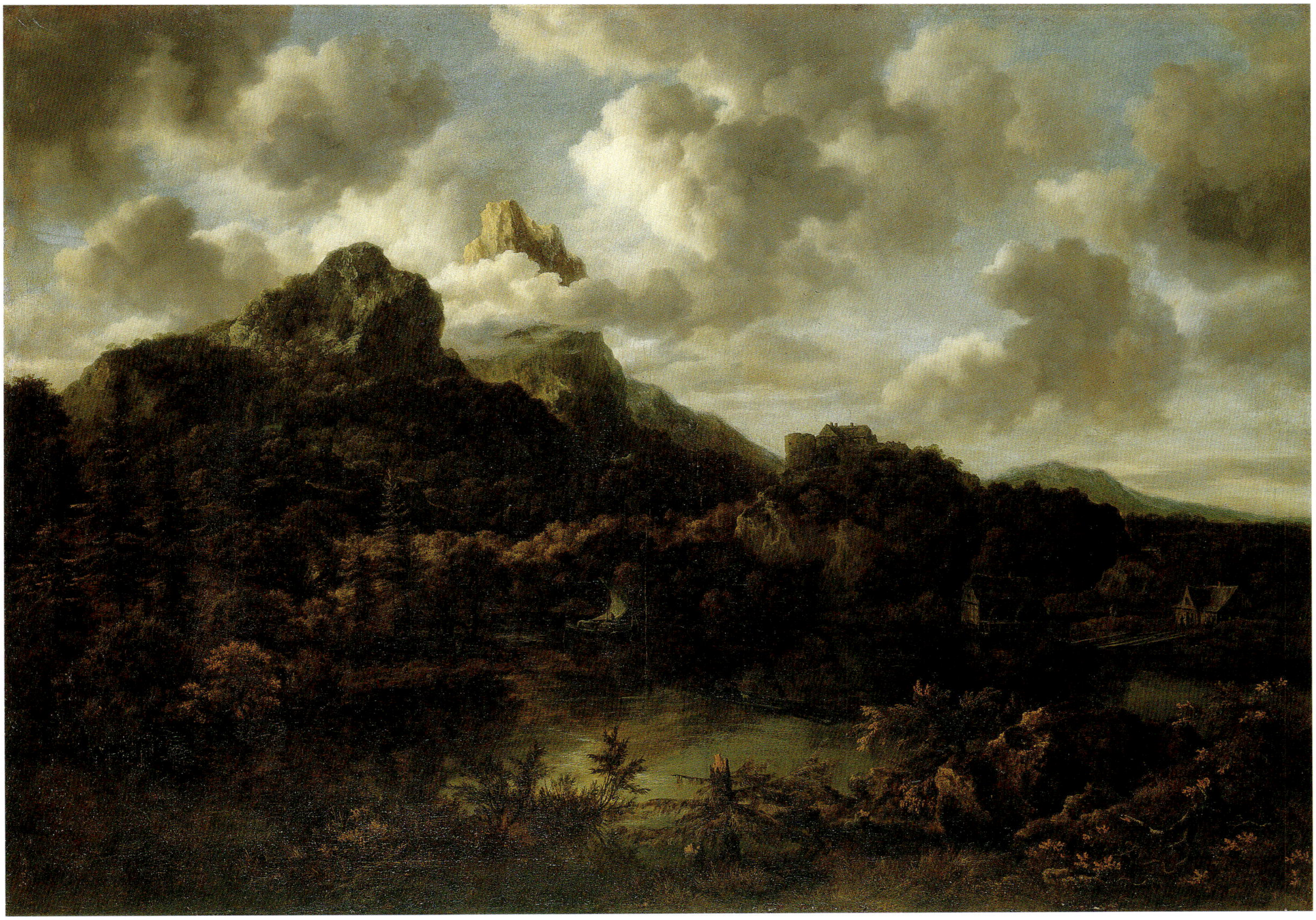

55

Winter Landscape with a Lamp-post and a Distant View of Haarlem

1670s. Canvas, 37 × 32 cm
Städelsches Kunstinstitut, Frankfurt am Main, 1109

PROVENANCE: Sale, C. Sedelmeyer, Vienna (Sedelmeyer), 20 December 1872, no. 144; sale, Joseph Ritter von Lippmann-Lissingen of Vienna, Paris (Drouot), 16 March 1876, no. 38 (fr.1960); acquired for the Städel by the Frankfurter Kunstverein, 1876.

EXHIBITION: Vienna 1873, no. 165 (lent by von Lippmann-Lissingen).

LITERATURE: HdG 992; Ros 609; Städelsches Kunstinstitut, Frankfurt a. M., Catalogue, 1971, p.52, inv. no. 1109; Walford 1991, pp.182–85, repr.; Sander and Brinkmann 1995, p.50, repr.; Slive 2001, no. 670, repr.

RA

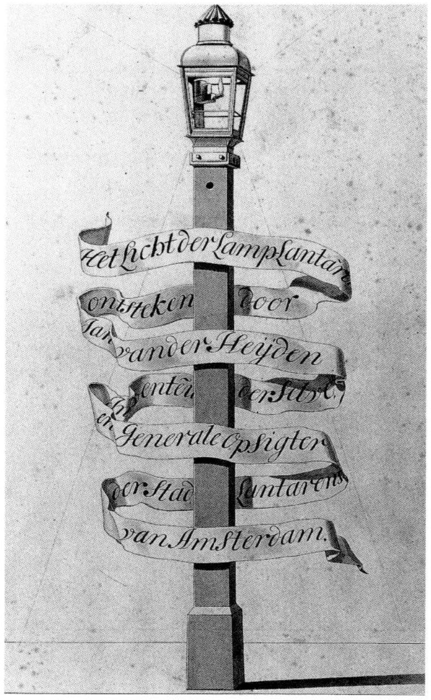

Fig. 55a Jan van der Heyden, title page of his manuscript *The Light of Lamp Lanterns*, c. 1679. Stadsbibliotheek, Haarlem.

The prominent lamp-post in this winterscape of the seventies is the type invented by the leading architectural painter Jan van der Heyden. In 1668 he presented Amsterdam's municipal authorities with a plan to light the entire city with glass lanterns and oil lamps similar to the one in the painting. Acceptance of his plan in 1669 to install more than 2,500 of his lamps made Amsterdam the first European city to enjoy street lighting; the year establishes a *terminus post quem* for the painting.

Van der Heyden's own drawing of his invention appears on the title page of his manuscripts on his street lamps (fig. 55a), which includes an explanation of how to mass produce them.[1] Amsterdam's city fathers appointed van der Heyden superintendent of the municipal lighting at the handsome annual salary of 2,000 guilders per year for life. His lamps were soon installed in Berlin, Leipzig and other cities – they even found their way to Japan. Those in Amsterdam continued to serve the city until 1840.

Though the silhouette of Haarlem's St. Bavo Church is dimly visible on the horizon of Ruisdael's painting, there is no reason to propose that we are looking at the city from an identifiable village that possessed one of van der Heyden's lamps. The picture, which does duty as the artist's homage to Jan van der Heyden, most probably depicts an imaginary winter scene.

1. Two virtually identical autograph copies of the manuscript exist: Stadsbibliotheek, Haarlem, no. 187 E37; private collection of a descendent of A. C. van Eck, Delden, who is a direct descendent of Jan van der Heyden (kind communication [1993] from L. de Vries). The title pages of the manuscripts differ, but both give clear images of the street lamps. For a survey of van der Heyden's work on street lamps and the equally important contribution he and his brother made to urban life when they constructed an improved fire engine with pump-driven flexible hoses see L. de Vries, *Jan van der Heyden*, Amsterdam, 1984.

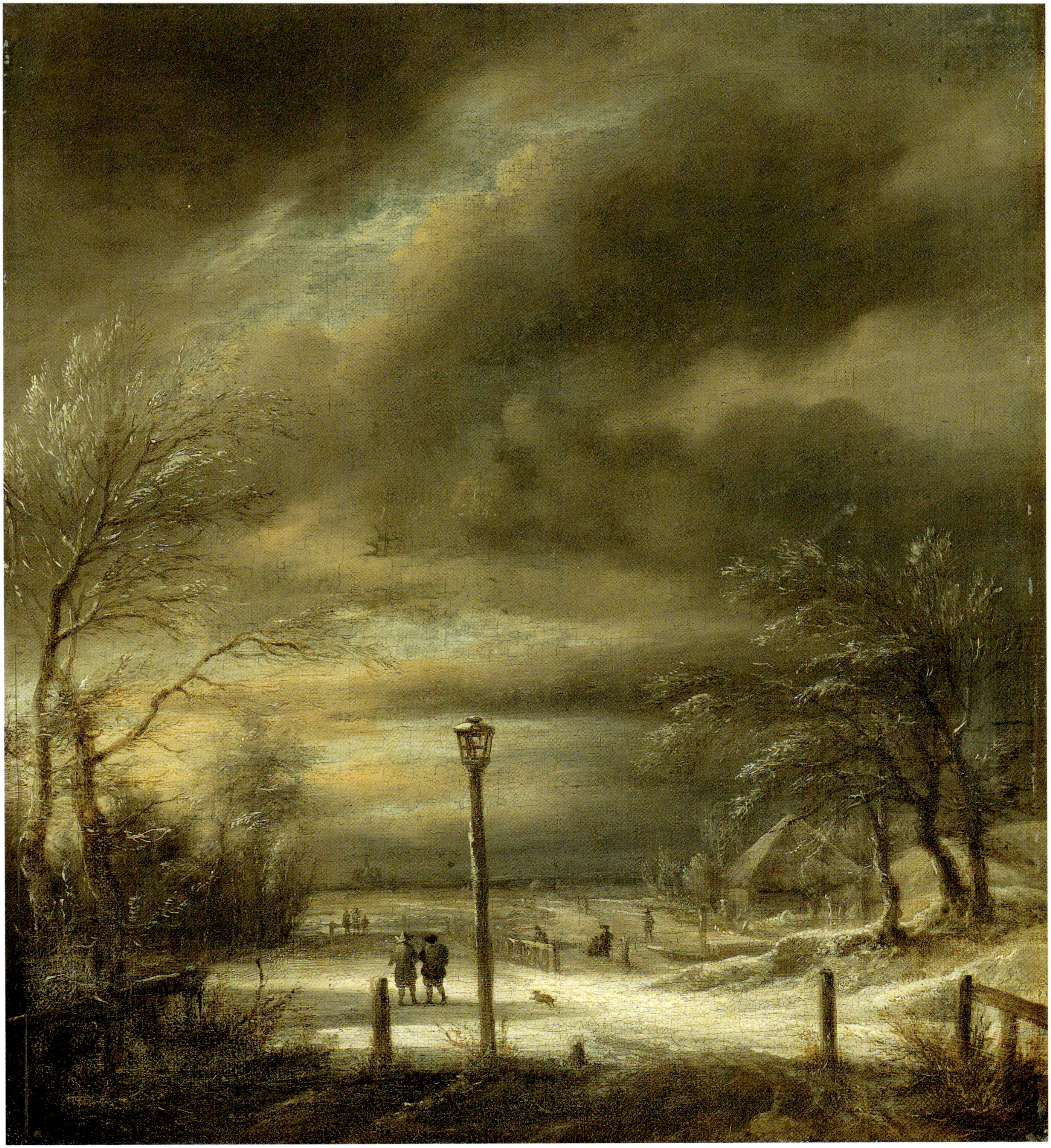

56

Winter Landscape with Two Windmills

Signed, lower right. About 1675–80. Canvas, 38 × 42.5 cm
Private Collection

PROVENANCE: Sale, Sabatier, Paris (Paillet), 20–21 March 1809, no. 47 (fr.1001); sale, John Maitland of Woodford Hall, Essex, London (Christie's), 30 July 1831, no. 88 (£47.5, Seguier; the compiler of the sale catalogue wrongly states the present painting was in the "Geldermeester Cabinet"; the winterscape that was in J. Gildemeester's collection appeared in his sale, 11–13 June 1800, no. 191, and is now in the Museo Thyssen-Bornemisza, Madrid, Slive 2001, no. 681); Sir Francis Cook (1817–1901), Doughty House, Richmond; by descent to his son Sir Frederick Cook (1844–1920), Doughty House, Richmond; by descent to his son Herbert Cook (1868–1939), Doughty House, Richmond; dealer Th. Agnew, London, 1956; private collection, England, from which it was sold, through Agnew, to a private collector in 1986, who, in turn, sold it to the present owner in 2004.

EXHIBITIONS: London, Guildhall Art Gallery, 1895, no. 94; Boston 1992, no. 127, repr.; Boston 2002, p.123, repr.

LITERATURE: Smith 120; HdG 1006, identical with HdG 1025; Kronig 1914, 2, p.93, no. 348, repr.; Ros 626; Slive 1981, p.149, repr. p.148; Slive 2001, no. 694, repr.

The striking sunset in this tender winterscape is unusual but not without precedence in Ruisdael's paintings. Rays of light emanating from the sun's orb also are depicted in the artist's exquisite *Sunset in a Wood* at the Wallace Collection (Slive 2001, no. 375, repr.). Equally unusual for the artist is the lovely, tiny anecdotal detail on the wide expanse of the frozen river of two small *kolf* players waiting for their companion to tie his skates. The long logs near the banks and shorter ones near the big shed adjacent to the prominent windmill indicate it is a saw mill.

According to Smith (120), the painting is a companion to a winterscape formerly in the Hibbert[1] and Hornstein collections (fig. 43a; Slive 2001, no. 683, repr.). Though both pictures passed through the Sabatier (1809) and Maitland (1831) sales as pendants and their dimensions are similar, the emphasis upon a windmill on the right of each picture would make them an unbalanced pair and suggests they were not conceived as companion pieces. Both works are datable to the mid- or late 1670s, and most probably postdate the winterscape at the Philadelphia Museum of Art (cat. 43). Beautiful variations on the theme of the present picture are at Fondation Custodia, Paris, and in a private collection (figs. 43b, c).

1. Hofstede de Groot (1025) makes the same comment; he copied that entry from Smith (120) and was unaware that he double-listed the painting (see HdG 1006, which makes no reference to an alleged pendant).

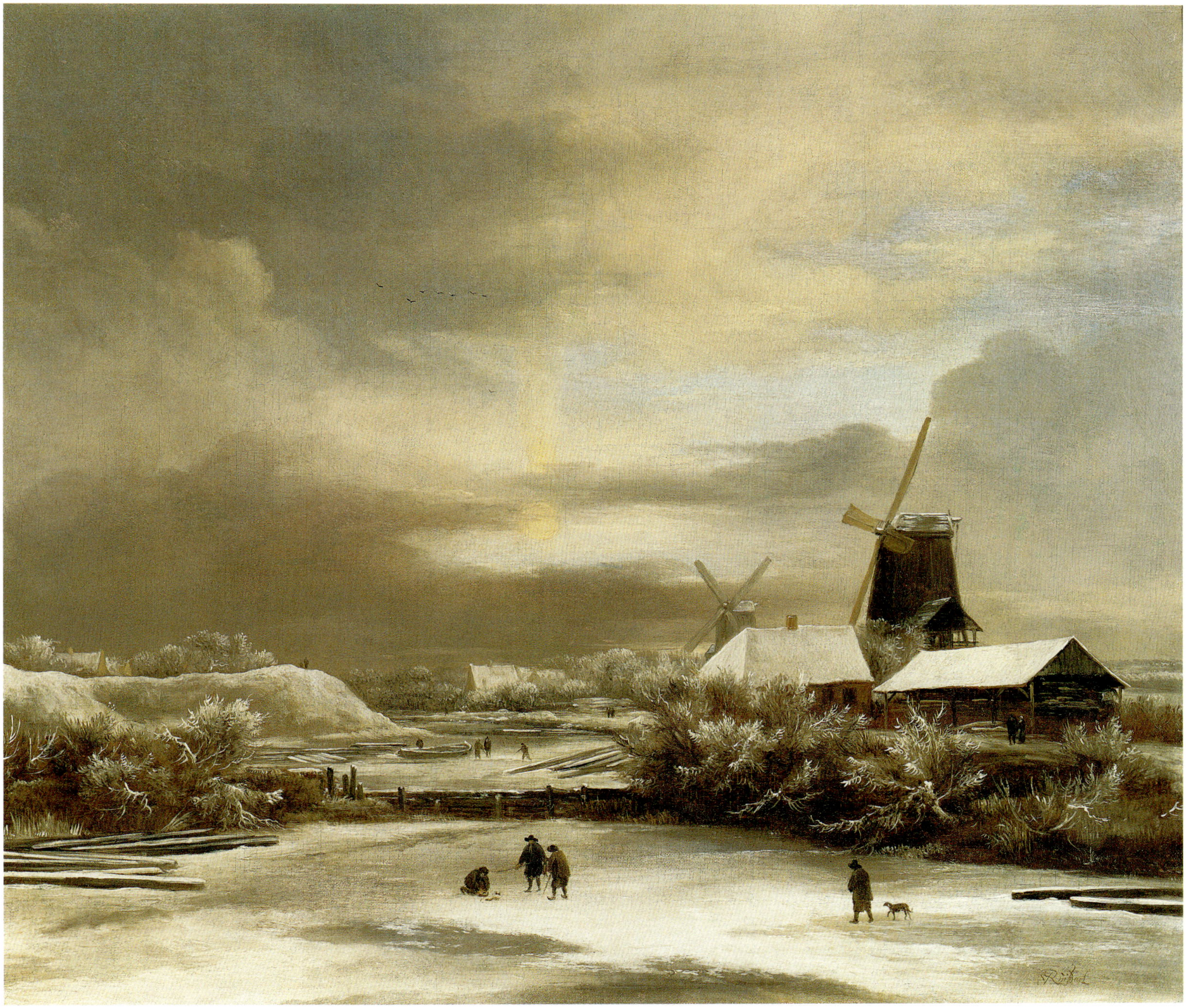

57

The Dam with the Weigh House at Amsterdam

Signed, lower left. Late 1670s. Canvas, 54.2 × 66.3 cm
Staatliche Museen zu Berlin, Gemäldegalerie, 885D

PROVENANCE: Possibly sale, Jeronimo de Bosch, Amsterdam (Jan de Bosch Jsz), 5 October 1767, no. 22 (fl.186, P. Yver); possibly sale, V [. . .], Amsterdam (v.d. Schley), 19 May 1779, no. 134 (fl.69, Nijman); possibly sale, Hendrik van Eyl Sluyter [Helsleuter], Paris (Paillet, Delaroche), 25 January 1802, no. 146 (figures by G. Terburg [*sic*]; fr.500, Paillet); sale, Engelberts and Tersteeg, Amsterdam (v.d. Schley), 13 June 1808, no. 128 (fl.260, with presumed pendant [*View of the Dam* at Rotterdam; see commentary], to Nieuwenhuys); collection Pastor, Burtscheid, 1820; collection B. Suermondt, Aachen, from which it was acquired by the museum with the Suermondt collection in 1874.

EXHIBITIONS: Munich 1869; Brussels 1873a, no. 25 (figures by Eglon van der Neer); Brussels 1873b, no. 150 (figures by Eglon van der Neer); Amsterdam 1925, no. 436; The Hague–Cambridge 1981–82, no. 55, repr.

LITERATURE: Bürger 1869, pp.184–86 (staffage by van Battem); Wurzbach 1906–11, 1, p.64 (staffage probably by van Battem); HdG 8 (staffage by Ruisdael) and possibly HdG 13f; Ros 1 (staffage by Gerard van Battem); W. F. H. Oldewelt, "Ruisdael en zijn Damgezichten," *Algemeen Handelsblad*, 23 April 1938; Roggeveen 1948, p.92; Staatliche Museen Preussischer Kulturbesitz, Berlin, Catalogues, 1975, pp.378–79, no. 885D (*c.*1670); 1986, pp.66–67, no. 885D, repr.; Walford 1991, pp.181–82, repr.; Slive 2001, no. 1, repr.

A drawing at Brussels, cut into two sheets at an unknown date (cat. 97, 98), served as a preliminary study for this view of Amsterdam's principal square, looking toward the former Weigh House, the inner harbour (Damrak) and the tower of the Old Church rising on the right above the city. Fig. 97a is a reconstruction of the drawings joined. A notable difference between the drawing and the painting is the change in the direction of the light.[1] The shift enabled Ruisdael to show the façade of the Weigh House in full light.

The Berlin painting has been dated traditionally about 1670. Although it is hazardous to try to draw a hard and fast line between works Jacob did early in the 1670s and those done later, the cool greyish tone of the high sky, and refined and rather thin brushwork in the vista of houses and boats seen along the inner harbour recall some of his beach scenes and panoramic views of Haarlem datable toward the end of the decade. The style of the Brussels drawings also tends to support the later date.

The figures in the Berlin picture of the expansive square play a more prominent role than those in most of Ruisdael's existing paintings. The small figures in the middle ground are most likely by Ruisdael. Hofstede de Groot (8) states that the larger, more carefully executed ones in the foreground are also by the artist. Other cataloguers have offered different opinions (see Exhibitions and Literature).

Following the suggestion Lamme made in his 1867 catalogue entry on Ruisdael's *View of the Damrak* at Rotterdam (Slive 2001, no. 8) that its figures are by "Jan van Battum" [*sic*], W. Bürger (1869, pp.185–86) concluded that the figures in the present work are by a certain "van Battem". Today we know that the van Battem who Bürger mentioned is the Rotterdam painter Gerrit van Battem (Rotterdam, *c.*1636–84). Bürger's conclusion that he was the artist who often furnished the carefully executed, elegantly dressed figures in various of Ruisdael's late paintings has been generally accepted. However, the attribution to him is not compelling. Moreover, how and where did they meet? Van Battem, a Rotterdammer, travelled in the Netherlands in his early years but settled in his native city by 1668 and to our knowledge remained there until his death in 1684.[2] As for Ruisdael, there is no evidence that he ever visited Rotterdam.

When we consider how brilliantly Jacob incorporated figures into his landscapes from the onset (*e.g.*, the hunter and his three dogs in the drawing dated 1646 at Berlin, cat. 65) and how he continued to create figures that contribute so much to the mood of his works, Hofstede de Groot's conclusion that all the staffage in the pictures is by Ruisdael is probably correct.

1. A painted variant (private Spanish collection; Slive 2001, no. dub2, repr.) by an unidentified hand in which the light is in accord with its direction in the reconstructed Brussels drawing and may reflect a lost original.
2. Van Battem was possibly Abraham Furnerius's pupil in Amsterdam between 1648 and 1654. He was married in Utrecht in 1667 and recorded in Rotterdam in 1668; see Ackley 1981, pp.218f.; Giltay 1983, pp.99ff.; Andrews 1983, pp.24ff.; Rotterdam 1994–95, p.168, nos. 3, 270.

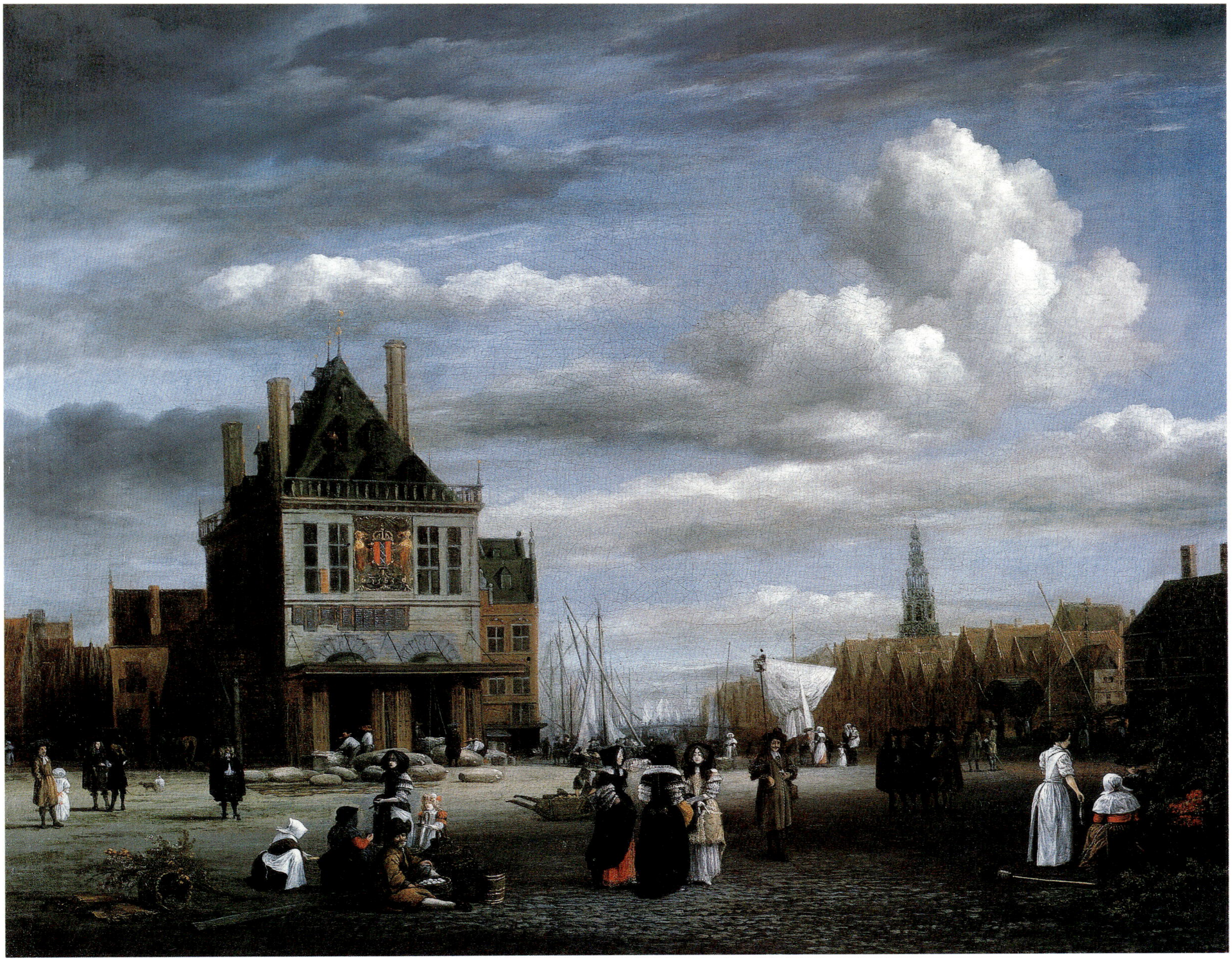

58

Panoramic View of the Amstel Looking towards Amsterdam

Signed, lower left. About 1675–81. Canvas, 52.1 × 66.1 cm
Lent by the Syndics of the Fitzwilliam Museum, Cambridge, 74

PROVENANCE: Collection Edward King; bequeathed to his widow, Susanna King, 1807; bequeathed to her late husband's niece, Anne Windsor, later Countess of Plymouth, 1820; bequeathed in 1860 to her great-nephew Augustus Arthur van Sittart, who gave it to the museum in 1864.

EXHIBITIONS: Amsterdam–Toronto 1977, no. 122 (exhibited in Amsterdam only); The Hague–Cambridge 1981–82, no. 56, repr.

LITERATURE: Smith 269 (in the collection Henry Windsor, 1835); E. W. Moes in *Bulletin van den Nederlandschen Oudheidkundigen Bond* (1902/3), 4, pp.164–65; HdG 10; Ros 4; Simon 1930, pp.66 (original), 79–80 (old copy based on the Philips version); Simon 1935, p.192 (not by Ruisdael; a copy); Simon 1939–40, p.24 (hardly by Ruisdael); Roggeveen 1948, p.94, note 13; van Regteren Altena [n.d.], p.321, note 16 (appears to be a copy after the Philips painting); d'Ailly 1953, pp.68–69, no. 138; Fitzwilliam Museum, Cambridge, *Catalogue of Paintings*, 1960, p.111f., no. 74 (1675–80); Stechow 1966, p.128 (after 1675); Slive 1973, pp.275–76; Walford 1991, pp.163, 182, repr.; Walsh 1991, pp.103–06, repr.; Slive 2001, no. 3, repr.

Gerson, an author of the Fitzwilliam catalogue (1960), rightly stresses that the quality of the painting is excellent; neither Simon (1930, pp.79–80; 1935; 1939–40) nor van Regteren Altena [n.d.] gives cogent reasons for the doubts expressed about its authenticity. A less well preserved variant of the composition is in the Philips–de Jongh Collection, Eindhoven (Slive 2001, no. 4). The drawing that served as a preliminary study for both paintings is at Leipzig (cat. 99).

These extensive bird's-eye views of Amsterdam seen from the south, after the completion of the city wall, may have been possible from the tower of the Pauwentuin. Both paintings show more of the vast expanse of Amsterdam than the drawing, which has probably been cut. The paintings include the Weesperpoort, which was set in the city wall. The Utrechtsepoort can be seen in the wall on the left. The large arched bridge linking the walls is the Amstelbrug (Hogesluis); beyond it the high spires of the Zuiderkerk and the more distant Oude Kerk are recognizable. The large building with a domed tower left of the centre on the horizon is the imposing New Town Hall.

Of special interest is the rectangular building with a low-pitched roof a little to the right of the centre beyond a windmill (it appears in the far right of the drawing). It is the Portuguese Synagogue. It was consecrated on 2 August 1675,[1] providing a highly probable *terminus post quem* for these views. A building that may be Het Besjehuis (Home for Old Women) can be seen; it is probably the long rectangular building behind the arched bridge in the centre. If it is that structure, Ruisdael provided it with many more dormers and chimneys than it actually had. The pavilion at the south end of the building in the Fitzwilliam version also appears to be Ruisdael's invention.[2] Firm identification of the structure in Ruisdael's paintings as Het Besjehuis would pinpoint 1681 as the *terminus post quem* for both versions. Since Ruisdael died in March 1682, it would also establish them as the artist's latest existing documentable works.

We shall probably never know when Ruisdael laid down his brushes for the last time. If this event occurred before the shell of the structure was completed, it could explain why parts of the building in his paintings do not correspond with the old women's home that was actually built. It would not have been the first time he allowed his fancy to play a role in his topographical paintings.

A notable feature of the Fitzwilliam painting is the very tall cloud on the right which meteorologists readily recognize as a cumulonimbus cloud. It is apparently the only accurate portrayal of the cloud in seventeenth-century Dutch art (Walsh 1991). With it is a gigantic cloud which is not found in nature; the meteorologist George Siscoe has baptized it "pseudocumulus codalis Ruisdaelis" (*ibid.*).

1. J. d'Ancona, "De Portugese Gemeente 'Talmoed Tora' te Amsterdam tot 1795," *Geschiedenis der Joden in Nederlands*, eds. H. Brugmans and A. Frank, Amsterdam, 1940, pp.287–89.
2. A print of Het Besjehuis done *c.*1700 by V. Smith is reproduced in D. C. Meijer, "Groei en Bloei der Stad," *Amsterdam in de zeventiende eeuw*, vol. 1, The Hague, 1897, p.187; an anonymous eighteenth-century print of it is illustrated in Kruizinga 1973, fig. 303.

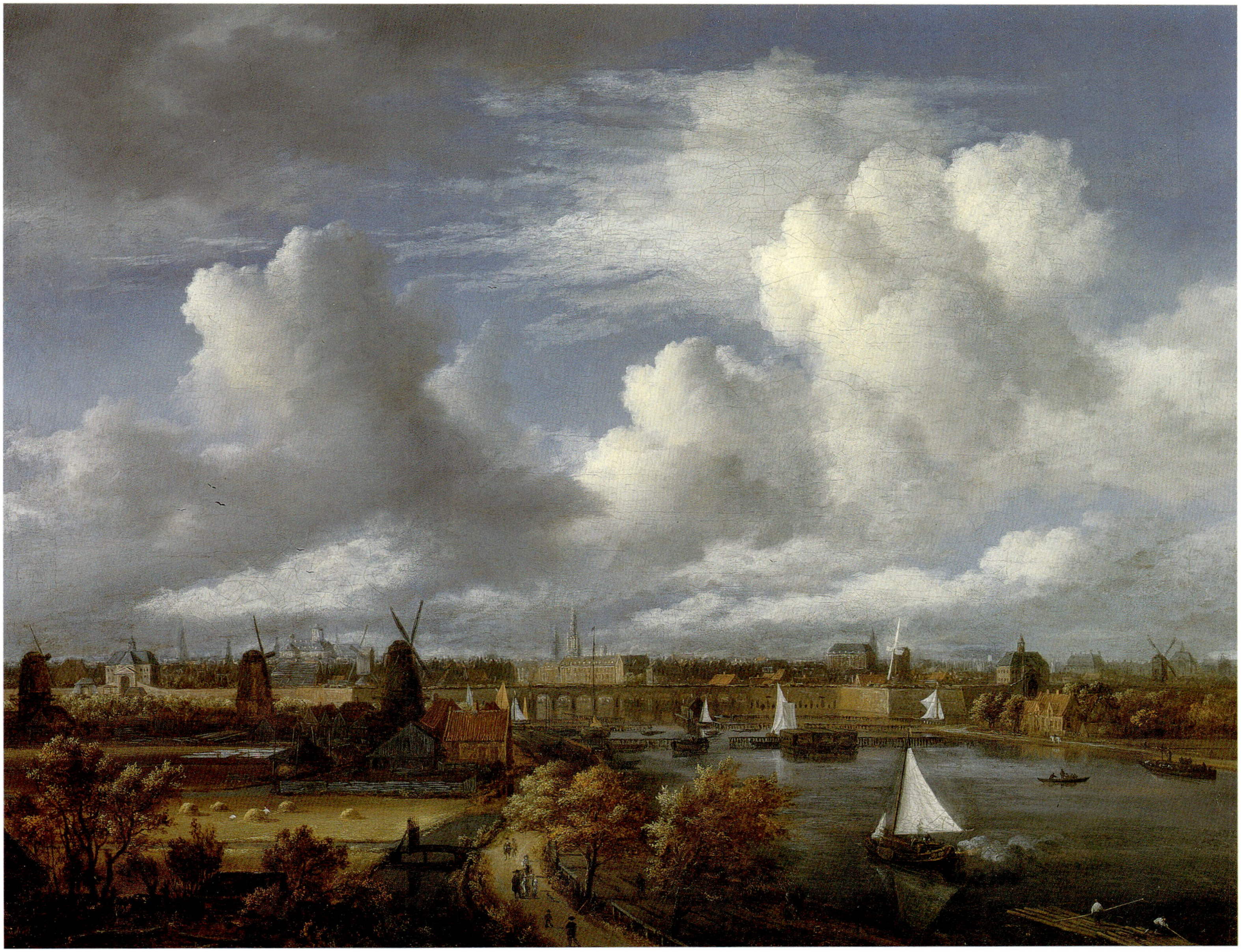

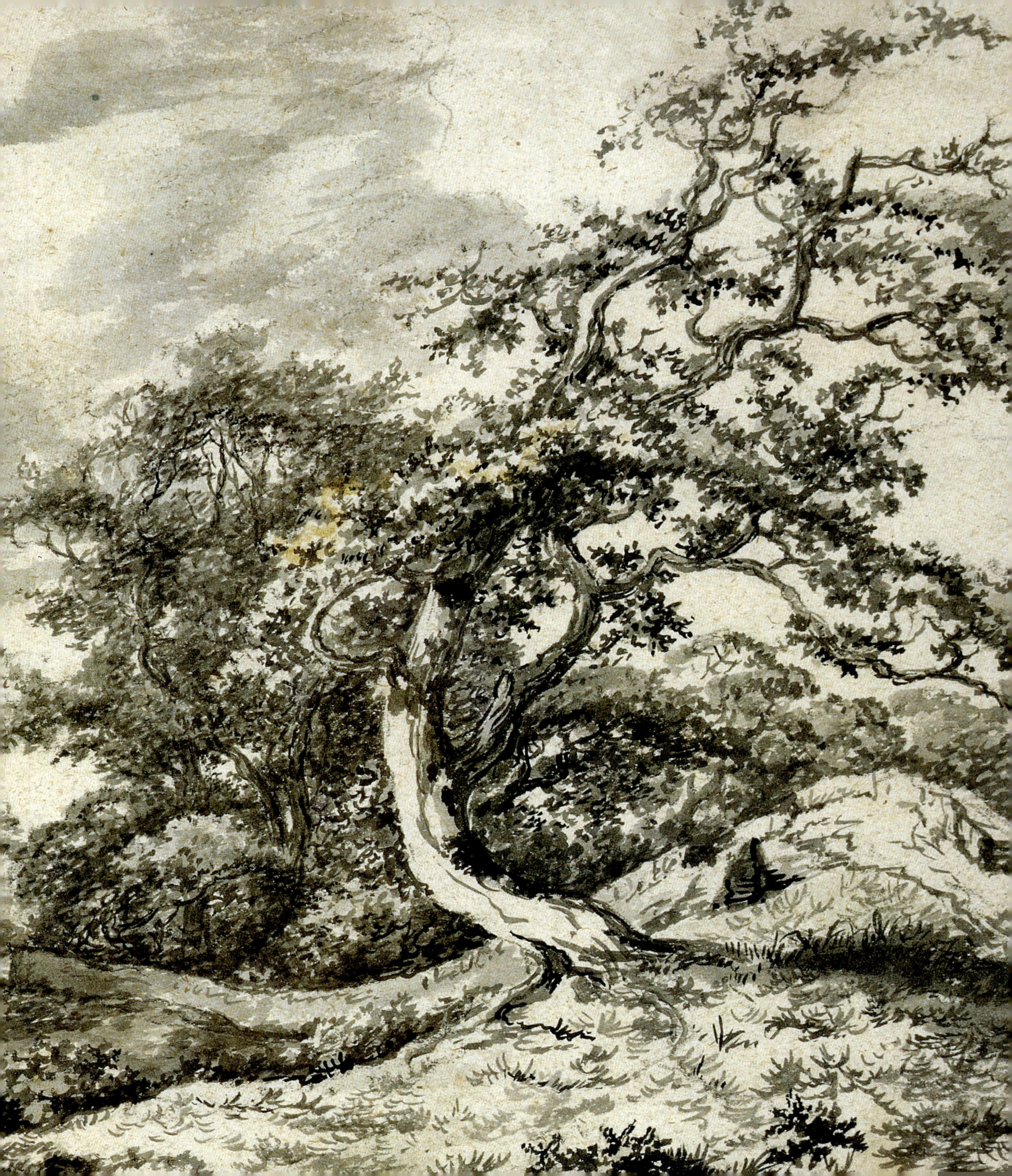

Dawings

Merely six of Ruisdael's more than one hundred and thirty drawings bear autograph dates. Three are inscribed 1646, the year we first recognize his hand as a seventeen- or eighteen-year-old independent artist; the remaining ones were done two or three years later.[1] Only a handful of others can be given more or less firm dates on the basis of topographical or other probative evidence. With so few firm reference points to help establish a chronology, the dates assigned to the artist's work as a draughtsman, like the dates given to his production as a painter, cannot be more than approximate. The arrangement of the drawings in the catalogue is roughly chronological.

About thirty of the existing sheets are highly finished and were most probably intended as autonomous works of art. A few of these were embellished with watercolour and a couple are on parchment, a support that usually indicates a drawing was designed as an independent work.

As for preparatory drawings, pedantically speaking, there exist no sheets by him of this type. Squared, indented,[2] or drawings pricked for transfer by his hand are unknown, and exact painted or etched copies by him of his sketches do not exist. Nevertheless, some qualify as preparatory studies, while others, more or less related to his painted compositions, can reasonably be classified as preliminary sketches, *aides-mémoires*, or *premières pensées*. Around thirty sheets can also be assigned to this category. Remarkable in this group are four drawings of the same water mill seen from different viewpoints (see cat. 74, 75), which were used as studies for four paintings.

When we consider that the artist made four drawings of the same water mill and left us only a single sketch of a waterfall in a northern landscape (cat. 90), but one of a marine (cat. 64), and none of winter scenes or mountain views, the conclusion that our sample of his surviving work as a draughtsman is badly skewed is unavoidable. Further support for this inference is the mysterious absence of drawings of any sort of Bentheim Castle. We know that his sight of it atop its low hill on his journey to the Westphalian town in *c.*1650–51 impressed him even more deeply than the water mills he saw *en route* to Bentheim or on his return to Haarlem. As early as 1651 he made the castle the subject of a painting (cat. 14), and soon afterward he incorporated it in pictures that appear to be topographically accurate, as well as patently imaginary landscapes. He continued to use the castle, seen from various sides and vantage points, in paintings up to his very last phase. Where are the initial and composition studies and other drawings he must have made of the picturesque motif? What did they look like? There is reference to an untraceable one in Sybrand Feitama II's 1758 sale.[3] Was the attribution correct? Will it ever surface?

And where are the artist's drawings that show how he managed to paint close-ups of scrupulously observed grasses, weeds, shrubs, and the distinctive architecture of various species of trees? None exist.

Only hypothetical answers can be given to these queries but a clue to the way some of his preliminary drawings appeared before a final composition was completely worked out is offered by a black chalk drawing in the Albertina (cat. 68) that Jacob used as a study for his monogrammed painting at the Ashmolean of a *Landscape near the Ruins of the Old Church at Muiderberg* (fig. 68a; Slive 2001, no. 77). The Albertina sheet has the distinction of being Ruisdael's only known preliminary drawing for his more than one hundred fifty wooded landscape paintings (because of significant changes he introduced into the painting it served, I term it a preliminary rather than a preparatory study but I would not quibble with anyone who prefers the latter label). We can only surmise how many similar

Facing page Detail of cat. 66, *Shore of the Zuider Zee with Three Anglers and a View of the Ruined Church at Muiderberg and Naarden*

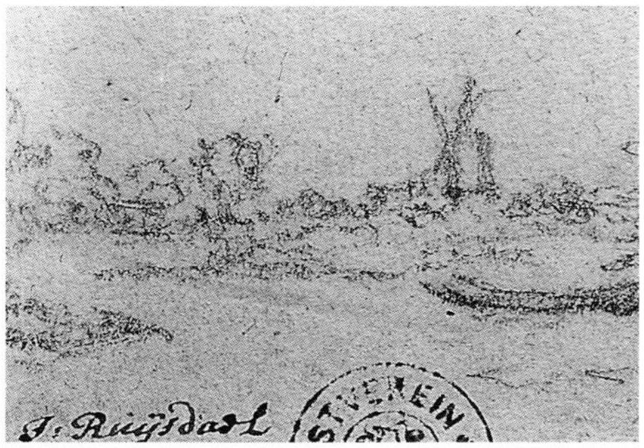

Fig. 46 Enlarged detail of the "J. Ruisdael" inscription (pen, brown ink) on *Windmills near a Body of Water* and a fragment of the collection stamp of the "Bremen Kunstverein" on the drawing illustrated p.21, Fig. 26.

Facing page Detail of cat.87 *The Blauwbrug over the Amstel River at Amsterdam.*

working drawings the artist made before touching the support for a painting of the most beloved subject in his wide repertoire.

The Albertina drawing and the Ashmolean painting are both datable to the early or mid-1650s. The date assignable to the sheet as well as its size, medium, technique and style places it with eighteen closely related small studies that Jeroen Giltay grouped together in 1980 as "black chalk sketches".[4] None are dated but, as he has shown, they are variously datable from the late 1640s to about 1655. Today more than thirty are known. Each measures approximately 15 by 20 centimetres and is mainly in black chalk, some being touched with a light grey wash and ink. A few were worked up by later hands. Many are probably quick drawings done from nature, though it would be rash to swear this was the case. Ruisdael and his contemporaries were fully capable of producing landscape drawings as well as paintings in the studio that can easily seduce us into believing they were done *naar het leven*. Take the Albertina sketch of the countryside near Muiderberg, for example: was it done *in situ* or in the studio? There is no cut-and-dried answer but it is unquestionable that the subject of this drawing and of other sheets belonging to the group were mainly derived from scenes that attracted the young artist as he explored the environs of his native Haarlem and nearby places: country roads flanked by scrubby dunes and thickets, woodland views, modest farmhouses and villages, ponds and canals, windmills and ruins.

An indication that some of these early efforts were given special attention more than a century before the artist began to win his reputation as the greatest seventeenth-century Dutch landscapist is offered by the careful inscription "J. Ruijsdael" written on their rectos in brown ink by an unidentified collector or dealer[5] (fig. 46). It has been established that some of these unmistakable inscriptions and possibly a few on drawings related to the black chalk group date from 1690 or before, and probably after 1682, the year of Jacob's death.[6] On the other hand, none bear Ruisdael's own autograph signature, though three are signed with his authentic monogram, which makes them important sheets that help secure the ascription of the entire group to the artist (Slive 2001, nos. D74, D100, D134). The Albertina's *Muiderberg* sketch employed by Ruisdael for a painting at the Ashmolean (see cat. 68) and two black chalk sketches at Bremen which were used by the artist as working drawings for paintings,[7] give further support for the attribution of the group to Ruisdael.

1. 1646: cat. 65; Slive 2001, nos. D55, D132; 1648: cat. 66; 1649: cat. 67; Slive 2001, no. D109.
2. Ruisdael's four existing drawings for his series of *Small Views of the Amstel* (*Amstel-Gesichjes*) etched by Abraham Blooteling (see cat. 86) and his two views of *The Portuguese-Jewish Cemetery at Ouderkerk on the Amstel* engraved by Blooteling (cat. 79, 80) are indented with a stylus and, except for cat. 80, rubbed with red on their versos but they are not exceptions; their indentations and rubbed backs were made by the printmaker or an assistant to facilitate transfer to plates.
3. Sale, S. Feitama, Amsterdam (de Bosch), 16 *sqq.* October 1758, no. N.60: "Jacob Ruisdaal. Een gesicht by de Poort te Benthem; 4¾ × 8¾ d; (P. Kalkoen, Dfl.25)". Frits Lugt identified it as identical with no. 1331 in a list compiled of Sybrand II's *Notitie der Teekeningen* when the latter was in the J. Six collection (RKD files). The item reads: "Jacob Ruisdael . . . 1 Landschapje, aan het Kasteel van Benthem, gehan^{d} of Gekocht omtr.: a^{o} 1735 f1.-.-." Lugt's identification may be correct. If not, it is safe to say that two drawings of Bentheim attributed to Ruisdael passed through Sybrand II's hands. For evidence derived from the artist's Bentheim paintings that include an unmistakable geological formation at the site from various points of view which indicate Ruisdael must have drawings of the place on the spot that he later incorporated in his paintings see cat. 15.
4. Giltay 1980, pp.148–49.
5. Giltay (1980, p.184 and note 107) first called attention to the significance of the inscription. He cited it on ten drawings. Today eighteen sheets are known which have it or traces of it. Two are in the exhibition: cat. 68, 70 – both have inscriptions that have been virtually obliterated. The others are Slive 2001, nos. D2 (partially obliterated), D22, D27, D34, D35, D41, D75, D90, D110, D123 (virtually obliterated), D124, D125, D126, D128, D129, SD137 (see Slive 2001, p.788, "Supplement" for SD137).
6. Broos (1987, pp.176, 199, notes 50–53) made a significant contribution to the early history of the collecting of Ruisdael drawings when he recognized that two black chalk sketches inscribed with the "J. Ruijsdael" signature at Bremen (Slive 2001, nos. D34 [illustrated p. 21, fig. 26 above], D35. Recovery of the drawings after they were presumed lost in World War II is discussed p.262, note 31) are identical with two items in Sybrand Feitama II's *Notitie der Teekeningen*. The entry establishes they entered the Feitama family collection *c.*1690 with the "J. Ruijsdael" inscription already on them and indicates how early the unknown collector or dealer was active. Proof that they had the inscriptions by *c.*1690 is offered by their unbroken history from *c.*1690 to 1782, and by the fact that the other sixteen drawings inscribed "J. Ruijsdael," cited in note 5 above, were in different collections and were never part of the Feitama family's holdings. Broos's supposition that the author of the inscriptions acquired all of the sketches *en bloc* (in a sketchbook?) soon after Ruisdael's death in 1682 – or even earlier – is not improbable.
7. One Bremen drawing (Slive 2001, no. D34; illustrated p. 21, fig. 26 above) served as a preliminary sketch for a painting in a private collection (*ibid.*, no. 136, repr.); the other (*ibid.*, no. D35) is related to a picture in The Detroit Institute of Arts (*ibid.*, no. 129, repr.).

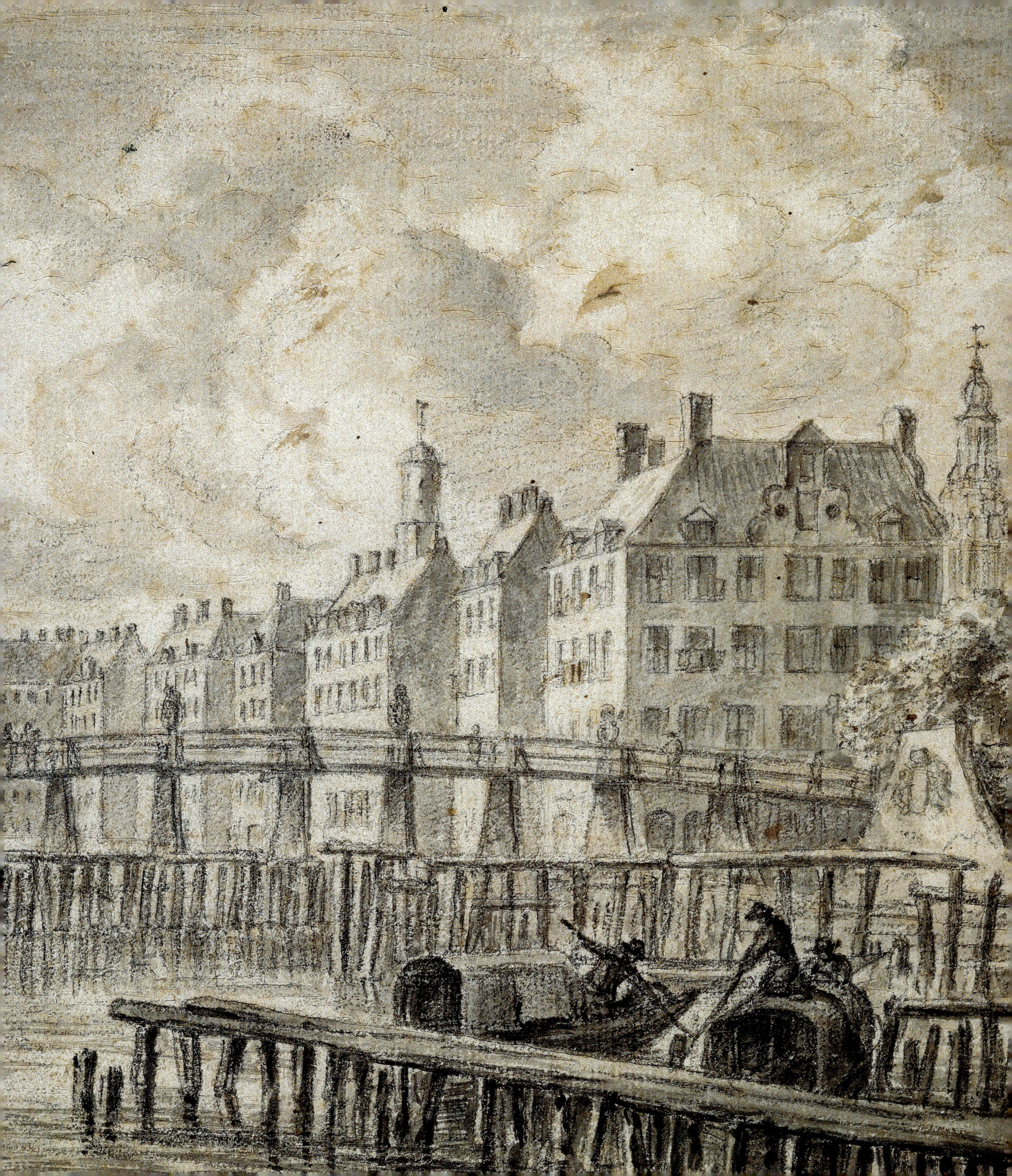

59

Landscape with a Toppled Willow

About 1646. Black chalk, 14.4 × 19.4 cm
Kupferstich-Kabinett, Staatliche Kunstsammlungen, Dresden, c 1285

PROVENANCE: In the collection by 1756.

EXHIBITIONS: The Hague–Cambridge 1981–82, no. 57, repr.; Dresden–Vienna 1997–98, no. 94, repr.

LITERATURE: Woermann 1896–98, 9, pl. 16, bottom; Ros Z18a; Simon 1930, pp.67, 83; Giltay 1980, p.147; no. 37; Slive 2001, no. D44, repr.

RA

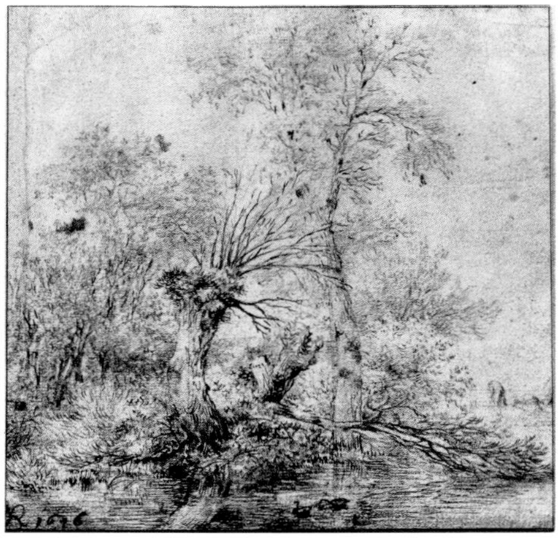

Fig. 59a Jacob van Ruisdael, *A Willow and Other Trees near a Pond*, 1646. Black chalk, pen, brush, grey wash. Formerly Feldsburg, Prince Johann Liechtenstein.

This little black chalk sketch and another five in the exhibition (cats. 60–64) are closely related to three other drawings also at Dresden.[1] Close similarities of size, medium and style indicate they were done about the same time and belonged to the same sketchbook, hence their name, the Dresden sketchbook drawings.[2] All are listed as part of the collection's *Altebestand* which establishes they were in Dresden by 1756. Possibly they were among the staggering number of 10,202 drawings Dresden acquired in 1728 from Gottfried Wagner, the largest acquisition ever made by the Kupferstich-Kabinett.[3]

There is a consensus that the sketches were done about 1646. They are a precious part of Jacob's incunabula that mainly introduce motifs to which he returned in drawings done during the following decades: trees and shrubs near water, windmills in a flat landscape, a simple farmstead, bridges, and ruins. The pronounced exception is a sketch of a calm body of water (cat. 64). No other marine drawings by the artist are known.

The spaciousness, luminosity and airy atmosphere of the countryside, often achieved with sensitive stippled touches of chalk, is stressed in the sketches, as differences between buildings, land and sky are slurred over. These qualities link them more closely to works done by artists of Jan van Goyen's generation than to Ruisdael's own early paintings. Yet, in drawings also datable *c.*1646 the massiveness and solidity of forms can receive great emphasis and there is no trace whatsoever of the pointillist-like technique of some of the Dresden sketches. Perhaps while still at the very beginning of his career Jacob experimented with more than one technique as he strived to achieve different landscape effects. Alternatively, some of the drawings may be a little earlier than has been traditionally proposed.

The very close connection of the present sketch to Ruisdael's monogrammed drawing of a *Pollard Willow and Thicket near a Pond*, dated 1646, formerly Liechtenstein collection (fig. 59a; Slive 2001, no. D55) provides a reasonable date for the work. Ruisdael added touches of pen and wash to the latter sheet, but the black chalk drawing underlying these additions is strikingly similar to the suggestive touch used in the sketch.

1. Slive 2001, nos. D49, D50, D51.
2. The Metropolitan Museum of Art's *House amidst Trees near a Footbridge* is classifiable as part of the group, and the Albertina's *Landscape with Windmills* may have belonged to the series as well (Slive 2001, nos. D90, D121).
3. Kind communication (1991) from Christian Dittrich, Curator, Kupferstich-Kabinett, Dresden.

60

Farmstead with the Ruins of Brederode Castle

About 1646. Black chalk, 14.5 × 19.5 cm
Kupferstich-Kabinett, Staatliche Kunstsammlungen, Dresden, no. c 1277

PROVENANCE: In the collection by 1756.

LITERATURE: Ros Z18d; Simon 1930, pp.67–68, 83; Giltay 1980, p.147; no. 40, repr. (in reverse); Slive 2001, no. D47, repr.

PMA

Giltay (1980, p.147) recognized the sketch includes the ruins of Brederode Castle, located a few kilometres northwest of Haarlem, a favourite subject for Dutch artists since the early seventeenth century. For a note on the castle's history, reference to artists who depicted it and Ruisdael's painting that concentrates on its remains (Philadelphia Museum of Art, John G. Johnson Collection) see cat. 29.

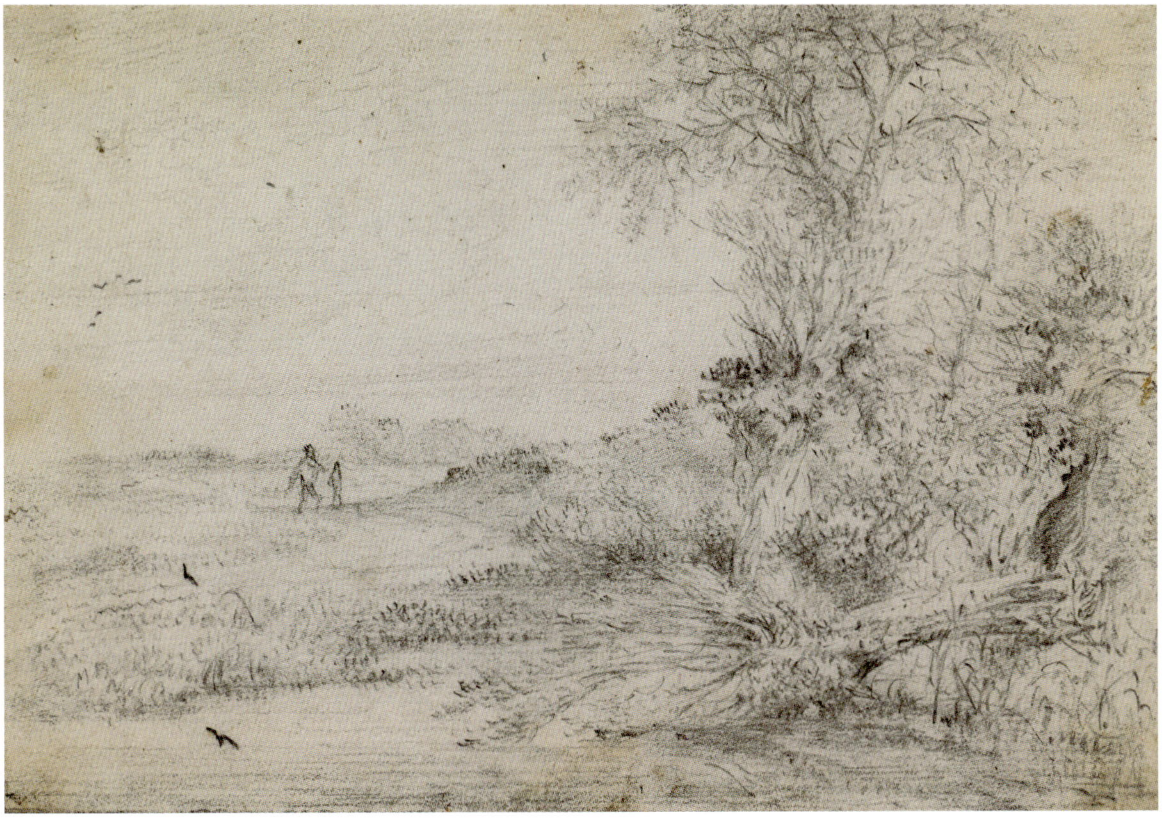

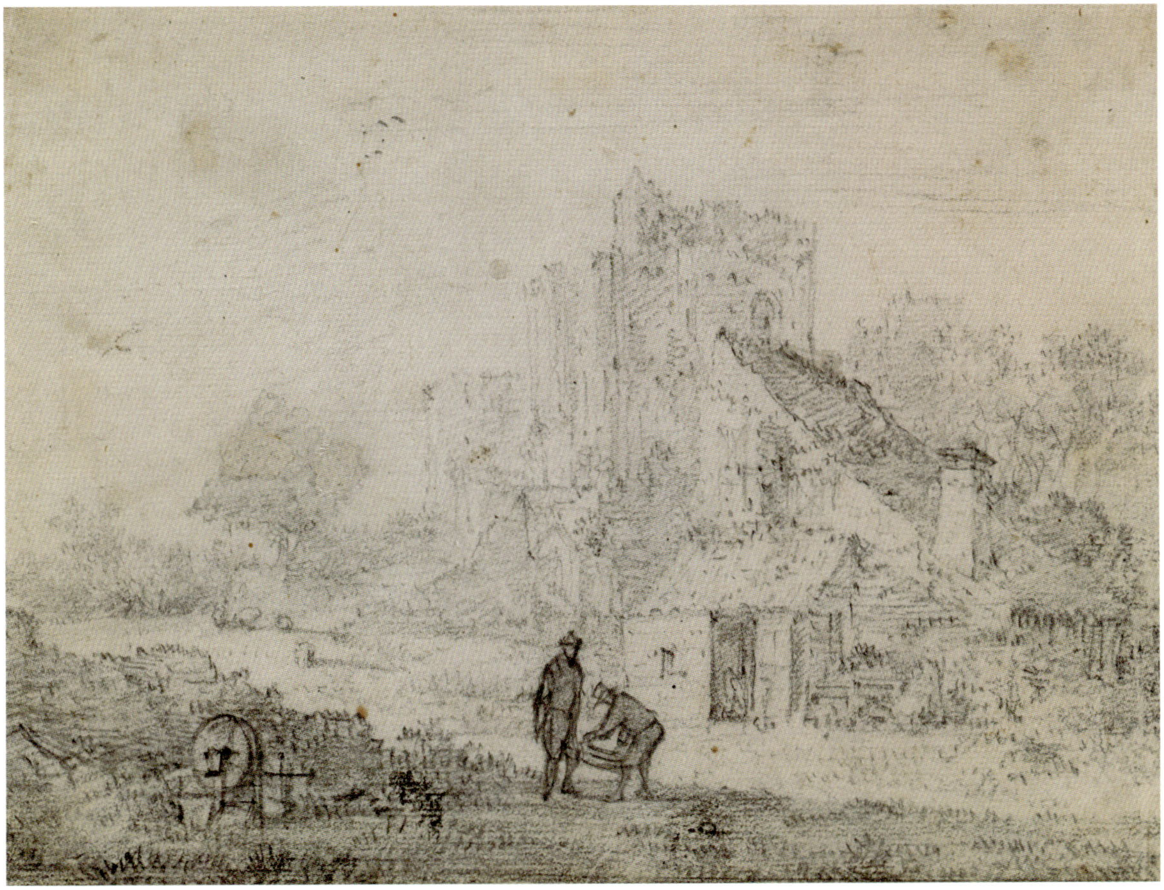

In the drawing the young artist did not focus on the picturesque wreck; he was equally interested in the cottage. Both serve as a backdrop for the activity of a pair of workmen. A foretaste of his genre-like approach to his subject is offered in a drawing at Berlin by Jacob Matham (1571–1631), dated 1603, that shows the grounds of the castle used as a spacious farmyard.[1]

1. Berlin, Staatliche Museen, Kupferstichkabinett; Bock and Rosenberg 1930, 1, p.41, no. 13326, as "View of a Farm Yard"; identified as Brederode by van Gelder 1933, p.21, fig. 6.

61

Windmill at the Edge of a Village

About 1646. Black chalk, 14.7 × 19.8 cm
Kupferstich-Kabinett, Staatliche Kunstsammlungen, Dresden, no. c 1286

62

Landscape with a Windmill and a Cottage

About 1646. Black chalk, 14.5 × 19.5 cm
Kupferstich-Kabinett, Staatliche Kunstsammlungen, Dresden, no. c 1279

CAT. 61

PROVENANCE: In the collection by 1756.

EXHIBITIONS: The Hague–Cambridge 1981–82, no. 58, repr.; Dresden–Vienna 1997–98, no. 95.

LITERATURE: Woermann 1896–98, 9, pl. 15, upper left; Ros Z18c; Simon 1930, pp.67, 83; Giltay 1980, p.147; no. 39; Walford 1991, p.57; Slive 2001, no. 46, repr.

RA

CAT. 62

PROVENANCE: In the collection by 1756.

EXHIBITIONS: The Hague–Cambridge 1981–82, no. 59, repr.; Munich–Bonn 1993, no. 48.

LITERATURE: Woermann 1896–98, 9, pl. 15, bottom; Ros Z18e; Simon 1930, pp.67, 83; Giltay 1980, p.147; no. 41; Slive 2001, no. D48, repr.

PMA

On young Jacob's sketching trips to Haarlem's environs windmills were a favourite subject. In addition to these two, which make a mill their principal motif, one other is in the Dresden group (Slive 2001, no. D49). Another is at the Albertina (Slive 2001, no. D121), which may be part of the "sketchbook" series; a fourth, datable *c.*1646, is at the Museum Bredius, The Hague (Slive 2001, no. D70). As Ruisdael grew older he did not neglect windmills in his drawings, but they do not occur with the same frequency in his paintings.

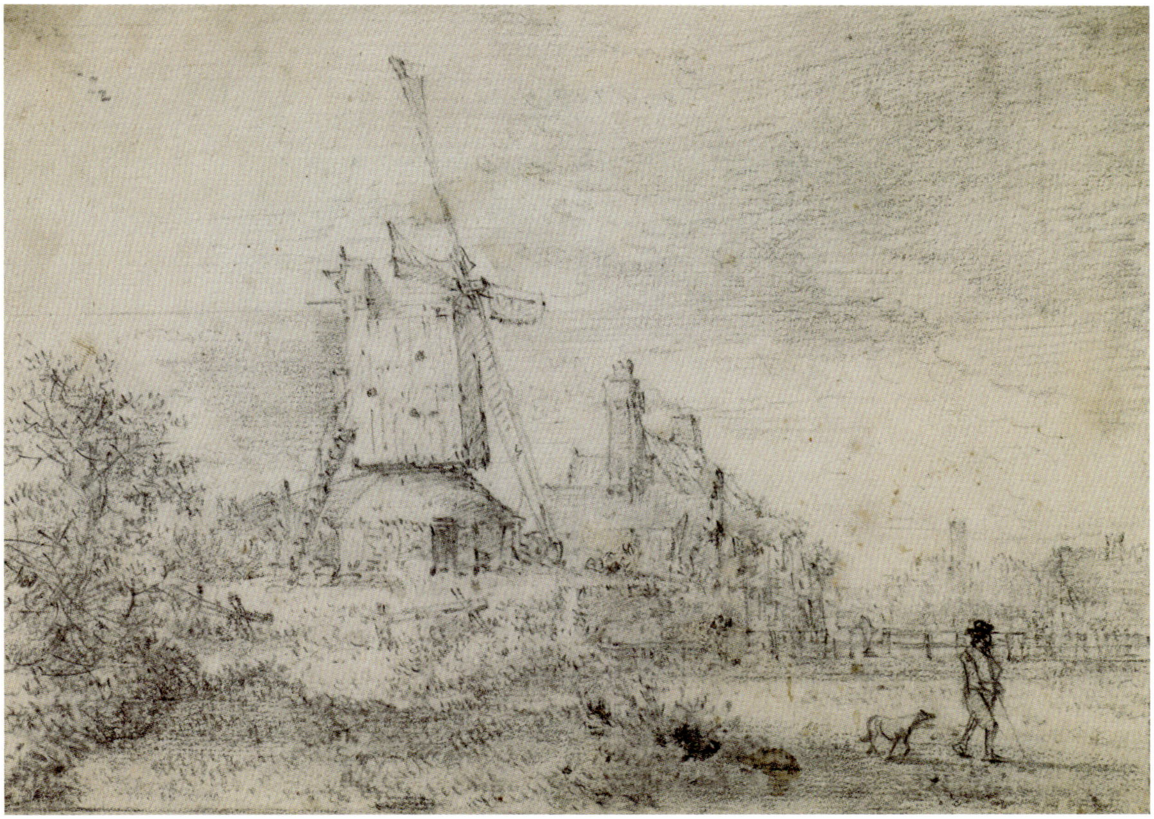

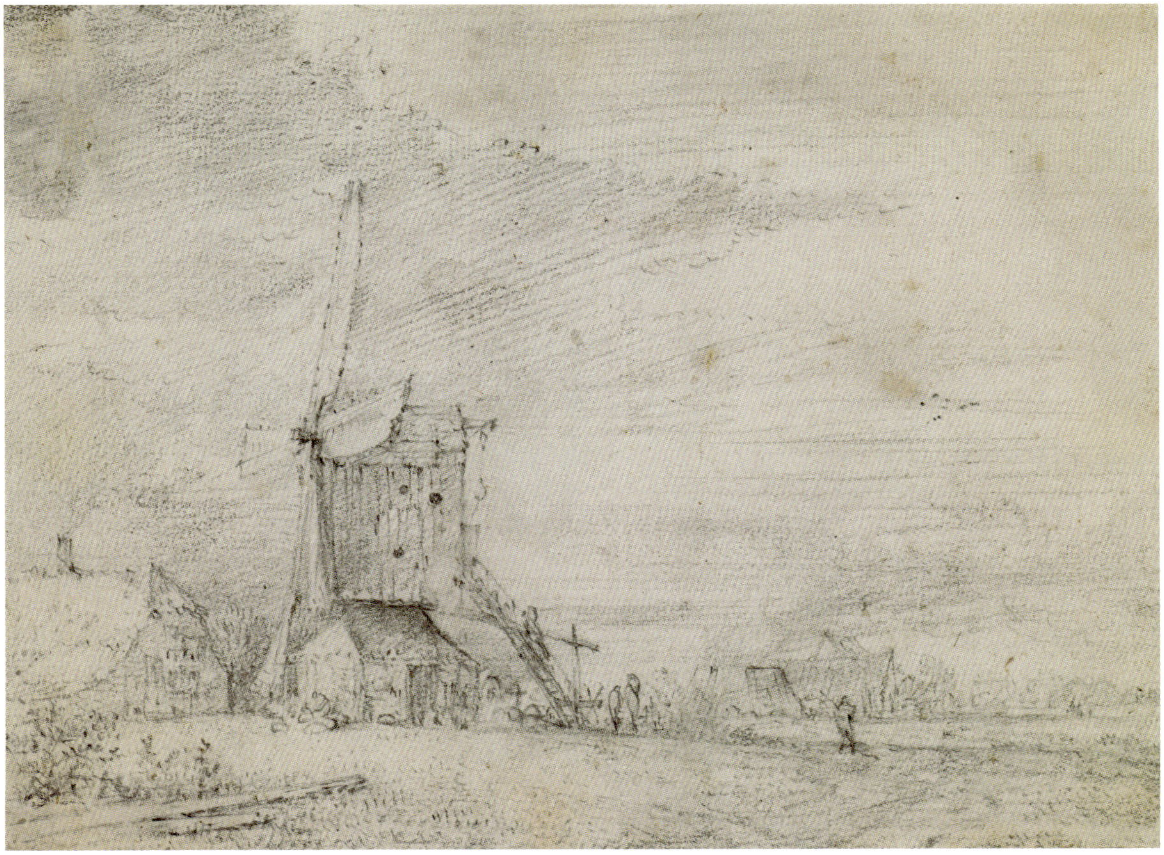

63

High Stone Bridge

About 1646. Black chalk, 14.5 × 19 cm
Kupferstich-Kabinett, Staatliche Kunstsammlungen, Dresden, no. c 1284

PROVENANCE: In the collection by 1756.

EXHIBITION: The Hague–Cambridge 1981–82, no. 61, repr.

LITERATURE: Ros Z18b; Simon 1930, pp.67–68, 83; Giltay 1980, p.147; no. 38; Slive 2001, no. D45, repr.

PMA only

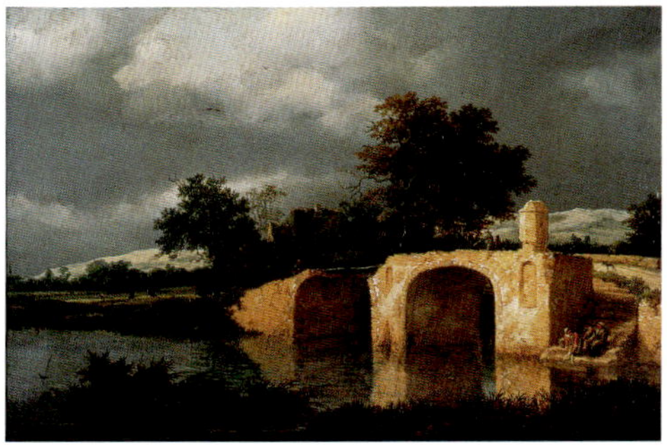

Fig. 63a Jacob van Ruisdael, *River Landscape with a Ruined Stone Bridge*. Philadelphia Museum of Art, John G. Johnson Collection.

Simon (1930, pp.67–68) noted a connection between the stone bridge in the drawing and Ruisdael's *Ruined Stone Bridge*, Philadelphia Museum of Art, John G. Johnson Collection (fig. 63a). The connection is a loose one. Apart from the steps that swing down to the water, there is no similarity between the two structures. In fact none of the "Dresden sketchbook" drawings can be related to any of Jacob's existing paintings or prints. However, Ruisdael made an effort to translate into etched lines the rich tonal effects he achieved with gradations of black chalk in this sheet as well as a few other Dresden sketchbook drawings in his 1646 print *Farmstead in the Dunes* (cat. 101). He never repeated the experiment in his etchings. It is noteworthy that the print exists in only an unique impression.

64

Seascape with Sailboats

About 1646.Black chalk, 14.8 × 19.5 cm
Kupferstich-Kabinett, Staatliche Kunstsammlungen, Dresden, no. c 1276

PROVENANCE: In the collection by 1756.

LITERATURE: Woermann 1896–98, 9, pl. 16, upper right; Ros Z18l; Simon 1930, p.83; Giltay 1980, p.147; no. 47; Slive 2001, no. D52, repr.

PMA and RA

This extensive view of a calm body of water under threatening clouds, with a few large boats unobtrusively arranged in diagonal formation with a distant view of the shore, recalls the broad sea and riverscapes by Salomon van Ruysdael and Jan van Goyen. However, this "Dresden sketchbook" sheet strikes an unique note in Ruisdael's *oeuvre*. It is his only known drawing of a seascape. Moreover, to our knowledge, he hardly ever painted such marines. Calms or waters stirred by gentle breezes seldom interested him; his marines almost invariably depict agitated seas.

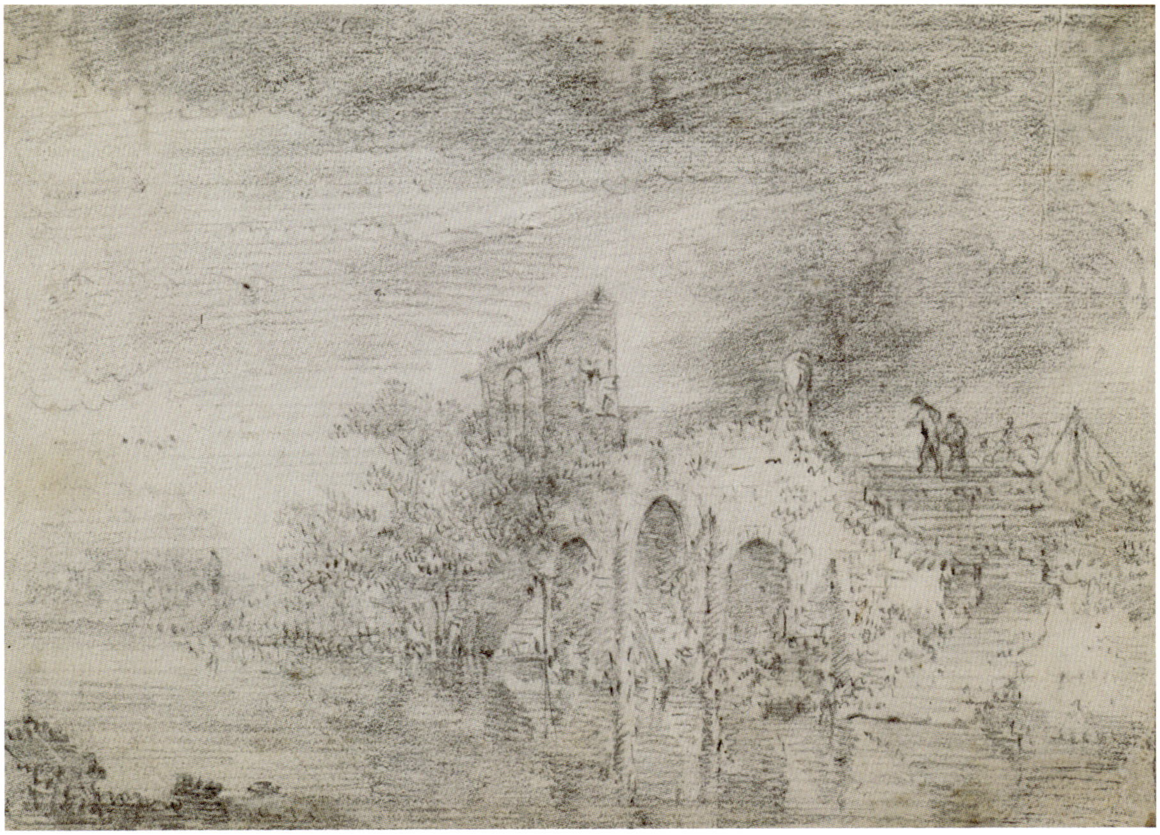

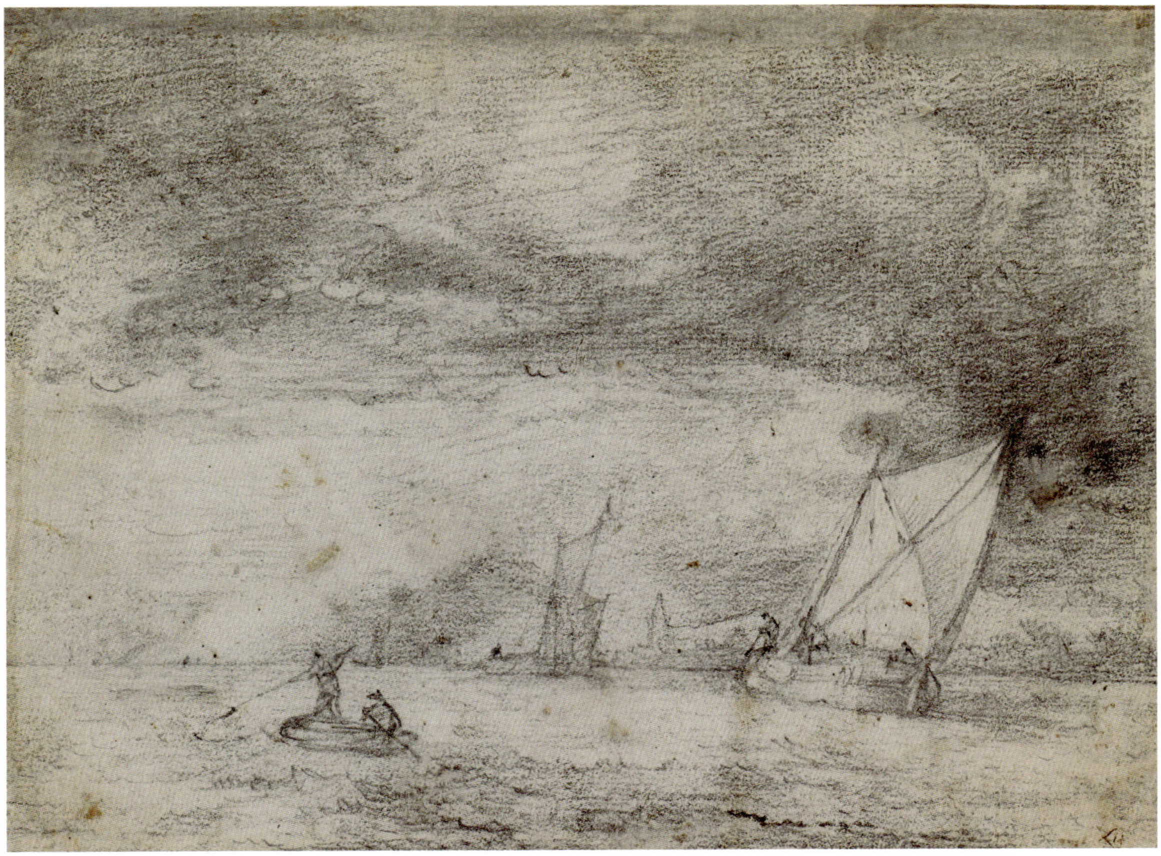

65

Hunter with Three Dogs Entering a Wood

Monogrammed and dated 1646, lower left. Black chalk, brush, pen and grey wash, 28.4 × 38.5 cm
Staatliche Museen zu Berlin, Kupferstichkabinett, KdZ2618

PROVENANCE: Sale, Earl Spencer, London (Philipe), 10–17 June 1811, no. 701; collection A. Donnadieu; collection B. Suermondt, Aachen; acquired by the museum in 1874.

EXHIBITIONS: Berlin 1974, p.73, no. 158, repr.[1]; The Hague–Cambridge 1981–82, no. 63, repr. (shown in The Hague only).

LITERATURE: Ros Z6; Simon 1930, pp.67, 83; Bock and Rosenberg 1930, 1, p.256, no. 2618; Giltay 1980, p.142, no. 16, repr.; Slive 2001, no. D21, repr.

PMA and RA

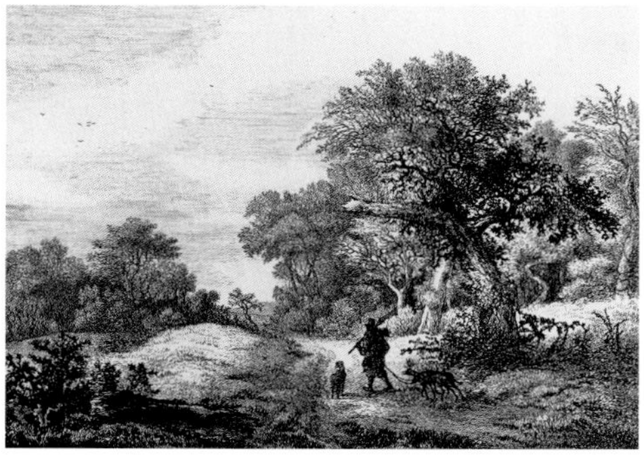

Fig. 65a Unidentified artist, etching after cat. 65.

This peaceful scene of a hunter approaching a sunlit meadow in a wood is the most ambitious and largest by far of the three surviving drawings the seventeen- or eighteen-year-old artist dated 1646, to our knowledge the first year he inscribed a date on his drawings (for the others see fig. 59a, and *Dune Landscape*, private collection, Slive 2001, no. D132, repr.).

Ruisdael began the sketch with black chalk and then worked up the entire foreground with pen, the tip of a brush and wash, taking obvious delight in portraying the kind of tangled growth and dense vegetation also found in his early paintings. The drawing of the hunter and his lean dogs indicates that from the beginning he was skilful at depicting figures and animals, a point to recall when debating whether Ruisdael himself or another artist provide staffage in his paintings.

Although Ruisdael himself may have stumped passages of black chalk in the middle ground and distance, when the drawing was fresh the contrast between these passages and the foremost plane may have been less sharp. An etching after the drawing by an anonymous artist probably gives an indication of some of the detail that has been lost[2] (fig. 65a).

1. W. Schulz, the author of the catalogue entry, calls the sheet, dated 1646, Ruisdael's earliest drawing. As noted below, there are two other drawings that bear the same date. The current state of our knowledge of Ruisdael's juvenilia makes it impossible to determine whether they were done before or after the Berlin drawing.
2. An impression of the etching is at the British Museum, no. 1861-5-18-193. Perhaps the same hand did the etchings after the artist's *Oak Trees at the Edge of a River*, Chantilly (Slive 2001, fig. D40a) and *Landscape with a Man Ploughing*, British Museum (Slive 2001, fig. D86a).

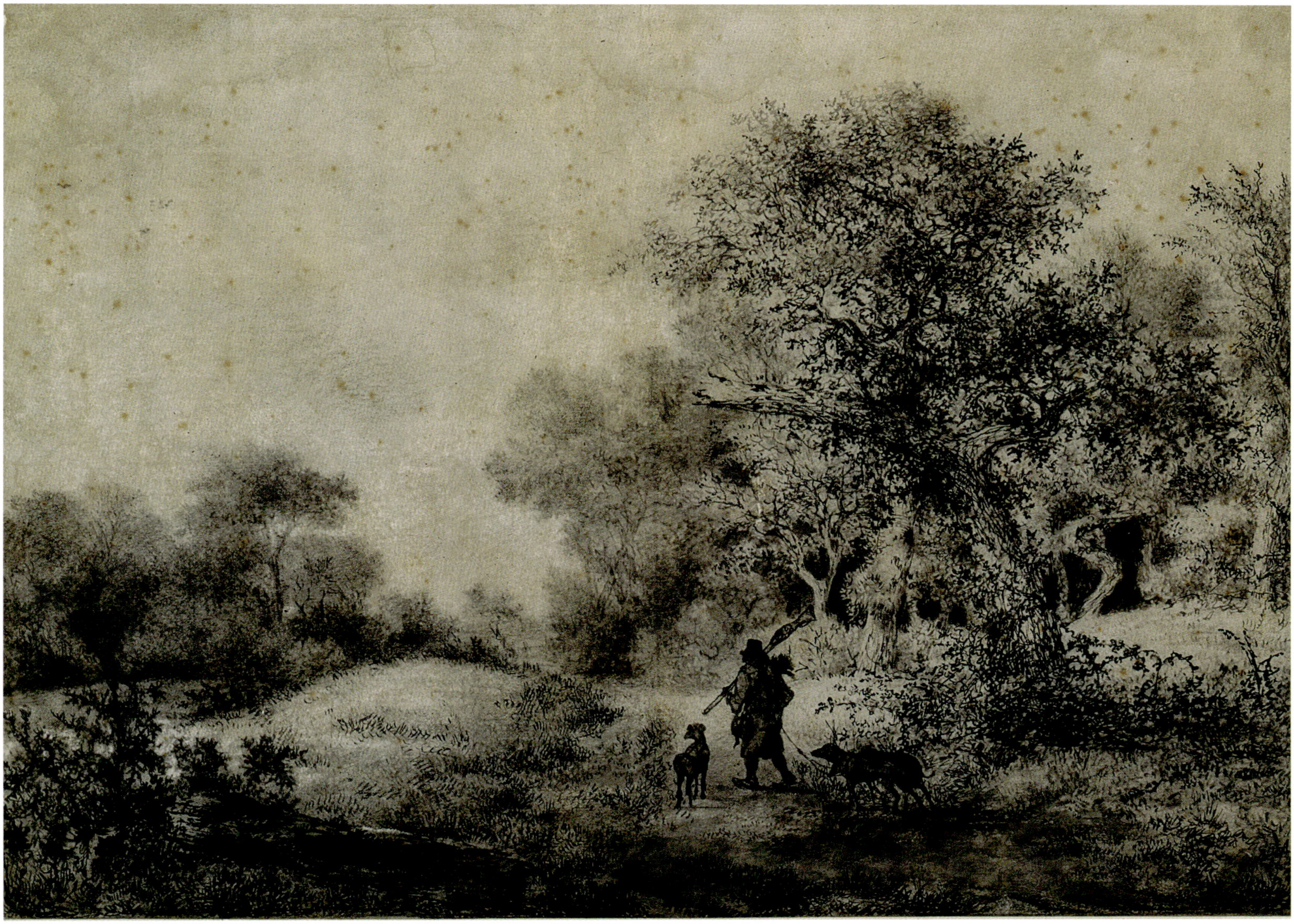

66

Shore of the Zuider Zee with Three Anglers and a View of the Ruined Church at Muiderberg and Naarden

Monogrammed and dated 1648, bottom left centre.[1] Black chalk, pen in grey ink, grey wash, touches of red, green and yellow watercolour, 17.6 × 29.4 cm
The British Museum, London, 1895.9.15.1299

PROVENANCE: Sale, Benjamin West, London (Christie's), 9 *sqq.* June 1820, no. 57 (30gns.); sale, E. Galichon, Paris (Drouot), 10–14 May 1875, no. 141 (fr.1,000); sale, B. Suermondt, Frankfurt a. M. (Prestel), 5 May 1879, no. 124; John Malcolm (1805–93); by descent to his son John Wingfield Malcolm; purchased 1895.

EXHIBITION: The Hague–Cambridge 1981–82, no. 64, repr.

LITERATURE: Josi 1821, 2, [n.p.] under "Jacob Ruisdael"; Ros Z45; Simon 1930, p.84; Hind 1915–31, 4, p.40, no. 1; Giltay 1980, p.142; no. 74, repr.; Slive 2001, no. D80, repr.

PMA and RA

In the distance of this grand drawing of 1648 there is a view of the ruined church of Muiderberg and beyond it, on the left, the tower of the church of Naarden can be seen. For Ruisdael's painting of a panoramic view of Naarden, dated a year earlier, and two drawings related to it, see cat. 6.

As in some other works done in the forties, Ruisdael uses the time-honoured diagonal compositional pattern for the expansive landscape. In his hands the scheme never becomes trite. Extraordinary is his use of light to isolate the trunk of the huge, back-bending tree while unifying the forms of its hoary, twisted crown with the richly foliated grove beyond it. The tall pole on the left makes a new structural accent.

The high finish of the drawing is found in others Ruisdael made about the same time.[2] They were most likely intended as autonomous works; the fact that two of the group are on parchment bolsters this supposition.[3] Jacob usually began them by first sketching the general outlines of the landscape with very light touches of chalk. He then worked them up with pen and more extensively with crisp strokes of the point of the brush. Their washes, like those in all of Ruisdael's existing washed drawings, are grey, ranging in value from deep darks to the most delicate, transparent tints.

A few faint touches of red, yellow and green watercolour are seen in the present drawing, the last remnants of more extensive passages of watercolour that have disappeared indicating that the beautiful sheet, at some time during the course of its history, was overexposed to the destructive effects of light. They must have been more conspicuous as late as 1820 when the drawing appeared in Benjamin West's 1820 sale since the compiler of the sale catalogue emphasized them: "N.B. In this drawing the artist has given his memorial tints for a picture".[4] Today these colours, interpreted as visual notes for a painting not as a worked-up watercolour that has faded, have virtually vanished.

The slight traces of watercolour in Ruisdael's *Landscape with a Ruined Church* (cat. 67), dated 1649, suggest that it also had larger areas of fugitive colour that vanished because it was overexposed to light.

1. The "8" of the date is a horizontal one; for other works that employ a "lazy eight" see Slive 2001, nos. 566, 578.
2. *E.g.*, Slive 2001, nos. D40, D81, D92, D94, D98, D109.
3. Slive 2001, nos. D40, D109.
4. Josi (1821) also wrote the drawing appeared in the 1820 West sale and its colours were only partially indicated, and noted it fetched 30 guineas – an astronomical price for a Ruisdael drawing in 1820. He added he knew four other watercolours in the Netherlands by the artist.

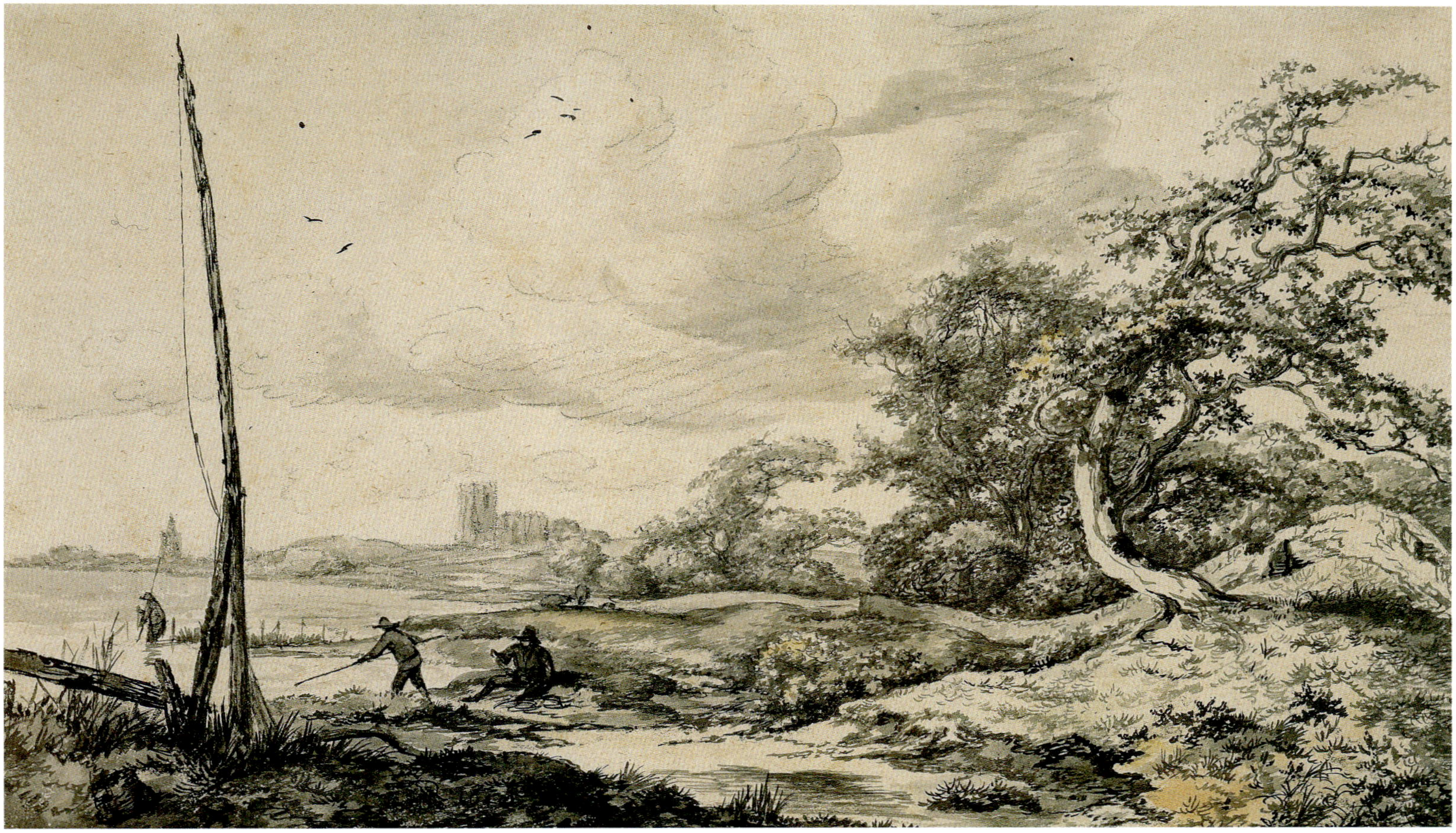

67

Landscape with a Grainfield and a Church with a Ruined Choir (at Soest?)

Monogrammed and dated 1649, lower left. Black chalk, pen in grey ink, grey wash and touches of yellow and green watercolour, 18.2 × 29.8 cm
The British Museum, London, Oo 11-248

PROVENANCE: Sale, Earl Spencer, London (Philipe), 10–17 June 1811, no. 702; collection R. Payne Knight, who bequeathed it to the museum in 1834.

EXHIBITION: The Hague–Cambridge 1981–82, no. 65, repr.

LITERATURE: Kleinmann [n.d.], 2, p.17, repr. (in reverse); *Ruysdael, Original Abbildungen* [1920?], repr. (in reverse); Ros Z46; Simon 1930, pp.67, 84; Hind 1915–31, 4, p.40, no. 2; Giltay 1980, p.142; no. 75, repr.; Slive 2001, no. D81, repr.

PMA

Rosenberg (Z46) and Hind (1931, 4, p.40, no. 2) expressed doubts about the reading of the last digit of the 1649 date on the drawing. Simon (1930, p.67) and Giltay (1980, p.142) have correctly read it as a "9". Even if the landscape were not dated, its strikingly close similarity to the conception, style and technique of the *Shore of the Zuider Zee* (cat. 66), dated 1648, would place it in the late forties. For comment regarding the faint touches of yellow and green watercolour on the drawing, see cat. 66. Although Ruisdael continued to make drawings during the course of the following three decades, the present landscape and his untraceable *Oaks on a Hillock*, also inscribed 1649 (Slive 2001, no. D109), are the latest known dated ones.

G. Hos (note at the RKD) has suggested that the ruined church in the drawing may be the one at Soest,[1] a town about thirty-five kilometres southeast of Naarden, where Jacob's grandfather settled and where his father was born. Ruisdael included views of Naarden in other works done in the forties (see cat. 6, 66).

1. Hos's identification is based on its similarity to a print in *Het verheerlykt Nederland of Kabinet van hedendaagsche gezigten*, 7, Amsterdam, 1745–74, no. 210.

68

Landscape with the Ruins of the Old Church at Muiderberg in the Distance

Inscribed by a later hand, lower right: *J. Ruijsdael* (vigorous scratching has virtually obliterated the inscription). About 1650–55. Black chalk, 15.1 × 19.3 cm
Albertina, Vienna, 10116

PROVENANCE: The "J. Ruijsdael collector" (see p. 168); Duke Albert von Sachsen-Teschen (1738–1822; founder of the Albertina).

EXHIBITIONS: Vienna 1993, no. 58, repr.; New York–Fort Worth 1995, no. 50, repr.

LITERATURE: Slive 1991, pp.602–04, repr; White 1999, pp.135–37, under no. A875; repr. p. 207, fig. 19 (inadvertently in reverse); Slive 2001, no. D122, repr.

PMA

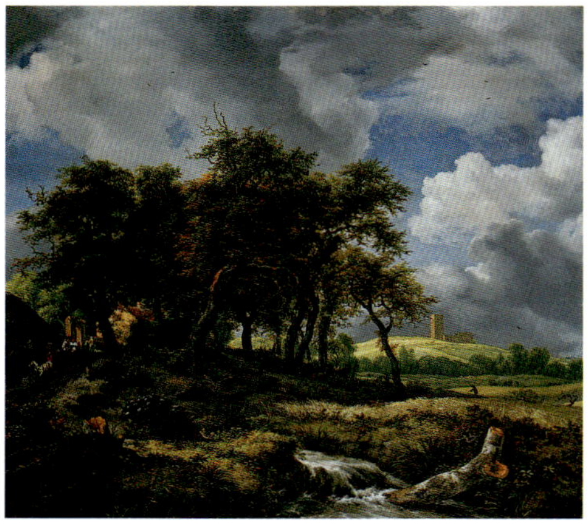

Fig. 68a Jacob van Ruisdael, *Landscape near the Ruins of the Old Church at Muiderberg*. Oxford, Ashmolean Museum.

The drawing, datable to the early or mid-fifties, belongs to the group of rapid, black chalk sketches Ruisdael began to make in the late forties (see pp.167–68). It served as a study for his *Landscape with the Ruins of the Old Church at Muiderberg* at the Ashmolean (fig. 68a; Slive 2001, no. 77) and is the only known preliminary study for his wooded landscapes, which number about one hundred fifty. We only can surmise how many similar working drawings the artist made before touching the support for a painting of one of the subjects that was so close to his heart.

The sketch includes the major elements of the painting and gives a clear indication of their position in space. In the foreground, the broken stump, the dead beech in the small rushing stream, and the elder bushes are indicated with pronounced saw-toothed and curly touches of black chalk characteristic of these sketches. The touch becomes lighter in the middle ground and distance, where there is an indication of the ruins of Muiderberg's Old Church. The wheeling birds and a suggestion of clouds are not missing, and even the solitary traveller has been given his place above the rapid, jagged strokes that serve as Jacob's shorthand for a grainfield. The staffage on the left in the Ashmolean painting does not appear; it is a later, rather incongruous addition. The principal changes in the finished work are the enrichment of the middle distance and, of greater consequence, the elaboration of the sky and the transformation of the grove of oaks. In Ruisdael's studio, where the painting was almost certainly done, the sky became more spacious and cloud filled, and the prominent trees more than doubled in number and acquired more towering, luxuriant crowns.

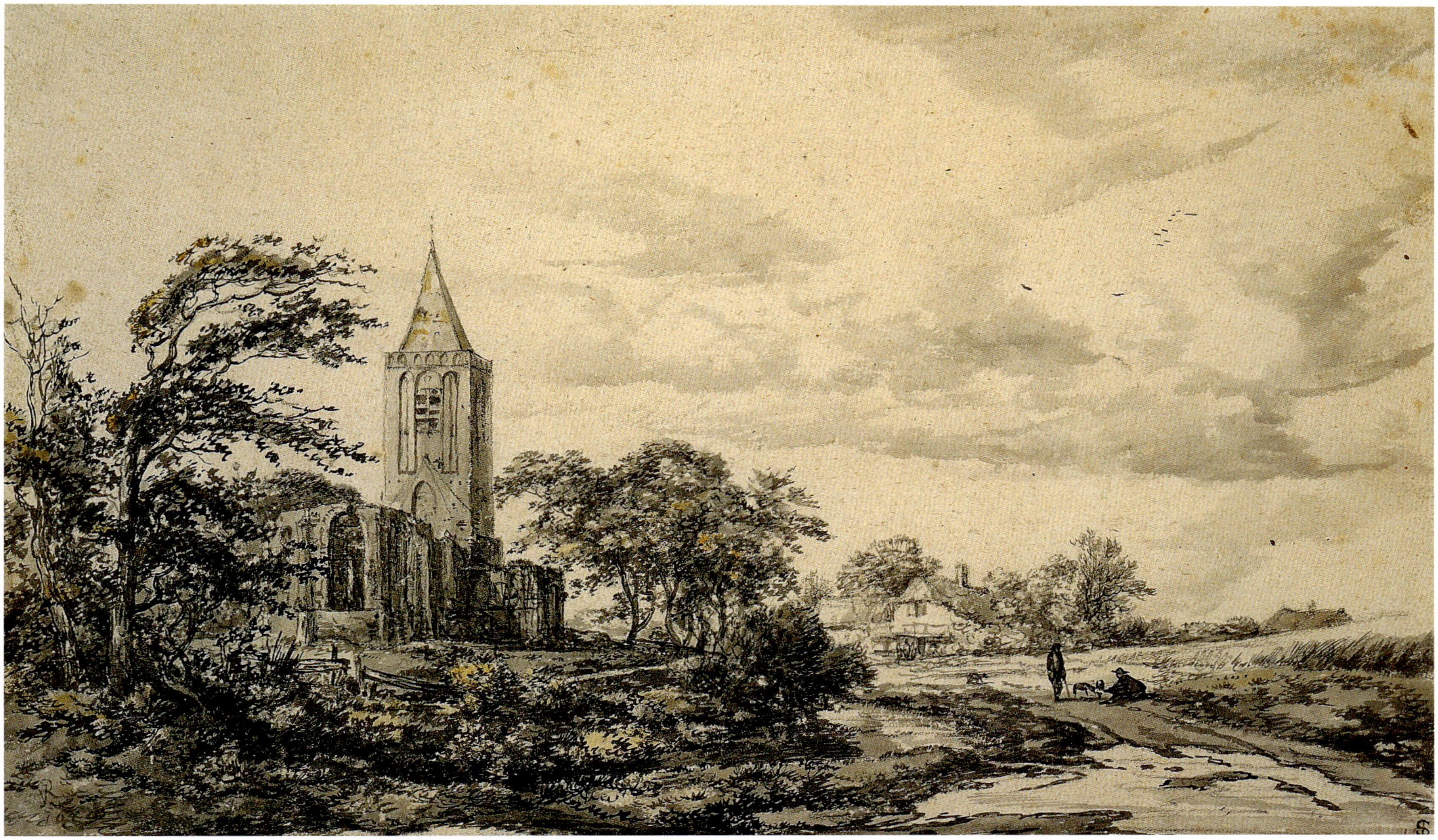

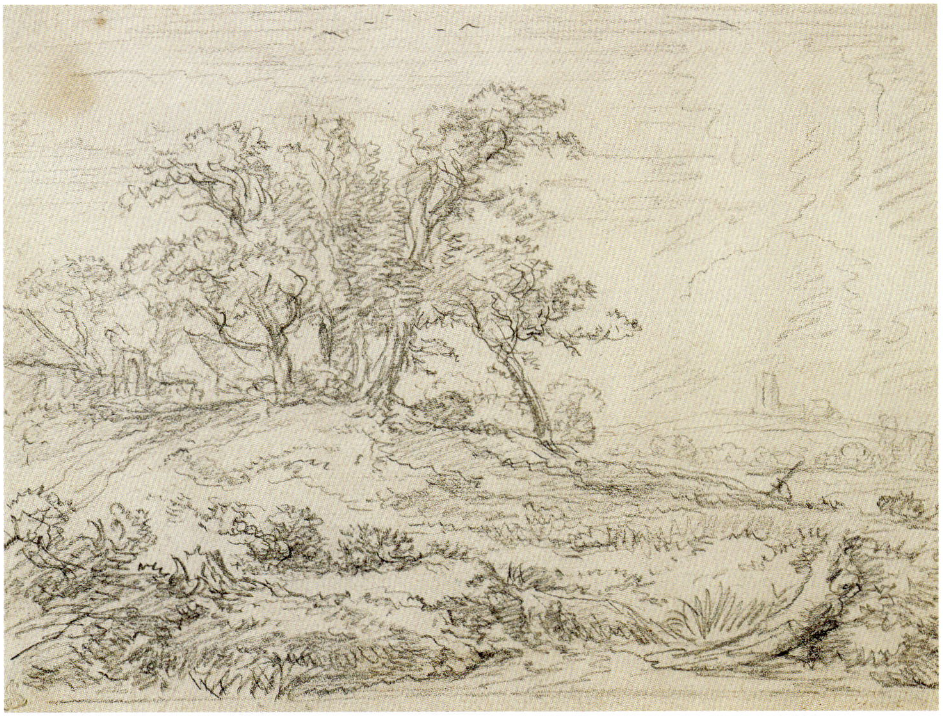

69

Landscape with the Heiligewegspoort at Amsterdam

About 1655–58. Black chalk, grey wash, pen and brown ink framing lines, 15.1 × 20.4 cm
Gemeentearchief, Amsterdam, v.E.32

PROVENANCE: Sale, Amsterdam (de Winter), 12 *sqq.* February 1770, no. 279; sale, Hendrik Busserus, Amsterdam (v.d. Schley), 21 October 1782, no. 2619; Baron van Leyden van Vlaardingen; sale, C. F. Roos, Amsterdam (Bom), 3 March 1866, no. 232 (Dfl.24, Bom); sale, [Atlas van Amsterdam], Amsterdam (Muller), 27–28 November 1879, no. 232; sale, J.P., Paris (Drouot), 8 December 1937, no. 96, repr. (wrong dimensions; Beets for Christiaan Pieter van Eeghen). Collection van Eeghen, which has been on deposit at the Gemeentearchief, Amsterdam, since 1980.

EXHIBITION: Amsterdam 1955, no. 36, repr.

LITERATURE: Giltay 1980, pp.149–50; no. 14; Bakker *et al.* 1988, pp.85–86, no. 32, repr.; Davies 1992, p.224, under no. d4; Slive 2001, no. D13, repr.

PMA and RA

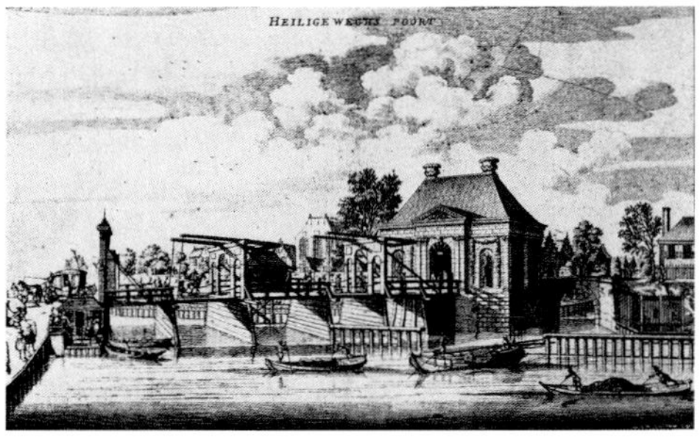

Fig. 69a Jacob van Meurs (attributed to), *Heiligewegspoort at Amsterdam.* Engraving in O. D[apper]., *Historische beschrijving der Stadt Amsterdam*, Amsterdam, 1663.

The site of the Heiligewegspoort on the southern side of Amsterdam's old city wall, in the vicinity of what is now the Koningsplein, had only a simple gate since *c.*1540 when one constructed in *c.*1427 was torn down (d'Ailly 1963, p.282). In about 1636 the city fathers commissioned Jacob van Campen to build a new one. Construction began in 1636. It was the first assignment Amsterdam gave the man who became Holland's leading seventeenth-century architect. His design provided Holland with its first classical gate, and, like projects done for some of his early private clients, already shows his mastery of the style that found its most magnificent seventeenth-century Dutch expression in the plans he made *c.*1650 for Amsterdam's monumental New Town Hall.

Judging from contemporary representations and descriptions the gate must have made a splendid effect. It was faced entirely with white sandstone and embellished with ionic pilasters, large niches that held allegorical figures, high-relief ornaments, polychrome coats of arms, and a blue slate roof. However, the new gate did not ornament Amsterdam for very long. It was demolished in 1664, a victim, as other structures in the area, sacrificed for the construction of the new Herengracht during the course of Amsterdam's vast expansion that began in the early sixties. Removal proceeded rapidly; the order for its demolition was signed in July, 1664, and less than two months later some of its hard stone was employed for the construction of the portcullises of the city's new Muider and Weesper Gates (Kannegeiter 1965, p.58).

Ruisdael shows the gate from the southeast but he does not offer a topographically accurate view of it as is apparent when his drawing is juxtaposed to the engraving attributed to Jacob van Meurs (*c.*1619–*c.*1680) of the structure seen from the same direction[1] (fig. 69a). To be sure, the gate is recognizable in Ruisdael's sketch – early compilers of sale catalogues had no difficulty identifying it – but it is obvious that in his hands the building became the subject of a capriccio in which light and atmospheric effects of an early morning or evening sky play a dominant role. Instead of showing the gate in its urban setting Ruisdael placed it on an imaginary lush wooded embankment suggesting it serves as a noble entrance to a grand country estate or garden. There are other changes. The arched stone bridge and the canal it spanned on the gate's right side have both disappeared. The canal served as an entrance from the Singel to the city's inner canals but the story of the movement of boats and their cargoes on Amsterdam's waterways was not Ruisdael's concern in this idyllic scene. One of the gate's two drawbridges designed to facilitate the passage of large vessels plying the Singel also has vanished. The drawbridge that remains has lost its triumphal arch-like support; two straightforward posts have taken its place.

1. The print attributable to Jacob van Meurs (fig. 69a) is in Dapper 1663, after p.511; the same print is in von Zesen 1664, after p.202 (Hollstein, 14, p.22, under no. 27).

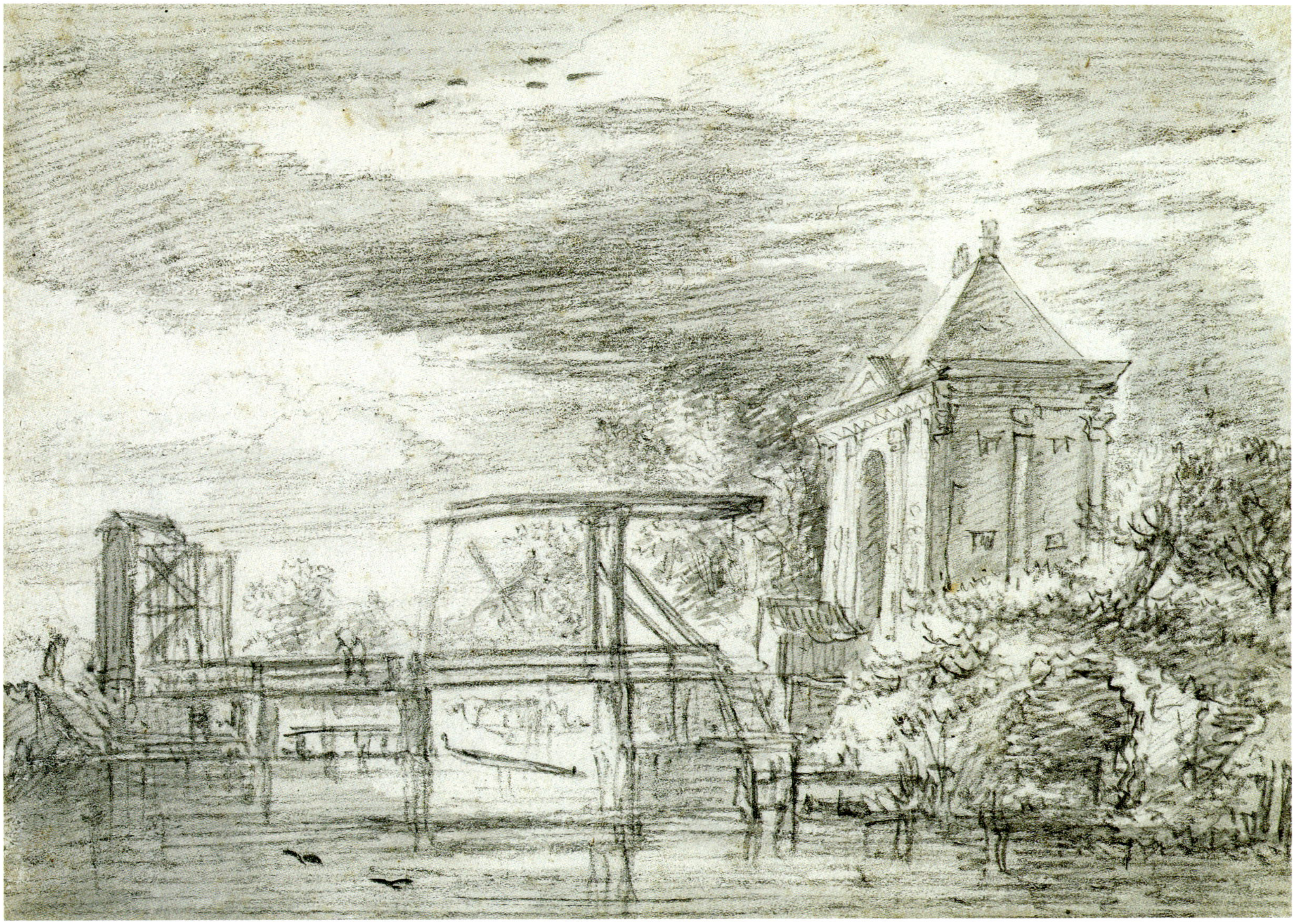

70

The Montelbaanstoren at Amsterdam

About 1655–58. Inscribed by a later hand, lower right: *J. Ruijsdael* (vigorous scratching has virtually obliterated the inscription). Black chalk, grey wash, 14.5 × 19.5 cm
Département des Arts Graphiques, Musée du Louvre, Paris, Collection Edmond Rothschild, 3532 DR

PROVENANCE: "The J. Ruijsdael collector" (see p. 168); most probably C. Josi; sale, J. H. Molkenboer, Amsterdam (de Vries), 17 October 1825, no. H.22 (as Ruisdael); sale, J. Goll van Franckenstein, Amsterdam (de Vries), 1 July 1833, no. GG.7; sale, G. Leembruggen, Amsterdam (Roos), 5 *sqq*. March 1866, no. 546 (as Ruisdael; Dfl.31, Pool); sale, Henri Duval of Liége, Amsterdam (Muller), 22–23 June 1910, no. 169, repr. (as Hobbema; Dfl.810); Edmond de Rothschild (1845–1934); bequeathed by his heirs to the museum, 1935.

LITERATURE: Josi 1821, 2, [n.p.] under "Jacob Ruisdael"; Broulhiet 29 (Hobbema); Simon 1940, p.209 (to judge from a reproduction, not good enough for Hobbema); Giltay 1980, pp.149–50; no. 88, repr.; Amsterdam–Paris 1998–99, pp.156–57, repr.; Slive 2001, no. D96, repr.

RA

Rightly related by Giltay (1980, pp.149–50) to three of Ruisdael's other drawings identifiable as views of Amsterdam (cat. 69; Slive 2001, nos. D2, D97, both reproduced); all are datable soon after the mid-fifties. The four sheets are among the latest black chalk sketches Ruisdael began to make in the late forties. This one is particularly close in style to his *Wooden Tower and Houses on the Bank of a River (probably the Amstel)*, also at the Louvre (Slive 2001, no. D97).

The Montelbaan Tower was built some time after 1516 as part of the fortifications outside the walls of Amsterdam; it lost its original function after the city's expansion in 1591–93 placed it inside the walls. In 1606 an octagonal brick structure and tall wooden spire, designed by Hendrik de Keyser, was added to it; the addition was enhanced by the installation of a prominent clock, vanes, and bells. The way the tower and its additions looked on an embankment of the Oude Schans in Ruisdael's time, and still does today, is seen in an engraving attributed to Jacob van Meurs (*c*.1619–*c*.1680) that appeared in a lavishly illustrated historical-topographical description of Amsterdam published in 1663[1] (fig. 70a). But as far as Ruisdael was concerned the grand spire did not exist. He completely ignored it. So did Rembrandt in a reed pen and wash drawing he made of it *c*.1644–45[2] (fig. 70b).

Although precise dates cannot be assigned to either Ruisdael's or Rembrandt's drawing of the tower *sans* spire, there can be no doubt that Jacob's sketch postdates the older master's. Was Ruisdael inspired to make the radical change in the city's well-known landmark by a glimpse of Rembrandt's drawing? Though the answer to the question must remain speculative, I lean toward a negative answer to the query; "influence" is not the only explanation for similar pictorial decisions.

Yet another question should be posed: Why did both artists omit the spire? There is no cut-and-dried answer to this query either. But it is not news that both artists, like so many of their contemporaries, did not have an unalterable commitment to making exact transcriptions of architectural monuments. Consider Ruisdael's sketch of Amsterdam's *Heiligewegspoort* (cat. 69), one of the drawings related in subject, style and date to the present one. It alters the gate and shows it in an imaginary landscape. And when Rembrandt made a drawing in *c*.1655 of a view that focuses upon the city's late medieval tower *Swijgh Utrecht*, originally part of its fortified wall, he left off its prominent spire *cum* gable, which were later additions.[3] Ruisdael's quick sketch changes the monument and gives equal attention to its setting on one of Amsterdam's busy, broad waterways. What the artists share is a preference for the ancient structure without its later addition. This is not the only case where they chose to ignore modern architecture. Neither of them ever made Amsterdam's brand-new Town Hall, by far the city's most conspicuous and imposing architectural glory, the major motif in their work.

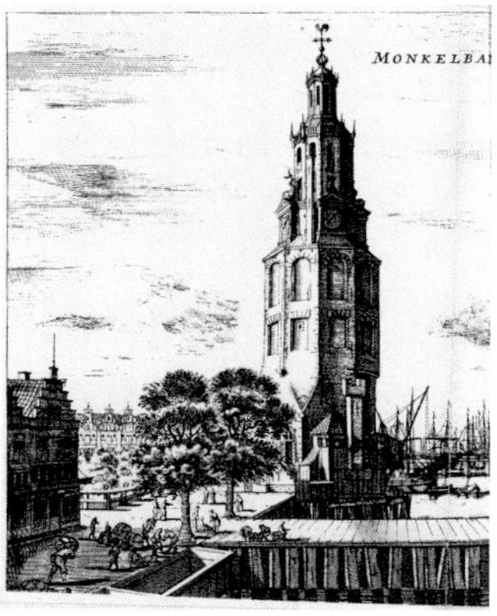

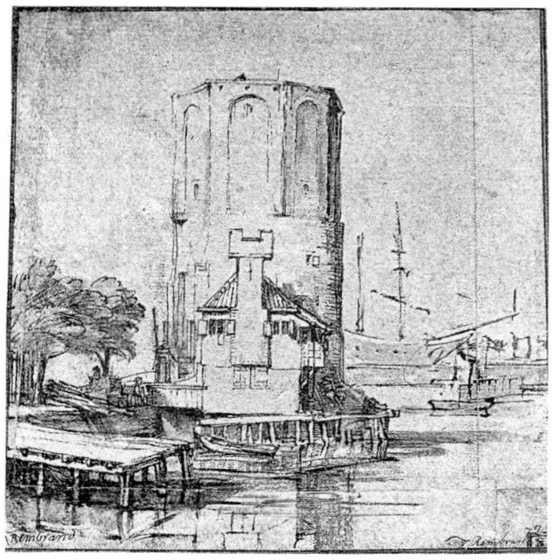

Fig. 70a Jacob van Meurs (attributed to), *Montelbaanstoren at Amsterdam*. Detail of an engraving in O. D[apper], *Historische beschrijving der Stadt Amsterdam*, Amsterdam, 1663.

Fig. 70b Rembrandt, *Montelbaanstoren at Amsterdam*. Reed pen, brown ink and wash. Het Rembrandthuis, Amsterdam.

1. Dapper 1663, after p.173; the same print is in von Zesen 1664, after p.150 (Hollstein, 14, p.22, under no. 27).
2. Het Rembrandthuis, Amsterdam; Benesch no. 1309; Washington 1990, no. 49; Amsterdam–Paris 1998–99, pp.156–59. Notice of the omission of the additions was first published by Lugt 1915, pp.31–32; thereafter it has been cited frequently in the Rembrandt literature. The drawing has been variously dated from *c*.1640 to the mid-fifties; for convincing reasons to date it *c*.1644–45 see Amsterdam–Paris 1998–99, pp.157–59.
3. Rijksmuseum, Amsterdam; Benesch no. 1334; Schatborn 1985, no. 34.

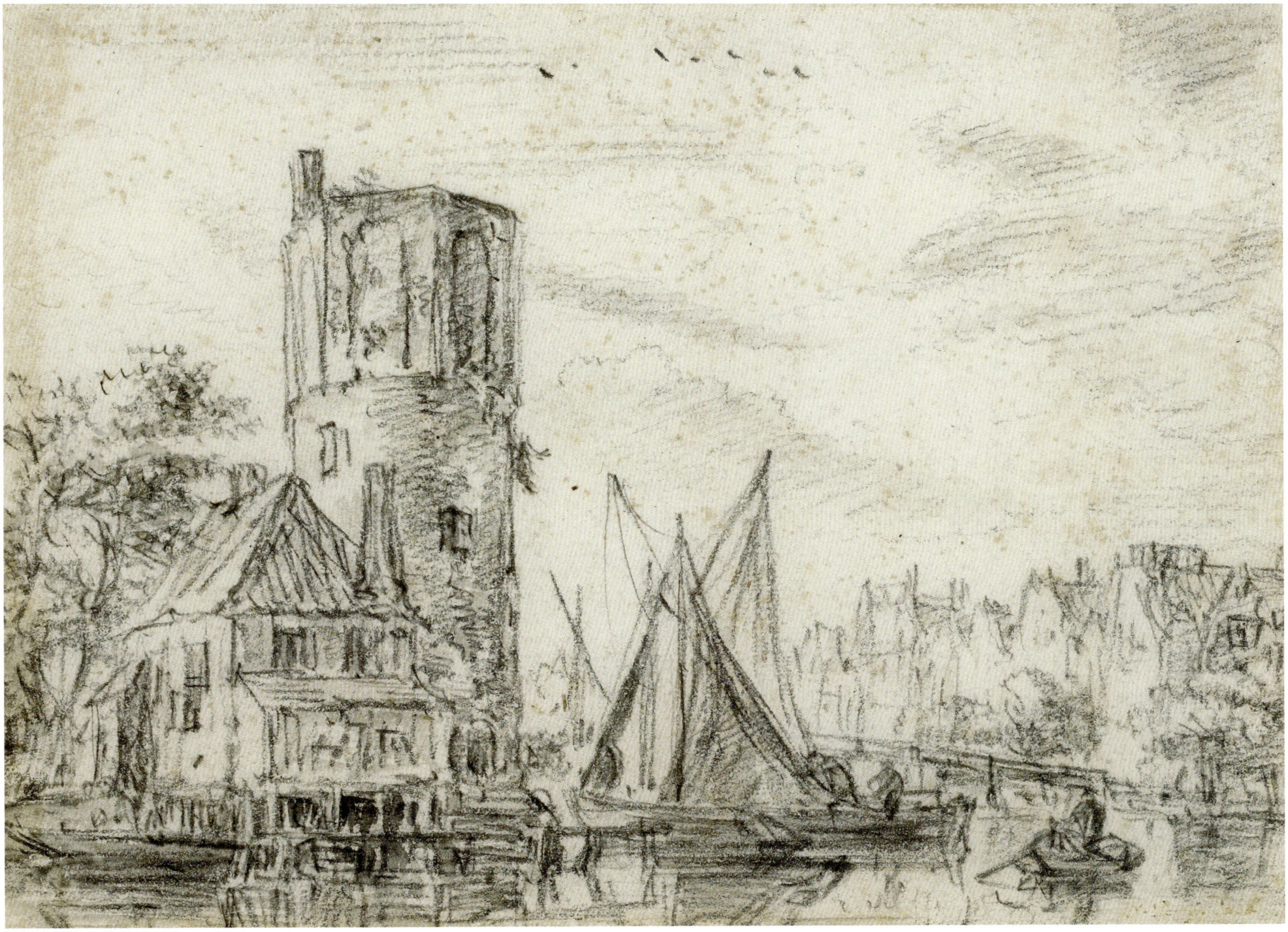

71

View of Rhenen from the East

Early 1650s. Black chalk(?), grey wash, 12.5 × 19.5 cm
The State Hermitage Museum, St. Petersburg, OP 5531

PROVENANCE: Sale, D. Muilman, Amsterdam (de Bosch), 29 March 1773, no. K.741 (Fouquet); Paul I; acquired for the Hermitage by 1797.

EXHIBITIONS: St. Petersburg 1867, p.67, no. 297; The Hague–Cambridge 1981–82, no. 69, repr. (shown in The Hague only).

LITERATURE: J. W. Niemeijer, "Varia Topographica: I. Ruisdael in Noord Brabant?," *O.H.*, 77, 1962, p.61; Giltay 1980, p.165; no. 72, repr.; Deys 1981, p.27, repr.; Walford 1991, p.71, repr. (perhaps 1649); Slive 2001, no. D112, repr.

PMA and RA

The conspicuous stamp bearing the large Cyrillic initial of Czar Paul I (reigned 1791–1801) below a crown in the lower right of the sheet was put on almost 8,000 drawings in the Imperial Russian collection that were inventoried in 1797. It also appears on the Hermitage's *Bulwark with a Wooden Footbridge* by Ruisdael (cat. 88) and the museum's six other drawings by the artist, establishing that they too were in the Imperial collection by 1797.

There may be an ever-so-slight underdrawing in black chalk beneath the grey wash of this panoramic view of Rhenen. Whether it is there or not, in this instance, is of little consequence. The effect of the drawing is of one solely done in brush and wash. Though the sheet shows some effects of over-exposure to light,[1] it still impresses by the extraordinary range of its tonal richness, luminous transparency and suggestiveness.

Less unusual is the subject of the drawing. The beautiful late Gothic tower of St. Cunera, which soars above the town of Rhenen and dominates the surrounding plain, was made the focal point of landscapes done by many Dutch artists, including Hercules Segers, Rembrandt, Jan van Goyen and Aelbert Cuyp.[2] The town was easily accessible, lying on the Rhine, about thirty-five kilometres southeast of Utrecht. Ruisdael himself made another drawing that shows Rhenen's skyline seen from the west, which was formerly at the Hermitage and is now at Berlin (cat. 72). Although wash is used more sparingly in the St. Petersburg sheet, close similarities in its treatment to the Berlin drawing indicate that both works were done at the same time.

1. Alexei Larionov, curator of drawings at the Hermitage, informed me (June 2002) the sketch was uninterruptedly exhibited in a gallery of the museum from 1867 until about 1900.
2. For a rich selection of illustrations of their views and those by other landscapists see Deys 1981, pp.24–44. The present drawing was erroneously catalogued as *Vue de Flessingue, à l'embouchere de l'Escaut* when it was placed on exhibit in St. Petersburg in 1867 (no. 297); it bore its wrong title at the Hermitage until J. W. Niemeijer (1962, p.61) recognized, almost a century later, that it is not a view of Flushing at the mouth of Schelde, but a panorama of Rhenen.

72

View of Rhenen from the West

Early 1650s. Black chalk, grey wash, 11.4 × 18.8 cm
Staatliche Museen zu Berlin, Kupferstichkabinett, Berlin, KdZ 14712

PROVENANCE: Sale, D. Muilman, Amsterdam (de Bosch), 29 March 1773, no. K.742; Paul I, acquired for the Hermitage by 1797 (inv. no. 5539); sale, Handzeichnungen alter Meister . . . aus den . . . Sammlungen der Sowjet Union, Leipzig (Boerner), 29 April 1931, no. 210, repr.; acquired by the Berlin museum in 1931.

EXHIBITION: Berlin 1974, no. 160, repr. (1660s; wrongly called Ruisdael's only existing view of Rhenen).

LITERATURE: Rosenberg 1928, p.22; Z35; Rosenberg 1931, p.111, repr. (1650–53); Simon 1935, p.192 (probably done in 1660s); Giltay 1980, p.165; no. 21 (1650–53); Slive 1981, p.180 under no. 69, repr. (early fifties); Deys 1981, p.24, repr.; Walford 1991, p.71 (1649); Slive 2001, no. D19, repr.

PMA

This view of Rhenen and another view of the town, now at the Hermitage (cat. 71), appeared in the Muilman sale held at Amsterdam in 1773. Both were acquired for the Hermitage by 1797 along with a half-dozen other Ruisdael drawings that were in Muilman's collection. They were separated when the present drawing was auctioned by the Soviet Union in 1931; it was acquired for Berlin at that sale.

An inscription by a later hand on the drawing's old mount correctly identifies the site and artist: "Rhaenen door J^B Ruysdael". The town's skyline is dominated by St. Cunera, a late Gothic church with a high, elaborate church tower erected 1492–1531.

The Berlin sheet was first assigned to the early 1650s when Rosenberg published it in 1928 (p.22; also see Rosenberg 1931, p.111). He proposed that it was

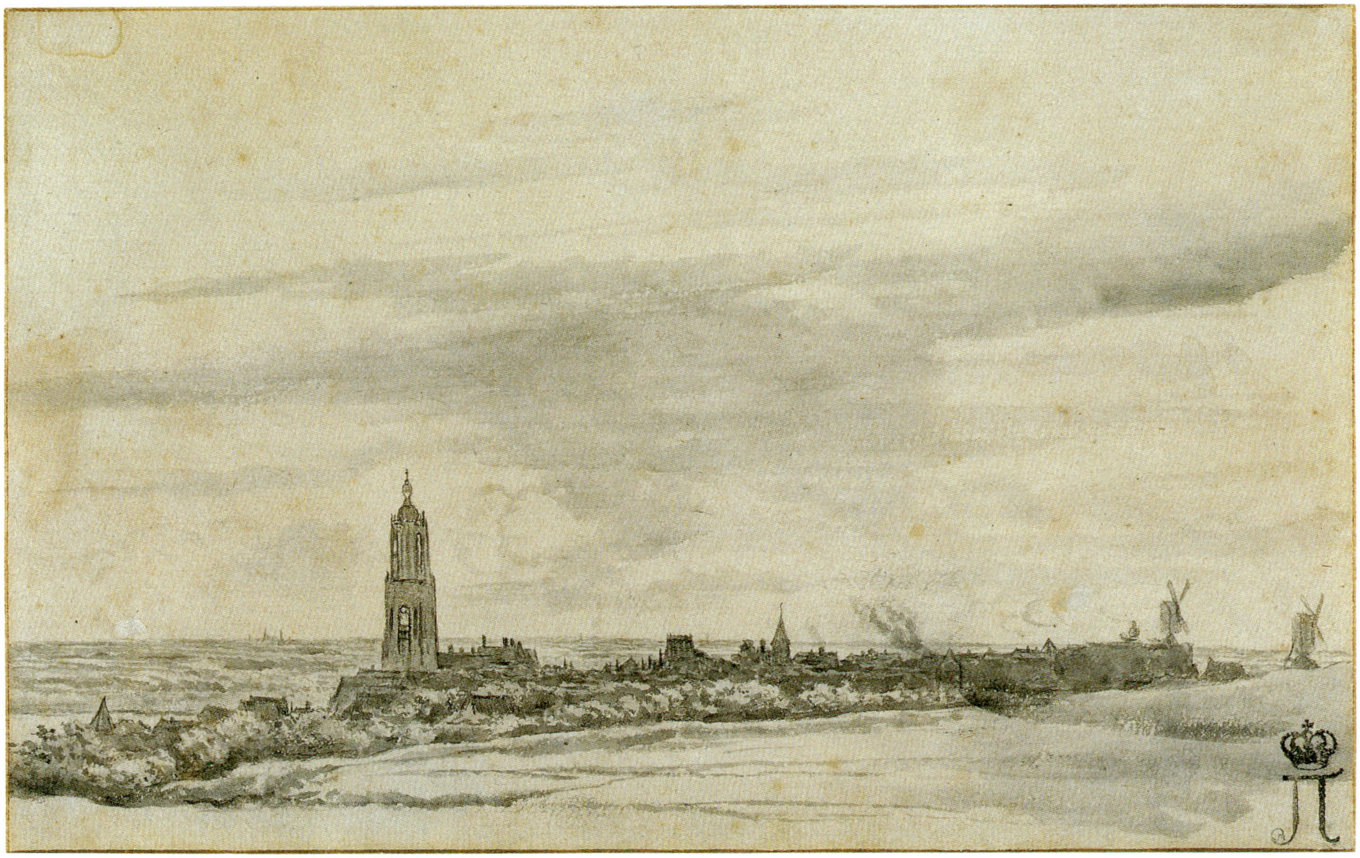

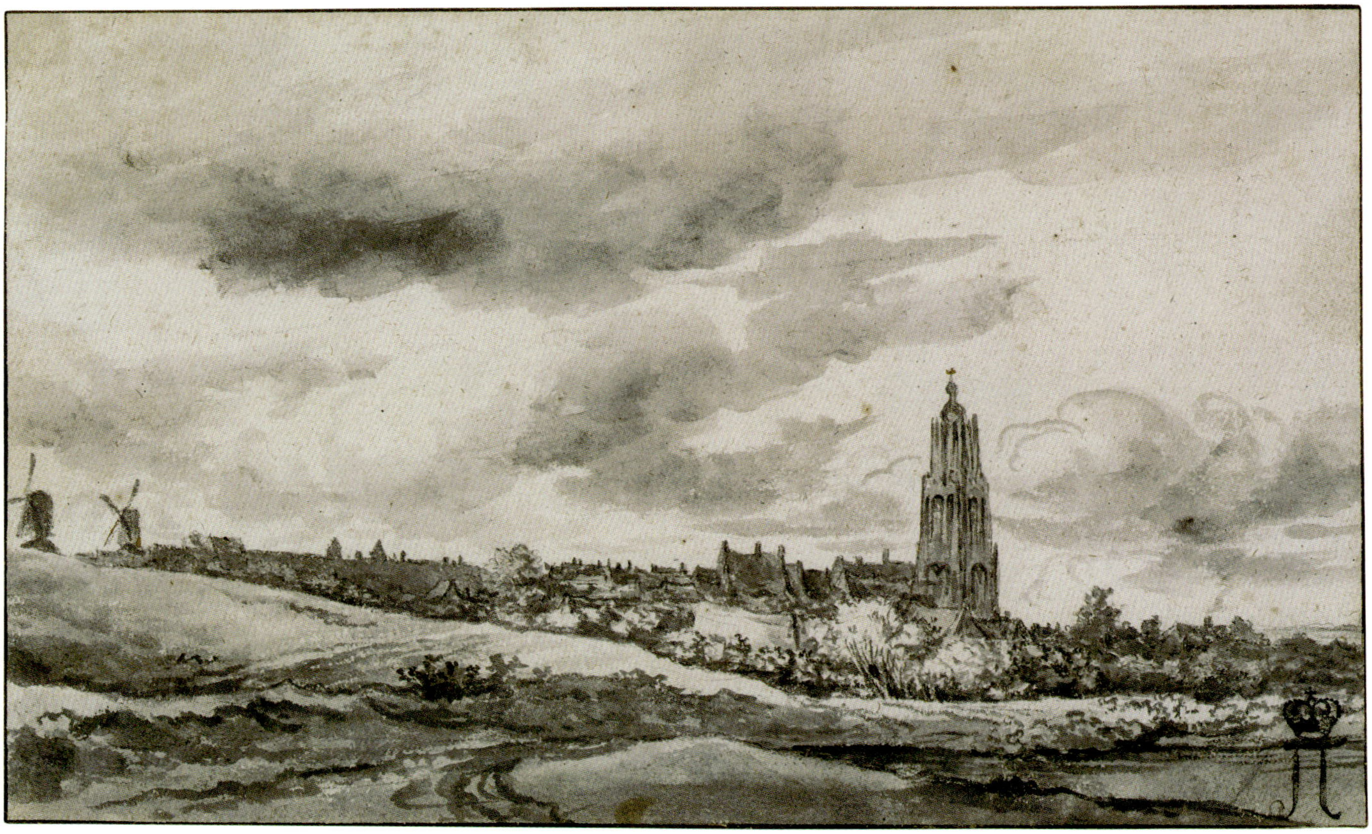

probably made by Ruisdael during the course of a visit to Rhenen when he was on his travels to the Dutch–German border region. Rosenberg did not catalogue Ruisdael's second drawing of Rhenen that is still at the Hermitage (cat. 71), his *View of Vianen* at the Amsterdam Historical Museum or his *View of Wijk bij Duurstede* at the British Museum (Slive 2001, nos. D11, D82, respectively). Close analogies of their compositional schemes and handling of the medium place them at the same time. All four townscapes probably were done during the course of the artist's travels along the Rhine and Lek River in the early fifties.

Walford (1991) proposes that the present drawing and the *View of Rhenen* at St. Petersburg served as the point of departure for the artist's *Banks of a River* at Edinburgh (cat. 12). Since the latter is dated 1649, he assigns a date of 1649 to both drawings. Since I do not see a connection between the compositions of the drawings and the masterwork at Edinburgh, and I am not convinced the tower in the painting is based on St. Cunera, Rhenen's prominent church, I find no reason to abandon the date in the early fifties assigned to them by Rosenberg.

73

Wooded Landscape with a Pond

Monogrammed, lower left. Early 1650s. Black chalk, grey and black wash, 19.8 × 31 cm
Rijksmuseum, Amsterdam, RP-T-1984-11

PROVENANCE: C. Ploos van Amstel; probably his sale, Amsterdam, 3 March 1800, no. T.9 (Dfl.76, Boddens, with T.10, which is identical with Slive 2001, no. D62); Jhr. J. A. Repelaer collection; sale, the heirs of J. A. Repelaer, The Hague, 7–8 November 1967, no. 168; W. van Dalfsen, Arnhem; acquired by the Rijksprentenkabinet, 1984.

EXHIBITIONS: Amsterdam 1987, no. 53, repr; Amsterdam 2000a, no. 72.

LITERATURE: Laurentius *et al.* 1980, p.358; Giltay 1980, pp.155 (early fifties); 158, repr.; no. 113; *Bulletin van het Rijksmuseum*, 32, 1984, no. 2, p.90, repr. (early fifties); Broos 1989, pp.48–50, repr.; Davies 1992, p.86, fig. 67; Slive 2001, no. D8, repr.

PMA

This exceptionally well-preserved, highly finished sheet ranks with the artist's most beautiful wooded landscape drawings. It is safe to say it was done as an autonomous work.

The proposal (Broos 1989) that it is identical with a sheet Sybrand Feitama II records in his notes as a Ruisdael landscape drawing, with a peasant cottage, which he inherited from his grandfather or father and that he had J. de Moucheron retouch in about 1710 and then, in 1742, employed Nicholaas Verkolje (1673–1746) to add the staffage, is unconvincing.[1] The drawing does not show a trace of a cottage and it is impossible to spot the work of more than one hand in the magnificent work.

1. "J." de Moucheron is certainly a reference to Isaac de Moucheron (1667-1744). In Slive 2001, no. D8, "J." de Moucheron is erroneously called Jacob de Moucheron.

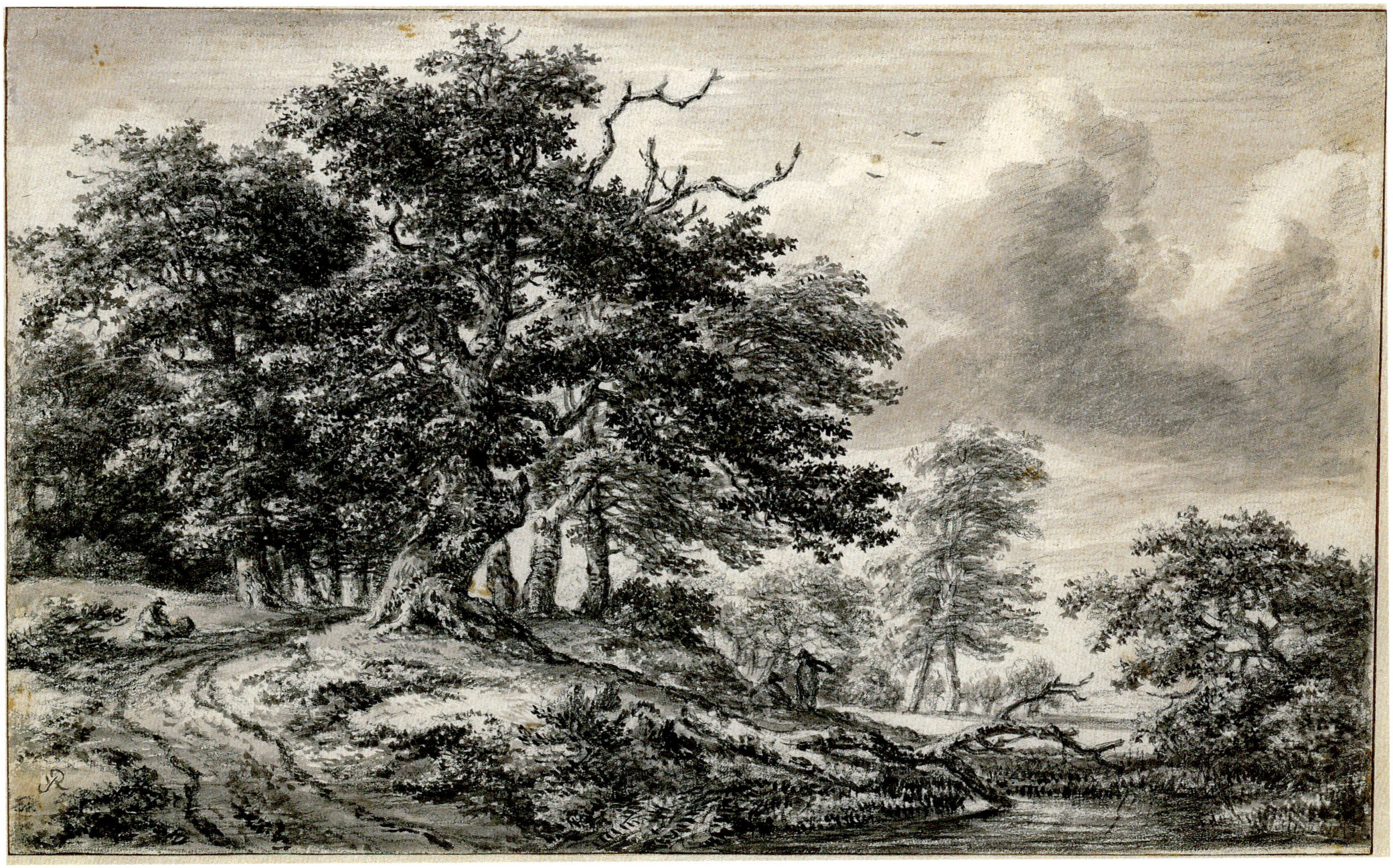

74

Water Mill

Signed in pen on the verso in a later hand: *Ruysdal*. 1650s. Black chalk, grey wash, 20 × 31.3 cm
Rijksmuseum, Amsterdam, RP-T-1887-A-1392

PROVENANCE: Sale, J. de Vos Jbsz., Amsterdam (Roos), 22–23 May 1883, no. 465; Vereniging Rembrandt, transferred to the Rijksmuseum, 1887.

EXHIBITION: Amsterdam 1987, no. 54, repr.

LITERATURE: Moes [1906], 2, no. 69, repr. (Ruisdael); Lugt 1927, p.22 under no. 42 (Hobbema or Ruisdael); Broulhiet 1, repr. (probably Ruisdael); Frerichs 1963, no. 73, repr. (Hobbema); Giltay 1980, pp.169–72; no. 8, repr. (Ruisdael; 1650–60); Slive 1991, pp.601–02 (Ruisdael); Slive 2001, no. D6, repr.

RA

This sensitively worked-up drawing of an overshot water mill of a type found in the eastern province of Gelderland was used as a preparatory study for the artist's painting now at the Toledo Museum of Art (fig. 74a)[1]. A painted copy of the composition by Ruisdael's pupil Meindert Hobbema datable to the late 1650s provides a probable *terminus ante quem* for both works.[2]

Ruisdael made three other drawings datable to the fifties of the same mill showing it from different points of view. They also were used as preparatory studies for paintings. The one at Haarlem (cat. 75) is a study for a painting in Melbourne (fig. 75a). The others, at the Amsterdam Historical Museum and the British Museum[3] are studies for paintings in the collection of the heirs of Hans P. Wertitsch, Vienna and at the Netherlands Institute for Cultural Heritage, Amsterdam.[4]

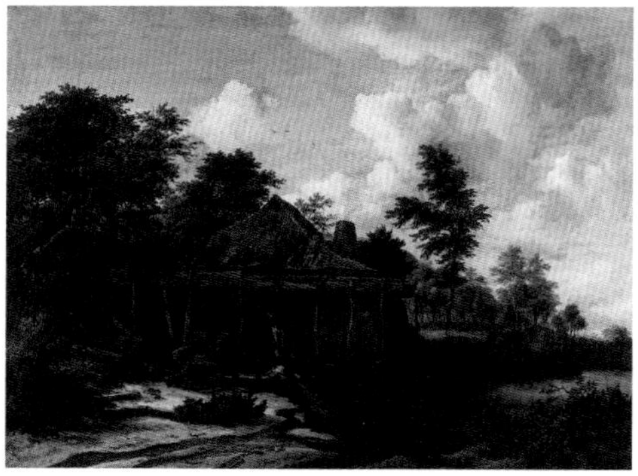

Fig. 74a Jacob van Ruisdael, *Water Mill at the Edge of a Wood*. The Toledo Museum of Art.

1. Slive 2001, no. 124.
2. Panel, 52 × 67.5. Signed, lower right. Illustrated *ibid.*, fig. 124a. In the 1957 Summer Exhibition, P. de Boer, Amsterdam, [n.p.], repr. De Boer kindly informed me it was sold to an Austrian collector *c.*1958; its present whereabouts are unknown.
3. Slive 2001, nos. D12, D83.
4. *Ibid.*, nos. 125, 116.

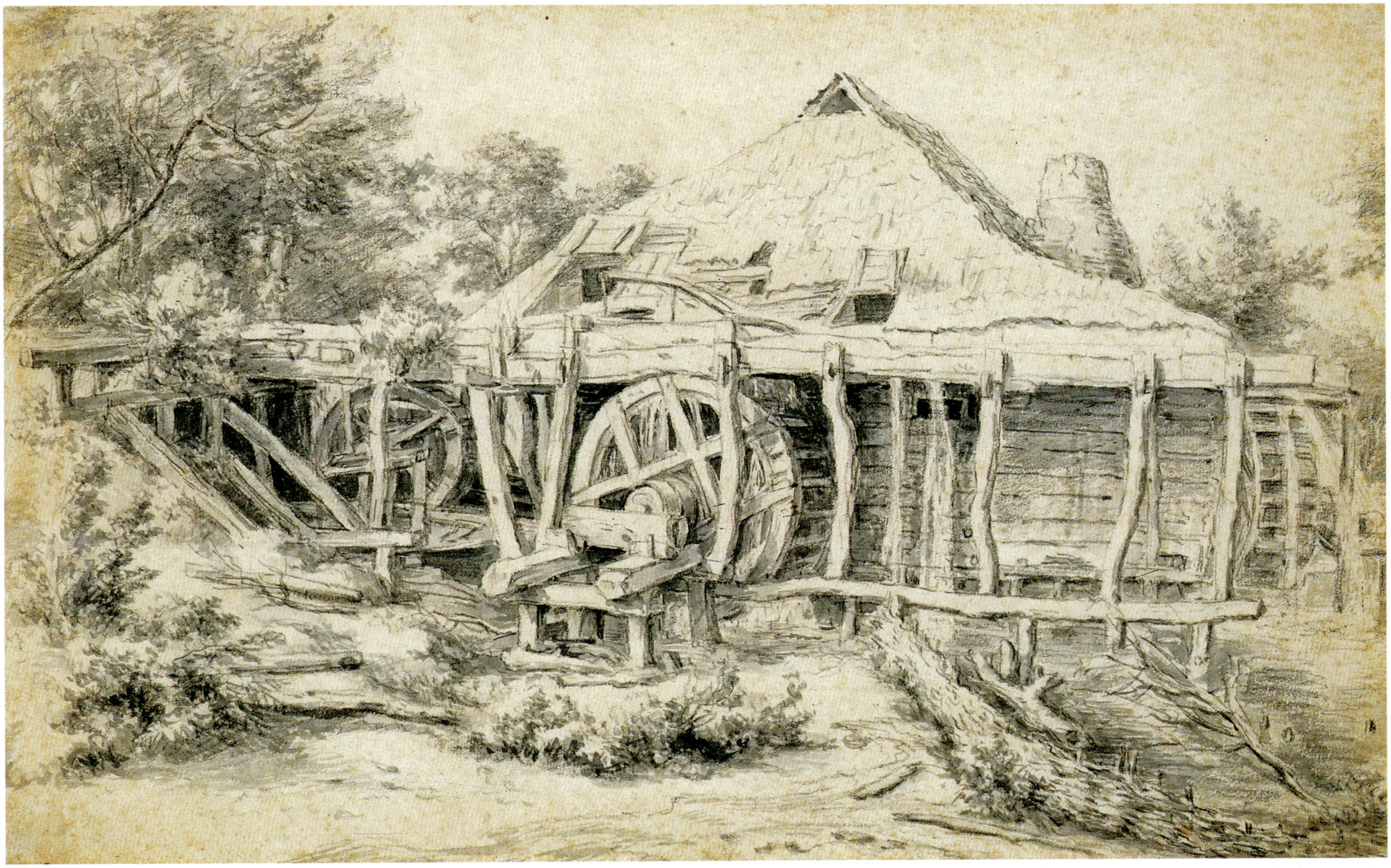

75

Water Mill in a Wooded Landscape

About 1651–55. Black chalk, brush and grey ink, framing line in pen and brown ink, 20.1 × 31.4 cm
Teyler Museum, Haarlem, R38

PROVENANCE: Collection E. Valckenier-Hooft; sale, A. van der Willigen and A. van der Willigen Pz, The Hague (de Visser), 10–11 June 1874, no. 122 (as Hobbema; Dfl.825, van der Vlugt for the museum).

EXHIBITIONS: Washington and elsewhere 1958–59, p.43, no. 106 (Hobbema); Brussels–Hamburg 1961, no. 148 (late Hobbema[1]).

LITERATURE: Ms. catalogue of the Teyler collection, 1864, no. P79a (added; Hobbema); Scholten 1904, p.255, no. R38 (Hobbema); Kleinmann [n.d.], 1, pl. 5 (Hobbema); Mellaart 1926, no. 27 (Hobbema); Rosenberg 1927, p.142 (Hobbema); Lugt 1927, p.22, under no. 42 (Hobbema or Ruisdael); Broulhiet 3 (Ruisdael; preparatory study for *Water Mill* now at Melbourne); Melbourne, National Gallery of Victoria, Catalogue, 1967, p.116, under no. 1249/3 (probably by Ruisdael and a study for the gallery's painting, an attribution endorsed by I.Q. van Regteren Altena); Kusnezow 1975, pl. 37 (Hobbema); Giltay 1980, pp.169–71; no. 60, repr. (Ruisdael; 1650–60); Slive 1991, pp.601–02 (Ruisdael; 1650s); Walford 1991, p.123, repr. (Ruisdael; 1660s); Plomp 1997, pp.357–58, no. 410 (Ruisdael); Slive 2001, no. D63, repr.

PMA

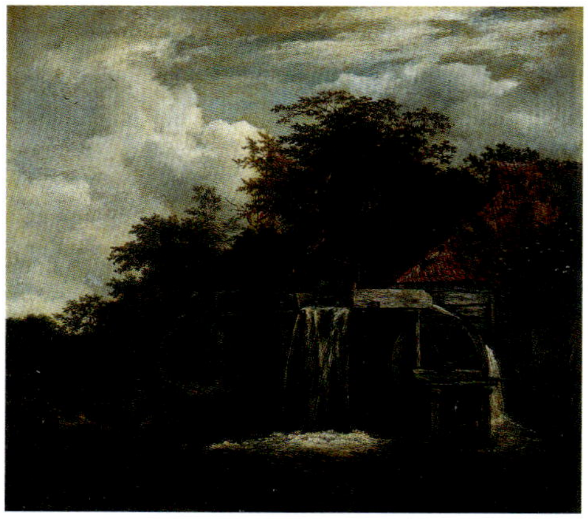

Fig. 75a Jacob van Ruisdael, *A Water Mill*. National Gallery of Victoria, Melbourne.

The stain in the lower right corner of the drawing hardly detracts from the impact of the magnificent sheet which is one of the four drawings Ruisdael made of the same overshot water mill seen from different angles that were used as preliminary studies for paintings. For the other three sheets and the paintings related to them see cat. 74.

The present fully worked-up drawing served as preliminary study for a painting at Melbourne (fig. 75a; Slive 2001, no. 120). It is notable for its vigorous, yet meticulous, differentiation of foliage and convincing depiction of rushing and still water. These qualities are not immediately apparent in the Melbourne painting which has darkened considerably; however, detailed inspection reveals that the correspondences between them is strikingly close. The compactness of their compositions speaks for a date in the first half of the fifties.

1. In the Dutch edition of the catalogue (p.145), L. C. J. Frerichs writes the drawing is on paper that has a watermark (Villandry [a variant spelling of Villedary?]) that was first used in Holland in the late seventeenth century. The observation lent support to her opinion that the work is a late Hobbema and, if correct, would rule out the possibility that it was done by Ruisdael *c.*1651–55, the date offered here. However, in the later German edition of her catalogue (p.110), Frerichs notes the paper bears the Seven Provinces mark, dating after the middle of the century. The correction admits an attribution to either the master or his pupil.

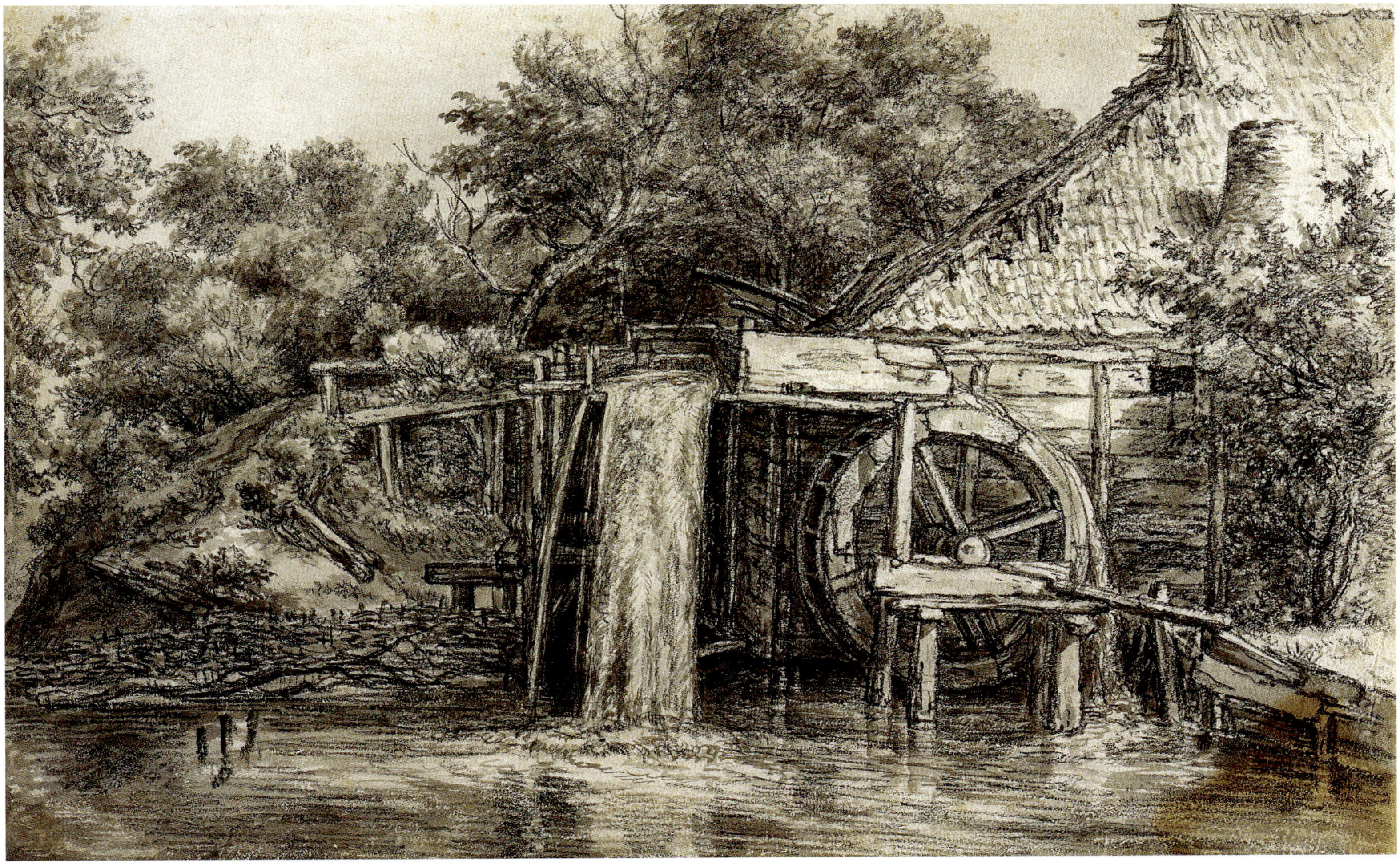

76

The High Bridge over a Sluice near the Schermerpoort at Alkmaar

Monogrammed, lower left, in pen by a later hand over the original monogram. Inscribed on the verso by a later hand in pencil: *bij Alkmaar JvRuisdael*. About 1652–55. Black chalk, grey wash, 19.91 × 27.4 cm
Amsterdams Historisch Museum. Bequest C. J. Fodor, TA 10305

PROVENANCE: Possibly Dirk Dalens by 1687(?); acquired by Sybrand Feitama I or his son Isaac by *c.*1690; by descent to the latter's son Sybrand Feitama II (Feitama II, NdT 1296: "1 Bruggetje by Alkmaar, door Ruisdael begonnen omtr.: a° 1670: opgemaakt door Dirk Dalens, omtr: a° 1687: Op oudste Notitie, omtr: a° 1690 gesteld op f7."; Broos 1984, pp.23–24; Broos 1987, p.210). Sale, Sybrand Feitama II, Amsterdam (de Bosch), 16 *sqq.* October 1758, no. H.15 (Dfl.40, Jan van Dijk, probably for Ploos van Amstel); sale, C. Ploos van Amstel, Amsterdam (v.d. Schley), 3 *sqq.* March 1800, no. T.6 (Dfl.191, Josi; sold as a lot with no. T.7, *The Excise House at Alkmaar*, Slive 2001, no. D39); C. Josi; collection Helmolt, Haarlem; sale, B. de Bosch, Amsterdam (v.d. Schley), 10 *sqq.* March 1817, no. B.5 (Dfl.310, de Vries for Molkenboer); sale, J. H. Molkenboer, Amsterdam (de Vries), 17 October 1825, no. H.4 (Dfl.440); sale, H. van Cranenburgh, Amsterdam (Roos), 26 *sqq.* October 1858, no. G.148 (Dfl.300, Lamme for Fodor); collection C. J. Fodor; bequeathed to Amsterdam in 1860.

EXHIBITIONS: London 1929, no. 698; Amsterdam 1932a, no. 63; Paris 1950–51, no. 156; Cologne 1955, no. 75; Haifa 1959, no. 48; Tel-Aviv 1959, no. 99; Jerusalem–Belgrade 1960, no. 77; Brussels–Hamburg 1961, no. 125; Amsterdam 1963, no. 35, repr.; The Hague–Cambridge 1981–82, no. 74, repr.; Cambridge–Montreal 1988, no. 82, repr.; Amsterdam 1992, no. 165, repr.; Amsterdam 1998, p.66, repr. (*c.*1658–60).

LITERATURE: Feitama II, *Notitie der Teekeningen*, p.45; Feitama II, NdT 1296; Josi 1821, 2, [n.p.] under "Jacob Ruisadel" (Josi writes that he purchased the present sheet and Jacob's drawing of *The Excise House at Alkmaar* [Slive 2001, no. D39] at Ploos van Amstel's sale in 1800 [20 louis], and that the pair then passed to Helmolt of Haarlem and afterwards to de Bosch of Amsterdam, at whose 1817 sale they were sold separately. Josi then erroneously states that the present drawing was bought at de Bosch's sale by de Haas [25 louis] and *The Excise House at Alkmaar* was purchased by Molkenboer [35 louis]; in fact, de Vries acquired the present sheet for Molkenboer and de Haas bought *The Excise House* drawing at the sale). *Beschrijving der schilderijen, teekeningen etc., in het Museum Fodor . . .*, Amsterdam, 1863, no. 189; Gower 1875, p.126; Kleinmann [n.d.], 3, p.23, repr.; *Ruysdael, Original-Abbildungen* [1920?], repr.; *Honderd teekeningen naar oud hollandsche meesters*, Bloemendaal, 1924, pl. 80; Ros Z4; Parker 1929, p.10; Simon 1930, pp.68 (mid-fifties), 83; Laurentius *et al.* 1980, p.358; Giltay 1980, p.159; no. 9, repr. (1655–60); Broos 1984, pp.23–25, repr.; Broos 1987, pp.176; 199, note 48; 210; Broos 1989, p.54; Broos and Schapelhouman 1993, pp.148–49, no. 110, repr.; Couprie 1998, pp.40–49, repr. (*c.*1658–60); Slive 2001, no. D10, repr.

RA

Sybrand Feitama II's *Notitie der Teekeningen* states this drawing of a bridge in Alkmaar was retouched by Dirk Dalens II (1658/59–88) in about 1687 (see Provenance), and that his drawing now in Budapest of Alkmaar's excise house (Slive 2001, no. D39, repr.) was redrawn by Dalens around the same year. Word that Dalens worked on these two sheets merely five years after Ruisdael's death (and around a year before he himself died) as well as stylistic evidence that he embellished other drawings by the artist led Broos (1984, p.24; 1985, p.111) to make the reasonable suggestion that Dalens had some of Jacob's drawings in his possession and possibly acquired them directly from Ruisdael or from his estate. In any event, it is evident that Dalens had both drawings in his hands before they were acquired for the Feitama family collection *c.*1690 and that the subsequent history of the present sheet is virtually unbroken.

Discovering Dalens's hand in the two drawings is another matter. Giltay (1980, p.159) understandably states that it is hard to see the hand of another artist in the present sheet. Broos (1984, p.25) agrees that it is not possible to establish Dalens's touch in it and suggests that perhaps he only added the light brown ink border around the image and the monogram. I concur with both conclusions, and have equal difficulty finding an indication of Dalens's work in the Budapest drawing or in Ruisdael's drawing of the *Ruins of the Manor Kostverloren on the Amstel*, Teyler Museum, Haarlem, yet another sheet Feitama states was retouched by Dalens (for a discussion of the latter see Slive 2001, no. D62 repr.).

Feitama's *Notitie* succinctly describes the drawing as "1 Bruggetje, bij Alkmaar". An inscription by an unknown hand on the verso of the sheet gives the same information. Various efforts to identify the precise location of the bridge were unsuccessful until Couprie (1998) established that the drawing represents the high bridge near the Schermerpoort in Alkmaar. He notes the break in the middle of the bridge's railing indicates that it is an *oorgatbrug*, a fairly common type in the Netherlands during the seventeenth century. These stationary bridges had narrow splits across the middle of their decks which were covered with planks; before a vessel with a tall mast passed through, the planks were removed or folded back.

A Ruisdael drawing of the same high bridge done from the opposite bank is at Windsor Castle (Slive 2001, no. D127); this fact was published by K. T. Parker (1929) when he introduced the sheet to the literature.[1]

In addition to Ruisdael's two views of this bridge at Alkmaar and his drawing of the city's excise house (Budapest; Slive 2001, no. D39), he also drew *The Gasthuis Street behind the Grote Kerk at Alkmaar* (cat. 77). All four drawings are datable to the fifties. Especially notable in the present one, probably done during the first years or middle of the decade, is the aggrandizement of the simple motif and the strong daylight effect. The peaceful view is undisturbed by the anglers and other figures that he himself, his contemporaries, and later artists often added to their pictures of such scenes.

1. Couprie's conclusions (1998) that the Windsor drawing is not by Ruisdael but a follower, probably Jan van Kessel, and that it was done on the very same day Jacob did the Amsterdam sheet and at the very same time (between one and four in the afternoon) are rejected in Slive 2001, no. D127.

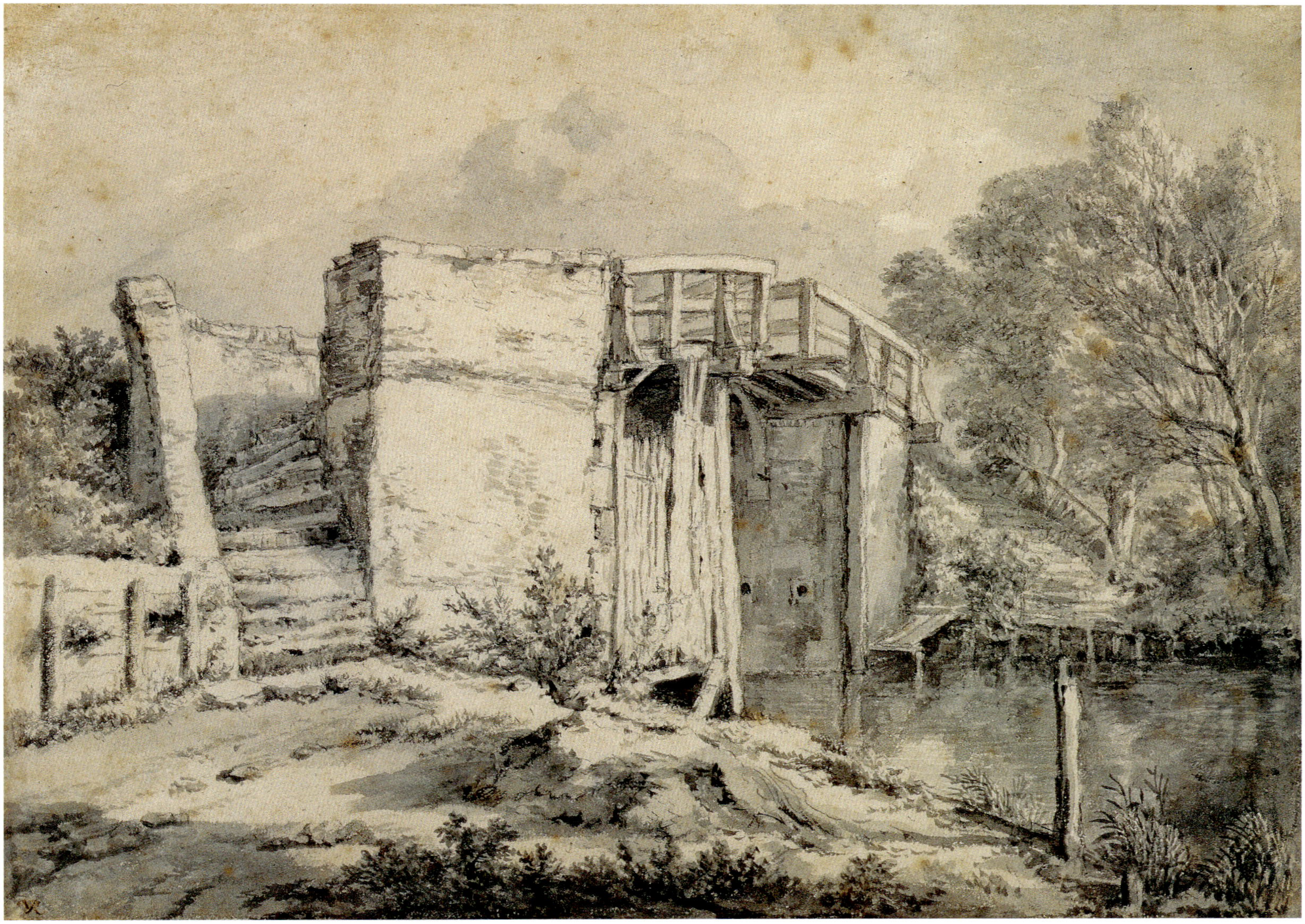

77

The Gasthuisstraat behind the Grote Kerk (Sint Laurenskerk) at Alkmaar

Signed by a later hand at the lower right: Ruisdaal. Inscribed on the verso in a later hand: *Te Alkmaar agter de Groote Kerk*. About 1655. Black chalk, grey wash, 20 × 31 cm
The British Museum, London, 1895.9.15.1926

PROVENANCE: Acquired by Sybrand Feitama I or his son Isaac by *c.*1690; by descent to the latter's son Sybrand Feitama II (Feitama II, NdT 1299: "1 Gezicht achter de Groote Kerk te Alkmaar, omtr: a° 1690 f7" [Broos 1987, p.210]). Sale, Sybrand Feitama II, Amsterdam (de Bosch), 16 *sqq.* October 1758, no. H.11 (Dfl.49; according to a copy of the catalogue at the RKD the buyer was van Dyck; the FARL copy states the buyer was Huquier); sale, H. van Eyl Sluyter, Amsterdam (van der Schley), 26 September 1814, no. F.10; sale, J. G. Verstolk van Soelen, Amsterdam (de Vries), 22 March 1847, no. 217; sale, G. Leembruggen, Amsterdam (Roos), 5–8 March 1866, no. 543 (Dfl.160, Robinson); John Charles Robinson (1824–1913); John Malcolm (1805–93); by descent to his son John Wingfield Malcolm; purchased 1895.

EXHIBITIONS: Amsterdam–Toronto 1977, no. 78; The Hague–Cambridge 1981–82, no. 81, repr.; London 1996–97, no. 95, repr.

LITERATURE: Feitama II, *Notitie der Teekeningen*, p.45; Feitama II, NdT 1299; Josi 1821, 2, [n.p.] under "Jacob Ruisdael"; Ros Z47; Simon 1930, p.84 (*c.*1655); Hind 1915–31, 4, p.40, no. 5; Giltay 1980, p.154; no. 76, repr. (*c.*1655); Slive 1982, p.29, repr.; Broos 1987, pp.176, repr.; 210; Slive 2001, no. D79, repr.

PMA and RA

Particularly beautiful in the drawing are the delicate gradations of grey wash which capture the quality of strong sunlight permeating the shadows and almost dissolving the forms of the town's Grote Kerk seen at the end of the street. The rectangular group of buildings is the Middelbegijnhof. The bridge in the foreground spanned the Geestwater (now called the Geest). The cropped signature indicates that the lower edge of the sheet has been cut off; it may also have been cut slightly along the left side.

Like Ruisdael's three other views of Alkmaar (Amsterdam Historical Museum, Budapest and Windsor Castle; cat. 76, Slive 2001, nos. D39, D127, respectively), the sheet is datable to the fifties. On the basis of style, especially the emphasis on the massiveness of its closely packed buildings, it appears to have been done in the mid-fifties. However, the presence of the scaffolding on the Grote Kerk's small tower suggests it may have been done a few years earlier. In a private communication (1982), W. A. Fasel, director of the Alkmaar archives, reported that a rather drastic repair of the church took place in the first years of the decade. In a letter preserved in the Stadsarchief (inv. no. 1846), the warden of the church wrote to the city government early in 1651 asking for financial support because they had paid 6,574 guilders in the previous year for a most necessary renewing of the roof and slating of the church; furthermore, they anticipated in the coming year the additional expense of 2,500 guilders for work on the roofs of four chapels and a part of the choir. Such high costs indicate that substantial work was done and, although the tower itself is not mentioned in the letter, Fasel notes that it seems likely that scaffolding was set up on it for the repairs described. This topographical information does not fully resolve the date of the drawing. How long was the conjectured scaffolding in place? Was it still up in the mid-fifties, or even later? Was the drawing done in the studio after a sketch made *naar het leven* a few years earlier?

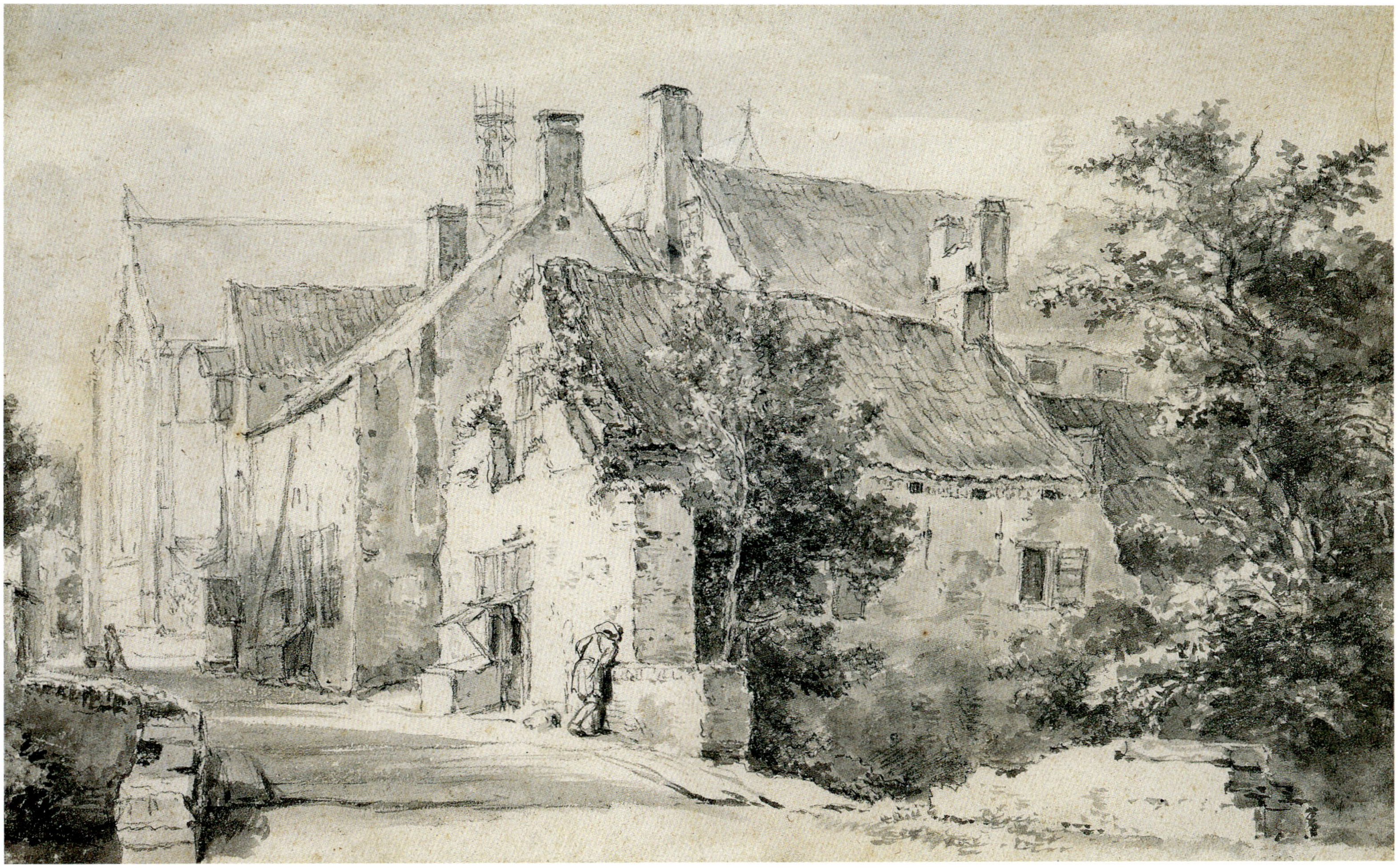

78

Interior of the Oude Kerk [Old Church] at Amsterdam

Inscribed at the lower left in faded ink: *d'oude kerk*; over this inscription, in a darker ink, a later hand has written: *J. Ruisdael*. About 1655–60(?). Black chalk, lead pencil, grey wash, 48.2 × 41.5 cm
Ecole Nationale Supérieure des Beaux-Arts, Paris, Mas 1962

PROVENANCE: J. Masson (as Pieter Saenredam), who presented it to the École des Beaux-Arts.

EXHIBITIONS: Utrecht 1953, Addenda, no. 131a; The Hague–Cambridge 1981–82, no. 82, repr.

LITERATURE: Lugt 1950, 1, p.65, no. 519; J. G. van Gelder, *Prenten en tekeningen*, Amsterdam, 1958, p.96, no. 107, repr.; Kusnezow 1975, p.85, pl. 34; Giltay 1980, pp.155–56; no. 91; Slive 2001, no. D104, repr.

RA

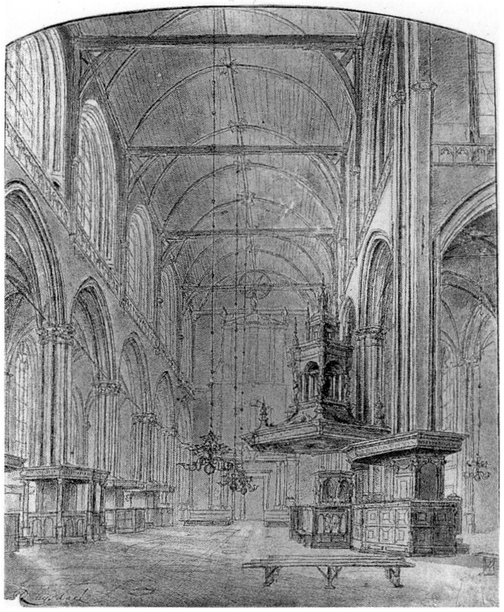

Fig. 78a Unidentified artist, *Interior of the Nieuwe Kerk [New Church] at Amsterdam*. Black chalk, grey wash, reinforced with pen and brown ink. Staatliche Museen, Kupferstichkabinett, Berlin.

The exceptionally large drawing is made up of three pieces of paper: Two have been pasted together about seventeen centimetres from the top, and a strip about four centimetres wide has been added at the right. The drawing is exceptional in other ways. Apart from the many drawings of church interiors by Pieter Saenredam, who made a speciality of the subject, seventeenth-century Dutch drawings of the theme are relatively rare. One by Ruisdael is unexpected (the drawing entered the collection of the Ecole des Beaux-Arts as a Saenredam). Lugt (1950), who first published the sheet, observed that it was not done by an artist who was an experienced architectural draughtsman. The initial drawing was made with black chalk, Jacob's customary way of working, but evidently he found this medium too broad. He then used lead pencil, an unusual choice for him, to lay in the architectural details.

The only other drawing of a church interior that has been attributed to Ruisdael is of the Nieuwe Kerk (New Church) at Amsterdam, which is at Berlin (fig. 78a; Slive 2001, no. dubD6). I side with students who find its ascription to Ruisdael dubious. However, it has its defenders, among them Lugt.[1] He suggests that there may be a link between the drawings of the interiors of Amsterdam's two principal churches and Ruisdael's baptism into the Calvinist Reformed Church in 1657.[2] Even if the status of the Berlin drawing is disputable, Lugt's proposal remains intriguing. Is there a connection between Ruisdael's unusual drawing of the Oude Kerk and his commitment to a new faith? Does the year of his baptism help establish a date for the drawing? The delicate handling of the wash, which fuses with the lines that define forms of the structure of the church, while giving spaciousness and airiness to its vast interior is consistent with Ruisdael's other drawings datable to the mid- or late fifties; however, the absence of comparable studies by Jacob makes this suggested date even more provisional than many offered here.

1. Lugt 1931, p.66; Lugt 1950, 1, p.65, under no. 519.
2. See Chronology of Jacob Isaacksz van Ruisdael, 14 June 1657 and 17 June 1657, p.xii. Jacob came from a Mennonite family; however, nothing is known about his personal religious beliefs before his baptism in 1657.

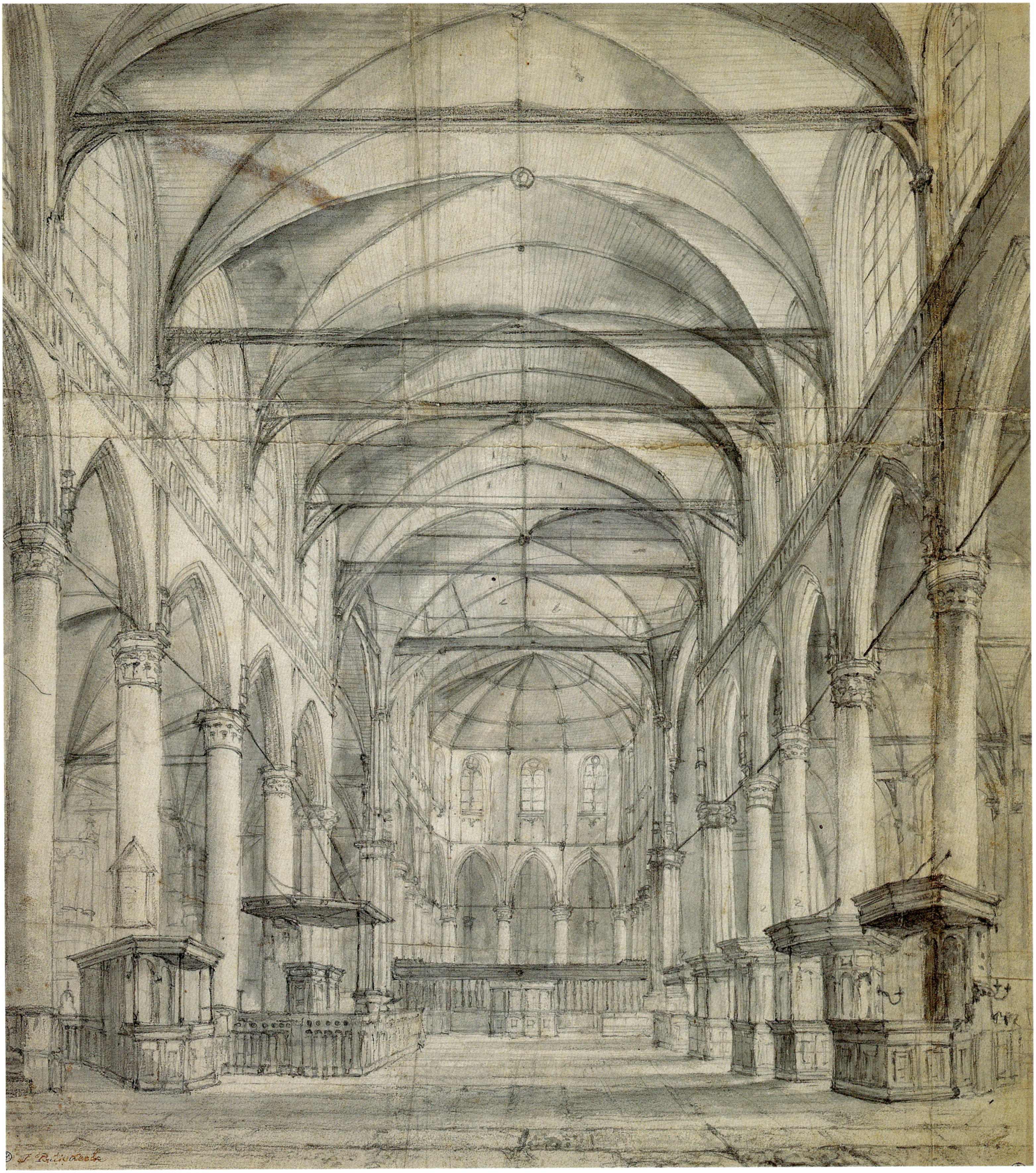

79

The Portuguese-Jewish Cemetery at Ouderkerk on the Amstel

Signed, lower right. Mid-1650s. Indented (but not rubbed with red chalk on the verso) for transfer. Black chalk, pen, brush in several grey tints, 19.3 × 28.5 cm
Teyler Museum, Haarlem, Q*49

PROVENANCE: See cat. 80.

EXHIBITIONS: Amsterdam 1925, no. 371; Brussels–Hamburg 1961, no. 124; Paris 1972, no. 88; The Hague–Cambridge 1981–82, no. 77, repr.; New York–Chicago 1989, no. 87, repr.

LITERATURE: Josi 1821, 2, [n.p.] under "Jacob Ruisdael"; ms. inventory of the Teyler collection, 1864, no. Q71; Scholten 1904, p.230, no. Q*49; *Ruysdael, Original-Abbildungen* [1920?], repr.; Ros Z28; Kusnezow 1975, p.92, fig. 34; Giltay 1980, p.151, no. 56, repr.; Plomp 1997, p.361, no. 413; Tax 1998, pp.26–28; Slive 2001, no. 61, repr.; also see cat. 80.

PMA and RA

The drawing shows tombs depicted in cat. no. 80 from another angle and a higher viewpoint. On the left is the tomb of Israel Abraham Mendez, next to that of Hakam Isaak Uziel, and on the right that of Eliahu Montalto. The sagging sarcophagus with a pagoda shape on a raised platform of which two steps are visible is that of Yshak Franco Medeyros[1] (d.1623). The tomb furthest to the right has not been identified. The spire and tower of St. Urban's Church at Ouderkerk is seen beyond the trees in the distance. See cat. 80 for further discussion of the drawing, its companion and copies made after both works.

1. *Alias* Francisco Mendes Medeiros, also called Isaac Mendes Franco. As a govenor of one of the Jewish communities in Amsterdam he signed the deed of purchase in 1614 for the cemetery's land. Tax (1998) convincingly shows that the pagoda-like shape of his tomb and others of the same type at Ouderkerk are derived from tomb monuments used in the late sixteenth century for Moroccan kings in Marrakesh (I am indebted to Marten Jan Bok for this reference).

80

The Portuguese-Jewish Cemetery at Ouderkerk on the Amstel

Signed, bottom, right centre. Mid-1650s. Indented and rubbed with red chalk on the verso for transfer. Black chalk, brush and black ink, grey wash, 19.1 × 28.3 cm
Teyler Museum, Haarlem, Q*48

PROVENANCE: C. Sennepart; his sale, Amsterdam, 1704, p.7 in Kunstboek no. 10 ("2 van Ruisdael, zijnde de Joodse Kerkhoven"); Valerius Röver [also van Reuver]; his manuscript catalogue, 1739, portfolio 46, no. 13 ("Begraafplaatze in een Lantschap van der Derzelve [Ruisdael]") or no. 14 ("Dito zijnde een Wedergae"); sale, Gerard van Berkel, Amsterdam (de Leth), 24 *sqq.* March 1761, no. 6 or 7; sale, Dionis Muilman, Amsterdam, 29 *sqq.* March 1773, nos. 1120, 1121 (Dfl.60 or 69, de Vos [with its companion]; Jacob de Vos Sr. (not in his sale); sale, [A. Saportas], Amsterdam, 14 May 1832, no. A.3 (Dfl.400, 410, or 465, Hulswit [with its companion]); sale, H. van Cranenburgh, Amsterdam (Roos), 26 *sqq.* October 1858, no. F.123 (Dfl.905, Buffa for the Teyler Museum [with its companion]).

EXHIBITIONS: Amsterdam 1925, no. 371; London 1929, no. 699; Brussels 1937–38, no. 132, repr.; Paris 1950–51, no. 159; London 1970, no. 43, repr.; The Hague–Cambridge 1981–82, no. 76, repr.; Cambridge–Montreal 1988, no. 81.

LITERATURE: Josi 1821, 2, [n.p.] under "Jacob Ruisdael"; ms. inventory of the Teyler collection, 1864, no. Q70; Castro 1883, pp.17–18, note 34; Scholten 1904, p.230, no. Q*48; *Ruysdael, Original-Abbildungen* [1920?], repr.; Ros Z27; Zwarts 1928, pp.232ff. (*c.*1664; the companion *c.*1667); Simon 1930, pp.31, 68 (mid-

Giltay (1980) established that the famous drawing and its companion, cat. 79, were listed in the 1739 inventory (not sale) of Valerius Röver's outstanding collection and that they remained together since they were in his collection.[1]

The principal lines of the drawing and of its pendant have been sensitively traced over with a stylus for transfer, almost certainly by Abraham Blooteling, who made engravings (in reverse) after both works in 1670[2] (figs. 80a, b). Some pen lines may have been added by Blooteling to facilitate transfer.

The large monuments in the central part of the present sheet are incorporated in Ruisdael's paintings of the *Jewish Cemetery* at Dresden and Detroit (cat. 22; fig. 22a). The tomb in the right foreground appears, seen from different points of view, on the left in both paintings. The most conspicuous monuments in the drawing and in its companion, which shows the opposite view of the tombs with St. Urban's Church at Ouderkerk rising in the distance, are still *in situ* at Beth Haim (House of Life), the Portuguese-Jewish cemetery at Ouderkerk on the Amstel, a village about eight kilometres from Amsterdam.

David Henriques de Castro (1883, pp.17–18) first recognized that the tombs in Ruisdael's drawings and Dresden painting are related to those at the cemetery (in Castro's day the Detroit painting was unknown).[3]

The sarcophagi that can be identified in the drawings are among the cemetery's oldest. They still exist, sunken and missing some fragments (fig. 80c). In the present

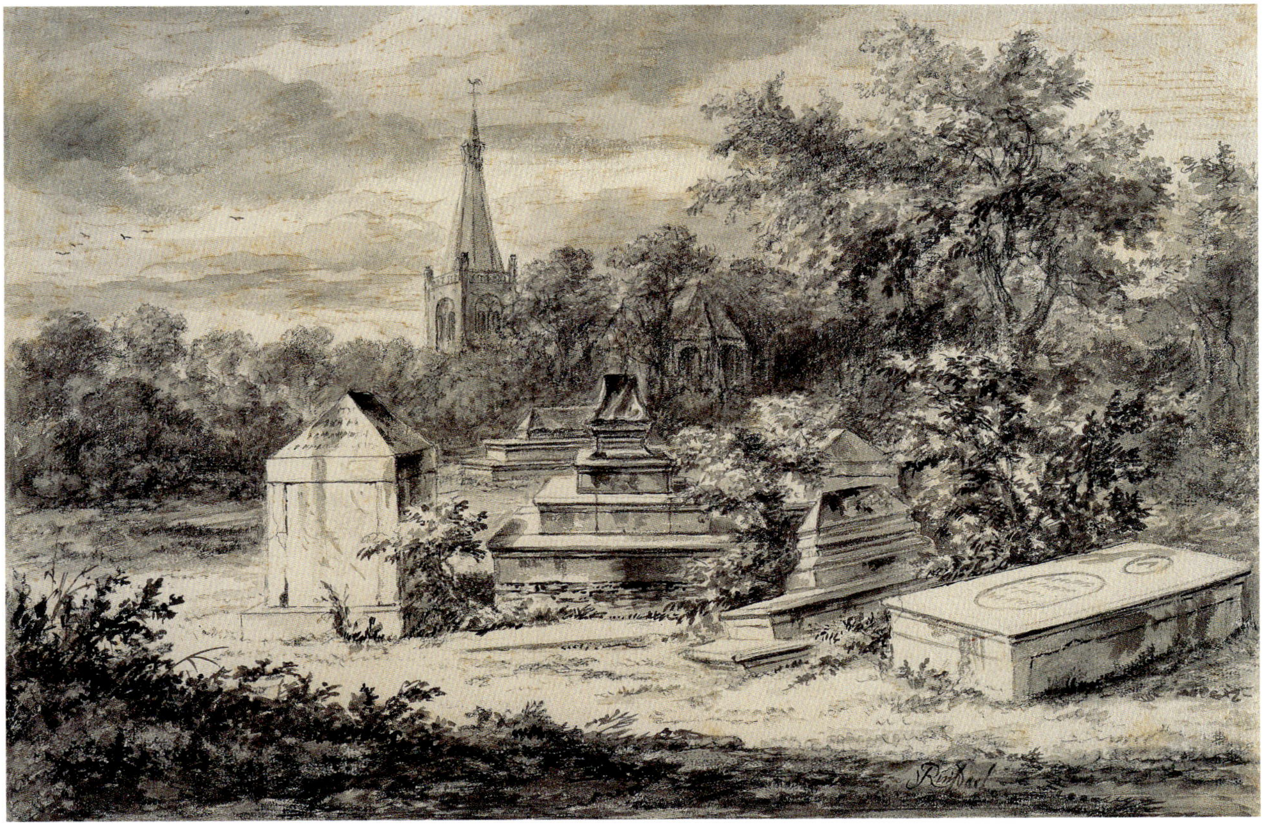

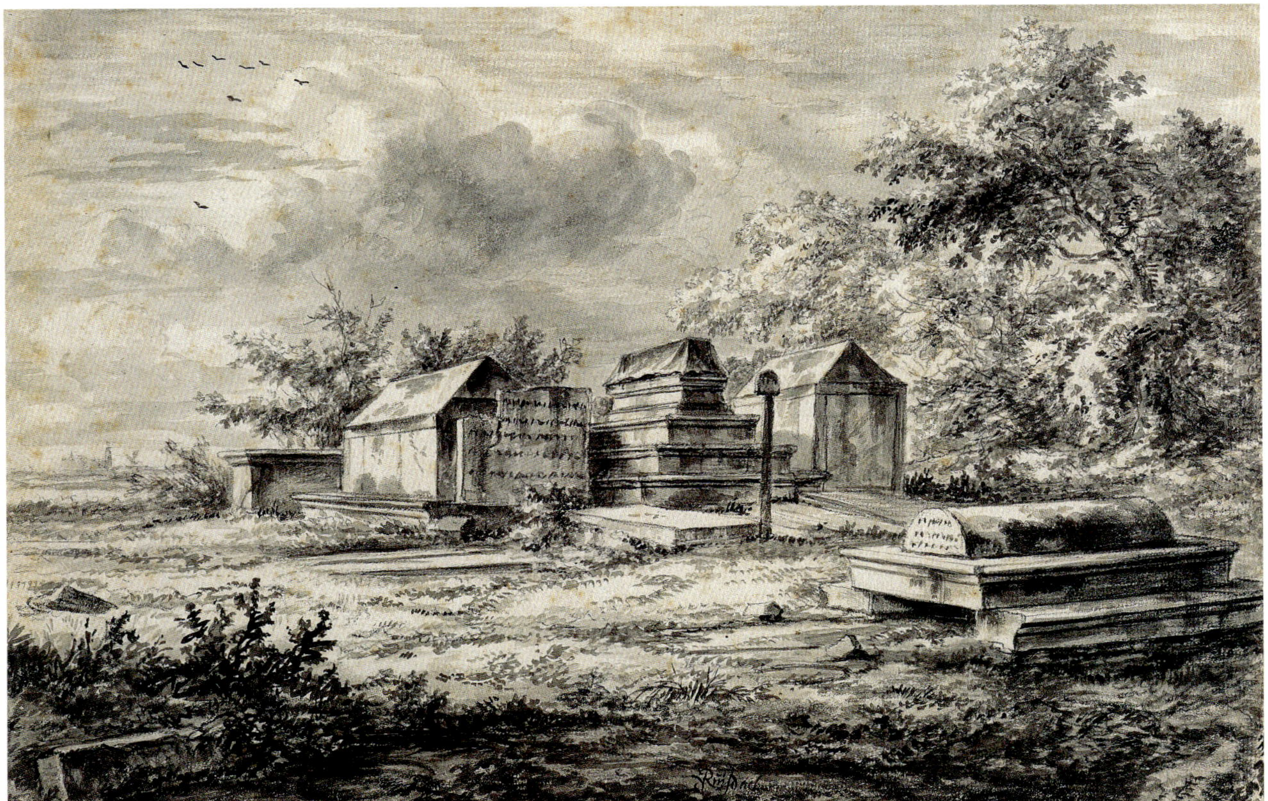

fifties), 84; Wijnman 1932, p.179 (after 1657); Rosenberg 1933, pp.217–18; Simon 1935c, pp.158–59 (mid-1650s); H. Friedenwald, "Montalto," *Bulletin of the Institute of the History of Medicine, The Johns Hopkins University*, February, 1935, p.145; I.Q. van Regteren Altena, *Dutch Master Drawings of the Seventeenth Century*, London, 1949, p.xxvi, no. 48; Rosenau 1958, pp.241–42 (shortly before 1670); Dubiez 1967, p.208 (shortly before 1670); Vega 1975, *passim*; Scheyer 1977, pp.133–34; Giltay 1980, p. 151; no. 55, repr.; Kusnezow 1981, under no. 183 (both drawings made after the paintings were finished); Walford 1991, p.99, repr.; Plomp 1997, pp.360–61, no. 412, repr.; Slive 2001, no. D60, repr.

PMA and RA

sheet the large tomb on the left, with a prismatic cover and a broken slab in front of it, belongs to Dr. Eliahu Montalto (d.1616). After leaving Portugal, his birthplace, Montaldo settled in Leghorn. He became physician to Ferdinand I, Grand Duke of Tuscany and later to Marie de' Medici.

The bierlike tomb behind and to the left of Montalto's monument belongs to Dr. David Farras (d.1624). The tomb with a stepped platform, over the sarcophagus of which a cloth is carved, holds the remains of Hakam Isaak Uziel. He was the Hakam (Chief Rabbi) of the Neweh Shalom congregation in Amsterdam from 1617 until his death in 1622. To the right of Uziel's monument is the tomb of Israel Abraham Mendez (d.1627). The tomb surmounted by a half-column in the right foreground has been identified as the monument that marks the plot where Melchior Franco Mendes (d.1614; also called Abraham Franco O. Velho [velho = the old one]) and members of his family were buried.

The broad touch employed in both drawings suggests they were done in the mid-fifties; however, the pronounced diagonal composition of this sheet and the compactness and emphatic *repoussoir* of its companion indicate that they may have been done earlier in the decade.

The style of the drawings rules out the possibility that they were done shortly before Abraham Blooteling engraved them in 1670. Blooteling, who also made prints after Ruisdael's six views of Amsterdam (see cat. 86), probably made them to help satisfy the great demand for topographical prints that arose in the Netherlands in the 1660s, and which continues in our day.

Evidence that there was enough interest in the cemetery to attract tourists even before the middle of the century is found in an entry in John Evelyn's *Diary* for 21 August 1641.[4] On that day, the first of four crowded days he spent in Amsterdam, Evelyn squeezed in visits to Amsterdam's Spin-house ("a kind of Bridewell, where incorrible and Lewd Women are Kept in Discipline and Labour [...]"), a privately endowed Gasthuis for the poor, another maintained by the city, the Old Town Hall, and the Kloveniersdoelen, the headquarters of one of Amsterdam's civic guard companies, where he made note of a group portrait of militiamen by Sandrart (if he had visited the Doelen a year later he would have seen Rembrandt's recently finished *Night Watch* mounted in the building). Evelyn records that he began his busy day with a visit "to a Synagogue of the Jewes (it being then Saturday)" and witnessed much that "afforded matter for my wonder and enquiry [. . .] From hence I went to a place (without the Towne) called Over-kirk [Ouderkerk], where they had a spacious field assign'd them for their dead, which was full of Sepulchers, and Hebrew Inscriptions, some of them very stately, of cost".

Black chalk and grey wash variants of each drawing by Dirk Dalens II are at The Israel Museum, Jerusalem.[5]

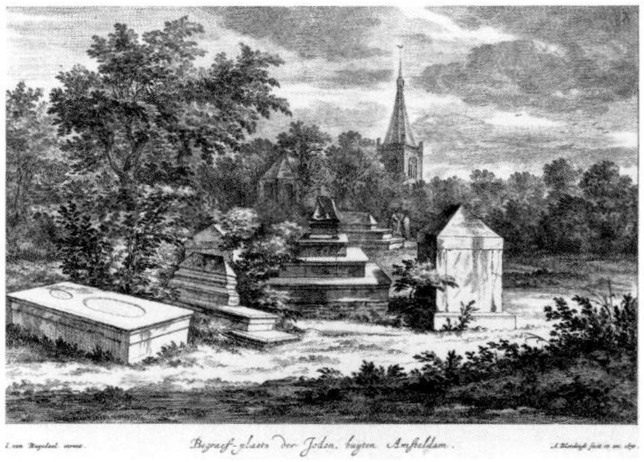

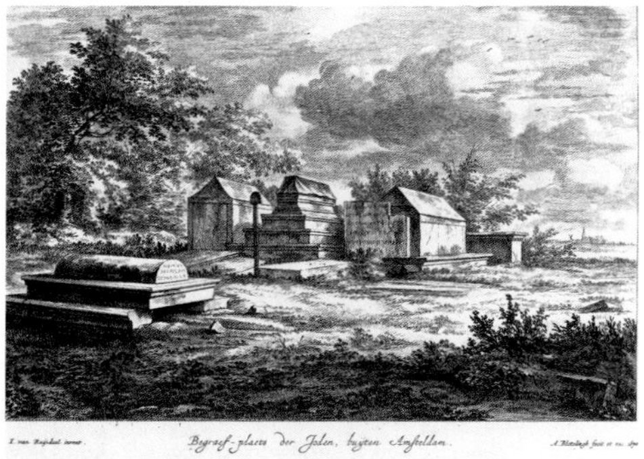

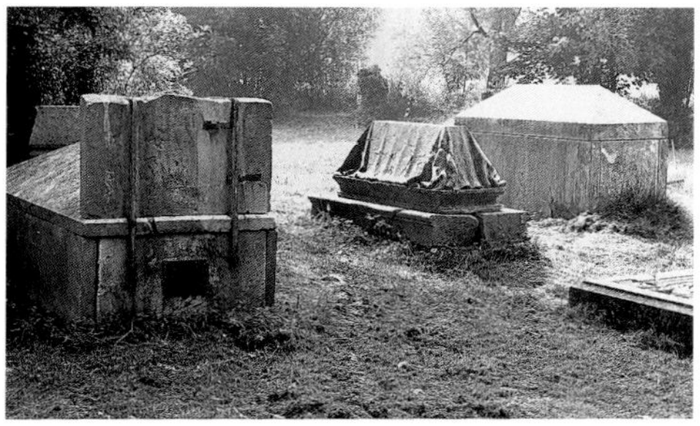

Fig. 80a Abraham Blooteling, engraving (in reverse) of cat. 79.

Fig. 80b Abraham Blooteling, engraving (in reverse) of cat. 80.

Fig. 80c Photograph of tombs at the Portuguese-Jewish Cemetery, Oudekerk, *c*.1980.

1. The manuscript of Röver's inventory is at the Amsterdam University Library, H.S. 1446 II A18.
2. Hollstein, 2, p.216, nos. 115, 116, reprs.
3. See Vega (1975) for an excellent survey of the cemetery's history. Land for it was purchased by the Sepharic communities Beth Jacob and Neweh Shalom of Amsterdam in 1614. Additional parcels of land adjacent to the original land were acquired later in the seventeenth century and still more was bought subsequently. By 1923 all the land available for burial was used. Since members of the Amsterdam Portuguese-Jewish community found it impossible to conceive of being buried elsewhere, an eighteenth-century part of the cemetery was raised, with rabbinical approval, with three metres of sand. It was projected that this action would enable the congregation to acquire enough new ground for forty years of burials. Thus it was anticipated that about 1960–65 the community would face the same problem it confronted in 1923. This did not happen. The Nazi death camps of World War II changed the situation completely. Now there is room enough for some time to come (Vega 1975, p.16).
4. *The Diary of John Evelyn*, ed. E. S. de Beer, 2, *Kalendarium, 1620–1649*, Oxford, 1955, pp.42–43.
5. No. 49.70 (19.8 × 28.8) and no. 48.70 (19.6 × 28.7); gift of Lola Kramarsky, New York. See Slive 2001, sub no. D60, both reproduced.

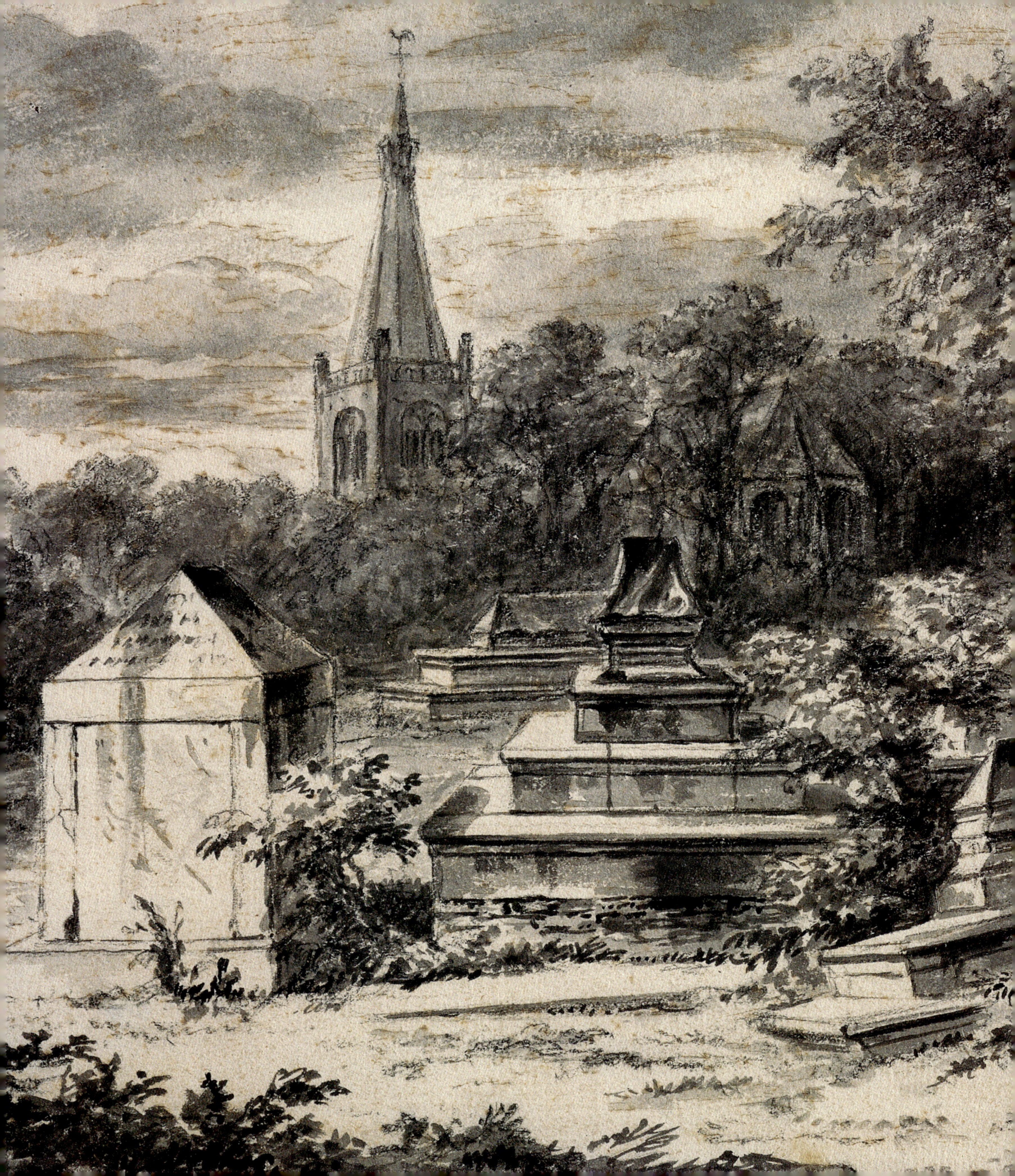

81

Ruins of Egmond Castle at Egmond aan den Hoef

Monogrammed, lower right. Mid-1650s.Black chalk, grey wash, 20 × 28.5 cm
Staatliche Museen zu Berlin, Kupferstichkabinett, KdZ 14726

PROVENANCE: Possibly one of the four drawings of the ruins owned by Sybrand Feitama II, which did not appear in his 1758 sale (see cat. 82); Oscar Huldschinsky, Berlin; his sale, Berlin (Graupe), 3 November 1931, no. 76, repr. (sold as a lot with another drawing of Egmond's ruins; see Slive 2001, no. D57, repr.); acquired by the Berlin museum in 1931.

EXHIBITIONS: Berlin 1974, p.74, no. 161; The Hague–Cambridge 1981–82, no. 78, repr. (shown in The Hague only).

LITERATURE: Ros Z13 (an old copy is in the Berlin Kupferstichkabinett); Simon 1930, p.85; Renaud 1940, pp.339–40; Rosenau 1958, p.242; Giltay 1980, pp.150–51; no. 20; Broos 1985, pp.118; 129, notes 74, 75; 148; Davies 1992, pp.40, 86, 125, under no. 15, 237, under no. d17, 255, under no. d52, 256, under no. d53, repr.; Slive 2001, no. D18, repr.

PMA and RA

Renaud (1940, p.339, note 1) established that the drawing represents the east side of the ruins of the inner court of the castle.[1] Rosenberg's (Z13) view that it is a preliminary study for the prominent ruins in the Dresden version of *The Jewish Cemetery* (cat. 22) was generally accepted until the reappearance of a drawing, now at Stuttgart, which depicts the same ruins, but from a viewpoint more to the right, almost the way they are seen in the painting.[2] Both studies and the Teyler Museum's celebrated drawing of tombs at the Portuguese-Jewish cemetery at Ouderkerk (cat. 80) unequivocally establish that Ruisdael incorporated key elements of identifiable sites separated by almost forty kilometres in his version of *The Jewish Cemetery* at Dresden.[3] A search for preliminary drawings used as studies for the more elaborate ruins in Detroit's *Jewish Cemetery* has been fruitless.

Major elements of the drawing, or one very similar to it, were incorporated in a landscape with ruins, formerly in the collection of the Prince of Hannover, Ernst August; for an extended period it was on loan to the Provinzialmuseum, Hannover (fig. 81a). The painting was traditionally attributed to Ruisdael, but it is almost certainly by Jan van Kessel.[4]

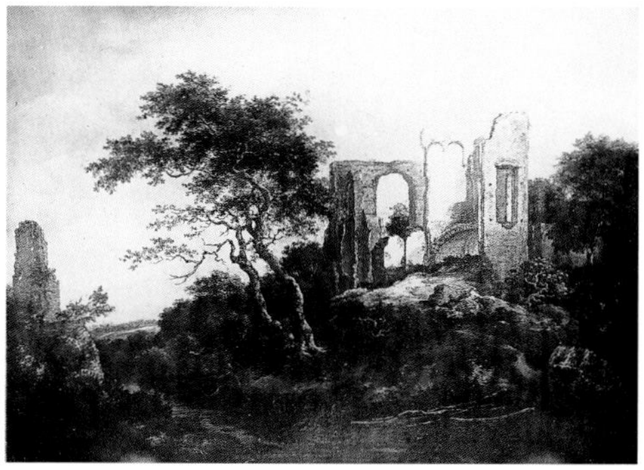

Fig. 81a Jan van Kessel (attributed to), *Landscape with the Ruins of Egmond Castle*. Formerly collection Prince Ernst August of Hannover.

1. A copy almost identical in size (19.5 × 30.8) is also at the Kupferstichkabinett, Berlin; see Slive 2001, p.508, fig. D18a.
2. Staatsgalerie, Stuttgart (no. C 64/1329); *ibid.*, no. D120, repr.
3. The relationship of Berlin's drawing to Dresden's *Jewish Cemetery* led Rosenau (1958, p.242) to propose that it depicts St. Urban's Church at Ouderkerk, which is near the cemetery, after it was damaged in 1674. Her proposal is unacceptable. The church was not a ruin in 1674. On 1 August 1674 it lost only its spire; later it was given a smaller one (van der Aa 1846, 7, p.678). Moreover, the drawing's style places it in the early or mid-fifties, not in the 1670s.
4. The untraceable painting (canvas, 46 × 61; reportedly monogrammed, lower right) was returned by the Hannover museum to the royal family of Hannover in 1924. LITERATURE: Provinzialmuseum, Hannover, Catalogues: 1891, no. 477 (Ruisdael); 1905, no. 360 (Ruisdael); HdG 756 (Ruisdael); Ros 471 (Ruisdael); Simon 1930, p.75 (doubtful as Ruisdael); Davies 1992, pp.124–25, no. 15 (judging from the photo, Kessel; *c.*1664). The monogram cited by Hofstede de Groot and Rosenberg is invisible on available photos.

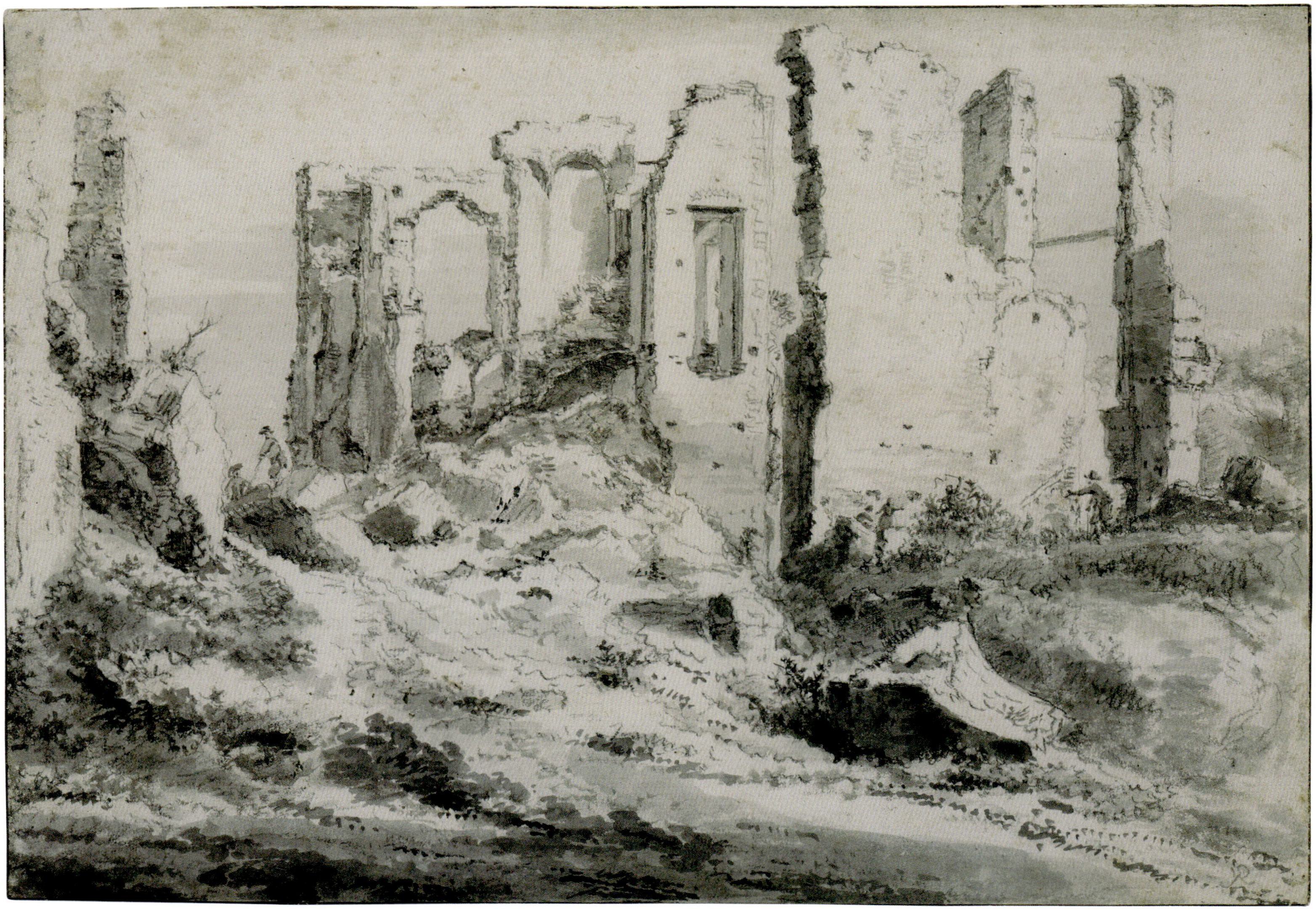

82

Ruins of Egmond Castle at Egmond aan den Hoef

Monogrammed, lower right. Inscribed, lower right, by a later hand: *Egmond op d hoef*. 1650s.
Black chalk, grey wash, 19.6 × 29.4 cm
Rijksmuseum, Amsterdam, RP-T-1902-A-4560

PROVENANCE: Sale, Sybrand Feitama II, Amsterdam (de Bosch), 16 *sqq.* October 1758, nos. H.44, H.45 (Dfl.62, the pair, Hoet); sale, G. Hoet, The Hague (Franken), 25 *sqq.* August 1760, nos. 272, 273 (the pair to Yver); sale, Jan Tak of Leiden, Haarlem (v.d. Vinne), 10 October 1780, nos. 56, 57; sale, J. Goll van Franckenstein, Amsterdam (de Vries), 1 *sqq.* July 1833, no. U.7; S. Woodburn; W. Esdaile; probably sale, W. Esdaile, London (Christie's), 18–25 June 1840, no. 1092 (£2.12.6); sale, W. N. Lantsherr of The Hague, Amsterdam (Muller), 3 June 1884, no. 284; sale, M. Baron de B[eurnonville], Paris (Drouot), 16 February 1885, no. 217; sale, W. Pitcairn Knowles, Amsterdam (Muller), 25–26 June 1895, no. 563; acquired by the Rijksprentenkabinet in 1902.

EXHIBITIONS: Amsterdam 1935, no. 130; Vienna 1936, no. 67; Brussels 1937–38, no. 31; Paris 1950–51, no. 158; The Hague–Cambridge 1981–82, no. 80, repr.; Amsterdam 1987, no. 55, repr. (1650s).

LITERATURE: Feitama II, *Notitie der Teekeningen*, p.45; Feitama II, NdT, 1300, 1301; Josi 1821, 2, [n.p.] under "Jacob Ruisdael"; de Vries 1915, p.38, no. 125; Huffel 1921, p.63, no. 143; Ros Z2; Simon 1930, p.85 (not authentic); Simon 1935, p.192 (probably by Dirk Dalens II); Renaud 1940, p.339, note 1, repr.; Frerichs 1963, p.52, no. 66, repr.; Giltay 1980, p.150f.; no. 1; Broos 1985, pp.118; 129, notes 74, 75; 148; Broos 1987, p.210; Slive 2001, no. D3, repr.

Engraved by Cornelis Ploos van Amstel (1726–98); his print is listed in Josi 1821, no. 95 and in Laurentius *et al.* 1980, p.289, no. 109.

RA

For the history of Egmond Castle see cat. 18. Renaud's (1940) fundamental account of its iconography emphasizes the importance of Ruisdael's drawings for knowledge of the interior organization of the structure; they are the oldest and virtually the only seventeenth-century source on the subject. In the present sheet the large ruins on the left shows the interior of the southwestern corner of the principal building of the castle; beyond it is the ruin of the southwestern corner tower of its outer structure (Renaud 1940, p.340). The latter ruin is the main motif of the drawing's companion (cat. 83). Like the artist's other studies of the remains of Egmond's fabric they amply satisfy the needs of both historians and connoisseurs, whose interests, of course, are not necessarily mutually exclusive.

To judge from Ruisdael's seven existing, large, highly finished drawings of Egmond's ruins there must have been a good market for them in the artist's time and at least one eighteenth-century collector showed a pronounced taste for them as well. Sybrand Feitama II acquired this drawing or its mate (cat. 83) as early as 1715[1] and before his death in 1758 another four passed through his hands.[2]

1. The drawing and its companion (cat. 83) are listed in the Notitie compiled by Feitama II: "2 [originally 3 was written] Gezichten aan de puinhoopen van 't Huis te Egmont op den Hoef, geteekend omtr: a° 1670: van welken 1 gehandeld is uit S. Schynvoets Collectie, a° 1715 f 8" (Feitama II, NdT 1300, 1301; Broos 1985, pp.118, 148); which sheet Feitama acquired from Simon Schijnvoets in 1715 is unknown. The drawings remained together from the time they were joined by Feitama.

2. In addition the two drawings Feitama notes he acquired in 1715, in his *Notitie* he writes he purchased a pair in 1743 (Dfl.4 each) and sold or traded them in 1756 (Dfl.12); another pair entered his collection in 1752 or thereabouts and left in 1755 (Dfl.21); see Broos 1985, pp.118; 129, notes 74, 75; 148. They may be identical with drawings of the castle's ruins at Berlin, formerly Bremen, private German collection, Groningen or Stuttgart (Slive 2001, nos. D18, D33, D57, D59, D120, respectively).

83

Ruins of Egmond Castle at Egmond aan den Hoef

1650s. Black chalk and grey wash, 19.8 × 30.3 cm
Rijksmuseum, Amsterdam, RP-T-1902-A-4561

PROVENANCE: See cat. 82.

LITERATURE: Feitama II, *Notitie der Teekeningen*, p.45; Feitama II, NdT 1301, 1302; Josi 1821, 2 [n.p.] under "Jacob Ruisdael"; Ros Z3; Simon 1930, p.85 (not authentic); Simon 1935, p.192 (probably by Dirk Dalens II); Renaud 1940, p.339, note 1; Giltay 1980, pp.150–51, no. 2; Broos 1985, pp.118; 129, notes 74, 75; 148; Davies 1992, pp.41, 237, under no. d17, 255, under no. d52, 256, under no. d53, repr.; Slive 2001, no. D4, repr.

PMA

The drawing shows the southwestern corner of the ruined outer structure of the castle (Renaud 1940). The same section of the ruins is seen from a different angle in the right part of the drawing's companion, which is also at Amsterdam (cat. 82).

The view of the ruins in the present sheet is closely linked to the ruins of the castle that are incorporated in Ruisdael's painting now in the collection of the Earl of Northbrook, two pictures by Hobbema, and a group of works that have been variously ascribed to Ruisdael and Hobbema (see Slive 2001, nos. 30 and dubD30).

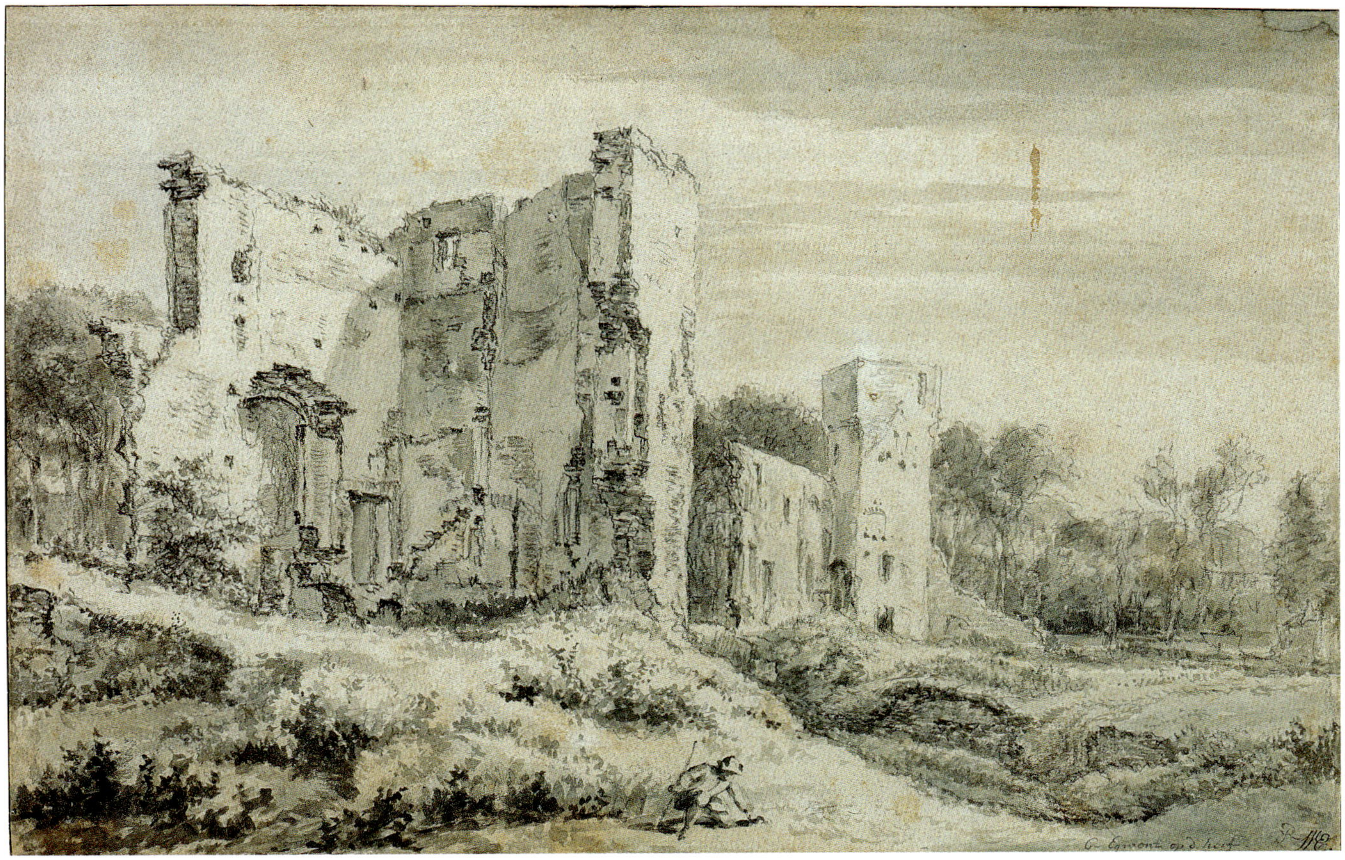

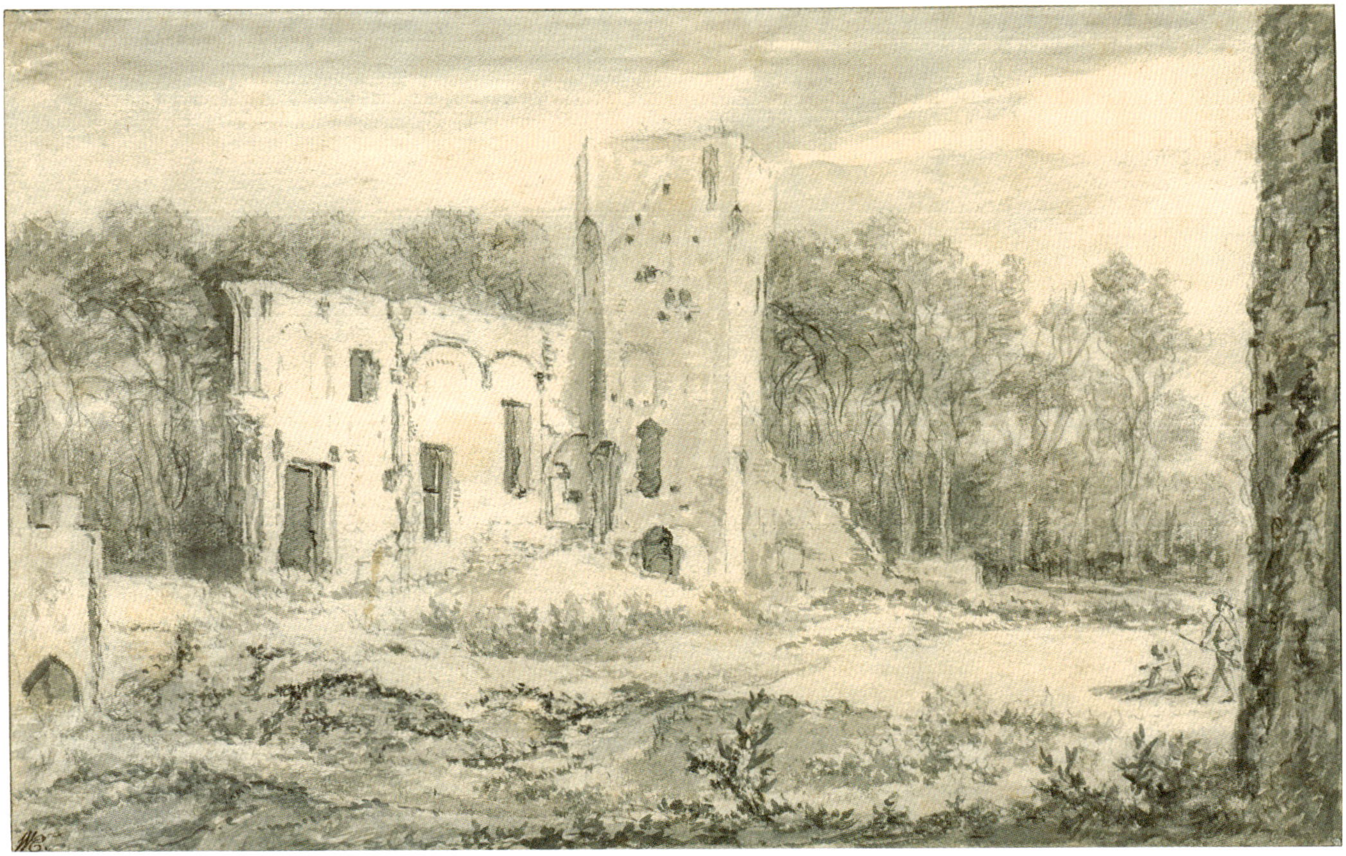

84

Ruined Cottage

Monogrammed, lower right corner. Mid-1650s. Black chalk, grey wash, 20 × 27.5 cm
Thaw Collection, The Pierpont Morgan Library, New York

PROVENANCE: Acquired by Sybrand Feitama I or his son Isaac, most probably by *c.*1690; by descent to the latter's son Sybrand Feitama II (Feitama II, NdT 1297: "1 Bouwvallige schuur, omtr: a° 1670. Op dezelfde [oudste] Notitie, [omtr: a° 1690 gesteld op] f3."; Broos 1987, p.210). Sale, Sybrand Feitama II, Amsterdam (de Bosch), 16 *sqq.* October 1758, no. L.44 (Dfl.25, Hoet); sale, G. Hoet, The Hague (Franken), 25–28 August 1760, no. 801 (Dfl.25, Yver); sale, Pieter Hendrik Goll van Franckenstein, Amsterdam (de Vries), 1 *sqq.* July 1833, no. S.9 (Dfl.90, Hulswit); sale, H. van Cranenburgh, Amsterdam (Roos), 26 October 1858, no. B.30 (Dfl.61); sale, Emile Galichon, Paris (Drout), 10–14 May, no. 143 (fr.415, to his twin brother, Louis Galichon); his sale, Paris (Danlos), 4–9 March 1895, no. 146 (fr.520); sale J. P. Heseltine, London (Sotheby's), 27–29 May 1935, no. 193 (£7, Reitlinger); sale, H. S. Reitlinger, London (Sotheby's), 22–23 June 1954, no. 699 (£130, Lütjens); Curtis O. Baer, New Rochelle, New York; by descent to Yvette Baer, Atlanta, Georgia; acquired by Mr. and Mrs. Eugene V. Thaw, New York and Santa Fe, *c.*1997.

EXHIBITIONS: Cambridge 1958, no. 33; Poughkeepsie 1976, no. 41; Washington–Denver–Fort Worth 1977, no. 71; The Hague–Cambridge 1981–82, no. 71, repr.; Washington and elsewhere 1985–87, no. 42, repr.; New York 2002–03, no. 9, repr. (entry by J. S. Turner).

LITERATURE: Feitama II, *Notitie der Teekeningen*, p.45; Feitama II, NdT 1297; Josi 1821, 2, [n.p.] under "Jacob Ruisdael"; de Vries 1915, p.39, no. 126; Huffel 1921, p.63, no. 144; Giltay 1980, p.156; no. 15, repr.; Broos 1987, p.210; Davies 1992, pp.75–76, repr.; Slive 2001, no. D95, repr.; *ibid.*, sub dub120.

A drawing after the sheet by C. Ploos van Amstel (1726–98) was engraved by Cornelis Brouwer (active 1781–1802). It is published in Josi 1821, no. 96; de Vries 1915, p.39, no. 126; Huffel 1921, p.63, no. 144; Laurentius *et al.* 1980, p.289, no. 110; Slive 2001, p.563, fig. D95a.
RA

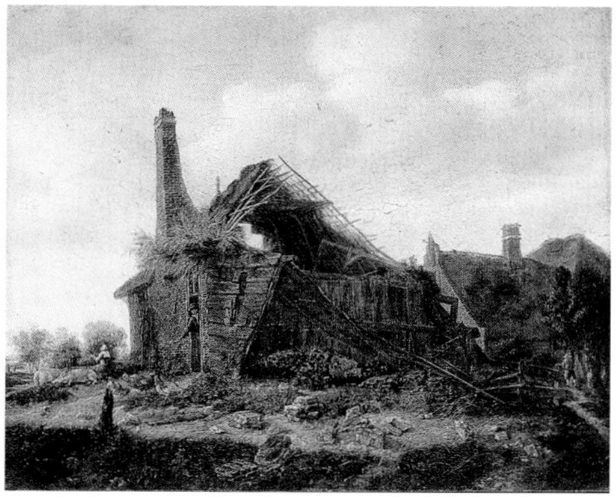

Fig. 84a Emanuel Murant, *Ruined Cottage.* Amsterdam, Rijksmuseum.

As the drawing shows, Ruisdael's special fascination with ruins during the early and mid-fifties was not confined to the remains of massive walls and arches of grand buildings. The deterioration of a modest cottage also attracted his attention. His depiction of the decayed house appealed to more than one of his followers. At least four paintings by different artists, which incorporate changes in the staffage but in other respects are close to the drawing, have been identified. The copies may have been based on his drawing, but perhaps Ruisdael himself used it as a preparatory study for a painting that is now untraceable. The existing variants may be based on his lost painting; alternatively, Cornelis Brouwer's print, which was based on C. Ploos van Amstel's faithful drawing after the Thaw sheet, could have established a model for late ones.

The copy by Emanuel Murant (1622–*c.*1700) is the most intriguing one (fig. 84a; Rijksmuseum, Amsterdam, no. SK-A-281; canvas, 31 × 41). In it the subject has hardly changed, but the style has shifted. Murant has translated the work into his own idiom, reminiscent of Jan van der Heyden's; he gives almost microscopic attention to every single brick, plank, and weed. Examples in seventeenth-century Dutch painting of a slavish imitation of a composition done in a completely different style, such as Murant's work, are rare. Normally copies are straightforward attempts to replicate both the subject and manner of execution of a work; these are usually done by pupils or followers. Those done by artists who use a work done by a predecessor or contemporary as the point of departure for their own personal creations usually introduce significant compositional as well as stylistic changes. Other painted versions by unidentified hands are cited under Slive 2001, no. dub120.

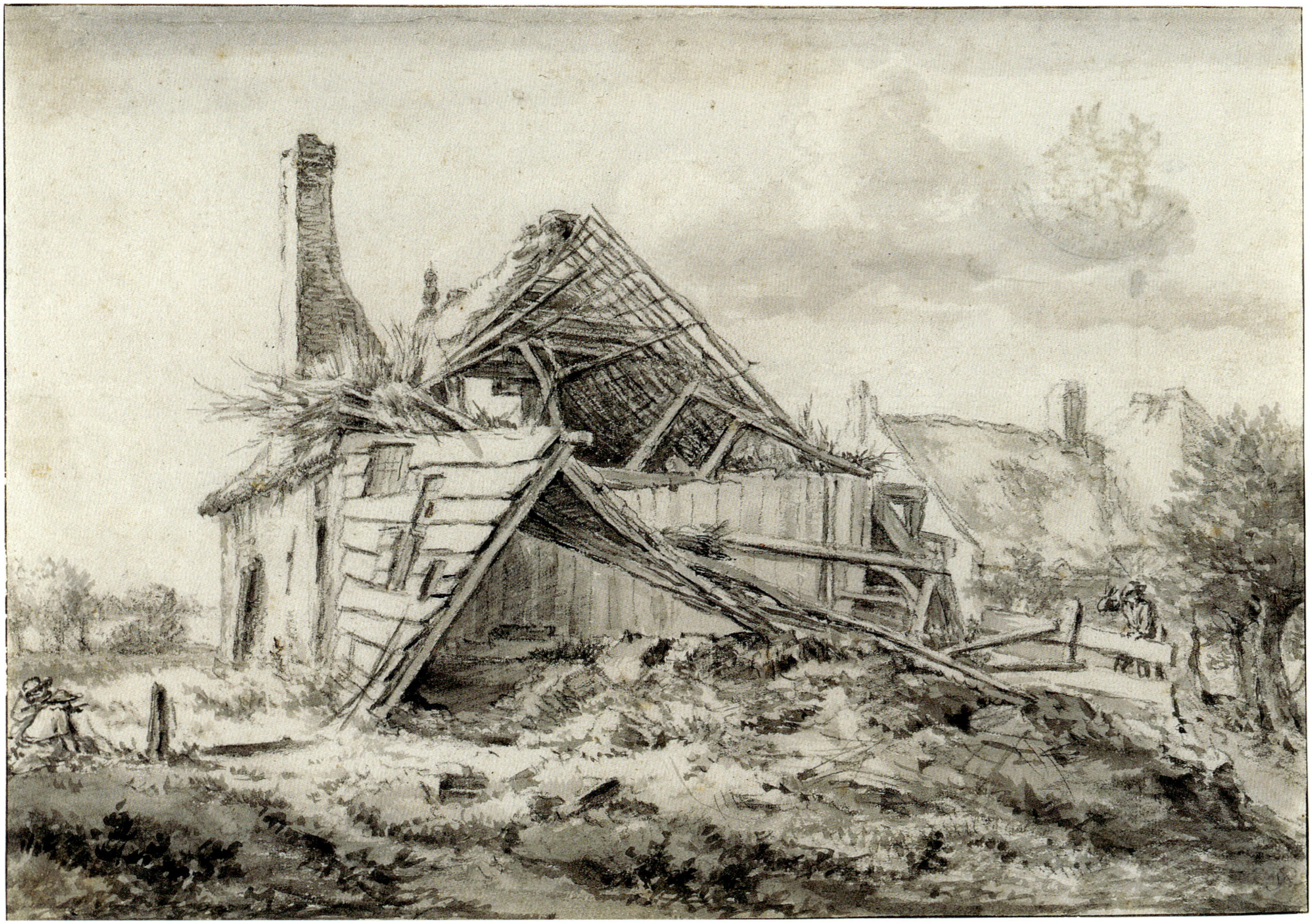

85

Mud-mill with a View of Buildings

1650s. Pen and black ink over black chalk, brush and grey wash, framing line in pen and brown ink, 9.1 × 15.1 cm
The Metropolitan Museum of Art, New York. Mrs. Carl L. Selden Gift in memory of Carl L. Selden, and Werner H. Kramarsky and Mr. and Mrs. Howard G. Leprow Giftsno, 1994, 1994.88

PROVENANCE: Jacob de Vos, Amsterdam; his sale, Amsterdam (F. Muller), 22–24 May 1883, no. 468 ("La Construction d'une êcluse"); Teodor de Wyzewa; sale, Paul Mathey, Paris (Drouot), 28 November 1924, no. 118 ("êchafaudages au bord de l'eau"); dealer Thomas le Claire, Hamburg, 1993, from whom it was purchased by the museum, 1994.

LITERATURE: H. B. Mules, "Recent Acquisitions: A Selection: 1993–1994," *The Metropolitan Museum Bulletin*, 52, no. 2, 1994, p.29 (as "Dredging a canal," probably early 1660s); Slive 1995, p.452, repr. (with wrong dimensions); Giltaij 1995, p.87; Haverkamp Begemann 1995, pp.98–99; Slive 2001, no. D91, repr.

PMA and RA

The drawing shows a mill (called *moddermolen* or *baggermolen* in Dutch) designed to dredge up mud or muck and then transfer it to a conveyor belt. In the sketch the contraption is operated by a horse, dwarfed by the machinery, on a treadmill. The evident delight the artist took in drawing the huge, complicated structure comprised of sturdy timber beams, piles and trusses is also seen in his depictions of the wooden apparatus of water and windmills, sluices, long footbridges, wharfs and jettys.

Mud-mills, sometimes operated by men on a treadmill, must have been a common sight in the Netherlands during the seventeenth century in areas where vast sections of land were drained and reclaimed from fresh water and the sea, but to my knowledge the number of existing representations of them can be counted on the fingers of one hand – good proof, if needed, that Dutch artists did not depict everything within sight. Among the rare representations of the motif is the mud-mill operated by two horses in Gerrit Berckheyde's *Construction of the New Ramparts at Haarlem*, datable to 1671, in the Fondation Custodia, Paris.[1]

The understandable impulse to relate the sketch to a set of drawings Ruisdael made of Amsterdam in the vicinity of the Amstel River near the city's old ramparts about the time of the dramatic expansion of the metropolis in 1663–64, which served as models for a series of six prints by Abraham Blooteling, is best resisted (for the prints see cat. 86). The present sketch is smaller in scale than Ruisdael's Amstel views and does not have their topographical character. Moreover, there is no compelling reason to place its unidentifiable buildings in Amsterdam or date it to the period of the drawings Blooteling used as *modelli*. Its free touches of wash and strong effect of light are not uncommon in the artist's drawings datable to the 1650s.

1. Illustrated Slive 2001, p.51, fig. a. A drawing by Renier Nooms (alias Zeeman) of *Ships Anchored* at The Boijmans Van Beuningen Museum, Rotterdam (no. R. Nooms 3), includes a mud-mill in a harbor filling a hopper with silt and mud brought up from the bottom on a conveyor belt. A cross section of this type, operated by horses, is discussed and illustrated with a double-spread engraving in the handsome folio *Groot volkomen moolenboek; of Naauwkeurig ontwerp van allerhande tot nog toe bekende soorten van moolens, met haar gronden en opstallen, en al het geene verder daar toe behoort . . . geteekent door Leendert van Natrus . . . Jacob Polly . . . en Cornelis van Vuuren; en zeer naauwkeurig in kooper gebract door Jan Punt*, 1, Amsterdam, [1734], p.6 and pl. 14.

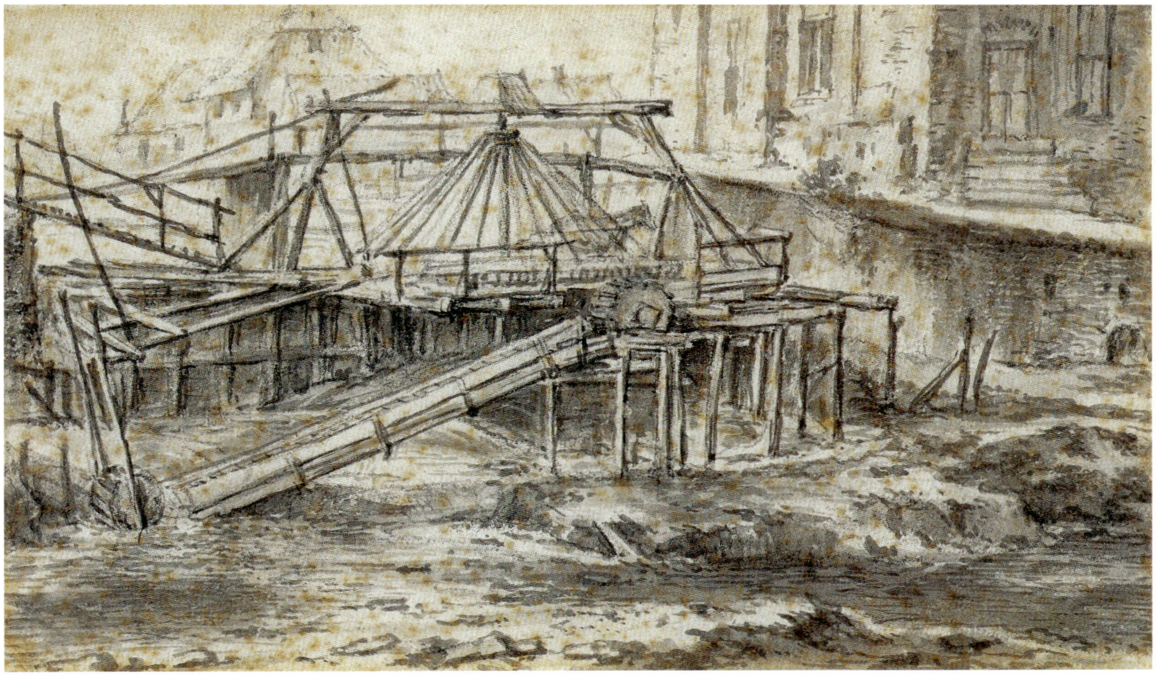

86

View of the Hogesluis Seen from a Bank of the Amstel River

About 1663. Indented and rubbed with red chalk on the verso for transfer. Black chalk, grey and black wash, 14.5 × 21 cm
Collection Noro Foundation, The Netherlands

PROVENANCE: Identifiable as one of the six views of old Amsterdam that Sybrand Feitama II states in his *Notitie* (p.45) he acquired about 1710: "6 oude Amsterdamsche gezichten, omtr. a° 1650 en 60, gekocht omtr: a° 1710; toen [the final word is crossed out] . . . f6.-.-." (Feitama II, NdT 1325–30). Sale, Sybrand Feitama II, Amsterdam (de Bosch), 16 *sqq.* October 1758, no. G.29 (Dfl.34.10, Fouquet); J. Goll van Franckenstein, Amsterdam; possibly his sale, Amsterdam (de Vries), 1 *sqq.* July 1833, no. S.10 or HH.10 (in each lot, two views of Amsterdam for the prints); sale, Prof. C. L. Wurfbain, Amsterdam (Muller), 20–22 November 1899, no. 3 (Dfl.220, Fr. Muller and Co. [sold with five other drawings presumably from the same series]); dealer Otto Wertheimer, Paris, in the 1960s; sale, anon., Paris (Drouot), 28 June 1996, no. 12 (fr.1,000,000).

EXHIBITION: Haarlem 2000, no. 55, repr. (entry by H. Verbeek).

LITERATURE: Feitama II, *Notitie der Teekeningen*, p.45; Feitama II, NdT 1325–30; Josi 1821, 2, [n.p.] under "Jacob Ruisdael"; Giltay 1980, pp.152–53; Slive 1981, pp.209–10, under no. 83; Slive 2001, no. D17, repr.

PMA and RA

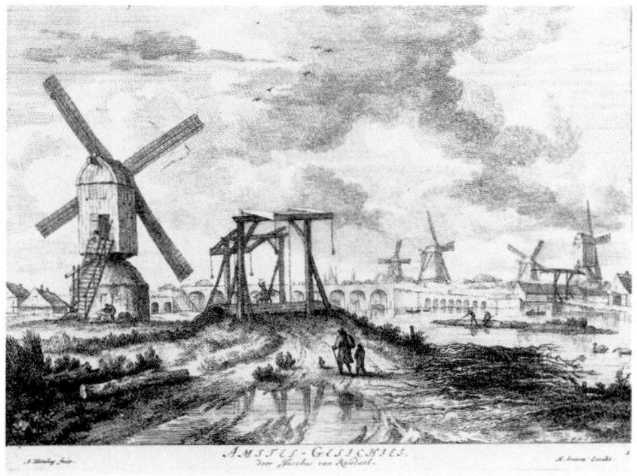

Fig. 86a Abraham Blooteling, *View of the Hogesluis Seen from a Bank of the Amstel River*, title page of *Small Views of the Amstel by Jacob Ruisdael.* Etching after cat. 86.

After laying fallow for about fifty years the interest in illustrated historical-topographical descriptions of Amsterdam was rekindled in 1662 with the publication of Melchior Fokkens's *Beschrijvinge der wijdt-vermaarde Koopstadt Amstelredam.* The volume found a ready market. Not only was it reprinted four times in the year it was published but its text and plates were pirated in the same year. The original publisher issued an enlarged edition of it, also in 1662, with a warning that a pirated edition was in the trade. The warning did not intimidate the pirates one iota. In 1663 they published a stolen edition of the enlarged work and in it they had the gall to reprint the warning as well.[1] Fokkens's volume was quickly followed by Olfert Dapper's *Historische beschrijvinge der Stadt Amsterdam*, published in 1663, Filips von Zesen's *Beschreibung der Stadt Amsterdam* in 1664, and Tobias van Domselaer's *Beschrijvinge van Amsterdam* in 1665. All of them were generously illustrated with engraved topographical views and maps, some of which were most probably sold loose as separate sheets.

Ruisdael also did his bit to help satisfy the new craze for topographical views of Amsterdam during these years by making six drawings of sites near the Amstel River in the vicinity of the city's old ramparts before and just after the metropolis's dramatic expansion began in 1663–64. Upon the basis of topographical evidence Simon (1930, p.65, note 67a) showed that the drawings were most likely done about this time. The Amsterdam printmaker Abraham Blooteling (1640–90) etched copies of them (fig. 86a, fig. 87a; see Slive 2001, p. 507, figs. D17 a–f; Hollstein, 2, nos. 109–114).

Sybrand Feitama II tells us in his *Notitie* that he acquired the six Amsterdam drawings in about 1710 for Dfl.6. They appeared as successive lots in his 1758 posthumous sale (nos. G.24–G.29) where they fetched a total of Dfl.218.30, an increase of more than 36 times the price he paid for them. C. Josi noted their presence in Goll van Franckenstein's collection in 1821, and according to the compiler of the Wurfbain auction catalogue of 1899 (no. 3) they were also grouped as a lot in that sale.

After the 1899 sale the series was dispersed. The present drawing, which reappeared in 1996, served Blooteling as a model for the first print of the set; it is inscribed: *Amstel-Gesichjes [Small Views of the Amstel] door Jacob van Ruisdael* (fig. 86a; Hollstein, 2, no. 109). The vista includes a view of the new Hogesluis that formed part of the new city wall.

Blooteling's prints after the known drawings do not reverse them, presumably for topographical accuracy. It should be noted, however, that topographical accuracy is not the strong suit of Ruisdael's *View of the St. Anthoniespoort* (Slive 2001, no. D32), one of his preparatory drawings of the series, and Blooteling's prints after Ruisdael's drawings of the tombs at the Portuguese-Jewish cemetery give mirror images of his models (see cat. 79, 80). Blooteling's etchings after Ruisdael's drawings have been copied often, and his print of the *Rear View of Mr. Huydecoeper's House* (Hollstein, 2, no. 114) was used as the basis of two forgeries by Karel la Fargue (1738–93) which have been identified by Dumas and Plomp (1998).[2]

1. The account of reprints and pirated editions of Fokkens's *Beschrijvinge* is from van Eeghen 1974 (pp.98–99); she (*ibid.*, p.102) also cites a third edition, issued without Fokkens's name, published in 1664.

2. Both forgeries are touched-up counterproofs of the print. One is at the Städel, Frankfurt a. M., the other is at the Museum of Fine Arts, Budapest; see Dumas and Plomp 1998, p.58, nos. 128, 129.

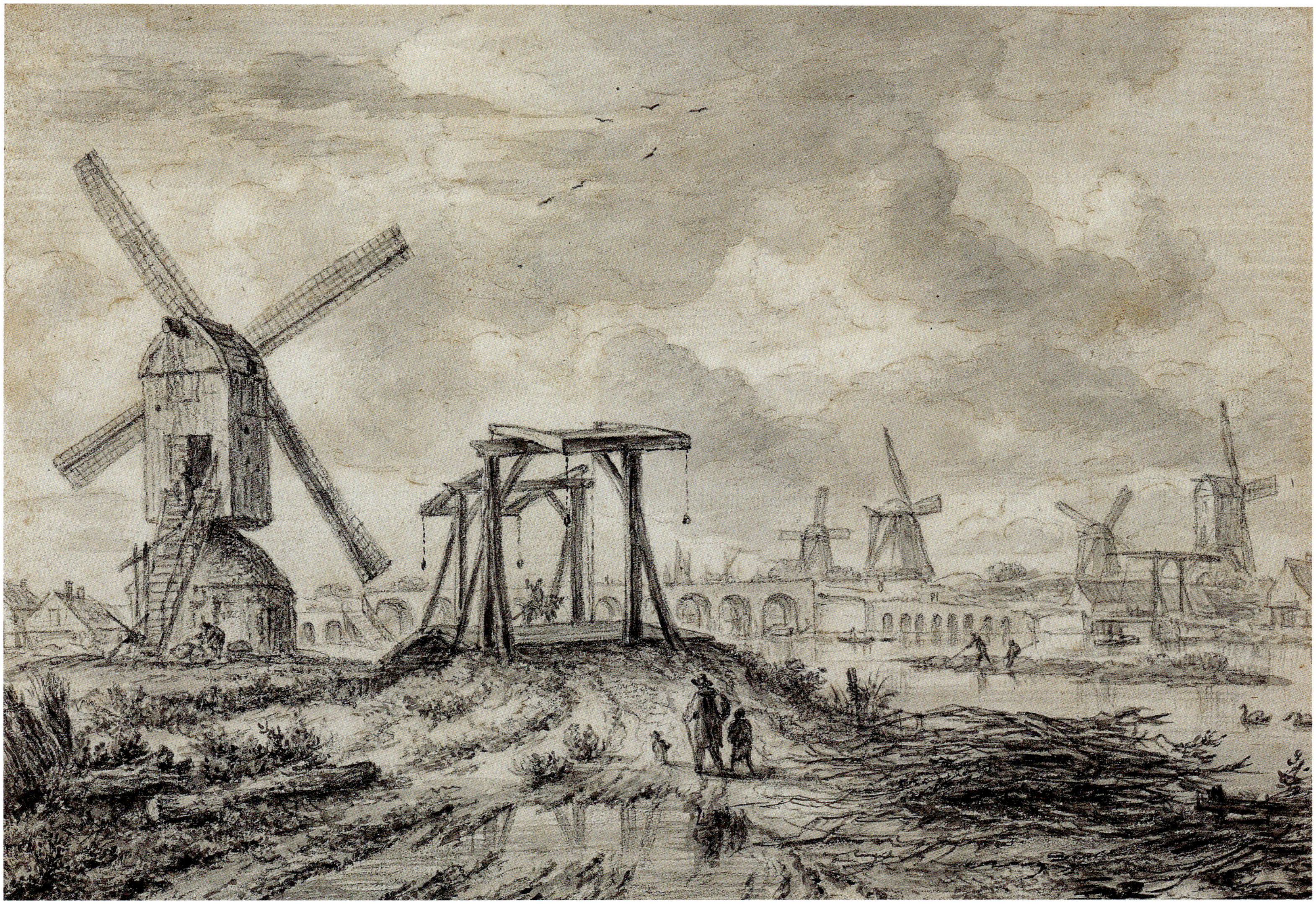

87

The Blauwbrug [Blue Bridge] over the Amstel River at Amsterdam

About 1663. Indented and rubbed with red chalk on the verso for transfer. Black chalk, grey wash, 15 × 21.2 cm
Ecole Nationale Supérieure des Beaux-Arts, Paris (no. Mas 1965)

PROVENANCE: Identifiable as one of the six views of old Amsterdam that Sybrand Feitama II stated in his *Notitie* (p.45) he acquired about 1710: "6 oude Amsterdamsche gezichtes, omtr: a° 1650 en 60, gekocht omtr: a° 1710; toen [the final word is crossed out] . . . f6.-.-" (Feitama II, NdT 1325–30). Sale, Sybrand Feitama II, Amsterdam (de Bosch), 16 *sqq.* October 1758, no. G.28 (Dfl.29, Yver); J. Goll van Franckenstein, Amsterdam; possibly his sale, Amsterdam (de Vries), 1 July 1833, no. S.10 or no. HH.10 (in each case, two views of Amsterdam for the prints); sale, L. Dupper, Dordrecht (Roos), 28–29 June 1870, no. 290 (sold with no. 291, "Vue sur l'un des ramparts d'Amsterdam (Blaawhoofd)"; both sold to Prestel, Dfl.38); A. J. Eyndhoven; sale, J. Werneck, Amsterdam (Muller), 23–25 June 1885, no. 254 (Dfl.110, Wurfbain); sale, Prof. C. L. Wurfbain, Amsterdam (Muller), 20–22 November 1899, no. 3 (Dfl.220, Fr. Muller and Co. [sold with five other drawings presumably from the series]); collection J. Masson, who presented it to the Ecole des Beaux-Arts.

EXHIBITION: The Hague–Cambridge 1981–82, no. 83, repr.

LITERATURE: Feitama II, *Notitie der Teekeningen*, p.45; Feitama II, NdT 1325–30; Josi 1821, 2, [n.p.] under "Jacob Ruisdael"; Lugt 1950, 1, p.65, no. 517, repr.; Giltay 1980, pp.152–54; no. 89; Davies 1992, pp.38–39, 221–22, under no. d1, 227 under no. d7, repr.; Slive 2001, no. D102, repr.

PMA

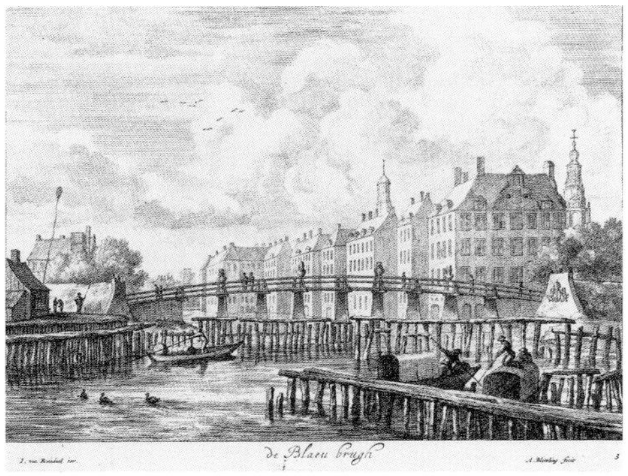

Fig. 87a Abraham Blooteling, *The Blue Bridge*, Etching after cat. 87.

The drawing belongs to the set of six preparatory drawings the artist made about 1663 as *modelli* for a series of etched *Amstel-Gesichjes* (*Small Views of the Amstel*) by Abraham Blooteling (fig. 87a). The present one depicts a view of the Blauwbrug from the yacht harbour looking toward the city. The foreground shows part of the yacht harbour; beyond it, on either side of the bridge, are the city's walls. The row of prominent large houses beyond the bridge are on an island called Vlooienburg. On the right is the tower of the South Church.

The name of the Blauwbrug was derived from its colour. It was also known as the Leeuwenbrug (Bridge of the Lions), an appellation that refers to the four statues of lions on its balustrade. As might be expected in cityscapes designed to be translated into prints for buyers with an interest in topography, a close look at the drawings of the *Blauwbrug* and the *Yacht Harbour* (Slive 2001, no. D103) shows the four statues on the well-known structure, and in general they exhibit greater attention to detail than is normally found in the artist's drawings. In light of their intent, it is notable that there is a difference in the large building seen on the right in both drawings and in the etchings made after them. In the scene of the *Blauwbrug* the long façade of the building is almost a third longer than it is in the *Yacht Harbour*. Either the drawings show the building before and after it had been extended or Ruisdael took liberties with the building in one of his drawings of it.

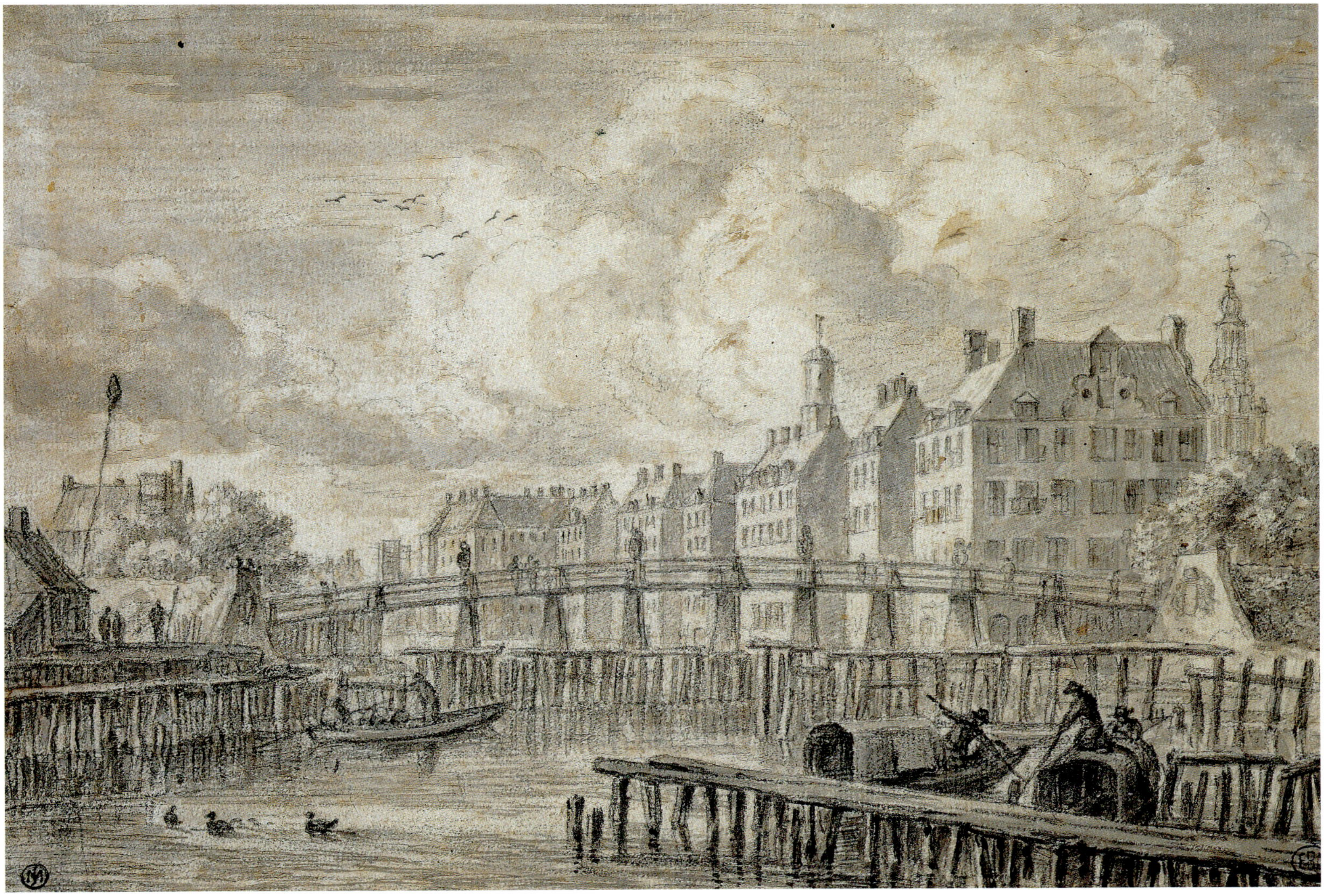

88

Bulwark with a Wooden Footbridge across a Moat

Monogrammed, lower left. 1660s. Black chalk, grey wash, 19.7 × 30.6 cm
The State Hermitage Museum, St. Petersburg, 5538

PROVENANCE: Sale, D. Muilman, Amsterdam (de Bosch), 29 March 1773, no. B.86 (Fouquet); Paul I, acquired for the Hermitage by 1797.

EXHIBITIONS: Leningrad 1926, no. 152; Brussels–Rotterdam–Paris 1972–73, no. 92, repr. (entry by Kuznetsov [also Kusnezow]; grey wash probably added by Dalens); New York 1998–99, no. 57, repr.

LITERATURE: Ros Z38; Agafonova 1935, p.183, repr. on p.179; Dobroklonsky 1961, no. 72; Giltay 1980, p.154; no. 69 (*c.*1660–70); Kusnezow 1981, no. 182 (drops the suggestion made in the 1972–73 exhibition catalogue [see above]); Slive 2001, no. D119, repr.

PMA and RA

Bridges fascinated Ruisdael. During the course of his career he depicted virtually every type found in seventeenth-century Holland. In this drawing he shows the full extent of a rickety wooden footbridge spanning a moat. The unusual angle permits us to share his interest in contrasting a full record of the structure's fragile appearance with the solid rampart it abuts.

The site has not been firmly identified. Giltay (1980, p.154) suggests the drawing may depict the ramparts of Amsterdam. The compiler of Muilman's 1773 sale catalogue was more specific; he suggests it may be a view of the partly ruined fortifications in the Oude Vest region of Amsterdam, but Jan van der Waals finds the proposal unlikely.[1]

1. Cited in New York 1998–99, no. 57 and p.256, no. 57, note 2 (entry by Alexei Larionov).

89

View of the Seashore and Boats from a Dune

1660s. Black chalk, brush in black, grey and white body colour, on prepared grey-brown paper, 23 × 37.8
Staatliche Museen zu Berlin, Kupferstichkabinett, Berlin, KdZ 2593

PROVENANCE: Sale, J. G. Verstolk van Soelen, Amsterdam (de Vries), 22 March 1847, no. 308 (Dfl.262); sale, J. de Vos Jbzn, Amsterdam (Roos), 22–24 May 1883, no. 462; collection B. Suermondt, Aachen; acquired for the museum in 1874 (not 1884).

EXHIBITIONS: Berlin 1974, p.75, no. 163, repr.; Munich–Bonn 1993, no. 23; Amsterdam 2000a, no. 74.

LITERATURE: Ros Z8; Simon 1930, pp.68, 83; Bock and Rosenberg 1930, 1, p.257, no. 2593; van Regteren Altena 1948, no. 49; J. G. van Gelder, *Prenten en Tekeningen*, Amsterdam, 1958, p.96, no. 108, repr.; Giltay 1980, p.165; no. 17, repr.; Slive 1981, p.215, under no. 86, repr.; Slive 2001, no. D26, repr.

PMA and RA

The economy of the wash that captures the light and atmospheric effects at the seashore on a calm, dull day combined with exquisitely placed accents of pen and brush that define the dunes' hardy grasses and details of the near and distant boats make the sheet one of Ruisdael's most impressive drawings. The extensive view appears to been done directly from nature or drawn after *naar het leven* studies with very little change.

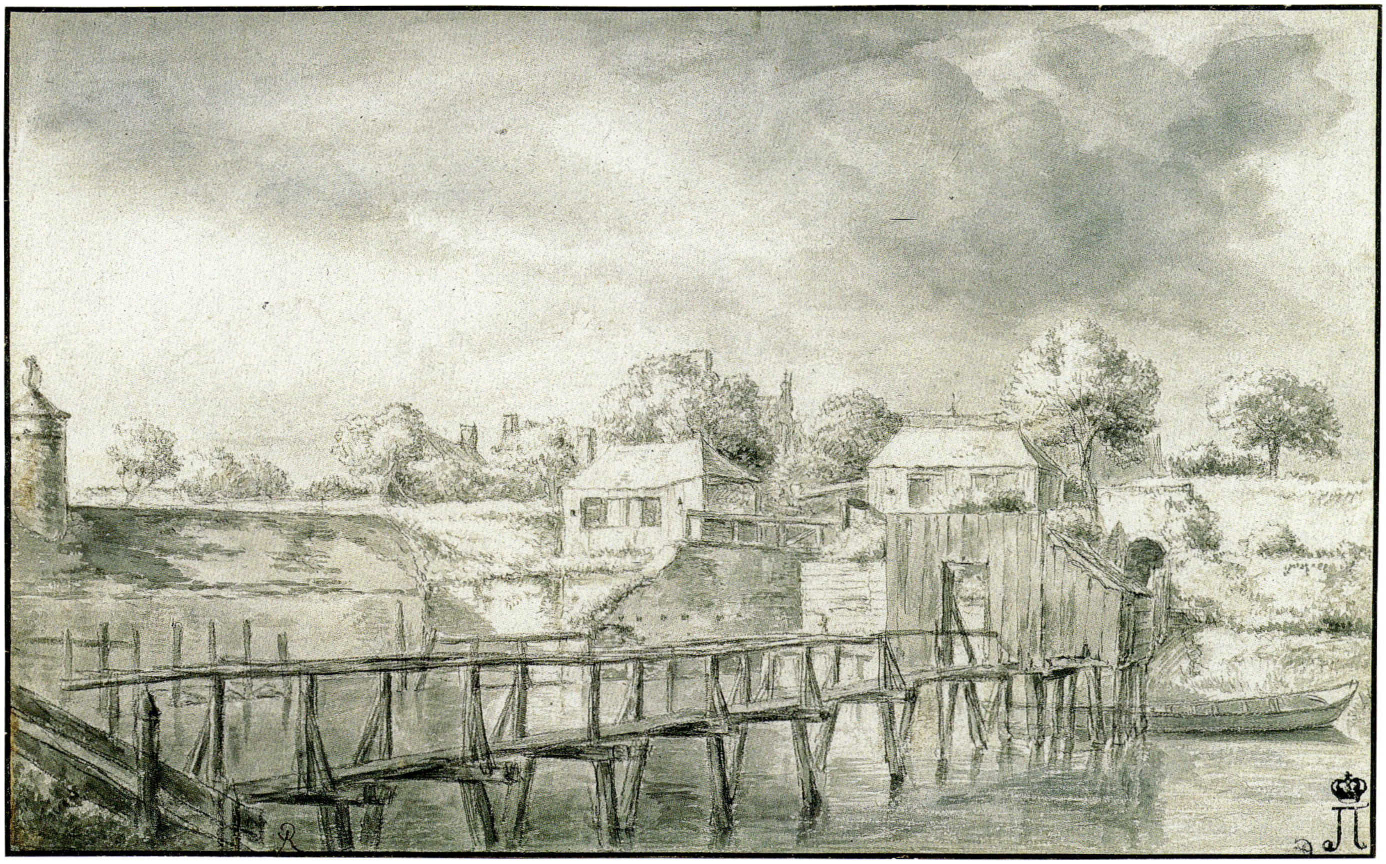

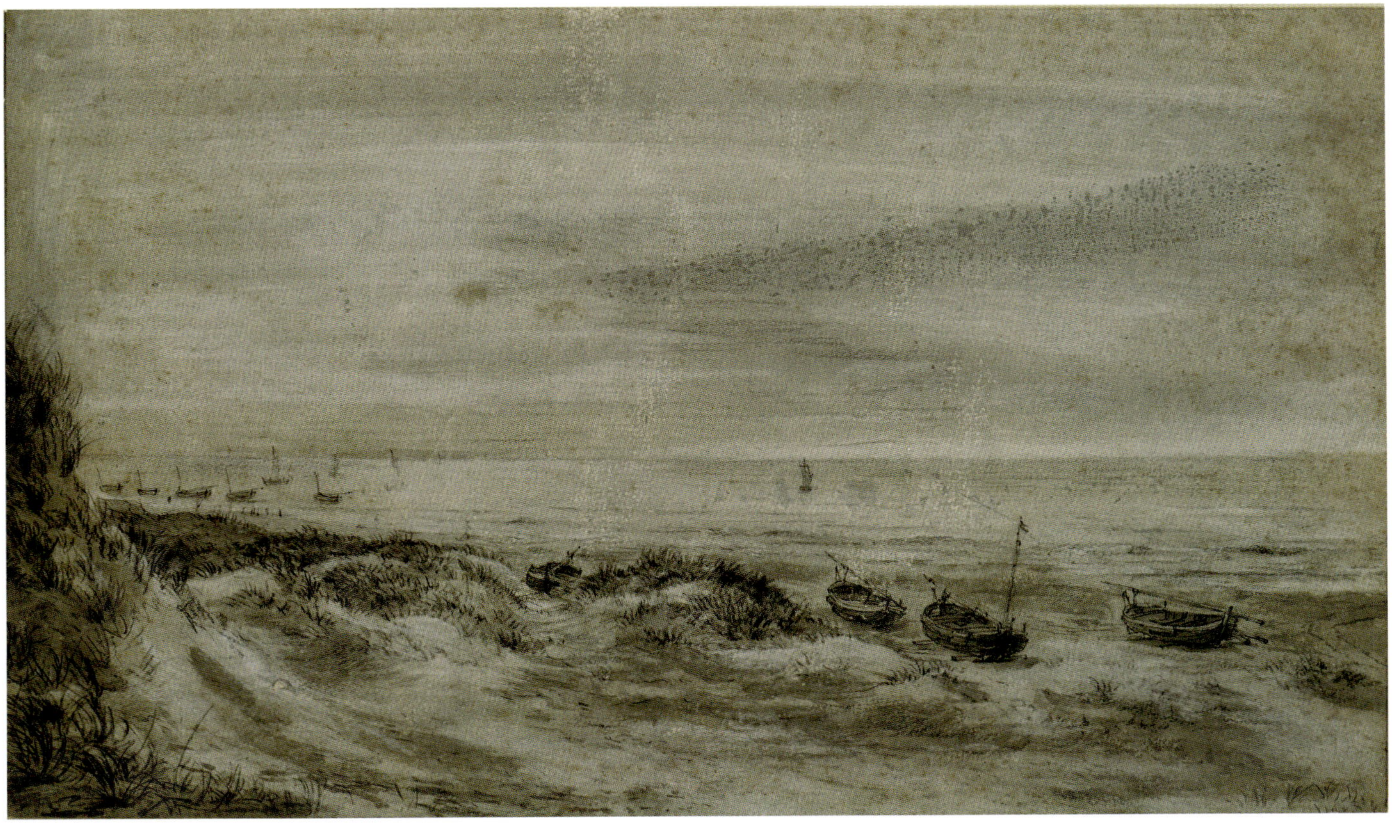

90

Cottage in a Northern Mountainous Landscape with a Waterfall

About 1665–70. Black chalk, grey wash, 19.7 × 23.2 cm
The Pierpont Morgan Library, New York. Purchased by Pierpont Morgan, 1909, III, 218

PROVENANCE: Sir Thomas Lawrence, London; probably sale, Miss James of Norfolk Square, London (Christie's), 22–23 June 1891, no. 242 (one of a pair: "Rocky Landscape"; £5.15.6, Tooth); sale, George Edward Habich, Stuttgart (Gutekunst), 27–29 April 1899, no. 590 (DM86, Colnaghi); Charles Fairfax Murray, London and Florence; The Pierpont Morgan Library, New York. Purchased by Pierpont Morgan, 1909.

EXHIBITIONS: New York, The Pierpont Morgan Library, *Landscape Drawings and Watercolors: Bruegel to Cézanne*, 1953, p.28, no. 77; Poughkeepsie 1976, no. 42.

LITERATURE: *J. Pierpont Morgan Collection of Drawings ... Formed by C. Fairfax Murray*, 3, London, 1912, no. 218; Giltay 1980, p.161; no. 81, repr.; The Hague–San Francisco 1990–91, p.401, under no. 55, repr. (entry by B. Broos); Walford 1991, p.104, repr.; Slive 2001, no. D93, repr.

PMA and RA

The sheet has a special place in Ruisdael's work; it is his only existing drawing of a waterfall or rushing torrent in a northern mountainous landscape. To our knowledge Ruisdael never laid eyes on such scenes. It is hardly conceivable that he did not make additional waterfall drawings and use some as preliminary or preparatory studies for his waterfall pictures which constitute the largest category of his painted œuvre – more than 160 are known today. The absence of waterfall drawings gives an indication of the number of his drawings that are lost.

The Morgan drawing's composition is comparable to a *Waterfall* by Ruisdael at Dresden (Slive 2001, no. 181, repr.) and, though the format differs, it is even more closely related to *Waterfall in a Mountainous Landscape* in a private collection, Scotland (cat. 34), the artist's most imposing painting of the theme. These relationships are worth stressing because they indicate that Ruisdael used the same preliminary drawing for more than one painting, not astonishing when we recall he employed it for views he had never seen.

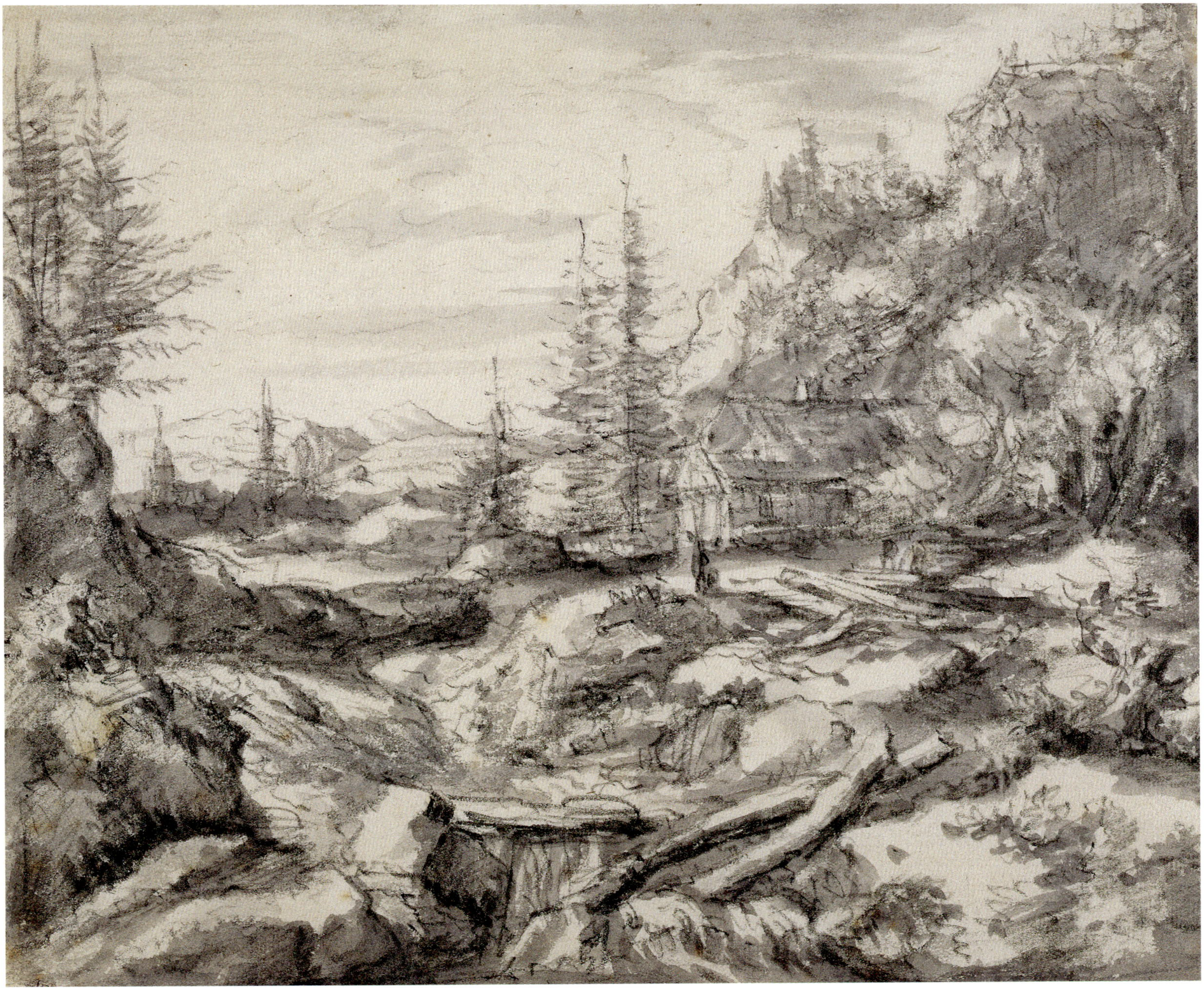

91

Extensive Landscape with a View of Haarlem

Late 1660s or early 1670s. Black chalk, grey wash, with figures in pencil, 9.9 × 16.1 cm
Museum Bredius, The Hague, T95-1946

PROVENANCE: Sale, Diderick, Baron van Leyden, Amsterdam (van der Schley, 13 May 1811, no. E.47 (sold as a lot with cat. 92, 93); A. Bredius, The Hague, by 1926.

EXHIBITIONS: The Hague–Cambridge 1981–82, no. 88, repr. (shown in The Hague only); Cambridge–Montreal 1988, no. 83a.

LITERATURE: Knuttel 1926, pp.35, 47, no. 147; Ros Z23a; Simon 1930, pp.68, 84 (rather later than 1663; the figures by another hand); Simon 1940, p.210 (not by Ruisdael; a copy); Blankert 1978, p.164, no. T 18 (with wrong Rosenberg reference); Giltay 1980, p.161; no. 49; Blankert 1991, p.267, no. T 18, repr.; Slive 2001, no. D67, repr.

PMA

The drawing belongs to the precious small group of panoramic sketches Ruisdael made in the late sixties or early seventies of the plain near Haarlem with the skyline of the town in the distance. Two others of the series, also at the Museum Bredius, are in the exhibition (cats. 92, 93). Another, closely related to them, is at the Rijksprentenkabinet, Rijksmuseum, Amsterdam (Slive 2001, no. D5). Perhaps all four sheets were part of the same sketchbook. All show St. Bavo from the northwest and were probably made from the Kopje in Bloemendaal; from left to right it is possible to make out the Bakenesser Church, St. Jans Church, the Clock Tower, the Town Hall and the New Church. The correspondences (some closer than others) that can be established between them and his *Haarlemjes* indicate that they were used as *aides-mémoires* for paintings that were worked up in the studio. In none of them is the proportion of sky to earth as great as it is in the paintings and only in the Amsterdam sheet is there a hint of the magnificent skies of the finished pictures.

Simon's (1940) rejection of the three Bredius sketches as copies is unjustified. Giltay (1980, p.161) notes a connection between this sketch and a problematic painting, *View of Haarlem*, formerly in the collection of the heirs of Ernest G. Rathenau and Ellen Rathenau Ettlinger (Slive 2001, no. dub20).

92

Extensive Landscape with a View of Haarlem

Late 1660s or early 1670s. Black chalk, grey wash, with figures in pencil, 9.2 × 15 cm
Museum Bredius, The Hague, T94-1946

PROVENANCE: Identical with cat. 91.

EXHIBITIONS: The Hague–Cambridge 1981–82, no. 89, repr. (shown in The Hague only); Cambridge–Montreal 1988, no. 83b.

LITERATURE: Knuttel 1926, pp.35, 47, no. 148; Ros Z23b; Simon 1930, pp.68, 84 (rather later than 1663; the figures by another hand); Simon 1940, p.210 (not by Rusidael; a copy); Blankert 1978, p.164, no. T17 (with wrong Rosenberg reference); Giltay 1980, p.161; no. 50; Blankert 1991, p.267, no. T 17, repr.; Slive 2001, no. D68, repr.

PMA

The cluster of houses on the left side of the sketch appear in the center of cat. 91, but the shift in its relationship to St. Bavo and other buildings on Haarlem's skyline indicates that Ruisdael did not make the drawing at precisely the same spot. Although the sketch cannot be related to a specific painting, the row of little houses recalls those seen near bleaching fields in other views of Haarlem by the artist.

Blankert (1978; 1991) sees a relation between the drawings and a sketch of Haarlem's plain at Berlin (Slive 2001, no. dubD8). However, apart from the motif, the connection between these works is negligible. For doubts regarding the attribution of the Berlin drawing to Ruisdael, see *ibid*.

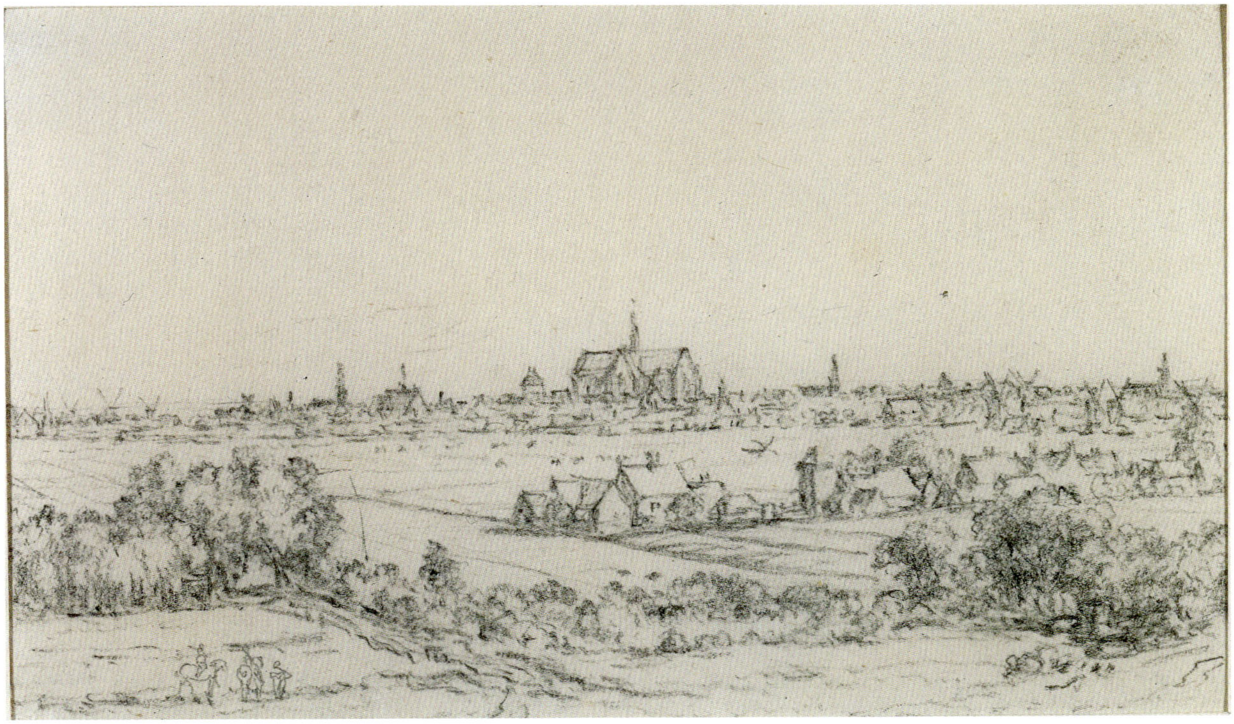

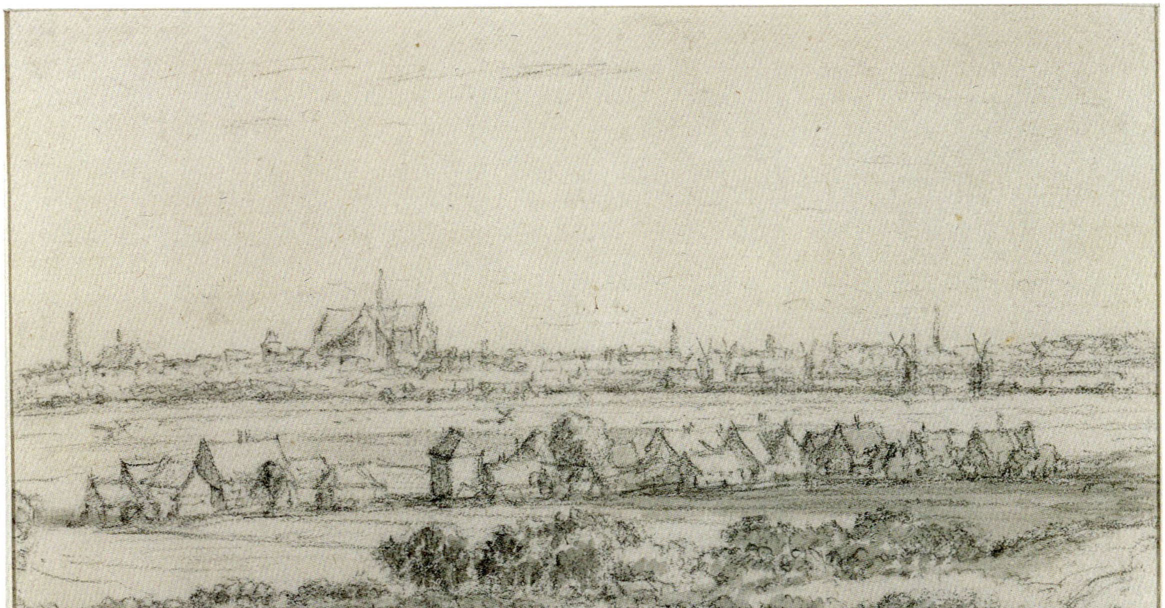

93

Extensive Landscape with a View of Haarlem

Late 1660s or early 1670s. Black chalk, grey wash, 10.7 × 15 cm
Museum Bredius, The Hague, T96-1946

PROVENANCE: Identical with cat. 91.

EXHIBITIONS: The Hague–Cambridge 1981–82, no. 90, repr. (shown in The Hague only); Cambridge–Montreal 1988, no. 83c.

LITERATURE: Knuttel 1926, pp.35, 47, no. 149; Ros Z23c; Simon 1930, pp.68, 84 (rather later than 1663; the figures by another hand); Simon 1940, p.210 (not by Ruisdael; a copy); Blankert 1978, p.165, no. T 19; Giltay 1980, p.161; no. 51; Blankert 1991, pp.267–68, no. T 19, repr.; Slive 2001, no. D69, repr.

PMA

Rosenberg (1928, p.58) recognized that the sketch was probably used as a study for Ruisdael's *View of Haarlem*, Mr. and Mrs. James C. Marlas collection, New York (Slive 2001, no. 54). He also related it to the artist's *Haarlemje* in the Guildhall Art Gallery, London (Slive 2001, no. 42). A generation after he published his observations another drawing of Haarlem's plain reappeared which is now at the Rijksmuseum (Slive 2001, no. D5). It is closer to the London painting than the present sheet.

A light graphite and wash sketch (10.6 × 16.2) similar to the present and Amsterdam sheets appeared in the Amsterdam art market in 1996 as a Ruisdael.[1] In my opinion it is by another hand.

1. Sale, anon., Amsterdam (Christie's), 11 November 1996, no. 97, repr. Provenance: Unknown.

94

Panoramic View of the Northern Part of Amsterdam and the IJ

About 1665. Inscribed on the verso in pencil in a seventeenth-century(?) hand: *Getekend van t dack der verbrande Niwe Kerk tot Amsterdam (naer 't Y)*. Black chalk, grey wash, 8.6 × 15.2 cm
Rijksmuseum, Amsterdam, RP-T-1960-116

PROVENANCE: Sale, Amsterdam (de Winter), 12 February 1770, no. 283; sale, Hendrik Busserus, Amsterdam (v.d. Schley), 21 October 1782, no. 2192 (sold as a lot with another Ruisdael drawing; see below); Friedrich August II of Saxony, Dresden; W. J. R. Dreesmann, Amsterdam; sale, Dreesmann, Amsterdam (Mensing), 22 *sqq.* March 1960, no. 24, repr. (Rijksmuseum).

EXHIBITIONS: Amsterdam 1932, no. 35; Washington and elsewhere 1958–59, no. 101a (*c.*1664–65); Amsterdam–Toronto 1977, no. 77 (*c.*1650); The Hague–Cambridge 1981–82, no. 87, repr.; Amsterdam 1997, pp.86–87, repr.; Amsterdam 1998, p.66 (*c.*1665), repr.

LITERATURE: H. W. Singer, *Zeichnungen aus der Sammlungen Friedrich August II*, Munich, 1921, no. 615; Ros Z20 (*c.*1665); Simon 1930, pp.68, 83 (by Ruisdael, *c.*1665); Simon 1940, p.210 (not by Ruisdael; a copy by another hand, after The Marquess of Lansdowne's painting); Regteren Altena [n.d.], pp.306–07, repr.; *Verzameling Amsterdam W. J. R. Dreesmann*, 3, 1951, p.770 (Ruisdael; panorama of Amsterdam from the Nieuwe Kerk); Stechow 1966, p.128 (*c.*1665); Slive 1973, p.275; Giltay 1980, pp.161–64; no. 3, repr.; Slive 2001, no. D1, repr.

PMA

Rosenberg (Z20) first noted that the drawing is a study for Ruisdael's magnificent *View of Amsterdam*, now in a private English collection (fig. 94a; Slive 2001, no. 5). There is general agreement that the painting was done during Ruisdael's maturity, but there are considerable differences regarding the date of the drawing.

The case for an early date was made by van Regteren Altena ([n.d.]), who called attention to the old inscription on the verso, which states that the panorama was drawn from the burned roof of the Nieuwe Kerk at Amsterdam looking toward the IJ. The fire that damaged the church occurred in January 1645. In view of the inscription, van Regteren Altena proposed that, if the drawing was indeed made from the roof of the Nieuwe Kerk, it must have been done about 1647 from the scaffolding that had been erected to repair the damage done to it. In the Amsterdam–Toronto 1977 exhibition catalogue, Bakker argues that there is no reason to doubt the veracity of the inscription and dates the drawing about 1650. Giltay (1980, p.153) agrees that topographical arguments (also see below) support a date of about 1647, but observes that in view of the style of the drawing perhaps it should be placed later, probably in the early fifties.

Despite the inscription, a date of about 1647–53 for the study is hard to square with drawings Ruisdael made during these years of his activity. The summary touch, the brilliant atmospheric effect, and the close connection of the drawing to Ruisdael's panoramic landscapes showing distant views of the horizon indicate that it should be assigned a later date. The observation made by Rosenberg (Ros 2; Ros Z20) that the scaffolding in the foreground of the sketch belongs to the construction of Amsterdam's New Town Hall, and L. C. J. Frerichs's (Washington and elsewhere 1958–59, no. 101a) conclusion that the drawing is datable to about 1665

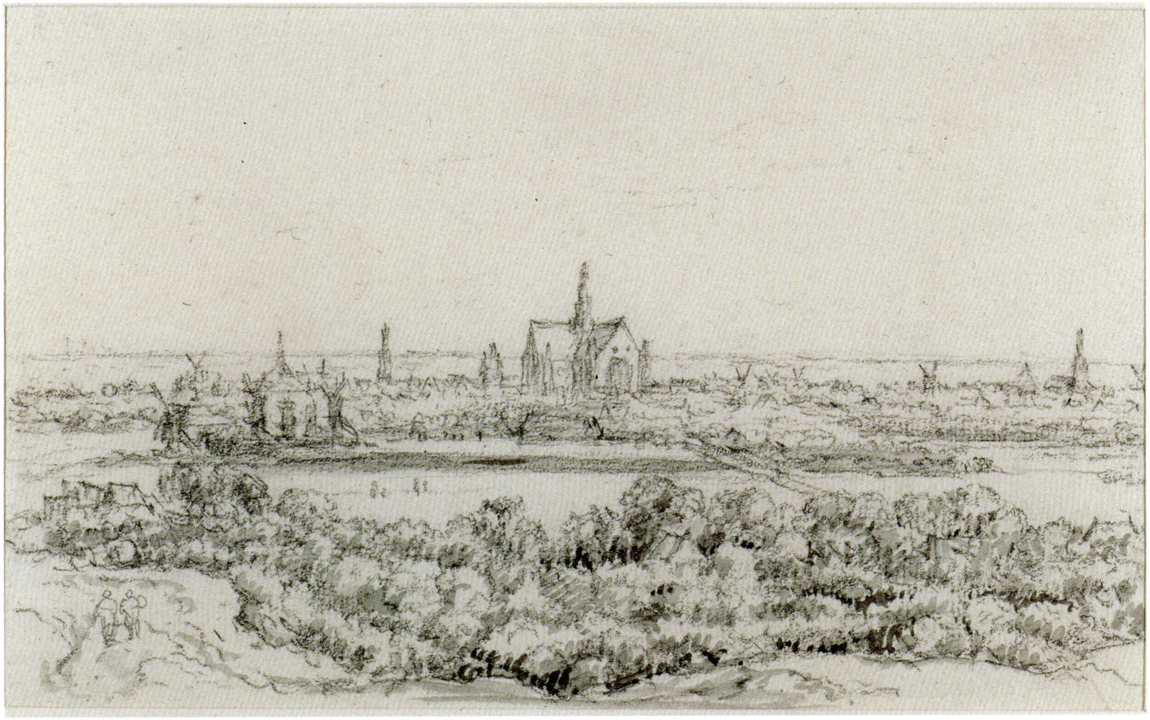

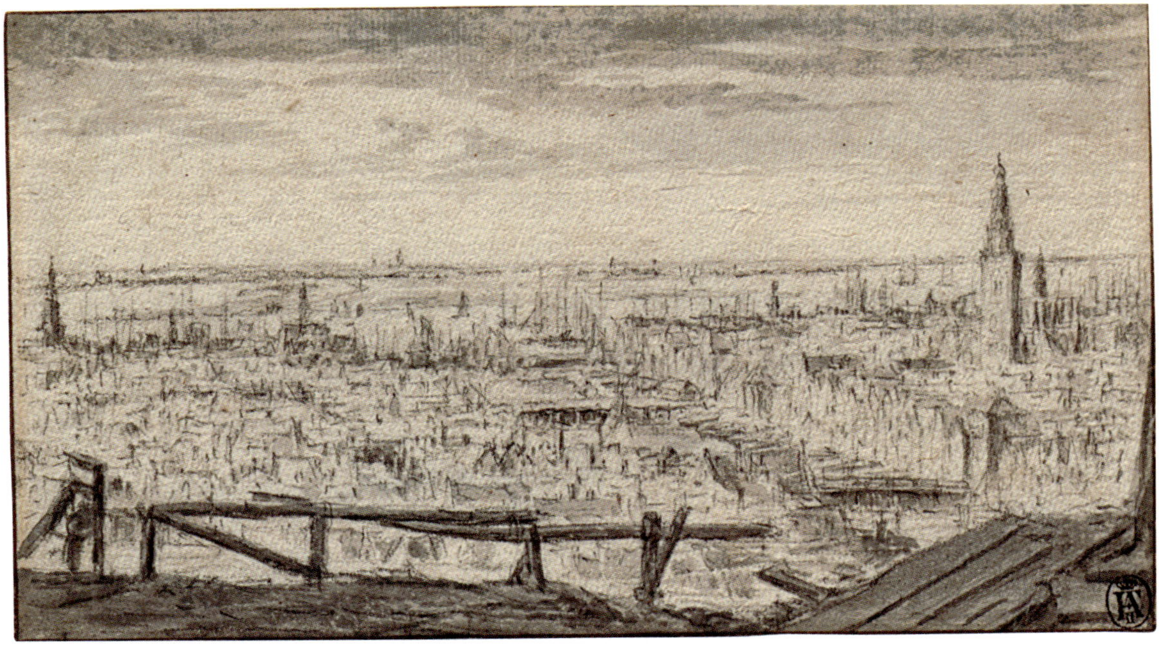

since the tower of the Town Hall was begun in 1664 and finished in 1665 is consistent with the style and conception of the little drawing. It is also noteworthy that it is virtually the same size and on the same paper as Ruisdael's drawing of the distant view of Haarlem at Amsterdam (Slive 2001, no. D5; kind communication from L. C. J. Frerichs), which is datable to the early seventies; perhaps both sheets came from the same sketchbook.

The tower on the extreme left is the Haringpakkerstoren on the corner of the Singel Canal. The high tower on the right belongs to the Oude Kerk, and behind it is the Montelbaanstoren. An additional point about the drawing's topography should be noted. As every Amsterdam school child knows, the New Town Hall was built on the Dam adjacent to the New Church. A view of the city from either height would have presented Ruisdael with very similar extensive views of the city – with one exception observed by van Regteren Altena ([n.d.]), a bird's-eye view of the city and its harbour from the top of the Town Hall should include the New Church in the foreground. Van Regteren Altena noted that, if the drawing was indeed made from the Town Hall, it is unclear why the church does not appear. The explanation may be that Ruisdael chose to concentrate on the vast panorama of Amsterdam, not on the architecture of the neighbouring church.

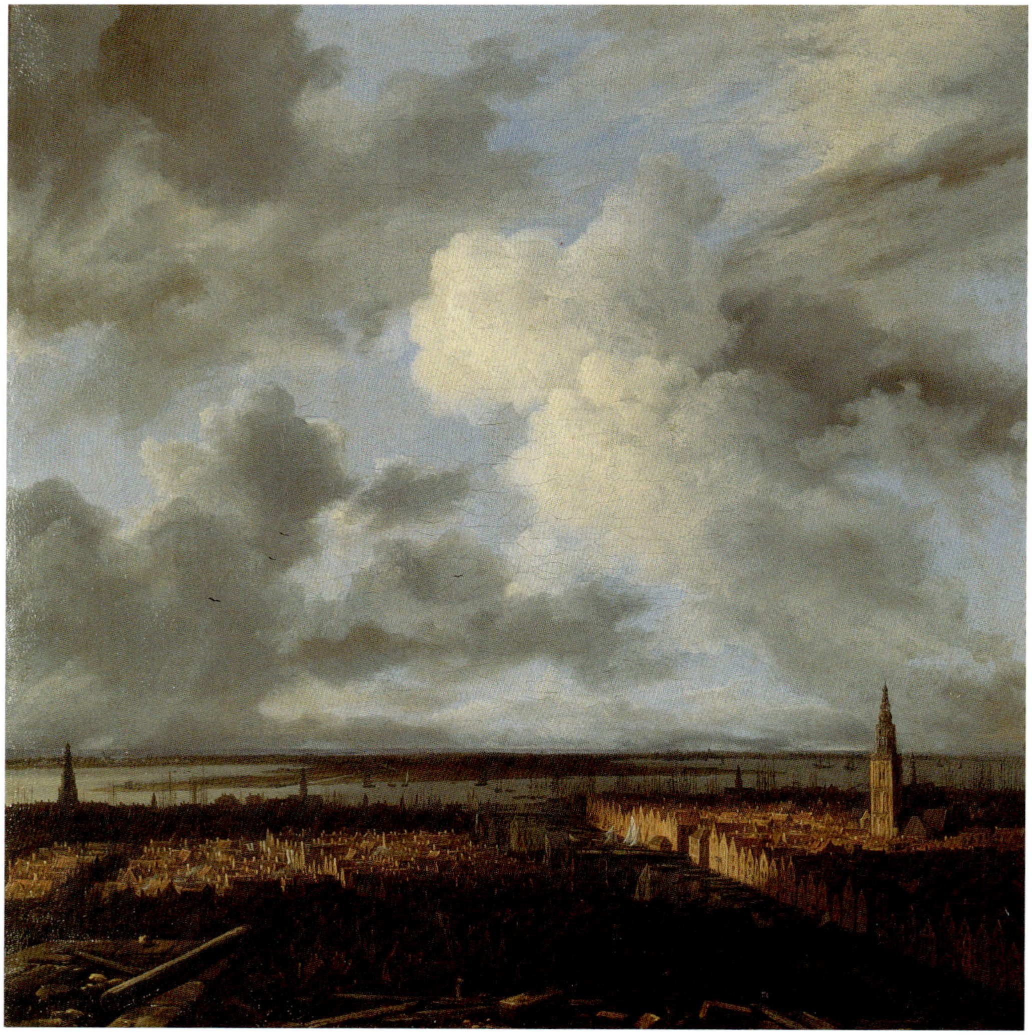

Fig. 94a Jacob van Ruisdael, *Panorama of Amsterdam, Its Harbour and the IJ*. England, private collection.

Facing page Detail of cat. 95 *Three Large Oak Trees at the Edge of a Wood.*

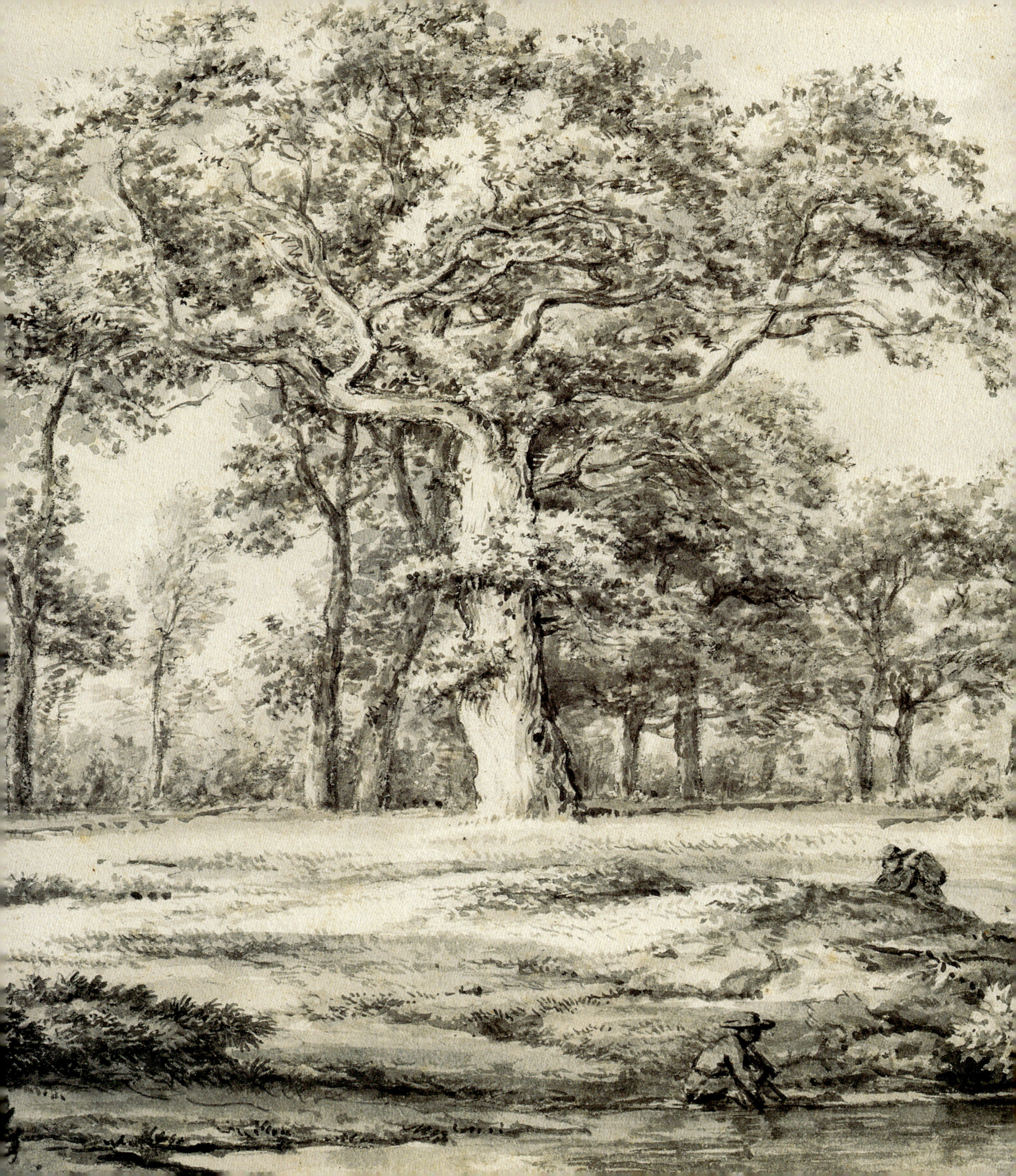

95

Three Large Oak Trees at the Edge of a Wood

About 1670. Inscribed by a later hand: *JvRuisdael*. Black chalk, brush and grey ink, grey and brown wash, 20.1 × 31.5 cm
Teyler Museum, Haarlem, no. Q*50

PROVENANCE: Identical with one of the "2 Gezichten in 't Haagsche Bosch, omtr: a° 1670; waarin de voorgrond is opgemaakt a° 1700, door J. de Moucheron: op oudste Notitie, omtr: a° 1690 gesteld a f14" listed in Sybrand Feitama II's *Notitie der Teekeningen* (Feitama II, NdT 1303, 1304; Broos 1984, p.24; Broos 1987, p.210). The other drawing is cat. 96. The *Notitie* entry establishes that both drawings were acquired by Sybrand Feitama I or his son Isaac by *c.*1690 and passed by descent to the latter's son Sybrand Feitama II. The two sheets appeared in Feitama II's sale, Amsterdam (de Bosch), 16 *sqq.* October 1758, as nos. H.13 and H.14. The former is identical with cat. 96; the latter is the present drawing. Both are described as works by Ruisdael with their foregrounds worked-up by Isaac de Moucheron and their staffage by Nicolaas Verkolje ("door Iz. de Moucheron in de voorgronden opgemaakt, en door N. Verkolje gestoffeerd" [cited by Giltay 1980, p.155, who first recognized the two sheets were identical with those that appeared in Feitama II's 1758 sale]). After the sale the drawings have different histories. For no. H.13 see cat. 96. The present sheet has an unbroken provenance from the time it was in the Feitama collection *c.*1690: Purchased at Feitama II's sale by G. Hoet (Dfl.40); his sale, Amsterdam (Franken), 25 *sqq.* August 1760, no. 513 (Dfl.22.15, Fouket); sale, Johan Goll van Franckenstein, Amsterdam (de Vries), 1 *sqq.* July 1833, no. GG.6 (Dfl.160, Michaëlis for the museum).

EXHIBITIONS: Washington and elsewhere 1958–59, p.41, no. 101, repr. (Ruisdael); New York–Chicago 1989, pp.136–37, no. 88, repr. (entry by Michiel Kirsten); Haarlem–Paris 2001–02, no. 97 (1655–60), repr.

LITERATURE: Feitama II, *Notitie der Teekeningen*, p.45; Feitama II, NdT 1303, 1304; ms. inventory of the Teyler collection, 1854, no. R15; ms. inventory of the Teyler collection, 1864, no. Q72; Scholten 1904, p.230, no. Q*50 (Ruisdael); *Ruysdael, Original-Abbildungen* [1920?], repr.; Giltay 1980, p.155; no. 58 (perhaps 1655–60); Broos 1984, p.24, repr. (Ruisdael, retouched in 1700 by Moucheron); Broos 1987, p.210; Broos 1989, pp.45; 53, note 41; 54, note 48, repr.; Davies 1992, p.89, repr.; Plomp 1997, pp.362–63, no. 414 (1655–60); Slive 2001, no. D64, repr.

RA

Whether this imposing drawing of giant oaks in a wooded landscape and one in the Maida and George Abrams Collection (cat. 96) are in fact views of The Hague Woods as they are identified in Sybrand Feitama II's *Notitie* cannot be determined (the title was a favourite for seventeenth-century Dutch wooded landscapes). In this instance, to judge from their style, I see no reason to question the date of *c.*1670 Feitama assigned to them. The forms of the drawing's monumental oaks set off from the broad expanse of space in their foregrounds and from the context of the woods beyond them as well as their numerous vistas into the distance are characteristic of Jacob's forest scenes datable to the late sixties and early seventies.

Despite Feitama's remark in his *Notitie* that the foregrounds of both the present and the Abrams drawings were worked up by Isaac de Moucheron (1667–1744) in 1700, in my opinion unequivocal recognition of his hand in the drawings is virtually impossible. To my eye, the more the drawings are studied, the greater their seamless impression.

An easier question to resolve is whether Nicolaas Verkolje (1673–1746) is responsible for the staffage in both drawings. This claim is found in Feitama's posthumous 1758 sale catalogue (see Provenance). Surely Broos is right to conclude that the compiler of the sale catalogue nodded when he made Verkolje a contributor to the sheet.[1] This was recognized by the compiler of Hoet's 1760 sale catalogue; his description mentions Moucheron's embellishment but omits a reference to Verkolje.[2] When the drawing appeared in Goll van Franckenstein's 1833 sale, Moucheron's name was dropped as well.[3] Neither cataloguer called the drawing a view of The Hague woods.

1. Broos 1984, pp.24; 34, note 44; Broos 1989, p.53, note 41. Feitama II makes no reference to Verkolje in his own entry on the drawings.
2. Sale, G. Hoet, Amsterdam (Franken), 25 *sqq.* August 1760, no. 513: "Een Boschje, uitvoerig met Zwartkryt en O.I. Ink. Door J. Ruisdael, en de Voorgrond door Moucheron opgemaakt. Uit het Kabinet van Feytama".
3. Sale, J. Goll van Franckenstein, Amsterdam (de Vries), 1 *sqq.* July 1833, no. GG.6: "De uitgang van een Bosch met trotsche eikenbomen; op den voorgrond eenig heestergewas aan eene waterplas, gestoffeerd met twee beeldjes, met zwart krijt en o.i. inkt".

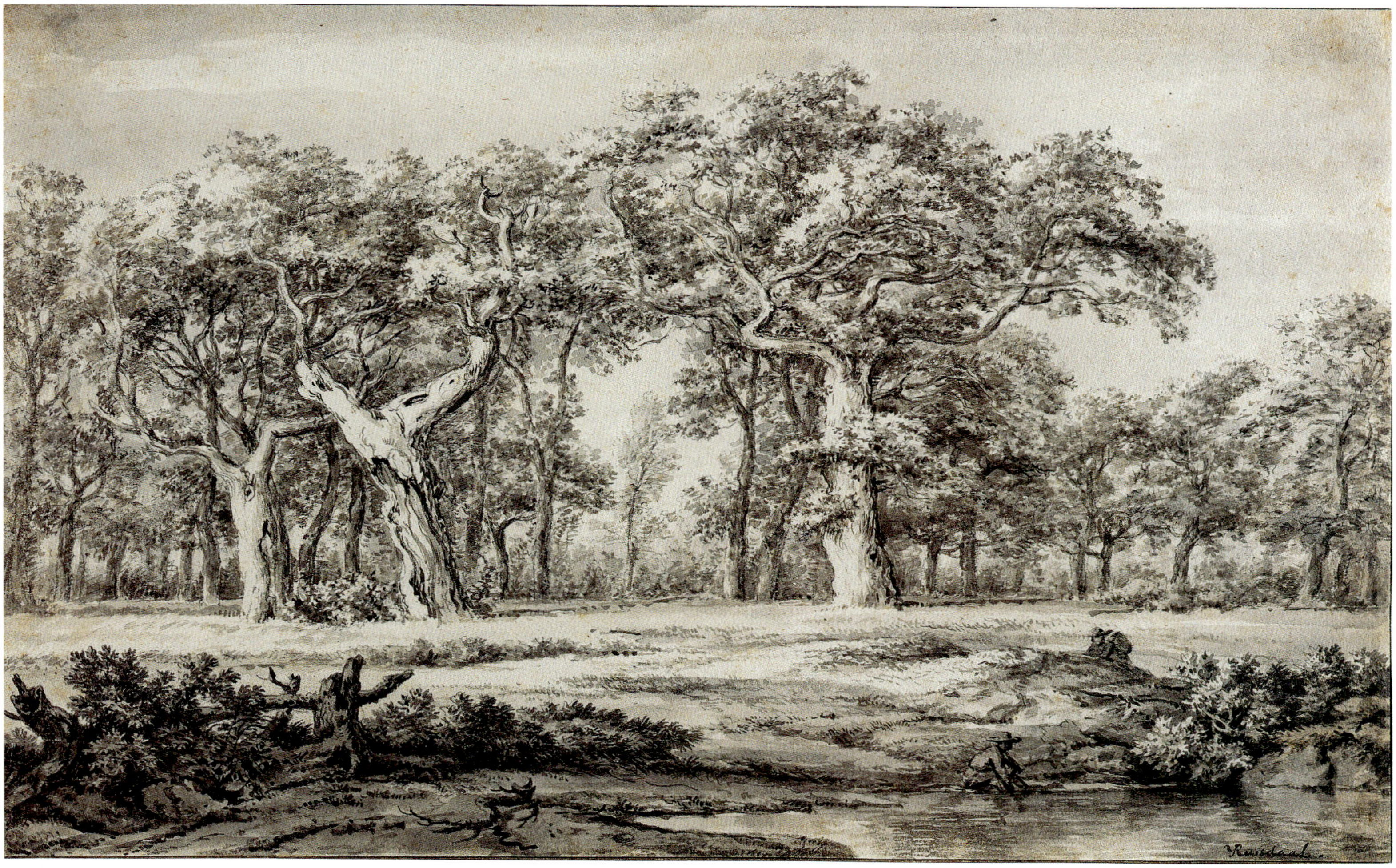
Ruisdaal.

96

Two Large Oaks and Two Deer at the Edge of a Wood

About 1670. Black chalk, grey wash, some later touches of graphite, 20.5 × 32 cm
Maida and George Abrams collection, Boston, Massachusetts. On loan to the Fogg Art Museum, Harvard University Art Museum, TL37587.19

PROVENANCE: Identical with one of the "2 Gezichten in 't Haagsche Bosch, omtr: a° 1670; waarin de voorgrond is opgemaakt a° 1700, door J. de Moucheron; op oudste Notitie, omtr: a° 1690 gesteld a f 14" listed in Sybrand Feitama II's *Notitie der Teekeningen* (Feitama II, NdT 1303, 1304; Broos 1984, p.24; Broos 1987, p.210). The other drawing is cat. 95. The *Notitie* entry establishes that both drawings were acquired by Sybrand I or his son Isaac by *c.*1690 and passed by descent to the latter's son Sybrand Feitama II. The two sheets appeared in Feitama II's sale, Amsterdam (de Bosch), 16 *sqq.* October 1758, as nos. H.13 and H.14. The former is the present drawing (purchased by Yver, Dfl.41), the latter is identical with cat. 95; both are described as works by Ruisdael with their foreground worked up by Isaac de Moucheron and their staffage by Nicolaas Verkolje ("door Iz. de Moucheron in de voorgronden opgemaakt, en door N. Verkolje gestoffeerd" [cited by Giltay 1980, p.155, who first recognized the two sheets as those that appeared in Feitama II's 1758 sale]). After the sale the drawings have different histories. For no. H.14 see cat. 95. The present sheet appeared subsequently in the sale, J. de Vos, Sr., Amsterdam (de Vries), 30 October 1833, no. C.11 (Dfl.161, de Vries); C. Fairfax Murray, London and Florence; his sale, London (Christie's), 30 January–2 February 1920, no. 140 (480 gns., Agnew); Victor Koch, London, by 1929 (cited in Lugt 1929, 1, p.71, under no. 170.487; I have been unable to verify references found in various sources that the drawing was in the coll. H.E. ten Cate, Amelo, in 1929 and with the dealer Katz, London, *c.*1959); Hertha Katz, London; sale, anon. [estate of Hertha Katz], New York (Christie's), 24 January 2001, no. 162; purchased by dealer Bob Haboldt who sold it to Maida and George Abrams in the same month.

EXHIBITION: London–Paris–Cambridge 2002–03, no. 70, repr. (*c.*1670; cat. by William W. Robinson).[1]

LITERATURE: Feitama II, *Notitie der Teekeningen*, p.45; Feitama II, NdT, 1303, 1304; *Collection of Drawings by the Old Masters, formed by C. Fairfax Murray*, 3, no. 19 [n.d.,.n.p.], repr. (Ruisdael); Lugt 1929, 1, p.71, under no. 170.487 (Ruisdael); Giltay 1980, p.155 (perhaps 1655–60); no. 107; Broos 1984, p.24 (Ruisdael, retouched in 1700 by Isaac de Moucheron); Broos 1987, p.210; New York–Chicago 1989, under no. 88 (entry by Michiel Kirsten); Broos 1989, pp.41–42, repr.; Plomp 1997, pp.362–63, under no. 414; Slive 2001, no. D87 and supplement, p.788, no. D87; Haarlem–Paris 2001–02, p.171.

PMA and RA

As noted in the provenance, this drawing of two gargantuan oaks and one of three equally huge oaks, now in the Teyler Museum (cat. 95), were in the Feitama family collection from *c.*1690 until both appeared in Sybrand Feitama II's sale in 1758. See the entry for the Teyler sheet for their topography, dates (*c.*1670) and what can be deduced from Feitama's *Notitie* and his posthumous sale catalogue about them.

The Teyler entry (cat. 95) indicates the compiler of the sale catalogue erred when he wrote Nicolaas Verkolje did the drawing's staffage but Feitama himself tells us that Isaac de Moucheron (1667–1744) worked up the foregrounds of both sheets in 1700, about a decade after they were acquired by his grandfather or father. In both Moucheron's hand is virtually impossible to distinguish, but he must have been impressed by the present drawing and perhaps had it in his hands more than once since he made a close copy of it, signed and dated 1716, which is now in the Louvre (fig. 96a). His copy, first recognized by Lugt (1929), faithfully reproduces the great oaks and some of the landscape beyond them. However, by offering a closer view of Ruisdael's two giant protagonists, eliminating the sky above their ancient crowns and stretches of the plain they dominate, he dissipates most of the power of Jacob's invention. His introduction of a conspicuous horseman and a couple of resting figures does not enhance the scale of the two oaks. Without them, particularly the rider, the trees gain in height as can be seen in an embellished offset of Moucheron's drawing which was made before he added the rider to his copy.[2]

Ruisdael's drawing was most probably used for the left half of a painted pastiche by an unidentified hand of a *Wooded Landscape with a View of the Castle of Bentheim*, formerly at the Hermitage, where it was erroneously attributed to Ruisdael; a second version of the pastiche is known (for both works see Slive 2001, no. dub3).

1. Robinson confirms that the sheet bears the arms of Amsterdam watermark.
2. Published by Broos 1989, pp.41–42, repr. The verso of the offset is inscribed: "Opgemaakt uijt de Schets van/I. Moucheron./1743" (*ibid.*, fig. 11b), establishing that it was worked up about a year before Moucheron's death. The artist who finished it had not been identified. The offset was in the collection W. B. Wouters, Delft, 1967. Also illustrated, Slive 2001, fig. D87b.

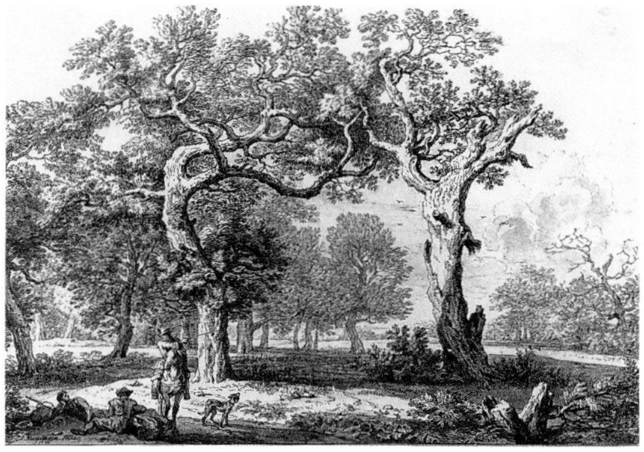

Fig. 96a Isaac de Moucheron, copy of cat. 96. Pen and wash. Musée du Louvre, Paris.

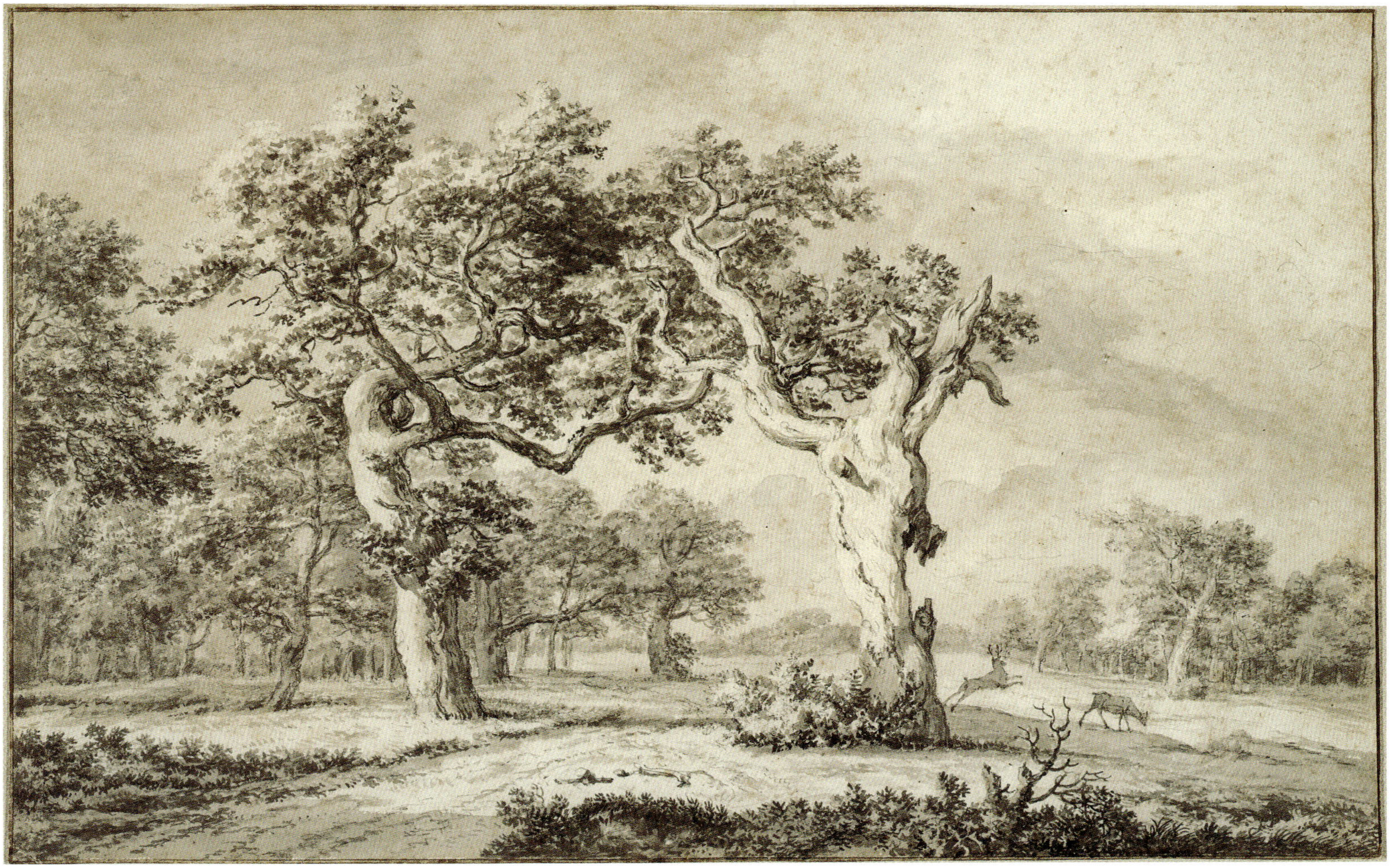

97

View of the Dam with the Weigh House at Amsterdam

About 1675–80. Black chalk, grey wash, 9 × 15.1 cm
Musées royaux des Beaux-Arts de Belgique, Brussels, 4060/169

98

View of the Dam and Old Church at Amsterdam

About 1675–80. Black chalk, grey wash, 8.7 × 12.3 cm
Musées royaux des Beaux-Arts de Belgique, Brussels, 4060/168

Cat 97

PROVENANCE: Collection de Grez.

EXHIBITION: The Hague–Cambridge 1981–82, no. 93, repr.

LITERATURE: Nève 1913, no. 169 (as "J. Beerstraten," erroneously called "Hôtel de Ville de . . . ,"); Giltay 1980, p.164, no. 32, repr.; Slive 2001, no. D37, repr.

PMA and RA

Cat 98

PROVENANCE: Collection de Grez.

EXHIBITION: The Hague–Cambridge 1981–82, no. 94, repr.

LITERATURE: Nève 1913, no. 168 (as "J. Beerstraten," erroneously called "La Grand'place à Harlem"); Giltay 1980, p.164, no. 33, repr.; Slive 2001, no. D78, repr.

PMA and RA

The present drawing and cat. 98 were formerly ascribed to J. Beerstraaten (Nève 1913). Frits Lugt (1925) and An Zwolle (1967) attributed both sheets to Ruisdael (notes at the RKD). Giltay (1980) published them as works by Jacob and correctly observed that they not only show unmistakable views of the Dam at Amsterdam but once formed a single sheet. When or why they were cut is unknown. Giltay also noted that the close correspondence of the joined drawings to Ruisdael's painting of *The Dam with the Weigh House at Amsterdam*, now at Berlin (cat. 57), indicates that they served as a preliminary study for the painting. Fig. 97a is a reconstruction of the drawing; the top and bottom edges no longer align but the left side of the present drawing makes almost a perfect fit with its mate.

The Berlin painting has been generally dated about 1670. However, as mentioned in the discusssion of it, its style suggests that it may have been painted toward the end of the decade. Similarities between the handling of the Brussels drawings and the artist's sketch at Leipzig (cat. 99), which was most probably used as a study for his late panoramic views of the Amstel looking toward Amsterdam (see cat. 58), tend to support this hypothesis. The Leipzig drawing could hardly have been done before 1675, and it may have been made as late as 1681 (see cat. 99). Like the cut one at Brussels, it also comprises two sheets of paper; whether its support was originally put together by the artist or was a single sheet that was cut, and later rejoined, is not known.

The artist made changes when he transposed his drawing of the Dam into a painting. Notable is the shift in the direction of the light. In the preliminary study the façade of the blocky Weigh House is in shadow. When the artist turned to his canvas he put it in full light and adjusted the light-dark effect accordingly. He also emphasized the massiveness of the Weigh House by reducing the height of the tower of the Oude Kerk and the building on the extreme left, a tavern and shopping center called *Het Huis onder't Zeil* (The House Under the Sail).

For a painting by an unidentified hand related to the Brussels drawing see Slive 2001, no. dub2, repr.

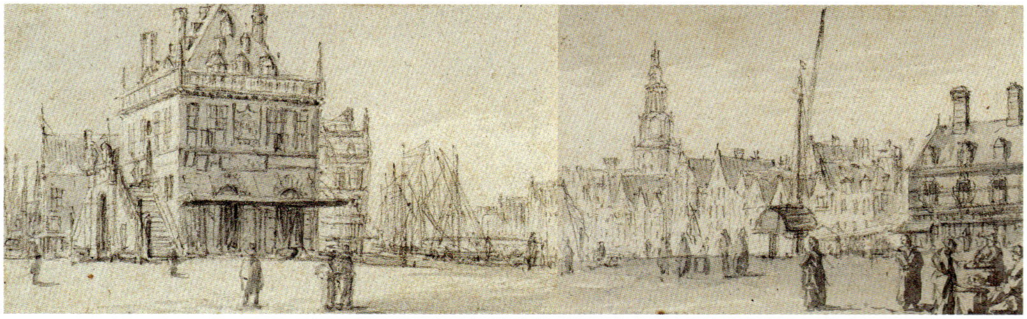

Fig. 97a Reconstruction of Ruisdael's drawing of the Dam (see cat. 97 and 98).

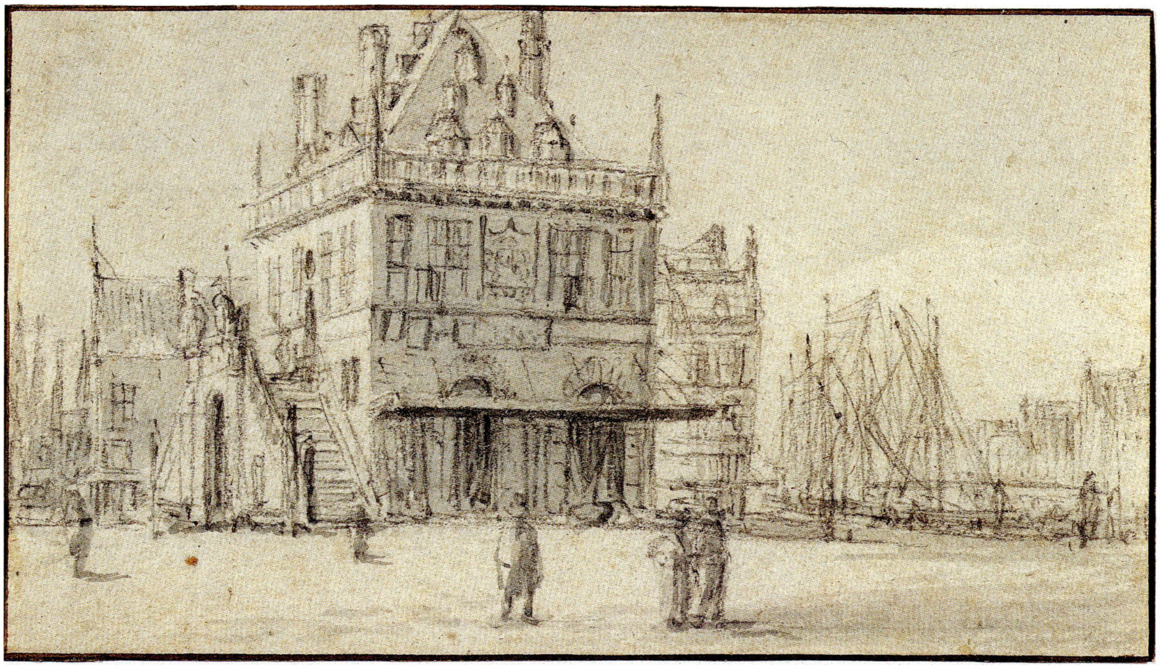

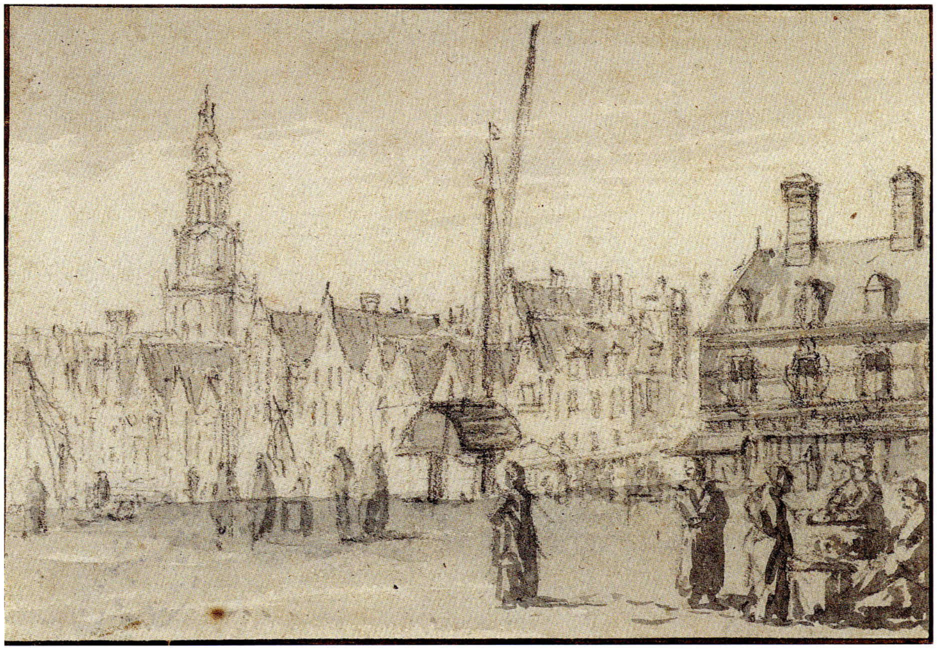

99

Panoramic View of the Amstel River Looking toward Amsterdam

About 1675–81. Black chalk, grey wash, 8.2 × 30.6 cm; the support is two joined sheets of paper (8.2 × 14.6; 8.2 × 16 cm)
Museum der bildenden Künste, Leipzig, J 413

PROVENANCE: J. de Vos, Sr.; not in his 1833 sale. (A "Vue panoramique" appeared as a lot with a more fully described "Profile d'un village" in the sale, J. de Vos Jbzn [1803–82], Amsterdam [Roos], 22–23 March 1883, no. 469; both drawings are now in the Amsterdam Historical Museum [see cat. no. D11].) Most probably K. E. von Liphart (d.1891) who bequeathed his collection to his grandson R. von Liphart who sold the drawing in a sale called Karl Eduard von Liphart of Florence, Leipzig (Boerner), 26 *sqq.* April 1898, no. 812.

EXHIBITIONS: Budapest 1969, no. 123; Yokohama–Sapporo–Hiroshima 1985–86, no. 105; St. Louis 1991, no. 43.

LITERATURE: Rosenberg 1928, p.73; no. Z33 (preparatory study for Cambridge and Philips paintings); Simon 1935, p.192 (copy by another hand after a painting); d'Ailly 1953, pp.68–69, no. 138 (*c.*1681); Slive 1973, pp.275–76, repr.; Giltay 1980, pp.163–64; no. 65; Slive 1981, p.156, repr.; *Meisterzeichnungen: Museum der bildenden Künste*, Leipzig, 1990, no. 51; Slive 2001, no. D77, repr.

RA

The drawing is a preliminary study for Ruisdael's painting at the Fitzwilliam Museum, Cambridge (cat. 58), and for a variant of the composition in the Philips-de Jongh collection, Eindhoven (Slive 2001, no. 4). The drawing's support is made up of two sheets of paper pasted together, which may have been contiguous pages in a sketchbook. The dark wash in the upper right part of the sky is probably a later addition. A black ink border (by another hand?) frames the top and two sides of the drawing; its absence at the bottom as well as the unusual cropped trees in the foreground suggest that the lower part of the drawing has been cut. The foremost parts of both the Fitzwilliam and Philips versions bolster this supposition. It hardly need be mentioned that the drawing does not include the vast expanse of sky and clouds seen in the paintings, but it should be noted that the Fitzwilliam picture shows a more extensive view of the distant city than is seen in the drawing, and the Philips version shows even a bit more of its skyline than is seen in the Fitzwilliam painting. These differences raise the possibility that the Leipzig drawing was originally larger and has been cut at the top and at both sides as well as at the bottom.

The bird's-eye sketch may have been made from the tower at the Pauwentuin, a seventeenth-century excursion site down the Amstel River. Although emphasis has been given to the foliated trees, buildings and windmills in the fore- and middle-grounds, and the distant view has been only lightly sketched, enough has been shown of the salient characteristics of the city's major buildings to make their identification possible. Amsterdam is seen from the south after the completion of the city wall. The Utrechtse Poort can be seen in the wall on the left. The large arched bridge linking the walls is the Amstelbrug (Hogesluis), beyond it the high spire of first the Zuiderkerk, and then the more distant Oude Kerk are recognizable. The large building with a domed tower left of center on the horizon is the monumental New Town Hall.

The rectangular building with a low-pitched roof on the far right is the Portuguese Synagogue. Its cornerstone was laid on 17 April 1671 and it was consecrated on 2 August 1675.[1] The year of the Synagogue's consecration provides a very probable *terminus post quem* for the drawing. D'Ailly (1953, pp.68–69) writes that in the drawing he can recognize the Reformed Church's Home for Old Women (Het Besjehuis) above the Amstelbrug and to the right of the tower of the Zuiderkerk. If he is correct, the *terminus post quem* for the drawing is pushed forward to about 1681, since the construction of the home began in that year; it was completed in 1683, a year after Ruisdael's death. However, the case for d'Ailly's date of about 1681 for the sheet is not conclusive. Although it is possible to distinguish a building that may be identical with the old women's home in both of the painted versions of the view (see cat. 58), it is exceedingly difficult, if not impossible, to spot it here. In any event, the drawing can serve as a safe touchstone for Ruisdael's latest drawing style. There is little reason to believe that his work as a draughtsman radically changed from about 1675 until 1681.

1. See J. d'Ancona, "De Portugese Gemeente 'Talmoed Tora' te Amsterdam tot 1795," in *Geschiedenis der Joden in Nederland*, edited by H. Brugmans and A. Frank, Amsterdam, 1940, pp.287–89.

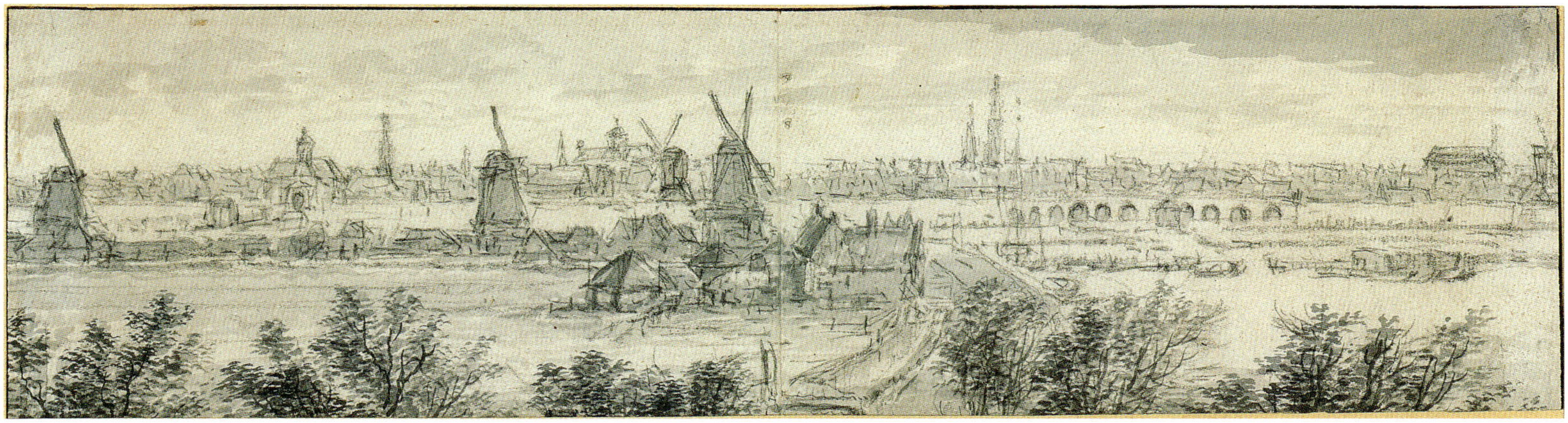

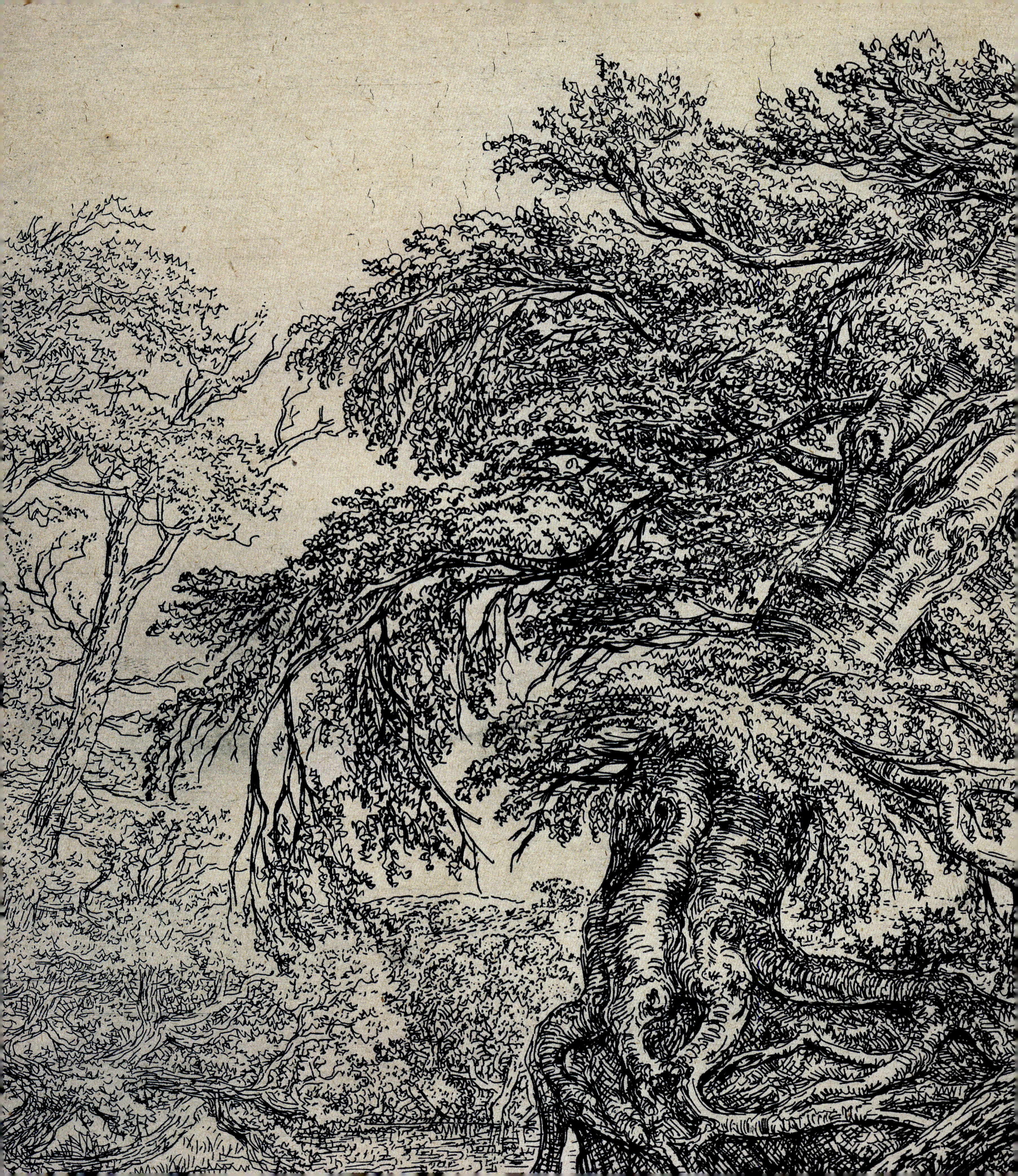

Etchings

It is abundantly evident that Ruisdael decided to try his hand at etching during the first phase of his career. Two prints are dated 1646 (cat. 100, 101), the year he appears on the Haarlem scene. Both are proudly signed: *JvRuisdael in.f.*.[1] Three tiny oval prints – they are about the size of calling cards – also are datable to Ruisdael's earliest years of activity in Haarlem (cat. 102–04). The unique impression of his etching of a heavily shaded thicket at the edge of a pond (cat. 105) probably belongs with this early group, or was made soon afterward. Another three are signed and dated 1647, 1648, 1649 (cat. 106–08). Ruisdael's best known etchings, the four landscapes that may have been designed as a set (cat. 109–12), are datable to the first half of the 1650s. They mark the end of his brief career as a printmaker. To our knowledge he did not etch another plate from about 1655 until his death in 1682.

Dates on five of his thirteen etchings have made it possible to attempt to catalogue them here in an approximate chronological order. Other aspects of his printmaking activity are less clear. It is not known who taught him the technique of etching or the elements of the graphic vocabulary of hatched lines, curly cues, hooks and dots that he employed with impressive competency by the time he made his two etchings dated 1646. To judge from their production as printmakers, his father Isaack, his uncle Salomon van Ruysdael or Cornelis Vroom, artists who stimulated him upon occasion in his youth, were not his mentors. Not a single print by these artists is known. Was he self-taught? The high order of artistic intelligence he shows in his early works seems to rule out that possibility. He was too bright to attempt to reinvent the wheel. Perhaps Allart van Everdingen helped him. After all, Everdingen settled in Haarlem early in 1645 after he left Scandinavia and remained there until 1652 when he moved to Amsterdam; these were precisely the years Ruisdael was active as an etcher. Moreover, Everdingen was a prolific printmaker (more than 100 landscape etchings, about fifty etched illustrations for *Renard the Fox* and a few mezzotints). But the connection between the two artists as printmakers remains hypothetical. It has not been possible to ascertain if Everdingen worked as an etcher during his Haarlem years; all of his prints are undated, and their uniformity of style has defied attempts to work out a relative chronology.

In view of what Ruisdael had achieved by the time he made his 1646 etchings and his ever increasing mastery of printmaking, his decision never again to touch an etcher's needle after about 1655 is puzzling. Knowledge that he moved from his native town to Amsterdam soon after he abandoned etching complicates matters. Surely Amsterdam would have offered him a much larger market for his prints than Haarlem. There is no reason to believe he was insensitive to the demands of the metropolis' thriving art market; its existence helps explain why he made the twenty kilometre move from Haarlem to Amsterdam. His prodigious output of Scandinavian landscapes, which begins not long after he settled in the largest city of the new republic, can be partially explained by his desire to capitalize on the vogue that Everdingen had established for them there. He also did his bit to help satisfy the demand for topographical views that suddenly blossomed in Amsterdam about 1660 by making six drawings (see cat. 86) of sites near the old city's ramparts before they were demolished to make land available for the dramatic extension of the city that began in the early sixties.

Facing page Detail of cat. 110, *The Great Beech, with Two Men and a Dog*

Abraham Blooteling, the prolific Amsterdam printmaker, made etchings after them and in 1670 Blooteling also engraved copies of Ruisdael's two drawings of views of the Portuguese-Jewish Cemetery at Ouderkerk on the Amstel (see cat. 79, 80).

Ruisdael was not the man for an engraving job. Like so many artists who made prints in The Netherlands in his time he never made one. He left the rigid discipline demanded by graving in cold metal to a highly skilled craftsman who specialized in making engravings after designs produced by other artists. But why did he cease to use the print technique that he had mastered? Why did he not make etchings for the large Amsterdam market? Perhaps he decided that the energy spent on polishing metal plates, sharpening needles, mixing grounds and preparing acid baths needed to bite plates, messing with printer's ink, struggling with presses and other paraphernalia used by etchers was simply not worth the effort involved. Moreover, consideration of what he had achieved in his paintings by the time he moved to Amsterdam suggests that he would have had to have put much more effort into his plates than he had done in the past if he had attempted to transpose into his etchings fundamental aspects of what he had accomplished in his paintings.

Support for this hypothesis is found if we take a close look at two of his latest etchings: *The Great Beech* (cat. 110, see detail, p. 234) and *Cottages on a Hill* (cat. 111). Both prints impress by the almost palpable presence of the verdant growth on the hills in the foreground and the gigantic trees that dominate the landscape. In these passages the etched lines are extremely dense and heavily worked. In contrast, he used more widely spaced lines and the white of the paper for the few light accents in the foremost parts of the landscapes and for their subordinate distant views. The result is a clear distinction between the powerful forms in the foreground and the airy vistas beyond them; the division between the two is rather sharp.

Now, even before he had made these etchings Ruisdael had achieved far less abrupt shifts between the near and far views in his paintings, and in his subsequent work, as the extent between the foreground and distant views in his landscapes increased, the transitions between the two became more subtle and gradual. To achieve similar effects in his etchings Ruisdael most likely would have had to resort to multiple bitings of his etched plates, the most common method used by printmakers of his time to obtain a wider range between the light and dark lines usually found in an etching.

A printmaker who desires to subject a metal plate to more than one biting normally etches his entire composition on a plate in the usual fashion. Then he covers his plate with transparent stopping-out varnish, which serves the same purpose as an opaque etcher's ground, but permits him to see the parts he wants to rework with his needle. After the reworking has been finished the plate is immersed in acid a second time. When done by a skilled etcher, the second biting introduces a greater range of gradations between the lightest and darkest etched areas of the print. The process can be repeated again and again until the desired effect is achieved.

Use of the multiple biting process would have enabled Ruisdael to translate more of his pictorial achievement into his etchings. But he never employed it. Indeed, he seems to have laid down his etcher's needle forever at the very time the process would have begun to serve him best. Perhaps he abandoned the technique because he decided that a single biting of a plate could not produce the effects he desired and never adopted the multiple biting process because it has too many objectionable features. It is slow and tedious. It is also risky. If the stopping-out varnish fails, all the etcher's previous effort has gone for naught. Third, fourth or more bitings compound the difficulties and risk.

Few public or private print collections offer visitors the pleasure of seeing many fine original impressions of Ruisdael's etchings and since five of his prints are unique impressions in three different collections no print room has a full set of his thirteen prints. A passing remark in a letter John Sheepshanks sent in 1833 to John Constable to thank him for two of his own etchings indicates that they already were scarce in his day:

. . . I can well imagine that these [etchings] will be sought for in another Century, as the rare Ruisdaels are now – What a pity, that dealers you will not live to see, must have the pecuniary advantage, & that you have only the prospective reputation.[2]

Of Ruisdael's unique impressions, the British Museum has two (both were in Sheepshanks's collection, and Constable made a pen drawing after one of them; see p.33 and fig. 41); two are at the Albertina; one is at Amsterdam. We also have seen that his most scarce prints are datable to the early years of his activity as an independent artist. Their rarity suggest that Ruisdael considered them trial essays that did not warrant large editions.

Nothing is known regarding the number of impressions the artist pulled from his plates, the prices they fetched, or the manner in which they were distributed for sale. A publisher's credit line on late states of two of his prints, *The Grain Field at the Edge of a Wood*, 1648 (cat. 107), and *The Three Oaks*, 1649 (cat. 108), informs us that they were printed by the Antwerp engraver and print publisher Frans van den Wyngaerde (1614–79), who had a knack for obtaining plates made by other artists (*e.g.*, Jan Lievens, Lucas Vostermann, Wencelaus Hollar) and publishing editions of them. But how or whether he managed to make contact with the Antwerp publisher and what arrangements were made with him remain unanswered questions.

The prints that turn up most often are three etchings that belong to the group made about 1650–55: *The Little Bridge*, *The Great Beech*, *Cottage on a Hill* (cat. 109–11). Impressions of first states of these outstanding prints, which show them before another hand added the hatched skies and clumsy, cotton batting-like cumulus clouds that appear in their second states, are uncommon.[3] The cumulus clouds in late states of *Forest Marsh with Travellers on a Bank* (cat. 112) also were added by another artist. For a view of Ruisdael's own sensitive and sometimes impetuous handling of skies and clouds we need only to turn to his other etchings that include them.

Late impressions of *The Little Bridge*, *The Great Beech* and *The Cottage on a Hill* made from reworked plates also have been recorded. According to Weigel[4] the printmaker, publisher and author Pierre François Basan (1723–93) had their plates and pulled impressions from them. Since they appear in *A Collection of [Two Hundred] Original Etchings . . .*, printed by J. McCreery, London, 1816, and in an 1816 edition of the *Collection* published in London by G. Schulze that postdates it,[5] the three plates were certainly available for use early in the nineteenth century. Their fate after 1816 remains a mystery.[6] Apparently no other plates have been preserved.

1. It is noteworthy that Rembrandt, who made more than 280 etchings and whose achievement in the medium was unmatched by any of his contemporaries, felt compelled to inscribe on only two of his that he was the author of the design (*in.* = *inventor*) as well as the maker of the print (*f.* = *fecit*); these inscriptions are found on his *Flight into Egypt*, 1633 (Bartsch 52), and *The Good Samaritan*, 1633 (Bartsch 90).
2. Parris *et al.* 1975, p.133.
3. Laurence Binyon (1895, pp.46–50) first recognized these later additions in the brief essay he published on the artist, and aptly described the added clouds as pudding shapes "with hard bulging edges (what a satire on this consummate master of clouds!)" and deplored "the presence of those inflated shapes inserted by a stupid publisher". Not all Binyon's observations regarding Ruisdael's etched work and achievement are equally acceptable. He (*ibid.*, pp.46–47) made a demonstrable muddle of their chronology and (*ibid.*, p.50) maintained that Ruisdael lacked John Crome's consummate style. Binyon's book devoted to Crome and John Sell Cotman appeared two years after he published his essay on Ruisdael.
4. Weigel 1843, pp.39–40.
5. For evidence that G. Schulze's edition postdates McCreery's see Mannocci 1988, p.28. McCreery's *Collection* is known for its inclusion of images struck from original plates by seventeenth-century artists including Ruisdael, Rembrandt, Hollar, Castiligione, Bega and especially Claude – the volume includes twenty-five very good impressions of Claude's prints struck from twenty-four original plates (see *ibid.*, pp.27–28).
6. They do not appear in an edition of the *Collection* datable 1819–22, published by W. Lewis, London, or in an edition printed in 1826 by J. Kay, London. For the possibility that the plates were in the hands of the dealer Samuel Woodburn before or after they were published by McCreery see Slive 1991, p.606. Weigel (1843, pp.39–40) writes in his time the plates for *The Little Bridge, The Great Beech* and *Cottage on a Hill* were in England, but he does not say more. In 1910 Wurzbach (1906–11, 2, p.521) wrote that the plate for *The Little Bridge* is still in existence ("Die Platte existiert noch"); however, he did not state where.

Cottages and a Clump of Trees near a Small River

1st state: Signed and dated bottom, centre left: [*Jv Ruisdael i*]*n f.1646.* 20.6 × 28.1 cm. Unique impression, Collection Frits Lugt, Institut Néerlandais, Paris, 7253
2nd state: Signed and dated, upper right: *JvRuisdael f.1646.* 20.4 × 28.1 cm. Albertina, Vienna, DG2004/4573; a band 2.3 centimetres in width has been trimmed at the top of this impression

1st state: The bottom left margin of this unique impression of the print, which included the artist's signature, is missing. It can be deduced from impressions of the second state that, before the lower margin was damaged, the inscription on it read: *JvRuisdael in. f.*1646.

2nd state: The bottom margin is extensively darkened with hatching, which makes it difficult to read the first signature and date. Foliage has been added to the highest tree; additional hatching on the cottage on the right and the tree near it.

LITERATURE: Bartsch 1803, 7 (described from a cropped impression); Regnault-Delalande 1817, 7 (first notes that the print is signed and dated 1646 at the bottom and again at the top); Smith 1835, p.104, no. 7; Weigel 1843, 7; Duplessis 1878, 8; Dutuit 1885, 7; Wurzbach 1910, 7 (dated 1645 in lower margin); Simon 1930, pp.14, 68 (dated 1645 in lower margin); Simon 1935a, p.7 (dated 1645 in lower margin); Stechow 1960, pp.250, 260, note 3 (apparently begun in 1645 and completed in 1646; the date was changed from 1645 to 1646); Keyes 1977, 1 (changes in the second state by another hand); Hollstein-de Hoop Scheffer 1978, 7; de Groot 1979, no. 221; Slive 1981, pp.238–39, no. 96; Ackley 1981, pp.184–85, no. 123; Ackley 1982, p.123, note 5; Walford 1991, pp.53–54; Keyes 1999, pp.157–59; Slive 2001, no. E1.

PMA 2nd state; RA 1st state

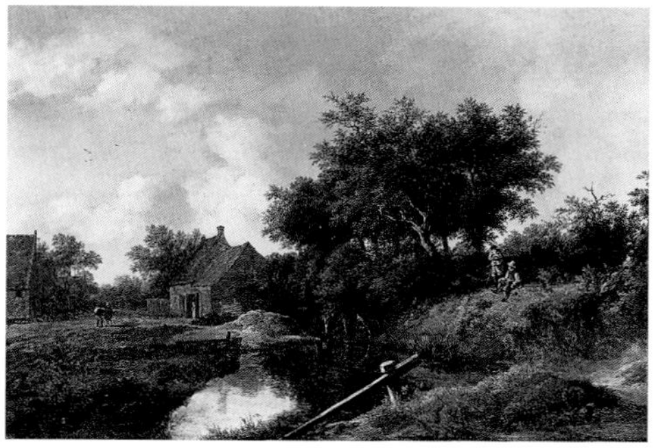

Fig. 100a Isaack van Ruisdael, *Cottages and a Clump of Trees near a Small River.* Detroit Institute of Arts.

Wurzbach (1910) and Simon (1930; 1935a) evidently knew only the second state and erroneously read the date in the lower margin as 1645. Stechow's (1960) statement that the print was begun in 1645 and finished in the following year because the date on it was changed from 1645 to 1646 is hard to follow; no existing impression shows the change he mentions. Since none of these authors cite the unique first state of the etching now at Collection Frits Lugt, Institut Néerlandais, Paris, it is reasonable to conclude that they did not know it; the date on its bottom margin is unmistakably 1646.

Widely spaced dots and irregular short lines help achieve the effect of sparkling sunlight in the print; Ruisdael used a similar pointillist-like technique in his early chalk drawings at Dresden that are datable about the time of the etching (cf. cat. 59–64).

A painting which gives a mirror image, with some modifications, of the same site is at the Detroit Institute of Arts[1] (fig. 100a). Hofstede de Groot, who did not know the original, listed it as Hobbema.[2] Simon correctly wrote the panel has a false Hobbema signature; he attributed the landscape to Isaack van Ruisdael.[3] Keyes reported that during the course of the painting's conservation treatment in the 1990s it was learned that underneath the false Hobbema signature there remain "substantial traces of what appears to be a genuine signature – that of Isaack van Ruisdael" (Keyes 1999, p.155). The style of the restored Detroit painting accords with other landscapes by and attributable to Isaack. It, as well as hardly decipherable remnants of the picture's monogram (not signature), support Simon's (1935a, p.8) contention that father and son worked together at the same site. Keyes (1999, pp. 156–59) argues that the son used his father's painting, not nature, as a point of departure for his early etching. Keyes's hypothesis is possible but in my opinion Simon's is more probable. Moreover, as Stijn Alsteens rightly notes, the young artist's own inscription on the print "Jv Ruisdael in [venit] f[ecit]" proclaims he is its author as well as its etcher.[4]

1. *Path Leading to Farms by a Wooded Bank*, no. F73.12. Panel, 53.3 × 78.7; remains of a signature, bottom right: *IvR* [. . .]. PROVENANCE: Sale, François Delessert, Paris, 15 March 1869, no. 34 (as Hobbema; fr.10,200); private collection, U.S.A.; gift of Joseph B. Schlotman to the Detroit Institute of Arts, 1973.
2. HdG, Hobbema 280; panel, 56 × 78. Hofstede de Groot does not mention a signature.
3. Simon 1935a, pp.7–8, repr. Before the landscape was restored, I did not find Simon's attribution compelling (Slive 1981, p.239).
4. Paris 2004, p.282.

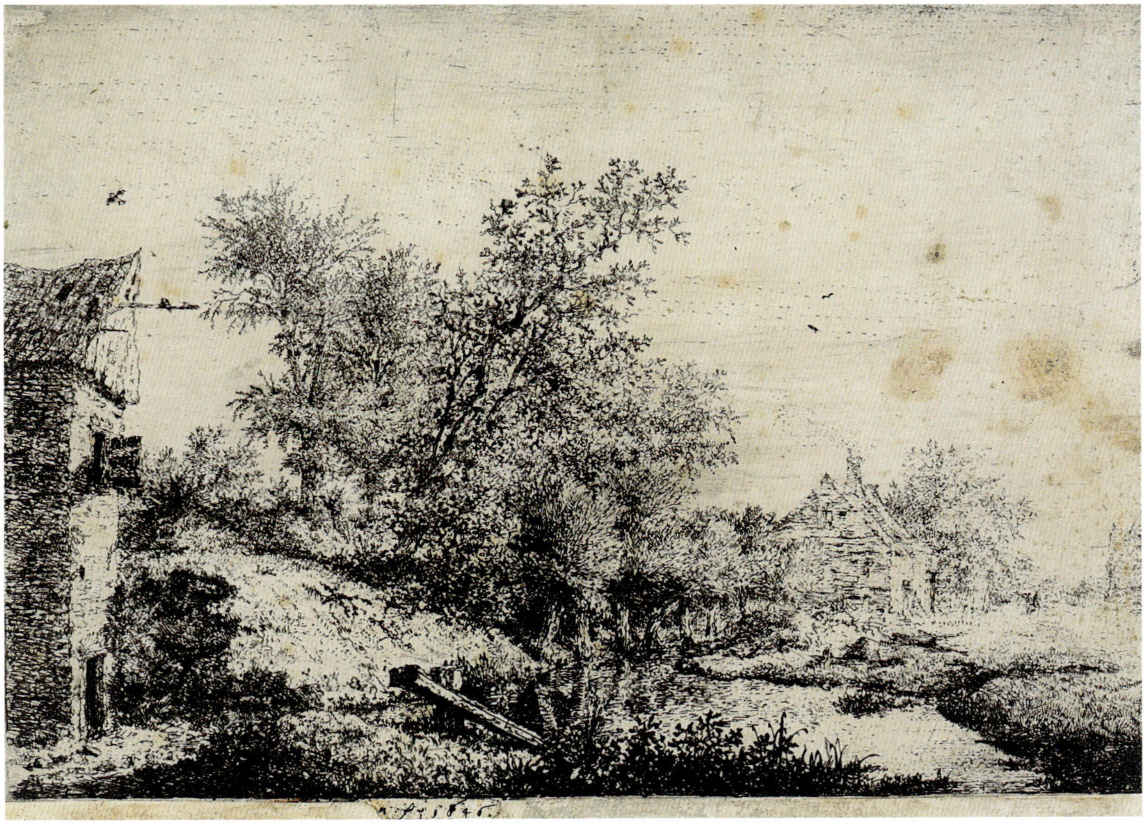

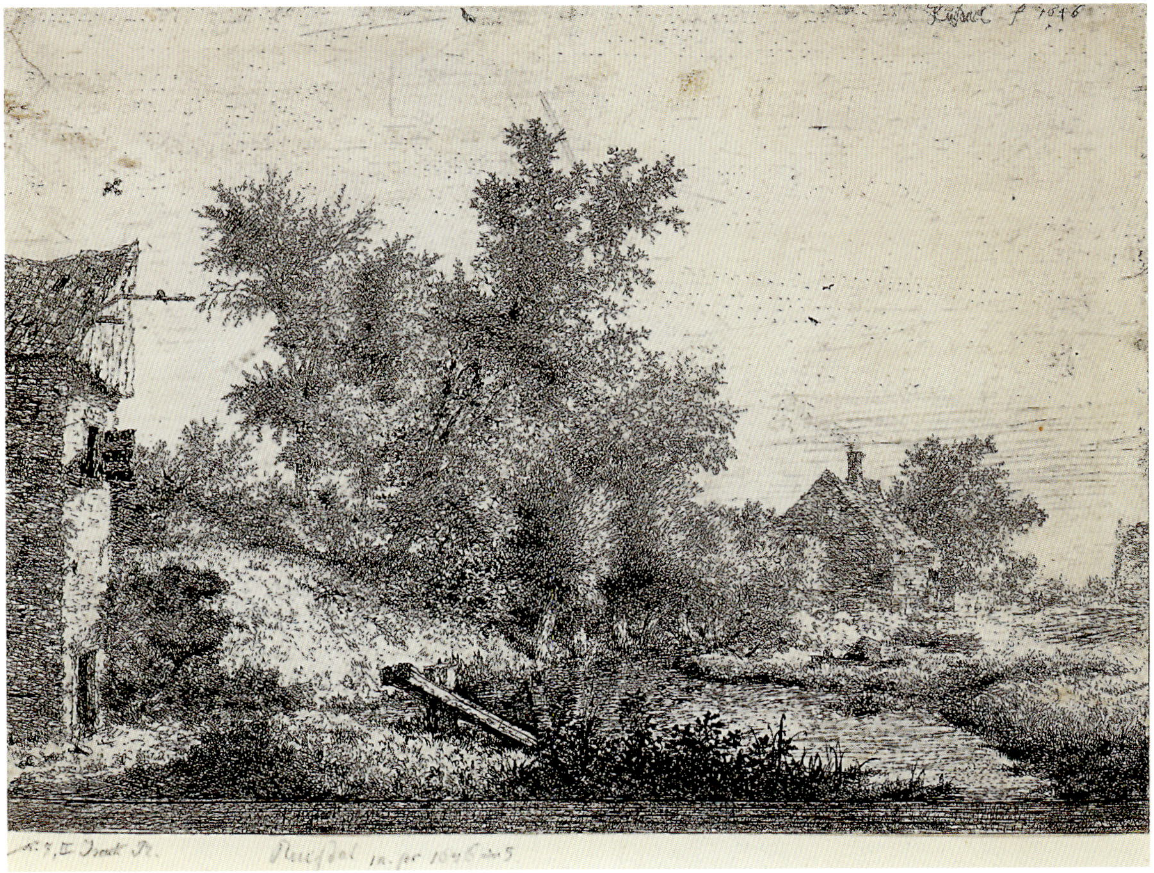
f 1646

101

Farmstead in the Dunes

Only state: Signed and dated on the bottom margin: *JvRuisdael in f. 1646.* 15.8 × 21.5 (15.9 × 21.7) cm
Rijksmuseum, Amsterdam, RP-P-OB-4867, unique impression

LITERATURE: Duplessis 1878, 9; Dutuit 1885, 11; Wurzbach 1910, 11; Keyes 1977, 2; Hollstein-de Hoop Scheffer 1978, 11; de Groot 1979, no. 216; Slive 1981, p.240, no. 97; Walford 1991, pp.53–54; Slive 2001, no. E2, repr.

PMA and RA

The print shows the sun breaking through a heavily overcast sky, a sharp contrast to Ruisdael's other etching dated 1646 (cat. 100) which depicts a clear, sparkling day. The fusion of the modest buildings and trees in the distance with the leaden sky recalls the tonal painting done by the landscapists of Salomon van Ruysdael and Jan van Goyen's generation, as well as a few of the artist's early black chalk studies at Dresden (see *e.g.*, cat. 63). It is an effect that Ruisdael did not attempt again in his etchings. The bold, impetuous hatching in the sky, which obliterates some of the wispy clouds he initially drew, also is unique to this print.

Duplessis (1878) and Dutuit (1885) list a faithful copy by Johannes Arnoldus Boland (1838–1922).

102

Willows on a Bank

Only state: Signed at the bottom: *JvRuisdael.* About 1646. 7.5 × 6.4 cm (oval)
British Museum, London, Sheepshanks 1145, unique impression

LITERATURE: Duplessis 1878, 12; Dutuit 1885, 12; Wurzbach 1910, 12; Simon 1935a, p.8; Keyes 1977, 12 (youthful work); Hollstein-de Hoop Scheffer 1978, 12; Slive 1981, p.241, no. 98; Keyes 1999, p.164; Slive 2001, no. E3, repr.

PMA

The close similarity of the handling of the trees in the little etching to those on the left side of Ruisdael's *Farmstead in the Dunes*, dated 1646 (cat. 101), supports a date of about the same time for the print. There are also similarities in the artist's rudimentary attempt to give tone to the sky. Format, scale and style connect the work to cat. 103 and 104. These three modest etchings are conceivably his first essays in the medium.

For Constable's pen drawing after the print done in 1827 when it was in the collection of John Sheepshanks see p.33 and fig. 41. Evidence that a close etched copy (7.4 × 6.4) at the British Museum which is tentatively ascribed to Benjamin Phelps Gibbon (1802–51) by Hollstein-de Hoop Scheffer (1978, p.182, repr.) is, in fact, by him is provided by an impression of it in Rotterdam that is inscribed on the verso in Sheepshanks's hand: "Copied by B. P. Gibbon/from the original Etching of/Ruysdael in the possession of JS/Aug: 1st 1832/JS".[1] For another etched copy of a Ruisdael print inscribed by Sheepshanks see cat. 103.

1. No. BdH 20170; formerly collection Willink van Collen. For the Rotterdam impression of Gibbon's copy see Slive 2001, p. 596, fig. E3a. Hollstein-de Hoop Scheffer (1978, p.182) illustrates both the original and Gibbon's copy, but reverses the captions; Klaus Demus kindly informed me of the error after he noticed it during the course of his study of an unpublished impression of Gibbon's copy at the Albertina.

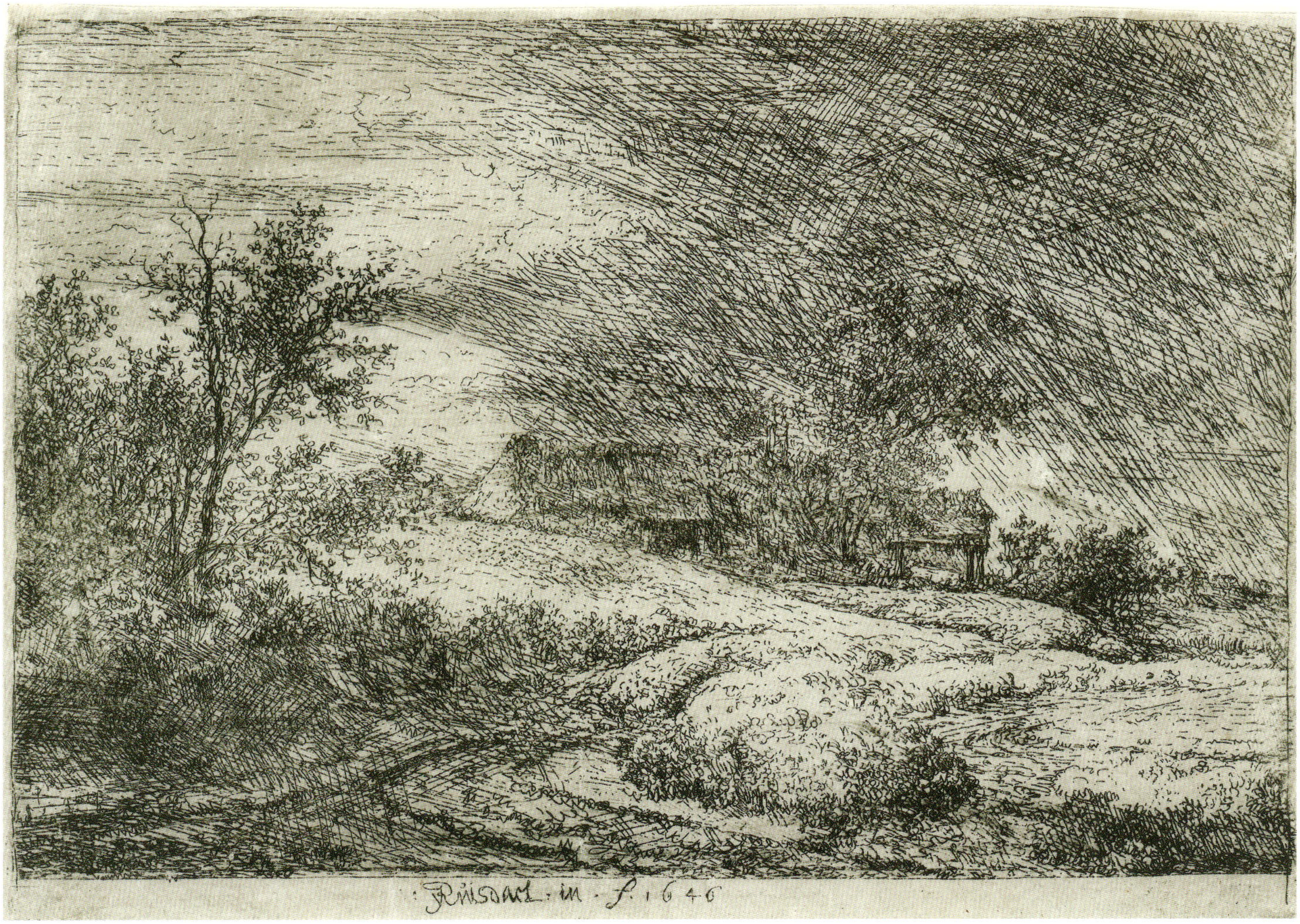
JRuisdael · in · f · 1646

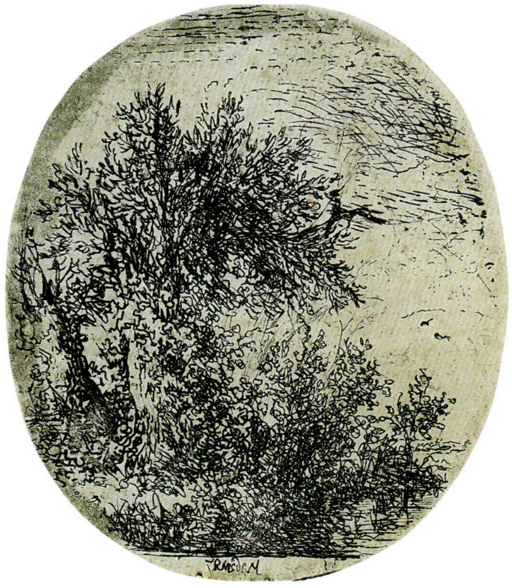

103

Landscape with a Brook and Willows

Only state: Monogrammed at the top, to the right: *JvR*. About 1646. 7.2 × 8.6 cm (oval)
Albertina, Vienna, DG2004/4575

LITERATURE: Regnault-Delalande 1817, 9; Weigel 1843, 9; Duplessis 1878, 11; Dutuit 1885, 9; Wurzbach 1910, 9; Keyes 1977, 11 (youthful work); Hollstein-de Hoop Scheffer 1978, 9; Slive 1981, p.242, no. 99; Keyes 1999, pp. 159–60; Slive 2001, no. E4, repr.

PMA

The etching is more densely hatched than cat. 102 and 104, but nevertheless it is related to them. Adam Bartsch, who knew the print from a cropped impression that did not include the monogram, wrongly attributed it to Allart van Everdingen (1803–21, 2, p.162, no. 3); Regnault-Delalande (1817) corrected his error. Keyes (1977, p.13) doubts the authenticity of the monogram. To be sure, it is rather awkwardly drawn and its prominent place in the sky also is unusual; however, its clumsy character and unusual position may be a consequence of young Ruisdael's inexperience as a printmaker.

John Burnett (1784–1868) made a deceptive copy;[1] impressions of it are in Hamburg, London and Rotterdam. According to Weigel (1843), Burnett's copy was commissioned by John Sheepshanks for a catalogue that was never published.[2] The verso of the impression of the copy in Rotterdam (no. BdH 20169; formerly collection Willink van Collen) is inscribed in Sheepshanks's hand: "Copy by John Burnett/J.S. 1830". For another copy of a Ruisdael print inscribed by Sheepshanks see cat. 102.

1. 7.4 × 8.4 (oval); illustrated Slive 2001, p. 597, fig. E4a.
2. In 1951, the British Museum was presented by Colnaghi's with an album of prints that Sheepshanks owned (nos. 1951-7-23-1 to 15; Royalton-Kisch 1996–97, p.77, note 13). Royalton-Kisch kindly informed me (written communication) that it includes a Burnett etching after Ruisdael (no. 1951-7-23-5); it is probably the one Weigel signaled.

104

Little Hut near a Pond and a Bridge

Only state: Signed at the bottom: *JvRuisdael f.* About 1646. 6.3 × 7.4 cm (oval)
Albertina, Vienna, DG2004/4572, unique impression

LITERATURE: Regnault-Delalande 1817, 8; Weigel 1843, 8; Duplessis 1878, 10; Dutuit 1885, 8; Wurzbach 1910, 8; Keyes 1977, 13 (youthful work); Hollstein-de Hoop Scheffer 1978, 8; Slive 1981, p.243, no. 100; Keyes 1999, p. 160; Slive 2001, no. E5, repr.

PMA and RA

Though the definition of forms in space is more clearly articulated and the foliage in the middle ground is airier in this print than in Ruisdael's two other small etchings done in an oval format (cat. 102, 103), it remains closely linked to them. Impressions of an anonymous copy are at Hamburg and London.[1]

An untraceable painting that shows similarities to the site (in reverse) was with the dealer Duits, London; it has been variously attributed.[2]

1. 6.2 × 7.2, oval on a rectangulare plate; see Slive 2001, p. 597, fig. E5a.
2. Panel, 36.5 × 31.5. EXHIBITION: Laren, Singer Museum, 1959, no. 69. Illustrated Slive 2001, p. 597, fig. E5b. None of the ascriptions given to the work (see *ibid.*, under E5) is fully convincing.

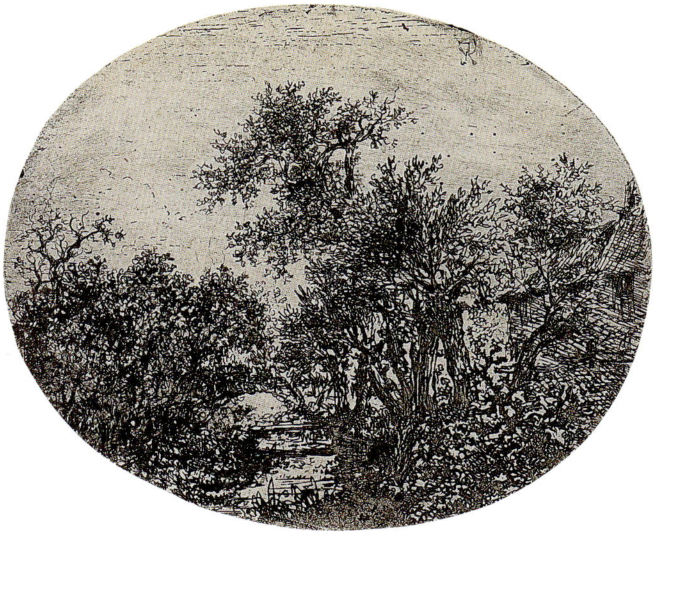

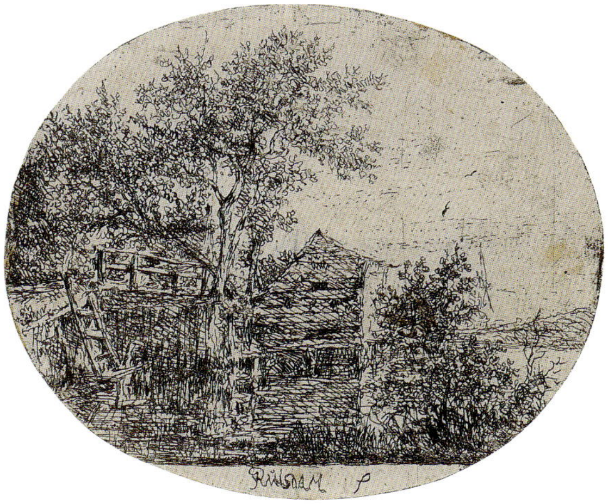
Ruisdael f

105

Trees and a Thicket on a Bank

Only state: About 1646–48. 10.2 × 7.8 cm
British Museum, London, Sheepshanks 1149, unique impression

LITERATURE: Dutuit 1885, 13; Keyes 1977, 10 (youthful work); Hollstein-de Hoop Scheffer 1978, 13; Slive 1981, p.244, no. 101; Ackley 1982, p.122; Slive 2001, no. E6, repr.

PMA and RA

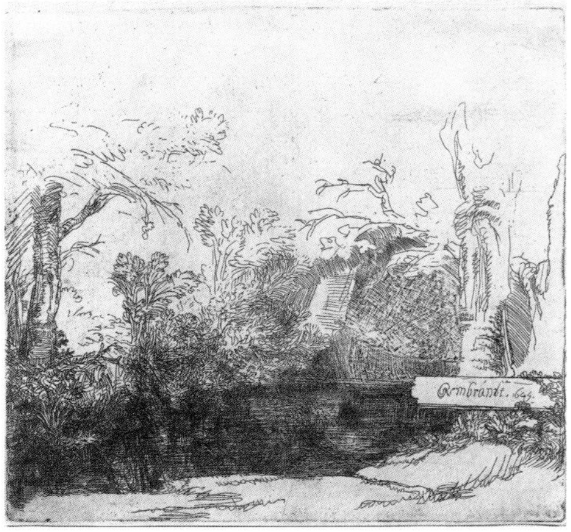

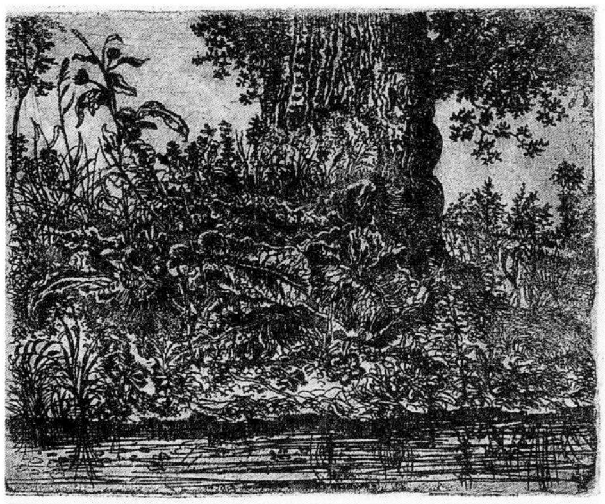

Fig. 105a Rembrandt, *The Boat House*, 1645. Etching and drypoint.

Fig. 105b Johannes Ruischer (attributed to), *Wild Plants and Trunk of an Oak on a Bank*. Etching (unique impression). Paris, Musée du Louvre (coll. Edmond de Rothschild).

The attribution of the unsigned etching to Ruisdael was made by Middelton and published by Dutuit (1885), with a slight reservation: "Il n'est pas impossible que l'auteur ne soit Ruisdael, mais cela est douteux."

Wurzbach (1910, 2, p.251) does not include the print in his list of the artist's etchings. Ackley (1982) rejects the attribution and suggests it was done by "someone close to Anthonie Waterloo". I find its style and techniques consistent with the artist's early etchings. The remarkable range of tonal values and control of spatial relations of the dense shrubbery suggest it may have been made a bit later than the small oval landscapes of about 1646 (cat. 102–04). Its compositional scheme bears some resemblance to Ruisdael's early painting of a close view of an *Oak Tree and Dense Shrubbery at the Edge of a Pond* in Budapest (cat. 5), but in the small print the sky has been darkened and the flickering light has become more intense.

Not many works of the period treat the subject. Among the few that depict it are Rembrandt's etching and drypoint called *The Boat House*, of 1645 (fig. 105a; Bartsch 231), and the unique impression of *Wild Plants and Trunk of an Oak on a Bank* (Paris, Rothschild) attributed to Johannes Ruischer (fig. 105b) by Trautscholdt.[1] Ruisdael's print also brings to mind Rembrandt's etchings in his dark manner, such as his *Rest on the Flight to Egypt: A Night Piece* of 1645 (Bartsch 57).

1. Rembrandt's black chalk drawing, a study related to Bartsch 231, is at the Library of the Ossolinski National Institute of the Polish Academy of Science, Wroclaw (Benesch 817, repr.). Trautscholdt's attribution of the etching *Wild Plants and Trunk of an Oak* to Ruischer is published in Trautscholdt 1973, p.119, no. Tr.6; he understandably rejects an earlier attribution of it to Hercules Segers. De Hoop Scheffer (Hollstein-de Hoop Scheffer 1978, Ruischer, p.150, no. 6) tentatively ascribes the print to Ruischer.

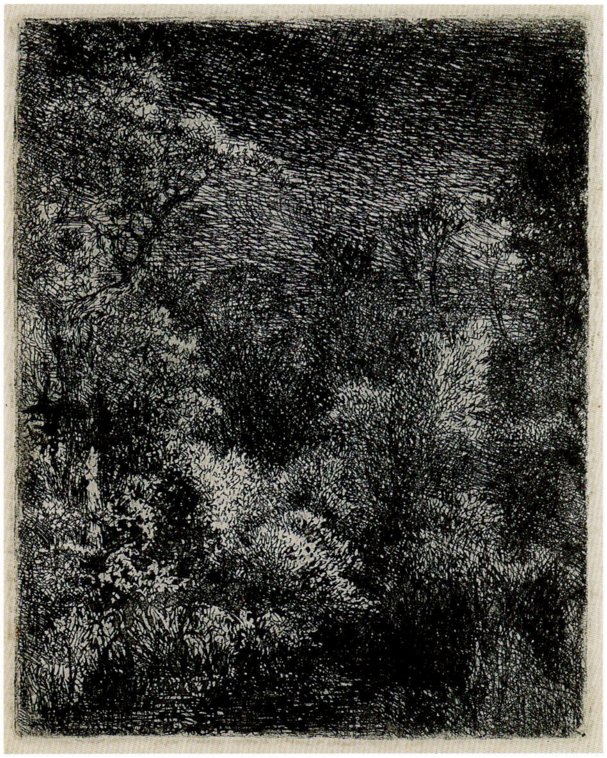

106

Landscape with Oaks, Houses and a Pond

Only state: Signed and dated, lower right: *JvRuisdael f 1647.* 14.5 × 20 cm
Albertina, Vienna, DG2001/1571, unique impression

LITERATURE: Regnault-Delalande 1817, 10; Weigel 1843, 10; Duplessis 1878, 7; Dutuit 1885, 10; Wurzbach 1910, 10; Keyes 1977, 3; Hollstein-de Hoop Scheffer 1978, 10, Slive 1981, p.245, no. 102; Slive 2001, no. E7, repr.

PMA

Weigel (1843) and Dutuit (1885) list an impression at the Museum in Amsterdam. There is no record of the existence of it at the Rijksprentenkabinet, Amsterdam (kindly confirmed by Dieuwke de Hoop Scheffer). The conspicuous scratches and burnish marks on the left and right of the trees may help explain why only a single impression of the splendid etching is known. Perhaps Ruisdael abandoned the print when he discovered burnishing failed to remove the plate's scratches.

Keyes (1977) lists a second state without the burnishing on the left and the right of the trees, and notes it is reproduced in the edition of facsimiles edited by Duplessis (1878); the facsimile is not a second state but made from the unique Vienna impression and touched up for the publication. Rosenberg (1928, pl. 18) reproduces the retouched facsimile, not the Albertina's unique impression.

The small hatched lines and dots used for passages of the light areas of the farmhouses and fields are similar to those Ruisdael employed a year earlier for his *Cottages and a Clump of Trees near a Small River* (cat. 100). However, the emphasis on the great oak, whose spiky crown virtually fills the sky, is a new note that anticipates the monumental works of the early fifties in which a single tree became his principal protagonist.

Weigel (1843) states that a copy of the print was etched by John Burnett for John Sheepshanks; the copy is untraceable.

A painted landscape, in a vertical format, that reverses the central part of the etching's composition was in the Earl Howe collection, Amersham, Bucks. (Slive 2001, no. 306, repr.); it is datable about the same time as the etching. Inspection of the painting may reveal that it was cut on both the left and right sides; if this proves to be the case, the painting was originally more closely related to the etching.

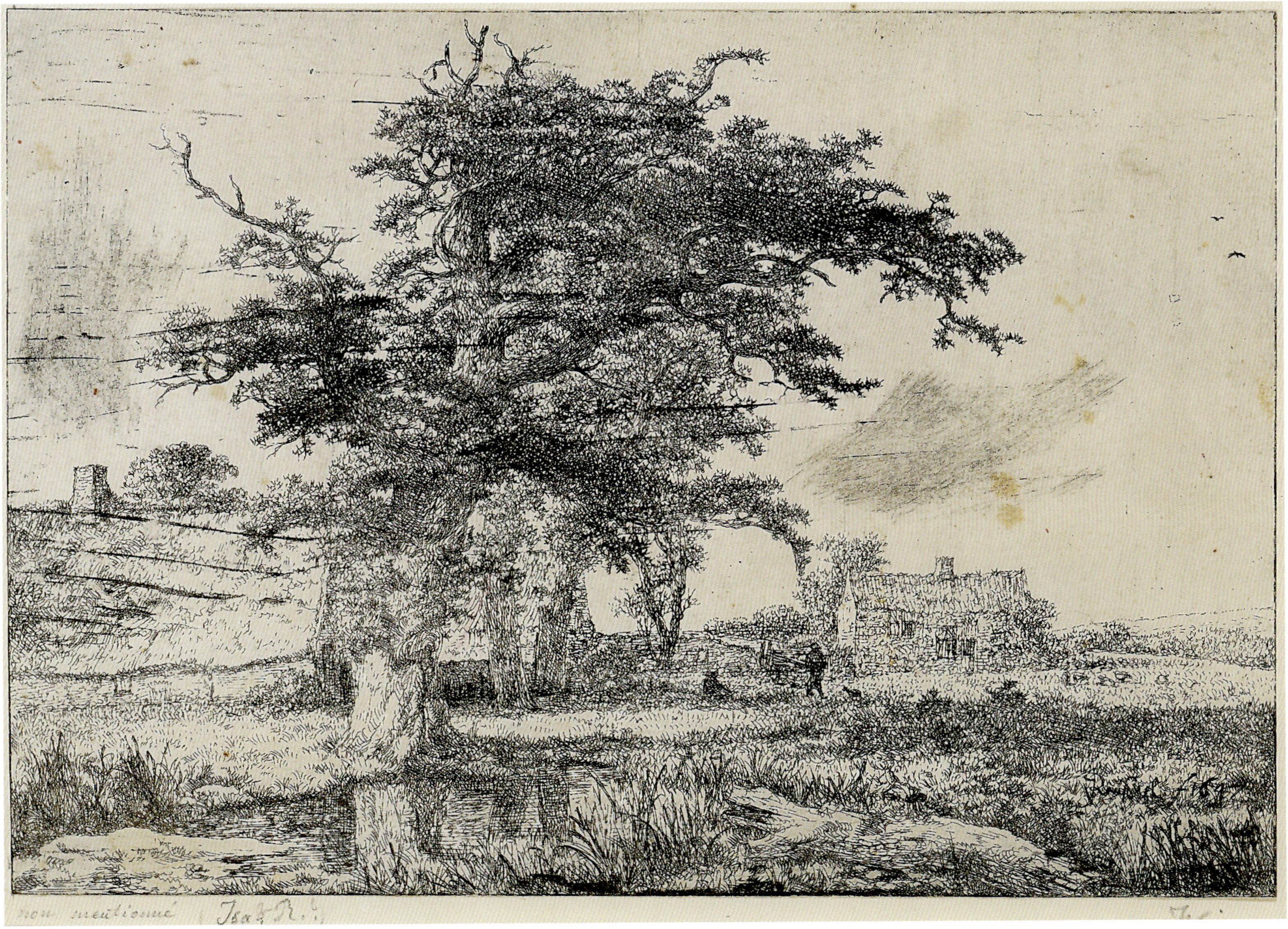
non mentionné

107

Grainfield at the Edge of a Wood

Signed and dated, lower right corner: *JvRuisdael (f ?) 1648.* 9.9 × 14.8 cm
1st state: British Museum, London, Sheepshanks 1137, unique impression
2nd state: Lent by The Metropolitan Museum of Art, New York, Harris Brisbane Dick Fund, 1925, 25.2.62

1st state: Before the lines in the sky and clouds were added with drypoint and before the foreground and trees were reworked.

2nd state: With the additions mentioned above.

LITERATURE: Bartsch 1803, 5; Regnault-Delalande 1817, 5; Smith 1835, p.104, no. 5; Weigel 1843, 5; Duplessis 1878, 5; Dutuit 1885, 5; Wurzbach 1910, 5; Keyes 1977, 4; Hollstein-de Hoop Scheffer 1978, 5; de Groot 1979, no. 214; Slive 1981, p.246, no. 103; Walford 1991, p.68; Slive 2001, no. E8 repr.

PMA 1st and 2nd states; RA 1st state

Wolfgang Stechow's sharp eye discovered the original signature and date of 1648 on the etching (private communication, 1968); it had been overlooked by earlier cataloguers. The coherence of the composition and intricate filigree-like treatment of the foliage show the influence of Cornelis Vroom's idyllic landscapes on the young artist, which is also recognizable in other works he made about the same time.

The initials *F.v.W.* in the bottom right margin of the third, fourth and fifth states are those of the Antwerp printmaker and publisher Frans van den Wyngaerde (1614–79); most likely he added the spurious "J v Ruysdael fe" signature that appears in the upper right of these states. Wyngaerde also published impressions of Ruisdael's *The Three Oaks*, 1649 (cat. 108).

The print served as the inspiration for an etching by the gifted Haarlem amateur Claes van Beresteyn (*c.*1629–84) of a *Grainfield.*[1] Two of his etchings are dated 1650;[2] judging from their style, his *Grainfield* was done about the same time. A pen drawing by Beresteyn of a grain field with a large clump of trees[3] is also related to Ruisdael's etching.

For Constable's pen and ink copy of a third or later state of the etching, monogrammed and dated on its verso: *J.C. fe: 1818*, Victoria and Albert Museum, see p.31 and fig. 35.

1. H. Gerson, *Leven en werken van Claes v. Beresteyn*, The Hague, 1940, in E. A. van Beresteyn, *Genealogie van het Geslacht van Beresteyn*, 2, The Hague, 1941, p.159, no. 5; Hollstein, 1, p.197, no. 5; Slive 2001, p.601, fig. E8a.
2. Gerson, *op. cit.* (as in note 1), p.159, nos. 6, 8, reprs.; Hollstein, 1, pp.198, 200, nos. 6, 8.
3. Collection Frits Lugt, Institut Neérlandais, Paris, no. 1971–T.17; see Slive 2001, p.601, fig. E8b.

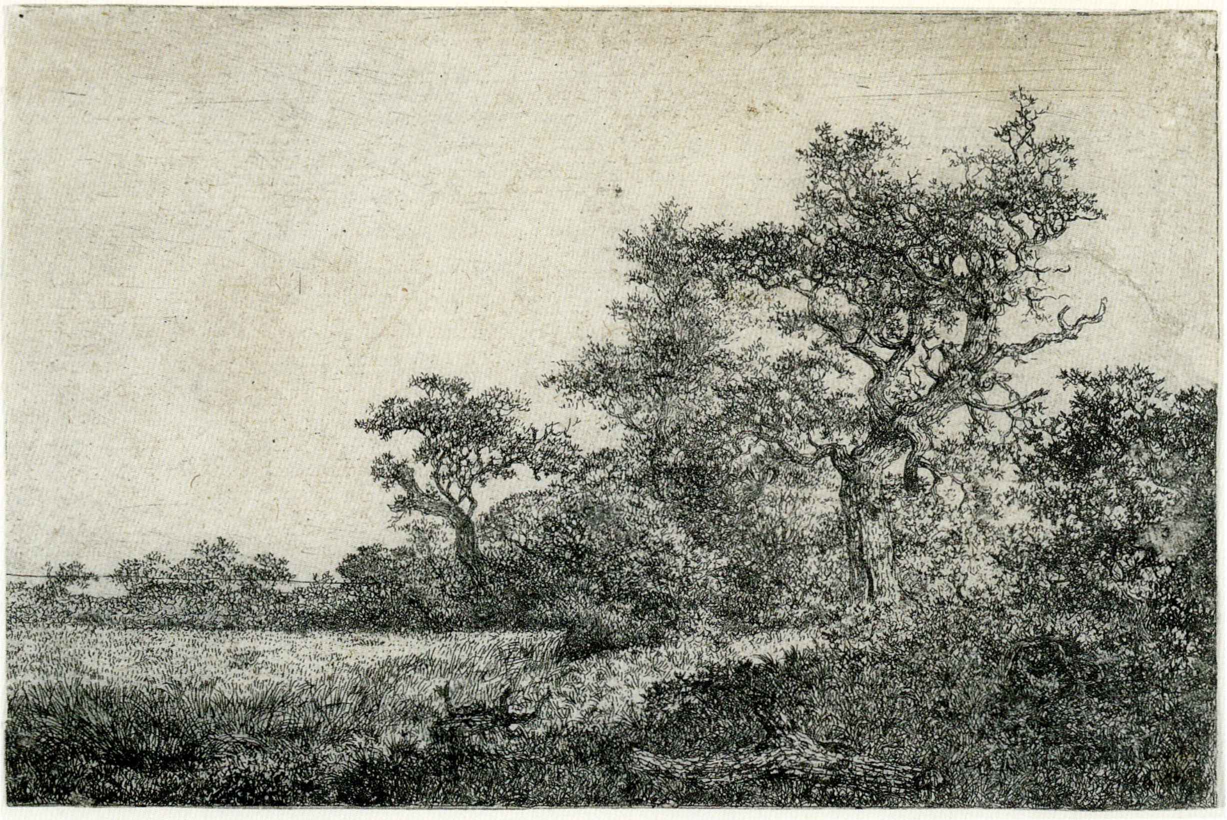

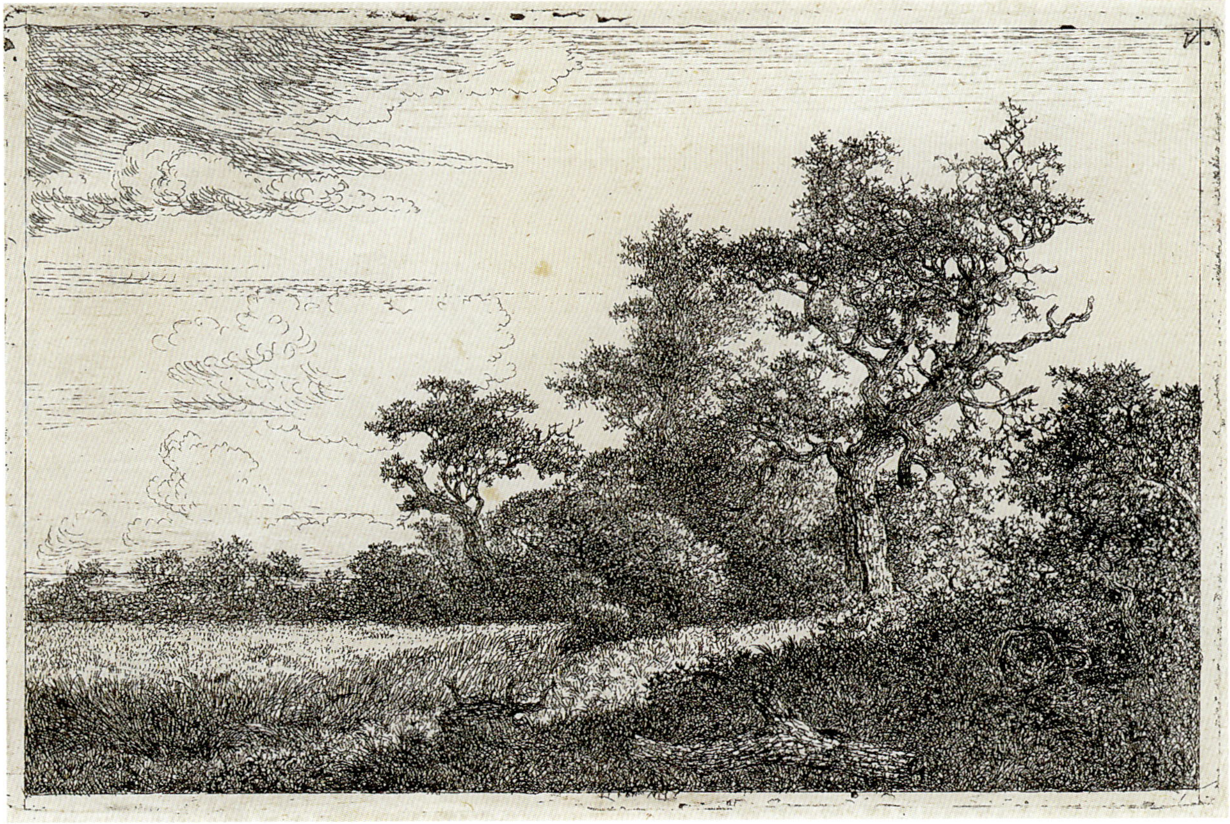

108

The Three Oaks

2nd state: Signed and dated on the lower margin: *JvRuisdael in.f. 1649*. 12.8 × 14.5 cm
Albertina, Vienna, DG2004/4576

2nd state: Borders strengthened with the burin; parallel lines in the tree on the extreme right, on the shaded bank and the willows at the foot of the bank; additional hatching on the stone to the right. Inscribed by another hand in the margin, bottom left: *F.V.W.ex.* (see text below).

LITERATURE: Bartsch 1803, 6; Regnault-Delalande 1817, 6; Smith 1835, p.104, no. 6; Weigel 1843, 6; Duplessis 1878, 6; Dutuit 1885, 6; Wurzbach 1910, 6; Keyes 1977, 5; Hollstein-de Hoop Scheffer 1978, 6; de Groot 1979, no. 220; Slive 1981, pp.250–51, no. 104; Walford 1991, pp.69–71; Slive 2001, no. E9 repr.

PMA

The inscription *F.V.W.ex* on the second state refers to the Antwerp printmaker and publisher Frans van den Wyngaerde (1614–79), who also published impressions of *Grainfield at the Edge of a Wood*, 1648 (see cat. 107).

Ruisdael's *Extensive Landscape with Trees, Grainfield, Dunes and a Distant View of a Town* at Springfield, Massachusetts (fig. 3), shows that a year earlier he dramatized a group of large trees by setting them against a distant panoramic view and a vast expanse of sky, a scheme reminiscent of Rembrandt's etching of *Three Trees* of 1643 (fig. 4; Bartsch 212). The present etching, dated 1649, of three towering oaks on a small hillock near a pond also recalls Rembrandt's *Three Trees*, but Ruisdael's virtual elimination of the effect of a distant view makes its concentration on the main motif more emphatic.

An untraceable drawing formerly in the A. Beurdeley collection, Paris, monogrammed and dated 1649 (Slive 2001, no. D109), and another sheet datable about the same time at the Musée Condé, Chantilly (Slive 2001, no. D40), are variations on the etching's theme. Both drawings are on parchment and done in ink, grey wash and watercolour. Similarities between the Chantilly drawing and the etching led Rosenberg (1928, p.19) to conclude that it is a preparatory study for the print. Strictly speaking, it is not. Its unusual parchment support and high finish indicate that it was intended as an autonomous work.

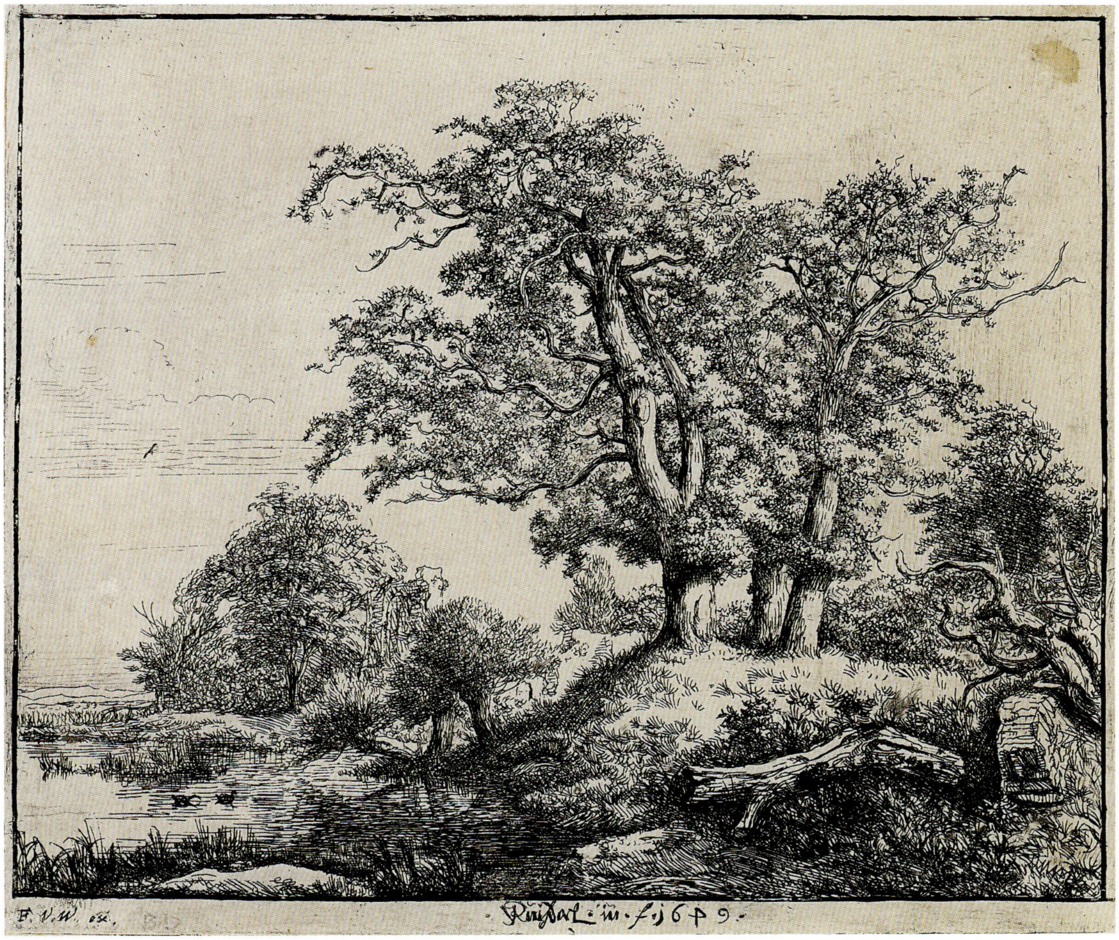
F. V.W. ex.
·Ruisdael·in·f·1649·

109

The Little Bridge

Signed on the bottom margin: *JvRuisdael f.* About 1650–55. 19.5 × 27.7 cm
1st state: Lent by The Metropolitan Museum, New York, Rogers Fund, 1922, no. 22.31 (illustrated opposite); Collection Frits Lugt, Institut Néerlandais, Paris, 1640
2nd state: Rijksmuseum, Amsterdam, RP-P-H- 1372

1st state: Before the clouds and sky.

2nd state: Clouds and sky etched in and retouched with drypoint. The foliage on the tree branch behind the fallen tree trunk enlarged; more hatching on the fallen tree trunk; more hatching on the sprouting willow on the left. In later impressions the drypoint on the lower clouds on the right is worn, and in some late impressions it virtually disappears.

LITERATURE: Bartsch 1803, 1; Regnault-Delalande 1817, 1; Smith 1835, p.104, no. 1; Weigel 1843, 1; Duplessis 1878, 1; Dutuit 1885, 1; Binyon 1895, pp.48, 50; Wurzbach 1910, 1; Bradley 1917, p.161; Simon 1930, p.69; Keyes 1977, 8; Hollstein-de Hoop Scheffer 1978, 1; de Groot 1979, no. 215; Slive 1981, pp.252–53, no. 105; Slive 2001, no. E10 repr.

PMA 1st state (New York), 2nd state; RA 1st state (Paris)

Similarity in size, style and technique of the etching to *The Great Beech*, *Cottage on a Hill*, and *Forest Marsh with Travellers on a Bank* (cat. 110, 111, 112) suggests that the four prints were conceived as a set, made not long after Ruisdael returned to Haarlem in the early 1650s from his journey to the border region between the United Provinces and Westphalia in Germany. The tie beam construction and vertical planks of the gable of the half-timbered cottage that fills the left side of the print are characteristic of the vernacular architecture of the region; half-timbered buildings of this type are not found in the western part of the Netherlands. Ruisdael first began to incorporate them in paintings and drawings that are related to the trip he made to Bentheim about 1650; he continued to employ them in works produced in the following decades.

Attempts have been made to establish a firm chronology for the four etchings. In my view, a date of about 1650–55 is a reasonable one for all of them; the limit of valid inference from the available visual evidence is strained by attempts to establish an incontestable chronology for the four prints.

Binyon (1895) rightly observed that the sky and clouds in the second state of the print as well as those in later states of *The Great Beech* (cat. 110) and *Cottage on a Hill* (cat. 111) were added by another hand.

Weigel (1843) mentions that Pierre François Basan (1723–93) had the plates for the present print and cat. 110, 111, and pulled impressions from them, but he does not provide evidence to support his statement. However, Basan's brief entry on Ruisdael in his *Dictionnaire des Graveurs . . . avec une Notice des Principales Estampes qu'ils ont gravées seconde partie* (Paris, 1762) shows that he was familiar with the artist's etchings; it is an early (the earliest?) printed reference to them.[1] It is evident from Basan's entry that, if he had the three plates by the time he published his *Dictionnaire* in 1762, he did not think prints pulled from them were worthy of special mention as *principales estampes*.

Impressions of the third state of the print mentioned by Weigel (1843), with the clouds hardly visible, were probably pulled from the worn second state of the plate. Weigel adds that in Basan's time, or later, the plate was etched again; he also notes that the modern impressions that often turn up in England are hard. Wurzbach (1910) also cites a third state, probably retouched by Basan; according to him the plate for *The Little Bridge* was still in existence in his time. I have not been able to trace the plate.

1. In his biography of Ruisdael in the supplementary volume to his *Abrégé de la vie des plus fameux peintres...* Paris, 1752 (vol. 3, p.152), Dézallier d'Argenville does not mention the artist's etchings but be cites the six little views of Amsterdam and the two cemetery views Abraham Blooteling did after Ruisdael's drawings (see cat. 86, 87, 80). In the revised edition of his work (1762, vol. 3, pp.211-12) he makes a muddle by attributing the Amsterdam and cemetery views to Ruisdael himself, not to Blooteling.

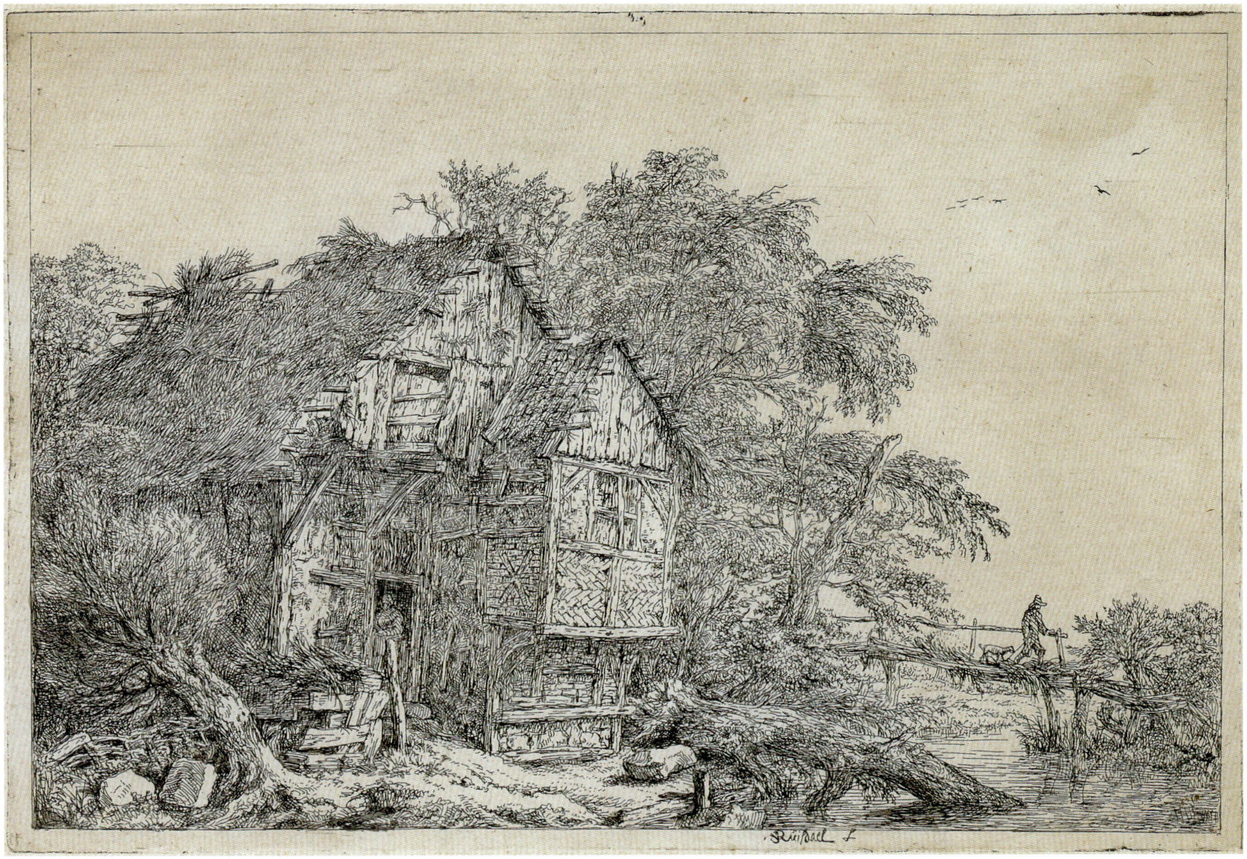

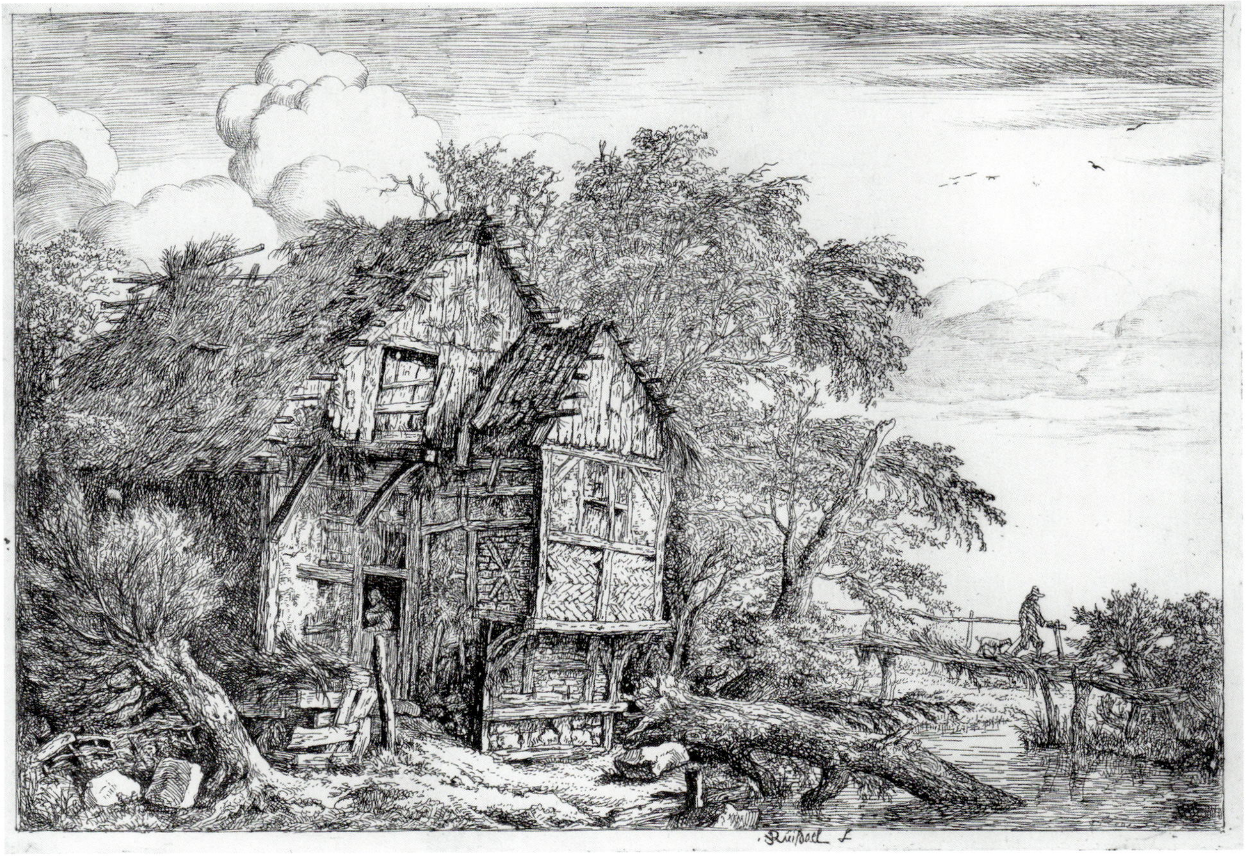

110

The Great Beech, with Two Men and a Dog

Signed on the bottom margin: *JvRuisdael f.* About 1650–55. 19.1 × 27.6 cm
1st state: Lent by The Metropolitan Museum of Art, New York, Harris Brisbane Dick Fund, 1926, 26.72.10 (illustrated opposite); Albertina, Vienna, DG2004/8505
2nd state: Rijksmuseum, Amsterdam, RP-P-OB-4861

1st state: Before the clouds and sky.

2nd state: The clouds and sky etched in; on the large tree trunk at the lower right, additional hatching; the area above and below it is strengthened with hatching. There also is additional hatching on the beech's trunk and roots.

LITERATURE: Bartsch 1803, 2; Regnault-Delalande 1817, 2; Smith 1835, p.104, no. 2; Weigel 1843, 2; Duplessis 1878, 2; Dutuit 1885, 2; Wurzbach 1910, 2; Simon 1930, p.69; Keyes 1977, 9; Hollstein-de Hoop Scheffer 1978, 2; de Groot 1979, no. 217; Slive 1981, pp.254–56, no. 106; Walford 1991, pp.81–82; Slive 2001, no. E11 repr.

PMA 1st state (New York), 2nd state; RA 1st state (Vienna)

De Groot (1979) notes that the craquelure in the upper right corner is due to breaks in the etching ground; she observes Rembrandt had a similar accident in the biting of his 1641 etching of a windmill (Bartsch 233; identified as *The Little Stink Mill on the Bulwark the Passeerden in Amsterdam* in Amsterdam–Paris 1998–99, p.194).

Ruisdael's particular emphasis on the growth of powerful natural forms is keenly felt in this etching of a gigantic beech, and in the predominant tree in his prints of *Cottage on a Hill* (cat. 111) and *Forest Marsh* (cat. 112). Here the ancient tree clings with its roots to the projection of a cliff; its broken top helps balance the weight of its heavily foliated branches. During the early 1650s Ruisdael showed a predilection in his paintings for variations on the theme of a monumental tree clawing into high ground or precariously balanced on a bank. Outstanding examples are seen in his *Wooded River Valley with a Footbridge*, dated 1652, at The Frick Collection (Slive 2001, no. 511) and *Large Pond with Cottages and Oak Trees*, datable about 1652, Indianapolis Museum of Art (Slive 2001, no. 502). *The Great Beech* was probably etched about the same time. A black chalk drawing related to the print and to cat. 111 was formerly in the collection of Friedrich August II, Dresden (see Slive 2001, no. D54, repr).

An impression of a much reduced etched variant of the print (9.1 × 11.3; in reverse) attributed to the German artist Jonas Umbach (*c.*1624–93) is at the Fogg Art Museum, Cambridge, Massachusetts.[1] Its clouds indicate the artist worked from the second state. If the ascription to Umbach is correct, his print establishes that the ungainly clouds in the print and its companions (cat. 109, 111) were added before the end of the seventeenth century.

Ruisdael's prints that exist in many impressions must have been copied often by budding artists. Constable was eager to copy *Forest Marsh* (cat. 112), or any other impression he could put his hands on, even before he began formal training at The Royal Academy Schools (see p.33 above); none of his early copies are known. The attrition of such works is understandably high. One that has survived is a pen and brush drawing after the present etching by Adrian Ludwig Richter (1803–84), the Dresden artist who became one of the most popular book illustrators of his time. He made his copy, dated 1818, when he was fifteen.[2] Richter describes how he began as a boy to make copies of the Netherlandish prints that were in his father's collection in his *Lebenserinnerung eines deutschen Maler*, Frankfurt a. M., 1885.

Weigel (1843) and Dutuit (1885) cite a third state that was etched again and reworked. Wurzbuch (1910) also lists a third, reworked state. According to Weigel the plate for the etching was in England in his day; it is untraceable today.

1. No. 22,068. The attribution was made by James A. Bergquist, Boston, Massachusetts. Illustrated Slive 2001, fig. E11c.
2. See dealer C. G. Boerner, Düsseldorf, catalogue, *Mit Kreide und Tusche*, 1977, no. 79, repr.

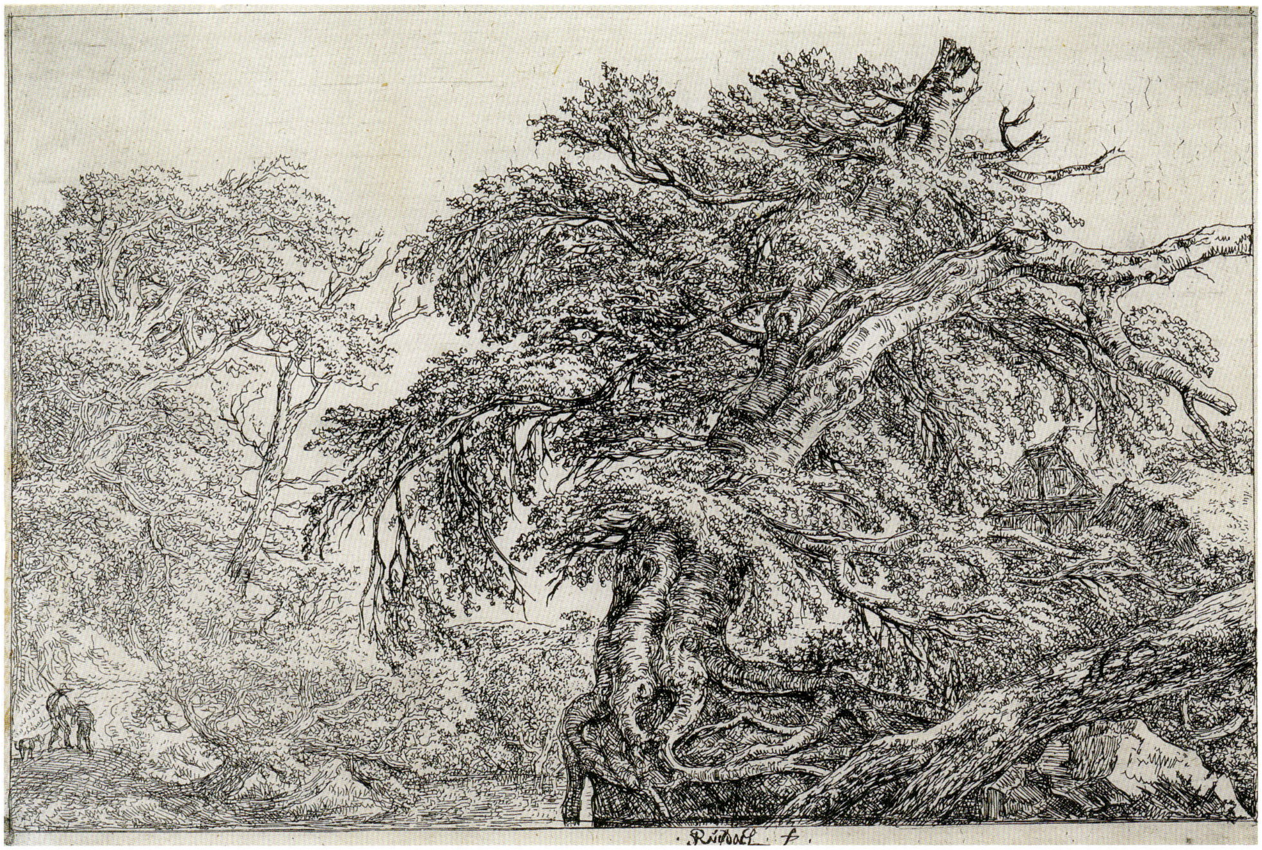
Ruisdael f.

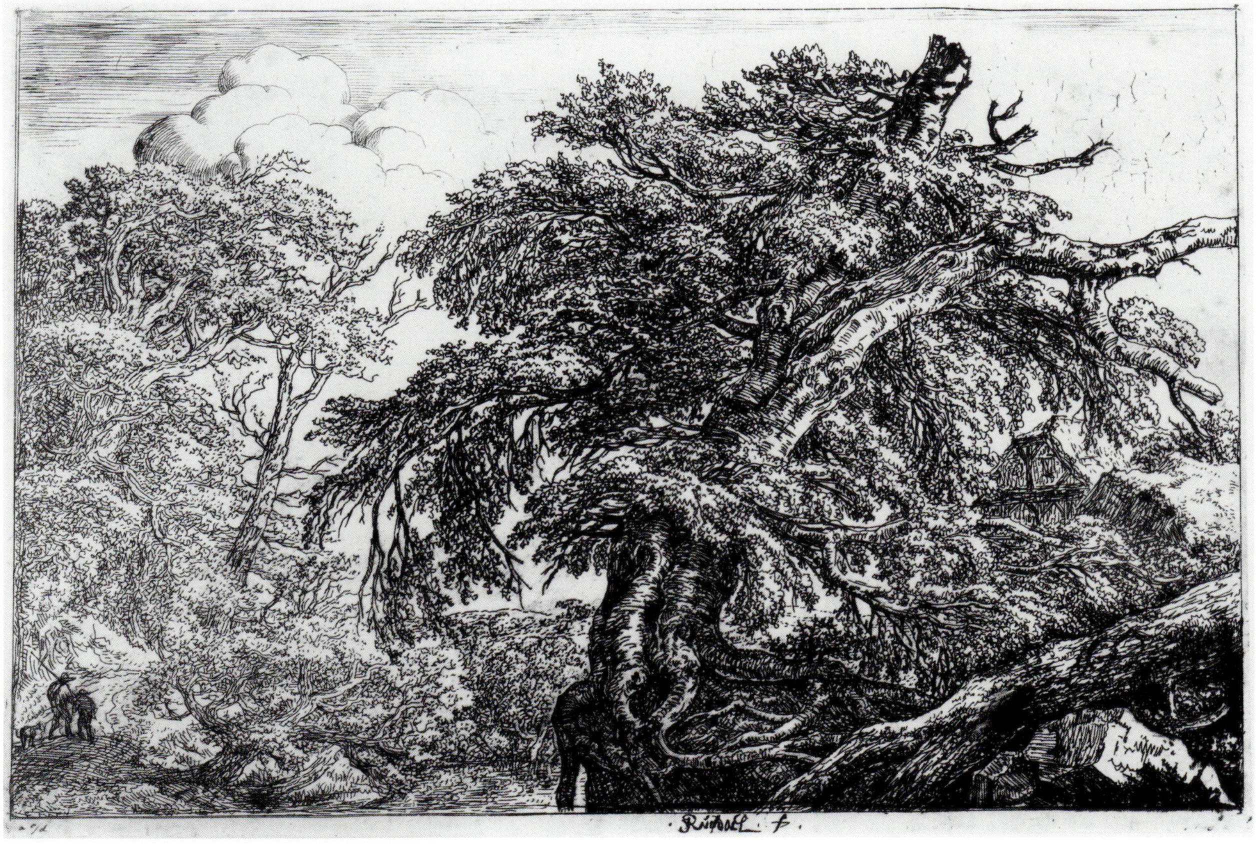
Ruisdael f.

111

Cottage on a Hill

Signed on the bottom margin: *JvRuisdael.* 19.4 × 27.9 cm
1st state: British Museum, London, Sheepshanks 1133[1]
2nd state: Rijksmuseum, Amsterdam, RP-P-OB-4862

1st state: Before the clouds and sky.

2nd state: The clouds and sky etched in and some touches of drypoint; foliage in the top of the trees to the right of the cottage burnished out; some burnishing in the lower trees beside the cottage. A black spot on the lower right margin.

LITERATURE: Bartsch 1803, 3; Regnault-Delalande 1817, 3; Smith 1835, p.104, no. 3; Weigel 1843, 3; Duplessis 1878, 3; Dutuit 1885, 3; Wurzbach 1910, 3; Simon 1930, p.69; Keyes 1977, 7; Hollstein-de Hoop Scheffer 1978, 3; de Groot 1979, no. 218; Slive 1981, p.257, no. 107; Walford 1991, p.81; Slive 2001, no. E12 repr.

PMA 1st and 2nd states; RA 1st state

See cat. 109 and 110 for comments on the print. A drawing related to it was formerly in the collection Friedrich August II, Dresden (see Slive 2001, no. D54, repr.).

A third state, with evidence of retouchings in the shaded areas and with the black spot in the lower margin faded, has been described by Weigel, Duplessis, Dutuit and Wurzbach. De Hoop Scheffer (Hollstein-de Hoop Scheffer 1978) notes it is probably a later impression of the second state.

Duplessis (1878) lists an etched copy (in reverse) that is signed in the left bottom margin: *D.L.sc.1759.* Weigel (1843) states that in his time Ruisdael's plate for *Cottage on a Hill* was in England; its present whereabouts is unknown.

1. Royalton-Kisch (1996–97, p.85, no. 27) rightly notes that four impressions of the first state are recorded. However, references to those in Berlin and Hamburg cited by Dutuit (1885) and de Hoop Scheffer (Hollstein-de Hoop Scheffer 1978) are wrong. Fedja Anzelewski of the Berlin print room informed me (17 February 1981) that the print is not there and Eckhart Schaar sent word (27 July 1980) that the etching's first state is not in Hamburg. To my knowledge only two impressions of the first state are known.

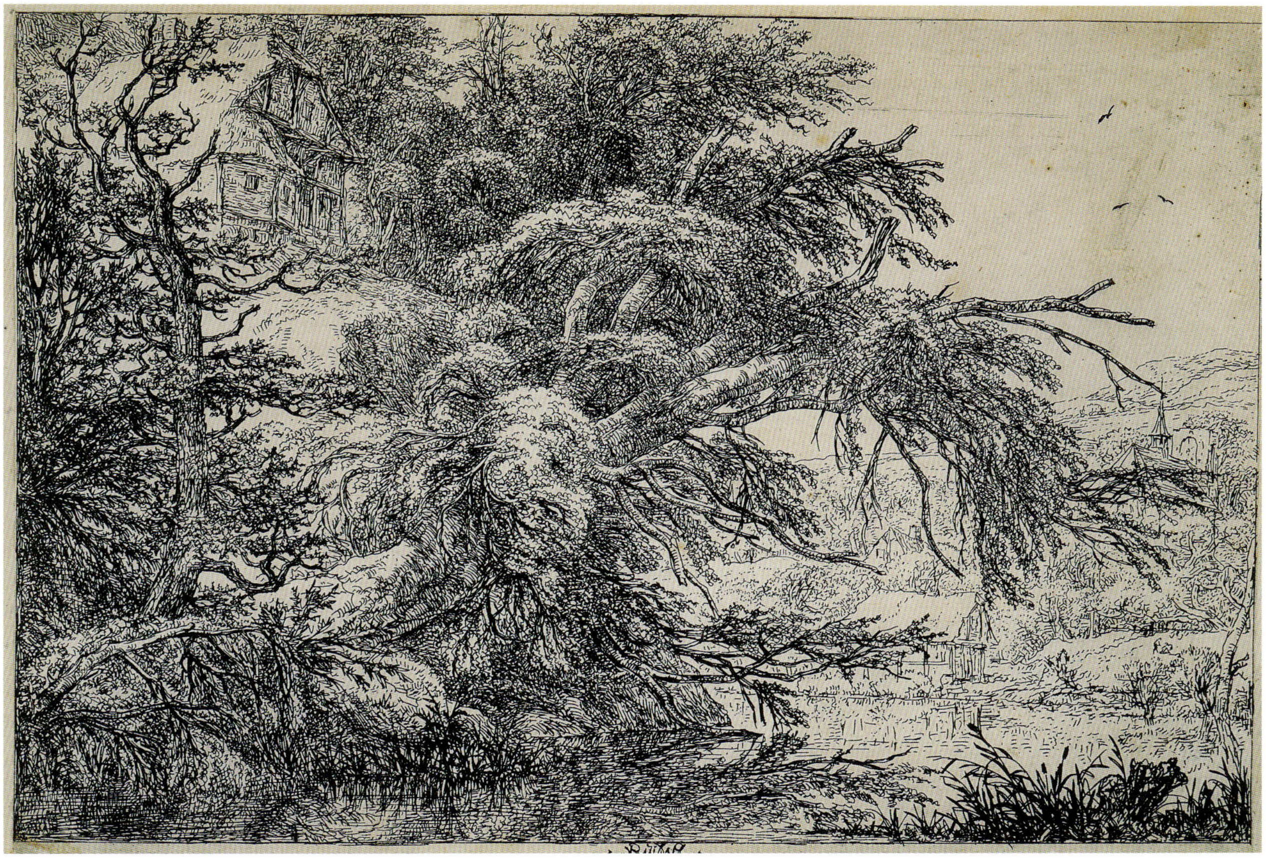

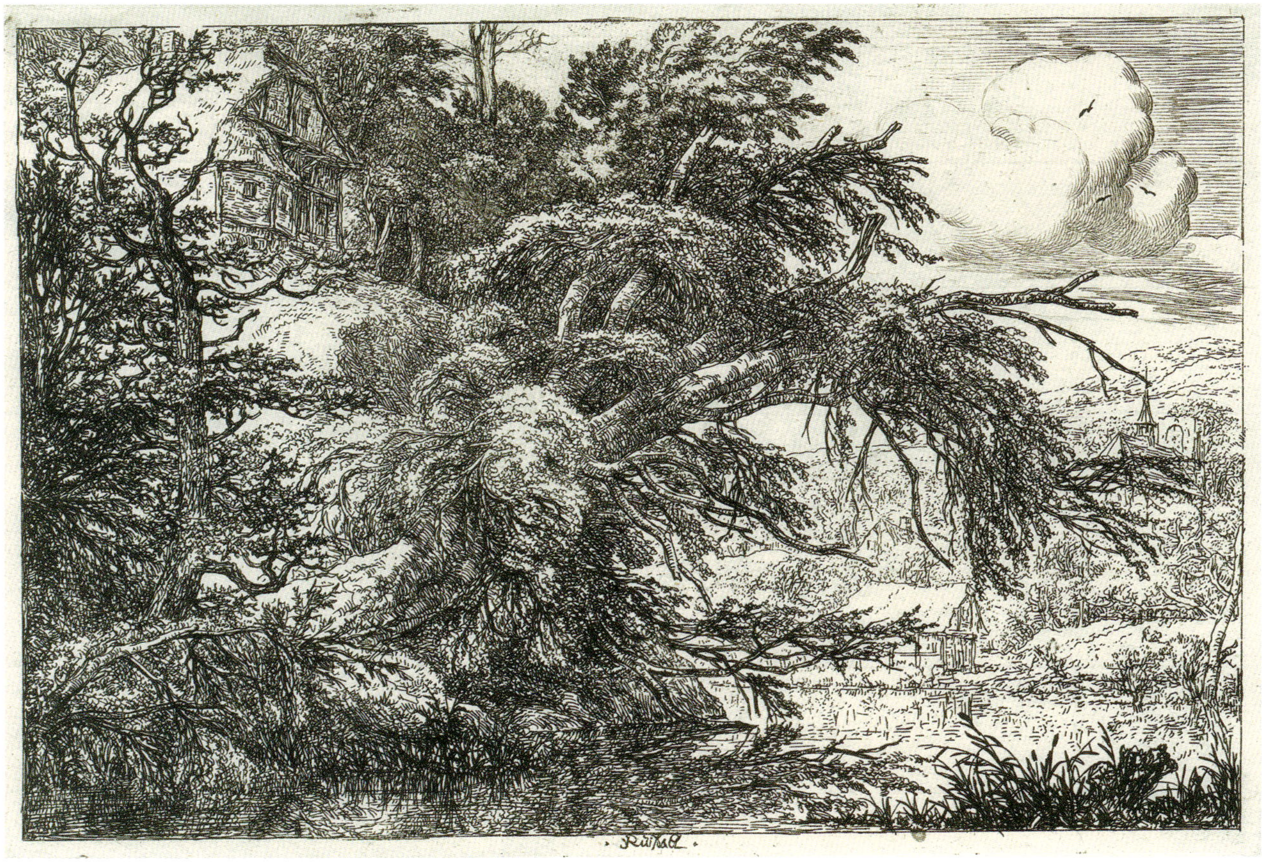

112

Forest Marsh with Travellers on a Bank

Signed at the lower right on the grassy bank: *JvRuisdael*. About 1650–55. 19.5 × 28 cm
1st state: Lent by The Metropolitan Museum of Art, New York, Harris Brisbane Dick Fund, 1926, 26.72.9
3rd state: Philadelphia Museum of Art, Bequest of Frederic L. Ballard, 1953, 1953-30-2.1
4th state: Rijksmuseum, Amsterdam, RP-P-OB-4864

1st state: Before the drypoint lines on the right in the sky; before the strengthening of the shadow of the large tree in the water.

3rd state: With drypoint on the right in the sky.

4th state: Clouds added and changed, the trunk of the oak reworked and foliage added, alterations made to the left and right of the oak tree, and hatching added to the reflections in the water on the left. Keyes (1977) ascribes all of the changes in this state to another hand.

LITERATURE: Bartsch 1803, 4; Regnault-Delalande 1817, 4; Smith 1835, p.104, no. 4; Weigel 1843, 4; Duplessis 1878, 4; Dutuit 1885, 4; Wurzbach 1910, 4; Simon 1930, pp.35, 60; Keyes 1977, 6 (p.17, erroneously states the print is dated); Hollstein-de Hoop Scheffer 1978, 4; de Groot 1979, no. 219; Slive 1981, pp.258–60, no. 108; Walford 1991, pp.81–83; Slive 2001, no. E13 repr.

PMA 1st, 3rd and 4th states; RA 3rd state

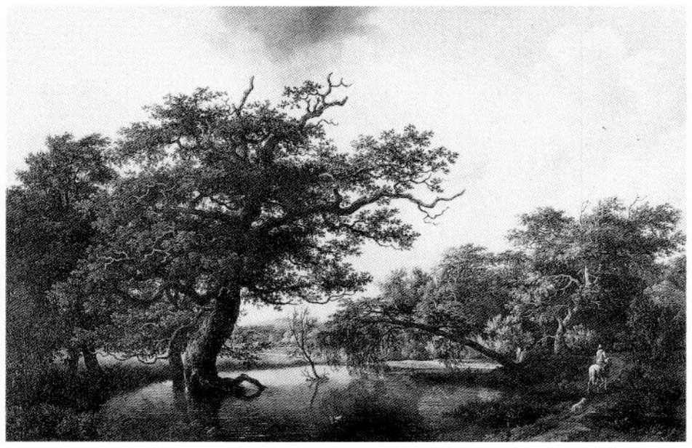

Fig. 112a Meindert Hobbema, *Forest Marsh*, 1662. Melbourne, National Gallery of Victoria.

In this outstanding etching of a forest scene a stout oak, which has clawed itself into the marshy ground, dominates the rich variety of growth reflected in the broad expanse of stagnant water. Comparison of the third state with the rare first one shows how Ruisdael's additional work on the plate heightened the massiveness and solidity of the oak and the high wall of trees beyond it without losing the lively play of light that permeates the landscape.

Hobbema painted three variants of the etching in the early sixties, when he often imitated his teacher's work; the one at the National Gallery of Victoria, Melbourne (fig. 112a) is signed and dated 1662. In these works he introduced modifications that make Ruisdael's composition more open in its spatial setting, changes that help account for the marked loss in mystery and intensity of the pupil's versions.[1]

Another contemporary painted variant after *Forest Marsh* is at Dresden where it was ascribed to Ruisdael from the time it was acquired for the gallery in 1743 until 1928 when Rosenberg firmly attributed it to Jan van Kessel after recognizing that remnants of Kessel's scratched-out signature still are visible under the spurious Ruisdael signature on the panel.[2]

For young Constable's request to borrow an impression of Ruisdael's etching in 1797 in order to copy it, see p.29, above.

1. For Hobbema's 1662 copy at Melbourne, and another, signed and datable about the same time, at the Museo Thyssen-Bornemisza, Madrid, see Slive 2001, under no. E13, p.609. A third one, untraceable and unpublished, reputed to have the remnants of a Hobbema signature and the date of 1661, was in a Dutch private collection; see *ibid.*, repr.
2. Slive 2001, no. dub67, repr.

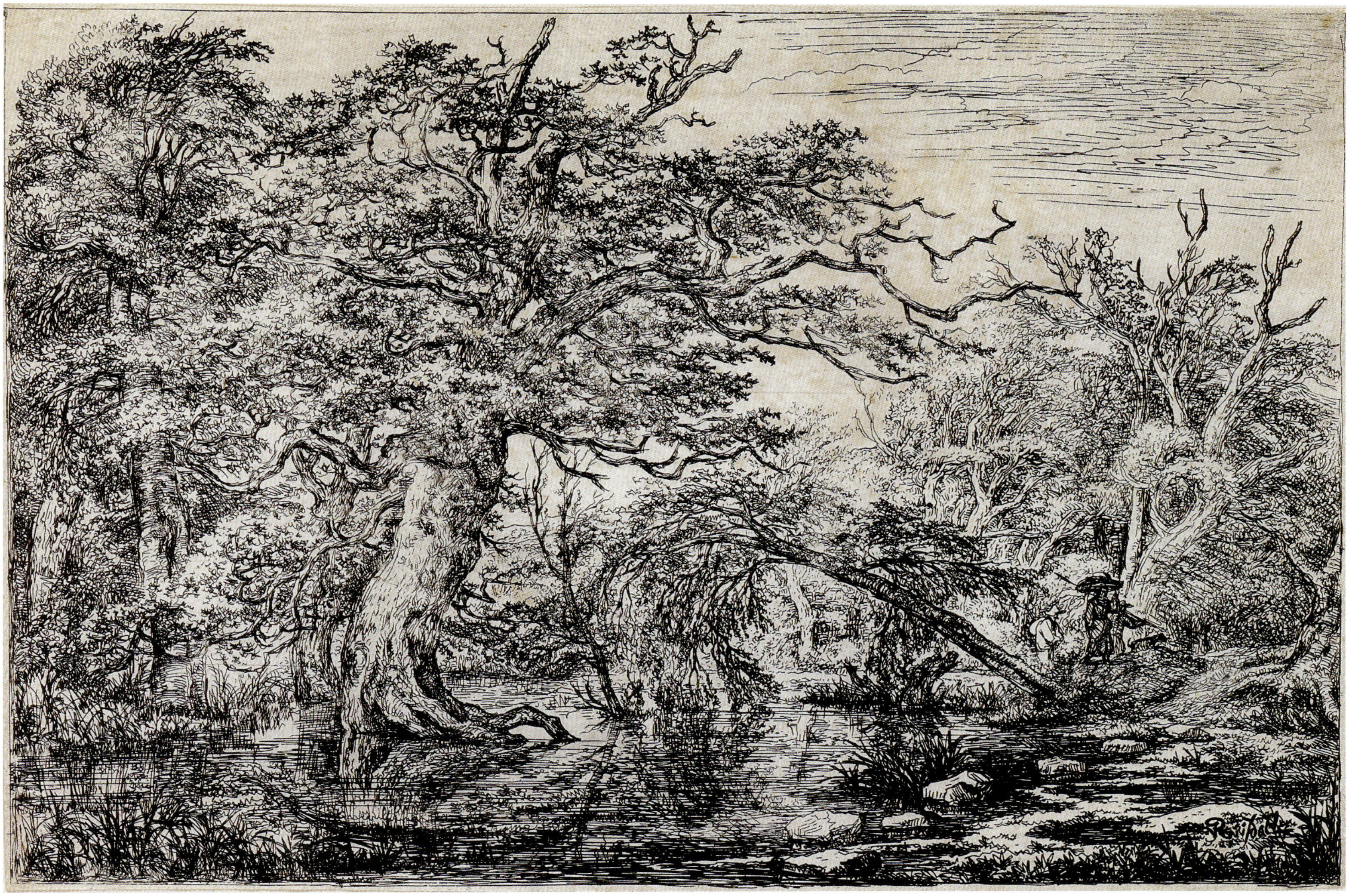

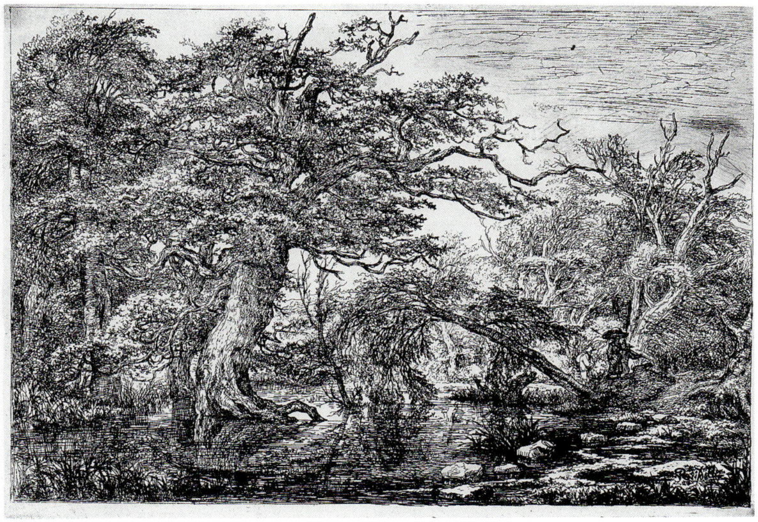

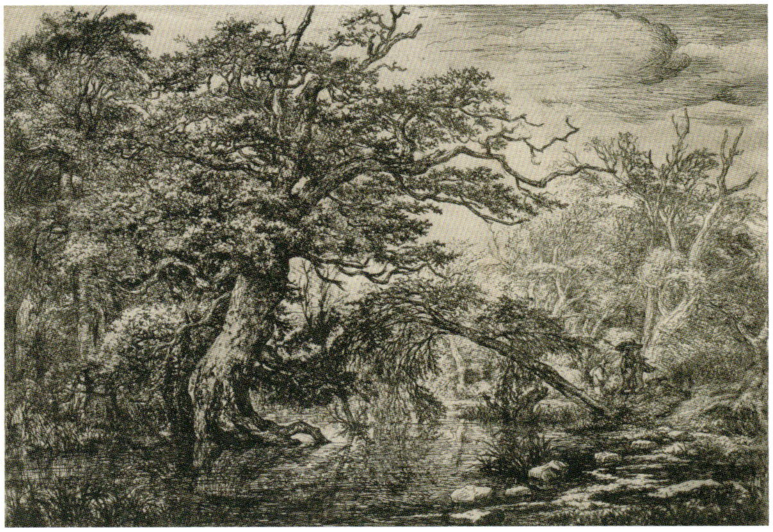

Appendix Ruisdael's Paintings in Seventeenth- and Early Eighteenth-Century Dutch Inventories and Sale Catalogues

Analysing Dutch references to Ruisdael's paintings in seventeenth- and early eighteenth-century inventories and sale catalogues is not a straightforward task because his surname, with various spellings (Ruyschdael, Ruisdalen, Ruisdaale, Ruijsdaal, Ruysdaal, etc.), occurs much more frequently without a first name and patronymic than with them. These references could refer to works by Jacob's father Isaack, his uncle Salomon van Ruysdael or his cousin Jacob Salomonsz van Ruysdael. There are also a few references to 'a landscape by the young Ruysdael' (*een landschap, gedaen bij de jonge Ruysdael*), which could refer to our Jacob or to his cousin Jacob Salomonsz. However, as will be seen, in more than 400 inventory and sale catalogues examined for this appendix, there is not a single specific reference to his cousin's works and those by his father and uncle do not turn up very often. Moreover, in some cases compilers offer a helpful clue when they do not use the neutral terms landscape (*landschap*) or piece (*stuk*) but cite subjects which were our protagonist's specialities: *e.g.*, waterfall (*waterval*), a painting of Haarlem with dunes (*een schilderije verbeeldende Haerlem met zijn landsdouwen*) or identify other sites he depicted (*e.g.*, Kostverloren, Amsterdam's Damrak, A Jewish Cemetery).

A summary of paintings by members of the Ruisdael family cited in Haarlem inventories compiled between 1636 and 1745 follows.[1] There are merely three or four references to pictures by Jacob van Ruisdael (the same painting may be cited in different inventories of the same family's possessions; hence the reference to 'three or four'). Two of these works are valued, one at Dfl. 7, the other at Dfl. 6.10. Five landscapes by Isaack van Ruisdael are listed; not one is appraised. Five or six references are made to paintings by Salomon van Ruysdael. Only one is valued; it is appraised at Dfl. 1.10. Fourteen works are called 'Ruisdael' without a first name; three are valued, the highest at Dfl. 40, the lowest at Dfl. 1.50.

Amsterdam inventories made between 1653 and 1750 offer a larger sample than those complied in Haarlem.[2] They list eleven works by Jacob van Ruisdael; six are valued, the highest at Dfl. 60, the lowest at Dfl. 7. No works by Isaack van Ruisdael are cited. Just two by his brother Salomon appear; only one is appraised, at Dfl. 1.10. No less than ninety-six paintings are identified by 'Ruisdael' without a first name; the highest valuation given is Dfl. 85, the lowest is Dfl. 6.

Noteworthy is a reference to a copy of a Ruisdael waterfall that appears in an inventory compiled in Amsterdam as early as 1684, only two years after the artist's death.[3] Another waterfall copy, valued at Dfl. 3, is cited in a 1708 inventory.[4] There also are references to works done in his manner, one in a 1684 inventory, and two more in an inventory of 1706.[5] It is hardly necessary to add, if any of these works surface, they will pass with flying colours technical tests made to determine if their supports, grounds and pigments date from Jacob van Ruisdael's time. Other techniques will have to be employed to determine their relation to the master.

A review of 222 Dutch painting sale catalogues published from 1678 until 1739 reveals that during these decades Ruisdael's pictures did not often turn up on the art market.[6] Sixty-seven paintings possibly by him are catalogued in thirty-five (15.7%) of these catalogues. Forty-three paintings are assigned to 'Ruisdael' without a first name. Twenty-four are attributed to 'J.' or 'Jacob Ruisdael'. None of the sale catalogues include a single reference to works attributed to Jacob's father Isaack, his uncle Salomon or, as we have heard, his cousin Jacob Salomonsz. Finally, the prices of paintings ascribed to 'Ruisdael' and 'J.' or 'Jacob Ruisdael' were low. One sold in 1739 for as little as Dfl. 1.15.[7] Most went for prices that ranged between Dfl. 20 and Dfl. 50. Only one, knocked down in 1746, fetched a three figure price: Dfl. 151;[8] in the same sale a Philips Wouwerman *Horse Fair* brought Dfl. 2,125 and an Adriaen van Ostade genre scene of peasants was sold for Dfl. 1,200, not unexpected prices for works by these artists at this time.

Notes

JACOB VAN RUISDAEL: MASTER LANDSCAPIST

1. See Slive 2001, no. 549.
2. The picture (Slive 2001, no. 20) was lost in a disastrous fire at the Boymans Museum, Rotterdam, in 1864.
3. I am beholden to Francis Russell for informing me (June 2003) that the painting (panel, 31.7 × 46.8 cm) is in the collection of Viscount Allendale, Bywell Hall, Northumberland, and for subsequently arranging a first-hand examination and providing photos of it. The painting is listed in Slive 2001, no. 547, but unillustrated and without word of its location, support or dimensions. It is signed and dated 1646, bottom, right [not left] centre (fig. 2). Here Ruisdael used a long Gothic 's' in his signature; in some others done in the 1640s he employed a lower case italic 's' (see, for example, cat. 3). During the following decade he began using the long Gothic 's' more consistently. The entry on the painting in Slive 2001, no. 574, states it is signed and dated 164(?8) and notes the picture is possibly identical with one that appeared in the sale, Charles Scarisbrick, London (Christie's), 10–11 May 1861, no. 58, with a description that fits the Allendale landscape and listed as dated 1646. Reappearance of the painting indicates it is almost certainly identical with the Scarisbrick picture. Both Hofstede de Groot (810) and Rosenberg (511) catalogued the painting; they were overly optimistic when they attributed its figures to Adriaen van Ostade.
4. Fourteen works dated 1646 are listed in Slive 2001, 'Chronological List of Dated Works', p. 5. The fifteenth is the Allendale painting cited in note 3 above.
5. For their identity see *ibid.*
6. Salomon, Isaack's younger brother, spelled his surname 'Ruysdael'. Isaack normally spelled his surname 'Ruisdael' and, to our knowledge, his son Jacob, the protagonist of our story, invariably spelled it 'Ruisdael'.
7. Ashton *et al.* 1982, p. 21.
8. Ashton *et al.* 1982, pp. 8–9, observe: 'Ruisdael's spruces lack the detail of his other trees [e.g., their distinctive pendant lateral twigs] and we would not be able to distinguish them from other conifers were they not placed into landscapes we recognize as "Nordic".' Ashton notes that Ruisdael's drawing of a *Hilly Landscape with Norway Spruce Trees* at the British Museum (Slive 2001, no. D85, repr.) offers an exception; its spruces are unusually well portrayed with branches properly scruffy and characteristically horizontal and pointed upward. Another notable exception is the towering Norway spruce in the Fogg Art Museum's *Waterfall* (cat. 33). The suggestion that Norway spruces may have been introduced into the Netherlands in Rusidael's day (Ashton *et al.* 1982, p. 8) is substantiated by an anonymous engraving datable to the early 1650s of views of Hofwijk, Constantin Huygens's small country seat, which shows that its garden had Norway spruces (see Wheelock 1995, pp. 345; 346–47, note 4, and Kuyper 1980, p. 154, fig. 314). However, their setting in Huygens's manicured garden has nothing in common with those in wild northern landscapes by Everdingen and Ruisdael. For paintings done in the following decades of elite country houses and their gardens by Ruisdael that include spruces see Slive 2001, nos. 554, 559, 573, 576, 588; for one by Everdingen see Davies 2001, no. 178, repr., and for a couple by Ludolf de Jongh see Fleischer 1989, figs. 94, 95. They also appear in a series of nine drawings by Anthonie Waterloo of an estate, probably Spruytenburg near Maarssveen, datable *c.*1675–80 (see Broos 1984a, pp. 18–48).
9. Ashton *et al.* 1982, p. 5 and *passim.*
10. Art Gallery and Museum, Glasgow; the State Pushkin Museum of Fine Arts, Moscow; Nationalmuseum, Stockholm (Slive 2001, nos. 31, 33, 34, respectively).
11. Berchem's paintings that include the castle are in the collection of the Duke of Westminster, and Staatliche Kunstsammlungen, Dresden; illustrated Slive 2001, p. 24 and p. 25, respectively.
12. *Village with Half-timbered Houses Flanking a Road on a Hill*, 1653, Musée des Beaux-Arts et Musée David d'Angers, Angers (S 552) and *Landscape with a Half-timbered House and a Blasted Tree*, 1653, The Speed Art Museum, Louisville, Kentucky (S 577).
13. 'In Wien ist eine Landschaft. Vorne geht über Lehmgrund ein klares Wasser, dann sind Baüme, ein Wäldchen, zwischen dessen Stämmen man wieder in freie Luft sieht. Der Himmel hat ein einfaches Wolkengebäude. Das ist mehrere hundert Millionen Male auf der Welt gewesen, und doch ist die Landschaft die gewaltigste und erschütterndste, die es geben kann.' (Stifter 1982, vol. 2, p. 410). *Nachkommenschaften* was first published in *Der Heimgarten*, vol. 1, 1864, nos. 6, 7, 8; reprinted in Stifter 1982, vol. 2, pp. 377–443. Stifter cites neither the artist nor the landscape his protagonist acclaims; both were first identified by Novotny 1941, p. 12. The impression the Vienna landscape makes today would be enhanced by conservation treatment that includes removal of its present mat surface coating.
14. No. 3289; Schneider 1932 (reprint 1973), p. 235, no. Z 314.
15. *Luther's Works. Table Talk*, 54, ed. and trans. by T.G. Tappert, general editor, H.L. Lehmann, Philadelphia, 1967, pp. 46–47.
16. See J. Bruyn, 'Toward a Scriptural Reading of Seventeenth-Century Landscape Paintings', in Amsterdam–Boston–Philadelphia 1987–88, pp. 84–108, with bibliographical references to critics who endorse a similar view.
17. Davies 2001, *passim*, provides the most comprehensive discussion of Everdingen's Scandinavian landscapes and their impact on his followers and imitators.
18. The Albertina drawing is illustrated *ibid.*, fig. 42. Rosenberg (1928, p. 44, note 1) identified it as a preliminary study for Everdingen's Frankfurt painting; Bisanz-Prakken (New York–Fort Worth 1995, p. 150, no. 71, repr.) contends it was intended as an independent work. Davies (2001, p. 56) sensibly observes that the two are not necessarily mutually exclusive.
19. *Rough Sea*, 1640, formerly Senator Clark, Montana (*ibid.*, no. 1, repr.; *Shipwreck on a Rocky Coast*, 1643, formerly P.M. Fowlie, Toronto (*ibid.*, no. 2, repr.).
20. GAA, notarial archive, J. Hellerus, fol. 555 (film 2579). Bredius 1888, pp. 21–2; Wijnman 1932, p. 173. The putative Porcellis had been purchased by the Amsterdam collector Laurens Mauritz Douci whose 1669 inventory lists a view of Haarlem by Ruisdael (see note 25 below), three of Jacob's waterfalls as well as six Everdingen landscapes.
21. A date in the sixties also is bolstered by a Jan van Kessel landscape dated 1664; it is a copy, with minor differences, of an untraceable Ruisdael and provides a firm *terminus ante quem* of 1664 for a landscape by Jacob that can be placed in the same category (see Slive 2001, no. 404 and fig. 404a).
22. Prof. Allan Robinson, Massachusetts Institute of Technology, Massachusetts (private communication).
23. J.M. Drees, 'Blade Twist, Droop Snoot, and Forward Spars', *Vertiflite*, September/October 1976, pp. 4–9.
24. *Ibid.*, p. 8.
25. 'noch een lantschap schilderytge Haerlem door Ruysdael'; inventory of Catrina Luijs, 27 August 1664; Amsterdam; GAA inv.no. 2259 (unpublished reference kindly supplied by Patricia A. Teter, Getty Research Institute). 'een Haerlemje van Ruysdael'; inventory of Laurens Mauritsz Douci, 18 January 1669 (Bredius 1915–22, 2, p. 425).
26. Identification by Biesboer 1995, p. 38.
27. *Banquet of the Officers of the St George Civic Guards*, c.1627; Slive 1970–74, 3, no. 46. He appears again in another group portrait Hals painted for the same guard company *c.*1639; *ibid.*, 3, no. 124.
28. For Hals's portrait of de Clercq see Slive 1970–74, 3, no. 104. Identification of his bleachery was made by Biesboer 1995, p. 37.
29. Musée du Louvre, Paris; no. RF 2862; repr. Slive 2001, p. 55, fig. Haarlem q.
30. Regtdoorzee Greup-Roldanus 1936, p. 323.
31. *Ibid.*, p. 36.
32. Kalf 1980, p. 15.
33. *Ibid.*, p. 20.
34. *Ibid.*, p. 19.
35. Illustrations of more than fifty seventeenth-century profile views of Rhenen by other artists are in Deys 1981.
36. In the picture by Jan Andrea Lievens (1644–80) Gudlaugsson (1950, p. 154) saw recollections of the style of landscapes by Jan Lievens (1607–74), Jan Andrea's much better known father who was closely associated with Rembrandt from about 1625 to 1631. This may be the case for passages for the fore and middle grounds of the painting but surely the background view is closer to *Haarlempjes* by Ruisdael and his circle than to any known landscape by Jan Lievens the Elder.
37. Wiegand 1971, pp. 99–106. The questionable interpretation has been extended to bits of household linen in the entry on Isaack van Ruisdael's *View of Naarden*, 1645 [not 1646], in the exhibition catalogue Hamburg-Haarlem 2002, no. 1, repr. Isaack's townscape includes a woman laying out wash which the entry's author states may be emblematic references to the soul's purity and God's grace. It is equally probable that Isaack employed the scene to add anecdotal interest to his topographical view of his native city.
38. This convincing argument was first offered by Fuchs 1973, p. 285.
39. Regtdoorzee Greup-Roldanus 1936, p. 39, note 3.
40. Wijnman 1932, p. 267; Oldewelt 1942, p. 165.
41. GAH, Baptismal, Marriage and Burial Register 82, fol. 188. Van der Willigen 1870, p. 257; Wijnman 1932, p. 266; Oldewelt 1942, p. 165.
42. GAA, Wijk 24, fol. 220. Oldewelt 1942, p. 165.

43. GAA, notorial document, C. Akerboom Doedens 4036 (film 4108), unpaginated. The document, dated 5 October 1682, states that Maria, Jacob's sole beneficiary, will receive 150 guilders as partial payment of van Lamsweerde's debt to the late artist. Additionally, it notes the loan of 400 guilders to the doctor was made 9 July 1678 and gives the date Ruisdael started action to confiscate his debtor's goods. Also see Bredius 1915, p. 25, and Wijnman 1932, p. 266.

RUISDAEL'S CLIENTELE, EARLY COLLECTORS AND CRITICS

* Material on the artist's customers appeared in another form in Slive 2004, pp. 174–85.

1. S 80.
2. Analogies to the rather thick, tall woods set on a hill are seen in Ruisdael's *Wooded Landscape with a Bridge*, Philadelphia Museum of Art, and *Wooded Landscape with a Rocky Stream*, Stanton Harcourt Coll., Stanton Court Manor, Oxon., both monogrammed and datable *c.* 1660 (cf. S 409 and S 424). For his similar but unidentifiable country houses in parks datable to the 1670s see paintings in the Fisher Art Gallery, University of Southern California, Los Angeles, and National Gallery of Art, Washington, D.C. (*S* 567 and S 588).
3. *De Werken van Vondel*, ed. by J.F.M. Sterck *et al.*, vol. 6, Amsterdam, 1932, pp. 83–87.
4. S.A.C. Dudok van Heel kindly informed me (private communication) that the three standing men on the left are possibly portraits (reading from left to right) of Cornelis de Graeff's brother-in-law Pieter Trip (1597–1655; hence a posthumous portrait), his brother-in-law Willem Schrijver (1608–61) and his younger brother Andries de Graeff (1611–78).
5. '*4 voet en 2 duim hoog en 6 voet lang van de schilderije van Keyser, sijnde een landschap van Zoestdijck met mijn vader Sal. karos en eenige conterfeijtsels*'. The note, dated 1 November 1670, is in Pieter de Graeff's V.O.C. almanac, Amsterdam Municipal Archives, de Graeff archives; Dudok van Heel 1983, p. 68, note 12.
6. '*1 groot stuck waarin de heer burgemeester Cornelis de Graeff met desselfs huysvrouw Catharina en beijde haare soone d'heeren Pieter en Jacob de Graeff noch jongh sijnde*'. Estate inventory, 27 October 1691, Amsterdam Municipal Archives, de Graeff family archives, no. 605, item 32.
7. Dudok van Heel 1975, pp. 146–59, establishes the identity of the sitters and the painting's early provenance. Also see the entry on the Berlin double portrait in Slive *et al.* 1989, p. 154, no. 9.
8. 8 March 1709: '*1 Groote schilderije waarin Pourtraicten van wijlen d'Hr Burgemeester Cornelis de Graeff, sijne vrouw en twee zoonen*'; Amsterdam Municipal Archives, NA, M. Servaes 5001, fol.511; Dudok van Heel 1983, p. 68, note 12.
9. 8 March 1709: '*Op de kamer van Vrouwe Agneta de Graeff* [Pieter's daughter]: *Een schilderij van zuijdpolsbroek door Jacob Ruijsdael f.36. – Een dito van Soesdijk f.36*'; Amsterdam Municipal Archives, NA, M. Servaes 5001, fol.485; Bredius 1912, p. 199; Dudok van Heel 1983, p. 68, note 12. One of Cornelis de Graeff's properties was a seigniory at Zuidpolsbroek (also Polsbroek). Ruisdael's painting of it may be an existing landscape which we fail to recognize as the place. In the attempt to identify it (which, in the end, was fruitless), consideration was given to his paintings of country houses constructed in a classicizing style that are set in gardens embellished with fountains. They are at Berlin, The Fisher Gallery of the University of Southern California, Washington, D.C., and one surfaced in the sale, anon., The Hague (Vendue Huis der Notarissen), 25 April 2002, no. 327 (S 554, 576, 588, 573, respectively). As noted, nothing was found to link any of them with Polsbroek. Information provided by the indefatigable Amsterdam archivist I.H. van Eeghen (private communication), which may help students who want to resume the search, is that the house at Polsbroek was not large. On 24 July 1674 Pieter de Graeff notes in his V.O.C. almanac that he contracted with Ruisdael before a notary to repaint and improve his landscapes of Soestdijk and Polsbroek, the former for *f.*30, the latter for *f.*40. ('*met Ruysdael, schilder, in presentie van de notaris Padhuysen afgesproken om twee landschappen, 't een van Zoesdijck 't ander van Polsbroeck door hem te doen overschilderen en hebben op 't eene toe af tot verbeteringh geboden f.30 — gl. en op 't tweede f.40 — gl. 't saeme 70 gl.*'); Amsterdam Municipal Archives, de Graeff family archives, no. 194; Dudok van Heel 1983, p. 68, note 12. The Soestdijk painting that was valued at *f.*36 in 1709 is probably identical with '*Een dito [schilderije] van Soesdijk*' cited in an inventory, dated 10 October 1710, which lists pictures given to Jacobus de Fremeri in the name of Cornelis de Graeff (Pieter's son, d.1719; since the son was said to be mentally incompetent, Fremeri probably received them on his behalf): '*...aan de heer Jacobus de Fremeri voor de Ed. heer en mr. Cornelis de Graeff, heer van Pumerland en Ilpendam ... Een dito [schilderije] van Soesdijk.*'
10. '*Een schilderije van de heerlijkheid van Ilpendam en 't Hof, door de jonge Moucheron f.20 — Een dito van de heerlijkheid van Zuid Polsbroek*'; Amsterdam Municipal Archives, NA, M. Servaes 5001, fol.485; Bredius 1912, p. 199.
11. Dudok van Heel 1975, pp. 157, 159, note 20.
12. Smith 1835, pp. 81–82, no. 258.
13. See Slive 2001, p. 25; for sources of the different interpretations see *ibid.*, p. 27, note 10.
14. Amsterdam Municipal Archives, NAA 2636 (film 2663); notary Gerrit Steeman (private communication from Burton B. Fredericksen, Getty Provenance Index).
15. Data about Pieter van Lutsen (also Lutzen, Lutselen) and his family was kindly provided by M.J. Bok who combed Amsterdam's archives for references to him.
16. S. Alsteens states (Paris 2004, p. 365, note 7) the title *Reconstruction of the Ruins of the Manor Kostverloren* is unwarrented because no element in the painting tells us if deconstruction or reconstruction work is underway. In my view the pristine white paint on the tower speaks for reconstruction (also see text and note 17 below).
17. According to I.H. van Eeghen (1969 [n.p.]), restoration work on Kostverloren began by May 1658 and finished November 1658. Her speedy schedule has been accepted by all authors cited in LITERATURE on the painting. But according to Alsteens (Paris 2004, p. 356, note 6) Erik Schmitz has established that van Eeghen's May 1658 date should read between March 1659–64. Schmitz also has shown that van Eeghen's terminal date of November 1658 merely refers to the completion of reconstruction of the manor's privies; he is unaware of a document that provides a date for the completion of the manor's full reconstruction. Schmitz's data is published in P. van Gent *et al.*, *Kostverloren Revisited. Een onderzoek naar de (bouw-) geschiedenis van huis Kostverloren*, Utrecht, 1995, p. 20; I have not seen the volume which is privately printed and unavailable in the trade.
18. Biesboer 1995, pp. 36–39.
19. Rijksmuseum, Amsterdam, no. SK-A-1510. Canvas, 192 x 254.5 cm; datable after 1649. Davies 2001, p. 239, no. 120, Pl. 120; her Everdingen study offers the best discussion of the work, pp. 125–27, 164–67.
20. Frans Hals Museum, Haarlem, no. 206. Pen and brown ink on panel, 71 x 116 cm. Illustrated Slive 2001, p. 516, fig. D30a.
21. Biesboer 2001.
22. The inventory of the estate of Laurens Mauritsz Douci assessed at Amsterdam, 18 January 1669, lists '*een Haerlempje van Ruysdael*' (Bredius 1915–22, vol. 2, 1916, p. 425). Seven more paintings of views of Haarlem are cited in Amsterdam inventories in a compilation of Dutch inventories made from 1664–1740 in a Getty Provenance Index print-out, dated 26 June 2002, helpfully provided by Patricia A. Teter. In the Getty print-out not one is listed in inventories compiled in Haarlem. It is pertinent to add in 1995 Biesboer writes he has 'found the title "Haerlempje" specifically identifying a painting by Jacob van Ruisdael in a Haarlem inventory' (Biesboer 1995, p. 38, note 1). He also states he has found a reference to a *Haarlempje* by Ruisdael in a Haarlem inventory dated as early as 1663 (see Slive 2001, p. 51). Yet no *Haarlempje* by Ruisdael is listed in Biesboer's *Collections of Paintings in Haarlem 1572–1740* published in 2001.
23. Martin 1935–36, vol. 2, p. 304.
24. Scheyer 1977, p. 138.
25. *Ibid.*
26. Concern for literal transcriptions of Hebrew inscriptions by Jewish patrons is found in the drawing Romeijn de Hooghe (1647–1708) made in 1668 of a group portrait of a Jewish family in a richly appointed interior of a circumcision scene (Wilson 1975, pp. 250ff., reprs. pls. 22, 23). De Hooghe's transcription of a Hebrew inscription over the doorway in the interior is clearly legible. Alexander-Knotter (1999, pp. 131–59) offers a fine survey and bibliography on the use of Hebrew inscriptions in Netherlandish Biblical paintings and prints. Her emphasis is on Rembrandt; however, she also considers some of his predecessors and contemporaries. She notes artists used both meaningless letters and correct Hebrew characters that occasionally make no sense. Readable inscriptions are found in Biblical works by Netherlandish artists that incorporate the Tetragrammaton, trilingual accusations pinned to the Cross, on garments and headgear, tablets of the law and texts that are part or provide a gloss on Biblical themes. Ruisdael's cemetery pictures are not part of Alexander-Knotter's brief.
27. For the inventory, see Bredius 1892, pp. 31–40; Russell 1975, pp. 50–57 (English translation).
28. A transcription of the complete inventory is in Strauss and van der Meulen 1979, pp. 349–88, no. 1656/12. The precise number of drawings and prints Rembrandt owned is impossible to determine because the inventory lists them as groups in albums, books, boxes and baskets; the 2,000 figure cited here is a conservative estimate.
29. Two works by Ruisdael are in a 1656 inventory compiled in Leiden of the effects of the genre painter Abraham van Pape, one valued at Dfl. 10, the other at Dfl. 15 (Bredius 1915–22, vol. 5, p. 1860). A landscape by Ruisdael is cited in an inventory of 64 paintings and drawings that were part of the contract Rembrandt's successful pupil Ferdinand Bol made upon the occasion of his second marriage in 1669 in Amsterdam (Blankert 1982, pp. 78–79). The Amsterdam inventory of the deceased wife of the marine painter Ludolf Bakhuizen compiled in 1680 lists a landscape by Ruisdael, appraised at Dfl. 15 (Bredius 1915–22, vol. 1, p. 101). An inventory of no less than 682 lots that were in the possession of the Haarlemer Cornelis Dusart after his death in 1704 lists just one Ruisdael landscape (Biesboer 2001, p. 303).
30. Broos 1984, Broos 1985, Broos 1987 are exemplary, detailed studies of the collecting activities of the Feitama family.
31. For proposed identifications of the windmills in the sketches see S D34, S D35. Soon after they were catalogued (*ibid.*), both listed as presumably lost in World War II, they surfaced. Revelations regarding their post-war history could serve, with little embellishment, as a script for a melodrama. During the war they and about 1,500 other works were hidden in a castle in Nazi Germany until Soviet troops stole the cache during their invasion of the country. Subsequently they were acquired by the KGB and deposited in the National Museum in Baku, Azerbaijen, where they were stolen again with other works in 1993. In 1997 they were in the possession of a former Japanese wrestler who attempted to sell them in Tokyo to pay for a kidney transplant. Later, in the same year, part of the trove was found in a closet and under a bed in a Brooklyn apartment. The two Ruisdael drawings finally were returned to the Bremen museum in July 2001 by USA officials along with precious drawings by Dürer, Rembrandt and Millet. Not a clue has been discovered regarding the fate of a third Bremen Ruisdael drawing presumably lost in World War II: *Ruins of Egmond Castle*

(S D33); the imposing sheet was possibly one of four drawings of Egmond's ruins owned by Sybrand II (see *ibid.*).

32. Giltay (1980, p. 184 and note 107) first called attention to the significance of the inscriptions. He cited it on ten drawings. As noted in the text, today eighteen are known; two are in the exhibition (cat.68, 70). Broos (1987, pp. 176, 199, notes 50–53) recognized that the two Bremen drawings entered the Feitama collection by *c.*1690 and that they must have borne the 'J. Ruijsdael' signature before they were acquired by the Feitamas.
33. The three drawings are: *The High Bridge over a Sluice near the Schermerpoort at Alkmaar*, Amsterdam Historical Museum, cat. 76; *The Excise House at Alkmaar*, Museum of Fine Arts, Budapest, S D39; *Ruins of the Manor House Kostverloren on the Amstel*, Teyler Museum, Haarlem, S D62. Regarding the Amsterdam Historical Museum's sheet Sybrand Feitama II wrote: '[...] door Ruisdaal begonnen [...] opgemaakt door Dirk Dalens, omtr: a° 1687.' Of the Budapest sheet he wrote: '[...] begonnen [by Ruisdael] omtr. A°. 1670, en opgeteekend door D. Dalens, a° 1687.' Regarding the Haarlem drawing he wrote: '[...] door ᵛR. begonnen; doch opgeteekend door Dirk Dalens omtr: 1687 [...].'
34. Giltay (1980, p. 159) states it is hard to see the work of another artist in the Amsterdam drawing (cat. 76); Broos (1984, p. 25) concurs and suggests Dalens may have added the brown ink border and the monogram. I agree with their conclusions. For references to vain attempts by Giltay, Broos and me to find unquestioned work by Dalens in the other two drawings see S D39, S D62.
35. Lairesse 1707, p. 349.
36. Luiken 1708, pp. 90–93.
37. This point is made by Porteman 1992, p. 148. I am indebted to Leeflang (2002, p. 414) for signaling Porteman's article.
38. Houbraken 1718–21, vol. 3, pp. 65–66. Vols. 1 and 2 were published for the author in 1718, 1719, respectively; vol. 3 was published for the author's widow in 1721.
39. These numbers are compiled from Hoet 1752 and Terwesten 1770.
40. Both are now in the Staatliche Kunstsammlungen, Dresden; see S 182, S 183.
41. For the two waterfalls, now in the Herzog Anton Ulrich-Museum, Braunschweig, see S 156, S 157.
42. The picture is now in the Staatliche Kunstsammlungen, Kassel; see S 167. When Cornelia's husband Valerius Röver (1686–1739; also called van Reuver) died his Rembrandt holdings were remarkable. He had eight paintings attributed to Rembrandt, two portfolios of drawings by him and members of his school, and what he called a complete set of the master's etchings and their various states (435 impressions); he also compiled the first *oeuvre* catalogue of Rembrandt's prints (see Slive 1953, pp. 173–76).
43. For a discussion of the question, see 'Appendix 1: Dr. Jacob van Ruisdael,' Slive 2001, pp. 693–94.
44. Van der Willigen 1870, p. 260.
45. Descamps 1753–64, vol. 3 (1760), p. 12.
46. *Ibid.* Two can be identified. One is *River Landscape with an Angler, a View of a Town and Windmills*, private coll., U.S.A.; S 521, repr.; Descamps's reference pushes its presence in the Horntener (also Horunter) coll., Rouen, back to 1760. Perhaps Descamps, who spent much of his long career in Rouen, knew the picture well. The other painting is *Windmill on a River Bank*, Staatliche Museen, Berlin. It was generally accepted as an original until 1975 when Jan Kelch expressed justifiable reservations about its traditional attribution; see Slive 2001, under no. 136, repr.
47. Descamps 1753–64, vol. 3 (1760, p. 11). In this passage he repeats Houbraken's error of wrongly calling Salomon the brother of Jacob not his uncle. Descamps tells us he himself owned a van Goyen (*ibid.*, vol. 1 [1753], p. 422). It and another painting by van Goyen that was in his collection entered the Musée des Beaux-Arts de Rouen in 1818 (inv.nos. 818–1–7, 818–1–8; Beck 1972–91, vol. 2 [1972], nos. 572, repr. and 776, repr., respectively) with a group of his other Dutch, Flemish and French pictures.
48. S 397. The painting, the artist's largest existing picture, is possibly identical with 'A large landscape by Ruijsdael with staffage by Berchem' cited in an inventory of 7 February 1702 of the deceased Amsterdam merchant Adolf Visscher (no. 72, GAA). Judging from Ruisdael's painting Gainsborough's close copy of it has been cut on the bottom and at both sides. For the possibility that the picture in the 1702 inventory is identical with one offered in a 1746 Amsterdam sale see Notes to the Appendix, p. 264 note 8 below.
49. *Wooded Landscape with Cattle at a Watering Place*, *c.*1747, São Paolo; *Landscape with a Peasant Resting Beside a Winding Track*, signed and dated 1747, Philadelphia Museum of Art; *Gainsborough's Forest*, *c.*1746–47, National Gallery, London; Hayes 1982, vol. 2, nos. 20, 22, 17, reprs., respectively.
50. The two volume manuscript transcript of English sales, 1711–1759, is at the Victoria and Albert Museum Library, London (MS 86.00 18–19). They are known as the Houlditch transcripts, after Richard Houlditch sen. and jun. who probably made them. The late Neil MacLaren kindly provided photocopies of pages of the transcriptions that include Ruisdael references.
51. Simpson (1953, pp. 40–42) offers a survey of Dutch material in the transcripts.
52. For the location of printed copies of John van Spangen's sale, London (Cock and Langford), 10–12 February 1748, see Lugt 681.
53. The principal posthumous painting sale was held in London (Christie's), 13, 14, 16, 17 March 1795. For the best study of the sale's protracted history, correction of errors made by earlier students, an account of sales Reynolds himself organized of works he had collected and his other posthumous painting sales, see Broun 1987, vol. 1, esp. chap. 3, 'The Dispersal of the Collection,' pp. 60–81. Reynolds's first drawing sale, held in the form of an exhibition organized by the dealer A.C. de Poggi, began 26 May 1794. The second sale was held in London (Philips), 5–26 March 1798. Royalton-Kisch 1978, pp. 61–91, is a rewarding essay on Reynolds as collector of drawings which includes comments on his painting collection as well as observations on the conditions under which his vast holdings were assembled and sold.
54. Sale, John Glover, London (Sutton), 7 *sqq.* March 1745, nos. 133, 135, 136, 148, 149, respectively. Lugt (11032) notes that a copy of the sale catalogue is in the collection of Seymour de Ricci, Paris; I have not seen it. The above lot numbers are derived from the handwritten copy of the sale catalogue in the Houlditch transcripts (V. and A. Library). Broun (1987, vol. 1, p. 108, note 4) rightly observes the layout of the manuscript makes it difficult to determine the exact number of works acquired by Reynolds at that sale. The landscapes by van Goyen and Dalens (nos. 133 and 148) are listed as 'Companions' to the previous lots. In each case Reynolds's name is placed only below the second item, and there is no buyer or price for the 'prime' lot. Thus, he may have bought four pictures in those instances rather than two. Reynolds is definitely cited as the buyer of both the Rembrandt and the Lievens which are also said to be companions. Royalton-Kisch (1978, p. 65) cites Reynolds as the purchaser of the Rembrandt and two pairs of landscapes for a total of 15 gns. He erred when he omitted Reynolds as the buyer of the Lievens (£1 14*s.*) and the Wouwerman (£9 9*s.*).
55. Broun (1987, vol. 1, p. 19) first suggested that Reynolds may have acted as Hudson's agent at Glover's sale. He overstates his case when he subsequently writes, without qualification, that Reynolds bid at auctions on Hudson's behalf (*ibid.*, pp. 33, 46).
56. *Ibid.*, pp. 23, 135–36 (Appendix A. Chronological List of Acquisitions).
57. According to a note in Reynolds's Sitter Book for 1755 (12–18 May) he bought 'A little Rysdale' from Mr. Charlton for £1 9*s.* (Waterhouse 1966–68, p. 128). The four other works were acquired at the following auctions. Sale, John de Pester, London (Prestage), 1–2 April 1756: no. 10. 'A Landscape with Figures,' 18″ × 22″ £15 15*s.*; no. 11. 'Its Companion,' ditto £13 2*s.* 6*d.* (also see note 58 below). Sale, Dr. Robert Bragge, 1757, 2nd day: no. 56. 'Landscape with a Waterfall,' £21 10*s.* 6*d.* Sale, Dr. Bragg, 1759, 2nd day: no. 25. 'A Landscape. Figs, Crabbi' [Krabbetje=Jan Asselyn], £21 10*s.* 6*d.* A review of the activities and unfavourable reputation of the auctioneer-dealer Dr. Robert Bragge (also Bragg) in London around the middle of the century is in Pears 1988, pp. 92–96. Pears states 'The 'Doctor' frequently attached to his name does not appear to have been genuine' (*ibid.*, p. 92).
58. Broun (1987, vol. 2, pp. 74–7) provides data for Reynolds's most probable ownership of the Metropolitan's *Grainfield* which I learned after cataloguing the painting (S 100). He observes that Reynolds purchased two Ruisdaels at Pester's sale, 1 April 1756: no. 10, 'A Landscape with Figures' and no. 11, 'Its Companion' (see note 57 above). In the catalogue for the exhibition and sale Reynolds organized to benefit his servant Ralph Kirkley (called 'Ralph's Exhibition,' 28 Haymarket, London, opened 4 April 1791), nos. 91 and 93 are listed as 'Ruysdael–Landscape.' In Reynolds's posthumous sale, 17 March 1795, no. 46 is described: 'A Pair, Beautiful Landscapes, scenes from Nature, in high preservation'; they were bought by Hardman for 50 gns. In the sale, Thomas Hardman, Manchester (Winstanley and Sons), 19 October 1838, no. 54, canvas, 18″ × 22″, is described as a Ruisdael: 'A Landscape, with the effect of a Showery Day. On the right is a Field of Standing Corn, protected by a broken Bank from a Public Road, on which a Peasant with his Dog are traveling towards a Mill; in the distance is seen a Village Church [... the picture] was in the Collection of Sir Joshua Reynolds, and more recently in that of the late William Hardman, Esq.' It was purchased by Edwards for 87 gns. For the appearance of the painting in the collection of Louis Viardot, Paris, its sale before his 1863 auction and its subsequent history see S 100. Regarding the provenance and attribution of the putative companion to Ruisdael's *Grainfield* see Broun 1987, vol. 2, p. 76, no. 2. The pair is identical with Smith 73, HdG 1070 and Smith 74, HdG 1071.
59. Reynolds 1996a, p. 111.
60. Sale, P. Calkoen, Amsterdam (v.d. Schley), 10 September 1781, no. 116 (Dfl. 450, Wubbels); for additional provenance, see S 659. Reynolds's instructions to his Amsterdam agent Pierre Yver and the latter's response are discussed in Broun 1987, vol. 1, pp. 31, 114, note 42, and Reynolds 1996a, pp. 109, 174, note 592. A complete transcription of the letter (2 October 1781) Yver sent to Reynolds that includes references to the bidding he did for Reynolds at the Calkoen sale is cited *ibid.*, pp. 209–11.
61. For details of the provenance of Getty's *Sluice*, see cat. 7. The *Sluice* and an unidentified landscape that sold for Dfl. 310 are listed in the sale of the late Willem Lormier, The Hague (Franken), 4 *sqq.* July 1763; the latter is no. 277: 'Een Landschap met een fraay verschiet, door denzelven [Jacob Ruysdael]; D. breet 2 voet 3 duim, hoog 1 voet 8 duim'.
62. Pott 1782, pp. 41–43. Efforts to discover whether Pott himself collected Ruisdael's landscapes or works by other artists have been unsuccessful. His obituary in *The Gentleman's Magazine* (n.s., 1847, vol. 28, part 2, pp. 210–11) gives considerable particulars of the bequests stipulated in his will, but no mention is made of pictures he owned. His DNB biographer (vol. 16, p. 207) writes he died 'leaving considerable personalty and a valuable library, which was sold by auction'; an endeavour to find a copy of his posthumous sale catalogue failed.

CONSTABLE AND RUISDAEL

1. Beckett 1968, 6, p.229. For more about the Ruisdael landscape (Slive 2001, no. 121) that captivated Constable see p. 37 below and fig. 39.
2. Beckett 1964, 2, p.9.

3. Constable's etching is illustrated in Parris and Fleming-Williams 1991, p.388, fig. 188. See *ibid.*, p.388, no. 221, for the relation of the print to Smith's etchings.
4. Beckett 1964, 2, p.22.
5. I am beholden to Charles S. Rhyne for clarifying this passage's ambiguity and for generously sharing his knowledge of works by Constable and members of his circle.
6. Farington 1978–84, 4, p.1166.
7. *Ibid.*, p.1202.
8. Beckett 1964, 2, p.24.
9. *Ibid.*, pp.25–6.
10. Leslie 1951, p.4.
11. Beckett 1968, 6, p.44.
12. *Ibid.*, p.45.
13. Beckett 1970, pp.35, 56.
14. Leslie reported the exchange; see *ibid.*, p.56, note 6.
15. Becket 1964, 2, p. 90, 15 October 1812. Until MacLaren (1960, pp. 365–66) correctly identified the National Gallery's *Shore at Egmond aan Zee* it was wrongly called *Shore at Scheveningen*; also see Slive 2001, no. 631, repr. An anonymous engraving of it, which does not bear a title or verse, appears in Pierre François Basan, *Recueil d'estampes gravés d'après le Cabinet de Monseigneur le duc de Choiseul*, Paris, 1771, no. 117; see Slive 2001, fig. 631a.
16. Victoria and Albert Museum, London, no. 288–1888; 10.3 × 15.2. Reynolds 1984, p.23, no. 18.31. Monogrammed and dated on the verso: *J.C. fe: 1818.* Although Reynolds (*ibid.*) notes the inscription is perhaps by another hand, he catalogues it with Constable's works of 1818.
17. Parris *et al.* 1976, pp.107–8, no. 104.
18. Beckett 1952, pp.38–9.
19. Beckett 1968, 6, p.83.
20. 8.9 × 11; inscribed on the verso: 'V.W. [= vd Velde] 1 foot 4 1/2 1d.o 7 1/2/ hight of Hor[izon] 3 inches/Ruysdael/ 1 foot 6/ 1d.o 91/2/ British Gallery July 13. 1819.' PROVENANCE: By descent from the artist; acquired by David Thomson, 1992. EXHIBITIONS: London 1976a, no. 167, repr.; London–New York–Toronto 1994–95, no. 49, repr. LITERATURE: Fleming-Williams 1976, p.64, repr.; Reynolds 1984, p.34, no. 19.18, repr.; Fleming-Williams 1990, pp.166–69. The drawing is trimmed. David Thomson kindly provided a transparency of the sketch.
21. Parris *et al.* 1976, p.110, no. 167.
22. Fleming-Williams 1990, pp.166–69; London–New York–Toronto 1994–95, pp.184–86, no. 49.
23. Beckett 1968, 6, p.74. See also note 42, below.
24. Parris *et al.* 1975, p. 57.
25. Beckett 1968, 6, p. 229. For the provenance of Rotterdam's *Water Mill* see Slive 2001, no. 121. Fisher was intimately acquainted with Constable's *Perne's Mill*; Constable give him a small oil sketch of the undershot water mill in 1824 (now in the Fitzwilliam Museum, Cambridge; Reynolds 1984, 1, no. 24.4, repr.). For Constable's other versions of it (also known as 'Parham's Mill' and 'The Mill at Gillingham in Dorset') see *ibid.*, nos. 23.22, 26.4, 27.5, all illustrated.
26. Beckett 1968, 6, p.77.
27. The drawing surfaced in the sale, anon., London (Sotheby's), 13 November 1997, no. 3, repr. (£2800). Pen and black ink, 7.8 × 6.3 (oval).
28. See Martin Royalton-Kisch, 'John Sheepshanks (1787–1863) and his Dutch and Flemish Etchings,' *Landmarks in Print Collecting. Connoisseurs and Donors at The British Museum since 1753*, ed. Antony Griffiths, London, 1996, pp.65–79 and Appendix H, 'Purchases by John Sheepshanks and Sales from his Collection,' pp.190–94. Royalton-Kisch offers an excellent, detailed discussion of Sheepshanks's activities as a collector of the graphic arts and account of the acquisition of this part of his holdings by the British Museum.
29. For Swanevelt's etching of *Satyr Playing the Pipes* and Constable's pen, ink and grey wash drawing after it see *ibid.*, pp.70, 71 (figs. 2 and 3), 77, note 13.
30. Panel, 33 × 33. Reynolds 1984, p.242, no. 32.44.
31. The Hague–London 1970–71, no. 2. Reynolds 1984, no. 32.44, catalogues the copy with works done by Constable in 1832, but writes: 'There is no clue to the occasion on which this copy was made.'
32. Ruisdael's *Windmills* was part of the 1811 bequest of Sir Peter Bourgeois RA (1756–1811) of more than three hundred pictures to Dulwich (in a posthumous 1813 inventory of his holdlings [no. 246] it is listed as by Rembrandt). Bourgeois, in turn, acquired the Ruisdael and many of his other paintings from the bequest of the dealer Noel Desenfans (1744–1807), his close friend. Nothing indicates that Constable had an opportunity to study or copy the Ruisdael when it belonged to Bourgeois or Desenfans.
33. Beckett 1966, 4, p.330. Pictures were being lent from the Dulwich Picture Gallery to the Royal Academy; *ibid.*, note 2. Also see Reynolds 1996, 1, p.252, no. 32.44.
34. Beckett 1966, 4, pp.349–50.
35. Beckett 1966, 6, pp.264–65.
36. Canvas, 58.1 × 70.8. Signed, lower right, with an imitation Ruisdael signature. PROVENANCE: Trustees of the Will of H. G. Howe; dealer Noortman, Maastricht, who sold it to a private collector, 2002. LITERATURE: Reynolds 1984, p.242, no. 32.43.
37. No support has been found for the claim made in the early literature that the *Winter Landscape with a View of the Amstel River and Amsterdam*, now in the Girardet Collection, Kettwig (Ruhr), was also in Peel's collection; see Slive 2001, no. 676, repr.
38. Parris *et al.* 1975, pp.61–2. Lucas's annotated copy of Leslie's *Memoirs of the Life of John Constable* is in the Huntington Library, San Marino, California.
39. Beckett 1970, p.64. Constable never published the ten discourses he delivered on landscape painting between 1833 and 1836; they are known chiefly from his original drafts and second-hand accounts, mainly by Leslie; cf. Beckett 1970, pp.28–37; Parris *et al.* 1975, pp.6–10. In a letter the artist wrote in 1833 there is a tantalizing reference to: 'My character of Ruysdael' which he cannot find; he adds: 'but I can always write it out . . . and better and better . . .' (Beckett 1970, p.32). Constable's sketch of the character of Ruisdael's work remains untraceable. Perhaps the comprehensive list he made in 1832 of the varieties of Ruisdael's landscapes is related to it. He lists: 'Rural Landscapes, such as/ Woodlands, & Woods./ Cottages, & Villages./ Cornfeilds [*sic*]./ Water & Windmills./ Ruins of/ Old Houses./ Churches./ Castles and Chateaux./ Sea Pieces/ Fishing Towns./ Sea Storms./ Boats and Fishermen./ Storms &c./ Waterfalls – Rural Scenery and Winter peices [*sic*]/ Sometimes moon lights./ John Constable – 1832.' (Beckett 1970, p.88). Apart from 'moon lights,' which are unknown today, the list is strikingly similar to the typology of Ruisdael's landscapes made by later cataloguers. The single notable omission is reference to identifiable topographical views.
40. Beckett 1970, p.64.
41. The sale catalogue is reprinted in Holmes 1902, pp.227–33.
42. Possibly the *Cornfield* is related to Constable's 1819 pencil drawing of Ruisdael's *Grainfield* (see fig. 37). Absence of a copy of Ruisdael's *Evening Landscape: A Windmill by a Stream*, now at Buckingham Palace, which Constable admired and stated he wanted 'to procure a memorandum of it' may indicate that he never fulfilled his wish (see above and Slive 2001, no. 130).
43. Beckett 1967, 5, p.67 (12 November 1833).
44. Beckett 1964, 2, p.301 (18 November 1823).
45. Holmes 1902, p.229.

APPENDIX: RUISDAEL'S PAINTINGS IN 17TH AND EARLY 18TH-CENTURY DUTCH INVENTORIES AND SALE CATALOGUES

1. The information on Haarlem is primarily derived from 105 probate inventories published by Biesboer 2001, pp. 72–354, and data pertinent to this investigation which are cited *ibid.*, pp. 34, 390; corrections have been made silently to material related to 'Ruisdael (no first name)' and 'Isaak Ruisdael', *ibid.*, p. 34. Additional data on Haarlem inventories is culled from Bredius 1915–22 and from an unpublished Getty Provenance Index Printout 'Dutch Inventories Ruisdael & Ruysdael Paintings,' 26 June 2002, kindly provided by Patricia A. Teter. An additional reference to 'a landscape with a river' by 'Ruysdael' valued at Dfl. 10 in a 1667 Haarlem inventory which was missed by Biesboer (2001, p. 188, no. 13) is noted by J. van der Veen (2004–05, p. 112); as will be seen, the oversight hardly modifies the findings of this appendix a trifle.
2. A systematic study of Amsterdam's inventories is not available. References cited here are principally from the sixty-seven pertinent Amsterdam inventories included in the unpublished Getty Provenance Index cited in Note 1 above. Bredius 1915–22 also offers material.
3. Inventory, Jacob van Dael, Amsterdam, 12 June 1684, 'een dito [landtschappie] sijnde een water valletje nae Ruijschdael in een dito [swarte] leijst'; cited in an unpublished Getty printout (see Note 1 above).
4. Inventory, Judith Elpen, Amsterdam, 20 December 1708, 'Een watervalle Ruijsdaels, copy [*sic*] Dfl. 3'; cited in an unpublished Getty printout (see Note 1 above).
5. Inventory, Hendrick Meyeringh, Amsterdam, 8 June 1687, 'Een waterval op de manier van Ruisdael'; see Bredius 1915–22, vol. 1, p. 339. Inventory, Thomas de Letter and Rebecca Anna van Tongeren, Amsterdam, 'Een schilderije verbeeldene een Ruijsdaeltje' and 'een dito [schilderije verbeeldene een Ruijsdaeltje]'; cited in an unpublished Getty printout (see Note 1 above).
6. The sale catalogues are published in Hoet 1752 (reprint; Soest, 1976). A sale at Amsterdam, 10 May 1664, which escaped Hoet's net, included a Ruisdael landscape which sold for Dfl. 60. More than twenty other paintings in the same sale by seventeenth-century Dutch artists, including Adriaen van de Velde and Jan van der Heyden, fetched prices that ranged from Dfl. 12 to Dfl. 42. Only a pair of pictures attributed to 'Bassant' (Bassano?) brought more; they sold for Dfl. 400 (Bredius 1900, pp. 182–84).
7. Sale, Amsterdam (Beukelaar), 16 September 1739, no. 100, 'Een fraai Landschap, van dito [Ruisdael], gestoffeert door denzelven'. Although the compiler does not say so, the painting may very well have been a copy or done in the artist's manner, since the sale included eighteen other paintings called 'Ruisdael' [nos. 84–99, 142], of which a half-dozen fetched significantly higher prices, ranging from Dfl. 20 to Dfl. 54.10. On the other hand, another half-dozen brought dismally low prices, ranging from Dfl. 2 to Dfl. 6; perhaps this group included dubious or poorly preserved works. In any event, to my knowledge, the paintings comprise the largest clutch of paintings called Ruisdael offered in an eighteenth-century auction (were they part of a dealer's stock?). The group included: no. 88. 'A Jewish Cemetery, very natural, by the same artist [Ruisdael]. Dfl. 11.10' (Een Joode Begraafplaats, zeer natuurlyk, door dezelven [Ruisdael]. Dfl. 11.10). If the painting was identical with the version of *The Jewish Cemetery* at Detroit or Dresden, it was one of the great bargains of the century.
8. Sale, Lambert Witsen, Amsterdam (Lambert), 25 May 1746, no. 83. 'A ditto [large landscape], by Ruisdael, with staffage by Berchem' Dfl. 151 (Een dito [groot Landschap], van Ruysdael, door Berghen gestoffeert). We have seen that Ruisdael's works never attained over-heated prices during the first half of the eighteenth century, but the price the Witsen Ruisdael fetched indicates that Altes's (2000–01, p. 267, note 60; 2003, p. 78, note 60) claim that none of the sixty-five or so paintings by Ruisdael listed in Hoet for the period 1676–1752 cost more than Dfl. 80 is too low by Dfl. 71. Another point about Witsen's 'Large landscape by Ruisdael with staffage by Berchem': perhaps it is identical with the painting given the very same description in a 1702 Amsterdam inventory (see Essay 2, p. 263, note 48 above). If so, both references may belong to the provenance of the Louvre's *Wooded Landscape with a Flooded Road* (fig. 30; S 397).

Select Bibliography and Abbreviations

A.Q.: *Art Quarterly*
van der Aa 1839–51: Abraham Jacob van der Aa, *Aardrijkskundig woordenboek der Nederlanden*, 13 vols., Gorinchem, 1839–51
Ackley 1981: Clifford S. Ackley, *Printmaking in the Age of Rembrandt*, Museum of Fine Arts, Boston – The Saint Louis Art Museum, 1981; includes an essay by William W. Robinson, " 'This Passion for Prints': Collecting and Connoisseurship in Northern Europe during the Seventeenth Century," pp.xxvii ff.
Ackley 1982: Clifford S. Ackley, "Ruisdael Reconsidered: Paintings & Prints," *The Print Collector's Newsletter*, 13, no. 4, September–October, pp.121–23
Adams 1985: Ann Jensen Adams, "The Paintings of Thomas de Keyser (1596/7–1667): A Study of Portraiture in Seventeenth-Century Amsterdam" (diss.), 3 vols., Harvard University, 1985
Agafonova 1935: K. Agafonova, "Ruisdael's Drawings in the Hermitage," *Iskusstvo*, 1935, no. 3, pp.177–84 (Russian text)
d'Ailly 1953: A.E. d'Ailly, *Repertorium van de profielen der stad Amsterdam en van de plattegronden der schutterswijken*, Amsterdam, 1953
d'Ailly 1963: A.E. d'Ailly, *Historische gids van Amsterdam*, ed. H.F. Wijnman, Amsterdam, 1963
Alexander-Knotter 1999: Mirjam Alexander-Knotter, "An Ingenious Device: Rembrandt's Use of Hebrew Inscriptions," *Studia Rosenthalia*, 33, 1999, pp.131-59
Altes 2000-01: Everhard Korthals Altes, "The eighteenth-century gentleman dealer Willem Lormier and the international dispersal of seventeenth-century paintings," *Simiolus*, 28, no. 4, 2000-01, pp.251-311
Altes 2003: Everhard Korthals Altes, *De verovering van de internationale Kunstmarkt door de zeventiende-eeuwse schilderkunst: enkele studies over de verspreiding van Hollandse schilderijen in de eerste helft van de achtiende eeuw* (University of Utrecht, Ph.D. diss.), 2003
Andrews 1983: Keith Andrews, " 'Ein Rotterdamer Maler und Radierer geringer Ordnung': on Some Gouaches by Gerrit van Battem," *Essays in Northern European Art Presented to Egbert Haverkamp-Begemann*, Doornspijk, 1983, pp.24–26
Apostool 1793: Cornelis Apostool, *The Beauties of the Dutch School: Selected from Interesting Pictures of Admired Landscape Painters*, London, 1793
Ashton *et al.* 1982: Peter Ashton, Alice I. Davies and Seymour Slive, "Jacob van Ruisdael's Trees," *Arnoldia*, 42, no. 1, Winter, 1982, pp.2–31
B.M.: *The Burlington Magazine*
Bachrach 1976: A.G.H. Bachrach, "Turner's Holland," *Dutch Quarterly Review*, 6, no. 2, 1976, pp.87–115
Bachrach [1980]: A.G.H. Bachrach, "Turner, Ruisdael and the Dutch," *Turner Studies*, 1, no. 1, [1980], pp.19ff.
Bakker *et al.* 1988: B. Bakker, E. Fleurbaay and A.W. Gerlagh, *De verzameling Van Eeghen Amsterdamse tekeningen: 1600–1950*, Zwolle–Amsterdam, 1988
Bartsch; Bartsch 1797: Adam Bartsch, *Catalogue raisonné de toutes les estampes qui forment l'oeuvre de Rembrandt . . .*, 2 vols., Vienna, 1797
Bartsch 1803; Bartsch 1803–21: Adam Bartsch, *Le Peintre-graveur*, 21 vols., Vienna, 1803–21 (Bartsch's catalogue of Ruisdael's prints are listed vol. 1, 1803, pp.311–18, nos. 1–7); 2nd ed., Leipzig, 1818–76
Bartsch 1978–: *The Illustrated Bartsch*, sometime general editor, Walter L. Strauss, New York, 1978–(in progress)
Basan 1771: Pierre François Basan, *Recueil d'estampes gravées d'après les tableaux de cabinet de Monseigneur le Duc de Choiseul*, Paris, 1771
Beck 1972–91: Hans-Ulrich Beck, *Jan van Goyen 1596–1656. Ein Oeuvreverzeichnis*, vols. 1 & 2, Amsterdam 1972; vol. 3, Doornspijk, 1987; vol. 4, *Die Künstler um Jan van Goyen*, Doornspijk, 1991
Beckett 1952: R.B. Beckett, *John Constable and the Fishers. The Record of a Friendship*, London, 1952
Beckett 1964: R.B. Beckett (ed.), *John Constable's Correspondence: II. Early Friends and Maria Bicknell (Mrs. Constable)*, Ipswich, 1964
Beckett 1965: R.B. Beckett (ed.), *John Constable's Correspondence: III: The Correspondence with C.R. Leslie*, Ipswich, 1965
Beckett 1966: R.B. Beckett (ed.), *John Constable's Correspondence: IV: Patrons, Dealers and Fellow Artists*, Ipswich, 1966
Beckett 1967: R.B. Beckett (ed.), *John Constable's Correspondence: V: Various Friends, with Charles Boner and the Artist's Children*, Ipswich, 1967
Beckett 1968: R.B. Beckett (ed.), *John Constable's Correspondence: VI: The Fishers*, Ipswich, 1968
Beckett 1970: R.B. Beckett (ed.), *John Constable's Discourses*, Ipswich, 1970
Beening 1963: Theo Jan Beening, *Het landschap in de Nederlandse letterkunde van de Renaissance* (diss.), Nijmegen, 1963
Beenken 1943: Hermann Beenken, "Die Landschaftsschau Jakob van Ruisdaels," *Neue Beiträge deutscher Forschung. Wilhelm Worringer zum 60. Geburtstag*, Königsberg, 1943, pp.lff.
Benesch; Benesch 1973: Otto Benesch, *The Drawings of Rembrandt: Complete Edition in Six Volumes*, enlarged and edited by Eva Benesch, 6 vols., London, 1973
van Berge-Gerbaud 1997: Mària van Berge-Gerbaud, *Rembrandt et son école. Dessins de la collection Frits Lugt*, Paris, 1997
Bergvelt 1998: Ellinoor Bergvelt, *Pantheon der Gouden Eeuw. Van Nationale Konst-Gallerij tot Rijksmuseum van Schilderijen*, Zwolle, 1998
Biesboer 1995: Pieter Biesboer, "Topographical Identifications for a Number of 'Haerlempjes' by Jacob van Ruisdael," *Shop Talk: Studies in Honor of Seymour Slive*, Cambridge, Massachusetts, 1995, pp.36–39
Biesboer 2001: Pieter Biesboer, *Collections of Paintings in Haarlem: 1572–1745*, ed. Carol Togneri. Documents for the history of collecting. Netherlandish inventories: 1. The Provenance Index of the Getty Research Institute, 2001
Bille 1961: Clara Bille, *De Tempel der Kunst of het kabinet van den Heer Braamkamp*, 2 vols., Amsterdam, 1961
Binyon 1895: L. Binyon, *Dutch Etchers of the Seventeenth Century*, London, 1895
Blanc 1857–58: Charles Blanc, *Le Trésor de la curiosité*, 2 vols., Paris, 1857–58
Blanc 1861: Charles Blanc, *Histoire des Peintres de toutes les Écoles: École Hollandaise*, 2 vols., Paris, 1861
Blankert 1978: A. Blankert, *Museum Bredius: Catalogus van de schilderijen en tekeningen, met een biographie van Abraham Bredius door Louise Barnouw-de Ranitz*, The Hague, 1978
Blankert 1982: Albert Blankert, *Ferdinand Bol. Rembrandt's Pupil*, Doornspijk, 1982
Blankert 1991: Albert Blankert, *Museum Bredius: Catalogus van de schilderijen en tekeningen*, Zwolle, 1991 (revised and enlarged ed. of cat. published in 1978)
Bock and Rosenberg 1930: Elfried Bock and Jakob Rosenberg, *Die Zeichnungen niederländischer Meister im Kupferstichkabinett zu Berlin*, 2 vols., Berlin, 1930
Bode 1872: W. Bode, "Die Künstler von Haarlem," *ZfbK*, 7, 1872, pp.164–77
Bode 1890: W. Bode, "Ausstellung von Werken der niederländischen Kunst veranstaltet durch die kunstgeschichtliche Gesellschaft in Berlin, II, Die Gemälde aus Berliner Privatbesitz," *Jahrbuch der königlich preussischen Kunstsammlungen*, 11, 1890, pp.199ff.
Bode 1909: W. Bode, *Die Sammlung Oscar Huldschinsky*, Frankfurt a. M., 1909
Bode 1910: W. Bode, *Die gemäldegalerie des herrn. A. de Ridder*, Berlin, 1910
Bode 1913: Wilhelm von Bode, *The collection and pictures of the late Herr A. de Ridder in his villa at Schoenberg near Cronberg in the Taunus*, Berlin, 1913 [Trans. by Harry Virgin for the exhib. and private sale at F. Kleinberg Galleries, New York, 1913.]
Bode 1913a: W. Bode, *Catalogue of the collection of pictures and bronzes in the possession of Mr. Otto Beit*, London, 1913
Boekhoff and Winzer 1968: Hermann Boekhoff and Fritz Winzer (eds.), *Das grosse Buch der Graphik*, Braunschweig, 1968
Boers 1991: O. Boers, "Burg Bentheim op gevelstene," *Ons Amsterdam*, 43, 1991, pp.102–04
Bol 1969: Laurens J. Bol, *Holländische Maler des 17. Jahrhunderts nahe den grossen Meistern: Landschaften und Stilleben*, Braunschweig, 1969
Bol 1973: Laurens J. Bol, *Die holländische Marinemalerei des 17. Jahrhunderts*, Braunschweig, 1973
Bowron 1990: Edgar Peters Bowron, *European Paintings before 1900 in the Fogg Art Museum. A summary Catalogue including Paintings in the Busch-Reisinger Museum*, Cambridge, Massachusetts, 1990
Bradley 1917: William Aspenwall Bradley, "The Etchings of Jacob Ruysdael," *The Print Collector's Quarterly*, 7, 1917, pp.153–74
Bredius: A. Bredius, *The Paintings of Rembrandt*, 3rd ed. (revised by H. Gerson), London, 1969
Bredius 1883: A. Bredius, "Dutch pictures recently exhibited at Edinburgh," *The Academy: A Weekly Review of Literature, Science, and Art*, vol. 24, 29 December 1883, pp.439–40
Bredius 1888: Abraham Bredius, "Het geboortejaar van Jacob van Ruisdael," *O.H.*, 6, 1888, pp.21ff.
Bredius 1890: A. Bredius, "Die Ausstellung alter Gemälde aus sächsischem Privatbesitz in Leipzig," *ZfbK*, N.F. 1, 1890, pp.189–93
Bredius 1892: A. Bredius, "De schilder Johannes van de Cappelle," *O.H.*, 10, 1892, pp.31-40
Bredius *et al.* 1897–1904: A. Bredius *et al.*, *Amsterdam in de zeventiende eeuw*, 3 vols., Amsterdam, 1897–1904
Bredius 1900: A. Bredius, "Schilderij-prijzen te Amsterdam omstreeks 1664," *O.H.*, 18, 1900, pp.181–84

Bredius 1912: A. Bredius, "De nalatenschap van Jan van der Heyden's weduwe," *O.H.*, 30, 1912, pp.129ff.
Bredius 1912a: A. Bredius, "Iets over de copie van Gerrit Lundens naar Rembrandt's 'Nachtwacht,' " *O.H.*, 30, 1912, pp.197ff.
Bredius 1915: A. Bredius, "Twee testamenten van Jacob van Ruisdael," *O.H.*, 33, 1915, pp.19ff.
Bredius 1915a: A. Bredius, "Nog een en ander over Hobbema," *O.H.*, 33, 1915, pp.193–98
Bredius 1915–22: A. Bredius, *Künstler-Inventare: Urkunden zur Geschichte der holländischen Kunst des XVIten, XVIIten und XVIIIten Jahrhunderts*, 8 vols., The Hague, 1915–22
Bridgewater Collection 1851: *Catalogue of the Bridgewater Collection of Pictures Belonging to the Earl of Ellesmere at Bridgewater House, Cleveland Square, St. James's*, 4th ed., London, 1851
Britton *et al.* 1801–16: John Britton *et al.*, *The Beauties of England and Wales; or Delineations, topographical, historical and descriptive, of each county*, 18 vols. in 34 parts, London 1801–16
Britton 1808: John Britton, *Catalogue raisonné of the pictures belonging to the Most Honorable the Marquis of Stafford, in the gallery of Cleveland House*, London, 1808
Broos 1984: B.P.J. Broos, " 'Notitie der Teekeningen van Sybrand Feitama': de boekhouding van drie generaties verzamelaars van oude Nederlandse tekenkunst," *O.H.*, 98, 1984, pp.13–39
Broos 1984a: B.P.J. Broos, "Antoni Waterloo f(ecit)' in Maarsseveen", *Jaarboekje van het oudheidkundig genootschap "Niftalake,"* 1984, pp.18–48
Broos 1985: B.P.J. Broos, " 'Notitie der Teekeningen van Sybrand Feitama,' II: 'verkocht, verhandeld, verëerd, geruild en overgedaan,' " *O.H.*, 99, 1985, pp.110–34
Broos 1987: B.P.J. Broos, " 'Notitie der Teekeningen van Sybrand Feitama', III: der verzameling van Sybrand I Feitama (1620–1701) en van Isaac Feitama (1666–1709)," *O.H.*, 1987, pp.171–213
Broos 1987a: Ben Broos, *Meesterwerken in het Mauritshuis*, The Hague, 1987
Broos 1989: Ben Broos, "Improving and Finishing Old Master Drawings: an Art in Itself," *Hoogsteder-Naumann Mercury*, 8, 1989, pp.34–55
Broos and Schapelhouman 1993: Ben Broos and Marijn Schapelhouman, *Nederlandse tekenaars geboren tussen 1600 en 1660. Oude tekeningen van het Amsterdams Historisch Museum, waaronder de collectie Fodor*, Amsterdam–Zwolle, 1993
Broulhiet: Georges Broulhiet, *Meindert Hobbema*, Paris, 1938
Broun 1987: Francis Broun, *Sir Joshua Reynolds' Collection of Paintings*, 3 vols. (Princeton University, Ph.D. diss.), 1987
Brugmans 1930–33: Hajo Brugmans, *Geschiedenis van Amsterdam van den oorsprong af tot heden . . . Amsterdam*, 4 vols., Amsterdam, 1930–33
Brugmans and Frank 1940: Hendrick Brugmans and A. Frank, *Geschiedenis der Joden in Nederland*, Amsterdam, 1940
Brugmans and Peters [n.d.]: H. Brugmans and C.H. Peters, *Oud-Nederlandsche steden in haar ontstaan, groei en ontwikkeling*, 3 vols., Leiden [n.d.]
Bruyn 1987–88: Josua Bruyn, "Toward a Scriptural Reading of Seventeenth-Century Dutch Landscape Paintings," in Amsterdam–Boston–Philadelphia 1987–88, pp.84–103
Buchanan 1824: W. Buchanan, *Memoirs of Painting, with a Chronological History of the Importation of Pictures by the Great Masters into England Since the French Revolution*, 2 vols., London, 1824
Buisman 1924: Hendrik Buisman, *Museum Teyler Haarlem, Handzeichnungen alter Meister der holländischen Schule . . .*, Leipzig, 1924
Bulletin K.N.O.B.: *Bulletin van de(n) Koninklijke(n) Nederlands(ch)e(n) Oudheidkundige(n) Bond* with *Nieuwsbulletin*; started in 1899 as *Bulletin van den Nederlandschen Oudheidkundig Bond*; 1921–47, called *Oudheidkundig Jaarboek*
W. Bürger: Pseudonym of Étienne-Joseph-Théophile Thoré
Bürger 1857: W. Bürger, *Trésors d'art exposés à Manchester en 1857 et provenant des collections royales, des collections publiques et des collections particulières de la Grande-Bretagne*, Paris, 1857
Bürger 1858–60: W. Bürger, *Musées de la Hollande*, 2 vols., Paris, 1858–60 (1. *Amsterdam et La Haye*; 2. *Musée van der Hoop à Amsterdam et Musée de Rotterdam*)
Bürger 1865: W. Bürger, *Trésors d'Art en Angleterre*, 3rd ed., Paris, 1865
Bürger 1867: W. Bürger, "Les Collections Particulières" in *Paris guide par les principaux écrivains et artistes de la France*, 10th ed., Paris, 1867, pp.536–54
Bürger 1869: W. Bürger, "Nouvelles études sur la Galerie Suermondt: XIII. Les Ruisdael," *G.B.A.*, 1869, 1, pp.179–87
Burgess 1754: J[ames]. B[urgess]., *The Lives of the Most Eminent Modern Painters, Who have lived since, or were omitted by Mons. De Piles*, London, 1754
Burke 1974: James D. Burke, "Ruisdael and his Haarlempjes," *M, A Quarterly Review of the Montreal Museum of Fine Arts*, 6, no. 1, Summer 1974, pp.3ff.
Büttner and Unverfehrt 1993: Nils Büttner and Gerd Unverfehrt, *Jacob van Ruisdael in Bentheim. Ein niederländischer Maler und die Burg Bentheim im 17. Jahrhundert*, Bielefeld, 1993
Butlin and Joll 1977: Martin Butlin and Evelyn Joll, *The Paintings of J.M.W. Turner*, 2 vols., New Haven–London, 1977; rev. ed., New Haven–London, 1984
Carus: C. G. Carus, *Neun Briefe über Landschaftsmalerei, Geschrieben in den Jahren 1815 bis 1824*, Dresden [1955]
de Castro 1883: De Henriques de Castro, *Keur van Grafsteenen op de Nederl.-Portug.-Israël. Begraafplaats te Ouderkerk aan den Amstel*, Leiden, 1883
de Castro 1950: D.H. de Castro, *De Synagoge der Portugees-Israëlietische Gemeente te Amsterdam*, ed. J. Meyer, Amsterdam, 1950
de Chennevières 1880: Marquis [Philippe Pointel-] de Chennevières, *Les dessins de maîtres anciens exposées à l'École des Beaux-Arts en 1879*, Paris, 1880
Churchill 1935: W.A. Churchill, *Watermarks in Paper in Holland, England, France, etc., in the XVII and XVIII Centuries and their Interconnection*, Amsterdam, 1935
Clément de Ris 1859–61: L. Clément de Ris, *Les Musées de province*, 2 vols., Paris, 1859–61
Clément de Ris 1872: L. Clément de Ris, *Les musées de province. Histoire et description*, 2nd ed., Paris, 1872
Cleveland 1982: *The Cleveland Museum of Art Catalogue of Paintings. European Paintings of the 16th, 17th, and 18th Centuries*, part 3, Cleveland, 1982
Couprie 1998: Leendert D. Couprie, "Met Jacob van Ruisdael en zijn metgezel bij de Schermerpoort in Alkmaar," in Amsterdam 1998, pp.40–49
Cust 1903: Lionel Cust, *The Bridgewater Gallery. One Hundred and Twenty of the Most Noted Paintings at Bridgewater House . . .*, Westminster, 1903
Czobor 1967: Ágnes Czobor, *Holland Mestermüvek a XVII. századból*, Museum of Fine Arts, Budapest, 1967
Dapper 1663: O[lfert]. D[apper]., *Historische beschrijving der Stadt Amsterdam*, Amsterdam, 1663 (N.B., pagination of the volume is muddled in two places: pp.44–56 appear twice; pp.449–56 appear four times); reprint, Amsterdam, 1975
Davies 1972: Alice I. Davies, "Allart van Everdingen's Drawings of the Twelve Months," *The Register of the Museum of Art*, The University of Kansas, Lawrence, Kansas, 4, no. 9, 1972 [n.p.]
Davies 1978: Alice I. Davies, *Allart van Everdingen*, New York–London, 1978
Davies 1992: Alice I. Davies, *Jan van Kessel (1641–1680)*, Doornspijk, 1992
Davies 1993: Alice I. Davies, *16th- and 17th-Century Dutch and Flemish Paintings in the Springfield Museum of Fine Arts*, Springfield, Massachusetts, 1993
Davies 2001: Alice I. Davies, *Allart van Everdingen: First Painter of Scandinavian Landscape*, Doornspijk, 2001
Demont 1922: Louis Demonts, *Catalogue des peintures exposées dans les galeries, 3, Écoles Flamande, Hollandaise, Allemande et Anglaise*, Musée National du Louvre, Paris, 1922
Denison and Mules 1981: Cara D. Denison and Helen B. Mules, *European Drawings 1375–1825, The Pierpont Morgan Library*, New York, 1981
Deperthes 1822: J.B. Deperthes, *Histoire de l'art du paysage, depuis la renaissance des beaux arts jusqu'au dix-huitième siècle*, Paris, 1822
Descamps 1753–64: J.B. Descamps, *La vie des peintres flamands, allemands et hollandais*, 4 vols., Paris, 1753–64
Deys 1981: H.P. Deys, *Achter Berg en Rijn: Over boeren, burgers en buitenlui in Rhenen*, Wageningen, 1981
Dézallier d'Argenville 1745: [Antoine Joseph Dézallier d'Argenville], *Abrégé de la vie des plus fameux peintres . . .*, 2 vols., Paris, 1745
Dézallier d'Argenville 1752: [Antoine Joseph Dézallier d'Argenville], *Supplement a l'abrégé de la vie des plus fameux peintres . . .*, Paris, 1752
Dézallier d'Argenville 1762: [Antoine Joseph Dézallier d'Argenville], *Abrégé de la vie des plus fameux peintres . . .*, 3 vols., Paris, 1762
Dingeldein 1969: W.H. Dingeldein, *Singraven: Beelden uit verleden en heden van een Twentse havezate*, Enschede, 1969
DNB: *Dictionary of National Biography*, ed. Leslie Stephen *et al.*, 22 vols. London, 1885–1901
Dobroklonsky 1961: M.V. Dobroklonsky, *Grafika, Dessins des maîtres anciens*, Hermitage, Leningrad, 1961
Dodsley 1761: *London and its Environs Described. Containing an Account of Whatever is most remarkable for Grandeur, Elegance, Curiosity or Use, in the City and in the Country Twenty Miles round it . . .*, 6 vols., London, printed for R. and J. Dodsley, 1761 (published in the autumn of 1760; see Simpson 1951, p.356, note 15)
Döhmann and Dingeldein 1934: K. Döhmann and W.H. Dingeldein, *Singraven, de geschiedenis van een Twentsche havezate*, vol. 3, Brussels, 1934
van Domselaer 1665: [Tobias van Damselaer], *Beschryvinge van Amsterdam . . . Aemstel en Aemstellant . . .*, Amsterdam, 1665 (the volume is comprised of six books by T. van Domselaer, A. Montanus, *et al.*)
DRVK: Dienst voor 's-Rijks Verspreide Kunstvoorwerpen, The Hague
Dubiez 1967: F.J. Dubiez, "Beth Haim, Huis des Levens: de Portugees Israëlietische begraafplaats te Ouderkerk aan de Amstel," *Ons Amsterdam*, 19, 1967, pp.178–86; 205–12
Duchesne ainé [n.d., *c.*1825]: [Jean] Duchesne ainé, *Musée Français. Recueil des plus beaux tableaux, statues, et bas-reliefs qui existaient au Louvre avant 1815 . . .*, 4 vols., Paris–London [n.d., *c.*1825], texts in French and English
Duchesne ainé and Réveil 1828–34: *Musée de peinture et de sculpture, ou recueil des principaux tableaux, statues et bas reliefs des collections publique et particulières de l'Europe dessiné et gravé à l'eau-fort sur acier par [Étienne Achille] Réveil, avec des notices descriptives, critiques et historiques, par [Jean] Duchesne ainé*, 17 vols., London–Paris, 1828–34 (French and English texts)
Dudok van Heel 1969: S.A.C. Dudok van Heel, "Het Maecenaat De Graefen Rembrandt," *Amstelodamum*, 56, 1969, pp.150–55
Dudok van Heel 1975: S.A.C. Dudok van Heel, "Een minne met een kindje door Frans Hals," *Jaarboek Central Bureau voor Genealogie*, 29, 1975, pp.146–59
Dudok van Heel 1983: S.A.C. Dudok van Heel, "In presentie van de Heer Gerard ter Borch," *Essays in Northern European Art Presented to Egbert Haverkamp-Begemann on his Sixtieth Birthday*, Doornspijk, 1983, pp.66–71
Dumas and Plomp 1998: Charles Dumas and Michiel C. Plomp, "Karl la Fargue (1738–1793) as a forger of seventeenth-century Dutch drawings," *O.H.*, 112, 1998, pp.1–76
Dunlap 1965: William Dunlap, *A History of the Rise and Progress of the Arts of Design in the United States*, ed. Alexander Wyckoff, 3 vols., New York, 1965 (1st ed. 1834)
Duparc 1981–82: F.J. Duparc, " 'Het Joodse Kerkhof' van Jacob van Ruisdael," *Antiek*, 15, 1981–82, pp.225–30
Duplessis 1878: Georges Duplessis, *Eaux-Fortes de J. Ruysdael*, Paris, 1878
Dutuit 1885: E. Dutuit, *Manuel de l'amateur d'estampes*, vol. 6, Paris–London, 1885
DVR: Dienst Verspreide Rijkscollecties, The Hague
Eckermann 1955: Johann Peter Eckermann, *Gespräche mit Goethe in den letzten Jahren seines Lebens*, ed. F. Bergermann, Wiesbaden, 1955
Edwards 1996: JoLynn Edwards, *Alexandre-Joseph Paillet, Expert et marchand de tableau à la fin du XVIIe siècle*, Paris, 1996
van Eeghen 1953: I.H. v[an]. E[eghen]., "De Geschiedenis van het Eiland Vlooienburg," *Amstelodamum*, 40, 1953, pp.17–23
van Eeghen 1969: I.H. van Eeghen, "Rembrandt aan de Amstel" in *Rembrandt aan de Amstel*, published by Genootschap Amstelodamum, Amsterdam, 1969 [n.p.]

van Eeghen 1973: I.H. van Eeghen, "Archivalia betreffende Jan van der Heyden," *Amstelodamum*, 60, 1973, pp.29–36, 54–61, 73–79, 99–106, 128–34
van Eeghen 1974: I.H. van Eeghen, "Illustraties van de 17de eeuwse beschrijvingen en plaatwerken van Amsterdam," *Jaarboek Amstelodamum*, 66, 1974, pp.96–116
Eigenberger 1927: Robert Eigenberger, *Die Gemäldegalerie der Akademie der bildenden Künste in Wien*, 2 vols., Vienna–Leipzig, 1927
Ellis 1826: George Agar Ellis [1st Baron Dover], *Catalogue of the principal pictures in Flanders and Holland 1822*, London, 1826
Emperius 1816: J.F.F. Emperius, "Über die Wegführung und die Zurückkunft der Braunschweigischen Kunst- und Bücherschätze," *Braunschweigisches Magazin*, 28, 1816, cols. 1–64
Engerand 1901: Fernand Engerand, *Inventaire des tableaux commandés et achetés par la direction des bâtiments du Roi (1709–1792)*, Paris, 1901
Eudel 1882–91: Paul Eudel, *L'Hôtel Drouot en 1881–88*, 9 vols., Paris, 1882–91
Evelyn 1955: John Evelyn, *The Diary of John Evelyn*, ed. E.S. de Beer, vol. 2, *Kalendarium, 1620–1649*, Oxford, 1955
Farington 1978–84: *The Diary of Joseph Farington*, ed. Kenneth Garlick and Angus Macintyre (vols. 1–6), Kathryn Cave (vols. 7–16), New Haven–London, 1978–84
FARL: Frick Art Reference Library, New York
Fechner 1958: E. Fechner, *Paintings by Jacob van Ruisdael in the Hermitage*, Leningrad, 1958 (Russian text)
Fechner 1963: E. Fechner, *Seventeenth-Century Dutch Landscapes in the Hermitage*, Leningrad, 1963 (Russian text)
Feitama II, NdT + number: Refers to Fritz Lugt's typed copy (at the RKD) after the ms. (also at the RKD) of Sybrand Feitama II, *Notitie der Teekeningen . . .*, see entry below
Feitama II, *Notitie der Teekeningen:* Sybrand Feitama II, *Notitie der Teekeningen uit de oudste en latere aanteekeningen, sedert de jaren 1685 en 1690, tot 1746, somtyds met volle zekerheid, somtyds naar de beste gissinge, of naar myn geheugen, opgemaakt*. A manuscript of the *Notitie* is at the RKD. It is an annotated inventory of the drawings Sybrand II (1694–1758), his grandfather Sybrand I (1620–1701) and his father Isaac (1666–1709) acquired and, in some cases, includes references to their subsequent history. Extended studies of large parts of it, that include scrupulous transcriptions, are in Broos 1984, 1985, 1987; also see Broos 1989. Among the 41 (not 38) Ruisdael drawings listed in it, 13 are recorded as entering the collection *c.*1690. It is not certain if these sheets were acquired by Sybrand I or Isaac
Filhol 1804–15: *Galerie du Musée Napoléon, publiée par [Antoine] Filhol . . . redigée par [Joseph] Lavalée . . .*, 10 vols., Paris, 1804–15 (originally issued in 120 livraisons, each including 6 plates and an explanatory text on pages that begin with number 1 in each livraison; see Filhol 1828 for a volume bearing a different title that was published as vol. 11 of the set)
Filhol 1828: *Galerie du Musée France, publiée par [Antoine] Filhol . . . le texte redigée par [Joseph] Lavalée . . . et continué par A. Jal . . .*, vol. 11, Paris, 1828 (published as vol. 11 of Filhol 1804–15; originally issued in 12 livraisons, each including 6 plates and an explanatory text on pages that begin with number 1 for in each livraison)
Finberg 1909: A.J. Finberg, *A Complete Inventory of the Drawings of the Turner Bequest arranged chronologically*, 2 vols., London, 1909
Fink 1954: A. Fink, *Geschichte des Herzog Anton Ulrich-Museums in Braunschweig*, Braunschweig, 1954
Fleischer 1989: R.E. Fleischer, *Ludolf de Jongh (1616–1679). Painter of Rotterdam*, Doornspijk, 1989
Fleming-Williams 1990: Ian Fleming-Williams, *Constable and His Drawings*, London, 1990
Fleming-Williams *et al.* 1994–95: Ian Fleming-Williams *et al.*, *Constable, a Master Draughtsman*, exhib. cat., Dulwich Picture Gallery, London–Art Gallery of Ontario, Toronto–The Frick Collection, New York, 1994–95
Fodor Collection 1863: *Beschrijving der schilderijen, teekeningen, prenten en boeken, in het Museum Fodor te Amsterdam*, Amsterdam, 1863
Fokkens 1662: Melchior Fokkens, *Beschrijvinge der Wijdt-vermaarde Koop-stadt Amstelredam*, Amsterdam, 1662
Foucart 1969: Bruno Foucart, "La fortune critique d'Alexandre Lenoir et du premier musée des monuments français," *L'Information d'Histoire de l'Art*, 14, no. 5, 1969, pp.225–32
Frerichs 1963: L.D.J. Frerichs, *Keuze van tekeningen bewaard in het Rijksprentenkabinet, Rijksmuseum, Amsterdam*, Amsterdam, 1963
Frimmel 1891–92: Theodor Frimmel, *Kleine Galeriestudien*, 2 parts, Bamberg, 1891–92
von Frimmel 1896: Theodor von Frimmel, *Kleine Galeriestudien*, N.F., 3, *Die Gräflich Schönborn-Buchheimsche Gemäldesammlung in Wien*, Leipzig, 1896
von Frimmel 1901: Theodor von Frimmel, *Geschichte der Wiener Gemäldesammlungen, viertes Capitel: Der Galerie in der Akademie der bildenden Künste*, Leipzig-Berlin, 1901
von Frimmel 1913: Theodor von Frimmel, *Lexikon der Wiener Gemäldesammlungen*, vol. 1, Munich, 1913
Fromentin 1876: Eugène Fromentin, *Les Maîtres d'autrefois*, Paris, 1876 (frequently reprinted and translated; see following entry)
Fromentin 1963: Eugène Fromentin, *The Old Masters of Belgium and Holland*, translation of *Les Maîtres d'autrefois* by Mary C. Robbins, 1882, intro. by Meyer Schapiro, New York, 1963 (Schapiro's brilliant introduction is reprinted in his *Theory and Philosophy of Art: Style, Artist and Society*, New York, 1994)
Fuchs 1973: R.H. Fuchs, "Over het landschap. Een verslag naar aanleiding van Jacob van Ruisdael, 'Het Korenveld'," *Tijdschrift voor Geschiedenis*, 86, 1973, pp.281–92
G.B.A.: *Gazette des Beaux-Arts*
GAA: Gemeentearchief, Amsterdam
Gage 1980: John Gage, *Goethe on Art*, Berkeley–Los Angeles, 1980 (selected, edited and translated by John Gage)
Gage 1980a: John Gage, *Collected Correspondence of J.M.W. Turner*, Oxford, 1980
GAH: Gemeentearchief, Haarlem
Galerie du Musée Napoleon: see Fihol 1804–15 and Landon 1805
Gaskell 1990: Ivan Gaskell, *The Thyssen-Bornemisza Collection: Seventeenth-century Dutch and Flemish Painting*, London, 1990
Geffroy [1905]: Gustave Geffroy, *Les Musées d'Europe, la Hollande*, Paris, [1905]
van Gelder 1922: H.E. van Gelder, "De Verzameling-Bredius," *Med.*, 4, 1922, pp.127–33
van Gelder 1933: J.G. van Gelder, *Jan van de Velde. 1593–1641. Teekenaar-Schilder*, The Hague, 1933
van Gelder and Kistemaker 1983: Roelof van Gelder and Renée Kistemaker, *Amsterdam: 1275–1795, De ontwikkeling van een handelsmetropol*, Amsterdam, 1983
Gerson 1934: H. Gerson, "The Development of Ruisdael," *B.M.*, 65, 1934, pp.76ff.
Gerson 1936: H. Gerson, *Philips Koninck*, Berlin, 1936
Gerson 1941: H. Gerson, *Leven en werken van Claes v. Beresteyn*, The Hague, 1940 (in E.A. van Beresteyn, *Genealogie van het Geslacht van Beresteyn*, vol. 2, The Hague, 1941, pp.143–74)
Gerson 1942: H. Gerson, *Ausbreitung und Nachwirkung der holländischen Malerei des 17. Jahrhunderts*, Haarlem, 1942; 2nd ed., enlarged by B.W. Meijer, Amsterdam, 1983
Gerson 1952: H. Gerson, *De Nederlandse Schilderkunst, 2, Het Tijdperk van Rembrandt en Vermeer*, Amsterdam, 1952
Gerson 1953: H. Gerson, "Dutch Landscape," review of London 1952–53 exhibition, *B.M.*, 95, 1953, pp.47ff.
Gerson [n.d., *c.*1966]: H. Gerson, *Jacob van Ruisdael: Maestri del Colore, no. 183*, Milan [n.d., *c.*1966]
Gerson 1971: H. Gerson, "Le Siècle de Rembrandt," (review of exhib. Paris 1970–71), *Kunstchronik*, 24, 1971, pp.148ff.
Gerszi 1986: Teréz Gerszi, "Jacob van Ruisdael und die Bruegel-Nachwirkung," *Orient und Okzident im Spiegel der Kunst, Festschrift Heinrich Gerhard Franz zum 70. Geburtstag*, ed. Günther Brucher *et al.*, Graz, 1986, pp.139–46
Getty Research Institute: The Getty Research Institute for the History of Art and the Humanities, Los Angeles, California
Giltay 1977: J. Giltay, "Guillam du Bois als tekenaar," *O.H.*, 91, 1977, pp.144ff.
Giltay 1980: J. Giltay, "De tekeningen van Jacob van Ruisdael," *O.H.*, 94, nos. 2–3, 1980, pp.141–208
Giltay 1983: J. Giltay, "Abraham Furnerius en Gerrit van Battem," *Essays in Northern European Art Presented to Egbert Haverkamp-Begemann*, Doornspijk, 1983, pp.97–101
Giltaij 1992: J. Giltaij, "The problem of Isaack van Ruisdael (1599–1677)," *B.M.*, 134, 1992, pp.180–82
Giltaij 1995: J. Giltaij, "Further Additions to Jacob van Ruisdael," *Shop Talk: Studies in Honor of Seymour Slive*, Cambridge, Massachusetts, 1995, pp.87–88
Goedde 1989: Lawrence O. Goedde, *Tempest and Shipwreck in Dutch and Flemish Art: Convention, Rhetoric and Interpretation*, University Park, Pennsylvania, 1989
Goethe 1790: Johann Wolfgang von Goethe, [notes in a 1771 Dresden Gallery catalogue], 1790, in *Goethes Werke*, vol. 47, Weimar, 1896, pp.368–87
Goethe 1816: Johann Wolfgang von Goethe, "Ruysdael als Dichter," *Morgenblatt für gebildete Stände*, Tübingen, no. 107, 3 May 1816, reprinted in *Goethes Werke, Hamburger Ausgabe*, ed. E. Trunz *et al.*, 7th rev. ed., vol. 12, Munich, 1973, pp.141–42; 611–13 (commentary by H. von Einem)
van Gool 1750–51: J. van Gool, *De nieuwe schouburgh der Nederlantsche kunstschilders en schilderessen*, 2 vols., The Hague, 1750–51
Gore 1957: St. John Gore, "Pictures in National Trust Houses: II," *B.M.*, 99, 1957, pp.175ff.
Götker, 1964: H. Götker, "Beitrag zur Baugeschichte der Burg Bentheim," *Jahrbuch des Heimatvereins der Grafschaft Bentheim*, 1964, pp.96–100
Gower 1875: Lord Ronald Gower, *A Pocket Guide to the Public and Private Galleries of Holland and Belgium*, London, 1875
Graves 1912: Algernon Graves, *Summary of and Index to Waagen*, London, 1912
Grimschitz 1957: Bruno Grimschitz, *Ferdinand Georg Waldmüller*, Salzburg, 1957
Groesbeek 1966: M.J. Groesbeek, *Amstelveen: Acht eeuwen geschiedenis*, Amsterdam, 1966
Groesbeek 1981: J.W. Groesbeek, *Middleeuwse kastelen van Noord-Holland, hun bewoners en bewogen geschiedenis*, Rijswik, 1981
de Groot 1979: Irene de Groot, *Landscape Etchings by the Dutch Masters of the Seventeenth Century*, Maarssen, 1979
Gudlaugsson 1950: S.J. Gudlaugsson, "Jan Andrea Lievens als schilder van ruiterportretten," *O.H.*, 65, 1950, pp.123–24
Gudlaugsson 1959–60: S.J. Gudlaugsson, *Gerard ter Borch*, 2 vols., The Hague, 1959–60
van der Haagen 1932: J.K. van der Haagen, *De schilders van der Haagen en hun werk*, Voorburg, 1932
Haak 1981: B. Haak, "Het Huis Kostverloren aan de Amstel, Jacob van Ruisdael, 1628/29–1682," *Vereniging Rembrandt, Nationaal Funds Kunstbehoud*, 1981, pp.91–93
de Haan 1966: Tj.W.R. de Haan (ed.), *Zeven heerlijkheden. Over geschiedenis en volksleven der voormalige gemeente Schoten*, The Hague, 1966
Hagels 1968: Herman Hagels, "Die Gemälde der niederländischen Maler Jacob van Ruisdael und Nicolaas Berchem vom Schloss Bentheim im Verhältnis zur Natur des Bentheimer Landes," *Jahrbuch des Heimatvereins der Grafschaft Bentheim*, 1968, pp.41ff.
Hagens 1979: H. Hagens, *Molens, Mulders, Meesters*, Hengelo, 1979
Hagens 1982: H. Hagens, "Jacob van Ruisdael, Meindert Hobbema in de identificatie-zucht," *'t Inschein*, 14, no. 1, January 1982, pp.7–12
Hagens and Elling 1991: H. Hagens, "Van Religie tot Romantiek; de watermolen in kanon, kerk en kunst" in H. Hagens and W. Elling, *Watermolens*, Oldenzaal, 1991
Haskell 1976: Francis Haskell, *Rediscoveries in Art. Some Aspects of Taste, Fashion and Collecting in England and France*, London, 1976
Hauke 1969: W. Hauke, "Der Landschaftsmaler Johann Jakob Dorner der Jüngere," *Oberbayerisches Archiv*, 91, 1969
Hausmann 1831: Bernhard Hausmann, *Verzeichniss der Hausmann'schen Gemählde Sammlung in Hannover*, Braunschweig, 1831
Haverkamp Begemann 1973: E. Haverkamp Begemann, *Hercules Segers. The Complete Etchings*, suppl. on Johannes Ruischer by E. Trautscholdt, Amsterdam–The Hague, 1973

Haverkamp-Begemann 1995: Egbert Haverkamp-Begemann, "Jacob van Ruisdael's Interest in Construction," *Shop Talk: Studies in Honor of Seymour Slive*, Cambridge, Massachusetts, 1995, pp.97–99

Hayes 1966: John Hayes, "British Patrons and Landscape Painting: 2. Eighteenth Century Collecting," *Apollo*, 83, 1966, pp.188–97

Hayes 1970: John Hayes, *The Drawings of Thomas Gainsborough*, 2 vols., London, 1970

Hayes 1982: John Hayes, *The Landscape Paintings of Thomas Gainsborough*, 2 vols., London, 1982

HdG: see Hofstede de Groot

Heseltine Collection 1910: *Original Drawings by Old Dutch Masters in the Collection of J.P. H[eseltine].*, London, 1910

Heyns 1625: Zacharias Heyns, *Emblemata, emblemes chrestienes, et morales. Sinne-beelden streekende tot christelicke bedenckinghe ende leere der zedicheyt*, Rotterdam, 1625

Hijmans 1951: H. Hijmans, *Wijk bij Duurstede*, Rotterdam–The Hague, 1951

Hind 1915–31: Arthur M. Hind, *Catalogue of Drawings by Dutch and Flemish Artists . . . in the British Museum*, 4 vols., London, 1915–31

Hinterding and Horsch 1989: Erik Hinterding and Femy Horsch, " 'A small but choice collection': the art gallery of King Willem II of the Netherlands (1792–1849)," *Simiolus*, 19, 1989, pp.5–122

Hoet; Hoet 1752: Gerard Hoet, *Catalogus of naamlyst van schilderyen, met derzelver pryzen zedert een langen reeks van Jaaren zoo in Holland als op andere plaatzen in het openbaar verkogt* . . . , 2 vols., The Hague, 1752; Hoet's transcriptions of sale catalogues and collections were continued by Pieter Terwesten [Terw.; Terwesten 1770], *Catalogus of naamlyst van schilderyen, met derselver prysen, zedert den 22. Augusti 1752. tot 21. November 1768* . . . , The Hague, 1770 (reprint, 3 vols., Soest, 1976)

Hoetink *et al.* 1985: H.R. Hoetink *et al.*, *The Royal Picture Gallery Mauritshuis*, Amsterdam – New York, 1985

Hofstede de Groot 1893: C. Hofstede de Groot, "Hollandsche kunst in Schotland," *O.H.*, 11, 1893, pp.129ff., 211ff.

HdG; HdG Zus.; HdG, Hobbema; Hofstede de Groot 1911: C. Hofstede de Groot, *Beschreibendes und kritisches Verzeichnis der Werke der hervorragendsten holländischen Maler des XVII. Jahrhunderts*, vol. 4, Esslingen a. N.–Paris, 1911. The Supplement = Zusätze [HdG Zus.] to the Ruisdael entries in the volume are listed pp.334–54

HdG, 1–10; Hofstede de Groot 1908–27: C. Hofstede de Groot, *Beschreibendes und kritisches Verzeichnis der Werke der hervorragendsten holländischen Maler des XVII. Jahrhunderts*, 10 vols., Esslingen, a. N.–Paris, 1907–28. English trans. of vols. 1–8 by E.G. Hawke, London 1908–27

Hollstein: F.W.H. Hollstein, *Dutch and Flemish Etchings, Engravings and Woodcuts*, 1–, Amsterdam, 1947–(in progress)

Hollstein–de Hoop Scheffer 1978: Dieuwke de Hoop Scheffer, *Hollstein's Dutch and Flemish Etchings, Engravings and Woodcuts*, vol. 20, Amsterdam, 1978 (includes a catalogue of Ruisdael's etchings)

Holmes 1902: C.J. Holmes, *Constable and His Influence on Landscape Painting*, Westminster, 1902

de Hoop Scheffer 1978: see Hollstein–de Hoop Scheffer 1978

Houbraken 1718–21: A. Houbraken, *De groote schouburgh der Nederlantsche konstschilders en schilderessen*, 3 vols., Amsterdam, 1718–21; 2nd ed. The Hague, 1753

Houlditch V+A: MS 86.00 18–19 [Richard Houlditch, Jr.] Sale Catalogues of the Principal Collections of Pictures (One Hundred and Seventy-one in number). Sold by Auction in England within the years 1711–1759, the greater part of them with the Prices and Names of Purchasers. The catalogues are at the Victoria and Albert Museum, London

Huffel 1921: N.G. van Huffel, *Cornelis Ploos van Amstel Jacob Corneliszoon, en zijne medewerkers en tijdgenooten. Historische schets van de techniek der Hollandsche prentteekeningen gemaakt in de tweede helft der 18e eeuw*, Utrecht, 1921

Imdahl 1968: Max Imdahl, *Die Mühle von Wijk*, Stuttgart, 1968

Ingamells 1981: John Ingamells (ed.), *The Hertford Mawson Letters: The 4th Marquess of Hertford to his agent Samuel Mawson*, London, 1981

Ireland 1796: Samuel Ireland, *A Picturesque Tour through Holland, Brabant, and part of France; Made in the Autumn of 1789*, 2 vols., London, 1796

Ivy 1991: Judy Croesly Ivy. *Constable and the Critics: 1802–1837*, Woodbridge, 1991

Jal, A.: see Filhol 1828

Jameson 1844: Mrs. [A.B.M.] Jameson, *Companion to the most celebrated private Galleries of Art in London*, London, 1844

de Jongh 1995: E. de Jongh, *Kwesties van betekenis. Thema en motief in de Nederlandse schilderkunst van de zeventiende eeuw*, Lieden, 1995 (includes "Bergen in de Lage Landen," a lecture delivered in 1988)

Josi 1821: C. Josi, *Collection d'imitations de dessins d'après les principaux maîtres hollandais et flamands, commencée par C. Ploos van Amstel, continuée et portée au nombre de cent morceaux* . . . , 2 vols., London, 1821

Jowell 1977: Frances Suzman Jowell, *Thoré-Bürger and the Art of the Past* (diss.), New York–London, 1977

Kalf 1980: E.J. Kalf, "De 'Val van Damiate' of het nut van vergissingen," *Haerlem Jaarboek* 1980, Haarlem, 1981, pp.7–26

Kalff 1919: S. Kalff, "De Ruisdael-familie," *Elsevier's Geïllustreerd Maandschrift*, 1919, pp.321–38, 377–86

Kamp 1968: R.D. Kamp, "Jacob van Ruisdael, Nicolaes Berchem und Schloss Bentheim. Ein kunsthistorischer Beitrag über zwei holländische Landschaftsmaler der 17. Jahrhunderts," *Jahrbuch des Heimatvereins der Grafschaft Bentheim*, 1968, pp.53–56

Kannegieter 1965: J.Z. Kannegieter, "Uit de wordingsgeschiedenis van de Leidsegracht en haas naaste omgeving," *Jaarboek Amstelodamum*, 57, 1965, pp.48–69

Kauffmann 1977: Hans Kauffmann, "Jacob van Ruisdael: 'Die Mühle von Wijk bei Duurstede,' " *Festschrift für Otto von Simson zum 65. Geburtstag*, ed. L. Grisebach and K. Renger, Frankfurt a. M., 1977, pp.379–97

Keyes 1975: George Shepard Keyes, *Cornelis Vroom: Marine and Landscape Artist* (diss.), 2 vols., Utrecht, 1975

Keyes 1977: George (not Roger) S. Keyes, "Les eaux-fortes de Ruisdael," *Nouvelles de l'Estampe*, no. 36, November–December, 1977, pp.7ff.

Keyes 1989: George Keyes, review of "Landscape in Perspective... [Cambridge–Monreal 1988]", in *Master Drawings*, 27, 1989

Keyes 1999: George Keyes, "Isaack van Ruisdael: further Reconsiderations", *Ex Fumo Lucem. Baroque Studies in Honour of Klara Garas*, ed. Z. Dobos, 2 vols., Budapest, 1999, vol. 1., pp.155–66

Kistemaker *et al.* 1987: *êxodo. Portugezen in Amsterdam: 1600–1680*, ed. Renée Kistemaker and Tirtshah Levie, Amsterdam Historical Museum, 1987

Kleinmann [n.d.]: H. Kleinmann, *Handzeichnungen alter Meister der hollaendischen Schule* . . . , 4 vols., Haarlem [n.d.]

Klessmann 1983: Rüdiger Klessmann, *Herzog Anton Ulrich-Museum Braunschweig, Die holländischen Gemälde*, Braunschweig, 1983

Kloek and Niemeijer 1990: W.Th. Kloek and J.W. Niemeijer, *De kasteeltekeningen van Roelant Roghman*, vol. 2, Alphen aan den Rijn, 1990

Klynder 1873: A.Y. Klynder, *Dessins de grand maîtres conservés au Musée de L'Ermitage Impérial, Reproduits par la photographie* . . . , St. Petersburg, 1863

Knoef 1948: J. Knoef, "De verzamelaar A. van der Hoop", *Jaarboek van het Genootschap Amstelodamum*, 42, 1948, pp.51–71

Knuttel 1926: G. Knuttel Wzn., *Museum Bredius, Gids met beknopten catalogus van de schilderijen en teekeningen*, [The Hague], 1926

Kolks 1980: Z. Kolks, "Zwei wenig bekannte Gemälde vom Schloss Bentheim," *Jahrbuch des Heimatvereins der Grafschaft Bentheim*, 1980, pp.105ff.

Kolloff 1841: Eduard Kolloff, *Beschreibung der Königlichen Museen und Privat-Galerin zu Paris*, Pforzheim–Paris, 1841

Korn 1978: U.D. Korn, "Ruisdael in Steinfurt," *Westfalen: Hefte für Geschichte, Kunst und Volkskunde*, 56, 1978, pp.111–14

Kouznetsov 1973: Iouryi Kouznetsov, "Sur le symbolisme dans les paysages de Jacob van Ruisdael," *Bulletin du Musée National de Varsovie*, 14, 1973, pp.31ff. (N.B. This Russian author's names are transliterated differently in French [as seen here], German [Juri Kusnezow], English [Yury Kuznetsov], and Estonian [Jurii Kuznetzov]; for the last three, see below.)

Kronig 1914: J.O. Kronig, *A Catalogue of the Paintings at Doughty House, Richmond and Elsewhere in the Collection of Sir Frederick Cook, Bt.*, vol. 2, *Dutch and Flemish Schools*, ed. Herbert Cook, London, 1914

Kruizinga 1973: J.H. Kruizinga, *Amsterdam, stad der duizend bruggen*, Naarden, 1973

Krul 1956: H. Krul, "Das Schloss zu Bentheim und die Ereignisse im Jahr 1795," *Jahrbuch des Heimatvereins der Grafschaft Bentheim*, 1956, pp.73–82

Kusnezow 1975: Juri Kusnezow, *Holländische und flämische Meisterzeichnungen*, trans. J. Rehork, Munich, 1975

Kusnezow 1981: *Ermitage. Westeuropäische Zeichnungen*, ed. Juri Kusnezow, Leningrad, 1981

Kuyper 1980: W. Kuyper, *Dutch Classicist Architecture*, Delft 1980

Kuznetsov 1960: Jurii Kuznetsov, "Hollandi Maastrkumaalija– Meindert Hobbema (1638–1709)," *Kunst: Kujutava ja Tarbekunsti Almanahh*, 1960, no. 3, pp.34–39 (in Estonian)

Kuznetsov 1975: Y. Kuznetsov, "Zabytaia kartina Jakoba van Reisdaly" (Russian text: "A Forgotten Painting by Jacob van Ruisdael"), *Pamiatniki Kultury: Nooye Otkrytiia. Pis'-mennost Iskusstvo. Arhiologiia Ezhegodnik AN SSR.M.: Nauka*, 1975, pp.377–80

Kuznetsov and Linnik 1982: Yury Kuznetsov and Irene Linnik, *Dutch Painting in Soviet Museums*, New York–Leningrad, 1982

L; Lugt 1921–56: Frits Lugt, *Les marques de collections de dessins et d'estampes*, Amsterdam, 1921; Supplement, The Hague, 1956

Lafenestre and Richtenberger 1897: Georges Lafenestre and Eugène Richtenberger, *La peinture en Europe. La Hollande: La Haye*, Paris, 1897

Lairesse 1707: Gérard Lairesse, *Groot Schilderboek, Waar in de Schilderkonst in al Haar Deelen Grondig werd onderweezen* . . . , 2 vols., Amsterdam, 1707 (2nd ed., 1712)

Landon 1805: C.P. Landon (ed.), *Paysages et tableaux de genre*, 4 vols., Paris, 1805–8 (the volumes are part of Landon's *Annales du Musée et de l'École moderne des Beaux-Arts. Recueil de gravures du trait, conterant la collection complète des peintures et sculptures du Musée Napoléon; les principaux chefs-d'oeuvre du Musée de Versailles; et de celui des Monuments français, aux petits-Augustins de Paris; les productions des Artistes vivants* . . . , 42 vols., Paris, 1800–22; a 21 vol. edition of the *Annales* was published in London–Paris in 1815; a 2nd ed. appeared in Paris, 1825; title pages of the vols. vary)

Landon 1815: see Landon 1805

Landon 1825: see Landon 1805

Landwehr 1973: John Landwehr, *Romeyn de Hooghe the Etcher*, New York, 1973

Laurentius *et al.* 1980: Th. Laurentius, J.W. Niemeijer, G. Ploos van Amstel, *Cornelis Ploos van Amstel 1726–1798. Kunstverzamelaar en prentuitgever*, Assen, 1980

Lavalée, Joseph: see Filhol 1804–15

Le Brun 1777–90: J.B.P. Le Brun, *Galerie des peintres flamands, hollandais et allemands*, 12 fascicles, Paris, 1777–90

Le Brun 1792–96: J.B.P. Le Brun, *Galerie des peintres flamands, hollandais et allemands; Ouvrage enrichi de deux cent une planches gravées d'après les meilleurs Tableaux des ces Maîtres*. . . , 3 vols., Paris, 1792–96

Lebrun 1809: J.B.P. Lebrun, *Recueil de gravures au trait à l'eau forte et ombrées* . . . , 2 vols., Paris, 1809

Leeflang 1997: Huigen Leeflang, "Dutch landscape: the urban view. Haarlem and its environs in literature and art, 15th–17th century," *N.K.J.*, 48, 1997, pp.52–115

Leeflang 2002: Huigen Leeflang, "Ruisdael," *Print Quarterly*, 19, 2002, pp.413–16 (review of Slive 2001)

Leeflang 2002a: Huigen Leeflang, "Ruisdaels Natur," in Hamburg–Haarlem 2002, pp.21–27

Lehninger 1782: [Johann August Lehninger] *Abrége de la vie des peintres, dont les tableaux component la galerie electorale de Dresde. Avec le détail de tous les tableaux de cette collection et des éclaircissements historiques sur ces chefs-d'oeuvres de la peinture*, Dresden, 1782

Leslie 1951: C.R. Leslie, *Memoirs of the Life of John Constable*, edited text of the 2nd edition (1845) by J.H. Mayme, London, 1951

Liedtke 1989: Walter Liedtke, "Dutch and Flemish Paintings from the Hermitage: Some notes to an exhibition catalogue with special reference to Rembrandt, van Dyck and Jordaens," *O.H.*, 103, 1989, pp.154–68

Lillie 2003: Sophie Lillie, *Was ein war – Handbuch der enteigneten Kunstsammlungen Wiens*, (vol. viii in the series *Bibliothek des Raubes*), Vienna, 2003

Linnik 1989: Irina Linnik, *Old Master Paintings in Soviet Museums*, Leningrad, 1989

Lippmann 1910: Friederich Lippmann, *Zeichnungen alter Meister im Kupferstichkabinet der K. Museen zu Berlin*, 2 vols., Berlin, 1910

London 1930: *Commemorative Catalogue of the Exhibition of Dutch Art Held in the Galleries of the Royal Academy, Burlington House, London, January–March 1929*, London, 1930

von Lorck 1936: Carl von Lorck, "Goethe und Lessings Klosterhof im Schnee," *Westdeutsches Jahrbuch für Kunstgeschichte, Wallraf-Richartz-Jahrbuch*, 9, 1936, pp.205–22

Louvre 1922: *Musée National du Louvre. Catalogue des Peintures Exposées dans les Galeries*, vol. 3, *Écoles Flamande, Hollandaise, Allemande et Anglaise*, by Louis Demonts, Paris, 1922

Louvre 1979: *Catalogue sommaire illustré des peintures du Musée du Louvre*, 1, *Écoles flamande et hollandaise*, by Arnauld Brejon de Lavergnée, Jacques Foucart, and Nicole Reynaud, Paris, 1979

Lugt 1915: Frits Lugt, *Wandelingen met Rembrandt in en om Amsterdam*, Amsterdam, 1915 (2nd enlarged edition, September 1915)

Lugt 1920: Frits Lugt, *Mit Rembrandt in Amsterdam*, trans. Erich Hancke, Berlin, 1920

Lugt 1927: Frits Lugt, *Les dessins des écoles du Nord de la collection Dutuit au Musée des Beaux-Arts de la Ville de Paris* (Petit Palais), Paris, 1927

Lugt 1929: Frits Lugt, *Musée du Louvre, Inventaire général des dessins des écoles du Nord, Ecole hollandaise*, 1, Paris, 1929

Lugt 1931: Frits Lugt, *Musée du Louvre, Inventaire général des dessins des écoles du Nord, École hollandaise*, 2, Paris, 1931

Lugt 1931a: Frits Lugt, "Beitrage zu dem Katalog der niederländischen Handzeichnungen in Berlin," *Jahrbuch der preussischen Kunstsammlungen*, 52, 1931, pp.36–80

Lugt *Répertoire*: Frits Lugt, *Répertoire des catalogues de ventes publiques*, 4 vols., The Hague–Paris, 1938–87

Lugt 1950: Frits Lugt, *École nationale supérieure des Beaux-Arts, Paris, Inventaire générale des dessins des écoles du Nord*, vol. 1, *École hollandaise*, Paris, 1950

Luiken 1708: Jan Luiken [also Luyken], *Beschouwing der Wereld, Bestaande in Hondert konstige Figuren, Met Godlyke Spreuken en Stichtelyke Verzen*, Amsterdam, 1708 (reprint, 2 vols., Leiden, 1891)

Luyken: see Luiken

MacLaren 1960: Neil MacLaren, *National Gallery Catalogues. The Dutch School*, London, 1960

MacLaren and Brown 1991: Neil MacLaren, *National Gallery Catalogues. The Dutch School*, revised and expanded by Christopher Brown, 2 vols., London, 1991

Magnin [n.d., 1922?]: Jeanne Magnin, *Un Cabinet d'Amateur Parisien en 1922*, vol. 1, *Peintures et Dessins des Écoles Étrangères, Sculptures*, Dijon [n.d. 1922?]

Mannocci 1988: Lino Mannocci, *The Etchings of Claude Lorrain*, New Haven–London, 1988

Martin 1911: W. Martin, "Ausstellung altholländischer Bilder in Pariser Privatbesitz," *Monatshefte für Kunstwissenschaft*, 4, 1911, pp.433–41, 502–08

Martin 1935–36: W. Martin, *De Hollandsche schilderkunst in de 17de eeuw*, 2 vols., Amsterdam, 1935–36; 2nd ed., 1942

Martyn 1767: [Thomas Martyn] *The English Connoisseur: containing an account of whatever is curious in painting, sculpture, etc., in the palaces and seats of the nobility and principal gentry of England, both in town and country*, 2 vols., Dublin, 1767 (1st ed., London, 1766)

Maschmeyer 1978: Dietrich Maschmeyer, "Jacob Isaackszoon van Ruisdael und Meindert Hobbema malen Motive aus der Grafschaft Bentheim und ihres Umgebung," *Jahrbuch des Heimatvereins der Grafschaft Bentheim*, 1978, pp.61ff.

Mayer-Meintschel 1985: A. Mayer-Meintschel, *Staatliche Kunstsammlungen Dresden, Gemäldegalerie Alte Meister*, Tokyo, 1985 (in Japanese)

Med.: *Mededeelingen van den Dienst voor Kunsten en wetenschapen*, The Hague; after 1955: *Mededelingen Gemeentemuseum van Den Haag*

Melchior 1957: S.W. Melchior, "Amersfoort of Rhenen?," *Maandblad van Oud-Utrecht*, 30, 1957, pp.51–54

Mellaart 1926: J.H.J. Mellaart, *Dutch Drawings of the Seventeenth Century*, London, 1926

Michel 1887: Émil Michel, "Le musée de Brunswick," *G.B.A.*, 35, 1887, pp.5–25

Michel 1890: Émile Michel, *Jacob van Ruysdael et les paysagistes de l'école de Harlem*, Paris, 1890

Michel 1906: Émile Michel, *Les maîtres de paysage*, Paris, 1906

Michel 1910: Émile Michel, *Great Masters of Landscape Painting*, London, 1910

Miedema 1980: Hessel Miedema, *De archiefbescheiden an het St. Lukasgilde te Haarlem*, 2 vols., Alphen an den Rijn, 1980

Moes [1906]: Ernst Wilhelm Moes, *Original drawings of the Dutch and Flemish school in the printroom of the State-museum at Amsterdam*, 2 vols., The Hague [1906]

Moes 1909: E.W. Moes, "De Dam in schilderij en teekening," *Jaarboek Amstelodamum*, 7, 1909, pp.197–207

Moes 1913: E.W. Moes, review of C. Hofstede de Groot, *Beschreibendes . . . Verzeichnis der Werke der höllandischen Maler*, vol. 4, Esslingen–Paris, 1911, in *Monath. Kunstw.*, 1913, pp.294–97

Moes and van Biema 1909: E.W. Moes and Eduard van Biema, *De Nationale Konst-Gallery en Het Koninklijk Museum*, Amsterdam, 1909

Monatsh. Kunstw.: *Monatshefte für Kunstwissenschaft*

Moore 1988: Andrew W. Moore, *Dutch and Flemish Painting in Norfolk*, London, 1988 [pub. in conjunction with the commemorative William and Mary Tercentenary exhibition at Norwich Castle Museum, 10 September–20 November 1988]

Münz 1948: L. Münz, *Katalog des wiedereröffneten Teils der Gemäldegalerie*, Vienna, 1948

Münz 1955: L. Münz, *Katalog und Führer der Gemäldegalerie*, Vienna, 1955

Murphy 1985: Alexandra Murphy, *European Painting in the Musuem of Fine Art, Boston: An Illustrated Summary Catalogue*, Boston, 1985

Musée Napoléon: see Fihol 1804–15 and Landon 1805

NdT: see Feitama II, *Notitie der Teekeningen*

Neale 1820–29: *Views of the seats of noblemen and gentlemen, in England, Wales, Scotland and Ireland*, from drawings by J.P. Neale, 11 vols., London, 1820–29

Nève 1913: Joseph Nève, *Inventaire des dessins et aquarelles . . . de Grez*, Brussels, 1913

Nicholas 1994: Lynn H. Nicholas, *The Rape of Europa: The Fate of Europe's Treasures in the Third Reich and the Second World War*, New York, 1994

Niemeijer 1959: J.W. Niemeijer, "Het topografisch element in enkele riviergezichten van Salomon van Ruysdael nader beschouwd," *O.H.*, 74, 1959, pp.51–56

Niemeijer 1962: J.W. Niemeijer, "Varia Topografica: I. Ruisdael in Noord Brabant?," *O.H.*, 77, 1962, pp.61–62

Niemeijer 1980: J.W. Niemeijer, "De kunstkamer; bezoekers van de verzameling" in Th. Laurentius *et al.*, *Cornelis Ploos van Amstel: 1726–1798, Kunstverzamelaar en prentuitgever*, Assen, 1980, pp.103–11

Nivaagaard: see Smidt 1983

NKJ: *Nederlands Kunsthistorisch Jaarboek*

Nöldeke 1919: A. Nöldeke, *Die Kunstdenkmäler der Provinz Hannover*, 4, no. 4, *Die Kreise Lingen und Grafschaft Bentheim*, Hannover, 1919

Northbrook Collection, Catalogue 1889: W.H. James Weale and Jean Paul Richter, *A Descriptive Catalogue of the Collection of Pictures Belonging to the Earl of Northbrook*, London–Sydney, 1889

Notitie der Teekeningen: see Feitama II, *Notitie der Teekeningen*

Novotny 1941: Fritz Novotny, *Adalbert Stifter als Maler*, 2nd ed., Vienna, 1941

Nugent 2003: Charles Nugent, *British Watercolours in the Whitworth Art Gallery, The University of Manchester. A summary catalogue of drawings and watercolours by artists born before 1880*, London, 2003

O.H.: *Oud Holland*

Obreen 1877–90: F.D.O. Obreen [ed.], *Archief voor Nederlandsche Kunstgescheidenis*, 7 vols., Rotterdam, 1877–90

Oldewelt 1938: W.F.H. Oldewelt, "Ruisdael en zijn Damgezichten," *Algemeen Handelsblad*, 23 April 1938

Oldewelt 1942: W.F.H. Oldewelt, "Jacob Ruisdael en zijn Damgezichten," *Amsterdamsche Archiefvondsten*, Amsterdam, 1942, pp.163–67

Ottley, William Young: see Stafford Gallery 1818

Pappé 1926: A. Pappé, "Oversicht der litteratuur betreffende Nederlandsche kunst: Sowjet-Rusland," *O.H.*, 43, 1926, pp.197–200

Parker 1929: K.T. Parker, "Jacob van Ruisdael," *Old Master Drawings*, 3, June 1928–March 1929, p.10

Parris *et al.* 1975: Leslie Parris, Conal Shields and Ian Fleming-Williams, *John Constable: Further Documents and Correspondence*, London–Ipswich, 1975

Parris *et al.* 1976: Leslie Parris, Ian Fleming-Williams and Conal Shields, *Constable: Paintings, Watercolours & Drawings*, exhib. cat., Tate Gallery, London, February–May 1976

Parris and Fleming-Williams 1991: Leslie Parris and Ian Fleming-Williams, *Constable*, exhib. cat., Tate Gallery, London, 13 June–15 September 1991

Parthey 1863–64: Gustav Parthey, *Deutscher Bildersaal. Verzeichniss der in Deutschland vorhandenen Oelbilder verstorbender Maler aller Schulen*, 2 vols., Berlin, 1863–64

Pears 1988: Iain Pears, *The Discovery of Painting. The Growth of Interest in the Arts in England, 1680–1768*, New Haven–London, 1988

Pauli, G.: see Prestel-Gesellschaft

Pérignon 1826: A.N. Pérignon, *Description . . . le cabinet de feu M. Le Baron V. Denon. . . . tableaux, dessins et miniatures*, Paris, 1826

Perkins and Gavin 1980: Robert F. Perkins, Jr., and William J. Gavin III, *The Boston Athenaeum, Art Exhibition Index: 1827–1874*, Boston, 1980

Philadelphia 1994: *Paintings from Europe and the Americas in the Philadelphia Museum of Art. A Concise Catalogue*, ed. Curtis R. Scott *et al.*, Philadelphia, 1994

Pieterse 1970: W. Chr. Pieterse, *Livro do Bet Haim*, Assen, 1970

Pilkington 1770: M[atthew]. Pilkington, *The Gentleman's and Connoisseur's Dictionary of Painters. Containing a Complete Collection and Account of the Most Distinguished Artists . . . from the Year 1250 . . . to the Year 1767 . . .*, London, 1770

Plietzsch 1951: E. Plietzsch, "Randbemerkungen zur Ausstellung holländischer Gemälde im Museum Dahlem," *Berliner Museen, Berichte aus den ehem. Preussischen Kunstsammlungen*, N. F., 1, nos. 3 and 4, 1951, p.42

Plomp 1997: Michiel C. Plomp, *The Dutch Drawings in the Teyler Museum*, vol. II, *Artists born between 1575 and 1630*, Haarlem–Ghent–Doornspijk, 1997

Plomp 2001: Michiel C. Plomp, *Hartstochtelijk Verzameld. 18de-eeuwe Hollandse verzamelaars van tekeningen en hun collecties*, Paris–Bussum, 2001 (see Haarlem–Paris 2001–02)

Poortenaar [1938]: Jan Poortenaar, *Hollandsche etsers van de gouden eeuw*, Amsterdam [1938]

Popham 1929: A.E. P[opham]., review of Jakob Rosenberg, *Jacob van Ruisdael*, Berlin, 1928, in *B.M.*, 55, 1929, pp.52ff.

Porteman 1992: K. Porteman, "De waterval in de Nederlandse cultuur van de zeventiende eeuw", *Verslagen en Mededelngen van de Koninklijke Academie voor Nederlandse Taal- en Letterkunde*, no. 1, 1992, pp. 141–52

Pott 1782: [Joseph Holden Pott] *An Essay on Landscape Painting, with remarks general and critical, on the different schools and masters, ancient or modern*, London, 1782

Potterton 1986: Homan Potterton, *Dutch Seventeenth and Eighteenth Century Paintings in the National Gallery of Ireland*, Dublin, 1986

Prestel-Gesellschaft-Veröffentlichungen, 3–5, Bremen, Kunsthalle: *Zeichnungen alter Meister in der Kunsthalle zu Bremen*, 3 vols., ed. Gustav Pauli, Frankfurt, 1914–16
Prestel-Gesellschaft-Veröffentlichungen, 8, Hamburg, Kunsthalle: *Zeichnungen alter Meister in der Kunsthalle zu Hamburg*, ed. Gustav Pauli, Frankfurt a. M., 1924, (vol. 1., *Niederländer*)
Preston 1937: Sir Lionel Preston, *Sea and River Painters of the Netherlands*, London–New York–Toronto, 1937
van Puyvelde 1944: L. van Puyvelde, *The Dutch Drawings . . . at Windsor Castle*, London, 1944
Rademaker 1725: Abraham Rademaker, *Kabinet van Nederlandsche outheden en gezichten: Vervat in 300 konst-plaaten, verzamelt, getekend en in 't koper gebragt door den konst-ryken Abraham Rademaker. Met eene korte beschryving der zelve in het Duitsch, Fransch en Engelsch*, Amsterdam, 1725
Rademaker 1730: Abraham Rademaker, *Hollands Arcadia, Of de vermaarde Rivier den Amstel; vertonende alle deszelfs lust-plaatzen, herenhuizen en dorpen . . . van Amsterdam af door Ouderkerk . . . naar 't leven getekend . . .*, Amsterdam, 1730
Raupp 1980: Hans-Joachim Raupp, "Zur Bedeutung von Thema und Symbol für die holländische Landschaftsmalerei des 17. Jahrhunderts," *Jahrbuch der Staatlichen Kunstsammlungen in Baden-Württemberg*, 17, 1980, pp.85–110
RBK: Rijksdienst Beeldende Kunst, The Hague
Regnault-Delalande 1817: François Léandre Regnault-Delalande, *Catalogue raisonné des estampes du Comte Rigal*, Paris, 1817
Regtdoorzee Greup-Roldanus 1936: S.C. Regtdoorzee Greup-Roldanus, *Geschiedenis der Haarlemmer Bleekerijen*, The Hague, 1936
van Regteren Altena 1948: J.Q. van Regteren Altena, *Holländische Meisterzeichnungen des siebzehten Jahrhunderts*, Basel, 1948 (English trans., London, 1949)
van Regteren Altena [n.d.]: J.Q. van Regteren Altena, "Het gelaat van de stad," in *Zeven Eeuwen Amsterdam*, ed. A.E. d'Ailly, vol. 3, Amsterdam [n.d.]
Renaud 1940: J.G.N. Renaud, "De iconografie van het slot te Egmond," *Maandblad voor beeldende Kunsten*, 17, 1940, pp.338ff.
Répertoire: see Lugt *Répertoire*
Réveil, Achille: see Duchesne aîné and Réveil 1828–34
van Reyen 1965: Paul E. van Reyen, *Middeleeuwse kastelen in Nederland*, Bussum, 1965
Reynolds 1970: Graham Reynolds, "Turner and Dutch Marine Painting," *N.K.J.*, 21, 1970, pp.383–90
Reynolds 1984: Graham Reynolds, *The Later Paintings of John Constable*, 2 vols., New Haven–London, 1984
Reynolds 1996: Graham Reynolds, *The Early Paintings and Drawings of John Constable*, 2 vols., New Haven–London, 1996
Reynolds 1996a: Sir Joshua Reynolds, *A Journey to Flanders and Holland*, ed. Harry Mount, Cambridge–New York, 1996
Riat [1905?]: Georges Riat, *Ruysdael* (*Les Grands Artistes*), Paris [1905?]
Rich 1948: Daniel C. Rich, "Two Great Romantic Landscapes," *Bulletin, The Art Institute of Chicago*, 43, 1948, pp.20–22
Riegel 1882: H. Riegel, *Beiträge zur niederländischen Kunstgeschichte*, vol. 2, *Die Niederländischen Schulen in herzoglichen Museum zu Braunschweig*, Berlin, 1882
Riegel 1885: H. Riegel, *Die vozüglichsten Gemälde der herzoglichen Museums zu Braunschweig. 100 Blatt in photographischen Kupferdruck*, Berlin, 1885
Rijksdienst Catalogue 1992: *Old Master Paintings, An Illustrated Catalogue. Rijksdienst Beeldende Kunst. The Netherlands Office for Fine Arts*, The Hague, 1992
RKD: Rijksbureau voor Kunsthistorische Documentatie, The Hague
Roggeveen 1948: L.J. Roggeveen, "Een gezicht op het Damrak van Jacob van Ruisdael," *Phoenix*, 3, 1948, pp.91–94
Roh 1921: Franz Roh, *Holländische Malerei*, Jena, 1921
Ros: see Rosenberg 1928
Rosenau 1958: Helen Rosenau, "The Dates of Jacob van Ruisdael's 'Jewish Cemeteries'," *O.H.*, 73, 1958, pp.241f.
Rosenberg 1926: Jakob Rosenberg, "'The Jewish Cemetery' by Jacob van Ruisdael," *Art in America*, 14, 1926, pp.37ff.
Rosenberg 1927: Jakob Rosenberg, "Hobbema," *Jahrbuch der preussischen Kunstsammlungen*, 48, 1927, pp.139ff.
Ros; Rosenberg 1928: Jakob Rosenberg, *Jacob van Ruisdael*, Berlin, 1928
Rosenberg 1928a: Jakob Rosenberg, "Cornelis Hendricksz Vroom," *Jahrbuch der preussischen Kunstsammlungen*, 49, 1928, pp.102–10
Rosenberg 1931: Jakob Rosenberg, "Neuerworbene Zeichnungen des Kupferstichkabinetts," *Berliner Museen*, 52, 1931, pp.108–12
Rosenberg 1933: Jakob, Rosenberg, review of M.F. Wijnman (*O.H.*, 1932) and Jacob Zwarts (*Oudheidkundig Jaarboek*, 1928) in *Zeitschrift für Kunstgeschichte*, 2, 1933, pp.237–38
Rosenberg 1958: Jakob Rosenberg, "A Seascape by Jacob van Ruisdael," *Bulletin, Museum of Fine Arts, Boston*, 56, 1958, pp.144–46
Rowlands 1984: John Rowlands (ed.), *Master Drawings and Watercolours in the British Museum*, London 1984
Royalton-Kisch 1978: Martin Royalton-Kisch, "Reynolds as a Collector" in *Gainsborough and Reynolds in the British Museum*, British Museum, London, 1978
Royalton-Kisch 1996–97: "John Sheepshanks (1787–1863) and his Dutch and Flemish Etchings," in *Landmarks in Print Collecting. Connoisseurs and Donors at the British Museum*, ed. Antony Griffiths, exhib. cat., Museum of Fine Arts, Houston, and elsewhere, 1996–97, pp.65–89
Royalton-Kisch 2002: Martin Royalton-Kisch, "Dutch Drawings Abroad: Aspects of the History of Collecting," *Bruegel to Rembrandt: Dutch and Flemish Drawings from the Maida and George Abrams Collection*, Cambridge, 2002, pp.15–24
Russell 1975: Margarita Russell, *Jan van de Cappelle, 1624/6–1679*, Leigh-on-Sea, 1975
Russell 2004: Francis Russell, *John, 3rd Earl of Bute. Patron and Collector*, London, 2004
Ruysdael, Original-Abbildungen[1920?]: Jacob van Ruysdael, *Original-Abbildungen nach seinen besten Gemälden, Handzeichnungen und Radierungen*, 3rd ed., Leipzig, [1920?]; the 2nd ed. of this work (one with a German text, another with a French text) was published in Leipzig, c. 1912; the 1st ed. is unknown to me
S: see Slive 2001
Sander and Brinkmann 1995: J. Sander and B. Brinkmann, *Niederländische Gemälde vor 1800 im Städel*, Frankfurt a. M., 1995
Schaar 1958: Eckhard Schaar, *Studien zu Nicolaes Berchem* (diss.), Cologne, 1958
Schatborn 1985: Pieter Schatborn, *Drawings by Rembrandt, His Anonymous Pupils and Followers*, Rijksmuseum, Amsterdam 1985
Scheltema 1861: P. Scheltema, "Namen der schilders, die in de tweede helft der zeventiende eeuw te Amsterdam poorters zijn geweest," *Aemstel's Oudheid*, 4, 1861, pp.59–70
Scheltema 1872: P. Scheltema, "Jacob van Ruijsdael," *Aemstel's Oudheid*, 6, 1872, pp.95ff.
Schepers 1976: Josef Schepers, *Haus und Hof westfälischer Bauern* [1960], 3rd ed., Münster, 1976
Scheyer 1977: Ernst Scheyer, "The Iconography of Jacob van Ruisdael's *Cemetery*," *Bulletin of the Detroit Institute of Arts*, 55, 1977, pp.133ff.
Schmidt 1981: W. Schmidt, *Studien zur Landschaftskunst Jacob van Ruisdaels: Frühwerke und Wanderjahre*, Hildesheim–New York, 1981
Schneider 1932: H. Schneider, *Jan Lievens: sein Leben und seine Werke*, Haarlem, 1932 (reprinted with a supplement by R.E.O. Ekkart, Amsterdam, 1973)
Scholten 1904: H.J. Scholten, *Catalogue raisonné des dessins . . . au Musée Teyler à Haarlem*, Haarlem, 1904
Schönbrunner and Meder 1896–1908: J. Schönbrunner and J. Meder, *Handzeichnungen alter Meister in der Albertina und anderen Sammlungen*, 12 vols., Vienna, 1896–1908
Schrevel 1754: Dirk Schrevel, *Harlemias of eerste stichting der stad Haarlem. Vermeerdert met historische aantekening tot den jaare 1750*, Haarlem, 1754 (enlarged ed. by an unnamed editor of Theod. Schreveli, *Harlemias, ofte, om beter te segen. De erste stichlinghe der stadt Haerlem*, Haarlem, 1648)
Schreveli: see Schrevel 1754
Schuchardt 1848: Christian Schuchardt, *Goethe's Kunstsammlungen*, 3 vols., Jena, 1848
Schwartz and Bok [1990]: Gary Schwartz and Marten Jan Bok, *Pieter Saenredam. The Painter and His Time*, New York [1990]
Sedelmeyer 1898: C. Sedelmeyer, *Catalogue of 300 Paintings by Old Masters*, Paris, 1898
Semenov 1906: Petr Petrovich Semenov-Tian'-Shanskii, *Études sur les peintres des écoles hollandaise, flamande et néerlandaise qu'on trouve danes la collection Semenov et les autres collections publiques et privées de St. Petersbourg*, St Petersburg, 1906
Shcherbachova 1924: M. Shcherbachova, "On the New Arrangement of Pictures by Dutch Artists in the Hermitage: 17th Century Landscape," *Sredi Kollektsionerov*, 1924, nos. 9–12, pp.3–24 (Russian text)
de Silva Rosa 1925: J.S. de Silva Rosa, *Geschiedenis der Portugeesche Joden te Amsterdam*, Amsterdam, 1925
Simon 1930: K.E. Simon, *Jacob van Ruisdael* (diss.), Berlin, 1927; trade edition reprinted with additions and corrections, Berlin, 1930
Simon 1935: K.E. Simon, "Isaack van Ruisdael," *Thieme-Becker*, 29, 1935, pp.188–89, "Jacob Isaackzoon van Ruisdael," pp.190–93, and "Jacob Salomonszoon Ruysdael," pp.193–94
Simon 1935a: K.E. Simon, "Isaack van Ruisdael," *B.M.*, 67, 1935, pp.7–23
Simon 1935b: K.E. Simon, " 'Doctor' Jacob van Ruisdael," *B.M.*, 67, 1935, pp.132–35
Simon 1935c: K.E. Simon, "Wann hat Ruisdael die Bilder des Judenfriedhofs gemalt?," *Festschrift zum 70. Geburtstag von Adolph Goldschmidt*, Berlin, 1935, pp.158–63
Simon 1939–40: K.E. Simon, "Ruisdael aanschouwt Amsterdam," *Historia*, 5, 1939/40, pp.23–25
Simon 1940: K.E. Simon, review of G. Broulhiet, *Meindert Hobbma*, Paris, 1938, in *Zeitschrift für Kunstgeschichte*, 9, 1940, pp.205ff.
Simon 1958: Maria Simon, *Claes Jansz. Visscher* (diss.), Freiburg, 1958
Simpson 1951: Frank Simpson, " 'The English Connoisseur' and its Sources," *B.M.*, 93, 1951, pp.355–56
Simpson 1953: Frank Simpson, "Dutch Pictures in England before 1760," *B.M.*, 95, 1953, pp.39–42
Slive 1953: Seymour Slive, *Rembrandt and His Critics: 1630–1730*, The Hague, 1953
Slive 1965: Seymour Slive, *Drawings of Rembrandt, with a Selection by His Pupils and Followers*, 2 vols., New York, 1965
Slive 1970–74: Seymour Slive, *Frans Hals*, 3 vols., London–New York, 1970–74
Slive 1973: Seymour Slive, "Notes on Three Drawings by Jacob van Ruisdael," in *Album Amicorum J.G. van Gelder*, The Hague, 1973, pp.274–76
Slive 1981: Seymour Slive, *Jacob van Ruisdael*, exhib. cat., Mauritshuis, The Hague–Fogg Art Museum, Cambridge, New York, 1981; Dutch ed., Amsterdam, 1981
Slive 1983: Seymour Slive, "An Unpublished Drawing by Jacob van Ruisdael" in *Essays In Northern European Art Presented to Egbert Haverkamp-Begemann*, Doornspijk, 1983, pp.249–50
Slive 1987: Seymour Slive, "Dutch pictures in the collection of Cardinal Silvio Valenti Gonzaga (1690–1756)," *Simiolus*, 17, 1987, pp.169–90
Slive 1988: Seymour Slive, "The Manor Kostverloren: Viscissitudes of a Seventeenth-Century Dutch Landscape Motif," *Papers in Art History from the Pennsylvania State University*, 3, 1988, pp.132–68
Slive *et al.* 1989: Seymour Slive *et al.*, *Frans Hals*, exhib. cat., National Gallery of Art, Washington D.C.–Royal Academy of Arts, London–Frans Hals Museum, Haarlem, 1989–90
Slive 1991: Seymour Slive, "Additions to Jacob van Ruisdael," *B.M.*, 133, 1991, pp.598–606
Slive 1995: Seymour Slive, "Additions to Jacob van Ruysdael: II," *B.M.*, 137, 1995, pp.452–57
Slive 1995a: Seymour Slive, *Dutch Painting: 1600–1800*, New Haven–London, 1995
Slive 1997: Seymour Slive, "Jacob van Ruisdael's variation on a theme by Rubens at Bilbao," *O.H.*, 111, 1997, pp.187–90

Slive 2001: Seymour Slive, *Jacob van Ruisdael: A Complete Catalogue of His Paintings, Drawings and Etchings*, New Haven–London, 2001
Slive 2004: Seymour Slive, "Jacob van Ruisdael's Clientele," *Collected Opinions. Essays on Netherlandish Art in Honour of Alfred Bader*, eds. V. Manuth and A. Rüger, London, 2004, pp.174–85
Sluijter-Seijffert 1984: N. Sluijter-Seijffert, "Cornelis van Poelenburch, ca. 1593–1667" (diss.), Leiden, 1984
Smids 1711: L. Smids, *Schatkamer der Nederlandsse Oudheden*, Amsterdam, 1711
Smith; Smith 1835; Smith Suppl.: John Smith, *A Catalogue Raisonné of the Works of the Most Eminent Dutch, Flemish and French Painters*, vol. 6, London, 1835; *Supplement*, vol. 9, London, 1842
Smith 1950: E. Smith, "An Early Landscape by Ruisdael," *Bulletin, Currier Gallery of Art*, December 1950, pp.1–4
SNK: Stichting Nederlandsch Kunstbezit, The Hague
Snowman 1966: A. Kenneth Snowman, *Eighteenth-Century Gold Boxes of Europe*, London, 1966 [includes an appendix by F.J.B. Watson on the Choiseul snuff-box; also see Watson 1963]
Stafford Gallery 1818: William Young Ottley and Peltro William Tomkins, *Engravings of the Most Noble The Marquis of Stafford's Collection of Pictures in London, arranged according to schools and in chronological order with remarks on each picture*, 4 vols., London, 1818
Stafford Gallery 1825: John Young, *A Catalogue of the Collection of Pictures of the Most Noble the Marquis of Stafford, at Cleveland House, London, containing an etching of every picture, and accompanied with historical and biographical notices*, 2 vols., London, 1825
Stechow 1938: Wolfgang Stechow, *Salomon van Ruysdael, eine Einführung in seine Kunst*, Berlin, 1938 (see Stechow 1975)
Stechow 1959: Wolfgang Stechow, "The Early Years of Hobbema," *A.Q.*, 22, 1959, pp.3–18
Stechow 1966: Wolfgang Stechow, *Dutch Landscape Painting of the Seventeenth Century*, London, 1966; 2nd ed., London–New York, 1968
Stechow 1968: Wolfgang Stechow, "Ruisdael in the Cleveland Museum," *Bulletin of The Cleveland Museum of Art*, 55, no. 8, 1968, pp.250–61
Stechow 1975: Wolfgang Stechow, *Salomon van Ruysdael, eine Einführung in seine Kunst* (revised and enlarged ed. of Stechow 1938), Berlin, 1975
Steuart 1890: A. Francis Steuart, *Catalogue of the Pictures of Dalkeith House*, Dalkeith, 1890
Stifter 1982: *Adelbert Stifter Werke*, ed. Uwe Japp *et al.*, vol. 2, Frankfurt a.M., 1982
van Straaten 1977: Evert van Straaten, *Koud tot op het bot: De verbeelding van de winter in de zestiende en zeventiende eeuw in de Nederlanden*, The Hague, 1977
Strauss and van der Meulen 1979: W.I. Strauss, M. Van der Meulen *et al.*, *The Rembrandt Documents*, New York, 1979
Sutton 1986: Peter C. Sutton, *A Guide to Dutch Art in America*, Grand Rapids–Kampen, 1986
Sutton 1990: Peter C. Sutton, *Northern European Paintings in the Philadelphia Museum of Art from the Sixteenth through the Nineteenth Century*, Philadelphia, 1990
Sutton 1991: Peter C. Sutton, "A Brief History of the Collecting of Dutch Landscape" in *The Hoogsteder Exhibition of Dutch Landscapes*, dealer Hoogsteder, The Hague, 12 March–12 May 1991, pp.16–29
Taillasson 1807: Jean-Joseph Taillasson, *Observations sur quelques grand peintres [dans lesquelles on cherche à fixer les charatères distinctifs de leur talent, avec un précis de leur vie]*, Paris, 1807
Tax 1998: C.J.H.M. Tax, "De graven van Beth Haim," *Amstelodamum*, 85, 1998, pp.26–28
Terw; Terwesten 1770: see Hoet; Hoet 1752
Thieme-Becker: Allgemeines Lexikon der bildenden Künstlers von der Antike bis zur Gegenwart, established by Ulrich Thieme and Felix Becker, 37 vols., Leipzig, 1907–50
Thoré: also see W. Bürger
Thoré 1845: T. Thoré, *Le Salon de 1845, précédé d'une lettre à Béranger*, Paris, 1845
Thoré 1868: T.E.J. Thoré, *Salons de T. Thoré, 1844, 1845, 1846, 1847, 1848*, preface by W. Bürger (= Thoré), Paris, 1868
Tomkins, Peltro William: see Stafford Gallery 1818
Toynbee 1927–28: "Horace Walpole's Journals of Visits to Country Seats," ed. Padget Toynbee, *Walpole Society*, 16, 1927–28, pp.9–80
Trautscholdt 1973: Eduard Trautscholdt, "Johannes Ruischer" in E. Haverkamp Begemann, *Hercules Segers. The Complete Etchings*, The Hague, 1973
Trèves 1951: A. Trèves, "Le moulin de Ruysdael," *Le Peintre*, 18, 1951, p.5
Trnek 1992: R. Trnek, *Die holländischen Gemälde des 17. Jahrhunderts in der Gemäldegalerie der Akademie der bildenden Künste un Wien*, Vienna–Cologne–Weimar, 1992
van der Tuin 1950: H. van der Tuin, "Reproduction et imitation de vieux tableaux flamands ou hollandais sur porcelain de Sèvres (1756–1847)," *O.H.*, 50, 1950, pp.41ff.
Valentiner 1926: W.R. Valentiner, " 'The Cemetery' by Jacob van Ruysdael," *Bulletin, Detroit Institute of Arts*, 7, 1926, pp.55–58
Valentiner 1930: W.R. Valentiner, *Das unbekannte Meisterwerk in öffentlichen und privaten Sammlungen*, New York, 1930
van der Veen 2004–05: J. van der Veen, review of P. Biesboer, *Collections of paintings in Haarlem 1572–1745*, ed. C. Togneri, Los Angeles, 2001, and E. Duverger, *Antwerpse kunstinventarissen uit de zeventiende eeuw*, vol. 12, Brussels, 2002, in *Simiolus*, 31, 2004–05, pp. 111–15
Vega 1975: L. Alvares Vega, *Het Beth Haim van Ouderkerk: Beelden van een Portugees-Joodse begraafplaats. The Beth Haim of Ouderkerk aan de Amstel: Images of a Portuguese Jewish cemetery in Holland*, Assen–Amsterdam, 1975
Het verheerlykt Nederland 1745–74: *Het verheerlykt Nederland of Kabinet van hedendaagsche gezigten*, 9 parts in 3 vols., Amsterdam, 1745–74
Viardot 1855: Louis Viardot, *Les Musées d'Angleterre, de Belgique, de Holland et de Russie . . .*, 2nd ed., Paris, 1855; 3rd ed., Paris, 1860
Viardot 1860: Louis Viardot, *Les Musées de France*, 2nd ed., Paris, 1860
Villot 1852: F. Villot, *Notice des tableaux exposés dans les galeries du Musée national du Louvre, 2e partie, écoles allemande, flamande et hollandaise*, Paris, 1852
Vondel: *De Werken van Vondel*, ed. by J.F.M. Sterck et al., 10 vols., Amsterdam, 1927–37
de Vrankrijker [n.d., 1965?]: A.C.J. de Vrankrijker, *De historie van de vesting Naarden*, Bussum [n.d., 1965?]
de Vries 1915: R.W.P. de Vries, *Cornelis Ploos van Amstel et ses élèves, essai d'une iconographie*, Amsterdam, 1915
Waagen 1837–39: Gustav Friedrich Waagen, *Kunstwerke und Künstler in England und Paris*, 3 vols., Berlin, 1837–39
Waagen 1838: Gustav Friedrich Waagen, *Works of Art and Artists in England*, 3 vols., London, 1838
Waagen 1854: Dr. [Gustav Friedrich] Waagen, *Treasures of Art in Great Britain*, 3 vols., London, 1854
Waagen 1857: Dr. [Gustav Friedrich] Waagen, *Galleries and Cabinets of Art in Great Britain*, London, 1857, supplement (vol. 4) to Waagen 1854
Waagen 1864: Gustav Friedrich Waagen, *Die Gemäldesammlung in der Kaiserlichen Ermitage zu St. Petersburg*, Munich, 1864
Waagen 1866–67: Gustav Friedrich Waagen, *Die vornehmsten Kunstdenkmäler in Wien*, 2 vols., Vienna, 1866–67
Waagen 1870: Gustav Friedrich Waagen, *Die Gemäldesammlung in der Kaiserlichen Ermitage zu St. Petersburg*, 2nd ed., St. Petersburg, 1870
Wagner 1971: Helga Wagner, *Jan van der Heyden: 1637–1712*, Amsterdam–Haarlem, 1971
Walford 1991: E. John Walford, *Jacob van Ruisdael and the Perception of Landscape*, New Haven–London, 1991
Walsh 1991: John Walsh, "Skies and Reality in Dutch Landscape," in *Art in History/History in Art*, eds. David Freedberg and Jan de Vries, Santa Monica, 1991, pp.95–117
Waterhouse 1966–68: Ellis Waterhouse, "Reynolds's 'Sitter Book' for 1755," *The Walpole Society*, XLI, 1966–68, pp.112–64
Watson 1963: F.J.B. Watson, *The Choiseul Box*, London, 1963
Weale and Richter 1889: W.H. James Weale and Jean Paul Richter, *A Descriptive Catalogue of the Collection of Pictures belonging to the Earl of Northbrook*, London 1889.
Weigel 1843: Rudolph Weigel, *Suppléments au peintre-graveur de Adam Bartsch . . .*, vol. 1, Leipzig, 1843
Westmacott 1824: C.M. Westmacott, *British Galleries of Painting and Sculpture . . . Critical Catalogue . . . of every Work of Fine Art in the Principal Collections*, London, 1824
Weyerman 1729–69: Jacob Campo Weyerman, *De levens-beschryvingen der Nederlandsche konst-schilders en konst-schilderessen*, 3 vols., The Hague, 1729–69; vol. 4, Dordrecht, 179
Wheelock 1995: Arthur K. Wheelock, Jr., *Dutch Paintings of the Seventeenth Century. The Collections of the National Gallery of Art. Systematic Catalogue*, Washington, D.C., 1995
White 1969: Christopher White, *Rembrandt as an Etcher A Study of the Artist at Work*, 2 vols., London, 1969; 2nd ed., London, 1999
White 1982: Christopher White, *The Pictures in the Collection of Her Majesty the Queen. The Dutch Pictures*, Cambridge and elsewhere, 1982
White 1999: Christopher White, *Ashmolean Museum Oxford. Catalogue of the Collection of Paintings, Dutch, Flemish and German Paintings before 1900*, Oxford 1999
White and Crawley 1994: Christopher White and Charlotte Crawley, *The Dutch and Flemish Drawings of the Fifteenth to the Early Nineteenth Centuries in the Collection of Her Majesty the Queen at Windsor Castle*, Cambridge, 1994
Wiegand 1971: Wilfried Wiegand, *Ruisdael-Studien: Ein Versuch zur Ikonologie der Landschaftsmalerei* (diss.), Hamburg, 1971
Wiese 1963: Georg Wiese, *Jakob van Ruisdael*, Leipzig, 1963
Wijnman 1932: H.F. Wijnman, "Het leven der Ruysdaels," *O.H.*, 49, 1932, pp.49–60, 173–81, 258–75
van der Willigen 1870: A. van der Willigen, *Les Artistes de Harlem*, 2nd ed., Haarlem, 1870
Willis [1911]: F.C. Willis, *Die niederländische Marinemalerei*, Leipzig [1911]
Wilson 1975: William H. Wilson, "'The Circumcision,' A Drawing by Romeyn de Hooge," *Master Drawings*, 13, 1975, pp.250–58
Witt: Witt Library. Courtauld Institute, University of London
Woermann 1896–98: Karl Woermann, *Handzeichnungen alter Meister im Königlichen Kupferstichkabinett zu Dresden*, 10 vols., Munich, 1896–98
Woodall 1935: Mary Woodall, "A Note on Gainsborough and Ruisdael," *B.M.*, 66, 1935, pp.40–45
Woodall 1939: Mary Woodall, *Gainsborough Landscape Drawings*, London, 1939
Woodall 1949: Mary Woodall, *Thomas Gainsborough, His Life and Work*, London, 1949
Wright 1976: Christopher Wright, *Old Master Paintings in Britain*, London, 1976
Wright 1992: Christopher Wright, *The World's Master Paintings from the Early Renaissance to the Present Day*, 2 vols., London–New York, 1992
Wuestman 1996: Gerdien Wuestman, "Nicolaes Berchem in print: fluctuations in the function and significance of reproductive engraving," *Simiolus*, 24, 1996, pp.19–53
Wurzbach 1906–11: Alfred von Wurzbach, *Niederländisches Künstler-Lexikon*, 3 vols., Vienna-Leipzig, 1906–11 (Wurzbach 1910 refers to vol. 2 of the lexicon which includes the author's entries on Jacob van Ruisdael and members of the family.)
van der Wyck and Niemeijer 1989: H.W.M. van der Wyck and J.W. Niemeijer, *De kasteeltekening van Roelant Roghman*, vol. 1, Alphen an den Rijn, 1989
Young, John: see Stafford Gallery 1825
van Ysselsteyn 1946: Geradina Tjebberta van Ysselsteyn, *Van linnen en linnenkasten*, Amsterdam, 1946
von Zesen 1664: Filips von Zesen, *Beschreibung der Stadt Amsterdam . . .*, Amsterdam, 1664
ZfbK: *Zeitschrift für bildende Kunst*; with the supplement *Kunstchronik*
Zwarts 1928: J. Zwarts, "Het motief van Jacob van Ruisdael's 'Jodenkerkhof'," *Oudheidkundig Jaarboek*, 8, 1928, pp.232–49

List of Exhibitions

Amsterdam 1925: *Historische tentoonstelling der Stad Amsterdam*, 2 vols., Rijksmuseum–Stedelijk Museum, Amsterdam, 3 July–15 September 1925

Amsterdam 1932: *Kaaarten, profielen en panorama's van Amsterdam*, Museum Fodor, Amsterdam, 1932

Amsterdam 1932a: *Hollandsche winterlandschappen uit de 17e Eeuw*, dealer J. Goudstikker, Amsterdam, 10–20 March 1932

Amsterdam 1945: *Weerzien der meesters in het Rijksmuseum. Keur van schilderijen uit: Rijksmuseum, Mauritshuis, Frans Halsmuseum, Dordrechts Museum*, Rijksmuseum, Amsterdam, 15 July–30 September 1945

Amsterdam 1955: *Amsterdam in tekening 1600–1800. Verzameling Mr. Chr. P. van Eeghen*, Rijksprentenkabinet, Rijksmuseum, Amsterdam, 1955

Amsterdam 1963: *Fodor 100 Jaar*, Museum Fodor, Amsterdam, 12 July–30 September 1963

Amsterdam 1971: *Hollandse schilderijen uit Franse musea*, Rijksmuseum, Amsterdam, 1971

Amsterdam 1987: *Land & Water. Dutch Drawings from the 17th Century in the Rijksmuseum Print Room*, Rijksmuseum, Amsterdam 1987 (cat. by Marijn Schapelhouman and Peter Schatborn)

Amsterdam 1992: *De wereld binnen handbereik. Nederlandse kunst- en rariteiten verzamelingen: 1585–1735*, 2 vols, Amsterdams Historisch Museum, 26 June–11 October 1992 (eds. E. Bergvelt and R. Kistenmaker).

Amsterdam 1997: *Het Paleis in de schilderkunst van de Gouden Eeuw*, Royal Palace, Amsterdam, 6 June–7 September 1997 (cat. by J. Peeters *et al.*)

Amsterdam 1998: *Buiten tekenen in Rembrandts tijd*, Museum het Rembrandthuis, Amsterdam, 30 September–29 November 1998 (cat. by Bob van Boogert *et al.*)

Amsterdam 2000: *The Glory of the Golden Age. Dutch Art of the 17th Century. Painting, Sculpture and Decorative Art*, Rijksmuseum, Amsterdam, 15 April–17 September 2000 (cat. by Judikje Kiers *et al.*)

Amsterdam 2000a: *The Glory of the Golden Age. Dutch Art of the 17th Century. Drawings and Prints*, Rijksmuseum, Amsterdam, 15 April–16 July 2000 (cat. by Epco Runia)

Amsterdam–Toronto 1977: *Opkomst en bloei van het Noordnederlandse stadsgezicht in de 17de eeuw. The Dutch Cityscape in the 17th Century and its Sources*, Amsterdams Historisch Museum, Amsterdam, 17 June–28 August 1977–Art Gallery of Ontario, Toronto, 27 September–13 November 1977

Amsterdam–Boston–Philadelphia 1987–88: *Masters of 17th-Century Dutch Landscape Painting*, Rijksmuseum, Amsterdam, 2 October 1987–3 January 1988–Museum of Fine Arts, Boston, 3 February–1 May 1988–Museum of Art, Philadelphia, 5 June–31 July 1988 (cat. by P.C. Sutton *et al.*)

Amsterdam–Paris 1998–99: *Landscapes of Rembrandt. His favourite walks*, Amsterdam Municipal Archives, 30 September–29 November 1998–Institut Néerlandais, Paris, 17 December 1998–14 February 1999 (cat. by B. Bakker *et al.*)

Atlanta 1996: *Rings. Five Passions in World Art*, High Museum of Art, Atlanta, Georgia, 1996 (ed. Michael Schapiro)

Baltimore 1968: *From El Greco to Pollock, Early and Late Works by European and American Artists*, The Baltimore Museum of Art, Baltimore, Maryland, 1968

Basel 1945: *Meisterwerke holländischer Malerei . . . Ausstellung aus Privatbesitz in der Schweiz*, Kunstmuseum, Basel, 28 June–19 August 1945

Basel 1987: *Im Licht Hollands: Holländische Malerei des 17. Jahrhunderts aus den Sammlungen des Fürsten von Liechtenstein und aus Schweizer Besitz*, Kunstmuseum, Basel, 14 June–27 September 1987 (cat. by Petra ten-Doesschate Chu *et al.*)

Berlin 1906: *Ausstellung von Werken alter Kunst aus dem Privatbesitz der Mitglieder des Kaiser-Friedrich-Museums-Verein*, ehemalig Gräflich Redern'schen Palais, Berlin, 27 January–4 March 1906

Berlin 1925: *Gemälde alter Meister aus Berliner Besitz*, Kaiser-Friedrich-Museums-Verein, Berlin, July–August 1925

Berlin 1955–56: *Gemälde der Dresdner Galerie*, National-Galerie, Berlin, 1955–56

Berlin 1974: *Die holländische Landschaftszeichnung: 1600–1740*, Berlin-Dahlem, Staatliche Museen Preussischer Kulturbesitz, Berlin, April–June 1974

Bethnal Green 1882–83: *Catalogue of the Collection of Paintings lent for Exhibition by the Marquis of Bute*, Bethnal Green Branch of the Victoria and Albert Museum, London, 1883

Boston 1992: *Prized Possessions: European Paintings from Private Collections of Friends of the Museum of Fine Arts, Boston*, Museum of Fine Arts, Boston, 17 June–18 August 1992 (cat. by Peter C. Sutton *et al.*)

Boston 2002: *The Poetry of Everyday Life. Dutch Painting in Boston*, Museum of Fine Arts, Boston, 12 June–15 September 2002 (cat. by R. Baer)

Brooklyn 1945–46: *Landscape: An Exhibition of Paintings*, Brooklyn Museum, Brooklyn, 8 November 1945–1 January 1946

Brussels 1873a: *Exposition de tableaux et dessins d'anciens maîtres*, Société néerlandaise de bienfaisance à Bruxelles, Brussels, 1873

Brussels 1873b: *Catalogue d'une collection [B. Suermondt], de tableaux et dessins anciens et moderne*, Musée Royal, Brussels, 22 December 1873

Brussels 1935: *Exposition Universelle et Internationale*, vol. 1, *Cinq siècles d'art*, Brussels, 24 May–13 October 1935

Brussels 1937–38: *De Jérôme Bosch à Rembrandt, dessins hollandais du XVIe au XVIIe siècle*, Palais des Beaux-Arts, Brussels, November 1937–January 1938

Brussels 1971: *Rembrandt en zijn tijd*, Palais des Beaux-Arts, Brussels, 23 September–21 November 1971

Brussels 1977–78: *Mens en landschap in de 17de eeuwse Hollandse schilderkunst*, Musées Royaux des Beaux-Arts de Belgique, Brussels, 17 November 1977–15 January 1978

Brussels–Antwerp 1946: *De Hollandsche schilderkunst van Jeroen Bosch tot Rembrandt*, Palais des Beaux-Arts, Brussels, 2 March–28 April 1946–Koninklijk Museum voor Schone Kunsten, Antwerp, May 1946

Brussels–Hamburg 1961: *Hollandse tekeningen uit de gouden eeuw*, Bibliothèque Royale Albert 1er, Brussels, 22 April–24 June 1961–Kunsthalle, Hamburg, 8 September–15 October 1961

Brussels–Rotterdam–Paris 1972–73: *Dessins flamands et hollandais du dix-septième siècle, Collections de l'Ermitage, Leningrad et du Musée Pouchkine, Moscou*, Bibliothèque Royale Albert 1er, Brussels, 21 October–25 November 1972–Boymans-van Beuningen Museum, Rotterdam, 1 December 1972–7 January 1973–Institut Néerlandais, Paris, 12 January–18 February 1973

Budapest 1969: *Mesterrajzok a Lipcsei Képzömüveszeti Múzeumbol (Meister Zeichnungen aus dem Museum der bildenden Künste Leipzig)*, Szépmüvészeti Múzeum, Budapest, 1969

Cambridge 1958: *Drawings from the Collection of Curtis O. Baer*, Fogg Art Museum, Harvard University, Cambridge, 1958 (cat. by A. Mongan)

Cambridge–Montreal 1988: *Landscape in Perspective: Drawings by Rembrandt and his Contemporaries*, Arthur M. Sackler Museum, Harvard University, Cambridge–The Montreal Museum of Fine Arts, 20 February–29 May 1988 (cat. by Frederik J. Duparc)

Chapel Hill 1958: *Inaugural Exhibition*, The William Hayes Ashland Memorial Art Center, Chapel Hill, North Carolina, 1958

Chicago 1942: *Paintings by the Great Dutch Masters of the Seventeenth Century*, The Art Institute of Chicago, Chicago, 18 November–16 December 1942

Chicago and elsewhere 1992–93: *Master European Paintings from the National Gallery of Ireland: Mantegna to Goya*, Art Institute of Chicago, 6 June–9 August 1992, and other locations in the United States through 26 June 1993 (cat. by Raymond Keaveney)

Cologne 1954: *Meisterwerke holländische Landschaftsmalerei des 17. Jahrhunderts*, Wallraf-Richartz-Museum, Cologne, May–June 1954

Cologne 1955: *Rembrandt und seine Zeitgenossen, Handzeichnungen aus dem Museum Fodor, Amsterdam*, Wallraf-Richartz-Museum, Cologne, June–August 1955

Detroit 1929: *Catalogue of a Loan Exhibition of Dutch Genre and Landscape Painting*, The Detroit Institute of Arts, Detroit, 16 October–10 November 1929

Dresden–Vienna 1997–98: *Van Eyck, Bruegel, Rembrandt: Niederländische Zeichnungen des 15. bis 17. Jahrhunderts aus dem Kupferstich-Kabinett Dresden*, Albertinum, Brühlsche Terrasse, Dresden, 1997–Kunstforum, Vienna, 1997–98 (cat. by Christian Dittrich)

Düsseldorf 1886: *Ausstellung von Bildern alterer Meister aus Privatsammlungen in den Rheinlanden und Westfalen*, Kunsthalle, Düsseldorf, 1 September–17 October 1886

Düsseldorf 1929: *Alte Malerei aus Privatbesitz*, Düsseldorf, 1929

Edinburgh 1949: *Dutch and Flemish Paintings from the Collection of the Marquess of Bute . . .*, National Gallery of Scotland, Edinburgh, 6 August–25 September 1949

Edinburgh 1992: *Dutch Art and Scotland. A Reflection of Taste*, National Gallery of Scotland, Edinburgh, 13 August–18 October 1992 (cat. by Julia Lloyd Williams)

Eindhoven 1948: *Nederlandse landschapskunst in de 17de eeuw*, Stedelijk Van Abbe Museum, Eindhoven, 1948

Glasgow 1884: *Catalogue of Paintings Lent for Exhibition by the Marquess of Bute*, Glasgow, 1884 (cat. by Jean Paul Richter)

Greenwich, Connecticut 2002–03: *Pleasures of Collecting: Part 1, Renaissance to Impressionist Masterpieces*, Bruce Museum of Arts and Science, Greenwich, Connecticut, 21 September 2002–5 January 2003 (cat. by Peter C. Sutton and Jennifer Ambrose)

Greenwich, Connecticut 2005: *Old Master Paintings from the Hascoe Collection*, Bruce Museum of Arts and Science, Greenwich, Connecticut, 2 April–29 May 2005 (cat. by Peter C. Sutton)

Haarlem 2000: *Travels through Town and Country. Dutch and Flemish Landscape Drawings 1550-1630*, Teylers Museum, Haarlem, 7 October–3 December 2000 (cat. by Hans Verbeek; contributions by Robert-Jan te Rijdt)
Haarlem–Paris 2001-02: *Hartstochtelijk Verzameld. Beroemde tekeningen in 18de eeuwse Hollandse collecties*, Teylers Museum, Haarlem, 16 December 2001-17 February 2002–Institut Néerlandais, Paris, 28 February–28 April 2002 (cat. by Mària van Berge-Gerbaud *et al.*)
The Hague–Cambridge 1981–82: *Jacob van Ruisdael*, Mauritshuis, The Hague, 1 October 1981–3 January 1982–Fogg Art Museum, Cambridge, 18 January–11 April 1982 (cat. by Seymour Slive)
The Hague–London 1970–71: *"Shock of Recognition": The Landscape of English Romanticism and the Dutch Seventeenth-Century School*, Mauritshuis, The Hague, 24 November 1970–10 January 1971–Tate Gallery, London, 22 January–28 February 1971
The Hague–San Francisco 1990–91: *Great Dutch Paintings from America*, Mauritshuis, The Hague, 28 September 1990–13 January 1991–The Fine Arts Museums of San Francisco, 16 February–5 May 1991 (cat. by Ben Broos *et al.*)
Haifa 1959: *Holland's Golden Age*, Museum of Modern Art, Haifa, April 1959
Hamburg–Haarlem 2002: *Jacob van Ruisdael: Die Revolution der Landschaft*, Hamburger Kunsthalle–Frans Hals Museum, Haarlem, 2002 (cat. by Martina Sitt, Pieter Biesboer *et al.*)
Hove–Lincoln–Sudbury 1993: *The Romantic Windmill. The Windmill in British Art from Gainsborough to David Cox, 1750–1850*, Hove Museum and Art Gallery, 7 March–25 April 1993–Usher Gallery, Lincoln, 1 May–20 June 1993–Gainsborough's House, Sudbury, 10 July–September 1993 (cat. by T. Wilcox *et al.*)
Jerusalem–Belgrade 1960: *Master Drawings from the Fodor Collection – Crtezi majstora iz Kolekcije Fodor u Amsterdamu*, Bezalei National Museum, Jerusalem–Narodni Muzei, Belgrade, 1960
Krefeld 1938: *Deutsche Landschaften und Städte in der niederländischen Kunst des 16. bis 18. Jahrhunderts*, Kaiser-Wilhelm-Museum, Krefeld, 1938
Leeds 1868: *National Exhibition of Works of Art at Leeds in 1868*, Leeds, 1868
Leiden 1965: *17de eeuwse meesters uit Nederlands particulier bezit*, Stedelijk Museum "De Lakenhal," Leiden, 1965
Leningrad 1926: *Dessins des maîtres anciens*, Hermitage, Leningrad, 1926 (cat. by M. Dobroklonsky; published 1927)
Leningrad 1976: *Exhibition of Pictures from the United States of America*, Hermitage, Leningrad, 11 February–24 March 1976 (also shown at Moscow, Kiev, and Minsk; Russian text)
Lincoln 1946: *Dutch and Flemish Paintings of the Seventeenth Century from the Cook Collection*, Usher Art Gallery, Lincoln, August–September 1946
London 1924: *Lord Haig's Fund Exhibition*, dealer Thos. Agnew, London, 1924
London 1929: *Exhibition of Dutch Art, 1450–1900*, Royal Academy of Arts, London, 4 January–9 March 1929
London 1932: *An Exhibition of the Von Auspitz Collection of Old Masters by courtesy of Herr Walter Bachstitz*, dealer Thomas Agnew and Sons, London, November–December 1932
London 1938: *Exhibition of 17th Century Art in Europe*, Royal Academy of Arts, London, 3 January–12 March 1938
London 1945: *Dutch Painting of the 17th Century*, Arts Council, London, 1945
London 1947–48: *Cleaned Pictures Exhibition*, National Gallery, London, 1947–48
London 1949: *Richard Wilson and his Circle* (organized by the City Museums and Art Gallery, Birmingham), Tate Gallery, London, January 1949
London 1952–53: *Dutch Pictures: 1450–1750*, Royal Academy of Arts, London, 1952–53
London 1961: *From Van Eyck to Tiepolo: An Exhibition of Pictures from the Thyssen-Bornemisza Collection*, National Gallery, London, 2 March–20 April 1961
London 1970: *Drawings from the Teyler Museum, Haarlem*, Victoria and Albert Museum, London, 1970
London 1976: *Art in Seventeenth-Century Holland*, The National Gallery, London, 30 September–12 December 1976
London 1976a: *Constable: Paintings, Watercolours & Drawings*, The Tate Gallery, London, 18 February–25 April 1976 (cat. by L. Parris *et al.*)
London 1978: *Dutch and Flemish Pictures from Scottish Collections. A Loan Exhibition in Aid of the National Trust for Scotland*, dealer Thos. Agnew & Sons, Ltd., London, 8 November–8 December 1978
London 1986: *Dutch Landscape, the Early Years, Haarlem and Amsterdam 1590–1650*, The National Gallery, London, 3 September–23 November 1986 (cat. by Christopher Brown)
London 1996–97: *Old Master Drawings from the Malcolm Collection*, British Museum, 1996–97 (cat. by M. Royalton-Kisch *et al.*)
London–New York–Toronto 1994–95: *Constable, a Master Draughtsman*, Dulwich Picture Gallery, London, July–October 1994–The Frick Collection, New York, November 1994–February 1995–Art Gallery of Ontario, Toronto, May–July 1995 (cat. by Ian Felming-Williams)
London–Paris–Cambridge 2002-03: *Bruegel to Rembrandt: Dutch and Flemish Drawings from the Maida and George Abrams Collection*, British Museum, London–Institut Néerlandais, Paris–Fogg Art Museum, Cambridge, Massachusetts, 2002-03 (cat. by William W. Robinson)
Los Angeles 1992–93: *A Mirror of Nature. Dutch Paintings from the Collection of Mr. & Mrs. Edward William Carter*, Los Angeles County Museum of Art, 22 October 1992–17 January 1993 (cat. by J. Walsh and C. Schneider)
Los Angeles–Boston–New York 1981–82: *A Mirror of Nature. Dutch Paintings from the Collection of Mr. and Mrs. Edward William Carter*, Los Angeles County Museum of Art, Los Angeles, 13 October 1981–3 January 1982–Museum of Fine Arts, Boston, 20 January–14 March 1982–The Metropolitan Museum of Art, New York, 7 April–20 June 1982 (cat. by J. Walsh and C. Schneider)
Madrid 1994–95: *The Golden Age of Dutch Landscape Painting*, Thyssen-Bornemisza Museum, Madrid, 1994–95 (ed. P.C. Sutton, in collaboration with J. Loughman)
Manchester 1857: *Catalogue of the Art Treasures of the United Kingdom Collected at Manchester in 1857*, London, 1857. (The first edition gives provisional numbers to the works; the second edition cites different, definitive numbers. The latter numbers have been cited *passim* in the present catalogue.)
Milan 1954: *Mostra di pittura olandese del seicento*, Palazzo Reale, Milan, 25 February–25 April 1954
Minneapolis–Houston–San Diego 1985: *Dutch and Flemish Masters. Paintings from the Vienna Academy of Arts*, The Minneapolis Institute of Arts, Minneapolis–The Museum of Fine Arts, Houston–The San Diego Museum of Arts, San Diego, 1985 (cat. by George S. Keyes)
Minneapolis–Toledo–Los Angeles 1990–91: *Mirror of Empire: Dutch Marine Art of the Seventeenth Century*, The Minneapolis Museum of Art–The Toledo Museum of Art–Los Angeles County Museum of Art, 1990–91 (cat. by George S. Keyes *et al.*)
Montreal 1990: *Italian Recollections. Dutch Painters of the Golden Age*, Montreal Museum of Arts, Montreal, 8 June–22 July 1990 (cat. by F.J. Duparc and L.L. Graif)
Munich 1869: *Ausstellung von Gemälden älterer Meister*, Koniglichen Kunstausstellungsgebaude gegenüber der Glyptothek, Munich, [probably 20 July–31 October] 1869
Munich 1930: *Sammlung Schloss Rohoncz*, Neue Pinakothek, Munch, 1930
Munich–Bonn 1993: *Das Land am Meer. Holländische Landschaft im 17. Jahrhundert*, Staatliche Graphische Sammlung, Munich, 12 February–18 April 1993–Rheinisches Landesmuseum, Bonn, 6 May–4 July 1993 (cat. by Thea Vignau-Wilberg)
Neuchâtel 1953: *Semaine hollandaise*, Musée des Beaux-Arts, Neuchâtel, 1953
New York 1830: *Richard Abraham Collection*, American Academy of Fine Arts, New York, March 1830
New York 1909: *The Hudson-Fulton Celebration. Loan Exhibition of Paintings by Old Dutch Masters*, The Metropolitan Museum of Art, New York, September–November 1909
New York 1939: *Catalogue of European Paintings and Sculpture from 1300–1800, Masterpieces of Art*, New York World's Fair, New York, May–October 1939
New York 1942: *Paintings by the Great Dutch Masters . . . in Aid of the Queen Wilhelmina Fund . . .*, dealer Duveen Galleries, New York, 8 October–7 November 1942
New York 1985: *The Golden Ambience: Dutch Landscape Painting in the Seventeenth Century*, Minskoff Cultural Center, New York, April 1985 (cat. by Walter Liedtke)
New York 1988: *Dutch and Flemish Paintings from New York Private Collection*, National Academy of Design, New York, 1988 (cat. by Ann Jensen Adams)
New York 1998–99: *Master Drawings from the Hermitage and Pushkin Museums*, The Pierpont Morgan Library, New York, September 1998–January 1999
New York 2002–03: *The Thaw Collection. Master Drawings and Oil Sketches. Acquisitions Since 1994*, The Pierpont Morgan Library, New York, 27 September 2002–19 January 2003 (cat. by C.D. Denison *et al.*)
New York–Chicago 1988: *Dutch and Flemish Paintings from the Hermitage*, The Metropolitan Museum of Art, New York, 26 March–5 June 1988–The Art Institute of Chicago, 9 July–18 September 1988
New York–Chicago 1989: *From Michelangelo to Rembrandt: Master Drawings from the Teyler Museum*, The Pierpont Morgan Library, New York–The Art Institute of Chicago, 1989
New York–Fort Worth 1995: *Drawings from the Albertina. Landscape in the Age of Rembrandt*, The Drawing Center, New York–Kimbell Art Museum, Fort Worth, 1995 (cat. by M. Bisanz-Prakken)
New York–Toledo–Toronto 1954–55: *Dutch Painting, The Golden Age, An Exhibition of Dutch Pictures of the Seventeenth Century*, The Metropolitan Museum of Art, New York–The Toledo Museum of Art, Toledo–The Art Gallery of Toronto, Toronto, 1954–55
Norwich 1966: *Dutch Paintings from East Anglia*, City of Norwich Museums, Norwich, 20 July–29 August 1966
Oslo 1959: *Fra Rembrandt til Vermeer*, National Gallery, Oslo, 9 October–6 December 1959
Oxford 1975: *Dutch Pictures in Oxford*, Ashmolean Museum, Oxford, 10 May–27 July 1975
Paris 1911: *Exposition rétrospective des grands et petits maîtres hollandais*, Musée du Jeu de Paume, Paris, April 1911
Paris 1921: *Exposition hollandaise: tableaux, aquarelle et dessins anciens et modernes*, Musée du Jeu de Paume, Paris, April–May 1921
Paris 1945: *Exposition des chefs-d'oeuvre de la peinture*, Musée du Louvre, Paris, 1945
Paris 1950–51: *Le paysage hollandais au XVIIe siècle*, Musée de l'Orangerie, Paris, 1950–51
Paris 1970–71: *Le siècle de Rembrandt: Tableaux hollandais des collections publiques françaises*, Musée du Petit Palais, Paris, 17 November 1970–15 February 1971
Paris 1972: *Cent dessins du Musée Teylers, Haarlem*, Musée du Louvre, Paris, 1972
Paris 2004: *Regards sur l'art hollandais du XVIIe siècle. Frits Lugt et les Frères Dutuit, collectionneurs*, Institut Néerlandais, Paris, 18 March–16 May 2004 (cat. by S. Alsteens *et al.*)
Philadelphia 1950–51: *Diamond Jubilee Exhibition: Masterpieces of Painting*, Philadelphia Museum of Art, Philadelphia, 4 November 1950–11 February 1951
Poughkeepsie 1976: *Seventeenth Century Dutch Landscape Drawings and Selected Prints from American Collections*, Vassar College Art Gallery, Poughkeepsie, New York, 28 March–7 May 1976
Providence 1938: *Dutch Painting in the Seventeenth Century*, Rhode Island School of Design, Providence, RI, 1938
Rome 1928: *Mostra di capolavori della pittura olandese*, Galleria Borghese, Rome, 1928
Rome 1954: *Mostra di pittura olandese del seicento*, Palazzo delle Esposizioni, Rome, 4 January–14 February 1954
Rotterdam 1985: *Meesterwerken uit de Hermitage, Leningrad, Hollandse en Vlaamse schilderkunst van de 17e eeuw*, Museum Boymans–van Beuningen, Rotterdam, 19 May–14 July 1985
Rotterdam 1994–95: *Rotterdamse Meesters uit de Gouden Eeuw*, Historisch Museum, Rotterdam, 15 October 1994–15 January 1995 (ed. Nora Schadee)

Rotterdam–Berlin 1996–97: *Praise of Ships and the Sea: The Dutch Marine Painters of the 17th Century*, Museum Boijmans Van Beuningen, Rotterdam, 21 December 1996–23 February 1997–Gemäldegalerie im Bodemuseum, Staatliche Museen zu Berlin, 21 March–25 May 1997 (cat. by J. Giltaij *et al.*)
Rotterdam–Essen 1959–60: *Collectie Thyssen-Bornemisza (Schloss Rohoncz)*, Museum Boymans-van Beuningen, Rotterdam, 14 November 1959–3 January 1960–Museum Folkwang, Essen, 1960
St. Louis 1991: *Five Centuries of Drawing: Masterpieces at the Museum of Fine Arts, Leipzig*, St. Louis Art Museum, 2 February–24 March 1991 (cat. by Barbara Butts)
St. Petersburg 1867: *Collection des dessins, Ermitage Impérial*, Hermitage, St. Petersburg, 1867 (cat. by Baron B. de Koehne)
San Francisco–Toledo–Boston 1966–67: *The Age of Rembrandt. An Exhibition of Dutch Paintings of the Seventeenth Century*, California Palace of the Legion of Honor, San Francisco–The Toledo Museum of Art, Toledo–Museum of Fine Arts, Boston, 1966–67
Seattle 1962: *Masterpieces of Art*, Fine Arts Pavilion, World's Fair, Seattle, 21 April–4 September 1962
Tel-Aviv 1959: *Holland's Golden Age, Paintings, Drawings, Silver of the XVIIth Century*, Tel-Aviv Museum, Tel-Aviv, 1959
Tokyo 1992–93: *European Landscapes from Raphael to Pissarro. Museum of Fine Arts, Budapest. Hungarian National Gallery*, Mitsukoshi Museum of Art, Tokyo and four other venues in Japan, 20 November 1992–27 June 1993
Tokyo–Fukuoka–Kyoto 1983–84: *Masterpieces of Euopean Paintings from the Museum of Fine Arts, Boston*, Isetan Museum of Art, Shinjuku, Tokyo, 21 October–4 December 1983– Fukuoka Art Museum, Fukuoka, 6–29 January 1984–Kyoto Municipal Museum of Art, Kyoto, 25 February–8 April 1984
Tokyo–Kyoto 1968–69: *The Age of Rembrandt: Dutch Paintings and Drawings of the 17th Century*, National Museum for Western Art, Tokyo, 19 October–22 December 1968–Municipal Museum, Kyoto, 11 January–2 March 1969
Tokyo–Kyoto 1974–75: *Meisterwerke der Euopäischen Malerei aus der Gemäldegalerie alte Meister Dresden*, National Museum for Western Art, Tokyo, 21 September–24 November 1974–National Museum, Kyoto, 3 December 1974–26 January 1975
Tokyo–Osaka 1983: *Seventeenth-Century Dutch and Flemish Paintings and Drawings from the Hermitage, Leningrad*, Tokyo–Osaka, 1983
Tokyo and elsewhere 1992–93: *Tussen fantasie en werkelijkheid. 17de eeuwse Hollandse landschapschilderkunst*, Tokyo Station Gallery–Kasama Nichido Museum of Art–Kumamoto Prefectural Museum of Art–Stedelijk Museum De Lakenhal, Leiden, 1992–93 (cat. by E. Buijsen *et al.*; with English translation of text)
Utrecht 1953: *Nederlandse architectuurschilders, 1600–1900*, Centraal Museum, Utrecht, 28 June–28 September 1953
Utrecht 1961: *Catalogue Raisonné of the Works of Pieter Jansz Saenredam, Published on the Occasion of the Exhibition*, Centraal Museum, Utrecht, 1961 (cat. by P.T.A. Swillens and J.Q. van Regteren Altena)
Vienna 1873: *Gemälde alter Meister aus dem Wiener Privatbesitze*, Österreichischen Museum für kunst und Industrie, Vienna, August–September 1873
Vienna 1936: *Die holländsche Landschaften in Zeitalter Rembrandts*, Albertina, Vienna, 1936
Vienna 1993: *Die Landschaft im Jahrhundert Rembrandts*, Albertina, Vienna, 17 September–14 November 1993 (cat. by M. Bisanz-Prakken)
Washington 1985–86: *The Treasure Houses of Britain: Five Hundred Years of Private Patronage and Art Collecting*, National Gallery of Art, Washington, 3 November 1985–16 March 1986
Washington 1990: *Rembrandt's Landscapes: Drawings and Prints*, National Gallery of Art, Washington, 11 March–20 May 1990 (cat. by Cynthia P. Schneider *et al.*)
Washington–Denver–Fort Worth 1977: *Seventeenth Century Dutch Drawings from American Collections*, National Gallery of Art, Washington–The Denver Art Museum–Kimbell Art Museum, Fort Worth, 1977 (cat. by Franklin W. Robinson)
Washington–Fort Worth–Chicago–Los Angeles 1982–83: *Dutch Paintings of the Golden Age from the Royal Picture Gallery, Mauritshuis*, National Gallery of Art, Washington–Kimbell Art Museum, Fort Worth–The Art Institute of Chicago–Los Angeles County Museum of Art, 1982–83
Washington–New York–San Francisco 1978–79: *The Splendor of Dresden*, National Gallery of Art, Washington–The Metropolitan Museum of Art, New York–California Palace of the Legion of Honor, San Francisco, 1978–79
Washington and elsewhere 1958–59: *Dutch Drawings, Masterpieces of Five Centuries*, National Gallery of Art, Washington–The Pierpont Morgan Library, New York–The Minneapolis Institute of Art–Museum of Fine Arts, Boston–The Cleveland Museum of Arts–The Art Institute of Chicago, 1958–59
Washington and elsewhere 1975–76: *Master Paintings from the Hermitage and State Russian Museum, Leningrad*, National Gallery of Art, Washington–The Metropolitan Museum of Art, New York–The Detroit Institute of Arts–Los Angeles County Museum of Art–Museum of Fine Arts of Houston, 1975–76
Washington and elsewhere 1985–87: *Master Drawings from Titian to Picasso. The Curtis O. Baer Collection*, National Gallery of Art, Washington, D.C. and five other venues, 1985–87 (cat. by E. M. Zafran)
Worcester 1951: *Condition: Excellent. A Catalogue of a Special Exhibition of Paintings Notable for their State of Preservation*, Worcester Art Museum, Worcester, 22 March–22 April 1951
Yokohama–Sapporo–Hiroshima 1985–86: *Meisterwerke der Renaissance und des Barock aus dem Museum der bildenden Künste, Leipzig*, Sogo Museum of Art, Yokohama–Museum of Modern Art, Sapporo–Museum of Modern Art, Hiroshima, 1985–86
Zurich 1949–50: *Gemälde der Ruzicka-Stiftung*, Kunsthaus, Zurich, December 1949–March 1950
Zurich 1950: *Europäische Kunst, 13.–20. Jahrhundert aus Zürcher Sammlungen*, Kunsthaus, Zurich, 6 June–13 August 1950
Zurich 1953: *Holländer des 17. Jahrhunderts*, Kunsthaus, Zurich, 4 November–20 December 1953
Zurich 1971: *Kunstschätze aus Dresden*, Kunsthaus, Zurich, 28 May–18 September 1971

Index

References to illustrations are given in italics, and square brackets indicate catalogue numbers

Photographic Acknowledgements

All works of art are reproduced by kind permission of the owners. Special acknowledgements for providing photographs are as follows:

Reproduced by Gracious Permission of H. M. Queen Elizabeth II, fig. 38
Amsterdam: Amsterdams Historisch Museum, cat. 31, 76
Amsterdam: Gemeentearchief Amsterdam, cat. 69
Amsterdam: © Rijksmuseum, fig. 11; cat. 35, 39, 73, 74, 82, 83, 94, 101, 109, 110, 111, 112
Berlin: © Bildarchiv Preussischer Kulturbesitz, fig. 24; cat. 65, 72, 81, 89; Jörg P. Anders, fig. 22; cat. 25, 57
Bilbao: © Museo de Bellas Artes de Bilbao, fig. 5
Boston: © 2004 Museum of Fine Arts, cat. 51
Brussels: © Musées royaux des Beaux-Arts de Belgique/Speltdoorn, cat. 97, 98
Budapest: © Szépmüvészeti Múzeum/Józsa, cat. 5
Cambridge (MA): Widener Library Photographic Services, figs 27, 28; courtesy of the Fogg Art Museum, Harvard University Art Museums/Allan Macintyre, cat. 96; Photographic Services/© President and Fellows of Harvard College, cat. 33
Cambridge: © Fitzwilliam Museum, Universtiy of Cambridge, cat. 58
Chicago: © The Art Institute of Chicago, cat. 18
Cleveland: © The Cleveland Museum of Art, cat. 2
Detroit: © 1996 Detroit Institute of Arts, cat. 22a; © 2000 Detroit Institute of Arts, cat. 100a
Dresden: © SKD/Herbert Boswank, cat. 59, 60, 61, 62, 63, 64; H.-P. Klut, cat. 22; Klut&Estel, cat. 38
Dublin: © courtesy of The National Gallery of Ireland, cat. 16
Edinburgh: © The National Gallery of Scotland/Antonia Reeve, cat. 12
Enschede: © Rijksmuseum Twenthe, cat. 7a
Fort Worth: © 2004 Kimbell Art Museum/Michael Bodycomb, cat. 24
T.M. Gonzalez, cat. 40
Haarlem: © Teylers Museum, cat. 75, 79, 80, 95
Hamburg: © Hamburger Kunsthalle/Elke Walford, cat. 1
Perry Hastings, cat. 14, 15, 41
Karlsruhe: Staatliche Kunsthalle, cat. 36
Bernd-Peter Keiser, cat. 21
Leipzig: Museum der bildenden Künste Leipzig/Ursula Gerstenberger, cat. 99
London: Christies Images, figs. 1, 2
London: National Trust Photographic Library/Derrick E. Witty, cat. 52
London: © National Gallery, figs. 18, 52a; cat. 10, 45
London: © The British Museum, figs. 10, 53a; cat. 66, 67, 77, 102, 105, 107, 111
Los Angeles: courtesy of the J. Paul Getty Museum, cat. 7, 17
Los Angeles: © 2005 Museum Associates, LACMA, cat. 20, 34, 44
Madrid: © Museo Thyssen-Bornemisza, cat. 6
Melbourne: © National Gallery of Victoria, fig. 75a
New York: © 1994 The Metropolitan Museum of Art, cat 85; © 2004 The Metropolitan Museum of Art, fig. 31; cat. 107, 109, 110, 112
New York: © The Pierpont Morgan Library 2004/Joseph Zehavi, cat. 84, 90
Jeff Nintzel, cat. 8
Oxford: © reserved the University of Oxford, Ashmolean Museum, cat. 68a
Paris: Collection Frits Lugt, Institut Néerlandais, fig. 43b; cat. 100; Pascal Faligot, cat. 109
Paris: Ecole nationale supérieure des beaux-arts, cat. 78, 87
Paris: Institut de France - Musée Jacquemart-André, cat. 50
Paris: © RMN fig. 30; / © Thierry Le Mage, cat. 70; ©Hervé Lewandowski, cat. 53
Philadelphia: © Philadelphia Museum of Art, cat. 27, 43, 11; Graydon Wood, cat. 29
Antonia Reeve, cat. 13
St Petersburg: © The State Hermitage Museum, cat. 3, 37, 54, 71, 88
The Hague: Museum Bredius, cat. 91, 92, 93
The Hague: © Royal Cabinet of Paintings, Mauritshuis, cat. 48
Vienna: Fotostudio Otto, cat. 4
Vienna: KHM, fig. 12; cat. 11
Vienna: © Graphische Sammlung Albertina, cat. 68, 100, 103, 104, 106, 108, 110
Washington: Board of Trustees, National Gallery of Art, cat. 32
Worcester: © Worcester Art Museum, Theodore T. and Mary G. Ellis Collection, fig. 32
Weilheim: Artothek, cat. 55; Blauel Gnamm, cat. 42
Zürich: © 2004 Kunsthaus. All rights reserved., cat. 26, 49